THE THEATRICAL IMAGINATION

Second Edition

JEFFREY H. HUBERMAN
Bradley University

JAMES LUDWIG
Bradley University

BRANT L. POPE
Florida State University

HARCOURT BRACE COLLEGE PUBLISHERS
Fort Worth Philadelphia San Diego New York Orlando Austin San Antonio
Toronto Montreal London Sydney Tokyo

Publisher	Christopher P. Klein
Acquisitions Editor	Barbara J. C. Rosenberg
Developmental Editor	Terri House
Project Editors	Elizabeth Cruce Alvarez
	Elke Herbst
Manager of Art and Design	Pat Bracken
Production Manager	Jane Tyndall Ponceti
Art Program	Marco Ruiz
Photo Researcher	Lili Weiner
Permissions Editor	Eleanor Garner

Cover Photograph: The Hartford Stage Company production of *A Midsummer Night's Dream,* directed by Mark Lamos. Lighting designer: Pat Collins. Set designer: Michael Yeargan. Photo: © T. Charles Erickson. Hand tinting: Donna Buie.

ISBN: 0-15-503024-8

Library of Congress Catalog Card Number: 95-82110

Holt, Rinehart and Winston, Inc., may provide complimentary instructional aids and supplements or supplement packages to those adopters qualified under our adoption policy. Please contact your sales representative for more information. If as an adopter or potential user you receive supplements you do not need, please return them to your sales representative or send them to: Attn: Returns Department, Troy Warehouse, 465 South Lincoln Drive, Troy, MO 63379.

Address for Editorial Correspondence: Harcourt Brace College Publishers, 301 Commerce Street, Suite 3700, Fort Worth, TX 76102.

Address for Orders: Harcourt Brace & Company, 6277 Sea Harbor Drive, Orlando, FL 32887-6777. 1-800-782-4479, or 1-800-433-0001 (in Florida).

Printed in the United States of America

6 7 8 9 0 1 2 3 4 5   039   10 9 8 7 6 5 4 3 2 1

PREFACE

Imagination, being much neglected in the modern world, is little
understood.

John Masefield

Theatre is insistently the art of the present. Unlike other works of art that are fashioned with a permanence that makes them artifacts of their times, the live performances of theatre evolve virtually on a daily basis. A book that seeks to examine the theatrical imagination, then, must also evolve. As the world itself has changed in unimaginable ways since 1993 (when the first edition of this text appeared), so too has the theatre, which fulfills its mission by reflecting the human journey. There have been many entrances and exits on the stages of the world. There are many new plays and players—theatremakers and theatregoers.

New to This Edition

To embrace these new theatrical lives, every chapter has been rewritten in part. The focus of the text has been sharpened, new material has been added, and the latest scholarship has been incorporated. Excellent suggestions offered by the book's many users—students and faculty alike—are evident on every page in ways large and small. The new edition includes sections on the most current and, in many cases, most challenging issues facing theatre artists today, such as:

- The legal and economic impact of intellectual property;
- The latest research on art and creativity, including brain structure and talent, brain activity and imagination, and creativity and artificial intelligence;
- The effects of new technology on the delivery and practice of theatre art including digital performance and interactivity, virtuality, synthespians, virtual scenery, and sound design;
- Expanded coverage of theatre in African, Middle Eastern, and Asian societies, new material on multicultural acting styles, and the examination of global theatre marketing as the new model of commercial theatre production;
- A new section on musical theatre and an expanded section on dramatic genres;
- Disturbing trends in worldwide antitheatrical prejudice as well as the latest laws on stage censorship;
- Updates on the latest statistics and profiles of theatre attendance including an examination of how previously underserved populations are beginning to choose theatre as a leisure-time choice;
- A more concise "Theatregoer's Guide" that provides information on going to the theatre, finding out what's playing, and making reservations and getting tickets in today's online society;

- A double "Time Line" that lists major events of "The Theatrical Imagination" and "The World Reflected;" and
- By popular demand: more "Legendary Theatrical Zingers."

In all, there are references to 52 new artists and commentators, 47 new plays, 16 new films and television shows, and 80 new photographs including 5 photo essays.

Making Choices

Despite these revisions, the basic philosophy and mission of the book remain intact. *The Theatrical Imagination* examines the creative choices artists make in transforming ink on the page to art on the stage. Examples take the form of comparisons between successful and unsuccessful choices of the greatest theatre artists to demonstrate both the positive results and potential risks of provocative imaginations at work.

The book is organized according to the imaginative process. Part 1, "The Creative Imagination," provides the framework for examining drama and theatre within the larger contexts of imagination, creativity, and art. Part 2, "The Play," examines forces that make and shape the initial artwork, with chapters on theatregoers, playwrights, and producers. Part 3, "The Production," focuses on the choices of the company of artists assembled for the staging of the play, profiling directors, actors, and designers. Part 4, "The Performance," looks at the play as enacted live on stage, with chapters on the role of the audience, critics, and the life cycle of the theatrical imagination. Popular features such as the focused historical perspectives, choices questions, and the artists-at-work essays are also key aspects of this second edition.

While the text describes a sequential process, the chapters are self-contained units, and instructors may customize the assignment of topics as preferred. It is a basic tenet of *The Theatrical Imagination* that there is no theatrical orthodoxy; no one formula, process, or viewpoint prevails. This book highlights theatrical diversity and controversies among not only the viewers and critics, but among the practicing artists themselves. Theatre teachers, like theatre artists everywhere, ultimately make their own choices in presenting how word symbols on a page and empty space can be transformed into an artistic world that is rich, provocative, and entertaining.

Fiona Shaw is the award-winning British actor who was the first woman to play the title role in Shakespeare's *Richard II*. In performances on stage and on screen, she makes daring choices that are memorably—insistently—her own. "In a new century, the theatre can be a place of fabulous exploration into the imagination," she says. "Theatre has to change its form every time it's done. You can use elements of the old form, but it takes one stroke to change it utterly. That's me."[1] That is the theatrical imagination.

Acknowledgments

We are deeply indebted to many people for their assistance, advice, contributions, and encouragement in completing this book. We are grateful to Debbie Perry, Joan Wilhelm, Georgia Zaeske, Rob Beck, Julie Dempewolf, and Rebecca Crist for their assistance in verifying data, researching material, and transcribing copy.

For their encouragement as well as their expertise, we are very grateful to our friends and colleagues: Kathy St. George, Kenneth Freeburn, Richard Hansen, Mona Louise Hyre, Amir Al-Khafaji, Claire Etaugh, Ellen Watson, Patrick Spottiswoode, William J. Langley, Jr., Paul Kassel, Armella Nefzger, Ann Fink, Terry Dean, and Danny Newman. Their thoughts and their art fill the pages of this book.

For their guidance and wisdom, we owe a special debt of gratitude to pre-eminent theatre educators and artists who we are privileged to call our collaborators: Ralph G. Allen, Benjamin Mordecai, D. Terry Williams, Jon Farris, Frank Silberstein, Anatoly Smeliansky, and T. Charles Erickson.

Our editors at Harcourt Brace College Publishers—Barbara Rosenberg, Terri House, Beth Alvarez, Elke Herbst, and Lili Weiner—have been particularly supportive and tolerant.

The following reviewers saw drafts of the manuscript and offered helpful suggestions: Marya Bednerik, Kent State University; Pat Behrendt, University of Nebraska; James B. Randolf II, University of Miami; D. Terry Williams, Western Michigan University; Tom Mitchell, University of Illinois at Urbana-Champaign; and Larry Walters, University of Nevada.

The love and devotion of our families have kept us happy, healthy, and sane throughout this project (that, for them, must never seem to end): the Hubermans—Raquel, Jacob, David, Mark, Ruth, and Max; the Ludwigs—Rosemarie, Brian, and Jeffrey and Clare; and the Popes—Barbara and Olivia.

Without doubt, we owe our greatest thanks to the many teachers and students who responded so enthusiastically to the first edition. Their valuable feedback has enabled us to preserve, focus, and improve our message.

Jeffrey H. Huberman
James Ludwig
Brant L. Pope
August 1996

For

RAQUEL HUBERMAN

ROSEMARIE LUDWIG

BARBARA POPE

our partners in life

PREVIEW

Imagine you are an adventurous entrepreneur looking for an entertaining break from business as usual by investing $3 million in a new Broadway musical. By making the right choice, you could leave the boardroom and enter the heady artistic realms of show business as a theatrical "angel." But betting on the right combination of creative people who possess nothing more solvent than imagination and talent is a high-stakes game, more consequential than leveraged buyouts or foreign exchange derivatives. The risks are so great that you could lose everything the day after reviews dub the show a "flop," "turkey," "disaster," or "bomb." On the other hand, the payoff could be enormous: a "hit," "smash," or "blockbuster" could return your entire investment in a matter of months and continue in pure profit for years to come.

Well known for your wealth as well as for your thrill-seeking investment style, you are besieged with scripts, ideas, scenarios, and packaged deals from the best to the barely known of show business. Relying only on your own instinct for success, you narrow your search for a Broadway hit to the following two proposals.

Production No. 1 specs out as follows:

A musical thriller spectacular budgeted at $8.5 million. The plot is based on a novel by master of the macabre extraordinaire Stephen King that was so successful it has already been turned into a movie that became a cult classic. It depicts a young girl with telekinetic powers who heaps horrific revenge upon her mean-spirited schoolmates.

The personnel already signed for the project are a veritable who's who of international theatrical, video, and cinematic megahits, including Terry Hands, former artistic director of the Royal Shakespeare Company; Debbie Allen, Tony Award-winning actor and Emmy Award-winning director/choreographer; Michael Gore, Academy Award-winning composer of the film *Fame;* and the ensemble acting power of the Royal Shakespeare Company itself. The most promising song in the show—sure to hit the top of the pop charts— is the pounding hard rock "Out for Blood." The high-school setting, contemporary musical sound, along with the high-tech potential for horror and special effects, incorporate the most successful elements of such legendary hits as *Grease, Sweeney Todd, The Phantom of the Opera, Tommy, Joseph and the Amazing Technicolor Dreamcoat, Beauty and the Beast,* and *Peter Pan.*

Even King's original title is fittingly concise for the musical marquee and already part of the popular imagination: *Carrie.* Sounds terrific, yes?

Production No. 2 has somewhat more suspect specifications:

This show, costing out at $5 million, is a bittersweet musical drama based on little-known historical events.

The plot is based on an obscure short story in Yiddish by a nineteenth-century author who wrote under the pen name of Sholem Aleichem. It concerns a Jewish milkman in a small Russian village and the great difficulty he experiences in trying to marry off his five daughters. There is, as yet, no film version.

The production team so far assembled is made up of unknowns except for the famous choreographer Jerome Robbins. The star is an actor who has not worked in a major production since he was blacklisted during the political hysteria of the McCarthy era.

The production has few opportunities for spectacular visual effects. The "big number" consists of bearded men dancing with wine bottles balanced on their hats.

The producers recognize that even the title will have to be changed. *Tevye and His Daughters* will sell no tickets. The authors suggest *Fiddler on the Roof.* Sounds crazy, no?

So what's it going to be: Stephen King and his coed from hell or Sholem Aleichem and his milkman from Russia? The choice is yours.

To be sure, the theatrical folklore on this fantasy choice has already been settled. *Carrie* was one of the biggest bombs in theatrical history, having closed on Broadway after only one weekend, while *Fiddler on the Roof* has become a masterpiece of international stature with an initial record-breaking Broadway run and five major revivals, not to mention countless local, regional, and international productions. Even a hit movie has been made. This unlikely work of art has captured the imaginations of theatregoers throughout the world.

In hindsight, choosing *Carrie* or *Fiddler on the Roof* might seem easy. Yet, caught up in the intoxication of creating theatre, identifying the "better play" is not such a sure thing. Who knows? With different theatrical choices, we might all be humming "Out for Blood" instead of "If I Were a Rich Man."

The Flop

The Hit

CONTENTS

THE CREATIVE IMAGINATION

Actor Richard Iglewski in the title role in the Guthrie Lab production of Shakespeare's Pericles. *Directed by Bartlett Sher, setting designed by Thomas J. Truax, costumes designed by Kim Krumm Sorenson, and lighting designed by Marcus Dilliard.*

Romeo; now art thou what thou art by art as well as by Nature.

Romeo and Juliet, *Act II, scene iv*

CHAPTER 1

Art and the Creative Imagination

THE ARTIST'S CHOICES

PREVIEW

In Michael Crichton's science fiction novel *Sphere,* a psychologist, seeking to gain invincible mental powers, climbs into an alien vessel sent to Earth by a deep-space probe. As the door to the vessel closes, he finds himself floating in a mysterious darkness pierced only by strange flickering pinpoints of light. Amid his fear of the unknown and his anticipation of undreamed of power, the psychologist hears a telepathic voice speaking to him from the depths of the alien vessel. The secret of invincible mental power is about to be revealed as he listens to the voice of the alien intelligence.

On your planet you have an animal called a bear. It is a large animal, sometimes larger than you, and it is clever and has ingenuity, and it has a brain as large as yours. But the bear differs from you in one important way. It cannot perform the activity you call imagining. It cannot make mental images of how reality might be. It cannot envision what you call the past and what you call the future. This special ability of imagination is what has made your species as great as it is. Nothing else. It is not your ape-nature, not your tool-using nature, not your language or your violence or your caring for young or your social groupings. It is none of these things, which are all found in other animals. Your greatness lies in imagination.

The ability to imagine is the largest part of what you call intelligence. You think the ability to imagine is merely a useful step on the way to solving a problem or making something happen. But imagining it is what makes it happen.

This is the gift of your species . . . the ability to imagine.

I hope you enjoyed this speech, which I plan to give at the next meeting of the American Association of Psychologists and Social Workers which is meeting in Houston in March. I feel it will be quite well received.

What, he thinks, startled.

Who did you think you were talking to? God?

Who is this? he thinks.

You, of course.

But you are somebody different from me, separate. You are not me, he thinks.

Yes I am. You imagined me.

Tell me more.

There is no more.[1]

For this fictional psychologist, such self-discovery is startling. For writer Michael Crichton, the essence of human mastery over the world is the ability to make mental images of how reality might be—a distinctly human process we call imagination. This chapter examines art as a product of human imagination in terms of the art object, the artist, and the audience. The chapter provides a context for understanding theatre art by examining definitions and various manifestations of art, the nature of talent, the requirement of skill, and the value and power of purely imaginative creations.

The Human Power of Imagination

Imaginary applies to what could be existent or present but in fact is not. **Imagination** is the act or power of forming a mental image of something not present to the senses or never before wholly perceived in reality. The extent to which such images *can* be manifested is the power we call **creativity.** The essence of human endeavor is that we imagine something, and then we try to create it. Like no other creatures we have reshaped our world—the colors of flowers, the shape of the terrain, the flow of rivers, every manner of technological device from the wheel to the supercomputer, from the flavors of foods to the organs of our bodies, the genetic makeup of living cells, and the very movement of elementary particles—all according to our images of how reality might be.

But, unlike the power imparted by Michael Crichton's sphere, the human power to create is not unlimited. As George Burns explained to John Denver in the film *Oh God!,* "I'm God, and you're not."[2] Herein lies the essential human frustration: unlike the power to create, the ability to imagine is virtually limitless. The creative dilemma is that we can *imagine* other lives, other worlds, other dimensions, other times—other images of reality—many of which the human mind and body can never bring into actual existence.

A CHILD'S ART   *Even at the earliest stages of cognitive development, the doodlings of a 2- or 3-year-old child display an imaginative and cognitive power far beyond that of the most intelligent animals. No scientific evidence indicates that even the most advanced chimpanzee has any awareness that its scratchings or random markings bear any relationship to preexisting objects, let alone individuals, events, or ideas.*

Metaphysics notwithstanding, human beings have developed an intermediate—some say instinctive—but nonetheless essential method for resolving this creative dilemma. In effect, we manifest our images of altered reality through the process of *artistic* (as opposed to "actual") creativity, in which the products of our imagination are rendered in the less tangible, suggestive forms we call works of art. As the poet Joyce Kilmer wrote, "Only God can make a tree."[3] Human beings, however, *can* make paintings, sculptures, stories, poems, songs, and even plays about trees.

Defining Art

Defining art is one of the most difficult of all linguistic tasks. Ask what people mean when they use the word *art,* and you will get as many definitions and contradictory responses as there are persons in the group:

"A feeling."
"Something beautiful."
"Anything of very high quality."
"Whatever pleases me."
"The expression of an idea."
"You know. Things like painting and sculpture and stuff."
"It's too personal a thing to define."
"I can't define it, but I know it when I see it."

Many people also express a vague sense that art is something generally boring, old, not popular, very expensive, difficult to comprehend, and primarily associated with museums, symposiums, aficionados, and experts—something obscure. Even the formidable *Oxford English Dictionary* has a difficult time with the word. Referring to "many elusive phrases," it offers at least eleven different definitions of "art" in the space of two pages and three columns.

An examination of theatre art demands a workable definition of art itself that transcends mutually exclusive, extremely personal, or overly technical specifications.

Art as Imitation

Aristotle said it first. Art, he wrote in the *Poetics,* is **mimetic (mimetikos),** meaning "imitative." Henry Wadsworth Longfellow said it best. "Nature," he wrote in *Hyperion,* "is reproduced in Art."[4] In simple terms, the ancient philosopher and the modern poet recognized that *art is the imitation of something natural or imagined.* Art is not the real thing, but the human imitation of it. In fact, the word *art* itself is derived from the same root as "artificial" and "artifice." Understood in this way, a tree is not art. But a painting of a tree (Piet Mondrian's *The Red Tree*),

MAKING TREES ON BROADWAY   *On the stage of the Brooks Atkinson Theater, workers wrestle with 24-foot sections of the aluminum-framed "trees" that dominate the set of Lanford Wilson's play* Redwood Curtain. *The drama depicts an adopted teenager, the child of a Vietnamese mother and an American soldier, who desperately wants to find her real father. On a visit to an aunt, she comes upon a "bush vet," a Vietnamese war veteran who has retreated into the redwoods. Designer John Lee Beatty set the trees closer together than they would be in a real redwood forest. Were they real, the trunks would burst out of the theatre roof. Beatty also chose to have the bark darken as the trees rise to give the impression of height. "I wanted to make them a little magical," Beatty said. "Only God can make a tree."[5]*

a sculpture of a tree (the ever-popular artificial Christmas variety), a poem about a tree ("I think that I shall never see/ A poem lovely as a tree"), a novel about a tree (*A Tree Grows in Brooklyn*), a song about a tree ("Lemon tree, very pretty . . ."), or even a play in which trees figure prominently (Anton Chekhov's *The Cherry Orchard*)—all of these human creations qualify as art. They are imitations of the real thing.

The definition of art as imitation makes no reference to quality, genre, style, medium, purpose, or meaning—all of which make art as various as human experience, potentially as limitless in manifestation as the imagination itself.

Like all attempts to objectify aesthetics, the mimetic view of art is controversial. It is viewed by many as simplistic and exclusionary. Many contemporary notions of art, for example, formulate definitions based on subjective aspects of style, meaning, and application rather than the fundamental form. But the idea of art as imitation is not so restrictive as to imply a kind of exact copying. Personal vision and interpretation are essential aspects of every imaginative perception. Art, however defined, encompasses a broad range of creations from those that are realistic to those that are abstract and symbolic. The view of art as imitation is as old and instinctive as the human need to communicate.

A Historical Context

Aristotle maintained that imitation is a human instinct, and of all the animals, we are the most imitative. Art as imitation is evident in the earliest relics of human creativity. The most revealing of these are the cave drawings of ancient hunting parties and of masked ritualistic dancers. Primitive human beings ascribed sympathetic powers to such imitative creations—powers that were meant to assure success in the hunt, the change of seasons, and universal fertility for the sake of survival.

Art by the Rules.   From the first stirring of the artistic impulse great importance must have been attached to getting the imitation just right, so as not to jeopardize the desired effect. It is in this context that the long-standing tradition of art as having specific rules began. The legacy of this classical idea can be seen in the many "rule books" and "how-to" manuals for making art. Aristotle began the vogue for such rule books in the fourth century B.C. with his *Poetics,* a descriptive guide to making a tragic play. Modern versions are available for the making of every art and craft from basket weaving to acting and computer art. For much of civilized history, the quality of art has been judged by how strictly it adheres to the rules for its creation. For example, some of the greatest artworks of the seventeenth century were created according to a strict set of artistic standards known as **neoclassicism** that sought to codify the methods by which the classical art of ancient Greece and Rome was created. Strict verisimilitude, symmetry, and unity were the distinctive qualities neoclassicism prescribed for everything from painting and sculpture to poetry, drama, and even the layout of flower gardens. The French dramatist **Molière** (1622–73), author of some of the finest stage comedies ever written, followed these rules unerringly; his imagination was shaped, not restricted, by the artistic guidelines of his day. By contrast, Molière's contemporary and France's first great tragic dramatist, **Pierre Corneille** (1606–84), was publicly condemned for breaking these same rules and was so stung by the criticism that he quit writing plays for four years.

Art and Creative Freedom.   The demand for the universal freedoms of expression that swept the world in the revolutions of the late eighteenth and nineteenth centuries changed completely the notion of art as an imitative creation made according to systematic rules. The new **romantic** view was that art should be a free-form, unfettered expression of the human imagination produced by the instinctively talented through the mysterious process of inspiration. Mere imitation, the romantics believed, was the work of hacks. True art, the creation of geniuses, could be appreciated only by those possessed of cultivated taste and knowledge.

The legacy of the romantic view of art is responsible for the belief that art is primarily an expression of feelings, not something produced by reason or intelligence. The emphasis on individual reaction promotes the idea that personal preference, as opposed to inherent characteristics, is what defines art; *art* has become a term of praise. This subjective designation has produced an elitist view of art, leading many to believe that since they do not like classical music, go to ballets, understand Shakespeare, or see the point of abstract painting, art has nothing to do with their lives.

Art and the Question of Realism

Art, however lifelike, does not imply an exact re-creation of nature. To link art and reality is a contradiction in terms; they are at opposite ends of the creative spectrum. Turn-of-the-century Russian dramatist Anton Chekhov illustrated the difference between art and reality perfectly when he suggested taking a painting of a person, cutting out the nose, and substituting a real nose. The nose would be "realistic," but the picture would be ruined. The nose notwithstanding, it is obvious that in many works of art the image is easily recognizable; in many others, it is not.

Realistic Art.   Also referred to as *representational,* realistic art attempts to represent nature as closely as possible and achieves its pleasurable effect through the viewer's recognition of the familiar objects. Other terms associated with realism in art include *literalism, illusionism, naturalism,* and *believability.* Examples of realistic art include classical sculpture, Renaissance painting, nineteenth-century novels, photographs, and naturalistic plays.

Nonrealistic Art.   Also called *abstract* or *presentational,* nonrealistic art seeks to imitate with a minimum amount of recognizable references, often depending for its effects on the provocative use of imaginatively juxtaposed sounds, shapes, or words. Nonrealistic art is usually associated with such styles as *nonfigurative, postmodern,* and *minimalist.* Examples of nonrealistic art include classical tragedy, opera, and contemporary forms such as *cubism, futurism, surrealism, dadaism,* and *absurdism.* While there are those who maintain that nonrealistic art is anathema to imitation, cultural historians point out that the geometric patterns so evident in modern graphic art appeared shortly after the completion of the Eiffel Tower in 1889. For the first time in human history, significant numbers of people saw the lines and patterns of their world from a great height rather than from the earthbound perspective of a fading horizon. They have been "imitating" accordingly ever since. (See color plate 1.)

REALISTIC ART *The Korean War Veterans Memorial stands in a grove beneath the Lincoln Memorial, across the Reflecting Pool from the Vietnam Wall. Unlike Maya Linn's abstract, but powerful tribute to those Americans who died in Vietnam, Frank C. Gaylord's sculpture is dominated by nineteen large ultrarealistic steel statues of infantrymen—a silent patrol moving warily up a slope. The abundance of lifelike details—from the bones in their hands and the exhaustion apparent in their faces to the precise mechanisms of their equipment—combines in a haunting depiction of an anguished conflict. Off to the side there is a granite wall with hundreds of faces etched on it, faces taken from actual photographs of men and women who served in Korea as support troops.*

Artistic Conventions.   Pablo Picasso, who was always irritated by the criticism that his paintings were not realistic, was once approached by a young man who complained the great artist's paintings were too abstract and nonrealistic for him to understand. In the polite conversation that followed, the young man proudly showed Picasso a snapshot of his girlfriend. "She's very pretty," said Picasso, "but

HERMAN®

"Even I can paint better than that!"

is she really that small?" Like the size of a photograph, what is viewed as "realism" in art is often a matter of cultural conditioning in which commonly understood symbols or substitutes called **conventions** are accepted as part of the imitation. Our understanding of art, therefore, is not diminished by paintings that are two dimensional, characters who break into song in musical plays, or movie actors of gigantic size. For example, one of the most horrifyingly "realistic" scenes in screen history is in Alfred Hitchcock's masterpiece *Psycho* in which a woman is stabbed to death in a motel shower. The black-and-white convention of the film in no way diminished the effect. Movie critic Gene Siskel maintains just the opposite: the horror is enhanced by our imaginative connection to the emblematic convention. As Siskel points out, "We know what color blood is."[6]

High technology offers new perspectives on the concept of realism in art. The digital age has coined the term **virtuality** to describe the visual effect created by computer-controlled video as seen through special goggles. The unbounded, sense-stimulating experience gives the viewer the sensation of actually being within the artificially created world. While virtual reality raises imitation to a new level, the abstract conventions of such digital art are readily apparent.

In a sense, then, all art is abstract. Rendering something on canvas, in stone, in musical notes, in words, in a photographic emulsion, in pixels, or on stage—is abstraction itself.

NONREALISTIC ART   *While there are those who maintain nonrealistic art is anathema to imitation, the essential mimetic nature of the work is usually evident in its title. Picasso's controversial painting* Guernica *refers to the village of Guernica, a defenseless Spanish town, bombed into rubble by Nazi planes in 1937. Although abstract, Picasso's cubist rendering of figures torn apart is a powerful graphic rendering of the horrors of warfare.*

The Many Forms of Imitation

The Useful Arts

The idea of art as the application of skills to achieve a desired result has always pertained to more than purely aesthetic creations. In the eighteenth and nineteenth centuries the terms *applied arts* and *fine arts* arose to distinguish creations valued primarily for their specific uses from those with predominantly aesthetic values. The applied arts, also called "useful arts," or simply "crafts," include making furniture and clothing that may have great sensory appeal but are valued primarily for their functions. Also included in this category are such applied pursuits as military, healing, industrial, and mechanical arts. Creators of these arts, rather than being called artists, are customarily referred to as **artisans,** "craftspersons," or simply "professionals." Consider the book *The Art of War* by the ancient Chinese military tactician, Sun Tzu. Sun's discourse is the current manual of contemporary play-to-win strategists and has been studied by the Japanese military and the Russian army as well as by American politicians.

MANHOLE COVERS, A NECESSARY ART   *Since the 1840s foundries have produced manhole covers for city streets. In the nineteenth and early twentieth centuries, artisans created many cover patterns, especially in Victorian, art nouveau, and art deco styles. Even the apparently decorative aspects of these iron covers are functional: the raised surfaces kept horses from slipping and glass insets allowed light underground.*

The Fine Arts

The fine arts are traditionally classified by the medium in which they are rendered and by the ways in which they are understood and perceived by observers (see Figure 1-1). Fine arts fall into two broad categories: spatial and temporal arts.

Spatial Arts.   Spatial arts are created primarily by manipulating material in space. This category includes the **graphic arts** of drawing, painting, and printmaking that use line, shape, and color to imitate, and the **plastic arts** of sculpture, architecture, pottery, and weaving that manipulate form, mass, and material. Spatial arts make use of the principles of symmetry and radiation as well as balance, emphasis, measure, and harmony.

Space arts are also **autographic,** meaning the artist acts on the same physical materials—paint, ink, stone, cloth—that are subsequently perceived by observers. Spatial arts exist in space and can be appreciated from their display. With no intermediary between the observer and the original artwork, the connection is "automatically graphic"—a direct imaginative connection.

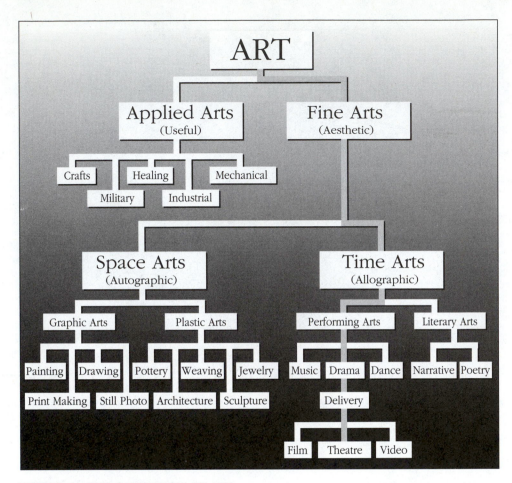

FIGURE 1-1   THE CATEGORIES OF ART

Temporal Arts.   Making up a more complex category, temporal arts are created by manipulating sound, symbols, or moving forms over a duration of time. Such art uses principles of rhythm, repetition, logical sequence, and melody to achieve its effects, as well as balance, measure, emphasis, and harmony to achieve unity. Included in this category are the **literary arts** of poetry, oratory, storytelling, and narrative that use written or spoken language, and the **performing arts** of music, dance, and drama. The audience for temporal arts, whether an individual or a group, must set aside time for perception, since these arts can be appreciated only in sequence.

Time arts are primarily **allographic,** meaning the artist renders them in a notation system (an "allograph" is a letter of an alphabet in a particular shape) that must be decoded and interpreted by those schooled in the symbol system used. Some notations, such as the written languages of literary arts, are commonly

FIGURE 1–2 ALLOGRAPHIC NOTATION *Beethoven said the first eight notes of his* Fifth Symphony *were meant to represent fate knocking at the door. Such a musical imitation is apparent to very few from "reading" the score. It is obvious, powerful, and affecting in its full symphonic performance.*

understood. Other symbol systems, especially those used for the performing arts, are not universally understood. Musical performers, for example, read **diatonic notations** of composers, which they then play on multitonal instruments in order to perform the musical imitations (see Figure 1-2). Dancers read the **laba notation** of choreographers to render in physical movements the steps and patterns originally conceived. Theatre artists interpret the staging codes written in playscripts to "physicalize" the actions imagined by the playwright.

Fine arts categories aid only in understanding general principles of art objects and the ways in which they achieve unity and effect. They are not absolute or pure. Many works of art are combinations that employ aspects from different categories. Sculptures may employ devices that enable them to move, giving them characteristics of time arts. Songs with lyrics have a literary component, whereas dance is almost always set to music. Operas, appreciated primarily for their musical aspects, contain dramatic plots and characters. Theatre art is always a composite, making use of literary, musical, choreographic, and dramatic principles, as well as many aspects of the spatial arts.

Artistic Delivery Systems

Many good works of art have failed and many bad ones have succeeded for reasons other than the inherent imagination and creativity of the artist in the making of the work. These reasons have to do with the methods used to present the work of art to an audience.

All art needs some sort of **delivery system.** Paintings and sculptures must be exhibited. Literary works must be published. Music, dance, and drama must be produced and performed. Delivery systems imply a place and a staff of others with technical or artistic expertise.

Delivering Spatial Arts.   When a painter puts down the brushes, the work is essentially complete. To reach the public the artist needs only to set up shop on a street corner to display the finished work. Better yet would be to find a gallery willing to exhibit the painting. While such expert display involves some staff—handlers, insurers, and the expert supervision of a curator—the autographic nature of

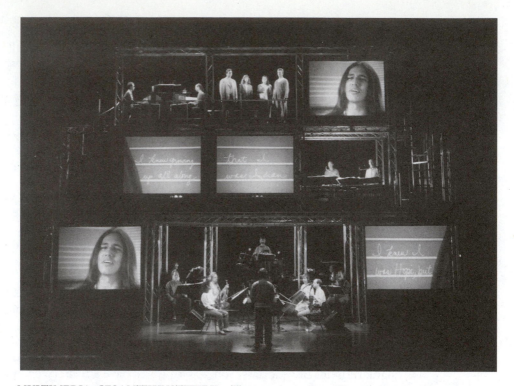

MULTIMEDIA *GESAMTKUNSTWERK*   *The great nineteenth-century opera composer Richard Wagner envisioned a "master artwork" he called a* Gesamtkunstwerk *that would meld music, poetry, drama, dance, and stagecraft into one unified magnificent spectacle. Twentieth-century* Gesamtkunstwerkers, *Steve Reich and Beryl Korot, pursued Wagner's ideal to create* The Cave, *a multimedia evocation of the Biblical story of Abraham that focuses on the patriarch's purported burial place in a cave— a symbolic site of rapprochement and deadly conflict between Arabs and Jews. In performance, the work consists of a wall of video screens set into a gigantic grid structure that also accommodates an ensemble of thirteen musicians and four choreographed singers. Video footage is of interviews with Israelis and Palestinians whose responses are used to punctuate and echo the music. The singers offer long recitatives based on Biblical or Koranic texts that also appear on the screens simultaneously in five or six languages. Modern high technology makes possible such multimedia creations that recombine elements of classic creations with the work of contemporary artists.*

space arts guarantees that the exhibited work communicates directly and wholly as the artist executed it. Aside from perhaps the picture frame and the way it is illuminated, nothing of the artist's work will be changed. In fact, the Visual Artists Rights Act of 1990, known as VARA, which is an amendment to the Copyright Act, provides that spatial artists have the right, subject to certain limitations, to prevent the "intentional distortion, mutilation, or other modification" of their creation that would be "prejudicial to his or her honor or reputation."

Delivering Literary Arts.   Delivering literary arts requires a method for multiplying and distributing the original work: the process of publication. The artist needs the skilled assistance of papermakers, typesetters, illustrators, printers, and binders. Literary artists submit their works to the scrutiny of editors who suggest changes before committing them to the printing press. Usually such changes are confined to aspects of phrasing and organization. Once published, however, the work communicates directly to its readers. The artist's work remains on the printed page with a kind of permanence that can span millennia. To reach an audience, the work requires only a person with the capability of reading the language in which it was written.

Delivering Performing Arts.   Delivering performing arts to an audience is the most complicated in terms of place, staff, and involvement of other artists. Public

MY WAY   *Paul Anka originally wrote "My Way" for Frank Sinatra. In 1993 BMI, the organization that licenses song rights, celebrated the song's 3 millionth performance. By interpreting the melody and lyrics in their own inimitable styles, Elvis Presley turned the song into a big hit for himself, as did the infamous "godfather" of punk, Sid Vicious (shown here), who recorded a bizarre version before his death in 1979. Said Anka of Vicious' version, "I loved it. I was shocked when I first heard it because I never imagined the song like that."[7] "I did it my way!" is a fitting refrain for all performing artists.*

assembly requires auditoriums of sufficient size, comfort, safety, acoustics, and visibility. Professional ticket sellers, ushers, electricians, movers, cleaners, wardrobe persons, accountants, promoters, and managers are also required.

Most importantly, others are needed to convert the written allographic notation into sound, movement, and action. Thus the performing arts are the only arts that *must* be delivered by other artists. **Performers,** by definition, are interpreters with their own artistic skills who can creatively translate and convey the sounds, movements, or actions imagined by the original artist. A work that calls for a group or **ensemble** of performers often requires the additional creative participation of a unifying, interpretive artist—a director, choreographer, or conductor.

In addition to creative skills, performing artists must have imaginative sensitivity to the tastes and conventions of the viewing audience, a knowledge of the period, style, and structure of the original work, and a commitment to the underlying intentions of the original artist. No matter how faithful the interpretation, the choices made by performing artists ensure that the work of the original artist—whether composer, choreographer, or dramatist—will be changed. The result is a unique work of art each time a performance takes place. The potential for such change is an aspect of the original work that must be present to ensure its success.

The Artist: A Talent for Making Choices

Although we may not know it, most of us are artists. When we doodle while carrying on a phone conversation, when we arrange a room to reflect our moods, personalities, or interests, or when we choose our clothes to impress others, we are designing our environments to imitate the particular images we have of what they ought to be. Such selection is precisely the chief business of the artist.

Most of us realize, however, that choices as simple as selecting the right necktie do not call for a complex intellectual process. The combination of instinct, rational intelligence, emotional sensitivity, and practiced motor ability for making imaginative choices is the **talent** that separates accomplished artists from everyday choice-makers like ourselves.

A Profile of Creativity

In his book *The Arts and Human Development,* Howard Gardner defines an artist as "an individual who has gained sufficient skill in the use of a medium to communicate through the creation of a symbolic object."[8] He describes a poet who, having undergone a deeply moving experience, seeks to communicate the emotional nature of the event through an effective arrangement of words, sounds, and images. The poet then becomes "immersed in the demanding task of selecting and combining words, phrases, and figures of speech suitable to the ideas and tones he wants to convey. Although many others may have shared the poet's moving experience, only one practiced in choosing words . . . will be able to have the sought-for effect upon others."[9] Similarly, other artists are practiced in the demanding tasks of choosing colors, shapes, sounds, body movements, or human actions.

Throughout history, the imagination of creative people has been deemed an enigma beyond the scope of rational analysis. Shakespeare wrote that "The lunatic, the lover, and the poet/Are of imagination all compact."[10] In recent years, however, researchers have begun systematic analyses of artists, and distinct psychological and physiological profiles of the creative personality have begun to emerge.

Using laboratory and abundant biographical data, psychologist David Perkins has developed what he calls the "Snowflake Model of Creativity."[11] The analogy refers to the six arms of a snowflake; Perkins' model is made up of six psychological traits of the creative person, all of which are crucial aspects in practiced choice making.

Trait 1—An instinct for unified arrangement is, according to Perkins, "the artist's drive to wrest order, simplicity, meaning, richness, or powerful expression from what is seemingly chaos."[12] An artist is one who can hear three notes that when played will make a melody, or one who can see three trees that create a vista, or one who can see and hear three characters that will render compelling human conflict.

Trait 2—The ability to excel at finding options reflects the artist's constant compulsion to increase the range of possible choices. In a study involving students at the Art Institute of Chicago, researchers discovered that young artists spent an inordinate amount of time contemplating a problem and investigating all the options for solving it before they chose a solution.

Trait 3—Mental mobility describes the tendency of artists to consider choices in terms of opposites and contraries in their attempts to achieve new unities, new

THE FAR SIDE cartoon by Gary Larson is reprinted by permission of Chronicle Features, San Francisco, CA.

perspectives, and new interpretations. This trait explains artists' tendencies to think in terms of analogies, emblems, imitations, and metaphors.

Trait 4—The willingness to take risks and accept failure is the price artists pay in order to achieve the rare creation of a masterpiece. A commonly held but mistaken notion is that master artists generate creative ideas instantly, produce only masterpieces, never have any failures, and, therefore, never need to risk bold choices. Picasso, for example, produced more than 20,000 works of art, many of which were mediocre.

Trait 5—Objectivity refers to the common trait artists share that compels them to seek advice and feedback in order to make the best choices from their many attempts and options. "Contrary to the popular image, the creative person is not a self-absorbed loner," says Perkins. Having made a detailed study of professional poets, he found that the ones who "sought feedback produced poetry that a panel of experts judged to be better than the poetry of those who didn't seek criticism."[13] In this sense, objectivity is a factor that goes beyond talent or inspiration. It involves the setting aside of ego, the seeking out of advice, and the constant testing of potential choices.

Trait 6—Inner motivation describes the driving force that compels artists to create for the enjoyment, satisfaction, and process of the work itself. Such impulses have been verified in lab studies that demonstrate creativity is inhibited when the range of choices is restricted by external constraints such as grades, work evaluation, supervision, or competition for prizes.

From this profile, the picture emerges of artists as choice makers who seek to expand their options by thinking in contrary and adventurous modes. When their choices are restricted, their creativity wanes. We who remain amateurs, dilettantes, hacks, copiers, and room arrangers stand in awe of those who have the rare ability—the talent—to make the choices that produce masterpieces.

The Sources of Talent

Referring to his apparent talent for painting, Picasso once remarked, "I can't drive a car, I can't repair the house, I can't even sing. All I can do is *this.*"[14]

Why was that all he could do, and why could he do it so well? What, specifically, was the source of his talent? Where did he get it? What was it about Pablo Picasso that endowed him with the talent for creating abstract art? Or Shakespeare for playwriting? Or Paul McCartney for songwriting? Or Glenn Close for acting? Is such talent instinctive, or learned and developed? Or is it a spiritual product of a special susceptibility artists have to inspiration, divine or otherwise? Or are there more scientific explanations for talent such as heredity, environment, or biochemistry?

The Case for Inspiration.   In Neil Simon's Tony Award-winning autobiographical play, *Broadway Bound,* Stanley and Eugene, two would-be comedy writers, beg God for some desperately needed help in coming up with an idea for a sketch they must write:

STANLEY: *[looking up]* Oh God. Give us an idea, God! I'm here, God. Tell it to me. Give us an idea for a sketch you're not using. Tell me an idea that makes you laugh.

[EUGENE looks up to see if God is going to do it][15]

The notion that the truly talented are constantly overcome by flashes of imaginative insight that erupt from some mystical source is an idea believed by many, understood by few, and most vigorously promoted by the artists.

There appears to be ample evidence, if mostly anecdotal, to support the idea of the inspired source of talent. Consider the case of "Heartbreak Hotel." It took Tommy Durden just twenty-two minutes to write this song that would become a number-one hit for Elvis Presley. But after a lifetime of trying, he has not been able to come up with another hit. Durden said he got the idea from a newspaper story about a man who committed suicide while clutching a note that read, "I walk a lonely street." He then came up with the idea of having Lonely Street lead to Heartbreak Hotel. "I have given it a lot of thought," he said. "I have come to the conclusion that the good Lord allows one 'Heartbreak Hotel' to the customer."[16] Many artists report that flashes of creativity are set off by unlikely stimuli. For example, Mozart claimed that traveling in a coach was necessary to enable him to compose entire pieces in his head. Paul McCartney maintained that, "I didn't write 'Yesterday,' I dreamed it."[17] Robin Williams is at a loss to explain the source of his comic genius: "It's hard to describe. There'll be moments when you get a spark, a gleam of light, and—boom! You're gone. It seems easy. But then it goes away, and it gets so incredibly hard. It's like having sex in a wind tunnel."[18]

The seemingly explosive, but entirely unpredictable nature of creativity has led many of the most talented artists to practice bizarre behavior and strange rituals in efforts to ensure the reliable flow of their creative juices. The eighteenth-century German dramatist Friedrich Schiller claimed the smell of rotten apples (which he kept in his desk) helped him write poetry. Richard Wagner put on perfume, scarves, and other feminine items while composing his operas. Chopin kept a supply of pencils on hand, not for writing, but for breaking; he claimed it helped stimulate his creativity. Too many artists have relied on alcohol and other drugs for inspiration.

Such tales of obsessive behavior are at least partly responsible for the perception of artists as megalomaniacs on the verge of insanity. Aristotle himself defined talent as either a happy gift of nature or a strain of madness. Or as William Blake put it,

> All pictures that's Painted with Sense and
>   with Thought
> Are painted by Madmen, as sure as a Groat;
> For the Greatest the Fool is the Pencil more
>   blest,
> And when they are drunk they always paint
>   best.[19]

There is disagreement even among artists that inspiration is the fundamental component of talent. The great Russian playwright Anton Chekhov insisted, "If an artist boasted to me of having written a story without a previously settled design, but by inspiration, I should call him a lunatic."[20]

The Case for Science.   Only recently has science begun to take on the challenge of penetrating the mystique surrounding artistic talent. While intriguing data have been uncovered, a full equation for a human physiology of talent is far from complete. Attracted to artists' obsessive tendencies, Freud attempted to determine the source of their creativity. Eventually he gave up in frustration. "The nature of artistic attainment," he wrote, "is psychoanalytically inaccessible to us."[21]

In the last few years, however, more sophisticated methods of neuroscience are revealing what parts of the brain function artistically. Positron Emission Tomography (PET) scans are being used to examine the brain during the creative process to actually "see" what areas are most active. These scans have shown the right side of the brain is more proficient at pattern recognition and spatial perception, indicating a preferred physiology for spatial artists. The left side of the brain controls reading, writing, and speech, favoring literary and performing artists. Both hemispheres, however, interact and share functions in many ways not yet fully determined. Surprisingly, research has uncovered evidence that the frontal lobe may be the region most crucial in overall creativity, primarily because of the high density of **opiate receptors,** nerve sites for the reception and processing of the body's natural and powerful pleasure chemicals called **endorphins.** Short for "endogenous morphines," endorphins are capable of producing natural highs similar to those induced by cocaine, opium, and alcohol. This biochemical link to talent has been investigated by Candace Pert at the National Institute of Mental Health. Pert notes that a variety of stimuli such as exercise, laughter, and even chocolate can cause the body to release endorphins producing a "creative high."[22] In his own inimitable fashion, comedian Robin Williams sees the connection between endorphins and creativity as magnificently Darwinian: "It's like *Bing!,* this is part of evolution. Eventually the brain figured out . . . 'If you create, we'll reinforce you. This and sex.' . . . That means creation is a drug! It is a drug and it was designed that way, evolutionwise, to make that *Bing!*"[23]

The PET scan's ability to "see" brain activity has also revealed other intriguing aspects of human imagination and creativity. Dr. Gottfied Schlaug of Washington's Beth Israel Hospital reports that brain scans of thirty classically trained musicians revealed that those with perfect pitch—the ability to identify the sound of an isolated musical note—have a greatly enlarged left brain structure called the panum temporale. Brain experts said the finding is the first that specifically and systematically relates a structure of the brain to an artistic talent.[24] At London's Institute of Neurology, Dr. Richard Frackowiak, a professor of cognitive neurology, used brain scans to discover an anatomical explanation for certain kinds of imagination experienced by athletes and performing artists. He found that subjects who imagined performing or playing turned on about 80 percent of the brain circuitry they used when they actually performed or played at their sport. "All the brain areas dealing with movement activate," explained Frackowiak, "except for the region associated with the final command that says 'Go.'" The scientific implication may be that imagination is 80 percent of reality.[25]

Another device being used to look for the source of creativity is the computer. Experts in "artificial intelligence" (AI) maintain the human mind is a kind of machine, and the artist's mind, by extension, is a machine that produces art. "Our goal is to come up with an *algorithmic* definition of creativity," write cognitive scientists Roger Schank and Christopher Owens. They seek to demystify talent, to break down what artists do into "a certain set of cognitive skills" that can be computerized.[26]

The brain is not the only organ that figures prominently in the creative profile of an artist. The rhythmic structure inherent in poetry, music, and dance is directly related to the heart, which beats in a strict iambic pattern. Artists who claim they put "heart" into their work may be revealing an important physiological component of talent. Metabolic rate and endocrine function have also been shown to affect the creative state. Of course, the intricacies of muscularity and physical coordination are crucial to spatial as well as performing artists: the former must have dexterous hands and fingers to manipulate the tools of painting, drawing, and sculpting; the latter must have the endurance and strength of legs, hands, and voices.

Complex psychology, chemistry, and physiology raise these questions: Are artists born, or are they made? Is talent inherent, or can it be developed? Some empirical studies have demonstrated a statistical hereditary link between the number of great artists who had similarly talented parents. Still, the complicated task of gene mapping has yet to find a specific location related to the capacity for creativity.

In the ongoing analysis, evidence shows the "gift" of artistic talent is determined by an interconnecting variety of factors as spiritual as the soul, as emotional as the heart, as mundane as rotten apples, and as physiological as the opiate receptors clustered in the frontal lobes of the brain.

Measuring Talent

Perhaps the best way to understand artistic talent is as a special kind of intelligence that empowers creative imagination. Intelligence is traditionally measured according to the IQ, or intelligence quotient scale, in which an individual's score is determined by standardized testing for mathematical reasoning and verbal comprehension. Versions of these intelligence tests have come under some sharp criticism because they fail to take into account culturally diverse backgrounds, conventions, and values. The tests also fail to account for the individualistic, optional/associational thinking of artists and the attendant skills they develop.

A person's "creativity quotient," if it could be measured, would be found to vary significantly from the IQ score. In fact, many great artists have done poorly in traditional school subjects. Playwright George Bernard Shaw and poet William

Butler Yeats were both poor spellers. John Lennon spoke for generations of young artists when he described his classroom frustration:

> People like me are aware of their so-called genius at ten, eight, nine . . . I always wondered, "Why has nobody discovered me? In school, didn't they see that I'm more clever than anybody in this school? That the teachers are stupid, too? That all they had was information that I didn't need." It was obvious to me. Why didn't they put me in art school? Why didn't they train me? I was different, I was always different. Why didn't anybody notice me?[27]

Like John Lennon's teachers, many scholars still have trouble believing that Shakespeare, who had no formal education beyond grammar school, could have been the author of such great plays; they are convinced only a more educated and therefore more cultivated person could have penned them.

In his book *Frames of Mind,* Howard Gardner presents his **theory of multiple intelligences** that seeks to account for the divergent mental and physiological proclivities—or talents—that define each person. Gardner proposes six categories of intelligence, each of which perceives the world in a different way, each deserving its own recognition.

> *Linguistic intelligence,* which is possessed by literary artists as well as writers of all types, understands the world in terms of words.
> *Musical intelligence* understands the world through a developed perception of the organization of sounds.
> *Logical mathematical intelligence* sees the world in terms of causal relationships between phenomena. It is possessed by philosophers, scientists, and mathematicians.
> *Spatial intelligence* is possessed by visual artists, designers, theatre directors, and athletic coaches who perceive the world in terms of the arrangement of objects.
> *Body/kinesthetic intelligence* is possessed by actors, dancers, and athletes who perceive and describe the world in terms of the people around them; they are acutely aware of the physical presence of others.
> *Personal intelligence* defines the perceptions of those who are primarily sensitive to the feelings of others. Caregivers such as doctors, nurses, social workers, and teachers are in this category.[28]

For parents concerned about the success of their children in school, the question should not be, "How smart is my child?" According to the theory of multiple intelligences it should be, "How is my child smart?"

For artists, their particular categories of intelligence are reflected not only in the ways they perceive and understand the world, but in the various ways they render it. Jean-Paul Sartre reported spending his childhood mimicking the talk of adults before fulfilling his destiny as a writer. The father of existentialist philosophy defined himself in terms of his talent: "By writing I was existing."[29]

Composer Igor Stravinsky's earliest memories of the street of his childhood home were of noises of wheels and horses and the whip cracks of coachmen. Michelangelo's spatial intelligence enabled him to see any object once—even the paintings of others—and re-create them later, totally from memory. It is said he never repeated anything of his own, since he remembered everything he had ever done. British actor Nicol Williamson says his mind is constantly filled with memories of the ways people fiddle with objects, such as a pack of matches.[30]

Skill, Training, and Practice

It does not seem to require much skill to fiddle with a pack of matches. The truth is that while part of an artist's talent is conceptual and lies within the imagination, the actual rendering relies on skills that are developed through training and practice. Thus a painter must have precise motor skills in the arm, hand, and fingers for brush manipulation, as well as expertise in paint chemistry and pigment combination. A musician must possess not only an ear for sound, but a mathematical knowledge of rhythm, timing, harmony, counterpoint, and orchestration, as well as accomplished motor skills for manipulating musical instruments. Writers must be practiced in word usage including the rules of grammar, syntax, composition, rhythm, and rhyme, and possess significant communication skills and a large vocabulary. Opera singers, in addition to other musical skills, must develop vocal elasticity, breath control, articulation, knowledge of foreign languages, and a perfect sense of pitch.

Such skills require training and continual, laborious practice—the least romantic aspect of artistic creativity. One need only think of childhood admonitions to "practice your piano" to elicit a groan of boredom and impatience. Composers such as Schubert, Tchaikovsky, and Beethoven perfected their talent by spending many hours practicing musical exercises including the incessant copying of the music of other composers. Theatre artists spend countless hours rehearsing a play before presenting it to the public. Writers claim their talent would atrophy without daily exercise; "No day without a line" is their oft-quoted motto.

While artists understand the necessity for training and practice, the public does not see this fundamental aspect of the creative process. When a work of art is skillfully rendered, the public perception of it is in the effortless form of a direct bond with the creative imagination.

Responding to Art

In the creative process the artist always imagines the presence of an ideal spectator. When the work is complete, the hope is that this hypothetical audience will appear. The spectator's response gives a work of art meaning, validates its worth, and gives potential immortality to the creative imagination.

The Question of Meaning

Because of the symbolic nature of art, one of the first responses to any work is in the form of a question: "What does it mean?" Variations of this question are "What's the artist trying to say?" "What's the point?" "What's the theme?" For most great works of art, it is impossible to get a single correct answer.

A great work of art is like a great moment in history; it means many different things to many different people. Consider the Crusades. Were they glorious battles waged to recapture the Holy Land for Christianity? Or were they inglorious invasions by infidel hordes bent on the desecration of Islam's holiest shrines? The answer depends on your point of view; the impartial historian, the devout Christian, and the Muslim will each have a different response.

The range of views concerning greater and lesser works of art is similarly divided. Are the patriotic marches of John Phillip Sousa more stirring than the symphonies of Beethoven? Is *The Adventures of Huckleberry Finn* a racist novel or a call for racial harmony and equality that was ahead of its time? Are the Rambo films jingoistic propaganda for American adventurism or depictions of the value of patriotism? Is *Death of a Salesman* a play about a son who was tragically let down by his father, or about a father who was let down by his son? Is the film *Wayne's World* an adolescent inanity or a clever satire on obsessive consumerism? Is the *Mona Lisa* smiling or smirking?

It might be thought the original artist should best be able to settle the question of meaning in the work. Inevitably, however, the explanations of artists concerning their works prove as unsatisfying as public interpretations. Isadora Duncan "spoke" for all artists when she responded to a question concerning the meaning of one of her dances by dancing it again. "If I could tell you what it is, I would not have danced it," she said.[31] For artists, their art *is* the explanation. Their creations are their most articulate forms of communication.

The Value of Art

While the question of meaning may be disputable or irresolvable, every work of art has some value. On one level a work of art has certain **formal values** in which its significance is defined in terms of the excellence of its structure, design, or composition. On a more subjective level, a work of art also has complex **functional values,** consisting of what it will generate in terms of enjoyment, instruction, inspiration, or monetary return.

Entertainment.   Much art is valued solely for its worth as entertainment, that is, as it helps us pass the time pleasantly. Pleasure refers to engaging our emotions compellingly. It means successfully provoking smiles, uproarious laughter, spine-tingling suspense, gripping horror, passionate romance, even cheap thrills. Marx Brothers films, the TV series *I Love Lucy,* and Stephen King novels are all highly regarded for their entertainment values alone.

Ironically, art that has high value as entertainment is often denigrated as a waste of time—like eating junk food when a balanced low-fat, high-fiber diet would be much healthier, if not as much fun. "Redeeming social value" is the artistic standard of those who find little worth in pure entertainment. Interestingly, recent scientific research has shown that pure emotional response such as laughing, crying, swooning, and even screaming in fright can be of substantial therapeutic value. Studies at Stanford University's medical school show that mirth and playfulness increase the release of endorphins, diminish fear, anger, and depression, and provide good aerobic exercise that ventilates the lungs, leaving the muscles relaxed. In fact, patients at Stanford are advised to take a "humor inventory," and then collect their own library of tapes, gags, books, and cartoons that can dependably trigger laughter.[32] Conversely, studies at the University of Minnesota have shown that tears play an important role in health. The studies conclude that tears are unique to human beings as our natural excretory response to strong emotions. Like all other bodily fluids, tears are involved in removing, or washing away, harmful substances that build up in the body.[33] Specifically, tears wash away biochemicals that build up during stress—an important therapeutic function. These physiological benefits suggest an evolutionary value of our insatiable pursuit of entertainment. Our diversions, it seems, are a necessary component of our survival.

Exaltation.   As a function of art, exaltation is closely related to the effect of entertainment, but on a more psychologically complex and enduring level. Exaltation refers to the spiritual response that can be aroused by a work of art. If entertainment is associated with fundamental emotions such as mirth, sadness, or fright, then exaltation is associated with such responses as joy, elation, exhilaration, rapture, and glory. Exaltation is the value many place on the religious artworks of Leonardo da Vinci and Michelangelo. Travelers to Rome who have stood in the presence of the city's overwhelming number of Renaissance artworks have reported being overcome by the **Stendhal syndrome,** which causes disorientation, amnesia, and dizziness in the face of so much inspirational beauty. Named for the French author and world traveler Henri Stendhal (1783–1842), the syndrome also explains the reaction of the millions of moviegoers who, from their repeated viewings, have made cult classics out of such films as *The Wizard of Oz* and *The Rocky Horror Picture Show.* It also explains the artistic exaltation—some say mania—of teenagers who scream, swoon, and otherwise go crazy in the presence of pop music superstars.

Economics.   Art that has either great exaltation or great entertainment value can also be worth a great deal of money. The idea of art as currency to be traded, invested, and merchandised is a reality of economics. In 1990, for instance, actor Jack Nicholson was paid $60 million for his performance as the Joker in the film *Batman,* listed in the *Guinness Book of World Records* as the largest paycheck for a single film. Steven Spielberg, the Academy Award-winning director of *ET, Raiders of the Lost Ark, Jurassic Park,* and *Schindler's List,* remarked not immodestly, "I have a pretty good imagination. I've made a fortune off my imagination."[34]

ART AND MONEY

The estimated gross incomes of the twenty highest paid entertainers in 1994, as compiled by *Forbes* magazine.[35]

1. Steven Spielberg, $355 million
2. Oprah Winfrey, $105 million
3. Barney (Richard Leach, publisher, Sheryl Leach, creator), $84 million
4. Pink Floyd, $62 million
5. Bill Cosby, $60 million
6. Barbra Streisand, $57 million
7. Eagles, $56 million
8. David Copperfield, $55 million
9. Rolling Stones, $53 million
10. Harrison Ford, $44 million
11. Garth Brooks, $41 million
12. Billy Joel, $40 million
13. Michael Jackson, $38 million
14. Charles Schultz, $37 million
15. Sylvester Stallone, $37 million
16. Kevin Costner, $37 million
17. Aerosmith, $36 million
18. Michael Crichton, $35 million
19. Grateful Dead, $35 million
20. Siegfried & Roy, $34 million

The top twenty "lots" sold at auction between 1987 and 1995 as compiled by Christie's:

1. Vincent van Gogh, *Portrait of Gachet,* $82,500,000
2. Pierre-Auguste Renoir, *Au Moulin de la Galette,* $78,100,000
3. Vincent van Gogh, *Irises,* $53,900,000
4. Pablo Picasso, *Les Noces de Pierrette,* $51,650,000
5. Pablo Picasso, *Self-Portrait: Yo Picasso,* $47,850,000
6. Pablo Picasso, *Au Lapin Agile,* $40,700,000
7. Vincent van Gogh, *Sunflowers,* $39,921,750
8. Pablo Picasso, *Acrobate et jeune Arlequin,* $38,456,000
9. Jacopo da Carucci, *Portrait of Duke Cosimo de'Medici,* $35,200,000
10. Leonardo da Vinci, the *Codex Hammer,* $30,802,000
11. Paul Cezanne, *Nature Morte: Les Grosses Pommes,* $28,602,500
12. Vincent van Gogh, *Self-Portrait,* $26,400,000
13. Edouard Manet, *La rue Mosnier aux drapeaux,* $26,400,000
14. Pablo Picasso, *The Mirror,* $26,400,000
15. Pablo Picasso, *Maternité,* $24,750,000
16. Claude Monet, *Camille in the Meadow,* $24,300,000
17. Paul Gauguin, *In Olden Times,* $24,200,000
18. Pablo Picasso, *Les Tuileries,* $23,500,000
19. John Constable, *Lock,* $21,100,000
20. Willem de Kooning, *Interchange,* $20,900,000

Indeed, combined ticket, video, broadcast, and merchandising sales of his films are calculated in the billions of dollars. Spielberg's 1994 personal income from his cinematic creations has been estimated at $355 million. Like most successful performing artists, Spielberg reaps the financial benefits of his creations in his lifetime. In 1990, however, Dutch impressionist Vincent van Gogh's painting of sunflowers became a record holder when it sold at auction for nearly $40 million. The economic value of van Gogh's art, which he never realized in his lifetime, continues to increase.

The legal designation for such revenue-generating art is **intellectual property,** and its impact is calculated on local, national, and international economies. For instance, according to a study titled "The Arts as an Industry," the arts had a total economic impact of $9.8 billion on the New York-New Jersey region in 1992. The study examined five areas of the arts: Broadway and Off-Broadway commercial threatres; film and television production; nonprofit institutions; art galleries and auction houses; and tourism.[36] A national study commissioned by the International Intellectual Property Alliance, a consortium of trade groups, determined that moviemakers, musicians, and other creators of copyrighted works make up one of the fastest growing sectors of the U.S. economy, accounting for 3.74 percent of the nation's gross domestic product. These artistic "industries" contributed at least an estimated $45.8 billion in foreign sales to the U.S. economy in 1993, second only to motor vehicles and automotive parts.[37]

Edification.   The capacity of art to reveal information has long been considered one of its most valued attributes. Educators have always known that formal lessons are easier to comprehend when they are presented in the imaginative forms of art—pictures, stories, poems, or plays. For example, Spielberg's Academy Award-winning film *Schindler's List* probably did more to inform large numbers of people about the horrors and heroism during the Holocaust than all the history books, articles, and courses on the subject. Spielberg's film follows in the educational tradition of *Roots, Gandhi,* and *Dances with Wolves*, which informed mass audiences about important historical subjects.

The Power of Art

The combined values of art give it substantial effective power as a major tool of communication, commerce, and public opinion. **Bertolt Brecht** (1898–1956), one of the most politically active playwrights of the twentieth century, noted, "Art is not a mirror, it's a hammer. It does not reflect, it shapes."[38]

The potential of art to affect has to do with the suggestive power of **artistic truth.** Scientific truth is based on *facts,* observable phenomena that can stand the regimen of objective testing. Artistic truth, however, involves human *intuitions* about the world. The truth contained in a work of art is subject only to the emotional, commercial, or intellectual confirmation of its audience. Thus a political cartoon can be far more devastating to the career of an elected official than any number of reasoned, well-supported editorials. Harriet Beecher Stowe was designated by Abraham Lincoln as "the little woman who started the Civil War" with her antislavery novel *Uncle Tom's Cabin*. Folksinger Bob Dylan convinced a generation of young people that "The Times They Are a-Changin'." Shakespeare portrayed Richard III (in his play of the same name) as one of the most murderous, malicious villains who ever lived. Investigations by twentieth-century historians have shown, however, that there is little truth to Shakespeare's characterization of the English monarch. Yet the art has so overshadowed the historical facts that "conventional wisdom" will probably always perceive Richard III as evil incarnate.

Such is the power of art that in many cases the effect is to reverse the imitative process itself. When this phenomenon occurs, art not only imitates life, but life returns the favor and imitates art. Famed trial lawyer William Kunstler observed that in an attempt to keep the interest of jurors who have seen every John Grisham film, watched *Law and Order* religiously, and think . . . *And Justice for All* is representative of the way a trial is conducted, real lawyers are now utilizing techniques they see in movies and on TV.[39] A whole population of young Americans took to wearing coonskin caps when Walt Disney put one on his television version of Davy Crockett in the 1950s. Successive generations have grown sideburns like Elvis, saw *Saturday Night Fever* and made a craze out of disco dancing, and named countless pets "Snoopy" and "Garfield."

POWERFUL ARTISTIC TRUTH
Shakespeare turned Richard III into a fiend, and John Barrymore's villainous portrayal is one of many since the seventeenth century that have perpetuated this image of the English monarch.

The substantial power of art to influence human behavior in beneficial ways also suggests the power to corrupt, deceive, and harm. Attorneys have filed lawsuits against record companies and screenplay producers claiming songs and dramas incited their clients to commit crimes. Hollywood has been blamed for, among other social problems, contributing to the increasing number of teenage pregnancies by depicting a world of sex without consequences in which no one gets pregnant, no one gets sick, and no one has to get up in the middle of the night to feed a baby. One outraged producer complained recently, "Can you imagine that people are lobbying to have Tom Cruise use a condom? Tom Cruise?"[40] Warnings about the corruptive potential of art go back to the earliest records of civilization. The second of the Ten Commandments adjures, "Thou shalt not make unto thee any graven image, any likeness of any thing that is in heaven above, or that is in the earth beneath, or that is in the water beneath the earth."

Art, Commerce, and Government

Perhaps no two segments of modern society have understood the power of art as have merchandisers and governments. Merchandisers have used every type of art to sell their products. And no politician of the media age is likely to be elected without a staff of artists who create pictures, songs, and small plays to create an image. It is no wonder so many artists find themselves in the service of advertising agencies.

Art and Government.   Governments from the dawn of civilization have sought to use (or suppress) the substantial power of art to ensure their survival. Such use is evident in the mild political socialization of elementary school "Thanksgiving" plays as much as it was in the coercive dictates of Josef Stalin, who, in 1934, decreed that the only permissible Soviet artistic style was "socialist realism." Soviet artists creating works in a style that failed to properly glorify the collectivist ideals of the workers' state often found themselves without a livelihood, jailed, or worse. Joseph Goebbels, Hitler's propaganda minister, spread murderous anti-Semitism by producing Nazi hate films such as *The Eternal Jew* and *The Rothschilds.* "What a good idea it was," Goebbels boasted, "to have taken possession of the film industry on behalf of the Reich several years ago!"[41] Sixty years later schools participate in a "Holocaust Education Program" in which Steven Spielberg permits children to see *Schindler's List* free of charge. To date, more than a million students from Germany to California have participated in the project.

At the same time governments have supported the arts with subsidies, they have often imposed strict censorship and suppression of the arts to serve their purposes. From 1558 until 1968, English law banned the unfavorable portrayal of the monarchy and the clergy in stage plays. During the fascist regime in Spain, dictator Francisco Franco forbade the display of Picasso's *Guernica* in the country. Picasso lived in exile until the generalissimo's death in 1976. For its 1994 U.S. study, "Artistic Freedom Under Attack," the advocacy group Artsave analyzed 104

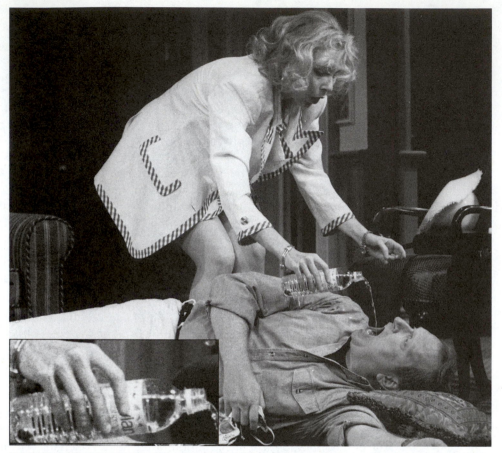

BOTTLED WATER ON STAGE *Merchandisers understand the power of art to persuade, and many pay exorbitant fees to have their products show up in films and recently stage plays with the potential to reach a mass audience. The makers of Evian bottled water paid a generous fee for a nightly appearance in Neil Simon's Off-Broadway hit* London Suite.

challenges to artistic expression in drawings, paintings, sculpture, photography, theatre, performance art, film, and television and found that censorship prevailed in 78 percent of the cases.[42]

Government attempts to impose its will on the creativity of artists have led to controversies and crises of national and even international dimensions. The most extreme recent example was the death sentence imposed on author Salman Rushdie for the sentiments expressed in his novel *The Satanic Verses,* which were officially decreed "blasphemous" by many Islamic governments in 1988. Yet at the same time that governments, fearing the power of art, seek to dictate, control, or ban it from creation and consumption, it is often through art that the records of

By permission of Mike Luckovich and Creators Syndicate.

great civilizations are preserved. The nineteenth-century American dramatist Booth Tarkington wrote,

> The degree of civilization to which a nation attains depends not upon its commerce, not upon its government, and not even upon its achievement in science. A country could be perfectly governed, immensely powerful and without poverty. Yet if it produced nothing of its own architecture, sculpture, music, painting and books, it would someday pass into the twilight of history leaving only the traces of a credible political record.[43]

Evaluating Art

In evaluating art, who is to say what is "good"? Governments, merchandisers, and artists themselves, it has been shown, have their own agenda and standards that are often at odds with those of their audiences. The judgments of critics, supposedly insightful, articulate, knowledgeable experts, are often sought to help consumers make decisions about investing time and money in works of art. But critics themselves must be evaluated to determine their standards and qualifications for making their judgments.

THE NATIONAL ENDOWMENT FOR THE ARTS

In 1965 Congress passed legislation to establish the National Endowment for the Arts as a federal agency to make grants of funds to individual artists, arts organizations, and projects with potential for growth and significant audience appeal. At the same time, the federal government encouraged each state and municipality to establish its own **arts council** for similar support on a local level. Most not-for-profit arts organizations such as regional and community theatres, symphony orchestras, dance companies, art galleries, and museums, as well as thousands of individual artists, have been subsidized by NEA grants. Government appropriations to the NEA have been in the range of $110 million to $175 million per year. That is less than .02 of 1 percent of the federal budget. It works out to a tax assessment of 55 cents per person. Other democratic governments spend far more per person: Sweden, $45; Germany, $39; France, $35; The Netherlands, $33; Canada, $29; and the United Kingdom, $16. These countries view the government subsidy of the arts as an essential investment in the cultural life of their citizens. Just as governments fund libraries to preserve and disseminate literary art, they must also support its visual and performing arts. The violin virtuoso Isaac Stern made the economic argument this way: "We are willing to have our mail subsidized. We are willing to have our roads subsidized. How much are we willing to pay to have the soul healthy?"[44]

Attempts to abolish the National Endowment for the Arts have been fueled by controversial grants that have become the center of national attention. Four particularly controversial projects—a display inviting patrons of an art institute to walk on an American flag, a gallery showing of homoerotic photographs, a color photo of a crucifix suspended in a jar of urine, and a "scarification ritual" by an HIV-positive performance artist prompted Congress to propose laws restricting the Endowment's discretion in awarding grants. In fact, since its inception only 40 of the nearly 100,000 projects funded by the NEA have proved controversial on moral or political grounds. The overwhelming majority of NEA grants have been allocated as seed money for not-for-profit community arts centers, to bring dance and theatre to children in rural areas, and to support promising unknown writers. Before the creation of the NEA in 1965 there were only 37 professional dance companies in America. Today, partly because of the NEA, there are nearly 300. Prior to the NEA, there were only 27 opera companies and 4 regional professional theatres. Today, there are 110 and 400, respectively. Still, attempts to abolish the agency continue, despite the fact that a 60 to 37 percent majority of the American people firmly support federal government financing of the arts.[45]

Many consumers are rightfully suspect of anyone—government official or otherwise—who presumes to tell them what is good art. They hold that the only real critic is the audience, who says what is good by its patronage. Popular success, however, as a standard for judging art can also be problematical. When applied, such creations as *Gilligan's Island,* Day-Glo-on-velvet paintings of Elvis Presley, Agatha Christie's long-running play *The Mousetrap,* and Bobby McFerrin's 1988 best-selling pop song "Don't Worry, Be Happy!" would rank among the greatest works of art ever created. For artists, popular success has proven a bane as well as boon. As Aldous Huxley once said, "Success—the bitch goddess, success . . . demands strange sacrifices from those who worship her."[46]

It remains to be seen if the tastes and judgments of either popular audiences or learned critics will extend over the long term to become the standards of an entire culture. Achieving the status of a **masterpiece** is an accomplishment reserved for precious few artworks. Such works, accorded the special protection of national treasures, are rightfully deemed "priceless" and "irreplaceable," and become some of the few artifacts of humanity to achieve immortality.

The Need for Artistic Literacy

Encountering, comprehending, and appreciating artistic masterpieces take preparation and education. For example, it is fairly easy to appreciate the physical comedy, exciting action, and bold passions in an expert performance of a Shakespearean play. But to savor the complete effect, a theatregoer must understand such aspects as idiomatic Elizabethan language, blank verse, the history of English monarchs, and other topical references. The reaction of the unprepared or artistically illiterate—those, for example, who do not study classical mythology, world history, or great literature—is often to dismiss great works of art as obscure.

The payoff of being prepared to encounter artistic masterpieces—that is, of achieving artistic literacy—is substantial and life altering. Artistic literacy opens up new realms of human understanding, emotional stimulation, and pure aesthetic pleasure of the highest order. Artistic literacy cements a bond with the original imaginative spirit through which the spectator becomes an inextricable part of the creative process. It is this love of the creative imagination that unites the patrons of *Gilligan's Island* with those of Shakespeare's *Hamlet.*

The Creative Process and Theatre Arts

Having established a context for understanding art, artists, audiences, and the creative process, the examination of the specifics of the theatrical imagination proceeds.

The method of this book is to promote theatrical literacy by identifying the theatrical imagination within the definition and various categories of art and by examining the making of theatre art as a function of the creative process, from

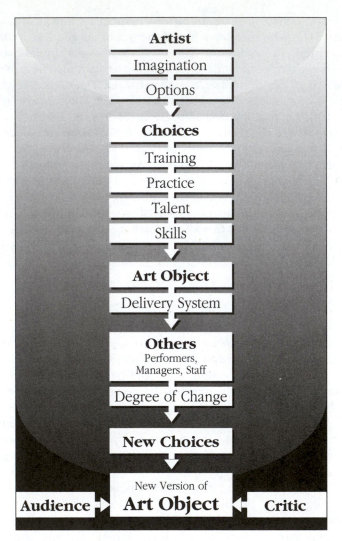

FIGURE 1–3   THE CREATIVE PROCESS

the initial dramatic images to the final choices delivered to and received by the audience (see Figure 1–3).

This method provides the artistic literacy for addressing important questions concerning the theatrical imagination:

What is the relationship between dramatic art (playwriting) and theatre arts (its delivery system)?
What kinds of art comprise theatre art?
How is theatre art imagined by the various artists?
What are the realms, the options, and the limits of the artists' choices?

How are their choices rendered?

What skills and training are needed to bring their choices to creation?

How is theatre art delivered to the audience?

What are the effects of new technology on the practice of theatre art?

How are these creations perceived by the audience and the critics?

What effects do they have on the audience?

How are theatrical creations ultimately valued?

Taken together, the answers comprise a detailed image of a performing art that is a composite creation of the imaginative best the fine arts have to offer.

AN ARTIST AT WORK

Pondering the Riddle of Creativity
by Daniel Coleman
[Excerpts reprinted from the *New York Times*][47]

In searching for an answer to the riddle of imagination—what makes creators create?—author Daniel Coleman interviewed psychologists who are taking a new approach to the quest: studying the moment of inspiration. Harvard Professor Howard Gardner found a pattern in the challenges artists face over a lifetime. By examining the lives of a handful of virtuosos, each of whose work transformed its field, Gardner formulated his "10-year rule" of creativity. Star Wars creator George Lucas was one of those virtuosos.

T. S. Eliot, who graduated from Harvard in 1910, had completed a draft of "The Waste Land" by 1921. Picasso, who left art school to live as a painter in Barcelona at 17, painted "Les Desmoiselles d'Avignon" at 26. Stravinsky, who began his apprenticeship as a composer with Rimsky-Korsakov in 1902, stunned the musical world with his score for "The Rite of Spring" just a decade later.

In the realm of American moviemaking, George Lucas entered film school in 1964 at the age of 20, finished his breakthrough movie *American Graffiti* just eight years later and turned to work on the *Star Wars* trilogy soon after that.

Typically high-level creators have come from geographical regions removed from the centers of power, and from families that valued discipline and achievement. "There's something to be said for being a big fish in a little pond when you're young," says Professor Gardner. "It gives you a certain feeling of invulnerability" that, along with self-discipline, shields an artist from the rebuffs that predictably assail every revolutionary creation.

Mr. Lucas, who grew up the son of a businessman in rural Modesto, Calif., stresses the importance of perseverance in his own success. "Persistence and tenacity are the reasons I've come this far," he said. "In film, especially when you are starting out, everyone says, no, you can't possibly do it that way."

That happened when Mr. Lucas was seeking financing for *American Graffiti*. "No one would touch it; it took two years of pounding on doors," said Mr. Lucas. "For one thing I was telling four separate stories simultaneously, intercutting them into a single whole. Now it's a standard style, especially on TV shows. Then it was an experiment in editing."

The second objection Mr. Lucas faced was to the film's soundtrack. "It was a musical montage. I structured each scene around a song. I took an operatic format and converted it to the modern cinematic medium. I was told it would be too disturbing, that people wouldn't sit still through 110 minutes of music."

But Mr. Lucas persevered, with the encouragement of close friends. That, too, Professor Gardner finds is a common element in the careers of the highly creative; they rapidly bond with a set of others who are exploring new terrain within their field, and who offer one another crucial support, exchanging ideas and boosting morale. For Mr. Lucas, the band included his mentor, Francis Ford Coppola, Steven Spielberg, Martin Scorsese, and Brian De Palma, all starting out as young filmmakers.

Until then, Mr. Lucas recalls, the film industry had been largely closed to those who were not shaped by the culture of the studios.

Such marginality is another theme in the lives of the highly creative, Professor Gardner finds, even after their breakthrough has won them acceptance and influence. Continuing to seek a marginal status helps the creator maintain crucial freshness. "Whenever they risked becoming members of the establishment in their field, they would again shift course," says Professor Gardner.

Professor Gardner finds another pattern: a second breakthrough, which, he says, is "also noteworthy, but less dramatic—a kind of coming home that places the person's work in a broader frame, reconciling it with basic values."

To be sure, Mr. Lucas has made several cinematic breakthroughs, not least is his *Star Wars* trilogy in which he created a modern myth.

KEEPING THE MAINSTREAM AT A DISTANCE   *George Lucas at Skywalker Ranch, his film studio in Marin County, far from Hollywood.*

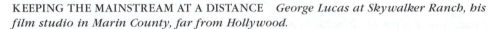

HARRY FENT, HUMAN BEING

DISCLAIMER: MR. FENT IS PURELY A CREATION OF THE ARTIST'S IMAGINATION, AND ANY RESEMBLANCE TO PERSONS LIVING OR DEAD IS PURELY COINCIDENTAL. ALSO, ONE SHOULD NOT ASSUME THAT THIS DEPICTION OF A HUMAN BEING IS AN INDICTMENT OF ALL HUMAN BEINGS PER SE. FURTHER, THE ARTIST DOES NOT ADVOCATE THE ABOVE MANNER OF DRESS, HAIR STYLE, OR BODY LANGUAGE. AND THE FACT THAT THIS DRAWING IS RENDERED TWO-DIMENSIONALLY AND IN BLACK-AND-WHITE DOES NOT PRECLUDE POSSIBLE FUTURE COLOR OR HOLOGRAPHIC RENDERINGS. FINALLY, THE ARTIST APOLOGIZES FOR WRITING THIS DISCLAIMER IN ENGLISH ONLY. TRANSLATIONS INTO OTHER TONGUES ARE AVAILABLE UPON REQUEST.

Drawing by Jack Ziegler © 1989 *The New Yorker* Magazine, Inc.

SUMMARY

1. Imagination is the human ability to make mental images of how reality might be. The extent to which such images can be manifested is called *creativity*.

2. Art is the imitation of something natural or imagined. It is not the real thing, but the human imitation of it.

3. Realistic art attempts to reproduce as closely as possible the appearances and/or sounds of things in nature. Nonrealistic art seeks to imitate with a minimum of recognizable references, depending for effect on the evocative use of symbolic patterns and juxtaposed sounds, shapes, or words.

4. Applied arts refer to creations valued for their usefulness. Fine art describes creations with primarily aesthetic qualities.

5. Only the performing arts require other artists to deliver the creation of the original artists to an audience.

6. Talent is the artist's instinct, rational intelligence, emotional sensitivity, and practiced motor ability for making successful, imaginative choices.

7. Art has both formal and functional values, the latter consisting of what it may generate in terms of entertainment, exaltation, economics, or edification. Art is a powerful tool of communication, commerce, and public opinion.

8. Appreciating artistic masterpieces often requires preparation and education. Artistic literacy allows new levels of understanding, stimulation, and aesthetic pleasure.

CHOICES

1. Make a list of the most important works of art you own. Describe what they imitate. Are they more realistic or abstract? Are they autographic or allographic? If allographic, do you understand the code sufficiently to comprehend the original work? How many persons were necessary to deliver each work of art to you? What makes you choose the kinds of art you possess?

2. Imitate one of your most powerful nightmares or an excruciating headache in either a painting, a poem, a sketch, or a scene. What is your choice for being the most effective? Which art form is the most difficult for you to work with?

3. Finding the meaning of art often involves translating an abstract form or code into recognizable objects and ideas. What does the Vietnam memorial wall in Washington, D.C., mean to you? What does it imitate? What is its value as exaltation? Can you learn anything from it? Research its cost and its present estimated monetary value.

4. What choices do you make in selecting your clothes every day? How would you characterize these choices? How would you characterize your instructor's choices? Is either selection "art"? How much inspiration is involved in your choices? How much do you credit to skill and practice?

5. Which of Howard Gardner's "multiple intelligences" best characterizes your perception of the world? Which best characterizes other members of your family? Is there a genetic connection? What is the most entertaining or creative thing you do?

6. Consider your position or belief on a controversial social or ethical issue. Choose an art form and describe or make a particular work of art that would be most effective in persuading those opposed to your position to change their minds and agree with you.

7. Take your humor inventory. Analyze your collection of tapes, gags, books, and cartoons that can dependably trigger your laughter. Do you ever use this collection for therapeutic purposes? Provide specific examples.

8. Take an endorphin test by imagining the following: the sound of chalk squeaking across a blackboard; embracing your favorite movie star; chocolate mocha mousse cake; a red rose sparkling with dew; smashing your thumb with a hammer. Describe in detail the physical and emotional reactions you have to each image. Were your reactions of such intensity that you would describe them as 80 percent of reality?

THE
Tragicall Historie of
HAMLET

Prince of Denmarke

By William Shake-speare.

As it hath beene diuerse times acted by his Highnesse seruants in the Cittie of London : as also in the two Vniuersities of Cambridge and Oxford, and else-where

At London printed for N.L. and Iohn Trundell.
1603.

Cover page from the 1603 published edition of Hamlet, *and Keanu Reeves as the Danish prince in the Manitoba Theatre Centre production.*

The play's the thing . . .

Hamlet, *Act II, scene ii*

The Dramatic Imagination

PREVIEW

Imagine that out of nowhere, a bolt of dramatic inspiration strikes you with a sure-fire, can't-miss idea for a blockbuster play.

Flushed from the release of a flood of endorphins to the opiate receptors of your frontal lobes, you rush to the office of a world-famous producer. Graciously admitted to the office by a kind and solicitous secretary (remember, anything is possible in your imagination), you meet the theatrical entrepreneur of countless Broadway hits, and of more than a few flops. The producer sits back in the chair and stares at the ceiling as you breathlessly explain the idea for your play.

"It's a new, updated, musical drama, comedy, adventure-type romance version of *The Adventures of Robin Hood.* It'll have terrific sword fighting, great love songs between Robin and Marian, and this chorus of merry men, dancing in tights and fighting with their swords, quarterstaffs, and longbows. And the title—wait'll you hear this—will be TWANG! Get it? TWANG, like, you know, the sound of a bowstring! What d'ya think?"

The grizzled impresario pauses thoughtfully, sighs deeply, and then tells you just like so many before you, "It's a great idea, kid. Put it on paper. 'Cause if it ain't on the page, it ain't on the stage."

Such crude but sage advice is a way of saying the dramatic imagination precedes the theatrical imagination; before unleashing the financial and artistic resources of the theatre, the original artwork—the play—must be complete.

But what exactly is this "it"—this play that is supposed to be put on paper if it wants to see light on a stage? And where and when is "it" a play? On the page? On the stage? This chapter addresses these fundamental questions concerning the nature of drama.

The Definition of Drama

Anyone who attempts to describe a play to someone else begins something like this:

"It's about these two young people who fall in love, get married, and commit suicide because their parents . . ."

"It shows this Danish prince who struggles to avenge his father's murder, but he just can't decide how."

"There's this salesman, see, who's trying to prove he's worth something, but his son . . ."

"It's about this religious hypocrite who dupes this guy out of everything he owns . . ."

"There's this psycho woman who tries to get her revenge on this married guy for this one-night stand . . ."

"This android from the future tries to terminate this woman named Sarah Connor because she . . ."

"This bomb-squad cop tries to save a speeding city bus full of innocent passengers from a mad bomber intent on revenge for . . ."

All of these descriptions *(Romeo and Juliet, Hamlet, Death of a Salesman, Tartuffe, Fatal Attraction, The Terminator, Speed)* contain the two definitive requisites of dramatic art: *human beings* engaged in *action.*

Imitating Human Action

The Human Factor.   All arts are capable of imitating human beings. Da Vinci's *Last Supper,* Michelangelo's *David,* Poe's "Annabel Lee," Dickens' *Oliver Twist,* Tchaikovsky's *The Nutcracker,* and Lennon and McCartney's "Eleanor Rigby" all testify to the potential of the graphic, plastic, literary, and performing arts to portray complex aspects of human life. On the other hand, practitioners of these arts have also created many works that have only marginal concern with human beings. One of van Gogh's best paintings is of sunflowers. For the city of Chicago, Claes Oldenburg created the "Bat Column," a gigantic sculpture that resembles a huge baseball bat. In her famous poem Gertrude Stein insists "a rose is a rose is a rose." Tchaikovsky's greatest ballet is about a dying swan; Rimsky-Korsakov used music to imitate the flight of the bumblebee; and one of the more distinctive American dances of the 1960s and 1970s was the "funky chicken." Drama, however, is distinctive in that it imitates *only* human beings. The titles of most plays refer to the activities of real or imagined persons. It is more than merely custom that published scripts always begin with a listing of the **dramatis personae,** the dramatic characters in the play. Imagining human beings, then, is the first order of business of the dramatic imagination.

THE ESSENTIAL HUMANITY OF DRAMATIC CHARACTERS   *Even animal and other nonhuman characters in drama are* **anthropomorphized:** *they are created and portrayed in terms of human qualities. The Cowardly Lion in* The Wiz *(the updated musical version of* The Wizard of Oz*) demonstrates the nature of human courage, not the instinctive feline variety. Similarly, Big Bird is an innocent, small child. And building a "droid" like R2D2 in* Star Wars, *with the capacity for adorable friendship, is still the stuff of science fiction.*

The Action Factor.   The word *drama* is derived from the ancient Greek *dromenon,* which means "the thing done," and from the Latin *dran,* which means "to do." Essential threatre terminology relates to the concept of drama as action: "acts," "acting," "actors"—even the more generic "show," "play," and "player"—all refer to doings and doers. When a director is ready to begin a rehearsal, the call is not for pictures, sound, poses, or dialogue but for "Action!"

Drama is the imitation of human actions. The dramatic imagination conceives of imitating with performers in order to capture a few moments of the human journey. Even the word *play* (which is a synonym for a drama) means "imaginative doings."

Dramatic Conflict.   The essence of dramatic action is conflict. It is not coincidental that the descriptions of plays at the start of this chapter use contentious, active verbs such as "struggle," "avenge," "battle," "fight," "prove," "dupe," "race," and "terminate." Unlike narrative literature, drama is not conducive to lengthy description. Drama is a cauldron for the struggle of opposing human urges carried out in limited space and limited time. Dramatic conflict is invariably a high-stakes struggle with life-and-death consequences. Thus Romeo and Juliet, like so many other "star-crossed lovers," fight a passionate but suicidal battle against their own families to consummate their love. Hamlet duels to the death—his own and those of his family and friends—to avenge his father's murder. Oedipus relentlessly pursues his father's murderer, only to discover that he, himself, unknowingly committed the crime. Even the characters in comic plays struggle desperately against each other in the belief they are fighting for their lives, loves, dignity, or reputations. In Neil Simon's *The Odd Couple* best friends and roommates Oscar and Felix fight to the point of "divorce" over the inanities of daily living:

OSCAR: If you want to live through this night, you'd better tie me up and lock your doors and windows.

FELIX: *(Sits at table with great pretense of calm.)* All right, Oscar, I'd like to know what's happened.

OSCAR: *(Moves towards him.)* What's *happened?*

FELIX: *(Hurriedly slides over to the next chair.)* That's right. Something must have caused you to go off the deep end like this. What is it? Something I said? Something I did? Heh? What?

OSCAR: *(Pacing.)* It's nothing you said. It's nothing you did. It's *you!*

FELIX: I see. . . . Well, that's plain enough.

OSCAR: I could make it plainer but I don't want to hurt you.

FELIX: What is it, the cooking? The cleaning? The crying?

OSCAR: *(Moving towards him.)* I'll tell you exactly what it is. It's the cooking, cleaning and crying. . . . It's the talking in your sleep, it's the moose calls that open your ears at two o'clock in the morning. . . . I can't take it any more, Felix. I'm crackin' up. Everything you do irritates me. And when you're not here, the things I know you're gonna do when you come in irritate me. . . . You leave me little notes on my pillow. I told you a hundred times, I can't stand little notes on my pillow. "We're all out of

ELEMENTAL DRAMA   *The intense conflict in David Mamet's controversial* Oleanna *develops in a terrifyingly short time when a college professor and a female student sit down to discuss her grades. Innocuous remarks become damning accusations of sexual harassment that give way to heated, violent assault. "People might want to know," explained Mamet, "why these two characters are at each other's throats. Well, you have a two-character drama. One person is a man and one person is a woman. Two people in opposition. That's what drama means."*[1]

	Corn Flakes. F.U." . . . It took me three hours to figure out that F.U. was Felix Ungar. . . . It's not your fault, Felix. It's a rotten combination.
FELIX:	I get the picture.
OSCAR:	That's just the frame. The picture I haven't even painted yet. . . . I got a typewritten list in my office of the "Ten Most Aggravating Things You Do That Drive Me Berserk." . . .[2]

Rather than aberrations, the conflicts of drama are innate to the human struggle for survival in a world of hostile, changing forces.

The Origin of the Dramatic Impulse

The Drama of Thought

The impulse to portray the human journey with active, vocal characters is probably as old as the need to communicate on a higher functional level. Aristotle pointed out the uniquely human disposition for imitation, and researchers today have also concluded the impulse for drama is innate. In her book *Invisible Guests: The Development of Imaginal Dialogues,* psychotherapist Mary Watkins points out that the dramatic impulse is evident in the imaginary characters with whom we carry on all sorts of fanciful conversations. "All persons' thought is dramatic," Watkins writes. "It is inhabited by voices and filled with imaginal conversations. . . . Plays may be going on in our thoughts, but they haven't been written out, and there is no audience in attendance."[3]

Ritual Drama

Drama for an audience most likely started as campfire reenactments of successful hunts. Those who had participated in the pursuit and kill selected the most important and exciting parts for reenactment. Choosing incidents of action and assembling them into a unified portrayal constitute the origin of the dramatic imagination.

From campfire reenactments it is only a short leap of the imagination to the **ritual enactment** of an imaginary occurrence of a future event. Enactments that seemed to bring about the desired results developed into rituals, many of which evolved over centuries into complicated dramatic events tied to important religious observances. Studies of ancient artifacts indicate that Ice Age human beings may have performed rituals 30,000 years ago. Cave paintings from 20,000 years ago are the first actual records of important ceremonial performances. From about 2500 B.C. actual texts survive describing ritualistic dramas performed by ancient civilizations in Egypt, Sumeria, Babylon, and Canaan. Despite the fact that these societies existed for hundreds—in the case of Egypt, for thousands—of years, none ever took the crucial step of separating the dramatic function of their texts from the more important ritual purpose. It is not surprising, therefore, that the *dramatis personae* of these rituals were not persons at all, but the supernatural beings of their religions.

Drama as Art

To reach the point at which dramatic enactments were valued for their aesthetic qualities required a society more concerned with human aspects of existence than with the divine. Drama as art was invented by the world's first humanistic society—the ancient Greek culture that flourished from the sixth to the third century B.C. The classical Greek preoccupations were science, philosophy, egalitarian politics, sports, and art. Even their gods were conceived in entirely human terms, as opposed to the animal deities of other ancient civilizations. Centered in the city-state of Athens, the Greeks established popular dramatic festivals at which plays by such masters as Aeschylus, Sophocles, Euripides, and Aristophanes were performed.

It is not surprising that drama as art has flourished in humanistic societies willing to grant a degree of individual freedom to their citizens and has been suppressed by totalitarian or fundamentalist societies. Significant dramatic traditions developed in England, Spain, France, and Japan during the sixteenth and seventeenth centuries, in Germany and the countries of northern Europe during the eighteenth and nineteenth centuries, and throughout all of western and eastern Europe, Africa, the Middle East, South America, and North America during the twentieth century. Societies with little dramatic tradition include ancient Hebrew and Islamic societies, the Byzantine empire, early Christian cultures of Europe, and the Puritan societies of seventeenth-century England and America (in which plays were permitted only as didactic vehicles for teaching theological lessons). A concisely stated "Argument Against Plays" issued by the lord mayor of London in 1597 sums up the intolerant attitude:

> They are a special cause of corrupting their Youth, containing nothing but unchaste matters, lascivious devices, . . . and other lewd and ungodly practices. . . . They maintain idleness in such persons as have no vocation and draw apprentices and other servants from their ordinary works and all sorts of people from the resort unto sermons and other Christian exercises, to the great hindrance of trades and profanation of religion. . . .[4]

Drama has been considered a "special cause" of affecting human behavior precisely because of its powerful ability to capture the human imagination.

The Power of Drama

The Literal Metaphor

The distinctive power of drama derives not only from the object, but the mode of imitation—the human being. In the other arts, the objects of imitation may be human beings, but the modes in which they are rendered are either paint, patterns, cloth, stone, words, or sounds. In the other performing arts, the mode of imitation may be human beings, but the object need not be. In drama both object and mode are always the same: men, women, and children are the objects, and actors—human beings—are the mode. Drama is the most complete manifestation of the Aristotelian imitative imperative. In drama there is no escaping the object of imitation, however abstract. It is not a contradiction in terms to describe drama as a "literal metaphor" of human behavior: the human being as human being.

A well-conceived dramatic character that behaves like a real human being can illuminate behavior with a totality not possible through other means. Willy Loman, the dispirited protagonist of Arthur Miller's *Death of a Salesman,* provides a much more complex, but at the same time perfectly understandable, portrait of the desperate lives of the urban working class than can the most detailed sociological study, psychological profile, or statistical sampling. Willy Loman the salesman, like other great dramatic characters from Oedipus the king to Tevye the milkman, has become so imprinted on the popular imagination that he is often referred to as if he were a living human being instead of an artificial *dramatis persona.*

Of course, a dramatic portrayal with the power to illuminate human behavior in its totality can also be used to distort. The vicious portrayal of the teacher/philosopher Socrates as a hypocritical con man in Aristophanes' fifth-century B.C. comedy *The Clouds* so powerfully reaffirmed official accusations that it played a large part in Socrates' eventual execution. Shakespeare's creation of the Jewish moneylender Shylock in *The Merchant of Venice* provoked the patrons of the Globe Theatre to demand the execution of Queen Elizabeth's personal physician, Rodrigo Lopez (a Portuguese Jew), who had been falsely accused of spying for Spain. More recently, many crisis intervention groups have cautioned against the inclusion on student reading lists of Marsha Norman's award-winning play *'night, Mother.* The play depicts the desperate but futile attempts of a mother to prevent her daughter from carrying out her calm and reasoned plan to commit suicide. The fear is that the daughter is so thoroughly convincing that even reading the play could provoke unstable students to imitate the imitation.

Merchandisers of all sorts have discovered their products sell better when "dramatized." Most television commercials are essentially one-minute dramas. Even the news is regularly packaged into a compelling time art in which the real-life participants are presented as antagonists in an epic struggle for dominance—complete with attention-grabbing graphics and musical underscore. So "dramatic" was the NBC coverage of a devastating fire in Oakland, California, that former *New York Times* theatre critic Frank Rich wrote the following "review":

> "Today" packed the whole epic into . . . one morning's show, giving it a shrewdly paced beginning, middle, and end as adeptly as any screenwriter might. . . . Thus had the fire been turned into an entertainment with a full dramatic arc—from deadly inferno to paradise reborn—in a lean two hours. Could Darryl Zanuck have done it any better? . . . It's not only trash television that blurs the line between news and entertainment anymore. Almost everybody does, squeezing every last drop of blood out of every last disaster, war and crime. Such infotainment is as ubiquitous and, finally as numbing as the parade of wares on QVC.[5]

Drama and the Other Performing Arts

Compared to the other performing arts, drama is not so much better as it is different in what it portrays most effectively.

Music.   Shakespeare opens his comedy *Twelfth Night* with the lovesick Orsino indulging his appetite for the sentiments of passion by having his musicians play the most romantic strains they know. "If music be the food of love," he pines, "play on." He commands them to repeat a particularly sad refrain:

> That strain again! it had a dying fall;
> O! it came o'er my ear like the sweet sound
> That breathes upon a bank of violets,
> Stealing and giving odour.

Shakespeare, like everyone else who has ever come under the spell of a love song, understood the power of music is in its direct appeal to the emotions.

On the other hand, music has a limited potential for conveying action. The *1812 Overture,* in which Tchaikovsky used the fading strains of "The Marseillaise" and the rising intensity of a gentle Russian folk song to portray the annihilation of Napoleon's army, is more effective as patriotic inspiration than as a historical chronicle of events.

Dance.   The most physically active of the performing arts, dance can convey a significant range of emotions, but its overall impact is essentially abstract because it usually uses only the symbolic and rhythmic actions of coordinated human movements without words. The absence of language limits the potential of dance to convey more literal aspects of human behavior.

Composite Forms.   By adding a dramatic component to their compositions, musical artists create **operas**—grand (Verdi's *Rigoletto*), small (Menotti's *The Medium*), comic (Gilbert and Sullivan's *The Pirates of Penzance*), or rock (The Who's *Tommy).* Both composers and choreographers have adapted classic plays into full-length ballets that, like Prokofiev's *Romeo and Juliet,* rely on familiarity with the original drama to augment the storytelling power of the dance. Similarly, dramatists have sought to add the emotional and rhythmic power of music and dance to their plays—either in the form of underscoring of particularly passionate scenes, or as songs and dances producing the enormously popular performing art hybrids known as **musicals.**

ACTOR WITHOUT WORDS
Pantomime is a performing art that uses neither words nor props to portray short dramatic episodes. World-renowned mime Marcel Marceau wears the classic makeup of symbolic black tears painted on a white face, reflecting the ever-present pathos of speechless humanity.

MUSICALS

Classical Roots

Musicals seem to be a rather strange kind of imitation of human behavior: action built to an emotional crisis is resolved by characters breaking into song and dance. Historically, however, this phenomenon of the dramatic imagination is not so strange. From its very origins, the drama has had roots in singing and dancing. Drama, Aristotle tells us, developed from choral odes to Dionysus called *dithyrambs.* Greek tragedies resembled nothing so much as grand opera with much of the dialogue sung, danced, or recited to musical accompaniment. Roman comedies were bawdy musical farces, and even Shakespeare's plays invariably contained songs. Plays without music— "legitimate drama" or "straight plays" as they are known—are rather recent phenomena dating from the eighteenth century.

European Musical Diversions

In the nineteenth century straight plays took over the theatrical tradition, while musical entertainments evolved into comic operas, operettas, burlesques, and variety shows. These musical diversions were most popular in European renditions by Franz Lehar *(The Merry Widow),* by Johann Strauss *(Die Fledermaus),* and by the still-popular W.S. Gilbert and Arthur Sullivan *(The Mikado, The Pirates of Penzance).*

American Originals

The modern musical was born in the United States under ignoble theatrical circumstances. In 1866 a quick-thinking producer of a second-rate far-fetched melodrama called *The Black Crook* got the idea of extending his show's run by adding a chorus of a hundred or so immodestly garbed visiting French ballet dancers who had been rendered homeless when their theatre burned down. *The Black Crook* was an instant hit—if not a very unified dramatic concoction. At the turn of the century, **George M. Cohan** added happy patriotic plots to the "musical comedy" formula that demanded chorus girls, scenic spectacle, toe-tapping melodies, and the barest excuse for a story.

Big-Book Musicals

In 1927 Florenz Ziegfeld took a major step toward a unified musical when he produced Jerome Kern's and Oscar Hammerstein II's groundbreaking *Showboat,* which had a thoroughly American setting, a serious story, no chorus girls, and, for the first time, carefully integrated songs that grew out of the plot and revealed important aspects of character. In 1945 dance became an integral part of the plot, rather than a theatrical decoration, when Hammerstein teamed up with Richard Rodgers to create *Oklahoma!.* In this cowboy musical romance, everything that happened on stage, including Agnes de Mille's choreography, was essential to the plot. The 1960s mark the culmination of the big-book musical in such hits as *Fiddler on the Roof, Hello Dolly,* and *Mame.*

MUSICALS

Concept Musicals

In 1967 the big hit on Broadway was *Hair,* the "American tribal love rock musical," an antiwar extravaganza that had no real plot. Rather, it was a series of juxtaposed images, episodes, and musical numbers unified by its counterculture, antiwar polemics. The musical had more in common with the Beatles' film *A Hard Day's Night, The Monkees* TV show, and subsequent "music videos." Called "concept musicals" because they are unified by an idea rather than a story, the form has been used successfully by Stephen Sondheim *(Follies, Sunday in the Park with George),* Michael Bennett *(A Chorus Line),* Andrew Lloyd Webber *(Jesus Christ Superstar),* The Who *(Tommy),* and John Kander and Fred Ebb *(Chicago, Kiss of the Spider Woman).*

BIG-BOOK UNITY *Agnes de Mille's groundbreaking choreography for Rodgers and Hammerstein's* Oklahoma!.

MUSICAL FRIVOLITY *Four of the chorus dancers in the original production of* The Black Crook.

CONCEPT ROCK OPERA *The Who's* Tommy.

More Than a Genre.   In today's theatre, the musical is more than a genre of drama. It is a performing art composite of immense international popularity that encompasses big book musicals, concept shows, rock and traditional operas, and revues. They come in all sizes from the huge industrial extravaganzas like *Les Misérables* to small two-character plays like *I Do! I Do!*. They can be funny, frivolous, or most serious. The fundamental question is, Do the composite elements "harmonize"? That is, do all the parts work together to create a unified whole?

Genre and Point of View

Dramatic **genres** are distinctive categories of plays grouped according to their purpose, form, or content. For most, genres are useful for understanding plays with common attributes. For playwrights, the choice of genre is a consequence of their particular points of view—the varying ways in which they see the actions of human beings. The dramatic imagination expresses points of view that are tragic, comic, or some combination of the two.

Tragedy.   Tragedy is the choice of playwrights who see the consequences of human action as serious and ethically complex. In drama, tragedy results from the consequential errors—tragic mistakes—of admirable characters placed in impossibly difficult situations in which they are forced to make ethical decisions. The philosopher **George Wilhelm Friedrich Hegel** (1770–1831) wrote that tragedy has a disastrous outcome because it involves the life-and-death struggle between two "rights" or equally valid conflicting necessities. The tragedy, according to Hegel, is that one of the "rights" could not be realized.[6] Because the tragic view does not discern actions as simply right or wrong, there are no easily identifiable heroes or villains among the characters in the plays. The protagonists make serious mistakes in the pursuit of admirable goals, while the antagonists have justifiable reasons for their decisions. In a crucial scene in *Death of a Salesman,* the aging protagonist, Willy Loman, asks his young boss, Howard, for the desk job promised him. Instead of giving Willy the job, Howard fires him. But Howard is not a villain in this play. In the ethically complex world of tragedy, his decision is a "right:" his action is justifiable, if not admirable, for the financial well-being of his company and its other employees. For Willy, however, the consequences are tragic. For the audience, the result of playing out the ethical dilemmas of tragedy is the arousal and purgation of the sympathetic emotions of pity and fear.

Comedy.   The comic point of view results in the depiction of humorous actions that ridicule and laugh at human imperfections. As such, comic playwrights find no shortage of subjects to ridicule in the human condition. Codes of behavior and social etiquette are the targets of **comedies of manners.** Home and hearth are the settings for **domestic comedy.** Public figures and institutions are the subjects of **satire.** Performances, productions, and other works of art are lampooned in **burlesques,** and the average human being as an undeserving, universal victim of circumstances is the slapstick subject of **farce.**

Playwrights who choose comedy to ridicule *harmful* human follies take their humor seriously. Aristophanes used comedies to protest his nation's war-making and to call for peace. Molière pilloried religious hypocrisy in his controversial but very funny play *Tartuffe*. George Bernard Shaw drew attention to a whole range of social problems—from poverty and prostitution to war and nationalism—in his witty **comedies of ideas** like *Major Barbara* and *Pygmalion*. Wendy Wasserstein, the author of such award-winning plays as *The Heidi Chronicles* and *The Sisters Rosensweig,* uses comedy to dramatize the dilemmas of women in contemporary American society. "What interests me most," says Wasserstein, "is the idea of using humor to draw people into what is serious in the balance. That's what I call having it both ways."[7]

Of the two genres, comedy—perhaps unexpectedly—is the more pessimistic. Ralph G. Allen, scholar and translator of classic and modern comedies, points out that tragedy's viewpoint is essentially optimistic, since it presents the possibilities of human knowledge and power. The heroes of tragedy are at the zenith of human achievement. Comedy, on the other hand, addresses itself to human limitations. It contradicts our view of ourselves as free and rational human beings who solve problems by using our intelligence and reason. Comedy contrasts this self-congratulatory view of human behavior with the painful fact that we are creatures of flesh in the grip of irrational passion, behaving reflexively. Oedipus, Hamlet, and Willy Loman are rational and reasonable. In Neil Simon's *The Odd Couple,* Oscar Madison, the inveterate slob, and Felix Ungar, the hopeless anal retentive, are limited, mechanical, obsessed, and instinctual. Thus comedy always contrasts our flattering self-image as reasonable people with the sad (but laughable) fact that we are often in the grip of irrational compulsions.

For comedy to work—that is, to arouse laughter—the audience must view the subject of ridicule with a certain detachment or objectivity. In a society concerned with "political correctness," many traditional targets of comic ridicule are viewed as inappropriate. The overly serious always have a difficult time appreciating their behavior as ridiculous. "A sense of humor," Ralph Allen points out, "is not the prime trait of a revolutionary."[8] Viewed objectively, however, no subject is inappropriate for comedy. Mass murder and mental illness, for example, are the hilarious subjects of *Arsenic and Old Lace,* one of the most successful American stage comedies ever produced.

Melodrama.   **Melodrama** is the dramatization of a temporarily serious action that always upholds conventional morality. Unlike tragedy, the ethical conflicts of melodrama are simple and clear-cut, with good always prevailing over evil. Characters are drawn in the absolute terms of admirable heroes and despicable villains. In the film *Lethal Weapon II* the protagonists are two virtuous detectives: a devoted family man played by Danny Glover, and a brave, handsome, selfless adventurer played by Mel Gibson. Together they fight to defeat the evil designs of one of the most unredeemably bad villains ever created: a gluttonous, murdering, white supremacist, South African, neo-Nazi drug dealer who keeps pet sharks and piranhas. The outcome is assured by the inevitable defeat of this gross moral transgressor.

Whereas tragedy strives to arouse pity and fear, melodrama creates terror, horror, and spine-tingling excitement through suspenseful plotting, great spectacle effects, and evocative, heart-pounding music. (The original meaning of *melodrama* is "music drama.") Melodramas depicting heinous crimes and natural disasters constituted the most popular form of drama on nineteenth-century European and American stages. In the twentieth century the genre has been coopted by film and television in which the depiction of realistic spectacle and quick-cut suspense plotting is greatly enhanced.

Mixed Genres.   Historically, dramatists have specialized in either serious or comic plays. An aspect of Shakespeare's genius was his rare talent for writing in virtually all genres and subcategories of drama including tragedies, comedies, melodramas, tragicomedies, romances, farces, and histories. In modern drama, many playwrights mix aspects of different genres in a single play resulting in such labels as "tragicomedy," "dramedy," "tragic farce," and "American tribal love rock musical." Neil Simon, who made his reputation as a writer of comedy, described his tendency in his later plays such as *Broadway Bound, Lost in Yonkers,* and *Jake's Women* to create serious scenes amid humorous action: "It's like life; there are a lot of funny things in it, there are a lot of sad things and a lot of gritty things."[9] Recently, however, Simon has returned to pure comedy in such works as *Rumors, Laughter on the 23rd Floor,* and *London Suite.* Most playwrights specialize; their chosen genre is a consequence of their view of how the world operates.

Determining a play's category can sometimes draw more attention than the drama itself. For example, endless arguments go on among critics and theatregoers over whether or not *Death of a Salesman,* with its common, proletarian protagonist, is a "real" tragedy. Miller himself entered the fray with his own written defense called "Tragedy and the Common Man." Shakespeare (who wrote in all genres) ridiculed categorical obsessions in *Hamlet* when Polonius classifies plays as either "tragedy, comedy, history, pastoral, pastoral-comical, historical-pastoral, tragical-historical, tragical-comical-historical-pastoral" (Act II, scene ii). When labeling a play becomes more important than understanding it, classification by genre is not helpful. But as a way of analyzing the organizational principles of drama as well as clarifying a playwright's point of view and motivating impulses, genre classification can be useful.

Plays for the Page

Are Plays Literature?

The dramatic imagination is frequently misunderstood, since drama is often considered a literary rather than a performing art. There are several reasons for this misconception. Some of the greatest writers of all time—Sophocles, Shakespeare, Molière, Racine, Goethe, Ibsen, and Chekhov—wrote plays for the theatre. Their works are studied in classes that focus on distinctly literary elements such as language, verse, imagery, and narrative or poetic structure. The result is that prose plays are regarded as novels in dialogue, and older verse plays are viewed as grand epic-length poems. As drama critic Bernard Beckerman noted, "Between the drama-as-novel and the drama-as-poem, drama-as-drama got short shrift."[10]

Second, the terminology commonly used to refer to dramas and those who create them is confusing. The scholarly designation of "dramatic literature" reinforces the play-as-novel and the play-as-poem misconceptions. *Playwright,* which is the commonly used synonym for *dramatist,* is often misspelled as "play*write,*" which makes them *sound* like "writers." The actual derivation of "wright" comes from the category of "master maker" as in "wheelwright" or "shipwright." A playwright, therefore, is a master maker of actions. Of course, the greatest playwrights have also been great wordsmiths. But their literary talents have been put to use to serve the larger artistic purpose of creating compelling human actions. While a great play may also be a great work of literature, it is not always so: *Charley's Aunt,* a hilarious stage farce full of slapstick comedy, and *The Phantom of the Opera,* a blockbuster musical drama with spectacular scenery, costumes, and special effects, are great plays, but neither is very good literature. The dramatic imagination understands the basic truth of the old saying, "Actions speak louder than words." In the literary arts, the entire finished artwork is rendered in words. Such is the fundamental difference between the dramatic and the literary imagination.

Scripts

What playwrights make is a scheme of actions called a **script.** A script is not a book, even though it may be bound like one, look like one, bought like one in a bookstore, or checked out of a library. While a script may be published, it is almost never written for the general reader, and its success as a work of art is not measured by its appearance on the best-sellers' list. Playscripts are intended primarily for limited distribution to theatre artists—a "performership" rather than a "readership."

A script is the record of a performance that is rendered in a complex allographic code. Like all allographic arts, the original dramatic work is *not* a finished one, ready from the moment the playwright's ink dries on the page to be presented to an audience. It can reach the public only through those who are expert in decoding the script.

The Publication of Scripts.   Publication is one method of delivering plays, but it is not particularly satisfying. It is difficult for most general readers to imagine the full scale of the dramatic action because so much of it is hidden in the cryptography of the dialogue and the stage directions. For instance, except for entrances and exits, the original published versions of Shakespeare's playscripts contain almost no stage directions. Details of setting, costuming, and appearances of the characters are never directly stated. They must be inferred from the dialogue, the

PLAYS WITHOUT SCRIPTS
Many scripts of successful plays have never been published, and those of minor dramatic forms have never even been written down. **Burlesque** *and* **vaudeville** *routines and sketches were personally owned and sold only in verbal "editions" as they were passed from one performer to another. In this scene from Neil Simon's* The Sunshine Boys, *Sam Levine and Jack Albertson played aging vaudevillians Lewis and Clark trying to remember the dialogue and business for their famous "Doctor Sketch," which they have not performed for over thirty years.*

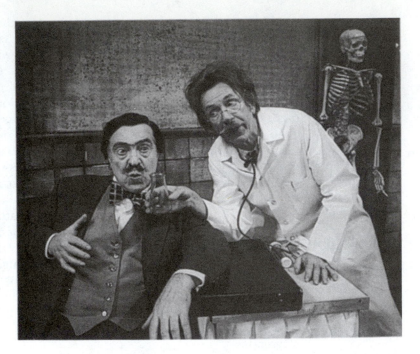

requirements of the action, and an expert knowledge of the customs of the period in which the play is set. The difficulty of reading classical texts has caused many to conclude that such plays are far from accessible, when, in fact, dramatic literacy has little to do with the ability to read. Like this textbook, published plays often include pictures to help "readers" visualize the dramatic action.

After-the-Fact Publication.   Few plays have achieved the status of a hit from publication alone. The irony is that a play does not have to be published at all for it to reach a wide audience. Most scripts are published as after-the-fact records of their performances. Shakespeare, for instance, never lived to see publication of his complete works, which were collected and set in print seven years after his death by John Heminge and Henry Condell, actors who performed with the Bard at the Globe Theatre. Shakespeare probably would have been astounded that there was a general readership for his plays. Reading a play for diversion in Shakespeare's time would be like reading a television or movie script for similar purposes in our own.

Plays for the Stage

To be fully realized, dramatic art must be performed. Dramatists know from the outset there usually can be no direct communication between themselves and their audiences. Each work of the dramatic imagination, therefore, presumes the services of managers and technicians as well as the creative choices of theatre artists to render it in its physical form.

The Flexibility of Dramatic Art

The addition of new creative choices means the original artwork will be changed in ways unique to each group of performers. The expectation of such change is an integral part of the musical, choreographic, and dramatic imaginations. The original artworks—compositions, dances, and plays—must be sufficiently *flexible* to accommodate a variety of interpretations. Rather than a limitation, flexibility is an important aspect of the staying power, even the immortality, of an original work of performing art.

The requirement of flexibility for plays is greater than that presumed for musical and dance compositions and is an aspect of drama that has attracted many artists and put off many others. **Richard Wagner** (1813–83) chose to compose operas for the musical stage so actors would not be free to change his original

CONTRACTUAL CHOICES   *Any theatre organization granted permission to produce* Fiddler on the Roof *must agree to follow the original choreography Jerome Robbins created for the Broadway production. Full notation and feet charts are provided for a fee.*

conceptions. The celebrated composer of *The Flying Dutchman, Lohengrin,* and *The Ring of the Nibelungen* used the precision of musical notation to control everything from the intonation of the singers' voices to their speed of delivery. Allowable change in opera is within very prescribed limits. Only physical movements, costumes, and settings can be handled with flexibility. Similarly, choreographers use dance notation, videotape, and even feet charts to protect the steps and movements of their dances from the imaginations of the dancers. Once recorded in such ways, dancers and future choreographers are limited in their freedom to reinterpret the original sequence of moves.

Drama, by its very nature, is the least specific and least restrictive performing art. Consider one of Shakespeare's most famous scenes from *Romeo and Juliet.* In Act III, Romeo, to avenge the murder of his best friend, viciously attacks his enemy Tybalt. Yet, Shakespeare chose to describe the great battle to the death with the simple notation:

[They fight: TYBALT falls.]

The particulars of the fight—the costumes, settings, weapons, choreography, the course of the battle, the wounds, the shouting, grunting, and accompanying dialogue, the musical underscore, the length of the fight, and the method of the final

MULTICULTURAL FLEXIBILITY   *Arthur Miller's American masterpiece,* Death of a Salesman, *proves its cultural flexibility in this successful 1983 production in the People's Republic of China.*

killing—are left to the imaginations of the many performing artists needed to stage and play this scene. Such flexibility is an opportunity. "The possible permutations," wrote playwright Elmer Rice, "are as infinite as the moves in a chess game, and the outcome as unpredictable."[11]

The flexibility of a playscript is the key to understanding the dramatic imagination and an important source of a play's greatness. Dramatists who insist their plays are inviolable works of art would not last long in the world of theatre. However interpreted and performed, Shakespeare's plays are so flexible they can accommodate any culture, race, nationality, gender, theatre space, or production style. "A play," Bernard Beckerman wrote, "does not have a single, ideal manifestation. Instead, it experiences a succession of manifestations."[12]

In the final analysis, the encoded actions set down by the dramatic imagination have no life until they are decoded, reimagined, and performed by theatre artists. Only then can the transformation from ink on the page to art on the stage be complete.

♦ THE DRAMATIC IMAGINATION AT WORK ····················

That *Is* the Choice

It's the most well known scene in all of drama. A blond actor in black doublet and tights steps alone onto the stage. He affects a troubled, indecisive demeanor. He draws his dagger, examines it intensely, and contemplates its form and purpose. After the most pregnant of pauses, he draws a great breath and speaks the most famous line of dramatic language ever conceived in the imagination of a mortal:

"TO BE, OR NOT TO BE,"—he intones ominously,
—"AYE, THERE'S THE POINT!"

"Aye, there's the point!"? What is this, anyway: an actor who muffed *the line?* An amateur drama group performing a burlesque satire?

Actually the line is a direct quote from the first *published* edition of *Hamlet,* which was sold in a cheaply bound version, called a **quarto,** in 1603. Some literary scholars dismiss this version as a pirated, spurious edition copied by a spy from a competing theatre company who tried, without success, to remember the play as heard in performance.

In fact, the version may reflect Shakespeare's original idea for the line, which was improved by the alternate choice *("that is the question")* by an actor who played the Danish prince.

Individual playscripts, which exist in many variant forms and editions, reflect not so much the indecision of the dramatist, but the variety of effective choices used in the most successful performances.

SUMMARY

1. Drama is the imitation of human action; it has roots in ritual and ceremony. Dramatic imagination becomes dramatic art when its aesthetic values supersede its utilitarian purposes.

2. In drama, both the object and the mode of imitation are the human being. This emphasis gives drama a power to both clarify and distort human behavior.

3. Plays are effective for conveying action, while the appeal of music is primarily emotional; and dance conveys both action and emotion, but in a more abstract manner. Composite forms seek to increase the range of their appeal by incorporating aspects of all the performing arts.

4. Musicals are composites of all the performing arts in which the challenge is creating an artistic harmony so that all the elements combine to create a unified whole.

5. The dramatic genres of tragedy, comedy, melodrama, and their hybrids are expressions of playwrights' points of view about the nature of human action.

6. Even though most plays are recorded in writing, drama is not primarily a literary art. Published scripts are after-the-fact records of performances.

7. Drama must be sufficiently flexible to incorporate the creative choices of the other artists needed to bring it to life.

CHOICES

1. Imagine the telling of an important event in your life through music, dance, poetry, and a play. Write a verse of melody and lyrics, describe the type of dance most appropriate, write a verse of poetry, and describe the opening scene of a play, each of which conveys the event.

2. Turn your favorite popular song into the scenario for a play. What elements must be added to accommodate a two-hour full-length drama?

3. Turn your favorite film or an episode of your favorite TV show into a song. What parts of the dramatic action can be conveyed in music and lyrics? Which parts must be left out?

4. Listen to the *1812 Overture*. What are its insights into human action? Human emotions? History?

5. *Drama* means "to do." How might you express the human feeling of elation through action, not words? Describe a brief scene that expresses this emotion entirely in stage directions—without dialogue.

6. What artistic expressions are best for teaching moral lessons? Is drama a good choice? Could a drama ministry be as effective as a music ministry? Why has so much more music than drama been written for religious reasons?

7. Examine television programming—news and commercials—for evidence of "dramatizing" in which the issues and participants have been simplified or manipulated to emphasize elemental human conflict. Does the resulting "play" use any of the terminology of drama? Does it resemble a play with which you are familiar? The plot? The characters? Does the result illuminate the issues involved or distort them with possible detrimental consequences?

Romeo and Juliet *directed by Jeffrey Huberman.*

[They fight: TYBALT falls.]

Romeo and Juliet, *Act III, scene i*

The Theatrical Imagination

PREVIEW

As Shakespeare laid it out, it is a scene of almost unbearable tragedy: Romeo discovers Juliet lying cold and motionless in the Capulet burial vault. Thinking her dead, he swoons with grief, swallows a vial full of deadly poison, and chokes horribly at the pain of oncoming death. In one last gesture of love he presses his lips to hers and whispers softly with his last breath, "Thus with a kiss I die."

Then, with the practiced craft of a master playwright, Shakespeare has Juliet awaken from her potion-induced coma. She sees Romeo and the empty vial in his lifeless hand. Desperately she tries to lick a few drops of the deadly liquid from his lips, and to her horror finds them still warm. Bearing the full weight of lasting happiness destroyed, she draws his dagger, pushes it into her heart, and joins her young husband in death.

It is tragic drama of the highest order—perfection on the page available for successive generations of theatre artists to put before the public. Yet, in 1759, barely four generations after it was first performed, **David Garrick** (1717–79), an English actor whose name had become inseparable from the performance of Shakespeare's greatest tragic figures, conceived a daring idea for *improving* this scene. The change in action was small, but the resulting increase in the magnitude of the tragic effect was substantial: Garrick, as Romeo, drank the poison, but *before* he died with that famous kiss, *Juliet woke up!* She saw him dying, and he saw her living, for one unspeakably awful, magnificently theatrical moment of irretrievable loss.

Change Shakespeare? *Improve* Shakespeare? The audacity of the suggestion is enough to make the high-minded literary purist burn with indignation. Yet theatre artists, with sensitive hands on the pulses of their publics and a sense of what plays on the stage, have been improving—delivering—the works of Shakespeare and his fellow dramatists for more than 2,500 years, with barely a blush beneath their stage makeup.

Whether or not Garrick's change is an improvement, it is surely not a desecration. It is the **theatrical imagination** at work, delivering the drama of a great playwright to an audience. Theatre art is the original artistic delivery system for dramatic art. The delivery of drama always involves change—for better or worse; theatre and dramatic artists alike always hope for the better.

Theatre art requires the participation of many different artists to translate old ink into the sights, sounds, and passions of new theatrical action. To realize his unique choice for playing the death scene, Garrick needed the imaginations of the actor playing Juliet, the scenic and lighting designers, a composer to write special music to emphasize the horrible moment of recognition, and writers to redo the dialogue.

This chapter examines that quality of imagination shared by the many different artists who deliver drama. It compares the theatre to other methods of delivering drama, such as film and video, includes historical perspectives on the origin and survival of the threatre, and describes the nature of the creative process theatre artists use to synthesize the products of their imaginations into a singular work of live performing art. Before proceeding with a chapter-by-chapter examination of each theatre artist's imaginative and creative processes, this chapter analyzes that which unifies their vision. Such an examination reveals an imaginative process rich in tradition, intricate in design, and universal in its human appeal.

Theatre as a Place

Terminology

It is appropriate that the ancient Greeks, who invented the art of theatre, should have given us the terminology to describe it. The word *theatre* is derived from *theasthai,* meaning "to view." The root word is *thea,* which means "act of seeing." Ancient Greeks called the place on the side of the Acropolis from which they watched plays the **theatron** or "seeing place." Considering our modern usage of the word, these derivations make sense. However, another often overlooked derivation of the word refers to the imitative power of the art—from the word *thauma,* which means "miracle."

The most common modern usage of "theatre" refers to the place, the space or structure designed for the display of dramatic action. Theatre spaces vary in size and arrangement to suit the variety of drama being performed. The military plans its strategies for **theatres of war,** continent-size areas of battle such as the "European theatre of war" of World War II. The **amphitheatres** of ancient Rome have evolved into modern sports stadiums where the "human drama of athletic competition" is played out with its resulting "thrill of victory" or "agony of defeat." As locations for the performing arts in which the conflicts of human drama are displayed, theatre spaces of a smaller scale are required so the range and complexity of human interaction can be perceived.

Movie Theatres

Movie theatres are places for the display of **screenplays,** dramas in which performances are recorded photographically, brought to the theatre on film, and delivered to the audience via the mechanical transmission of light and sound onto large two-dimensional surfaces. The scale of reproduction permits the use of very large spaces, up to several acres for the virtually extinct drive-in theatres. The huge size of the screen puts the emphasis in screenplays on panoramic depictions in which human beings are part of the overall vista. One of the most famous scenes ever filmed is in David Lean's *Lawrence of Arabia* in which a sheik played by Omar Sharif appears as a mere speck on the horizon of the Arabian desert. T.E. Lawrence (played by Peter O'Toole) and his youthful companion watch transfixed as the sheik rides into view, draws his rifle, and suddenly shoots down the boy. The stunning scene is panoramic film drama at its best.

Home Viewing

A television theatre is virtually a contradiction in terms. The theatre space need only be a room that accommodates the private viewing of drama on its smallest scale. In the "home theatre," **teleplays** and a variety of other events that have been recorded are delivered by electronic transmission into individual viewing devices. Easy access makes teleplays the perfect vehicles for the delivery of

SEVEN-LETTER WORD

[Reprinted with permission from *Stagebill* magazine]

In America, should theatre be spelled with an "er" or an "re"?

"We should spell it with an 're' because this keeps the word closer to its source, the Greek word *theatron,* which means 'the seeing place.' There's no reason for us in America to differ from the Latin or French spelling, 'theatre'; this just takes us farther away from the word's etymological roots."
—Robert Scanlan, literary director, American Repertory Theatre, Cambridge, MA; Lecturer on Dramatic Arts, Harvard University

"As far as I remember the history, after the American Revolution, Noah Webster made up an American dictionary to standardize spelling and to make spellings more logical, and one of the words that he changed was 'theatre' to 'theater.' The Organic Theater is officially with an 'er' because our founder, Stuart Gordon, felt strongly that we should use the American spelling. So as a patriot, I spell it with an 'er'—1776 and all that."
—Jeff Neal, general manager, Organic Theater Company, Chicago

"Depends, I guess, whether you picture theatre in America in a Huck Finn mode, lighting out for new territory ('er'), or as a New World extension of the European tradition ('re'). The fact is that the great majority of American theatres—nearly nine out of ten, by our calculations—opt for the latter, which is the main reason we retain that usage in *American Theatre* magazine. Otherwise we don't think about it much."
—Jim O'Quinn, editor, American Theatre

"Theatre is definitely an 're' word. It comes from the ancient Greek theatron. The only people who spell it with an 'er' are Germans, and it was never spelled that way in English until the big emigration of German scholars in the 1930s. Using the 'er' form in English represents the triumph of German pedantry over French professionalism."
—Michael Feingold, critic, The Village Voice

"This question has concerned me since I became a theatre/theater professional, and after much thought I have reconciled standards to determine when which form is used. If the actual building faces north, is in the center of town, has been in existence longer than the neighborhood 7-11, has a budget over $1,000,000 and a debt less than $500,000, the spelling 're' would apply. Only companies that do new work, classics, international mime troupes, and one-woman shows can correctly apply the term 'theater.' This should forever clear up this agonizing question."
—Pat Murphy Sheehy, producing artistic director, Source Theatre Company, Washington, D.C.

"THE HILLS ARE ALIVE!" *In the famous opening of the film* The Sound of Music, *the hills truly are "alive" as the camera, mounted on an airplane, pans across the Austrian Alps and then zooms in on a lush highland meadow just as Julie Andrews twirls into view singing the opening lyrics. In the original Broadway production, the focus was entirely on the actor, Mary Martin, who appeared as the curtain went up, standing spotlit on a bare stage in front of a backdrop with painted mountains.*

episodic dramas, or series. The emphasis in a video representation varies from the microscopic details of open-heart surgery and the "talking heads" of news broadcasts to medium-distance and long shots of locations. The panoramas of film can be shown, but the small size of the TV screen diminishes their sweeping effects.

The most enigmatic aspect of home viewing is that television converts everything into two-dimensional pictures, blurring the distinction between the reality of actual events and the fictional representations of drama. This blurring is evident when you turn on the TV in the middle of a "program," and after watching for a few moments, you still are not sure if you are seeing a teleplay or a news event. In many cases it is not clear that what you are watching is taking place *as* you watch (a "live" broadcast), or if it is "prerecorded" (a rather curious redundancy). NBC was denounced when it was revealed its 1994 broadcast exposé of the danger of gas tank explosions on some GM trucks contained footage of explosions produced by television-crew-installed detonators. CBS was severely criticized in 1989 when it was revealed some of its broadcasts of fighting in the Afghan civil war were faked enactments. From watching the "news," it was impossible to tell. It has also been reported that regular requests for medical advice arrived at the TV studio of *Doogie Howser, M.D.* Dr. Howser was a character played by an actor, but some viewers obviously failed to make the distinction between appearances and reality. "The world of television," wrote clinical psychologist John F. Gilligan, "demands more discipline, more discernment, more selection, more analysis, more responsibility and more choice about its use than all the other media technologies combined."[1]

Plays shown on movie or television screens can be shockingly realistic, but they are never, in any sense of the word, "real." They do not exist in present time. They are pictures of events that happened in the past, somewhere else. The viewer cannot be sure if what is seen ever really happened at all. Special-effects technicians and cinematographers are essential artists of these mechanical and electronic delivery systems.

Playhouses

A space designed for the delivery of **stage plays** is called a **playhouse.** Also called **legitimate theatres,** playhouses vary greatly in size, design, and location, but the definitive requirement is a **stage,** which is a space adjacent to those who are watching live actors performing drama. The emphasis is entirely on the performer, the only nonartificial element in view of the audience.

Plays on stage are performed in the present, in real time, in the "now," as theatre artists call it. Personal artistry as opposed to technical wizardry is on display. Artists of the theatre work in your presence. They, and the actions they perform, clearly illustrate the relationship between the art of drama and the art of theatre: drama is the play itself, an imitation of human action. When the drama is performed, it becomes theatre art, the imitation of an action (the play) by another action (the performance).

Live Theatre

For most of us, our first experience with theatre art is of the flesh—not of language, themes, or philosophy. You probably remember it something like this:

> Along with the rest of your grade-school class, you were bused on a field trip to the community playhouse where the local amateur theatre group was presenting *The Wizard of Oz.* While the show didn't have the special effects, songs, stars, and sophistication you remembered from watching the film on TV, it had something different. The actors were among you: they performed right in the aisles. When Dorothy asked the audience how to find the Wizard, you joined all the other kids in shouting out, "Follow the yellow brick road!" Even after the show ended, the relationship begun in the theatre continued in the lobby. The actors were there. You could see them. You could talk to them. You could touch them. You clamored for their autographs.

From such experiences, we know theatre art is something tangible and alive. Live theatre fulfills the expectation that audience responses are heard and seen. These are live actors available for interaction during the performance and perhaps for conversation afterward. When both the audience and the performers are live, communication and interdependence—no matter how dark the auditorium—are inevitable.

The Life Cycle of a Theatrical Production

Like all living things, live theatre performances have definite life cycles. A play begins as a glint in the mind's eye of a playwright. Conception is achieved with theatre artists, each of whom will contribute creative imprints of personal choices that together give life to the play. Gestation occurs in the rehearsal process. The birth, appropriately called an **opening,** can happen only in one place with a select few privileged to attend. The offspring is called a **production,** and each day of its life is called a **performance**—a one-of-a-kind event. (In contrast, every performance of a film is a clone of the original performance.) If the production is healthy and vigorous, it matures. In its prime, there is not a more physiologically complete imitation of human action available in the world of art. Like all living things, however, it will eventually die—the event is called a **closing**—even after a very long life.

The Immediacy of Live Theatre

Hamlet called stage actors "the abstracts and brief chronicles of the time." It is a reference not only to the fleeting immediacy of the live experience, but to the highly concentrated impact of theatre art.

Theatre Art Is Concentrated.   An evening in the theatre is relatively brief. Give or take thirty minutes, "the two hours traffic of the stage" that Shakespeare laid out for *Romeo and Juliet* is usual for the performance of a full-length play. The American actor Jason Robards, acclaimed for his towering performance as James Tyrone in Eugene O'Neill's searing autobiographical drama, *Long Day's Journey into Night,* best described the impact of theatrical brevity: "The theatre is uncluttered by the mechanics of progress. Life is boiled down from years to seconds, and you live an entire life in an evening."[2]

Theatre Art Is Passionate.   Television accommodates the kind of "cool" personalities that are welcome in our homes. Theatre art, which must fill larger spaces with the actions of living human beings—the audience can't zoom in for a closeup to hear an actor's whispered subtleties—requires "hot" performers. Consider that in its nonartistic usage, "theatrical" is used to describe those whose behavior is not only overly emotional, but also full of extravagant displays and exhibitionism.

Theatre Art Is Demonstrative.   *Romeo and Juliet* is a very good play to read. Its soaring poetry, vivid verbal images of lightness and dark, and universal themes can be very inspiring. But no reading can compare with seeing and hearing the stage performance—the opening brawl, the pageantry and music of the Capulet ball, the breathless passion of the first kiss, the ribald horseplay of Mercutio and his friends, the climactic swordplay and murder, and the tragic suicides in the dank shadows of the burial vault—all underscored by the most evocative music.

PROSCENIUM THEATRE *The New Amsterdam Theater on 42nd Street in midtown Manhattan is a classic* **proscenium theatre** *in which the audience sits facing the stage from one direction. This large-capacity opulent theatre is ideal for big, visually-splendid entertainment like the live stage version of Disney's* Beauty and the Beast. *The stage frame called the* **proscenium arch** *hides the machinery and rigging used for the complex scenery.*

THRUST THEATRE *With the audience on three sides of the stage, a* **thrust theatre** *is perfect for classical plays from Shakespeare to Shaw. The emphasis is on the actors and their intimate proximity to the audience rather than on the spectacle and special effects of proscenium theatres.*

ARENA THEATRE **In-the-round,** *or* **arena theatres,** *have a stage surrounded on all sides by the audience. They are the most intimate of all stage spaces, and scenery is at a minimum, confined to furniture and props. The emphasis is on the art of the actor, costume designer, and lighting designer.*

Making Theatre in Unlikely Places: Site-Specific Productions

The rusting piers near the PENN RAIL yards on the West Side of Manhattan and a rubble-strewn alley in Seattle may seem a million miles from the classic open-air Greek theatre, but not anymore. **Site-specific** productions find their theatre spaces "on location."

All of the productions of the En Garde Arts theatre company are site specific. They performed Orestes, *an updating of the Euripides play by Charles L. Mee Jr., near 59th Street and 12th Avenue in Manhattan. The Hudson River, the New Jersey skyline, and the twisted spines of two large piers are all part of the background against which the tragedy was enacted. Sites for other productions have included Central Park, the meatpacking district, and the Chelsea Hotel.*

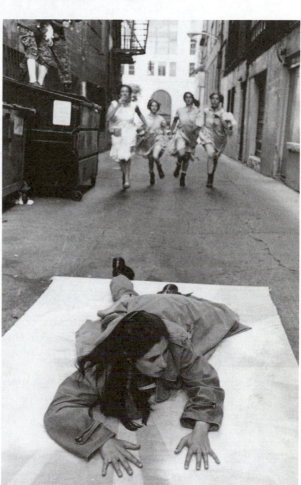

Seattle's Annex Theatre set its production of Erik Ehn's site-specific play Wholly Joan in the alley in back of its theatre.

ACTORS AND THEATRICAL ILLUSIONS *The truth of the living actor at the center of each stage picture never varies. Other aspects of theatrical illusion can exist on a variety of different levels. For instance, Alfred Uhry's award-winning play* Driving Miss Daisy *requires a minimum of visual elements—two stools and a chair to depict its multiple locations, including a moving car.*

Theatre Art Is Suspenseful.   Seeing a TV show in rerun or a movie for a second time, even a very exciting one, is entirely predictable. The dramas delivered by these technological systems are fixed and permanent, "wrapped," as they say in the trade. Even the so-called endless hyperlinked connections of digitized performances played out on computers eventually give up all their "remote-site" surprises. Seeing another stage performance of a play, however, is inherently suspenseful. Anything can happen. The drama may be familiar, but the live theatrical rendition—the theatrical imagination at work—is not. At each performance there may be improvised actions, extemporaneous speech, lapses of memory, even actual catastrophes. "We are not free," wrote the provocative theatre critic, Antonin Artaud, "and the sky can still fall on our heads. And the theatre has been created to teach us that first of all."[3] It is an axiom of the theatrical imagination that the greatest sin you can commit in the theatre is to bore an audience. For this reason, all theatre artists share the common motivation to conceive choices that are unpredictable, surprising, and astonishing.

Theatre Art Is Ephemeral. "The infinite sadness of the theatre," said Robert Brustein, "is that it is written in the flesh, and the flesh is mortal. . . . [Works of theatre art], intense as they may have been at the time—lose their physical life the moment the show closes."[4] It is for this reason that even major theatrical disasters, relegated to the fading memories of the performers and spectators present at the event, become the stuff of anecdotes, increasingly retold with a tinge of wistfulness, even sadness.

In recent years, projects have been launched to "preserve" theatrical productions by recording them on videotape. The New York Public Library Theatre Collection at Lincoln Center maintains a videotape collection of Broadway and Off-Broadway productions. Likewise, London's Theatre Museum has launched a program of recording London productions to store in a national video archive. Both collections, however, are intended for professional and scholarly use only—as records of productions, not as entertainments for audiences.

Possessing theatre art, except as a memory, is impossible. Theatre art is transient, fleeting, evanescent. When it dies, nothing is left but the ephemera of the event: photographs, programs, faded press clippings, articles and reviews relegated to microfiche—**artifacts,** they are appropriately called—which, like the bones of our ancestors, give only hints of their actual existence.

The Miracle of Theatre Art

As for all things of the spirit, there is the potential for reincarnation. In the theatre, reincarnation becomes a reality when new theatrical imaginations join with dramatic imaginations to resurrect old plays on new stages. When artistic reincarnation occurs, it is the miracle *(thauma)* to which the ancient Greeks referred.

Shakespeare expressed the nature of theatrical immortality in *Julius Caesar.* After stabbing Caesar, Brutus and Cassius gaze on what they have done. Then Cassius says, "How many ages hence shall this our lofty scene be acted over in states unborn and accents yet unknown!" On the other hand, in *Macbeth* Shakespeare described real life as "a walking shadow, a poor player that struts and frets his hour upon the stage, and then is heard no more. . . ."

Theatre as a Mirror. As the art form with a human being as both artist and artwork in a living performance that is immediate and ephemeral, theatre art mirrors human nature in a very sharply focused way. It is such a good reflector that many who have gazed at its powerful images have disliked what they have seen and have sought to keep the rest of us from looking.

The Survival of the Theatrical Imagination

From its beginnings as an artistic enterprise 2,500 years ago, the theatre has held a place in the civilized world that is as popular as any cultural phenomenon. At times echoing the dominant culture, it has also been an agent of unwanted ideas and change, viewed with suspicion by powerful authorities. As a public enterprise the theatre has been regulated in every area of its practice, from the nonartistic (building codes, child labor, fire laws, taxes, religious affiliations, political affiliations, Sunday laws, discrimination) to matters of fundamental artistic choice including bans and censorship. Throughout history, more restrictions have been imposed on theatre art than on harmful substances or firearms. Perhaps the miracle of theatre is that it has survived at all.

The Origin of the Theatre.   The origins of the theatre can be found in primitive rituals that make use of performing spaces, dance, music, chants, costumes, and impersonations. The rituals that evolved into theatre are those associated with the human life cycle and seasonal changes involving birth, maturity, death, and rebirth. The most direct line of development of theatre arts as a purely aesthetic enterprise extends from rituals associated with **Dionysus** (also called **Bacchus**), the ancient Greek nature god of wine and fertility. The most distinctive aspects of these rituals were the drunken orgies **(Bacchanalia)** of his devotees in the eighth and seventh centuries B.C. By the sixth century B.C., the ancient peoples of the Peloponnesian peninsula had learned to channel the enthusiasm of their orgiastic displays into choral competitions at festivals specifically honoring Dionysus. Prizes were given for singing, composing, and dancing—perhaps one of the first instances of the recognition of the aesthetic qualities of performing art.

Ancient Greek Theatre.   About 560 B.C. an Athenian named **Thespis** stepped out of the chorus, put on a mask, impersonated a character, and theatre was born. By 534 B.C. the Thespian invention was so popular that a contest was held for the best play. The record of Thespis' victory in that year is the first extant evidence in Western civilization of the theatrical imagination at work.

No sooner had Thespis stepped out than Solon, the lawgiver, condemned the new art as a dangerous deception. As the story is told, Solon went to see Thespis perform, and after the performance asked the actor if he was not ashamed to tell so many lies in front of such a large number of people. When Thespis answered there was no harm in doing so in a play, Solon vehemently struck the ground with his staff and replied, "Ah, but if we commend lies on the stage, some day we will find it in our politics."[5]

Despite such misgivings, by the fifth century B.C. the theatre had achieved overwhelming popularity in Athens. To accommodate the dramatic competitions of such playwrights as Aeschylus, Sophocles, Euripides, and Aristophanes, the government built a permanent theatre, a stone and wood structure on the side of the Acropolis that could hold 17,000 people. Not everyone was enthusiastic.

Plato (429–347 B.C.) viewed the theatre as a socially destructive force and would have banished it from his ideal Republic:

> And therefore when any of these pantomimic gentlemen, who are so clever that they can imitate anything, comes to us and makes us a proposal to exhibit himself and his poetry, we will fall down and worship him as a sweet and holy and wonderful being; but we must also inform him that in our state such as he are not permitted to exist; the law will not allow them. And so after we have anointed him with myrrh, and set a garland of wool upon his head, we shall send him away to another city.[6]

Banning of the Roman Theatre.   In the third century B.C. the Romans conquered Greece, absorbed its culture, and imitated its artistic pursuits. As for the theatre, they made slaves of the Greek playwrights and continued the classical tradition of theatre with a distinctly Latin style. Throughout their vast empire, the Romans built free-standing theatres in which a great variety of theatrical spectacles were performed including tragedies, comedies, musicals, bawdy improvisations, aquatic battles, gladiatorial matches, and the one-sided spectacle of lightly armed human beings fighting ferocious lions.

An increasingly powerful voice of protest came from the early Christians who viewed theatre as an obscene practice associated with pagan gods, as well as dangerous diversions in which they were often the victims. The objection of St. Augustine of Hippo (345–430) was typical of such attitudes: "Stage plays are the most petulant, the most impure, impudent, wicked, unclean, the most shameful and detestable atonements of filthy Devil-gods."[7] As Christian rulers took over the empire, their protests took on the force of official decree, and in 398 the Council of Carthage ordered excommunication for everyone attending the theatre. Actors were forbidden the sacraments. The 1,000 years of theatrical glory that was Greece and Rome came to an inglorious end.

The Theatre Is Dark.   The Christian ban remained in force throughout Europe from the fifth through the tenth centuries. There were no theatres, and no plays were written or performed. The theatrical imagination survived only in performances by strolling players—singers, jugglers, storytellers, and multitalented impersonators called *histriones*. The Western theatre was "dark" for more than 500 years.

Medieval Theatre—for Amateurs Only.   Ironically, it was the Church that reinvented the theatre in Europe. Recognizing the power of theatrical portrayals, the European clergy of the tenth century turned the "pagan" diversion to their own uses. They began the practice of using local volunteers to act out religious stories as a way to illustrate the miraculous nature of the Gospel. What started in the Church eventually burst forth to take Europe by storm in town-sized, week-long theatrical extravaganzas performed yearly from the thirteenth through the sixteenth centuries. The theatre of the Middle Ages was a wholly amateur community endeavor in which the performers and spectators were exempt from Church and civil

OTHER ORIGINS

As the theatre languished in the West from the fifth to the tenth century, it flourished in Asia. Ritual performances gained widespread popularity in West Africa in the seventeenth century.

India

Around 100 B.C. the ground rules for drama were laid out in a treatise, *Natyashastra,* by the sage Bharata. It dictates that theatre art should give pleasure as a means to the ultimate peace of meditation. Classical Indian drama, written in Sanskrit, dates from the first century.

China

As early as the eighth century B.C. there are records of Chinese entertainments at religious festivals combining pantomime, dancing, singing, and acrobatics. T'ang Dynasty emperor Ming Huang (713–756) established the first known formal acting school in the world in the eighth century. Chinese drama flourished during the Yüan Dynasty in the thirteenth century. Plays were performed in palaces, temples, and in open-air theatres not unlike those in Elizabethan England.

Japan

Like Rome, Japan assimilated the theatrical traditions of other cultures. From China, they imported masked dances based on mythological themes as early as 540. Native drama based on the Samurai code of honor and Zen Buddhism was established in the fourteenth century and flourished in imperial and aristocratic courts.

Africa

The Egungun Festival celebrated in Yoruban settlements in West Africa beginning in the seventeenth century contained many theatrical elements. The festival began with symbolic fertility dances by female devotees of the cult. Male performers impersonated animals, did magic tricks, and performed mimetic dances. They wore large woven masks to extend their height—much like actors in the ancient Greek theatre 2,000 years before.

restrictions against performing because of the newly revived theatre's didactic mission. Professional playing was still banned, with severe punishments meted out to violators. As late as 1572 traveling actors caught in the act of performing were "to be grievously whipped and burnt through the gristle of the right ear with a hot iron." Second offenses were considered felonies, and third violations were punishable by death "without benefit of sanctuary or clergy."[8]

PLATE 1.   VIEW OF REALITY   *This familiar bird's-eye view reflects images of the world that have found their expression in modern art. Seemingly abstract and patterned, such art has an actual basis in our contemporary views of reality.*

PLATE 2.   "ENTER PRINCE AND HIS TRAIN"   *When Shakespeare wrote the deceptively simple stage direction "Enter Prince and his train" in Act I, scene i, of* Romeo and Juliet, *he visualized a grand scene of major theatrical spectacle that would fill the playing space with pageantry, color, sound, and excitement.*

PLATE 3. SPORTS ENTERTAINMENT: HULK HOGAN VS. THE ULTIMATE WARRIOR *Highly skilled professional athletes performing their craft in an entertainment setting. It has all the elements of well-crafted popular drama and theatre: a hero and antagonist, confrontational dialogue, music, costumes, makeup, and a howling audience.*

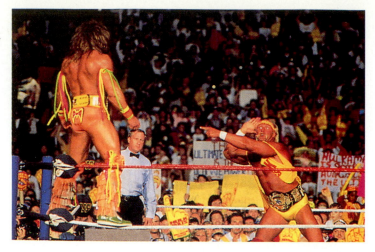

PLATE 4. THEATRICAL FUSION *The original Broadway production of* The Wiz, *written, directed, designed, and choreographed by Geoffrey Holder. This big-book musical played to capacity crowds in a long Broadway run, in many road shows, and in countless community and educational theatre productions. Its songs—ranked among the top 40 on soul and pop charts—and the show itself launched the career of its original Dorothy, Stephanie Mills.*

PLATE 5.   INTERCULTURAL PERFORMANCE   *An intercultural production fused from a variety of theatrical sources and traditions. The original Broadway production of David Henry Hwang's* M. Butterfly.

PLATE 6.   IS THERE A DOCTOR IN THE HOUSE?   *The forty-year "medical" history of the musical version of Voltaire's* Candide *has had a veritable hospital's worth of play doctors treat it in successive efforts to make it more stageworthy. Shown here is Harold Prince's 1973 "total theatre" version, which is credited with reviving interest in a piece originally received as D.O.A.*

PLATE 7. "IT JUST KEEPS ROLLIN' ALONG"   *In 1993 Harold Prince directed a restoration of Jerome Kerns' and Oscar Hammerstein II's* Show Boat, *produced by Livent Inc., that had its world premiere in Metropolitan Toronto, Canada, and opened on Broadway in 1994. Originally produced in 1927 by Florenz Ziegfeld,* Show Boat *revolutionized musical theatre. This production, which featured a new second act and incorporated material never before presented in previous productions, was a trend-setter in its own right: In New York, its top-ticket price was a record-breaking $75, and it became the most honored production of the 1994–95 season, winning, among its numerous awards, five Tonys including Best Musical Revival.*

PLATE 8.   A NINE-HOUR SANSKRIT EPIC   *Famed international director Peter Brook's staging of the Sanskrit epic* The Mahabarata *took more than nine hours to perform. A combination of history, legend, myth, and religion,* The Mahabarata (A.D. 250) *is central to the art, culture, and faith of Hindu India.*

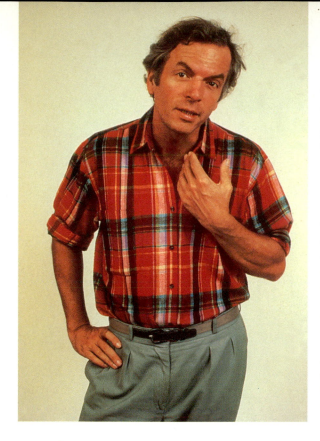

The Range of Theatre Arts

Theatre art is the mode used to render more than the traditional spoken drama, musicals, opera, or dance. There is a range of art forms—from the storytelling of monologists to the megatheatrics of modern circus spectacles—that depend on the imagination and skills of theatre artists. Plates 9 through 14 depict some of these forms.

PLATE 9.   MONOLOGIST   *A more basic, unadorned type of one-person show, monology has its roots in the most primitive of performing arts: storytelling. The very origins of the theatre are to be found in the monologist's art that depends exclusively on the storyteller's verbal skills. In African performance traditions, which grew out of spoken rather than written language, the* **griot,** *or storyteller, was the living repository of oral history. Off Broadway and on tour in the United States, monologist Spalding Gray recounted his Southeast Asian experience while he was an actor with a bit part in the film* The Killing Fields.

PLATE 10.   READERS THEATRE   *A cross between oral interpretation and traditional drama, readers theatre presents plays and other* literary *arts in a formalized, conventional setting. Actors dress in neutral costumes and "read" from scripts. Like monology, spectacle is at a minimum. In A. R. Gurney's* Love Letters, *two actors sit at a table and read the letters two characters have written to each other over the course of a lifetime—from childhood to old age. This bittersweet drama requires only the table, two chairs, loose-leaf notebooks containing the "letters," two actors, and a minimum of rehearsals. Its powerful emotional effect on audiences and its minimal production requirements combined to make* Love Letters *one of the most frequently produced plays of the 1990s.*

PLATE 11.   CABARET   *A cross between variety acts, musical theatre, and topical satire, cabaret had its roots in German performing clubs in the turbulent years between the first and second world wars. The subject of the John Kander and Fred Ebb musical starring Joel Grey (see photo, Chapter 7, p. 261), cabaret is making a comeback in the United States. Shown here is the Yale Cabaret production of "Niravanov."*

PLATE 12.   ARENA SHOWS   *Bigger than even the techno-pop musicals such as* Phantom of the Opera *are spectacle dramas made for family outings to local sports arenas to see live productions of their favorite TV shows or films. The multimillion-dollar* Mighty Morphin Power Rangers—Live *features lots of pyrotechnics, explosions, aerial stunts, illusions, magic, world-class martial arts, audience participations, and lots of diabolical monsters jumping off the stage. The producers have also been careful to add a good deal of comedy so the younger "arena-goers" are not frightened. Like the arena shows of ancient Rome, the goal is to offer something for everyone.*

PLATE 13. CIRCUS SUPERPRODUCTIONS *In just ten years Cirque du Soleil (Circus of the Sun) has expanded from a troupe of Montreal street performers to a $40 million corporation that takes its "tent shows" all over the world. Its mission is to blend traditional circus with theatre by adding a plot line and baroque costumes to "death-defying" aerial stunts, acrobatics, and clowning. With a cast of seventy-two performers, Cirque du Soleil's meta-Broadway superproduction* Mystère *is a fantasy of rebirth, from Adam and Eve to spaceship earth.*

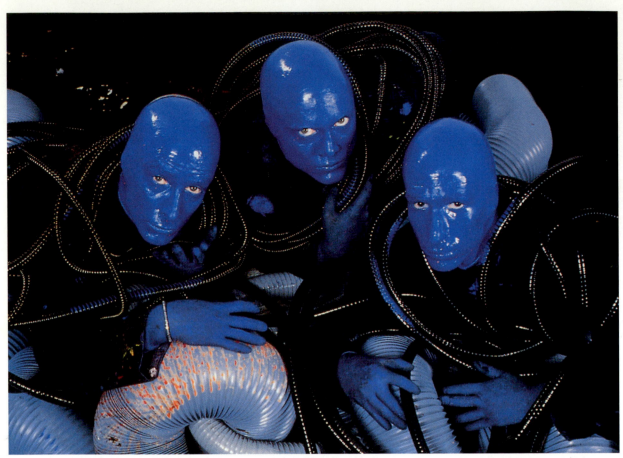

PLATE 14. PERFORMANCE ART   Tubes, *the performance art production of the Blue Man Group (Phil Stanton, Chris Wink, and Matt Goldman), has been a major Off-Broadway attraction. The group, which began performing pieces and events that dealt with the ways in which technology and humanity intersect, uses tubes (which are strung and intertwined throughout the lobby, auditorium, and stage) as a visual metaphor for their performance "bits." In one piece they bang on drums covered with wet paint that spatters onto white canvas, spit colored gumballs and marshmallows onto the canvas, and spurt goo from artificial orifices in their tubular costumes. Creating art—literary, theatrical, graphic, musical, and plastic—is the performance. Because the show is messy, audience members in the first few rows are covered with large plastic garbage bags.*

The Theatrical Renaissance.   By the late sixteenth century, after 1,000 years of dodging the authorities, *histriones* had become fairly resourceful in finding ways to practice their art. In France and Spain they aligned themselves with the fund-raising efforts of religious charities. In London and in Paris, the leading actors were successful at gaining the protection of royal patrons. Shakespeare's troupe, which did many command performances for Elizabeth I and James I, called itself **The King's Men.** English Renaissance players were also careful to give their performances outside the city limits of London, avoiding local jurisdictions.

A crucial event in the survival of the theatrical imagination occurred in 1576 when James Burbage, a former carpenter, borrowed money to construct a building he named **The Theatre.** It was the first time the word had been used in English to designate a building whose sole purpose was the presentation of plays. The venture was an immediate success. By the end of the seventeenth century, officially sanctioned—or "legitimate"—theatres, licensed by royal decree, were thriving in the major cities of England, France, Italy, and Spain. Despite the ravages of plagues, wars, zealous politicians, and the fall of empires, the survival of the theatrical imagination was assured.

Lingering Antitheatrical Prejudice

The important lesson of the theatre's survival is that trying to legislate against innate human desires will ultimately prove unsuccessful. History demonstrates that antitheatrical prejudice tends to increase in proportion to the strength and vigor of the theatrical institution.

It is not so much plays on the page that are considered dangerous, but plays on the stage, in the flesh. For instance, when the early romantic plays of the great nineteenth-century Scandinavian playwright **Henrik Ibsen** (1828–1906) were first staged, the Norwegian parliament voted him a lifetime pension. When he turned to writing his controversial "problem" plays that dealt with issues such as women's rights and venereal disease, he was publicly condemned. He gave up trying to get his plays produced and turned instead to writing them only for publication. From the sixteenth century until 1968, all British plays needed to pass official censorship by the Lord Chamberlain before they could be licensed for production. The common law of British theatre practice decreed that any play that ridiculed the Royal Family or the clergy, contained obscenities, or called for nudity would be refused a license. In 1994 and 1995 suits were filed to stop theatrical productions in Texas, Ohio, and Georgia because of nudity, simulated sex on stage, and homosexual content. In Korea, 1995 marked the first time a person had been indicted for allowing obscene scenes in a stage play; theatre director Choi Myong-gyu was arrested after he staged a version of a British play in which a female actor performed nude for about ten minutes. In the same year antitheatrical prejudice turned deadly in Algeria when a series of artists, including the head of the Algerian National Theatre, were assassinated in an intensified campaign of attacks by religious extremists.

IN THE FLESH: STATE OF THE LAW

"Censorship is when we stop people from reading or seeing what we do not want to read or see ourselves."

—Lord Diplock

Why We Fight Art

In its study, *Artistic Freedom Under Attack,* People for the American Way documented attempts to remove paintings from exhibitions, stop productions of plays, and revoke arts funding. Here is a breakdown of catalogued objections (categories may overlap):

- Nudity and/or sexual content   50%
- Offensive/inappropriate political content   31%
- Antireligious content   16%
- Homosexual content   13%
- Racist/ethnically insensitive content   7%
- Sexually harassing content   6%
- Aesthetically unpleasing/ugly   1.5%

In America the state of the law on nudity in theatrical productions is based on the 1991 Supreme Court ruling *Barnes v. Glen Theatres.* In the ruling, referred to as the "nude dancing decision," the court upheld a South Bend, Indiana, ordinance that prohibited nude barroom dancing. Even though the Court said there was no evidence the nude dancing had caused any harm such as crime or prostitution, the justices relied on a generalized community interest in "morality" to permit the ban. However, the justices also took pains to emphasize that they were not antagonistic to art. They wrote that if the nude dancing had occurred in an opera or play at Lincoln Center, it would have been protected. This reasoning prompted one lawyer to observe, "Whether you have a constitutional right to watch nude dancing depends on what you are drinking while you are watching the dancing. If you are drinking white wine, your viewing is constitutionally protected, but if you are drinking beer, it's not!"[9]

Another source of antitheatrical prejudices may not be so much the subjects or manner of the performances as the fact that theatre people earn their livings by selling their "wit," an entirely intangible commodity. After all, the product of their labors is called "playing," which is to many the very opposite of "working."

THEATRE PROSECUTION, 1994   *Because of a scene involving male nudity in its production of John Guare's award-winning* Six Degrees of Separation, *the Dallas Theater Center was accused of operating a sex business. Inspired by a true story, the play follows the trail of a young con man who insinuates himself into the lives of a wealthy New York couple. The title refers to a statistical theory that states that any two people in the world can be connected through only six other people.*

Theatre Artists

The Collaborative Imagination

Theatre is a collective endeavor, in contrast to the art of drama, which is more individualistic. As such, the theatre requires artists with collaborative imaginations and tendencies. Their choice making is interdependent and evolutionary. Individual artists, playwrights included, are free to pursue their images wherever their inspiration leads them. Theatre artists, however, must pursue a creative process that unifies their imaginations into a single coherent vision. Despite their various talents, they must seek what they have in common. Jule Styne, the composer of the music for such legendary Broadway musicals as *Peter Pan, Gypsy,* and *Funny Girl,* knew full well that a great measure of his success in the theatre derived from

THE GLOBE REBUILT   *A fitting symbol of the survival of the theatrical imagination is the construction of a nearly exact replica of Shakespeare's Globe Theatre where his greatest plays including* King Lear, Hamlet, *and* Julius Caesar *were first performed. (The old-fashioned thatched roof has been augmented by a modern sprinkler system.) Built in 1599, Shakespeare's theatre was pulled down in 1644 by Oliver Cromwell's republicans who disapproved of the arts. This 1990s reconstruction was built entirely on charitable donations of $37.7 million. It is the realization of a dream and twenty-five-year campaign by American actor Sam Wanamaker, who died in 1993 before the project was completed.*

his ability to collaborate. "In the theatre," he once said, "you need someone to talk to. You can't sit by yourself in a room and write. You gotta get along."[10]

Stagestruck Artists

It's an old joke:

> Question: How do you get an elephant out of the theatre?
> Answer: You can't. It's in its blood.

Actually, what is in the "blood," bones, genes, synapses—the imaginations of theatre artists—is a stage, the common factor of the theatrical imagination. Regardless of the particular size or shape of the stage, theatre artists envision dramatic action as occurring within the three-dimensional boundaries of this empty space. Their shared talent is for translating coded action into the full-bodied sights and resonant sounds of theatrical spectacle. In his hilarious stage farce *Footlight Frenzy,* playwright Ron House included the following suggestive stage direction:

[For the next two minutes the actors fall up and down the stairs]

"I only had a rather generic idea of what that meant," said House. "But I knew the actors and the director would latch right on to it. They love doing this stuff. If they're good, they know exactly what works on stage. It's their job. I depend on them to make my shows work."[11]

If the essence of the dramatic imagination is seeing the world in terms of human action, the essence of the theatrical imagination is seeing the play as specific action on the stage at hand. Those who have this ability to imagine life in a three-dimensional display, who are drawn inexorably to the theatre, are appropriately diagnosed as "stagestruck."

Relationships to the Stage

Each theatre artist relates to the stage in a different way. Some design for it; others tread upon it. Still others illuminate it, give it sound, build it, manage it, or organize it. The stagestruck are artists from all areas of the arts: the useful and fine, spatial and temporal, graphic and plastic, literary and performing. When they assemble to produce a particular play, they become a **theatre company.**

The Production Staff.   Applied arts are practiced by theatre managers, technicians, and crew workers. In a moderate-size theatre production they make up the majority of the personnel, outnumbering the artists by as many as six to one. Collectively they are referred to as the **production staff.** The managers include the producer, investors, accountants, executives, legal advocates, union officers, public relations personnel, box office staffers, house managers, ushers, and stage managers. The technicians include electricians, carpenters, welders, cutters, costumers, riggers, and equipment operators. Crew workers include dressers, builders, custodians, and running crews who work backstage during the performances.

The Artists.   The spatial artists of the theatre include the designers of scenery, costumes, lights, properties, and makeup, as well as scene painters and set decorators. Practitioners of the time arts include the writers (playwrights, literary advisors or **dramaturgs,** and play doctors), musical artists (musical directors, conductors, instrumentalists, singers, and sound designers), the dance artists (choreographers, dance captains, and dancers), and the actors and their understudies. Modern theatre practice also requires a director, the master artist able to unify the imaginations of the other creative personnel as well as work within the guidelines of the production staff.

IMAGINATIVE STAGING   King Lear, *at the Shakespeare Festival, Stratford, Ontario. Left to right: Carole Shelley as Regan, Powys Thomas as Gloucester, and Roland Hewgill as Cornwall. For the famous scene in which the noble Gloucester is viciously blinded by Cornwall, Shakespeare wrote simply: "[GLOUCESTER'S eyes put out]." In this production at the Festival Theatre in Stratford, Ontario, director William Hutt conceived the idea of having Cornwall tie Gloucester to a chair, tip it back, and gouge out the old man's eyes with his riding spurs. It was a shockingly effective example of the theatrical imagination at work.*

Whose Choice Is It, Anyway?

The Rehearsal Process.   Thought of by many as simply "play practice," rehearsal is actually an evolutionary process of testing, selecting, and rendering all the theatrical choices that comprise the staged play. As much as it is a collaboration, the rehearsal process is also a hierarchy in which the presumptive choices of one artist affect and actually limit the choices of another. All members of a theatre company must understand precisely where and when in the rehearsal and performance of a play the individual theatre artists make their own choices, and to what extent they must accept the choices of others.

Under normal circumstances the playwright, mindful of potential theatregoers, dictates aspects of plot, characters, and dialogue. The producer selects the major artists whose visions are felt to be most compatible with the style and requirements of the play. The director interprets the play and imposes a personal vision of the physical staging on the other artists. The designers accept this vision, but are usually free to decide on the colors, dimensions, materials, placement, and construction of their sets, costumes, props, lights, or makeup. It is the actors who are finally alone on stage with their voices, bodies, and emotions. The performers collaborate with the audience at each performance to complete the creative process of theatre. Critics affect the life cycle of the production by rendering judgments on the totality of choices.

Theatrical License

For his final appearance, or "swan song," in a Shakespearean role, Laurence Olivier (1907–89), considered by many as the greatest actor of his time, played King Lear. He performed the role almost exactly as written, changing little, but interpreting the tragic actions and conflicting emotions of the fallen monarch in a way that displayed a lifelong affinity with the Bard and his work. It was at once towering and tender, strong and devastating. It was also traditional in its interpretation. Shakespeare would surely approve.

But what of David Garrick? Shakespeare might be pleased with his new ending for *Romeo and Juliet,* but what about Garrick's preposterous happy ending for *King Lear?* And what of *avant-garde* director Peter Sellars who, for his Harvard University production, rewrote and rearranged much of the dialogue and had Lear drive on stage in a Lincoln Continental? Are these choices interpretations, or do they fall into a category of creativity so personal that they usurp the playwright's prerogatives, debase the original intentions, and violate the spirit of collaboration?

The answers are not simple. Shakespeare is dead and cannot disapprove of such choices. In rare cases, living playwrights have tried to file legal objections to radical alterations of their works, but most accept the reality of **theatrical license.** Similar to the poetic license invoked by writers to alter the rules of language for literary effect, theatrical license permits theatre artists to alter dramatic action for **histrionic effect,** or stageworthiness. The requirements of the license are to communicate, clarify, and astonish. Restrictions pertain to offending, confusing, and boring the audience, the final arbiter and court of last appeal for successful theatrical choices.

Theatremakers cannot complete their art without theatregoers. Without the audience in attendance there is no theatre event. A painting, sculpture, book, or recording can wait indefinitely for discovery, viewing, and sale. A theatrical production must have its audience in attendance at the very moment the curtain

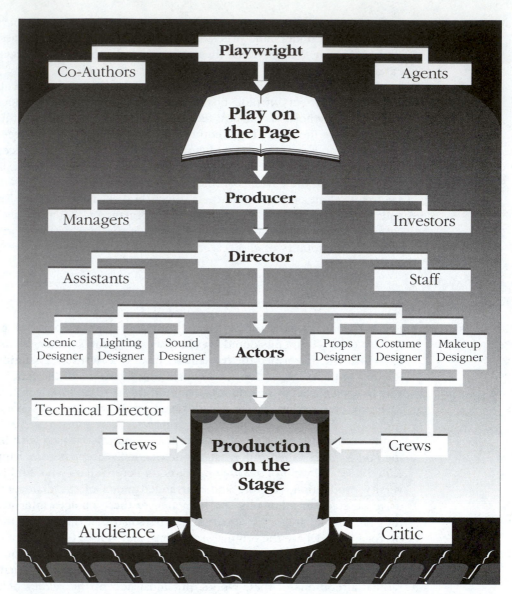

FIGURE 3–1 CREATING THEATRE ART   *Collaboration is essential for the play on the page to be transformed into art on the stage.*

rises. Without theatregoers there is no theatre art. That is why so much of the dramatic and theatrical imagination proceeds from an understanding of the public imagination.

Previewing Part 2

Part 1 provides a framework for examining drama and theatre within the larger contexts of imagination, creativity, and art. Proceeding from the universal concepts of Part 1, Part 2 focuses on the choices of specific participants in the theatrical process. "The Play" examines forces that make and shape the initial artwork. The imaginations, choices, creative processes, and profiles of theatregoers, playwrights, and producers are the subjects of the chapters in this section.

THEATRICAL IMAGINATIONS AT WORK ·······························

Intellectual Property and Theatrical License

In 1984, the American Repertory Theatre (ART) in Cambridge, Massachusetts, hired JoAnne Akalaitis to direct its production of *Endgame*, Samuel Beckett's 1957 absurdist play of oppressive, inescapable meaninglessness and doom. Beckett's stage directions call for a bare interior lit with gray light, a door, two small windows with drawn curtains, and a picture on a wall. There is an armchair on casters for the blind and paralyzed protagonist, Hamm, and two ashcans inhabited by his vegetative parents, Nagg and Nell. Nothing more. Outside are lifeless lands and motionless waters. The effect is that of a barren, existential wasteland.

For the ART production, Akalaitis chose to reimagine the play's environment by setting it in a burned-out subway tunnel—a modern, urban, American vision of the postnuclear wasteland. Beckett was, to say the least, not pleased. Believing Akalaitis had violated the intentions of his play, he protested, demanding the ART cease production. The ART refused,

and *Endgame* opened in the fall of 1984 and ran for six weeks. Reprinted here are Beckett's and his publisher's official protests of the director's and designers' choices, as well as ART's written reply justifying its production according to the traditions of theatrical license and the requirements of dramatic flexibility. All three statements were published in the program for the production.

Statement by Samuel Beckett about The ART Production

Any production of *Endgame* which ignores my stage directions is completely unacceptable to me. My play requires an empty room and two small windows. The American Repertory Theatre production which dismisses my directions is a complete parody of the play as conceived by me. Anybody who cares for the work couldn't fail to be disgusted by this.

—Samuel Beckett

Statement by Samuel Beckett's Publisher

As personal friend and publisher of Samuel Beckett, Grove Press is charged with the

The ART production of Endgame, *conceived by director JoAnne Akalaitis and protested by author Samuel Beckett.*

obligation of protecting the integrity of Samuel Beckett's work in the United States. The audience of the American Repertory Theatre production can judge for itself how the stage before you differs from Beckett's directions as they are reproduced here from the printed text. In Beckett's plays the silences specified in the text, the lighting and the costumes are as important as the words spoken by the actors. In the author's judgment—and ours—this production makes a travesty of his conception. A living author of Beckett's stature should have the right to protect himself from what he perceives to be a gross distortion of his work. We deplore the refusal of the American Repertory Theatre to accede to Beckett's wishes to remove his name from this production, indicate in some way that this staging is merely an adaptation, or stop it entirely.

—Barney Rosset, President, Grove Press, Inc.

Statement by the American Repertory Theatre

Samuel Beckett's plays are among the most powerful documents of the modern age—but except in published form they are not etched in stone. Like all works of theatre, productions of *Endgame* depend upon the collective contributions of directors, actors, and designers to realize them effectively, and normal rights of interpretation are essential in order to free the full energy and meaning of the play. Each age, furthermore, brings fresh eyes to the works of the past—it was Beckett's *Endgame,* ironically, that inspired Peter Brook's radical new reading of Shakespeare's *King Lear.* We believe that this production, despite hearsay representations to the contrary, observes the spirit and the text of Mr. Beckett's great play— far more so, in fact, than a number of past productions, which to our knowledge evoked no public protests from Mr. Beckett's agents. One of these, recently performed in Belgium in 1983, was set in a warehouse flooded with 8,000 square feet of water; another, produced in New York in 1972, substituted American colloquialisms for Beckett's language. Indeed, when directing his work Mr. Beckett makes significant revisions in his own text and stage directions, suggesting that even he recognizes the need for changes with the passage of time.

But even were our own production far more revisionist or radical, it is the public that must be the final arbiter of its value. This is not the first appearance of *Endgame,* nor is it likely to be the last. Like all great works of theatrical art, the play is open to many approaches, and each new production uncorks new meanings. To threaten any deviations from a purist rendering of this or any other play—to insist on strict adherence to each parenthesis of the published text—not only robs collaborating artists of their interpretive freedom but threatens to turn the theatre into waxworks. Mr. Beckett's agents do no service either to theatrical art or to the great artist they represent by pursuing such rigorous controls.

—Robert Brustein, Artistic Director

SUMMARY

1. Theatre is the original artistic delivery system for dramatic art.

2. Screenplays, which are recorded photographically and delivered mechanically, emphasize panoramic depictions. Teleplays are delivered by electronic transmissions that often blur the distinction between actual events and fictional portrayals. Stage plays created for the legitimate theatre emphasize the live human being in a space adjacent to the audience.

3. A work of theatre art has a life cycle that begins with the conception by dramatic and theatre artists, is developed through rehearsal, and lives through its production in performances before the public.

4. Theatre art is concentrated, passionate, demonstrative, suspenseful, and ephemeral. The miracle of theatre art is that old plays are continually reborn—"revived"—on new stages.

5. In spite of 2,500 years of antitheatrical prejudice that has resulted in severe legal regulations, censorship, and bans, the theatre has survived and continues to be a vital part of the human experience.

6. The theatre requires artists with collaborative imaginations whose choice making must be interdependent and evolutionary. Individual creative imaginations are unified by their goal of filling the empty space of the stage.

7. Theatre artists must understand precisely where and when they make their own creative choices and to what extent they must accept the choices of others.

CHOICES

1. Invoke your theatrical license: consider your favorite serious drama, whether a screenplay, teleplay, or stage play. In what way could you "improve" it so its serious effect is increased and heightened for a modern audience? Can it be improved without changing the dialogue? Do the same for your favorite comedy.

2. Exercise your theatrical imagination: try your hand at *Footlight Frenzy* by writing a specific description of the stage action for two minutes of "falling up and down the stairs." Remember, the play is supposed to be very funny and full of sight gags.

3. If comedy is not your strong suit, try some permissible, harmless violence: plan the fight between Tybalt and Romeo in *Romeo and Juliet* in detail. Make choices concerning the weapons, dialogue, the "story" of the fight, the crowd participation, the blows, injuries, and the death of Tybalt. Choose music to underscore the fight. Remember, we have seen all the cliché moves many times. Do not bore us. How will your fight be unpredictable, suspenseful, and thrilling?

4. Compare and contrast the "chain of choices" in a typical theatrical organization to the chain of command of an organization in which you participate. How do the flow charts match up?

5. If you were to turn your favorite movie into a two-hour stage play, what aspects of the film would you leave out, change, or adapt to the dimensions of stage space? What scenes of the movie could not be shown?

6. Turn *Romeo and Juliet* into a weekly television series. Describe the plots for sixteen one-hour episodes that could comprise the first season. Remember that you must leave a sufficient number of the main characters alive in order to keep the series going, not to mention renewed.

7. Document local and state laws pertaining to nudity and content in stage plays. Are these laws enforced? Do "community standards" influence local practice? Consult nearby theatres for policies about depicting potentially offensive material on the stage.

8. How would you deal with a wonderfully written and humorous play that also contained stereotypical and offensive references to minority Americans? Would you censor the playwright? Include a program note? Change the dialogue?

Reprint courtesy of the Fort Worth Star-Telegram.

They are coming to the play;
    I must be idle:
Get you a place.

Hamlet, *Act III, scene ii*

CHAPTER 4

Theatregoers

THE CONSUMER'S CHOICES

PREVIEW

The Pursuit of Leisure

Historical Profiles of Theatregoers: Who They Were

Profiles of Contemporary Theatregoers: Who They Are

Why They Don't Go: Who They Aren't

Multicultural Theatregoers: Who They Ought to Be

Why They Choose Theatre

Satiating the Public Imagination

Going to the Theatre

The irony is that Willy Loman, the workaday American in Arthur Miller's *Death of a Salesman,* probably never went to the theatre. He got home too late and was always too tired from long days on the road selling. Working to pay off the "labor-saving" necessities he purchased didn't leave him much time for leisure pursuits. If he had the time, he would rather have spent it planting a garden or making home improvements. Furthermore, he would have said he couldn't afford to go to the theatre. He'd point out that, ticket prices aside, it costs more just to park his car in the city than it does to buy a ticket and refreshments at a neighborhood movie house.

In the world of *Death of a Salesman* only Bernard, the up-and-coming young attorney, and Howard, Willy's boss, had the time and income for attending the theatre.

There is no doubt about it, Willy Loman is not your typical theatregoer. This quintessential American hero is probably not even your typical American anymore. Today, the universal "low man" is just as likely to be a woman. And her name would more than likely indicate heritage other than that suggested by the Anglo-Saxon phonetic simplicity of "Loman." If Willy Loman doesn't go to the theatre, who does? And why?

For all the fine arts, an audience is essential. For some arts, an audience of one is sufficient. For the performing arts, an audience of one is a failure. It will not work. Theatre art must have **theatregoers**—plural—and the more plural, the better. Without theatregoers the creation of the art remains incomplete; the drama would be delivered to no one.

In our increasingly mobile, technology-reliant, culturally diverse society, the competition for our leisure time is fierce. This chapter examines consumers who choose theatregoing as a leisure-time pursuit. Also examined are the logistics, customs, and methods of theatregoing, both historically and in the modern context. The consumers' choices have much to do with the theatre the artists produce. Later, Chapter 10, "The Audience Plays Its Part," examines the role of theatregoers when they assemble at a performance.

The Pursuit of Leisure

Leisure, from the Latin *licere,* which means "to be permitted," is the freedom from the demands of work, unoccupied time waiting to be filled with pleasing pursuits. Aristotle, an avid theatregoer, wrote in *The Ethics* that "happiness depends on leisure because we occupy ourselves so that we may have leisure, just as we make war in order that we may live at peace."[1] But, like Willy Loman, most of us have the vague sense that despite all of the labor-saving technologies, fast foods, high-speed transportation systems, and flextime work arrangements, we have less leisure time at our disposal, not more. It is not the nostalgist, but the realist who laments, "If this is progress, give me the good old days."

The Evolution of Leisure

It was better in the old days. In his recent book *Waiting for the Weekend,* Canadian architect Witold Rybczynski points out that ancient Jews and Egyptians observed yearly series of two- and eight-day seasonal holidays, the Greeks held four-day festivals four times a year, the Romans had 200 annual public holidays, and in the Middle Ages the European Christians stopped all work for their many saints' days. In fact, until the eighteenth century, Europeans and Americans enjoyed more free time than they do today. Except for a few national holidays and our individual vacations, we moderns have only our weekends—two days off at the end of five increasingly longer workdays.

According to Rybczynski, the seven-day week was invented in the fourth century and, like the month, actually bears little relation to the movement of the planets or the phases of the moon. The two-day weekend has its roots in the Industrial Revolution when British workers took off "Saint Monday" to sober up from a hard-drinking Sabbath. The Saturday/Sunday version observed in America owes its existence to such twentieth-century reformers as the Early Closing Society and pioneers of assembly-line, mass-production thinking like Henry Ford, who saw the weekend as a regularly occurring opportunity for people to use automobiles.[2]

The American connection between commerce and leisure is more than historical. In our free-market, consumer society, time has become a more precious commodity than money. Today, time is a valuable "currency" to be "spent" and carefully managed. Productive time is demanded by one's job, quality time is owed to the family, and idle time is somehow suspect as a waste of time. Time management has become a necessary skill for everyone in our modern society, and we employ a variety of strategies to help us spend this precious commodity.

And the weekend? In today's market culture the days of rest have been turned by merchants into "consumption opportunities," a necessary part of the commodification of leisure. The apt historical comparison may be, as Rybczynski implies, that the ancients had their festivals, and we have our "coffee breaks." TGIF, indeed.

The Decline of Leisure Time: Life's Leisure Lost

Recent studies have charted the decline of leisure time as a modern reality. In its most recent poll, the National Research Center for the Arts, an affiliate of the Louis Harris organization, reports that over the fifteen years between 1973 and 1988, the number of hours per week spent at work rose 15 percent, from 40.6 hours to 46.8 hours.[3] Put another way, today's work year of 1,949 hours has increased 163 hours—almost a month longer than it was in 1973. During the same period, leisure time has been shrinking rapidly, down from 26.2 hours per week in 1973 to 16.6 hours by 1988. Those with less than average leisure time per week were women (14 hours), those in the 30 to 49 age group (14.6 hours), African Americans (15 hours), and Hispanics (13 hours). If current trends continue for another twenty years, the average worker would be on the job 60 hours a week, 50 weeks a year—for an annual total of 3,000 hours.[4]

Graph shows increasing workweek and decreasing leisure time since 1973. (Source: National Research Center for the Arts)

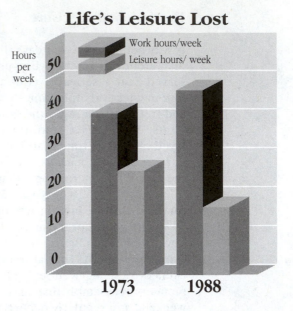

Life's Leisure Lost

Hours per week

■ Work hours/week
■ Leisure hours/ week

50
40
30
20
10
0

1973   1988

The only other rich industrialized country with longer working hours than the United States is Japan, which is also the only country that designates an official medical condition known as "death from overwork." In 1992 the Japanese government decreed that its citizens must work harder at leisure in order to make their country not only an economic superpower, but also a lifestyle superpower. The government set a goal of cutting working hours 9.5 percent by 1996.

The Competition for Leisure Time

Today, various diversions compete aggressively for the little time available for leisure pursuits in America. Everybody wants a piece of the inaction. Shopping malls have turned the purveyors of goods into profitable diversionary players. Gambling has become the fastest growing industry in the 1990s. Legal betting already totals some $330 billion a year: Americans spend more on gambling than reading, music, and movies combined.

Among spectator events, sports and the arts are the primary attractions. Most would assume the thrill of athletic competition is preferred by the majority of patrons with leisure time and money to spend. But the Harris poll has uncovered a curious phenomenon: while nearly 3 out of 4 people say they enjoy arts activities themselves, fewer than 1 in 3 firmly believes "most *other* people" share their pleasures. By contrast, 7 in 10 think "most people" enjoy sports, despite the fact that attendance at arts events is *greater* than at sporting events: in 1989 ticket sales to performing arts events surpassed spectator sports by $1.4 billion. Harris concludes that the popularity of the arts has been "undersold," with most people having to find out for themselves how much the public enjoys the arts.[5]

Those who choose to attend arts events can select from a veritable viewer's guide of exhibits, performances, and programs. Attendance at exhibitions and viewing of recorded performing arts have increased over the last decade, while the live performing arts have had to work to keep the seats in their auditoriums filled. Both the number of persons attending and their frequency of attendance are up for art museums (+24 percent) and for movies (+9 percent). Also up are the number who buy recordings of classical music (+2.3 percent). Hardly surprising is the phenomenal increase in the number of households owning VCRs: up almost 400 percent. More than 80 percent of American households now have them, renting an average of twenty five tapes per family per year and buying more than 100 million tapes annually.[6]

The live performing arts rely more heavily on fewer but more frequent attenders. They target market a smaller group. Not surprisingly, these arts enthusiasts

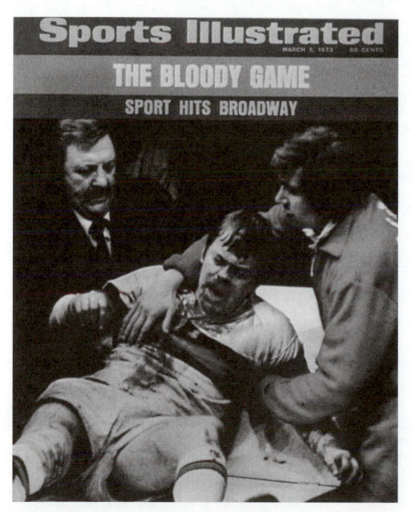

PLAYS ABOUT SPORTS   *In 1955* Damn Yankees, *by Richard Adler and Jerry Ross, was the first Broadway musical about baseball. It was based on the Faust story.* The Changing Room, *British dramatist David Storey's graphically brutal depiction of locker room activities before, during, and after a rugby match, actually made the cover of* Sports Illustrated.

are those reporting the most available leisure time: 18.3 hours per week as opposed to the national average of 16.6. The strategy is working. In the last ten years the American Symphony Orchestra League reports a 4 percent increase in concert attendance. Opera America also reports a 4 percent increase in attendance at professional opera productions. And the Theatre Communications Group's surveys show a 5 percent increase in the overall size of the theatre audiences at professional theatres in the United States over the last ten years.[7]

Who are these dedicated theatre enthusiasts and what are—and have been— the sources of their enthusiasm?

Historical Profiles of Theatregoers: Who They Were

The First Theatregoers

For many centuries before the first Greek drama festivals, ancient people attended elaborate ritual performances with all the trappings of theatre including performers, costumes, settings, properties, music, and scripts. Were the masses who attended these rituals in any sense theatregoers? Probably not. To the extent they watched performances, they share a common activity with their more aesthetically inclined descendants. As suppliants in powerful destiny-altering activities, they were participants in spiritual events, not in imitative performances valued for their aesthetic effects. One way of differentiating ritual and theatre is to observe that ritual performance is for the deity, whereas theatrical performance is for the benefit of the audience. Participation in rituals has usually been required, not voluntary, and certainly not diversionary. It was an obligation—not a choice.

Outdoor Theatregoing: Everybody Welcome

Ancient Greek Theatregoers.   The citizens of Attica were the first to actually go to the theatre—and in substantial numbers. In the sixth century B.C. they began crowding into the **theatron** or "seeing place," as the audience location was called at the Theatre of Dionysus in Athens, to see the newest in secular entertainments—plays—presented in artistic competitions, not ritual observances (see photo, p. 329). That they attended in large numbers is indicated by the need to introduce tickets as a way to control crowds and to obviate the first-come, first-served clamor of more than 17,000 Greeks trying to get into the theatre on a given day. In a four-day drama festival the theatre could accommodate up to 40 percent of the Attic population of 150,000 to 200,000.

Theatregoers were a cross section of the entire society, the theatre being open to *almost* everyone. At any given performance were dignitaries of government and religion, men, women, boys, and even some slaves. Not in attendance were unmarried women, who were considered too valuable a commodity for public view. Dignitaries had special front row seats, and married women had their own separate section.

Even by today's standards, theatregoing in ancient Greece was not a costly diversion. The price of a ticket was two *obols,* or about .6 percent of an average citizen's weekly wages. In today's dollars that translates to approximately $4—about what it costs to rent a videotape or go to a bargain matinee movie. The nascent democratic tendencies of these Athenians even led to the establishment of the *theoric* fund to provide free tickets for the poor. The institution of slavery provided the citizens of ancient Greece (as well as those of Roman and Asian empires) with a degree of leisure time virtually unknown to modern populations. Since they did not have to spend their time working, these "free citizens" had an abundance of leisure for recreational pursuits.

Evidence suggests that Greek theatregoers were an orderly, literate crowd. Laws decreed that violence (which was never depicted on stage) in the theatre was punishable by death. Theatregoers were offered ethically complex tragedies such as *The Oresteia, Oedipus the King,* and *Medea* as well as bawdy, yet politically sophisticated comedies like *Lysistrata, The Clouds,* and *The Frogs.* The ancient Greeks may have been the most theatrically literate theatregoers in history.

Roman Theatregoers: The Original Thrill Seekers.   Roman theatregoers were not so much less literate than the Greeks, just less sophisticated and less orderly. They had voracious appetites for entertainment made possible by having many more slaves *per capita,* which gave them more leisure time to attend more festivals. Viewing Greek entertainments as effete, the Romans pushed the limits of theatre beyond ethics, politics, and social commentary. Roman tragedies, with violence graphically depicted on stage, were more horrifying than thought provoking. Comedies were more domestic and bawdy, with definite anti-intellectual appeals.

These traditional dramatic forms had to compete with even more sensational spectacles. By the first century Romans crowded into huge amphitheatres like the Coliseum and the Circus Maximus to watch chariot, horse, and foot racing, mock cavalry battles, prize fighting, wrestling, and the ever-popular *venationes,* or animal fights in which the beasts were pitted against each other or against armed Romans or unarmed Christians. The most violent spectacles, however, were the infamous gladiatorial matches; in A.D. 80, in a most gruesome display, 9,000 gladiators were killed in one hundred days of matches. The most spectacular entertainments available to the Roman thrill seeker were the *naumachia,* or mock sea battles for which the amphitheatres were flooded and in which thousands of naval combatants on real battleships fought to the death.

Even in the face of such sensational competition, the Roman theatre fared well. One hundred days per year were reserved for theatregoing; only seventy-five were set aside for all other diversions.

Theatregoing vs. Theatremaking in Medieval Europe.   Theatregoing in medieval Europe was an anomaly. From the tenth to the sixteenth century, dramatic performances were permitted only under the didactic sponsorship of the Church. As such, theatregoing—to see religious stories acted out in festivals—was an extension of churchgoing. It was not exactly ritual and not exactly a secular choice either. A kind of enforced leisure operated in which the entire community was supposed to be at the theatre. Work was forbidden, and guards were posted to protect property against burglary. Performances lasted the entire day, and admission was free.

Renaissance Theatregoing: Theatregoers Become a Market.   Theatregoing as a leisure-time choice returned in the Renaissance as huge crowds elbowed their way into outdoor theatres in London and Spain. But now it cost money to attend. **Public theatres** such as the Globe and the Rose were built as commercial enterprises designed and priced to accommodate all classes of patrons from uneducated laborers to merchants and nobles.

Among the most popular amusements in Shakespeare's London were bearbaiting (in which a pack of vicious dogs was let loose to tear apart a bear tied to a stake), cockfighting, and public executions. In terms of cost, theatregoing was the bargain. A price of only 1 penny for standing-room admission to see a play at an outdoor theatre made theatregoing a better buy than drinking (4 pennies for a tankard of ale), smoking (3 pennies for a small pipe of tobacco), going out to dinner (20 pennies), or "whoring" (6 pennies minimum). One penny was approximately 1/84 of an average laborer's weekly wage. In today's currency that would put the cost of Elizabethan theatregoing at about $6 (based on weekly income of $500)—about the price of a movie ticket. (For the price of a $70 Broadway theatre ticket to be 1/84 of a weekly salary, a theatregoer today would have to earn about $364,000 per year.) If standing with the **"pennystinkers"** or **"groundlings"** as they were called was not to one's liking, a seat in the gallery could be had for a few pennies more. Private boxes with cushioned seats cost 20 pennies.[8]

The system worked well, drawing people from all classes to the outdoor theatres of the seventeenth century. During a typical week of the play season, 15,000 people or 12 percent to 20 percent of London's population could be found in these theatres. Even with segregated seating, outdoor theatregoing was a rowdy, egalitarian, leisure-time activity.

Theatregoing as Indoor Recreation: Refuge from the Roar of the Crowd

For members of the social elite of the English Renaissance, there was a more genteel, exclusive theatrical refuge from the roar of the outdoor theatre crowd. New indoor commercial theatres, smaller and higher priced, played to a restricted clientele. With one sixth the capacity of public theatres, seats at indoor theatres (there was no standing room) cost up to 46 pennies—more than double the highest priced admission to outdoor playhouses.

In the Puritan frenzy of the Commonwealth years (1642–61), the English public theatres were torn down as a stricter work ethic became the civil and religious law of the land. When the monarchy was restored twenty years later, the nobility and upper classes were eager to resume their ample leisure-time pursuits. By the end of the seventeenth century, theatregoing was an activity of the aristocracy who attended as an expression of their elevated social status. They went to see plays about themselves and their manners; they went as much to see others as to be seen—to carouse and make assignations. (It was a Restoration form of "club hopping.") One enthusiastic patron of the time described the benefits of theatregoing as including everything except watching plays:

> Playhouses, where all sorts of Company meet to laugh and talk Bawdy . . . 'Tis the pleasant'st Thing in the whole World to see a Flock of wild Gallants fluttering about two or three Ladies . . . and then they talk to 'em so wantonly, and so loud, that they put the very Players out of countenance—'Tis better entertainment, than any Part of the Play can be.[9]

JAPANESE THEATREGOERS   *Seventeenth-century aristocratic Japanese theatregoers attended exclusive performances of* **Noh** *plays, highly stylized dramas of soliloquies and reminiscence. Even today, audiences for Noh plays tend to be well educated and elderly. The more popular* **Kabuki** *drama drew theatregoers from the middle and lower classes to its more melodramatic, spectacular performances that mixed singing ("ka"), dancing ("bu"), and acting ("ki"). Shown here is a scene from the Grand Kabuki Theatre's 1969 production of* Chusingura. *First presented in 1748, it is the most popular play in the Kabuki repertoire.*

By the end of the seventeenth century theatregoing was not particularly decorous, but it was elitist.

Eighteenth-Century Theatregoing: Down 90 Percent.   Western democratic tendencies in the eighteenth century resulted in more dramas with merchant and middle-class characters. Thus theatregoing became less an exclusive pursuit of the aristocracy, but remained essentially an activity of the well-to-do. The European centers of theatregoing, London and Paris, had only three legitimate theatres apiece that were licensed to stage plays. As a result, only 1.7 percent of the population of these urban centers were **play-followers,** as regular theatregoers were called in the eighteenth century. The middle- and lower-class craze was for the new musical entertainments: grand operas, ballad operas, comic operas, satires, and burlesques that played at quasi-legal "minor" theatres.

The Nineteenth-Century Theatregoing Craze

Urban population explosions brought on by the Industrial Revolution resulted in the first potential mass market of theatregoers. By 1800 London was the largest city in the world; by 1840 its population had reached 2 million. The theatres were quick to develop mass-marketing practices that drew the working classes back to the theatre. First, existing theatres increased capacities—some in excess of 3,500. Second, theatre monopolies were abolished to encourage the opening of new theatres. By the 1860s, there were twenty-five theatres operating in London with a nightly capacity of 51,000 seats—not unlike the daily capacity of modern movie houses in similar-sized urban centers.[10] Third, seasons were extended and the evening's bill was increased to five or six hours, allowing patrons to come and go at various times with admission prices scaled accordingly (also similar to modern movie scheduling and pricing). Finally, the playbills themselves were expanded to include more popular, plebeian offerings such as spectacular melodramas, madcap farces, musicals, satires, and burlesques. More elitist theatricals, like Shakespearean revivals and serious dramas, were preferred by the more affluent and educated classes. Rather than one or two theatres for the well-to-do as in the eighteenth century, the nineteenth century had different theatres for different theatregoers. Significantly, 60 percent of London's theatres in this period were located in working-class neighborhoods.[11]

If the new entertainment consumers could not go to the theatre, the theatre went to them. Steamship and railroad transportation opened vast new markets of theatregoers as touring became another part of "show business" in the nineteenth century. In the United States, majestic showboats plied the navigable rivers bringing theatre to waterfront towns. Mining strikes like the Comstock Lode silver rush made theatregoing a diversion of choice in the American West; by 1859 five legitimate theatres and six variety houses played to audiences in Nevada alone.

In the nineteenth century there were more theatres thriving in Europe and America than at any other time in history. For a hundred years, theatregoing was at an all-time high.

The Theatre Market Crash

Twentieth-century theatregoing patterns were severely disrupted by the introduction of the first new delivery systems for drama in 2,500 years. The rapid ascendancy of moving pictures, broadcast television, and video recording devices is the dominant story of twentieth-century performing arts.

To an overwhelming extent these so-called media took over the more popular appeals of live theatre and did them better and cheaper. Film made an industry out of melodramas and farces, both of which are ideally suited to the panoramic scale, locations, and special effects of recorded drama. The movies even took over legitimate theatre buildings, which became "movie houses" with screens replacing actors on stage. Television brought the movies home.

The technological revolution quickly reversed the theatregoing patterns of the Industrial Revolution. Theatre lost its mass market of habitual customers; the middle- and working-class theatregoers of the nineteenth century are today's

---

THE RAPID RISE OF RECORDED DRAMA

1880	Moving pictures invented by Edison, who declared, "I consider that the greatest mission of the motion picture is first to make people happy . . . to bring more joy and cheer and wholesome good will into this world of ours. And God knows we need it."[12]
1895	Lumière brothers build first mechanism to project moving pictures onto a screen where they could be seen by an audience. Replaces penny arcade peep shows. Predicted Auguste Lumière, "My invention can be exploited for a certain time as a scientific curiosity, but apart from that, it has no commercial future whatsoever."[13]
1927	"Talkies" arrive with *The Jazz Singer* starring Al Jolson.
1932	Technicolor corporation introduces color films.
1950s	Television reaches mass market.
1970s	VCRs introduced as consumer product.
1994	*The Wizard of Oz* (via film, TV broadcast, and videocassette) seen by more people than any other entertainment in history—a total of 1 billion people since 1939.[14]
1995	65 percent of U.S. households subscribe to cable TV. *The Lion King* becomes best-selling videotape of all time with 26 million copies sold in first two weeks.
1996	VCRs owned by 85 percent of U.S. households.

moviegoers and "channel surfers." As in the eighteenth century, theatre once again relies on the attendance of its "play-followers," that 3 percent of the population who choose theatregoing as a regular part of their leisure-time pursuits.

Profiles of Contemporary Theatregoers: Who They Are

In recent years there has been much research on American patterns of theatregoing. Statistical studies chart attendance and preferences by such standard demographic measures as numbers attending, age, income, education, gender, and race. Other surveys attempt to examine more subtle criteria such as lifestyles and values. Taken together, both approaches provide important composites of not only those who go to the theatre regularly, but also those who do not.

How Many Go?

In its latest survey, the National Research Center for the Arts found that 60 percent of Americans over the age of 18—about 120 million adults—go to the theatre an average of 2.2 times per year to see some sort of live theatre.[15] This figure, however, includes all theatrical venues (except those given by children in connection with school or classes): community theatre, college and university productions, touring shows, tourist attractions, Broadway and other New York shows, dinner theatres, summer stock packages, and resident professional companies. Of these, approximately 55 million people attend professional theatre. (For comparison, fewer than 36 million people per year attend all NBA and NFL games combined.)

The League of American Theatres and Producers and the Theatre Communications Group (TCG) report that the percentage of the population *regularly* attending (four or more times per year) professional theatre—those who make theatregoing a lifestyle choice—is about 3 percent of the adult population, or 7.5

WHERE AMERICANS GO FOR DRAMA[16]

Yearly theatre attendance (all types)—120 million
Yearly professional theatre attendance—55 million
Yearly Broadway theatre attendance—8 million
Yearly touring show theatre attendance—17 million
Yearly dinner theatre attendance—5 million
Yearly regional professional theatre attendance—30 million
Weekly movie attendance at top ten films—25 million
Nightly TV audience for *Home Improvement*—25 million

million people. All told, these modern-day play-followers occupy about 30 million seats in America's professional theatres each year.[17]

The Demographic Profile

In its comprehensive study, *The Finances of the Performing Arts,* the Ford Foundation provided striking confirmation that the people who attend the theatre have been disproportionately middle aged, well-to-do, well educated, female, and white.

Income.   According to the study, the percentage of upper-income persons—those making more than $70,000 per year—who attend the live performances of plays is five times as large as the percentage of lower-income attendees.[18]

Education.   A similar relationship exists between theatregoing and education. The rate of attendance at live theatre productions (as well as at ballets, operas, and symphony concerts) among college graduates is more than five times as large as among those with a high school education or less.

As far as choosing theatre is concerned, education is much more important than income, gender, or race. Within the two educational groups, the percentage who attend theatre is only somewhat higher among upper-income people than among lower-income people. But, within each income group, the percentage attending is much larger among the more highly educated.

Theatrical Literacy.   Obviously, education is a factor strongly related to engaging the theatregoer's imagination. It is a key factor that opens the mind to the more complex appeals of the "classic" as opposed to the "popular" arts. In other words, knowledge results in a kind of theatrical literacy that substantially increases the range of appealing choices for the consumer.

Recently, much has been written and debated about what many view as the low state of American "cultural literacy." Many works critical of what is viewed as pervasive "Eurocentric bias" in Western thinking argue that cultural illiteracy accounts for the widespread inability to appreciate anything beyond the familiar or crassly entertaining.

The appeal of Shakespeare to modern audiences demonstrates the relationship of theatregoing and education. Teachers tell us Shakespeare was the greatest writer of all time, and his works demonstrate the greatest artistic use of language ever—on the stage or on the page. But for many today, Shakespeare's language has become an impediment to understanding the plays. As Hermione says in *The Winter's Tale,* "Sir, You speak a language that I understand not." Actor, director, and scholar Wandalee Henshaw maintained that the increasing problem of the decreasing appeal of Shakespeare to "general audiences" is a factor of religious education or what might be called "Biblical literacy." According to Henshaw, our difficulty in understanding Shakespeare's language is due in part to the fact that we no longer widely read the King James version of the Bible, which was written

REQUIRED LITERACY *To understand, let alone be willing to go see* The Resistible Rise of Arturo Ui *(1941), a certain degree of knowledge of world history and personalities is essential. The musical play by the influential German antifascist dramatist* **Bertolt Brecht** *(1898–1956) depicts the bloody rise to power of a fictional Chicago gangster. In a particularly powerful climactic scene, Ui is coached by an actor to use his voice and body to improve his speaking ability. As the scene unfolds, the audience sees the transformation of a crude thug into a dynamic, spellbinding orator with the vocal and physical characteristics of Adolf Hitler. This scene can work only if the imagination of the audience is engaged by their knowledge of the way the real Hitler looked and spoke.*

at the same time and in the same literary style as the Bard's plays. This seventeenth-century version of the Scriptures even bears the authorization of *the* monarch who was The King's Men's patron. Lending credence to Henshaw's claim is the fact that in the frontier towns of nineteenth-century America, the most popular varieties of theatrical entertainments were parodies of Shakespeare's plays. The implication is that these poorly educated pioneers had to be sufficiently familiar with Shakespeare's originals in order to appreciate the humor of such parodies as *Julius Sneezer, Hamlet and Egglet, Roamy-E-Owe and Julie-Ate,* or the frontier favorite, *Bad Dicky,* a takeoff on *Richard III.* In his record of travels across the United States in the 1830s, Alexis de Tocqueville observed that along with their King James versions of the Bible "there is hardly a pioneer's hut that does not contain a few odd volumes of Shakespeare."[19] Today, however, going to the theatre to see Shakespeare is considered by many to be the "highbrow" preserve of the overeducated.

Age. The average age of American theatregoers is 46.

On the other hand, everybody knows and likes trains—hence the popular appeal of Andrew Lloyd Webber's musical spectacle on roller skates, Starlight Express—*which is based on the children's story, "The Little Engine That Could."*

Gender and Race.   Current studies show that women are the best customers for the arts. Among theatregoers, women outnumber men by almost three to one. Retired women with more leisure time have been traditional mainstays of matinee performances and theatre parties, often employing "brokers" to arrange their theatregoing.

Polls are not needed to determine the racial profile of the typical American theatregoer. Since the founding of the country, the audience for professional theatre in the United States has been overwhelmingly white.

The demographic profile of modern theatregoers as high-income, well-educated, middle-aged, white, and mostly female renders an incomplete picture. Concerted initiatives by theatre managers to make theatre accessible to previously underserved populations are beginning to show results as more culturally diverse consumers are choosing theatre.

HIGHBROW, LOWBROW   *Historian Lawrence W. Levine points out that* highbrow *was a phrenological term first used in the 1880s to try to prove the intellectual or aesthetic superiority of certain racial types over the so-called* lowbrow *groups by measuring cranial shapes and capacities. This typical illustration from* Coombs' Popular Phrenology, *published in 1865, contrasts the high Caucasian brow of Shakespeare with the deplorably low brow of an "alien savage race." Such depictions became emblematic of the spurious attempts to link culture and race with intelligence.*

No. 32.   Portrait of Shakspeare.

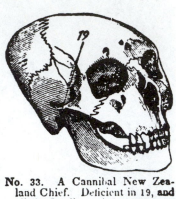

No. 33.   A Cannibal New Zealand Chief.   Deficient in 19, **and** all the Intellectual Organs.

Values and Lifestyles Profile

The objectification of such subjective qualities as values and lifestyles can be a controversial as well as a complex task. Done with care, however, the results can produce revealing profiles of arts consumers, illuminating ironies and disparities that empirical demographic data cannot accomplish.

In 1988 the Association of College and University and Community Arts Administrators (ACUCAA) commissioned a study by SRI International (underwritten by the National Endowment for the Arts) called *Value and Lifestyle Segments.* The VALS study identifies groups of people, not by demographic measures of income, education, race, status, and age, but by commonly held values and lifestyles. Groups are compartmentalized by the things they hold to be important that help determine choices concerning spending leisure time.[20]

The VALS groups follow a double hierarchy of psychological maturity in a graphic representation that looks very much like a candle flame (see Figure 4-1). At the base of the flame are two groups: "survivors" and "sustainers" who make up the 11 percent of the population closest to poverty, barely holding on to life, and for whom many arts are irrelevant. These groups are so occupied with the struggle for the basic necessities of life that they do not accept the arts as having much of a relationship to them. The largest group is made up of "belongers," at 39 percent of the population. Belongers are traditional, hard-working family people, concerned with meeting the hectic obligations of daily life. In earlier historical periods belongers regularly attended the theatre, but now they devote what leisure time they do have to passive pursuits like watching television or to an occasional movie. Heavy television watching, however, may not be so much an indication of less sophisticated tastes, less income, or less education. It may be that belongers are just too tired to choose "active" leisure pursuits such as theatregoing. A 1986 Gallup

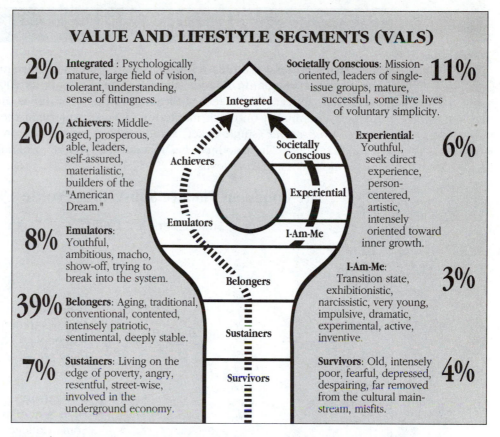

VALUE AND LIFESTYLE SEGMENTS (VALS)

2% **Integrated**: Psychologically mature, large field of vision, tolerant, understanding, sense of fittingness.

20% **Achievers**: Middle-aged, prosperous, able, leaders, self-assured, materialistic, builders of the "American Dream."

8% **Emulators**: Youthful, ambitious, macho, show-off, trying to break into the system.

39% **Belongers**: Aging, traditional, conventional, contented, intensely patriotic, sentimental, deeply stable.

7% **Sustainers**: Living on the edge of poverty, angry, resentful, street-wise, involved in the underground economy.

Societally Conscious: Mission-oriented, leaders of single-issue groups, mature, successful, some live lives of voluntary simplicity. **11%**

Experiential: Youthful, seek direct experience, person-centered, artistic, intensely oriented toward inner growth. **6%**

I-Am-Me: Transition state, exhibitionistic, narcissistic, very young, impulsive, dramatic, experimental, active, inventive. **3%**

Survivors: Old, intensely poor, fearful, depressed, despairing, far removed from the cultural mainstream, misfits. **4%**

FIGURE 4–1   THE VALS' DOUBLE HIERARCHY OF PSYCHOLOGICAL MATURITY.

poll found that the most popular ways to spend an evening are watching television, resting, and reading—all "low-energy" choices.[21]

The hierarchy of the groups diverges beyond the belongers into two paths. On the one side are the "emulators" (8 percent) and the "achievers" (20 percent), groups for whom measures of success are the completion of tasks, acquisition of material goods, and the recognition of accomplishment—the "builders of the American Dream." The achievers include such professionals as physicians, engineers, executives, and entrepreneurs. On the other side are the youthful, self-centered "I-am-me's" (3 percent), the artistic, inner-directed "experiential" (6 percent), and the "societally conscious" (11 percent). These are groups who value the *process* rather than the end results of human activities, for whom the *means* are more important than the *ends*. These groups are made up of activists who are more concerned about the treatment of workers, the conditions of humanity, and the burdens of affluence. They devote their time to causes and creative pursuits that promote important ideas rather than profits. Not surprisingly, it is the groups on these divergent paths of the VALS hierarchy that value the theatre most.

THEATRICAL DEMOGRAPHY

Like many professional theatres, Chicago's Goodman Theatre makes regular studies of its standard audience's profile. The results of its 1994 survey reveal what appear to be standard theatregoing demographics. However, due to new community-outreach marketing, African American theatregoers in the *nonsubscriber* (single-ticket) audience have increased from 4% in 1992 to 29% in 1994. The Goodman has inaugurated similar programs to attract Hispanic and Asian Americans.

The Goodman Theatre Subscriber Profile 1994

Subscribers for 1994[22]

Gender

Male	33%
Female	58%
No Answer	10%

Age

Under 25	1%
25–34	9%
35–44	17%
45–54	26%
55–64	19%
65+	19%

Race

Caucasian	84%
African American	5%
Asian	1%
Native American	1%
Hispanic	1%
No Answer	9%

Income

Under $30,000	5%
$30,000–60,000	22%
Over $60,000	54%
No Answer	20%

Education

High School or Less	3%
Some College	11%
College Graduate	29%
Advanced Degree	49%
No Answer	8%

Achievers and emulators make up the largest segment of the theatre*goers;* the societally conscious, I-am-me's, and the experiential make up the majority of the theatre*makers.* When Robert Brustein ran the Yale Repertory Theatre in the 1970s, he found that women and physicians constituted the largest audience for serious theatre. His explanation for this phenomenon has more to do with inner-directed values than with affluence or leisure time:

Drama, like a musical composition, really has no ultimate meaning until it has found some embodiment in the flesh of gifted, trained performers. . . . In addition to their intellectual and emotional capacities, [women and physicians] stand in a special relationship to the human body. The one to nature, through childbearing and nurturing, and the other to profession, through healing and care, have managed to develop a special sensitivity to the kind of natural shocks that flesh is heir to.[23]

The irony of the VALS profiles of theatregoers is that the societally conscious and experiential make plays about belongers, sustainers, and survivors that are attended primarily by achievers. *Death of a Salesman* was seen by few "Willy Lomans"; few, if any, farmers displaced by the hard economic times of the early 1990s could afford to see the Goodman Theatre's production of *The Grapes of Wrath.* Originally, *A Raisin in the Sun,* Lorraine Hansberry's Broadway hit about the struggles of a black family to move into an all-white neighborhood in the 1950s, did not play in the Chicago ghettos from which the Younger family fled; and there have been few revolutionary survivors or sustainers in the $70-a-seat crowds that have flocked to see *Les Misérables* on stage.

Why They Don't Go: Who They Aren't

The conundrum of modern theatregoing is that attending is a popular *preference* among consumers, but it is not a popular *choice.* Solving the riddle of why more people do not choose theatregoing is a major concern of theatremakers. Some answers such as high prices and prohibitive accessibility seem obvious. Other explanations are more complex, having to do with habits, background, upbringing, tradition, and culture. Solutions to social forces like those eroding leisure time are beyond the control of theatremakers. Most other barriers to theatregoing are not.

The major reasons people give for *not attending* theatre productions are these:

"Ticket prices are too high."
"I don't have enough time."
"Not very many performances given in this area."
"It's too difficult to get from here to places where performances are given."
"It's so difficult to find a parking place."
"The costs of hiring a babysitter, eating out, and other costs are more than I can afford."
"Going out at night is a real worry."
"Performances are usually given in neighborhoods that I prefer not to visit."
"I feel out of place in the theatres."

(Source: Americans and the Arts VI)

These reasons fall into the categories of costs, time, logistics, and habit.

Costs

Ticket Prices.   A groundling in Shakespeare's time may have spent 1/84 of a weekly salary to gain admission to a public playhouse. Today, 1/84 of most people's weekly salary will not buy a ticket to the theatre. In fact, you can go to ten movies, rent thirty videotapes, or take a family of four to an amusement park for the price of an orchestra seat ticket to a Broadway musical (which broke the $75 barrier in 1995). You can go to seven movies for the price of a touring show; three or four movies for the price of a resident professional production; and even two movies for the price of a community theatre performance.

Theatremakers argue that ticket price is primarily a psychological barrier and that "ticket shock" can be placed in perspective by considering the sharp rises in prices for other diversions of choice:

- Disneyland raised its admission prices for the eleventh time in eight years. Since 1982, adult tickets have gone up 132%.
- It's getting more expensive to play golf. Over the last ten years, the cost of golf balls has gone up 70%, golf lessons were up 67%, and the cost of a V-neck cashmere golf sweater rose 43%.
- The average cost of a Major League Baseball ticket has quintupled since 1950. Hot dog prices have bounced by a factor of 25! The average player salary has skyrocketed from $11,000 to $1.2 million.
- Even the cost of being a "channel surfer" has become a major budget item for most Americans: in 1990 the average family spent $46 per month on soft drinks, $46 per month on snack foods, $28 per month on candy and gum, and $30 per month for cable TV service for a monthly total "home theatre" expense of $150.

(Source: Community Antenna Television Association)

Of course, very few go to the theatre every week or even every month. Dedicated theatregoers attend an average of six performances per year. And as journalist Matt Wolf pointed out, "Broadway theatre long ago became associated with an unaffordable gourmet feast—a once-a-year splurge designed to assault the senses and empty the pockets."[24]

The market economy dictates that cost cutting is a prime strategy for staying competitive. For theatremakers, an empty seat is an omnipresent symbol of revenue unfulfilled. Therefore, most professional theatres offer a variety of discounts on their full-admission tickets. In major urban centers like New York, Chicago, and Los Angeles, same-day, space-available tickets can be purchased for half price to most big commercial shows. All resident professional theatres offer student and senior citizen tickets at substantial discounts.

Ancillary Costs.   Ticket price, of course, does not tell the whole story of the cost of going to the theatre. Other expenses can include parking, babysitting, dining out, and even formal attire. Such associated activities not only cost money, but require time and careful planning.

Time

Compared to attending recorded performances, theatregoing takes the most time. Movies range in length from an hour and a half to two hours and are shrinking in length proportionally to declining leisure time. Theatre performances may approach three hours including intermissions, intervals the movies dispensed with years ago.

Showtime.   Theatre, by its very nature, is determinedly "low tech." It is people intensive rather than technology dependent. Live performances cannot be distributed to mass markets like recordings of them can. Theatre takes place at one time per day (except on days with matinees), six days per week, at one place, with one cast and crew.

The usual curtain time is 8 P.M., which places the starting time for theatre performances between the movies' early and late shows of 7 and 9 P.M. Furthermore, theatregoers must arrive in enough time to park, find assigned seats, and read the program, which contains information crucial to understanding the production. Curtain times at many theatres are inflexible. Performances start exactly on time (there are no previews of coming attractions), and house managers often will not let latecomers into the theatre once the performance has started. Getting to the theatre on time can be a matter of complex logistics.

Logistics

Going to the theatre requires planning beyond that needed for other diversions.

Getting a Ticket.   Unlike the movies and television, a seat at the theatre is not always a sure thing. Getting a theatre ticket requires some doing. Purchasing it in advance is recommended before spending time and money on other necessary arrangements.

Seats at theatre performances are usually reserved; there is no open seating. Tickets are priced according to proximity to the stage and the night of the performance. To get good seats to popular productions, theatregoers must get their tickets as far in advance of the performance as possible. While a trip to the box office used to be required, reserving a ticket has been made easier through computerized telephone and credit card purchases. For example, the Shubert Organization, which owns sixteen Broadway theatres, sells most of its tickets through its sophisticated telemarketing center in midtown Manhattan. To see blockbuster hits such as *The Phantom of the Opera* has required planning and purchasing up to one year in advance of a chosen performance. Choosing seats by this method is "blind." Theatregoers pick the general section according to price, and the computer chooses the "best available seats." But the fee for the service is not inconsequential. Ticketmaster charges as much as $9.50 per ticket for the convenience of advanced purchase.

Season subscriptions are another popular strategy for ensuring a seat, but the theatregoer must choose the dates and seats for six performances spread over eight months, well before the first one opens.

Accessibility.   Theatrical performances do not accommodate spur-of-the-moment decisions to attend. At the movies there is almost always a seat available and a movie house nearby. For theatregoing, you must travel to one location to see the

GUTHRIE THEATRE GENERAL POLICIES[25]

LATECOMERS. Please plan to take your seats at least 15 minutes prior to the performance. Latecomers will not be seated until an appropriate break in the action. Latecomers will not be seated in the first five rows of the theatre until intermission. No refunds, exchanges or adjustments will be made for late arrivals.

TICKETS FOR GUTHRIE PLAYS MAY BE EXCHANGED until 4:00 P.M. on the day of an evening performance, and 12:00 noon on the day of a matinee performance. The tickets must be in the Ticket Office at that time. No refunds will be issued. A ticket exchange handling fee will be charged. The Ticket Office cannot handle any exchanges or business for future events during the one hour just before performance. There are no exchanges on past performance tickets. There are no exchanges, cancellations or refunds on special events or concert tickets.

CAMERAS AND TAPE RECORDERS are strictly prohibited in the auditorium—please leave them with an usher. PAGING DEVICES should also be left with an usher. If you are called, the House Manager will inform you immediately.

BAD WEATHER. The Guthrie Theatre generally does not cancel a performance because of weather. We urge all ticket holders to make every effort to attend. In the event that travel proves impossible at performance time, ticket holders may call the Ticket Office as soon as possible (no later than the following day). The theatre will then make whatever arrangements—short of a refund—that may be possible. However, we cannot guarantee that seats for an alternative performance will be available.

CHILDREN. Mainstage productions generally are not of interest to children under 8 years of age and they may not be admitted. Please discuss any exceptions to this policy with the Ticket Office personnel prior to the performance. Children as young as 3 are welcome to attend performances of A CHRISTMAS CAROL and you must have a ticket for each child. If your child proves disruptive or excessively restless you may be asked to leave.

PERFORMANCES are subject to change or cancellation.

TELEPHONE NUMBERS: Ticket Office 377-2224 Administration 347-1100

ABSOLUTELY NO LATE SEATING
BELOW ROW F.

The general policies of the Guthrie Theatre (provided with each ticket) are typical of the logistical restrictions of theatregoing.

play of choice. If the choice is moviegoing, the picture virtually comes to you. Today's multiplex movie houses are often located in outlying shopping centers with ample free parking. With as many as two dozen "screens" showing at least as many different films, each movie can be shown up to thirty times per week for six months or more. The best a theatrical production can do is eight performances per week for six weeks in repertory theatres or longer in commercial runs.

Geography. For theatregoers geography often is destiny. Major commercial productions play regularly only in the largest cities like New York, Chicago, and Los

Angeles. Most regional professional theatres are in metropolitan centers with populations of 1 million or more (see map on p. 233). For those outside these urban centers, one of the greatest impediments to theatregoing has less to do with price, time, or logistics than it does with the lack of cultural facilities. It is difficult to develop a theatregoing preference, let alone a habit, if there are no theatres to go to.

Developing the Theatregoing Habit

Acculturation to theatregoing is a habit best developed early in life. Studies show that people with rich backgrounds in the arts since childhood and adolescence tend to grow up to be regular arts patrons. The Harris survey reported that 60 percent of the American public say they want more children's theatre where they live. Most professional theatres offer special school performances, tours, and creative dramatics workshops to develop and nurture the theatregoers of the future. But competition for the limited attention spans of American children is fierce, and television, just a remote-control click away, is winning the battle.

British Theatregoers.   Probably no other society is as acculturated to theatregoing as the British, who consider accessible theatre a virtual birthright. The Italians have a passion for painting and sculpture rivaled by few. German music is world renowned. Parisians are the guardians of *haute couture,* both in *cuisine* and *cinéma.* The Chinese have achieved preeminence in expressive dance and acrobatics. Africans have raised storytelling and pantomime dance to high arts. But, whereas British cuisine may be an oxymoron, British theatre is a virtual redundancy, and it continues to exert worldwide influence on the theatrical imagination.

The London-based American journalist Matt Wolf noted with some amazement that a visitor need only strike up a casual conversation with the "Brits" to discover the intensity of their interest in and passion for the theatre.

> The saleslady at the Sketchley dry cleaners asks about Jonathan Pryce in the RSC *Macbeth* ("I'm a great fan of his, you know," she says sounding slightly proprietary) or the secretary at the International Press Center wonders what's worth seeing at Stratford. Theatre here is not solely the preserve of the middle and haute bourgeoisie. . . . Bankers and busboys alike attend Shakespeare as well as big musicals.[26]

In England, the theatre is easily accessible to nearly everyone. The sheer number of theatrical productions supports the widespread theatregoing habit. London, alone, sees the production of 350 to 400 plays per season; the average West End theatregoer sees ten shows per year. In virtually every city and town there is a professional theatre performing plays in a repertory rotation that offers a new production every one or two weeks. The establishment of these local theatres harkens back to the eighteenth century when Parliament chartered **Theatres Royal** in the provinces, thus developing the expectation that theatre is a community necessity and governmental entitlement not unlike libraries and museums.

THEATREGOING HABIT *British theatregoers packed into* their *Crucible Theatre in the northern city of Sheffield. In the United States such regional professional theatres were not widely established until after the 1950s. Even today, however, the American theatres do not attract the same cross section of society, nor the same degree of government support.*

Despite recent immigration, British theatregoers reflect a largely homogeneous culture that has been traditionally segregated by class rather than race, ethnicity, or national origin. To use the modern demographic lexicon, Britain is a **unicultural society.** On the other hand, the United States, which is a country of immigrants, is a **multicultural society** of many diverse races, origins, religions, and viewpoints. And for the first time in history, American theatregoers are beginning to "look more like America."

Multicultural Theatregoers: Who They Ought to Be

The United States of America, the original multicultural society, is becoming more multicultural at a rapid pace. The impact of this increasing pluralism affects all aspects of American society from commerce and international relations to education and the arts. Fundamental social institutions are all scrambling to adjust to the new demographic realities.

Multicultural Demographics

The Global Village.   In her essay "The Presence of the Future," Cynthia Mayeda notes that, in today's world, a representative global village of 1,000 people would include 564 Asians, 210 Europeans, 86 Africans, 80 South Americans, and 60 North Americans. Of these "citizens," 60 would control half of the total income, 500 would be hungry, 600 would live in Shantytown, and 700 would be illiterate.[27] And as everybody knows: they're coming to America.

U.S. Demographics.   A new reality fast approaching the United States is that by the year 2020, white Americans will be a majority minority—that is, the largest

THE THEATRE AS A MIRROR   *The young cast of playwright/composer Elizabeth Swados'* The New Americans. *For this bittersweet musical examination of cultural differences, Swados assembled nine children whose families recently immigrated to the United States. In a theatrical collage of songs and stories, the children recount the ridicule they have endured because of their accents, dress, and customs.*

minority in the United States. In many places the new demographics have already arrived. In Birmingham, Alabama, the public schools have an enrollment that is 80 percent African American. In the New York City schools, students speak an astounding babel of eighty-four different languages. San Diego's Filipino population is now second only to Manila's. The city also has a thriving Vietnamese business district and Laotian enclaves. The school system is made up of 65 percent "minority" students and 35 percent white students. Los Angeles is probably the only large urban center anywhere in the world where there is no racial majority at all. Asian immigrants (from Japan, China, Korea, Malaysia, Vietnam, Laos, and Cambodia), who have been coming to America for over a hundred years, now make up one of the country's fastest growing population groups.

As some groups increase demographically, others such as white Anglo-Saxon Protestants, Jews, and Native Americans are experiencing declines in population. Other groups, defined by nontraditional orientations or ideologies, such as homosexuals, feminists, environmentalists, veterans, and the disabled, also call for rights and recognition as valid segments of American society.

As society adjusts to rapidly changing social forces, all groups, large and small, advantaged and disadvantaged, empowered and unempowered, demand their rightful pieces of the "apple pie" that symbolizes American opportunity. **Multiculturalism** is the idea that today's demographic realities must be reflected in our public institutions. In the words of Linda Loman, the long-suffering character of Arthur Miller's *Death of a Salesman,* "Attention must be paid."[28]

The Cultural Mechanism of Theatre Art

One of the great clichés of America—that it is a "melting pot" for assimilating the diverse masses that have settled the land—was popularized by a 1908 Broadway play by Israel Zangwill. *The Melting Pot* ends with immigrant lovers, the son of a Russian colonel who had led a pogrom against a Russian Jewish *shtetl* and the daughter of a man from that little village, standing before the Statue of Liberty at sunset. The faint strains of "My Country 'Tis of Thee" underscore the climactic scene:

BOY: There she lies, the great Melting Pot— . . . *[taking the girl's hand]* Ah, what a stirring and a seething! Celt and Latin, Slav and Teuton, Greek and Syrian—black and yellow . . .

GIRL: *[Softly, nestling to him]* Jew and Gentile.

BOY: Yes, East and West, and North and South, the palm and the pine, the crescent and the cross . . . *[He raises his hands in benediction over the shining city.]* Peace, peace to all ye unborn millions, fated to fill this giant continent—the God of our children give you peace.[29]

When President Teddy Roosevelt saw this scene, he is reported to have jumped to his feet and shouted, "That's a great play, Mr. Zangwill. This is the stuff!"[30] In the years since President Roosevelt reiterated the ideal of *e pluribus unum,* integration has become the great social goal, while "separate but equal" has been discredited as the hypocrisy of oppressors.

In recent years there has been much debate as to whether or not the ideal is working well. When it comes to sharing access to the American Dream, some view the "melting pot" as a means of losing identity in a society in which certain groups are "more equal than others." This view evolved from the ethnic consciousness movements of the 1960s and has grown into what has been called a "cult of otherness." "The contemporary ideal is not assimilation but ethnicity," wrote noted historian Arthur Schlesinger, Jr. "We used to say *e pluribus unum.* Now we glorify *pluribus* and belittle *unum.*"[31]

In the theatre, however, the melting pot simmers. The theatre has a kind of cultural mechanism for adjusting to its potential consumers. American actor James Earl Jones points out, "If mankind is the first order of life to reflect upon itself, the theatre is its reflector."[32] Obviously, reflecting the images of today's America is not a unicultural picture. As groups converge, compete, appear, and decline in society, images on stage try to keep pace. The American stage itself becomes a bubbling artistic cauldron in which the ingredients are living imitations of the citizens themselves. As Asian American playwright David Henry Hwang observes, the United States is "the world's greatest experimental laboratory for cultural hybrids and convergences."[33]

Today's theatrical menu is made rich and exotic by the diversity of groups drawn to theatre as their first means of artistic expression. Theatremaking is the performing art of choice for traditionally excluded groups. Compared to big-budget film and television, producing theatre is attractively affordable. In addition, groups that produce their own plays can counterbalance the stereotyping that results when "others" portray them.

New Terminology.   Like "melting pot," "pluralism," and "integration," *multiculturalism* is an overused term, full of political connotations that do not accurately describe the new realities of American theatre art. Debate over theatrical diversity is refined as artists coin better terminology to describe cultural convergences on the stage. Among the new usages are "syncretic" and "creole." Director and critic Robert Brustein has suggested "transcultural blending"; *avant-garde* theatremaker Richard Schechner uses the nuclear age designation "fusion," which he says occurs when "elements of two or more cultures mix to such a degree that a new society, language, or genre or art emerges."[34] The word may be new, but the concept describes a process that has been going on in the theatre since the Romans found the Greeks performing plays in Sicily, imported them, and rendered the Attic art in distinctly Latin formulations.

The Process of Theatrical Fusion

Artistic fusion follows a pattern in the theatre that often runs concurrently with the emergence of a cultural group from isolation, oppression, and discrimination.

NATIVE AMERICAN DRAMA   *A member of the American Indian Dance Theatre nears the end of the* Hoop Dance, *in which reeds are used to depict flowers, a butterfly, and other creations of nature. According to legend, a dying man wanted to leave something on earth, and the Creator promised to give the man one hoop for each living creature he could make. The dance drama symbolizes how those creations are connected, yet grow and change on their own.*

AFRICAN PANTOMIME DANCE   *A Shilluk warrior of the Upper Nile enacts a passionate, violent war dance. Performed by one man, it depicts a fierce but graceful battle against a powerful unseen adversary.*

Enclave Theatres.   Theatrical fusion begins with the establishment of enclave theatres of a particular group, usually in its own community. Enclave theatres are based on native performing conventions. For instance, Asian theatrical traditions are tied to epic, mythic music dramas. Dance drama is the vital element in Native American performing arts, and storytelling and pantomime dance are central Africa's major theatrical forms. The artists of enclave theatres produce works in

BALINESE THEATRE   *In the storytelling dances of the Balinese theatre, children are trained from infancy in a unique vocabulary of dance movements that suggest fantastic birds, flowers, and even the architecture of Bali—all of which are rooted in Balinese folklore. Twelve-year-old Ni Gusta Raka portrays a bird of death poised to bring a prophecy of doom to a king. In the Western tradition, the messenger of doom, like Tieresias in* Oedipus the King, *would have delivered the prophecy in ringing tones of spoken drama.*

the cultural terms, images, characters, subjects of concern, and especially the language of their native cultures, usually making the work inaccessible to outsiders. As they might with an exotic cuisine, only the most committed mainstream theatregoers discover the hidden delights of enclave performances.

Assimilation and Liberation.   Because enclave theatre artists are on American, not native, soil, a degree of cultural assimilation is inevitable. Theatre art begins its emergence from the enclave in the creations of the first American-born generation. As native traditions mix with the conventions of contemporary American theatre practice, enclave performances become more accessible to mainstream theatregoers. Enclave theatre is finally liberated—"moved uptown," often in an attention-grabbing superior work that opens a new artistic window to multicultural America.

Absorption and Fusion.   The process is completed as culturally specific features of enclave art are absorbed into modern theatre practice. What was traditional becomes altered, fused into a new American theatrical experience. The fusion process is complete when a new definition of mainstream theatre has emerged.

The Fusion of Yiddish Theatre.   A case in point is the fusion of the Yiddish theatre into the American mainstream. Established in the 1870s, the Yiddish theatre reached its peak in the 1920s in the teeming Jewish enclave of New York's Lower East Side. This cultural phenomenon was so named because it was performed in Yiddish, a language that is a combination of medieval German, Hebrew, and the various Slavic languages spoken by European Jewish immigrants. For most of its history, Yiddish was scorned as a language for authors, but in the late nineteenth century it was developed as a literary medium in short stories by Sholom Aleichem and as a dramatic medium by Abraham Goldfadden (1840–1908), who founded the first Yiddish theatre in Russia in 1878. In America, Yiddish theatre drew on storytelling and folk music traditions to produce vibrant, touchingly comic plays about immigrants trying to scratch out their daily living in another of a long line of foreign lands. At its peak in the 1920s there were more than a dozen Yiddish theatre companies in New York.

Assimilation began as the American-born children of these enclave theatre artists became the first generation of Jewish American theatremakers. Directors like Harold Clurman, playwrights like Elmer Rice and Clifford Odets, composers like Irving Berlin and George Gershwin, and actors like Fanny Brice, Eddie Cantor, the Marx Brothers and Zero Mostel moved their art to the limelights of Broadway and from there to the searchlights of Hollywood. Liberation was achieved in the heavily ethnic-flavored comic performances of Ziegfeld Follies superstar Fanny Brice and in Clifford Odets' 1935 play *Awake and Sing,* a drama about a Jewish family in the Bronx struggling to survive the Depression. In his first draft of the play, Odets began Act I with the characters speaking entirely in Yiddish and had them gradually switch to English as action progressed. Harold Clurman, the play's director, talked Odets out of the idea. Clurman told him that the general public would not understand it. Odets changed it all to English, and the play became one of the first liberated hits of the Yiddish theatrical enclave.[36] With productions of the play running simultaneously on Broadway and in London, Odets was hailed as America's most promising young playwright.

Today, few people speak Yiddish. But in a sense, we all do. Parts of the language have been absorbed and fused with American English. *Webster's Unabridged Dictionary* lists over 500 Yiddish words including such common usages as "nosh," "kibbutz," "yenta," "klutz," "schnook," "schmooze," "schmuck," and "chutzpah." And where is the Yiddish theatre today? Like the language, it is everywhere—fused irrevocably into the modern American theatre. *Fiddler on the Roof,* one of the most

ETHNIC THEATRE

On the stages of immigrant enclave theatres the accents of the homeland were familiar melodies amid the strange sounds of the Americans. For poor immigrants, ethnic theatre helped to create a tolerable world.

"I do not go to the theatre to think," confessed one, "but to forget the crowded tenement, the littered wash. . . . [On stage I see] a beautiful room with expensive furniture and pretend that the star has invited me to his house."[35]

Performed by immigrants for immigrants, theatre met many needs. It expressed deep emotions, strengthened cultural bonds, kept traditions alive, educated the alien, and gave pleasure.

A sampling of enclave traditions:

The Finnish Stage

Wherever Finns settled, they were soon giving plays to raise funds for community projects. Believing in the instructional power of the theatre, Finnish American playwrights stressed leftist ideology. Finnish American audiences, on the other hand, preferred comedies, operettas, folk, and historical plays.

The Swedish Stage

Swedish immigrants preferred folk dramas on peasant life in the old country. They laughed heartily at the antics of their favorite stock character, "Olle Skratthult," Olle from Laughtersville, a country bumpkin who specialized in dialect parts.

The German Stage

German immigrants favored historical plays with large casts, choruses, horses, and battle scenes. These huge spectacles created living sagas that introduced their children to their ancestral heritage. Especially popular were the exploits of Frederick the Great.

The Greek Stage

Greeks in Chicago enclaves took special pride in staging ancient classics of Aeschylus, Sophocles, and Euripides, through which they felt they were showing the glory of Greece to uninformed Americans.

The Chinese Stage

Chinese immigrants preferred historical plays of epic proportions. A single performance could last five hours, while plays in hundreds of acts might take several weeks to complete. In gorgeous costumes and stylized makeup, men played all parts.

ETHNIC THEATRE

The Italian Stage

Italian immigrant theatre evolved from amateurs who met in cafés to sing. An immigrant named Eduardo Migliaccio became the comedian Farfariello who appeared in many plays as the quintessential immigrant greenhorn: the fruit vendor, the iceman, the garbageman. His audience laughed at his blunders, relishing the fact that they had learned better. They were Americans now.

YANKEE DOODLE BOY   *The son of Irish immigrant performers,* **George M. Cohan** *(1878–1942) was the "man who owned Broadway" at the turn of the century. He incorporated the exuberance of his Irish song-and-dance traditions into the new musical comedies that he wrote, produced, directed, and starred in. The flag-waving patriotism of "I'm a Yankee Doodle Dandy" and "You're a Grand Old Flag" became anthems for both new and old Americans.*

THEATRICAL FUSION *Jacob Adler, a star of the Yiddish theatre, in the role of Zelig Itzik the fiddler in the Broadway production of* Fiddler on the Roof. *Jacob Adler's daughter, Stella, became one of America's leading acting teachers and theorists.*

popular productions in American history, is only the most visible example. Fanny Brice's life was portrayed on Broadway in the hit show *Funny Girl,* starring Barbra Streisand, who also appeared in the film version. And Neil Simon continues to find universal American truisms in his personal journey from his Brooklyn enclave to Hollywood in the autobiographical trilogy of *Brighton Beach Memoirs, Biloxi Blues,* and *Broadway Bound.*

Fusion of African American Theatre. Throughout its history, Africa has been a continent rich in performance traditions associated with rituals, celebrations, ceremonies, and storytelling. However, unlike the Yiddish experience, African performing art did not coalesce around a common language. By the seventeenth century 800 local languages, most of which had no written form, were spoken on the continent. Words were often the least important element in African performances that stressed drumming, expressive dance, and pantomime. Lacking written languages, storytelling became an important part of African American life—to entertain and preserve their culture and history.

A SHAYNA MAIDEL   *Barbara Lebow's 1988 play,* A Shayna Maidel *("A Pretty Girl"), has a Yiddish title and the characters speak both Yiddish and English throughout. The play depicts a concentration camp survivor who immigrates to the United States in 1946 and struggles to form a family bond with her thoroughly assimilated American sister. The play had a long run in New York, followed by nationwide productions in regional and academic theatres. Theatregoers everywhere have recognized something essentially American in this immigrant family drama.*

And unlike other enclave experiences, the birth of African American theatre was long and painful, since so many Africans came to America not seeking a better life, but through forced emigration on slave ships. The first known company of African American actors, called **The African Company,** was founded in 1821 in New York, where it performed all-black versions of Shakespeare. The troupe was forever running into difficulties with city authorities who closed it down repeatedly. Its most lasting claim to fame was giving a start to the career of **Ira Aldridge,** the first black actor to achieve an international reputation. Prevented from pursuing a career in America, Aldridge went to Europe in 1825 where he was decorated by heads of state for his performances of Lear, Macbeth, Othello, and Shylock. He was one of the greatest actors of his age, but racial barriers prevented him from acting in his own country. Degrading stereotypes of African Americans were perpetuated on stage and then on film and television in such servile caricatures as Jim Crow, Stepin Fetchit, and "mammy roles."

True enclave theatres were finally established in Harlem in the 1920s and 1930s where black performers such as Bill "Bojangles" Robinson, Florence Mills, Josephine Baker, Bert Williams, and Lena Horne began to produce and appear in their own "Negro musicals" written by Eubie Blake, Thomas "Fats" Waller, and Duke Ellington. The civil rights struggles of the 1950s and 1960s lent new purpose to black theatre as active tools of social, if not artistic, liberation. By the late 1960s there were more than forty black theatre groups in New York alone. One of

HEALING THE WOUNDS OF CULTURE CLASH   *John O'Neal of Junebug Productions and Naomi Newman of A Travelling Jewish Theatre combined their theatrical traditions to produce* Crossing the Broken Bridge. *Their two-person play uses the lens of African American/Jewish relations to examine the forces that divide and unite the human community. Through stories and songs, the play attempts to address the volatile issues of stereotypes, racism, and anti-Semitism with humor and compassion.*

the most important was the **Negro Ensemble Company** (NEC) founded by Douglas Turner Ward in 1968 as a theatre dedicated to producing a wide range of plays meaningful to African Americans and to providing African American dramatists with an accommodating home in which to produce their works.

Artistic liberation was achieved in 1959 when *A Raisin in the Sun,* Lorraine Hansberry's famous play about the struggles of a hard-working black family to move into a white Chicago neighborhood, became a Broadway hit and then a major motion picture starring Sidney Poitier. Other significant productions that contributed to the liberation include *Purlie,* the first black musical to deal with racial problems; *The Wiz,* the urbanized version of *The Wizard of Oz;* and *Ain't Misbehavin',* in which a small talented ensemble sang and danced the music of the great enclave composer Thomas "Fats" Waller for the audiences of Broadway's "great white way." The special burden carried by African American theatre artists who feel trapped between the familiar world of the enclave and the expectations of the mainstream—neither fully liberated nor comfortably fused—was expressed

PERSECUTED ENCLAVE THEATRE   *Carlysle Brown's play,* The African Company Presents "Richard III," *chronicles the struggle against persecution and prosecution endured by the first African American theatre company. Whites who attended the company's productions of Shakespeare did so primarily to jeer. Claiming a fear for the public peace, the New York City constabulary arrested the company members and threw them in jail. Pictured here is Washington's Arena Stage production.*

by playwright, poet, novelist, and journalist **Langston Hughes** (1902–67) in his angry poem, "Note on Commercial Theatre":

> You've taken my blues and gone—
> You sing 'em on Broadway
> And you sing 'em in Hollywood Bowl,
> And you mixed 'em up with symphonies
> And you fixed 'em
> So they don't sound like me.
> Yep, you done taken my blues and gone.
>
> You also took my spirituals and gone.
> You put me in *Macbeth* and *Carmen Jones*
> And all kinds of *Swing Mikados*
> And in everything but what's about me—
> But someday somebody'll
> Stand up and talk about me,

And write about me—
Black and beautiful—
And sing about me,
And put on plays about me!
I reckon it'll be
Me myself!

Yes, it'll be me.[37]

Indeed, it was Langston Hughes—and other playwrights like Ossie Davis, Amiri Imamu Baraka, Ntozake Shange, George C. Wolfe, Suzan-Lori Parks, Adrienne Kennedy, and August Wilson—who created a diverse body of drama that fused

YALE REPERTORY THEATRE PRODUCTION OF *FENCES*   *Robert Brustein points out that* Fences, *one of August Wilson's most successful plays about the African American experience in the twentieth century, is written in the tradition of American family dramas like* Death of a Salesman. *Both plays depict the confrontation between an erring father and his indignant son. At the same time, however, Wilson's protagonist, Troy Maxson, faces off against death in a solitary battle not unlike that of the Shilluk warrior (see photo on p. 121), and the play concludes with an extraordinary ritual dance by Troy's brother Gabriel.*[38]

THE AMERICA PLAY   Reggie Montgomery as the Foundling Father in Suzan-Lori Parks' African American dramatic perspective on American history. "I take issue with history because it doesn't serve me," said Parks, "—it doesn't serve me because there isn't enough of it. In this play, I am simply asking, 'where is history?,' because I don't see it. I don't see any history out there, so I've made some up."[39] What she "made up" is a pun-filled allegory set sometime after Lincoln's death in which a black gravedigger who believes he resembles the late president digs a huge hole out West and opens a sideshow in it. For a penny, customers can shoot him with blanks as he sits in a rocking chair in a simulated theatre box.

their enclave experience to the American theatre, destroying the black stereotypes that had dominated the stage for over 200 years.

August Wilson writes plays that premiere at America's leading regional theatres and then transfer directly to Broadway, where they have won numerous awards. While drawing his characters from decades of African American experiences and crafting his dialogue in the cadences of blues music, Wilson creates actions in the conventionally recognizable tradition of American psychological realism. In an interview with Wilson, critic David Savran noted that each of his plays mixes European and African elements, keeping them intact, to create not a homogeneous synthesis but a complex and plural whole. It is as if each play, both formally and thematically, reflects Wilson's vision of a more equitable and respectful society, one that will not simply integrate African Americans by forcing them to renounce their cultural heritage and their history, but will encourage them to build upon and celebrate their past.[40]

New Fusion.   In the American theatre of the 1990s, the fusion process is under way as never before in cultural venues throughout the country. There are more culturally diverse "minority" actors, directors, producers, designers, and playwrights making theatre in America than ever before. Actors' Equity Association, the stage actors' union, reports that 50 percent of all plays produced by the League of American Theatres in 1990 had a significant number of actors belonging to ethnic and other minorities. In efforts to promote their visibility and employment in the art, many cultural groups have taken to publishing their own directories of theatre artists and organizations. Among the most consulted publications are *Asian American Arts Organization in New York, Black Theatre Directory* (second edition), *Deaf Artists of America* (divided into sections listing visual, performing, and literary artists), *Hispanic Theater Directory: United States, District of Columbia, and Puerto Rico, Directory of Native American Performing Artists,* and the *National Directory of Multi-Cultural Arts Organizations.* Playwright Ping Chong spoke for many theatremakers listed in these directories when he wrote,

> . . . I don't consider myself primarily as an Asian American artist. Recently, I was at a festival of Asian American culture at the Museum of Natural History where I showed slides of my work. I also talked about how Asian aesthetics functioned in my work. Kabuki and Chinese opera, for instance, incorporate elegant visual images and emphasize the beauty of gesture. While I was showing the slides someone in the audience said, "How come your performers are all white?" I do use ethnic people in my shows, but I wasn't going to say, I'll use three Japanese, one black, and one Hispanic—that's ridiculous. If you want to think in that narrow a way you can count me out. And second of all, I'm not going to allow myself to be ghettoized as an Asian American artist. I'm an *American* artist.[41]

At the same time, all groups, artistic and otherwise, include those who desire to maintain their original culture, reinterpret it, or leave it. Thus, even as theatre artists emerge from the enclaves, others steadfastly remain to stand in solidarity to preserve their traditions. Tina Howe, who has achieved a national reputation for her sensitive depictions of female/male relationships in such plays as *Coastal Disturbances, Painting Churches,* and *Approaching Zanzibar,* credits her own emergence to the important enclave productions of her work at New York's Second Stage:

> It wasn't until I went to a theatre that was run by women and found a director who was a woman, that my plays began to blossom. . . . if it weren't for my alliance with the Second Stage . . . and the nurturing atmosphere they create, I don't think I would be writing for the theatre anymore."[42]

Intercultural Performances. As new voices emerge fully from their enclaves, they will fulfill artistic destiny and change our ways of understanding theatre art. Some new adventurous creations are so fused to a variety of cultures that it is difficult to trace their exact ancestry. For instance, *The Gospel at Colonus,* Lee Breuer's hit play based on Sophocles' *Oedipus at Colonus,* is set in a black Pentecostal church, with the choral passages of the original adapted into gospel hymns that were sung on Broadway by Clarence Fountain and the Five Blind Boys of Alabama. In his international stage hit *M. Butterfly,* Asian American playwright David Henry Hwang took his title from *Madame Butterfly,* an Italian opera based on an American play, and combined it with the tale of a French embassy official who is duped by a Chinese spy who masquerades as a dancer in the Peking opera. The entire production was staged on a modified Japanese Kabuki stage.

Theatrical fusion is not always a happy or easy blending. Multiculturalism has never meant agreement, consensus, or feel-good art. Some see the movement as a kind of artistic segregation, a "new tribalism" that may result in a theatrical tower of Babel rather than new, universally appealing performances. In the effort to be heard as well as to destroy old stereotypes, some of the new work is narcissistic, fiercely preservationist, and confrontational. The immediacy of theatre art in which artist, artwork, and audience come together in real time and place can be a dangerous cauldron—a containment vessel in which meltdown is as likely as melting pot. As new groups add their voices and their choices to the theatrical mix, one thing becomes clear: cultural diversity is a reality of modern American theatre practice. On the country's stages, culturally diverse theatre artists are staging multicultural plays: new dramas with pluralistic *dramatis personae* and old plays envisioned from new cultural perspectives. The theatre is fulfilling its prime directive of reflecting the images of human action that make up multicultural America.

Looking for Multicultural Theatregoers

A Theatregoing Conundrum. The irony is that the cultural mechanism of theatre art works best on the stage. One of the biggest problems facing the American theatre today is that the cultures portrayed on *stage,* fused or otherwise, have not been in the *audience.* Many American plays have focused on the disempowered, disenfranchised, and disadvantaged of society. For most of the twentieth century, American theatregoers have been overwhelmingly homogeneous: the empowered elite who are white, middle aged, and affluent. The theatrical challenge of the 1990s is to attract audiences that more accurately reflect the cultural diversity of the plays being offered.

Producers everywhere recognize the urgency of solving this theatregoing dilemma. Gordon Davidson, artistic director of Los Angeles' Mark Taper Forum, considers audience development more than a simple matter of filling the seats of his resident professional theatre:

> I have devoted my life to the making of theatre which demands as much of its audience as it does from its artists. I have searched in my work to define and re-define in

Emerging Enclaves

SIGNS OF THE TIMES *Mark Medoff's* Children of a Lesser God *was one of the first plays since William Gibson's* The Miracle Worker *to dramatize the lives of the disabled and reach a wide mainstream audience. In the original production of the play, the protagonist and several members of the cast were played by hearing-impaired actors. Prior to this production, hearing-impaired actors practiced their craft with enclave companies such as the world-renowned National Theatre of the Deaf.*

A ONE-PERSON PANORAMA OF HISPANIC LIFE *In his one-person play,* Spic-O-Rama *writer/actor John Leguizamo depicts a panorama of New York Latino culture as he mutates into the entire Gigante family. Leguizamo, who has appeared in feature films and starred in his own TV show (*House of Buggin*), uses comedy as a weapon against cultural stereotypes. "America's a strange schizophrenic country," he says. "There's so much discrimination here, and yet it gives you that incredible self-pride. I want to help people see things and change things."*[43]

THE GREAT GAY WAY   *The 1990s have been the decade of gay theatre, on and off Broadway. Musicals, tragedies, comedies, and parodies on gay themes by gay writers have entered the mainstream. Most prominent is Tony Kushner's* Angels in America: A Gay Fantasia on National Themes, *a two-part, eight-hour epic that has been called "the most ambitious American play of our time." Kushner's theatrical juggernaut, which won the Pulitzer Prize, Tony Award, and New York Drama Critics' Circle Award, ranges from earth to heaven, with scenes in Washington, the Kremlin, the South Bronx, Salt Lake City, and Antarctica; focuses on sex, religion, and politics; deals with Jews, Mormons, WASPs, and blacks; switches between realism and fantasy, from the tragedy of AIDS to the camp comedy of drag queens.*[44]

A NATIVE AMERICAN SPEAKS IN A POWERFUL VOICE   Black Elk Speaks, *based on the 1932 book by John G. Neihardt and adapted for the stage by the late Christopher Sergel, is one of the first major plays to explore the Native American experience. The drama combines aspects of Sioux storytelling with American theatre performance traditions to depict the massacre of Native Americans in a series of flashbacks of bloody battles, each escalating in intensity and cruelty.*

INTERCULTURAL PERFORMANCE   *The intercultural connections of Peter Brook's production of* The Man Who *can only be described as global: the play was inspired by "The Man Who Mistook His Wife for a Hat," the best-selling collection of "clinical tales" by neurologist Oliver Sacks. In Brook's adaptation, four actors (the English Bruce Myers, the Japanese Yoshi Oida, the German David Bennent, and the African Sotigui Kouyate) play all of the patients and doctors. Brook, the celebrated English director, founded the transcultural International Center for Theatre Research, a Paris-based company of actors from all over the world dedicated to discovering theatrical paths to transcend barriers created by different languages and cultures.*

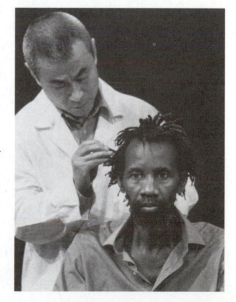

contemporary terms how a sense of community can be established in the theatre. I know that what happens on stage must be a truer reflection of what is happening in life and that the audience in the theatre be a truer representation of vast and nonhomogeneous society—that the mixture of age, race, sex, language and economic disparities all contribute vitality and energy to be shared by all.[45]

Adrian Hall, former artistic director of Trinity Repertory Theatre and the Dallas Theater Center, put it more bluntly: "The whole point of theatre is to develop new audiences. Without them, we're dead!"[46]

Attracting groups that feel uninvited is easier said than done. Joining an exclusive, homogeneous gathering like the typical American theatre audience is difficult for those who have long experienced exclusion. The difficulty is reflected by the respondents to the Harris poll who said they never go to the theatre because they "feel out of place."

With a sense of renewed urgency, theatres across the country are developing new, imaginative outreach programs designed to increase the diversity of their audiences—to make theatregoing more inviting, accommodating, and accessible to all.

Breaking the Price Barrier.   Many theatres are developing strategies to overcome the shock of theatre ticket prices. One very popular program is "Pay What You Can" ticket pricing that allows theatregoers to buy tickets to a specially designated performance (often a matinee) at any price they can afford. So popular is this program at San Diego's La Jolla Playhouse that it is not unusual for their "Pay What You Can" performances to sell out (at 25 cents to $25 for a ticket) less than an hour after the tickets go on sale. Surveys indicate that the program is successfully attracting a demographically diverse cross section of first-time theatregoers who are filling otherwise empty seats.

Other effective discount pricing strategies include student and senior **rush tickets** and half-price-day-of-show tickets. Some theatres have even found ways to admit first-timers and young patrons for free. The Actors Theatre of St. Paul gives free tickets to anyone under 18 who is accompanied by a paying adult. The Mark Taper Forum makes available theatregoing "scholarships," which are season subscriptions that adult donors purchase to be given to the students or schools of their choice.

Access.   In response to successful advocacy by groups representing citizens with disabilities, theatres are modifying their facilities and performances to make theatregoing more accommodating. For the hearing impaired, many theatres provide at least one performance at which sign language interpreters or projected subtitles run concurrently with the stage action. In addition, the **Americans with Disabilities Act** of 1992 mandates that all theatres and other public gathering places with fifty or more seats must provide free "assistive listening devices" to the hearing impaired. Most theatres have opted for wireless FM or infrared technologies that broadcast amplified sounds to earphones. Even visually impaired theatregoers now have the opportunity to enjoy live theatre. A special pilot program named

"Describe" has been inaugurated in several Broadway theatres as a joint venture of Hospital Audiences, Inc. (HAI) and the League of American Theatres and Producers. In advance of performances, "Describe" mails to its subscribers prerecorded audio cassettes that give descriptions of particular shows. At the performances, a live description is broadcast via a tiny earpiece, featuring a trained volunteer who sits in the technical booth and describes the stage action during pauses in the dialogue or singing.

Culture-Specific Outreach.   Some of the most imaginative and determined outreach programs are those dedicated to recruiting specific cultural, ethnic, and racial segments of communities in which theatres exist. For example, many not-for-profit theatres have rewritten their bylaws to mandate a diverse board of directors and artistic staffs. The San Diego Repertory Theatre runs an aggressive diversity program called *Teatro Sin Fronteras* ("Theatre Without Borders") that includes nontraditional casting, an advisory council of distinguished community leaders, door-to-door marketing by the managing director, one or two bilingual productions each season, and an administrative and artistic structure that mandates sharing decision making with "artists of color."

As these outreach strategies become successful in developing a culturally and demographically diverse audience, the new theatregoers may become dedicated play-followers for the same reasons as those long acculturated to the art.

Why They Choose Theatre

People choose theatre for many of the same reasons they select movies or television. But in several important ways the incentives are different. The **passive appeals** of theatre—entertainment and edification—are similar to those of film and television. The **active appeals** of theatre—social activities and participation—are better served by live performances.

In-the-Flesh Entertainment

The most obvious of the passive reasons people go to the theatre is *to be entertained.* "Let Me Entertain You," the signature song of the famous striptease artist Gypsy Rose Lee, has become an anthem for entertainers everywhere. Entertainment, however, means different things to different theatregoers.

To See a Star.   The audience comes to the theatre primarily to see the actors. This histrionic appeal is at the very heart of the art that presents human beings "in the flesh." Seeing a particular actor is also fundamental to film and television, but stars are literally a dime a dozen in recorded drama. The theatre, however, offers the rare opportunity to be with celebrities in the same space for a brief time. Tickets to *Waiting for Godot* at Lincoln Center were in demand because Robin Williams and Steve Martin played the title roles each night for seven weeks (see photo p. 115).

COMMUNITY OUTREACH *In 1966 Washington's Arena Stage created the Living Stage, a multiracial improvisational company as an outreach theatre to provide access to the art for the disadvantaged, handicapped, incarcerated, the young, and the elderly. Most of their work is with youth; the Living Stage has conducted more than 3,000 performances for audiences ranging in age from 2 to 18.*

Theatregoers love to see TV and movie stars on stage; the play is sometimes of secondary importance. The theatrical lives of the Broadway revivals of *Grease, Damn Yankees,* and *Kiss of the Spider Woman* were extended significantly when Brooke Shields, Jerry Lewis, and Vanessa Williams, respectively, joined the casts. The staple of many summer theatres is the star package—touring shows, usually musicals, built around a well-known film or television star.

To help sell their political drama on Broadway, the producers signed Glenn Close, Gene Hackman, and Richard Dreyfuss to star in the 1992 production of Chilean dramatist Ariel Dorfman's *Death and the Maiden.* The play is about a woman who kidnaps the man (Hackman) she believes raped her years before and puts him on trial in her home while her husband (Dreyfuss) defends him. While these actors may be good for the box office, they were not a hit with some segments of the theatre profession. Actors' Equity Association (AEA) and the Hispanic Organization of Latin Actors (HOLA) objected to the fact that although the events depicted in the play originated in Chile, and the play was originally written in Spanish, the production included no Hispanic performers in the leads or in understudy roles. Director Mike Nichols stated that the play's universal theme allowed it to be set anywhere, with anyone playing its characters. Responded HOLA, "Although we realize that this is a commercially driven venture, it's also a Catch-22 situation for our Hispanic actors: How can we have bankable Hispanic stars if there is no opportunity to attain this status? Help us insure that our Hispanic members will have the opportunity to advance their careers, break stereotypes, and become stars."[47] It has become conventional show business wisdom that big commercial productions can draw a substantial audience only with a **headliner,** an actor who is more of an attraction than the play itself.

STAR-CROSSED CASTING   *Broadway production of Ariel Dorfman's* Death and the Maiden, *starring Glenn Close, Gene Hackman, and Richard Dreyfuss.*

To See the Play.   Playwrights are sometimes as capable of achieving celebrity status as performers. Shakespeare is a perennial box office attraction. In the modern theatre, the plays of veteran dramatists Neil Simon, Arthur Miller, Edward Albee, and Andrew Lloyd Webber have a proven appeal and are generally recognized as star proof. Among the newer generation (all Tony Award and Pulitzer Prize winners), August Wilson, David Mamet, Wendy Wasserstein, and Tony Kushner can pack Broadway theatres on the strength of their names alone. Their new works are eagerly awaited, guaranteed to draw an advance audience.

A curious phenomenon of the contemporary theatre has been that the biggest hits, the longest running international sensations, the *things to see,* are shows that have never been known by their stars. *A Chorus Line, Cats, Les Misérables, Miss Saigon,* and *The Phantom of the Opera,* to name a few, have endured by title and reputation alone (and, some would say, clever marketing). The stage versions of

THIS IS ENTERTAINMENT   *The Flatrock Playhouse world premiere of* Gilligan's Island—The Musical, *directed by Stephen Rothman.*

There are times when people just aren't in the mood for Kafka, Sartre or Kierkegaard.

these productions have been far more popular than their screen versions: *A Chorus Line* is a good example.

The drawing power of "old favorites" is demonstrated by the fact that most stage productions are revivals of proven hits of the past. The theatre is unique in attracting those eager to see old plays rendered in new choices.

Relief and Release.   For many theatregoers entertainment is simple diversion, a fundamental consequence of weekend conditioning. They go to the theatre for release from the stresses of the workweek. Such theatregoers seek easy emotions: the hearty laughs of broad comedies, the tears jerked by sentimental romance, the thrills of good melodramas. More bang for your buck. No serious complex issues, please.

THEATRICAL EDIFICATION   *In* Terra Nova, *Ted Talley's drama on the nature of modern heroism, the audience learns of Robert Scott's doomed race against Roald Amundsen to the South Pole in 1907. Set in Antarctica, emotionally climactic scenes of survival and hallucination alternate with debates between Scott and Amundsen on the nature of heroism.*

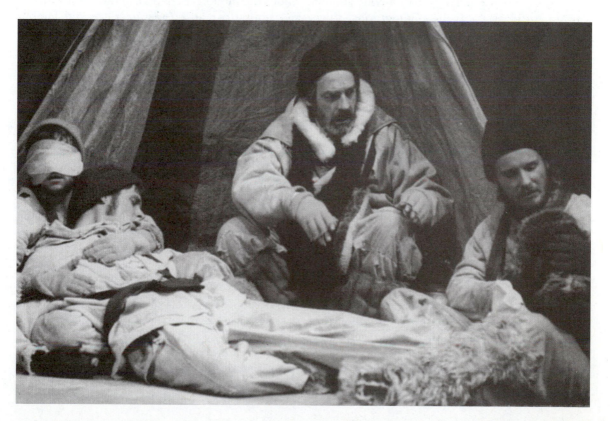

Edification

For others, pure entertainment is not enough. For them the theatre is a forum for the examination of serious issues, from psychology to sociology, from ethics to metaphysics, from the universal to the particular.

Theatre's advantage over the classroom is that the theatre shuns the cold, objective logic of impartial examination and reasoned discourse for the more imagination-charged, suspensefully crafted appeals to emotion *and* reason. In his biographical drama *Breaking the Code,* British playwright Hugh Whitemore set out to depict the tragically heroic life of Alan Turing, the British mathematician who helped turn the tide against the Nazis in World War II by breaking the ciphered code of the German Enigma machine. Whitemore chose to emphasize the personal trials of Turing's secret life as a homosexual rather than the math and science of his code breaking. He was surprised and delighted by the reactions of preview audiences who demanded "more math." The intellectually arcane became dramatic in its theatrical incarnation. In effect, the audience wanted "more brain for its bucks."

Television and film also play to these passive desires for entertainment and edification, and some would argue they do so more successfully. The popular MGM film retrospective of cinematic song and dance unabashedly declares "That's Entertainment!" The PBS miniseries *The Civil War* used the power of television to teach a huge nationwide audience about the bloodiest chapter in the country's history. Using photographs, songs, and actors to read correspondence and famous speeches, the series captured the imaginations of viewers as no Public Broadcasting System telecast (it used to be called "educational TV") had ever done before. Certainly, recorded drama competes well in playing to passive appeals, but the theatre has the advantage in playing to the active reasons for attending. Among the active appeals, social reasons dominate.

Socializing: The Need to Gather

Human beings exhibit a strong, innate need to gather. Our success as a species is enhanced by physical, emotional, and intellectual strengths that are experienced through the collective power of our social institutions. The family unit is basic, but does not fulfill our tribal instincts. Therefore, we organize ourselves into larger, increasingly complex groups—tribes, communities, nations—and into subsets of these structures—religious institutions, schools, and collective leisure pursuits.

Electronic Gathering.   In our modern electronic age, human gathering as traditionally understood is being redefined. Gathering via the cathode ray tube results in the literal manifestation of what was previously a metaphysical concept: the split whereby the body is in one place, while the mind is in another. As a result, "going out" to attend anything competes poorly with the convenience, safety, and economy of staying at home with a free broadcast, rented video, or computer network.

In ever-increasing numbers we tune in or log on to work, religion, conversation, and entertainment. Gathering has become a simple matter of staying put and pressing buttons.

The Privatization of the Performing Arts.   As for the performing arts, many believe we have already lost the will, habit, and need to gather as a live audience. The truth is we may have lost the habit and the will, but not the need. Syndicated talk-show host Sally Jessy Raphael refers to the innate human desire to gather as **"the pub mentality,"** and she maintains that Americans have few available places to develop it. According to Raphael, TV talk shows like hers are as good as it gets today:

> In Wales or England, after a day's work, people drop by the pub to hoist a pint and to say, 'Did you see in the news today?' Television has become the only pub we have, what with people rarely meeting, let alone developing relationships with, their neighbors. Every time I spend any time abroad, I always think how wonderful it is that a group can gather [to interact] that way. The talk shows—all of them—have brought the pub to TV.[48]

To join the token studio audience, one need only call in or, easier still, tune in. To drop by the "virtual pubs" available on the Internet, just log on. Some experts believe this technological transformation of leisure is, in the words of Harvard professor Robert Putnam, a dangerous sign of "the erosion of social capital."[49] Clifford Stoll, author of *Snake Oil—Second Thoughts on the Information Highway* (Doubleday, 1995), is more blunt in his assessment of electronic gathering:

> What's missing from this electronic wonderland? Human contact. Discount the fawning techno-burble about virtual communities. Computers and networks isolate us from one another. A network chat line is a limp substitute for meeting friends over coffee. No interactive multimedia display comes close to the excitement of a live concert. . . . this nonplace lures us to surrender our time on earth. A poor substitute it is, this virtual reality where frustration is legion and where—in the holy names of Education and Progress—important aspects of human interactions are relentlessly devalued.[50]

Theatre performance, on the other hand, is defined by gathering—the old-fashioned kind. You have to "go out" for it. It cannot come to you. Theatre, wrote critic and dramaturg James Leverett, "can do without *everything*—sets, props, costumes, even the stage itself—but it can't do without every*body* in order to fulfill a basic ritual of presence shared between performer and spectator."[51] With fewer opportunities to satisfy the pub mentality, the theatre has become for many a kind of refuge from the electronic crowd—an event completely structured for old-fashioned socializing. For these play-followers, the social occasion of going to the theatre is its primary attraction.

Few Go Alone.   Surveys show that very few go alone to the theatre. The VALS study reported that only 2 percent of those who attend the theatre go alone. Furthermore, theatregoers rarely attend with business associates (2 percent) or their children (2 percent). Their companions are usually their spouses (50 percent) or social friends (24 percent).[52] The survey demonstrates that theatregoing is viewed not as a business opportunity nor as a family occasion, but as a social event with a status and importance above the casual and spur of the moment.

Theatre as Café.   The theatre has always offered its patrons the opportunity to see and be seen as opposed to the more anonymous viewing of movies and the absolutely anonymous viewing of television. Polish drama critic Jan Kott calls this special opportunity **"theatre as café."**[53] So fundamental is this appeal of theatregoing, that producers structure the performances and provide dedicated facilities to enhance it. Many theatres have elaborate preshow, intermission, and postshow lobby activities. In some theatres, the lobbies themselves look like cafés, with gift shops, galleries, bars, tables, and even elegant food services. Arriving early at the theatre means social things to do. Arriving before the show starts at the movies means sitting in the dark and finishing the popcorn before they roll the previews.

Intermissions have always been the theatre's traditional time for café. In the eighteenth century there were four intermissions. By the end of the nineteenth century, only two intermissions were customary for a standard three-act play. Today, "full length" means two acts with one intermission.

Café also continues in postshow (après-theatre) activities from structured discussions with the theatremakers to the more informal opportunities to socialize with, or at least go backstage and congratulate (or commiserate with) the artists in person. Such artist-to-patron interaction has been going on in the theatre for 2,500 years. The performers expect it and crave it. They would feel like failures without it.

The Appeal of Participating

Theatre is the performing art at which your presence and *participation* are expected. People go to the theatre because they know they will participate in the performance—not only to interact with each other, but to interact with the artists. Like the actors, their reactions are seen and heard, their collective emotions are felt.

The live convergence of theatregoers and theatremakers, when it works well, goes beyond communication to synergy: the joint action of agents that, when taken together, increases each other's effectiveness. When the synergy is at its theatrical best, the result can be communion—not unlike that of the ancient ritualistic gatherings. "Theatre," wrote playwright Laura Shamas, "is a social arena; we experience this art—which is performed live—as part of a group. It's one of the few places left in America where 500 people can laugh or cry or sigh or breathe together, side by side, an acknowledgement of our humanity."[54]

Rounded Performers.   Theatrical communion can be a startling experience for those raised on recorded drama. Columnist Anna Quindlen describes such an ex-

CAFÉ TALK: A THEATREGOER'S GUIDE TO BACKSTAGE BANTER

Meeting actors backstage after a performance, especially one that has been less than boffo, can be a creative exercise in diplomacy for the experienced theatregoer. Following is a selection of the kind of *noncommittal* backstage banter guaranteed to be at least publicly accepted by thespians as congratulations at the backstage "café."

"Unbelievable!"

"Wow!" (Hug optional; repeat for effect)

"You really outdid yourself on this one!"

"You did it again!"

"You should have been in the audience!"

"Tonight I saw your work in a whole new light."

"You looked like you were having such fun up there!"

"I've always loved [name of play]!" (In response to actor's query: "How did you like it?")

"You really put a lot of work into this one!"

"How did you learn all those lines?"

"I'm speechless!"

"Where's the cast party?"

perience in her 5-year-old son's reaction to seeing his first stage play, Stephen Sondheim's fairy tale musical, *Into the Woods.* When she asked the youngster what he had liked best about the show, he said without hesitation, "I liked that it was real." "[He] was," wrote Quindlen, "deeply satisfied by the three-dimensionality of it all, by the rounded performers in a world that brings us most of our entertainment flat."[55] Most people have an innate, if not experiential, understanding of this appeal. The Americans in the Arts survey found that, despite the dominance of television, nine out of ten people felt that seeing something performed live on stage is more meaningful and exciting than seeing it on TV.

Satiating the Public Imagination

The public imagination is a powerful force with a voracious appetite. On the menu of performing arts, the theatre is increasingly the slow-cooked, made-from-scratch, gourmet, à la carte selection on a lengthening list of ready-made, fast-food choices. The potential market for the art is huge and diverse. Trying to determine the identities, proclivities, desires, tastes, and pleasures of a more inclusive clientele is part of the alchemy of choice making practiced by theatre artists.

The surveys, polls, studies, and analyses referred to in this chapter are only the latest strategies in the series of never-ending attempts to understand who theatregoers are and what they want. Surveys of arts consumers is big business. Television operates through electronic monitoring systems of its "viewers," basing everything from renewal and cancellation of programs to advertising prices on the rating points determined by Arbitron and Neilsen devices. The film industry does extensive test marketing in selected areas, and in recent years has come to rely on "test screenings" with audience members wired by electrodes to a computer that analyzes their positive and negative reactions to episodes in the film. The originally "sad endings" for such box office bonanzas as *Rocky II, Fatal Attraction, Pretty Woman,* and *Waterworld* were changed to their present "happy endings" based entirely on such testing. The video rental business has, in effect, become the "big brother" of arts consumers. Its computer lists of customers comprise vast databases of the rental habits, histories, and entertainment choices of virtually the entire population. The theatre, by comparison, is once again still relatively low tech and instinctive in its methodology: out-of-town tryouts, preview performances, and postshow discussions with the audience are standard practice.

Writing plays that will attract large diverse audiences who laugh, cry, or think together is the challenge. Theatremakers are acutely aware that theatregoers can "make" or "break" a play by attending or staying home. Two hundred years ago, the famous lexicographer Dr. Samuel Johnson took to verse to express the important lesson he learned about the public when his first play ended in failure at London's Drury Lane Theatre:

> Ah! let not censure term our fate our choice,
> The stage but echoes back the public voice;
> The drama's laws, the drama's patrons give,
> For we that live to please, must please to live.[56]

Theatrical Expectations

Imagine you have considered your options and have chosen an evening of theatregoing. You have cleared your weekend calendar and made a date with a similarly "free" companion. You have reserved your tickets, chosen your seats, and made dinner reservations that include others who will comprise your theatre party. You have arrived at the theatre early enough to find a place to park, pick up your tickets from the box office, have a bit of preshow "café," find your seats, and read your program. If all goes as planned, you should finish reading the cast biographies as the house lights dim for the start of the performance. You should feel the first stirrings of theatrical suspense as you wait expectantly for all the theatre promises—to have your imagination captured by something real, round, and live.

The first artist to make choices that anticipate your expectations and invite your communion is the playwright.

GOING TO THE THEATRE

A View from the Audience

by Lennore S. Van Ora
[Reprinted from *Playbill*][57]

"I arrived at the theatre to see Into the Woods *confined to a wheelchair, but I certainly didn't leave that way."*

I couldn't go *Into the Woods* until I got Out of My House. Because I've been an avid theatregoer for 30 odd years (all right, odd as in peculiar, bizarre and singular), a special friend decided that Stephen Sondheim would be an appropriate companion on my birthday. In the past, such news would have elated me. Broadway! Orchestra seats! Bernadette Peters! What could be bad?

Well, to make a long story short, I require a wheelchair now when I want to go somewhere. Have chair, will travel, so to speak. I lost the ability to walk 13 months ago, and although I'm determined to rise again like a Phoenix, I haven't quite succeeded—yet. What's worse, I also haven't garnered up the courage to brave Manhattan these many months, either. Maybe I wouldn't feel quite so conspicuous at *Starlight Express,* where everyone is on wheels, but a normal theatre, housing a normal (as in not disabled) audience rather intimidates me.

My friend, however, was unperturbed when I spoke about the obstacles that might deter us. She informed me, rather smugly, I thought, that she'd anticipated potential problems. She had specifically required an aisle seat, and the ticket agent had pointed out that if I could slide into a 36 inch wide, regular theatre seat (I could), the wheelchair would be stored away in a special spot, out of sight and out of mind. The words, "a special spot" reverberated inside of me for the rest of the day. Could it be that others "like me" had ventured out already?

Intellectually, of course, I know that the answers were decisively affirmative; viscerally, though, where my fears continued to imprison me, and my self-consciousness willed me to stay hidden (because I was after all, flawed and imperfect), I had deluded myself into believing that nobody in my condition had ever attempted such an excursion before. Imagine, then, my surprise when I discovered that the theatre had a special ramp entrance for wheelchairs. Picture, if you can, my astonishment when I realized that the ushers not only didn't leap over tall buildings in a single bound to escape from me, but rather went out of their way to be solicitous and kind throughout the show. Whenever possible, they asked newcomers to enter the row from the opposite aisle so as not to jostle me, and once, amazingly, they encouraged a man to climb into his seat from the row behind. He did!

Even the show (oh Lord, how I love the theatre, and oh Lord, how I had missed it) conspired to teach me a valuable lesson. I remembered from the reviews that many critics had complained about the disparity between the carefree, frivolous mood of the Act I and the somber, more serious tone of Act II. In many respects, however, this juxtaposition paralleled my own life. For 34 years I had played and frolicked and gamboled. (If only I'd fully appreciated that freedom at the time!) Yet, I'd had to learn, just as the characters did in *Into the Woods,* that we must regard adversity as a challenge, instead of as a punishment. It also became clear to me that innocence and experience are two sides of the same coin, and I understood William Blake's dictum at last that human beings must embrace both conditions, if they are to be truly free.

So you see, I may have arrived at the theatre confined to a wheelchair, but I certainly didn't leave that way. After the play ended, I was soaring higher than the birds, and the melody I sang was so sweet they paused in mid-air to listen to me.

Broadway, it's good to be back.
(PLAYBILL is a registered trademark of Playbill Incorporated, NYC. Used by permission.)

●●

SUMMARY

1. An audience is essential for all of the arts. Theatre art must have theatregoers. Without them, the creation of the art remains incomplete.

2. Leisure time is freedom from the demands of work, free or unoccupied time waiting to be filled with pleasing pursuits. In the last twenty-five years, leisure time has decreased per capita in America.

3. Competition among business, sports, and the arts for leisure-time dollars is fierce. Viewing of recorded performing arts has increased, while the live performing arts have had to struggle to maintain audiences.

4. Theatregoing was the most popular leisure-time pursuit in ancient Greece. Roman theatre had to compete with an almost modern selection of sensational spectator events. Renaissance theatre was the least expensive diversion attracting a cross section of 12 to 20 percent of society. Indoor theatregoing in the seventeenth and eighteenth centuries attracted fewer, while the nineteenth century experienced a theatregoing craze. In the twentieth century, competition from recorded drama has led to a decrease in dedicated theatregoing to 3 percent of metropolitan populations.

5. Today's theatregoers are disproportionately middle aged, well-to-do, well educated, female, and white. Among these demographic factors, education matters most.

6. Developing the theatregoing habit depends on access to theatre facilities, childhood experiences, and cultural traditions.

7. America, the original multicultural society, is becoming more culturally diverse at an increasing rate. Multiculturalism is the idea that today's demographic realities must be reflected in our public institutions.

8. Theatre has a cultural mechanism for reflecting society. The process of theatrical fusion begins in enclave performances that are assimilated, liberated, and ultimately absorbed into the mainstream to create new traditions and conventions of theatre art.

9. To attract a more diverse audience, theatremakers are using a variety of outreach strategies including lower prices, handicapped access programs and devices, and culture-specific targeting.

10. People choose theatregoing for its passive appeals of entertainment and edification and for its active appeals of socializing and direct participation.

11. In recent years, the entertainment industry has employed scientific, techno-logical, demographic, and psychological studies and surveys to try to gauge the public imagination.

CHOICES

1. Calculate the performing arts choices (excluding video) available in your community on a given weekend. Compare the number of films, stage plays, operas, symphony concerts, and dance events playing as well as the totals for all performances. Call the box offices for the various events to calculate the total number of available seats for all weekend performances. Calculate these available seats against the total population of the community. Compare the costs for each event including ancillary expenses of parking and refresh-ments.

2. Determine an entertainment/edification index for the film, television, and theatre choices available on a typical Saturday night in your community. Cal-culate the number of choices available in the following categories: Primarily Entertainment ("more bang for your buck"); Primarily Edification ("more brain for your buck"); or a combination of both ("a spoonful of entertainment makes the edification go down"). In calculating the television choices, con-sider only those network and cable programs shown in the prime-time hours of 8 P.M. to 11 P.M. Consider only plays, excluding sports, news, and other pro-grams.

3. Survey the multicultural choices available at the movies, at the theatre, and on television for a typical week in your community. Calculate the compara-tive number of choices that reflect the experience and lives of groups other than those of well-to-do white people of European descent. Use such factors as subject matter, casting, and writers or directors to classify a particular play as a multicultural choice.

4. Where are you on the VALS scale? Describe your values and lifestyle to deter-mine your place on the VALS scale. Where are you now? What are your ambi-tions? How do you expect your goals will affect your choices for acquiring and spending leisure time?

5. Research and describe other American examples of cultural fusion in the arts, language, fashion, and food. How do these new entities affect you personally? What are your preferences? How have they redefined American culture?

6. Do your own personal theatrical survey. How many times a year do you go to the theatre? What are the primary reasons you do or do not attend? Are you at-tracted to the passive or active appeals of theatregoing? Be specific. Compare your theatregoing profile to the number of times you go to the movies, con-certs, museums, and to the number of times you watch television and to the number of videocassettes you rent. For active or passive appeals? Be specific.

*Patrick Stewart as Shakespeare in the Royal Shakespeare Company
production of Edward Bond's* Bingo.

*Thus far, with rough and
    all-unable pen,
Our bending author hath
    pursu'd the story . . .*

King Henry V, *Act V, scene ii*

CHAPTER 5

Imitations of Action

THE PLAYWRIGHT'S CHOICES

PREVIEW

The 1991 *coup d'état* in the Soviet Union was one of the most suspenseful events of the century, and everybody, it seemed, likened it to a play. Newspaper headlines proclaimed the unfolding action "high drama." TV newscasts consistently interrupted regularly scheduled programming to provide the latest updates on the "unfolding drama" in the Soviet Union. Major networks ran specials with sensational titles underscored by ominous musical themes. The players were divided into colorless, grim-faced antagonists pitted against vibrant heroes supported by a chorus of brave, exuberant youths. In the aftermath of analysis, President Mikhail Gorbachev cast himself as the protagonist. "It's my drama," he said, unaware that the yet-to-be-played-out "last act" would contain his own downfall at the hands of his supposed ally, Boris Yeltsin. One editor of a midwestern daily paper called the event "great theater with the entire world as an audience. Let's hope there's no sequel." "Only a scriptwriter," he concluded, "might have told a better story."[1]

World politics aside, the pertinent *theatrical* questions are: What makes such a real-life situation highly dramatic? And what exactly is it that scriptwriters do better in making actions for the stage than real-life people do in playing out the course of human events? Is there a formula to the process, or does each new play have the potential for artistic innovation? This chapter answers these questions by examining playwrights making plays: who they are and have been, how they write, where they get ideas, how they combine their individual points of view with the rules of the stage, and how they protect their choices through the production process.

The Art of Playwriting: Historical Perspectives

Artists or Hacks: The Status of Playwrights

Although drama had its origins in a culture that revered playwrights among its most worthy citizens, the idea of plays as works of art (let alone playwrights as artists) has not always been a settled issue. In ancient Athens, the great playwrights were citizens of the highest social stature. They were military officers, priests, and elected officials. Families such as Aeschylus' established playwriting dynasties that passed the art from generation to generation. The city-state established festivals at which competitions for the best new play were held with prizes for the winning authors. Only later in the fifth century B.C. were prizes also established for actors. The tragedies of Aeschylus, Sophocles, and Euripides and the comedies of Aristophanes have survived the millennia like other great artworks of antiquity because they have been perceived as the masterpieces of master artists.

In the Renaissance, the commercial market for plays tended to turn playwrights into hacks. The dramatists of the seventeenth century competed not for prizes but for profits by selling their plays to acting companies. Once plays were sold, playwrights relinquished all future rights to them. Copyright protection did not exist. In addition, the need to turn out a new play every two weeks (not quite the schedule adhered to by television writers today) also diminished their standing when compared to "true" literary artists such as poets and philosophers who

Old News, New Dramas

As for events in the Soviet Union, the country that was saved from the coup no longer exists. The characters have either changed roles or faded from the scene, replaced by a new set of players. The real-life drama of the summer of 1991 is history. But no sooner had they exited than the "scriptwriters" began to make their own dramas out of those exciting images.

British actors David Calder and Russell Dixon portray Yeltsin and Gorbachev in the Royal Shakespeare Company production of Moscow Gold, *Tariq Ali and Howard Brenton's dramatized stage version of events in the former Soviet Union that shook the world.*

Mikhail Gorbachev and Boris Yeltsin confer before the Soviet Parliament shortly after the abortive coup attempt. (Photography by Allan Titmuss C., London)

Tony Kushner's Slavs! *is a ninety-minute, one-act play on the birth and eventual collapse of the Soviet Union told mainly through the satirical hijinks of aging party bureaucrats, cackling babushkas, disillusioned youths, and other assorted eccentrics. The play comes directly from* Perestroika, *the second half of his two-part, seven-hour epic,* Angels in America. *Other award-winning playwrights who have dramatized aspects of this earth-shaking event include Tom Stoppard* (Hapgood) *and Wendy Wasserstein* (The Sisters Rosensweig).

could write at a more leisurely pace. Renaissance playwrights made little attempt to preserve their plays. The first efforts at publishing the collected plays of even the most successful dramatists were met with ridicule. **Ben Jonson** (1572–1637), Shakespeare's contemporary and the poet laureate of England, was publicly derided for publishing an expensively bound "folio" edition of his plays and calling them "works." In the England of James I, plays were not art, and playwrights were not artists. Even Shakespeare never lived to see the publication of his collected plays; the folio of his "works" did not appear until seven years after he died. No copies of his plays were listed in his will or found among his possessions. They were not considered assets of significant value. As Elizabeth Kirkland notes in *Shakespeare Alive,* "the best play was the one that brought in the biggest audiences, not necessarily the one that would earn the praises of later critics as works of literary genius."[2]

In the nearly 400 years since Shakespeare stopped writing plays, several factors have served to restore the esteem of playwrights. First, widespread publication of plays improved their reputations; bound and titled, plays had the packaging of "real" books. By virtue of wide dissemination, productions, and study of his plays, Shakespeare enjoys a reputation he never could have imagined in his own day; only the Bible has been translated into more languages than the works of Shakespeare.

Second, in the eighteenth century playwrights succeeded in securing copyright protection for their works. Spearheaded by the comic dramatist **Pierre-Augustin Caron de Beaumarchais** (1732–99), the world's first copyright law was passed by the French National Assembly in 1791. The law gave authors and their estates complete control of their works until five years after death. In addition, playwrights were to receive **royalties**—fees for each performance based on a fixed percentage of the income. In 1886 the **International Copyright Agreement** was established by which each subscribing nation agreed to uphold the copyright laws of the others. The law also brought translations and adaptations under the same protections as original works. More than any other factor, these laws broke the stranglehold of actors on "their" playwrights. Eventually, the modern system of producing plays for long runs accorded playwrights the validity of making enduring works.

Today, the status of playwriting as an art is not in doubt. Dramatists are eligible for the most respected honors awarded to writers, including the Pulitzer Prize (which maintains a separate category for drama) and the Nobel Prize for literature (which has gone to a playwright eleven times since it was established in 1901). Significantly, screenwriting, which is more lucrative than writing for the stage, retains the diminished status of "unpublished" works. To date, no screenwriter has won the Nobel Prize, and screenplays are not eligible for the Pulitzer Prize in drama.

Dramatic Forebears

From Soyinka back to Brecht to O'Neill, Chekhov, Ibsen, Molière, Shakespeare, and Sophocles, it is easy to trace the patriarchal line of great dramatists back to Thespis.

DRAMA AS INTELLECTUAL PROPERTY

Copyright laws established the concept of **intellectual property**. The general rules pertaining to ownership of plays are as follows:

Copyrights protect authors' basic rights over their work:

> The right to perform or display it publicly,
> To reproduce and distribute it and produce other works based on it,
> To claim its authorship, and
> To make sure its integrity is not compromised.

A work is copyrighted by the act of writing something and is announced publicly by the act of publishing the text.

> A copyrighted play can then become a rentable property.
> Royalty is the author's income, the rental received for use of the property.

The original term of the copyright for works created prior to 1978 was 28 years, renewable for an additional 47 years. Current copyright term is limited to the life of the author plus 50 years.

It is safe to assume that intellectual property has fallen out of copyright—entered the **public domain**—if it was first published 75 years ago.

The average royalty for a play performed at a regional professional theatre for a one-month run is $20,000.

It is much more difficult to find matrilineal dramatic forebears, since women have been systematically excluded from theatre art for much of its history. The only female playwright whose works are commonly recorded in the histories of early European drama is **Hroswitha,** a tenth-century Benedictine nun who wrote six plays modeled on those of the Roman Terence. Even after most legal prohibitions against women acting in plays were lifted in Europe by the eighteenth century, the barriers that kept women from writing plays were still in place. Foremost were the denial of basic schooling to young women and the stifling chauvinism of male-dominated societies that restricted women to servile roles. The first Englishwoman to earn a living as a writer was playwright and novelist **Aphra Behn** (1640–89). Although she had several stage successes in her time, she was viciously reviled by her male counterparts as a woman of questionable virtue, and her plays disappeared from the stage until they were rediscovered in the 1980s. The untold story is that throughout the eighteenth and nineteenth centuries, European and American women wrote for the stage, although their work was not adequately chronicled. **Hannah Cowley**

NOBEL LAUREATE   *In 1986 Nigerian playwright* **Wole Soyinka** *(1934–) became the first African to win the Nobel Prize. His plays fuse his Yoruban tribal traditions and images with the structure of Western drama.* A Play of Giants, *shown here, satirizes the West's complicity with Africa's most corrupt dictators including Jean-Bedel Bokasa, Francisco Macias Nguema, Idi Amin, and Joseph Mobutu.*

(1743–1809), for example, was considered one of the top comic playwrights of the late eighteenth century. Her comedy of manners, *The Belle Strategem,* which was first produced in London in 1780, was one of the first plays to be staged in the United States (1794). Her thirteen plays, like those of her female contemporaries, were largely forgotten by the end of the nineteenth century. Playwriting, the Victorians felt, was not an appropriate activity for "decent ladies." Cowley's work has received new attention and productions since the publication of *Wicked Company,* an analytical biography by Ciji Ware. Today, many female dramatists and their plays are being recovered from the disregard of history.

Artists of Their Times

We are all creatures of our times, understanding the world through shared perceptions and behaving according to codes of common values. If female dramatists were victims of their times throughout most of cultural history, the male playwrights

YÜAN DRAMA: BY THE RULES
Chinese dramatists during the Yüan Dynasty of the thirteenth and fourteenth centuries also wrote according to strong traditional custom that dictated strict rules of construction including the use of music, dialogue, characters, and poetic justice. Their plays dealt with the entire spectrum of humanity, from emperors to peasants. One of the best known plays from this period is Kao Ming's Pi-Pa-Ki *(Lute Song) (c. 1350), a music drama in forty-two acts that depicts the story of a virtuous wife who reclaims her husband, who had abandoned her for a life of wealth and bigamy at the imperial court.* Lute Song *was produced on Broadway in 1946 with Mary Martin as the protagonist, Tchao-ou-niang, and with sets and costumes by Robert Edmond Jones.*

were just as surely prisoners of theirs. They all reflected their respective cultures, writing according to the fashions, conventions, and preoccupations—in a word, the styles—of their ages.

Style.   Dramatists fashion their plays to fit the distinctive architectures, sizes, and technologies of available theatres. They populate their dramas with characters that can be played by the available actors—according to the histrionic methods of the time. And they attune their plays to the tastes, fads, idioms, behaviors, and imaginations of the audiences. Taken together, these temporal, shared aspects of playwriting constitute theatrical **style,** a kind of imaginative signature of an age. Understanding style is a key to unlocking dramas of other times and places.

The ancient Greeks made plays depicting the human struggle with powerful emotional urges and the establishment of codes of social order. Roman playwrights provided theatregoers with a vast array of sensational entertainments that reflected the many colors, cultures, and curiosities of their vast empire. The clerical dramatists of medieval Christian Europe turned the Bible into huge epic plays that juxtaposed earthly travail with the miracle of heavenly bliss and the curse of eternal damnation. Renaissance writers portrayed a robust age of discovery and adventure. Their imaginations were expansive, encompassing all aspects of their world. Their *dramatis personae* were essential links in a perceived **great chain of being** that encompassed the whole of moral, spiritual, and physical existence. The emblematic theatre was the Globe, where plays illuminated all aspects of life.

Eighteenth-century playwrights depicted an age preoccupied with manners and rules for everything, including the writing of plays. The social hierarchy was as strictly enforced as the artistic code called **neoclassicism.** In the early nineteenth century, writers of all types rejected all rules considered oppressive. Freedom became the revolutionary battle cry in politics as well as in art. **Romanticism,** however, was much more accommodating to literary art than drama. The rules of the theatre tended to inhibit rather than free the romantic imagination.

By the late nineteenth century, many artists became caught up in the social utilitarianism of their age. Playwrights who adhered to illusionistic conventions of **realism** and **naturalism** adopted the empirical analysis of science as an artistic method, depicting their characters as helpless victims of heredity and environment.

Much of the art of the twentieth century has been shaped by new perceptions of reality, such as the theories of Freud and Einstein, and by apocalyptic events like world wars and their resulting horrors. **Expressionism** is the nonrealistic dramatic style in which human action is seen from the inner workings of a single human mind—as in Elmer Rice's *The Adding Machine,* Arthur Miller's *Death of a Salesman,* and Tennessee Williams' *The Glass Menagerie.* Distortions of time and perceptions are features of this popular style. Einstein's theory of relativity suggested to latter-day playwrights that they could break out of their temporal prisons and depict on stage the convergence of events and persons separated by time and space. In *Communicating Doors,* Alan Ayckbourn, one of the world's most widely produced playwrights, creates a portal between hotel suites that carries women who step through it either twenty years forward or twenty years backward in time. Tom Stoppard's *Arcadia* alternates between 1809 and the present, until the final scene when then and now mingle in a touching scene that links characters across the centuries. In Edward Albee's *Three Tall Women* the life of a 92-year-old coma victim is portrayed at different ages by three women on stage simultaneously. David Ive's *Sure Thing* lets two people who meet in a restaurant, at the ring of a time-altering bell, keep restarting their awkward encounter until they finally make a romantic connection.

The "being and nothingness" of **existentialism** is reflected in **absurdist drama** that portrays the meaninglessness of a world without discernible values. Samuel Beckett, Edward Albee, Harold Pinter, and Eugene Ionesco wrote plays that reflect this pessimistic philosophy. Playwrights on the verge of the twenty-first century often promote the multicultural trends of a consolidating world. Their plays reflect a multiplicity of beliefs and styles as diverse as the peoples of the world brought into face-to-face proximity by the wonders of instantaneous electronic communication.

WHEN ELVIS MET PABLO AND ALBERT   *In Steve Martin's hilarious* Picasso at the Lapin Agile, *Albert Einstein and Pablo Picasso meet accidentally in 1904 in a Paris café called the Lapin Agile (the Nimble Rabbit). The two future innovators of the twentieth century hurl drawings and equations at each other like intellectual custard pies. Martin gives the two geniuses a look at the future they helped to create when he lets Elvis Presley stroll out of the 1950s and into their bar.*

The Playmakers' Working Methods

The Solitary Writer

If theatre is thought of as the collaboration of many artists, playwriting can be thought of as a more private art, removed from the frantic scramble of creativity that is the rehearsal hall. Most imagine great playwrights sitting in quiet isolation writing with a quill, pen, or typewriter (an antique black Underwood is the cliché), alternately riding a surge of creativity and fighting off the ravages of writer's block. After a suitable interval the writer emerges to deliver the finished draft for production. There is some truth to this image. **Henrik Ibsen** (1828–1906), the great Norwegian playwright whom many consider the father of modern drama, wrote such masterpieces as *A Doll's House, Hedda Gabler,* and *The Master Builder* while seated at a great desk in a splendid study. The Russian naturalist Anton Chekhov, author of *The Seagull, Uncle Vanya, The Three Sisters,* and *The Cherry Orchard,* often wrote his plays at his secluded country estate, posting them to the Moscow Art Theatre, and showing up only for opening night. "Don't write a single line for the theatre unless it is a thousand miles away from you," he warned.[3] Arthur Miller writes plays in a small shack on his Connecticut farm. Compositional artists like painters, novelists, poets, musical composers, and dramatists find seclusion conducive to hearing the inner voices and conceiving the images they seek to render. The prolific output of these dramatists speaks for their successful methods.

Writer's Block.   Like all solitary artists, the playwright's nightmare is writer's block: the time when the inner voices do not speak, the images do not form, and the dramatic imagination falls into dysfunction. All artists are susceptible. Neil Simon, for instance, is one of the most commercially successful playwrights in the world. Between *Come Blow Your Horn* in 1961 and *London Suite* in 1995 he has had thirty-one plays on commercial New York stages—almost one per year. But, as Simon readily admits, he does not write them that fast or regularly; his creative process is a constant battle with writer's block. According to Simon, he has learned to accept it as a fact of life—to work with it, not against it:

> Do I ever get blocks? I have had enough blocks to fill in from 23rd Street to 89th Street. My blocks usually come about mid-way through the first act of a play. It's about this point that I begin to get nervous and ask myself, "Is this good enough to go on with, to spend another three or four months writing and another six months in rewriting, casting, rehearsing and going through the agonies of production?" Usually at that point I will put the work aside and let it sit for six weeks or six months . . . (even for six years but it has to be on a very low flame) and then go on to some other project. Then I will take it out and read it again. Sometimes I will be delighted and surprised at what I read and want to get at it again immediately. *Barefoot in the Park* and *The Sunshine Boys* sat in that drawer for over a year, rapping on the wood and squealing in a tiny voice to be let out. *God's Favorite* was in there for three years. . . . And some just sit in that manuscript *Graveyard* forever.
>
> The plays that I wrote "straight through" were *California Suite, Chapter Two, The Odd Couple* and *The Gingerbread Lady.* (For the last one, I rented a tiny room in the Plaza Hotel because I was stuck on the third act, and didn't come out for a week. The room service equalled my eventual royalties.)
>
> The longest writing time was for my first play, *Come Blow Your Horn.* It took three years and twenty complete revisions from page one on.[4]

One strategy for overcoming writer's block is to create a play jointly with another dramatist.

Co-authors

Perhaps taking their cues from the theatre artists with whom they eventually must work, playwrights often collaborate with one another to create a single play. In Elizabethan England, the demands of producing a new work every two weeks made co-authoring plays standard operating procedure for even the most successful dramatists. Shakespeare was one of the few who made a reputation for delivering the goods on his own; he is given credit for being the sole author of at least thirty-three plays. But several of "his" plays—*Titus Andronicus, Pericles, Henry VIII, Two Noble Kinsmen,* and a lost play, *The History of Cardenia*—were written in collaboration with others, among them **John Fletcher,** one of the great collaborators of his day. Fletcher and his main writing partner, **Francis Beaumont,** are credited with fifty-three plays that were produced in London in the early seventeenth century. In their time, works by "Beaumont and Fletcher" were even more popular than those by "Shakespeare."

In the twentieth century, **George S. Kaufman** (1899–1961) was known as "the great collaborator" because he wrote all but two of his forty-six plays as part of a two- or three-person team. His biggest hit was the 1936 Pulitzer Prize-winning family comedy *You Can't Take It with You,* which he wrote with his favorite collaborator, Moss Hart. "I've always been smart enough to attach myself to the smartest people in the theatre," Kaufman once said.[5]

Co-authoring is by necessity the "preferred" system of making musicals. Ever since Gilbert and Sullivan began making operettas in the late nineteenth century, the "bylines" of musicals have consisted of writing teams such as Richard Rodgers and Oscar Hammerstein II, Fred Ebb and John Kander, Betty Comden and Adolph Green, and Howard Ashman and Alan Mencken. Standard practice is for one to compose the music, called the **score,** and for the other to write the lyrics and the **book,** also referred to as the **libretto.** As for film and television, collaborating in writing teams is the usual system of making screen and teleplays. To produce 500 pages of new script per week for the soap opera *Days of Our Lives,* NBC employs a team of twelve writers: two head writers author the weekly "long story" in narrative form, five co-head writers put together one "daily outline" for each of the week's episodes. Finally, five subwriters turn the outlines into the week's five daily "dialogue scripts" of approximately a hundred pages each.

Play Doctors.   Some playwrights, Shakespeare and Molière among them, began their careers as **play doctors,** rewriters who are brought in to remedy problems with working drafts of plays. Their job is to fix something—a character, some dialogue, a plot problem—that the producers think is broken. Play doctors are not collaborators, since they do not work in tandem with the original authors. They are after-the-fact fixers and polishers, known for their theatrical instincts, which they use to make plays more playable. Take the case of the musical version of Voltaire's *Candide.* Since it first premiered on Broadway in 1956, the musical comedy has had at least seven different lyricists and four different scriptwriters, each doctoring the play into a more effective stage piece (see color plate 6):

1956: *Candide* opens on Broadway after a difficult rehearsal process. The original lyricist, John LaTouche, died before the show opened, so Richard Wilbur (known primarily for his poetic translations of Molière's plays) was hired to finish the lyrics for Leonard Bernstein's musical score. However, the book, originally written by Lillian Hellman, is lambasted by the critics as too long, ponderous, and heavy-handed.

1973: *Candide* remains unproduced until it is revived on Broadway in a new environmental production "conceived" and directed by Harold Prince. (See color plate 6.) Hugh Wheeler is hired to revise and streamline the book into a shorter under-two-hours version, and Stephen Sondheim *(Gypsy, West Side Story)* is brought in to add new lyrics. Even composer Bernstein gets into the act by adding some new lyrics of his own. However, because of copyright protections, the characters in the new script cannot travel to the same places as in Hellman's original. All the locales are changed.

PINTER'S LIST   *Acclaimed British dramatist Harold Pinter writes in isolation, but throughout his career has sent manuscripts of his works to other playwrights—such as Samuel Beckett, Simon Gray, David Mamet, and Ian Smith—for feedback and suggestions. Pinter refers to them as his "mailing list"—not exactly co-authors or play doctors, but more like "medical" consultation. Pictured above is Pinter's* Betrayal.

> 1982: After receiving inquiries from opera companies, Leonard Bernstein's manager gathers Harold Prince, Stephen Sondheim, and newcomer John Maurceri to "re-expand" *Candide* into a version suitable for the New York City Opera.
>
> 1988: The Scottish Opera produces *Candide* in London in yet another doctored version with new lyrics by John Wells. It wins the Olivier Award (the British version of the Tony Award) for best *new* musical.[6]

Play doctors are such a permanent fixture of the film and television industry that the old Hollywood joke is about the movie mogul who exclaims, "This is a great script! Who can we get to rewrite it?"

Developmental Ensembles

Perhaps the most collaborative method of playwriting is the contemporary practice of ensemble writing in which the script is generated by a company of actors during an improvisational rehearsal process. Such playwriting seems nontraditional, but the theatre probably had its origins in such practices as improvisations, scenarios, mimes, and interpolations. Many of the leading *avant-garde* theatre groups of the 1960s such as the Open Theatre, the Living Theatre, the Performance Group, and the San Francisco Mime Troupe organized themselves as developmental ensembles in order to break down traditional distinctions between playwrights and performers. Such groups focus on cooperative efforts in which the contributions of each company member are considered valid. By the 1970s, ensemble writing found its way into mainstream theatre companies. The most successful play initiated by a developmental ensemble was the record-breaking musical *A Chorus Line,* which has a plot based on the recorded conversations of a group of New York's "gypsy" dancers. The Royal Shakespeare Company used ensemble writing to turn Charles Dickens' novel *Nicholas Nickleby* into a monumental play by having a cast of actors improvise five-minute distillations of each chapter in the book.

In order to avoid total chaos and to bring playable structure to their improvisations, most developmental ensembles require the participation of a playwright to record, unify, and dramatize their improvisational choices. The Open Theatre relied on the talents of Jean-Claude Van Itallie for such purposes and actually credits him with the authorship of some of its works. The Royal Shakespeare Company relied on David Edgar to unify the company's improvisations on *Nicholas Nickleby;* Edgar is credited as the "adapter" of the finished script. Similarly, the New York Shakespeare Festival, which sponsored the development of *A Chorus Line,* turned over the recorded testimonials of the dancers to director Michael Bennett, writer James Kirkwood, lyricist Edward Kleban, and composer Marvin Hamlisch to make it a complete musical.

Regardless of the particular method used, once a playwright begins to write, as part of a team, an ensemble, or alone, each must finally turn inward to individual imagination, motivation, and style. Nothing, writers like to say, is as patient as a blank piece of paper.

Why They Write Plays

Much of Neil Simon's autobiographical *Broadway Bound* is concerned with co-authoring. Throughout the play, the young protagonist Eugene (Simon) learns the fine art of writing radio comedy sketches with his brother Stan (Simon's brother Danny). In one particularly instructive scene Stan tells Eugene the secret of writing a good sketch: "Conflict and wanting it bad."[7] Simon never forgot the lesson in playwriting; his string of phenomenally successful plays proves the wisdom of his brother's advice. These two essential requirements are basic to all dramas, whether comic or serious, musical or nonmusical, screenplay or stage play, full-length drama or short sketch. "Conflict and wanting it bad" describes not only the plays they write, but the personal turmoil that motivates many writers to become dramatists in the first place.

An Uncertain Romance

The renowned playwriting teacher Howard Stein describes the dramatist's motivating impulse this way: "They write plays in order to work out their own uncertain romances with the universe."[8] Stein recognizes that playwriting is the choice of those who have a need to play out "in the flesh" those inner conflicts that remain unresolved sources of personal turmoil. American dramatist **Elmer Rice** (1892–1967) similarly described the motivating impulse as a need to purge an "agitating idea":

> A [playwright] "has something on his mind:" an agitating idea or image or problem; we say he "has something he wants to get off his chest:" an exciting emotion, whether joyous or painful. In either case, he has a sense of constriction and uneasiness; he feels oppressed, obsessed even. He wants relief from tension, purgation. If he cannot get his trouble off his mind or off his chest by direct action, he must rid

AGITATING IDEAS   *Elmer Rice's own career as a dramatist is distinguished by plays that reflect his lifelong agitation for social justice in the causes of his time. His first major play was* The Adding Machine *(shown here in its original 1923 production), an expressionist fantasy that depicts the growing regimentation of human beings in the machine age through the life and death of the bookkeeper, Mr. Zero. Other plays chronicle life in the slums (*Street Scene, *1929), the futility of expatriation as an escape from materialism (*The Left Bank, *1931), and the Great Depression (*We, the People, *1933).*

himself of it by symbolically externalizing it. Thus, literally, he presses it out, or expresses it.[9]

In other words, rather than the direct action of real life, playwrights opt for the *artificial* action of drama. In imaginative terms, plays afford them the opportunities to play out the way the uncertain romance might happen. Each playwright's need to dramatize is animated by unique personal experiences. The only thing worth writing about, William Faulkner once said, is the story of the "human heart in conflict with itself."[10]

From his forty years of teaching at the University of Iowa, Yale, and Columbia, Stein observed that the first play of young dramatists is often a "kind of kill-your-parent play" that depicts a family crisis resolved with the death (often by suicide or disease) of a parent (usually the father). Actually doing the killing would be pathologically criminal. Having characters act it out on stage becomes therapeutic. During the late 1960s and early 1970s many of Stein's students were disaffected Catholics using drama to reconcile their inner conflict over strict religious upbringing with the liberal tendencies of Vatican Council II and society at large. In the 1980s more women enrolled in playwriting programs than ever before, seeking to make dramatic representations of the ever-increasing challenge of living effectively in a male-dominated society. Such uncertain romances and agitating ideas, which change over the course of a lifetime, are particularly apparent in the works of prolific dramatists. For Sophocles, Shakespeare, and Ibsen the verve of fearless, youthful romance and adventure so apparent in their early plays *(Antigone, The Taming of the Shrew, Peer Gynt)* changed to depictions of indecision and foreboding in the dramas of their middle-age years *(Oedipus the King, Hamlet, Hedda Gabler)* and finally resolved into portrayals of reconciliation, if not peace and understanding, in their final dramas *(Oedipus at Colonus, The Tempest, When We Dead Awaken)*.

With a clarity of self-examination possessed by the artists of the psychoanalytic age, playwrights today are unusually insightful in articulating their own uncertain romances. Consider the following testimonials:

Christopher Durang has used drama to express his agitating experiences with many of the "baby boom" issues. His merciless, darkly comic plays have pilloried psychoanalysis *(Beyond Therapy)*, raising children *(Baby with the Bathwater)*, marriage *(The Marriage of Bette and Boo)*, newspaper tabloids *(Laughing Wild)*, and even Peter Pan *('dentity Crisis)*. *Sister Mary Ignatius Explains It All for You* is his controversial dramatic response to the conflict of his Catholic upbringing with his mother's death from a long, debilitating disease:

> The last year of my mother's life I began *Sister Mary Ignatius Explains It All for You.* . . . I wrote the second half a few months after she died. The play was in no way written "because" my mother died. It was written partially in giddy recall (who can believe we once believed in limbo?), and partially in anger (the Church's teachings on sex have done nobody any good). And it's also written from a basic, and disappointed, non-belief—for even when one ignores and forgives the sillier rules that have been made up by generations of Irish and Italian men who thought they heard

God whispering in their ears, what still remains is the church's presentation of a paternal, watching-over-us Good Shepherd whose supposed power and concern for us simply does not correlate with the facts of human suffering. God knows that I'm not the first person to think these thoughts. Still when the myth of the Good Father in heaven is taught as fact and ingrained in you from early childhood, to realize much later that this is untrue is, frankly, very disappointing.[11]

David Mamet has written searing dramas that have revealed the abusive, brutal aspects of our social classes and institutions: the petty criminal underclass in *American Buffalo,* real estate brokers in *Glengarry Glen Ross,* teachers and students in *Oleanna,* and would-be Hollywood moguls in *Speed-the-Plow.* In *The Cryptogram,* his most personal work, Mamet presses out the pain of the psychological and physical brutality of his own family life with his sister, mother, and stepfather. The play's 10-year-old protagonist is Mamet's dramatic incarnation of his young self. The title refers to the hidden meaning of our lives that we never fully comprehend. In a personal reflection, he recalls an encounter between his young sister and his stepfather:

She told me that on weekends when I was gone my stepfather ended every Sunday evening by hitting or beating her for some reason or other. He would come home from depositing his own kids back at their mother's house after their week-

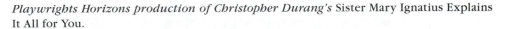

Playwrights Horizons production of Christopher Durang's Sister Mary Ignatius Explains It All for You.

end visitation, and would settle down tired and angry, and, as a regular matter on those evenings would find out some intolerable behavior on my sister's part and would slap or hit or beat her.[12]

Wendy Wasserstein, who won the Tony Award as well as the Pulitzer Prize for her Broadway hit *The Heidi Chronicles,* wrote her first play from an altogether liberated, but nevertheless theatrical motivating impulse:

I went to graduate school at Yale, and I remember all these Jacobean plays we would read about men kissing the skulls of women and then dropping dead. And I thought, I can't identify with this. And so I wrote *Uncommon Women* because part of me, maybe in a political way, wanted to see an all-women's curtain call at the Yale School of Drama. It was a vision—often I write a play because of an image and that was the image that I had.[13]

Suzan-Lori Parks is known for her imaginative use of dramatic language—a lover of words that "bang up against each other and do things." At the same time, she is reluctant to explain what her plays—darkly humorous, dreamlike allegories—mean. In *The Death of The Last Black Man in the Whole Entire World,*

The American Repertory Theatre's production of David Mamet's The Cryptogram.

The Phoenix Theatre production of Wendy Wasserstein's Uncommon Women and
Others *with Glenn Close, Meryl Streep, Jill Eikenberry, and Swoosie Kurtz.*

Parks parodies a string of stereotypical African American characters such as Old
Man River Jordan, Lots of Grease and Lots of Pork, and Black Man with Water-
melon and Black Woman with Fried Drumstick. The plot depicts an archetypal
black man who dies a dozen deaths as his wife feeds him soul food. In response to
questions about the play's meaning, Parks revealed more about herself than the
dramatic action:

> My experience on the planet as an African-American is fractured. There are notice-
> able gaps in tracing my family. And I think people in my plays come out of those
> gaps—they're my forebears. Then there is the gap between the promise and the real-
> ity of this country, and that is a wound.[14]

Samuel Beckett (1906–89), the author of the modern masterpieces *Waiting
for Godot* and *Endgame,* wrote plays depicting the existential wasteland, full of
lost characters, displaced in time and space, capable of little more than waiting
for the meaningless certainty of nonexistence. Beckett was always a reluctant subject of interviews, let alone outright self-examination, but the creatures of his
imagination testify clearly to the disillusion of his lost romance with the universe:

> I don't know when I died. It always seemed to me I died old, about ninety years old,
> and what years . . . I'm too frightened this evening to listen to myself rot, waiting for
> the great red lapses of the heart . . . So I'll tell myself a story . . .[15]

Yale Repertory Theatre production of Suzan-Lori Parks' The Death of the Last Black Man in the Whole Entire World.

A playwright's serious agitating idea or purpose does not always result in a serious play. Sophocles, Ibsen, and Miller wrote intensely serious plays that defined and redefined the meaning of tragedy. But Durang, Wasserstein, Parks, Mamet, and Beckett have dramatized their serious uncertain romances with the universe in some very funny plays.

An agitating idea is the motivation for playwriting, but it does not fully explain the source of the dramatic action.

Playwrights' Sources

The advice is so often repeated that it has become a virtual mantra: "Write what you know." It is a writer's best potential source of inspiration, an excellent context for understanding and perspective, and a rich resource of animating detail. "There's so much material in this house," budding playwright Eugene Jerome exclaims in amazement in Neil Simon's *Broadway Bound.*[16] To be sure, home and local environs have always been important playwriting resources. Some of Simon's best work is outright autobiography. His award-winning trilogy, *Brighton Beach Memoirs, Biloxi Blues,* and *Broadway Bound,* chronicles his own development as a playwright. *Chapter Two* depicts his personal struggle to deal with his guilt over

Beckett's Happy Days *is an absurdist play in which a character is progressively buried in earth until only her head remains visible.*

his quick second marriage after his first wife died. Before she married Simon, third wife Dianne asked for a prenuptial agreement stipulating he not use their lives as material for his plays. "I wanted him to be *in* the relationship with me," she said, "and not stuck in that observer person to write about me."[17] More the observer of others than of himself, **Anton Chekhov** (1860–1904) grew up in a small provincial village. Before turning to playwriting, he became a physician and practiced among the Russian peasantry. As an author his reputation was based on the memorable details and realism of his numerous stories and plays about small-town life. Like Chaucer *(Canterbury Tales)* before him and Garrison Keillor *(Lake Wobegon Days)* after him, Chekhov was able to find universal relevance in the seemingly insignificant corner of human existence he knew best.

Sometimes "what you know" is not enough, and, therefore, playwrights turn to other sources. Tina Howe's *Approaching Zanzibar* depicts a family on a long auto trip along roads and highways, passing by scenic vistas. "It was very hard," said Howe, "because I've never gone on a trip. I joined the AAA [American Automobile Association] and they plotted the route that the family would take."[18]

For playwright William Mastrosimone, a chance meeting and an offhand remark resulted in his need to dramatize a subject about which he knew very little. Months of research and self-education resulted in an intense, violent play he titled *Extremities:*

> In May of 1978 I met a fifty-five-year-old woman. For convenience let's call her Mary. Her face was cut, swollen, and bruised. I didn't realize it then, but our conversation would alter the course of my life.
>
> Mary was a rape victim. She told me she was raped the night before. Perhaps because I was a complete stranger, she told me about her bizarre ordeal. A nineteen-year-old man broke into her apartment with intent to rob. Thinking no one home, she startled him when she awoke. He raped her, beat her with a lamp, and fled. Hours later, when she was able to pick herself up, she called the police and gave a description. She was given a humiliating pelvic exam at the hospital and taken to police headquarters to look at several suspects. Out of a line-up of six, Mary made a positive identification of the rapist. He was arraigned and a court date was set.
>
> Months later the trial began. Mary was made to retell the rape before her peers, the public, the press. The rapist sat quietly in a three-piece suit, white shirt, and tie. He looked like the son of a minister. When he was cross-examined he made amusing remarks. The jury laughed. There was evidence of rape but no evidence that he was the rapist. The case was dismissed. Mary left the courtroom. On the courthouse steps the rapist walked up behind Mary and said, "If you think that was bad, wait until the next time."
>
> Mary informed the police. They told her that they would keep regular patrols near her home, that she should call them on the slightest suspicion. But there are many hours in a minute when you're waiting for the rapist to return. The house plays such cruel little pranks. A board creaks in the middle of the night. The dripping faucet sounds like a man coming up the stairs on tiptoes. The wind. A cat. Mary slept with the light on. Next to the phone was a butcher knife. It was too much. She quit her job, lost her pension, and bought a one-way ticket to the opposite coast.
>
> On her way to the airport, Mary stopped by to say goodbye to me. If she hadn't *Extremities* would not exist. She thanked me for listening. We shook hands and parted. As she walked through the door, something possessed her to stop and turn to say: "There was a moment during the rape when the animal stopped and reached for one of my cigarettes on the night table . . . He couldn't reach it . . . He put one foot on the floor . . . At that moment I knew I could kick him and hurt him . . . The moment waited for me . . . But I just lay there . . . Paralyzed . . . Maybe it was that I was too afraid that if I didn't hurt him enough, he'd kill me . . . I don't know . . . I did nothing . . . He lit a cigarette, raped me again and then beat me with a lamp . . . I will fantasize about what would have happened . . . Now I can see myself hurting him . . . And hurting him some more . . . It's hard for me to admit that I would love to hear his scream . . . I should have acted . . . I would've got real justice . . . Not to act is to have to live with a coward for the rest of your life . . . If I had five minutes in a locked room with him now . . ."
>
> Mary did not finish her sentence. *Extremities* was written to fill in the blank she left.[19]

Mastrosimone could have done a number of different things about the way he felt. He could have volunteered to work in a rape crisis center or written letters to legislators urging greater attention to justice for rape victims. Yet he chose to transfer this image into stage action because he wanted to, in his own words, "give thousands of women a fantasy that affects real behavior."[20] His desire was to give Mary her "five minutes." For Mastrosimone this meant attending countless rape trials, watching and listening to rapists and victims, talking to attorneys, interviewing the families of rapists and their victims—an exhaustive process of getting to know his characters and *their* motivating impulses.

Real-Life Events and Personalities as Sources.   It seems that no sooner does a story—crimes, battles, courtroom trials, heroic exploits, scandalous romance, disasters, and extreme human suffering—hit the headlines than agents are hired, the "rights" are sold, and it is dramatized. "Made-for-television" scripts promise the quickest turnover. Screenplays deliver the "epic" treatment, and stage plays provide intense, personal perspectives. Sensational real-life events have been important sources for playwrights since Aeschylus, a general in the Athenian military, wrote about a war he knew all too well in *The Persians* (472 B.C.). Such events at

A PLAYWRIGHT'S RESEARCH   *In* Extremities, *"Mary" became "Marjorie," the rape victim who got her chance to turn the tables on the "animal" that attacked her. Here, Farrah Fawcett and James Russo in the New York production.*

first seem ready-made for dramatic treatment. For example, courtroom trials seem easy to convert into dramas: a face-off of conflicting antagonists in dispute over moral, personal, and legal transgressions, withheld evidence, hidden motives, and the high suspense of an outcome in doubt until the last moment. And to be sure, many successful plays have used trials as sources. Yet gavel-to-gavel coverage of even the most lurid trials contains much that is of little interest to an audience. Legal procedure can be very boring, and courtroom decorum is intentionally low key, careful, and fair—except, of course, when the participants are "playing" to TV cameras. The challenge to playwrights dramatizing any real-life event is to select and arrange those incidents that are exciting—with the promise of capturing the imagination and holding the attention of a paying audience for about two hours. "Drama," said master of suspense Alfred Hitchcock, "is life with the dull parts left out."[21] Among the successful plays based on real-life events are Lawrence and Lee's *Inherit the Wind* (based on the Scopes "monkey" trial), Peter Shaffer's *Equus* (based on the ice-pick blinding of several horses by a young boy), and *M. Butterfly* (the story of real-life spy intrigue and shocking marital deception).

Writers of stage plays have always been drawn to real-life personalities as subjects of their works. Aristophanes lampooned many of his famous contemporaries, including fellow playwrights Aeschylus and Euripides in *The Frogs,* and the controversial Socrates in *The Clouds.* Shakespeare turned much of the British nobility into the heroes, villains, lovers, and malcontents of his epic "history" dramas; fully one fourth of his plays (all the history plays and *Macbeth*) were based on events reported in Raphael Holinshed's 1577 two-volume history, *Chronicles of England, Scotland, and Ireland.* In the twentieth century, such characters as Mark Twain, Adolf Hitler, Franklin Roosevelt, Eva Peron, Che Guevara, Richard Nixon, Malcolm X, Martin Luther King, Marilyn Monroe, Henry Ford, Boris Yeltsin, Abraham Lincoln, Albert Einstein, Pablo Picasso, and Elvis Presley have been dramatized.

Whether an event or a personality is the source, a playwright's rendering of the real-life subject is inherently personalized and subjective, and can be controversial. It is inevitable that a play made up of selected events from the lives of the famous and infamous mixed with invented scenes and dialogue will provoke argument over the validity of the portrayal. Controversy over Oliver Stone's *JFK,* a film about the Kennedy assassination investigation, ignited a nationwide furor that reached the halls of Congress. In the preface to his screenplay for the film *Nixon,* Stone confessed the portrayal of the former president as a pill-popping, scotch-swilling, epithet-spewing victim was based partly on imagined scenes and "incomplete historical findings."[22] **Docudrama** comprises a genre that promises more objective dramatizing, but this type of play may be a contradiction in terms. Selectivity and arrangement of events, however scrupulous, are still subjective. Leaving out the "dull parts" must be considered a kind of editorializing.

Dramatizing Novels.   Ancient Greek playwrights started the trend when they repeatedly used the epic poems of Homer as sources for their tragedies. In the Middle Ages John Heywood borrowed from Chaucer's *Canterbury Tales* for his short farces. In the Renaissance Shakespeare found an abundant resource for his romantic tragedies

MALCOLM X AS STAGE HERO   *Ben Holt in Anthony Davis' X. In recent years operas and musicals based on current events and personalities have become popular. Among the best are John Adam's* Klinghoffer *(1990), based on the murder of Leon Klinghoffer by Palestinian nationalists on the cruise ship* Achille Lauro, *and John Moran's* Manson Family *(1990), about the California mass murderer Charles Manson.*

in steamy Italian romances, and in the nineteenth century every popular dramatist, it seemed, made plays out of the works of Charles Dickens. Despite ready-made characters, plots, and settings, turning novels into stage plays can be difficult. The problem is one of scope and magnitude. A novel's expansive range of events and descriptive detail must be compressed into the confines of stage space and performance time. Much prose must be cut. Even when the Royal Shakespeare Company reduced each chapter in Dickens' *Nicholas Nickleby* to five minutes of stage time, the play still ran for eight and a half hours. When Alain Boublil and Claude-Michel Schonberg turned Victor Hugo's romantic novel *Les Misérables* into the famous musical spectacular, episodes such as the one in which Valjean steals the candlesticks, which occurs well into the novel, take place in the first five minutes of the play; a plot summary is printed in the program for theatregoers unfamiliar with the novel. Because of the huge theatrical

A PLAY FROM A PAINTING   *According to August Wilson, the source for his award-winning drama* The Piano Lesson *was a painting by Romare Bearden. "There is a painting of a little girl playing the piano with a woman standing over her—her piano teacher (but that became her mother), and so the mother and the little girl at the piano were in the play. So Bearden's art in particular has been influencing me because of the manner in which he treats Black life—in all of its richness and fullness in a formal artistic language, and he connects it to the great traditions in art, whether they are Dutch or whatever. But his subject matter is the Black experience in America."[23] Set in Pittsburgh in 1936, Wilson's Pulitzer Prize-winning drama depicts a sharecropper who wants to buy the land his grandfather worked on as a slave, and plans to sell the heirloom piano he and his sister inherited in order to help pay for the land.*

productions that dramatized novels often require, failures such as the musical versions of James Clavel's *Shogun* ($10 million) and Stephen King's *Carrie* ($7.5 million) rank among all-time theatrical financial disasters. Still, many have provided sources for hit stage plays and musicals such as Dale Wasserman's *Man of La Mancha* (based on Cervantes' *Don Quixote*), Jerry Herman's *Mame* (based on Patrick Dennis' *Auntie Mame*), Lionel Bart's *Oliver* (based on Dickens' *Oliver Twist*), and Andrew Lloyd Webber's *Phantom of the Opera* (adapted from Gaston Leroux's *Fantôme de l'opéra*).

Stage Plays as Sources for Stage Plays.   After the original ideas that spring from playwrights' own dramatic imaginations, the most readily available and frequently used sources for new plays are old plays. Since earliest times, playwrights have made translations, adaptations, sequels, and "prequels" out of the proven dramas of others. With other plays as the sources, compression and expansion are not problems, since the original work has already been "fitted" to the stage. The options, especially for those plays not protected by copyright, are many. Keep the plot, but change the characters and dialogue. Use the characters, but put them in new situations. Add additional characters and scenes. Add songs and dances to turn the play into a musical.

Some of our greatest plays are those modeled on other dramas. *Hamlet* is a distinct improvement on Thomas Kyd's *The Spanish Tragedy,* the play from which Shakespeare took the basic revenge premise and the royal family of characters. Roman tragedies were all based on Greek originals. Shakespeare and his contemporaries based many of their plays on Roman models. The most well-known example is Shakespeare's *Comedy of Errors,* which was based on Plautus' *The Twin Menaechmi,* a farce of mistaken identities involving a set of twins separated at birth. As was his style, Shakespeare improved on the original by adding another set of twins to double the fun. And Shakespeare's time-tested dramas have been used by subsequent playwrights as sources for their new plays, satires, films, and musicals. Among the most well-known examples are Tom Stoppard's *Rosencrantz and Guildenstern Are Dead* (*Hamlet* as seen through the eyes of its most inconsequential, disposable characters), Barbara Garson's *Macbird* (the murderous intrigues of medieval Scotland set in Lyndon Johnson's White House), Akiro Kirosawa's *Ran* (an epic film adaptation of *King Lear* set in samurai-era Japan), Cole Porter's *Kiss Me Kate* (the musical version of *The Taming of the Shrew*), and Leonard Bernstein and Stephen Sondheim's *West Side Story* (a musical updating of *Romeo and Juliet*). Shakespeare, no doubt, would not have objected. Using the written works of others to make his plays was his standard operating procedure. Of his thirty-six surviving plays, only one, the romantic comedy *Love's Labour's Lost,* was a Shakespearean "original." The others were based on all manner of previously written material including novels, histories, short stories, and other plays. "I have so written as I have read" was the motto of his profession. Judging from current dramatic practice, it still is. Consider the transfigurations of Austrian playwright Johann Nestroy's *A Day Well Spent,* which Thornton Wilder adapted into *The Merchant of Yonkers,* which Wilder then changed to *The Matchmaker,* which Jerry Herman then made into the legendary musical blockbuster *Hello, Dolly!*.

High-Tech Sources

Microchips promise to help us do everything more easily, if not better: driving cars, targeting smart bombs, washing dishes, reheating pizza. So why not writing plays? Computer programs with titles like Collaborator, The Idea Generator, Write Pro, IdeaFisher, Plots Unlimited, and Scriptor promise to help the novice as well as master dramatist come up with ideas for plays, generate scenarios for action, and turn them into finished plots. IdeaFisher (Fisher Idea Systems, Inc.) promises to

PLAYS FROM A PLAY   Amphitryon 38 *is the playful title French author
Jean Giraudoux gave his comedy because it is at least the thirty-eighth retelling of the
original by Plautus, which was most likely adapted from an uncredited Greek play by
Menander or Aristophanes. The English version pictured here was an adaptation of
Giraudoux by S. N. Behrman. Does that make it "Amphitryon 39"?*

"help speed up the creative process" by "offering more and better ideas quicker
and easier."[24] The program contains an IdeaBank of 28 Major Categories, 387 Topical Categories, and more than 60,000 Idea Words and Phrases to help the blocked
playwright free-associate. Plots Unlimited contains 13,900 "conflict situations"
ready for dramatic treatment. The program will not write the dialogue or make the
choices, but it does suggest possibilities and options, and it cautions about observing rules of selecting and arranging. Putting together the dramatic action, creating
characters, and giving them things to say and do are the real business of the dramatic imagination, not an electronic database.

MASTERPLOTS

The "Masterplot" option of Plots Unlimited displays a menu of basic plots, each offering an A clause (a character), a B clause (a conflict), and a C clause (a resolution).[25] By mixing and matching clauses from any column, the program promises the playwright's choices will be unlimited. Here are some samples:

Character	Conflict	Resolution
A person in love,	falling in love despite obligations, trying to prove love's power by a test of courage, compelled by excessive desire to exercise mistaken judgment in a romance,	suffers a heavy penalty as the result of an ill-fated venture.
A married person,	trying to make the best of a hopeless love affair, entering a love affair filled with unforeseen complications,	emerges happily from a serious involvement.
A criminal person,	being put to a test in which love is lost if riches are gained, facing a situation in which only courage and devotion can save a loved one,	outwits a scheming person and defeats an insidious plot.
A caring person,	rebelling against a power that controls and suppresses personal abilities, running into trouble and stranded in a primitive environment,	emerges from a difficult ordeal with hard-earned wisdom.
A resentful person,	fighting to achieve a cherished ideal, facing a situation in which the troubles of someone highly regarded call for courage and wise planning,	encounters a situation whereby a wrong is righted.
A person influenced by an obligation,	helping another to keep a deadly secret, selflessly aiding a needy person, leading a lonely, unhappy life and looking for companionship,	gains a spiritual victory.
An average person,	involved in a puzzling complication that concerns an object with mysterious powers, involved in an exotic complication and trying to make the best of a bizarre experience, testing the value of a mysterious communication and being drawn into bizarre complications,	achieves a permanent character change.

The Theatre as a Source

A primary source for many of the most successful playwrights is the theatre itself. This imaginative foundation of the art of drama provides a unique perspective on the dictum "write what you know." What the master makers of dramatic action have always known best is the theatre. You cannot make plays if you do not know the theatre. Thus the theatrical imagination is a crucial component of the dramatic imagination.

The ancient Greek dramatists all staged, rehearsed, and (except for Sophocles) acted, danced, and sang in their own plays. The Roman **Plautus** (c. 254 B.C.–184 B.C.), who wrote bawdy, exuberant musical comedies, turned to writing plays as vehicles to enhance his primary career as one of the great classic-era "zanies": his stage name, "Titus Maccius Plautus," means "Titus the Big-footed Clown." Shakespeare and Molière were among the most theatrically immersed playwrights ever. For over twenty years, Shakespeare wrote plays for a company of actors (of which he was a member) that performed in a theatre (of which he was an owner). Molière toured the French provinces for twelve years with his Illustrious Company before arriving in Paris, where he became the toast of king and court, writing and acting in the brilliant, witty comedies for which he is famous. Henrik Ibsen stage-managed more than 150 plays for several Norwegian theatre companies before turning full-time to playwriting. **Bertolt Brecht** (1898–1956) began his theatrical career as a cabaret performer in 1922 and then served for two years as the assistant to world-famous stage director Max Reinhardt. Absurdist playwright **Harold Pinter** (1930–) studied acting at England's Royal Academy of Dramatic Art and had a successful career on the stage under the name David Barron. August Wilson learned about the theatre by running his own community theatre, the Black Horizon's Theatre, and producing his own plays there. Tony Kushner started out as a director in college before someone asked him to doctor a play.

Continuing the tradition, many playwrights today are also actors. Among the most well known are Ann Meera, Wallace Shawn, Christopher Durang, Sam Shepard, Athol Fugard, Eduardo Machado, and Steve Martin. Others have gained their theatrical experience through college and university theatre programs.

Dramatic Limitations and Possibilities

Stage director Edward Stern recounts the following lesson he learned as a graduate student in a playwriting class: "The professor told us, 'Never write live animals into your plays.' So I went home and wrote my first play, which started like this:

> *The curtain rises on a bare stage. A whale crosses from right to left and disappears in the wings.*

I did it because I didn't like to follow rules. I thought it was funny as hell. The teacher was not amused. So I became a director."[26]

Every art has its conventions and limitations. Consider the creative limitations of a comic strip artist for a daily paper. The entire artwork is one to three panels of black lines, a bit of gray shading, a balloon or two of thirty words or less, all within an area of 11 square inches. In terms of space, color, characters, time, and dialogue, drama is obviously less restricted than the comics, but the rules of play-writing impose limitations all the same.

Limited Time

In the ***Poetics*** Aristotle warns that a play must take place within "a single circuit of the sun."[27] While many take this to mean that not more than a single day should be portrayed in the dramatic action, it may be the practical advice that the play must be short enough to end before the sun goes down. It would have been a strict requirement, since Greek plays were performed outdoors in sunlight. Shake-speare, who also wrote for an outdoor crowd, promised patrons of *Romeo and Juliet* "the two hours traffic of our stage," and then pleaded,

> The which if you with patient ears attend,
> What here shall miss, our toil shall strive to mend.

Signs in today's theatre lobbies carry on the tradition by telling theatregoers, "This performance ends at approximately . . ." For the "time art" of drama, time it-self is its most definitive limitation. Whether because of atmospherics, human at-tention span, necessary biological functions, or the ability of blood to circulate in a human body confined to a sitting position, playwrights must observe rules of time, and as a consequence, length. Traditionally plays come in two standard ver-sions: **one-act** and **full-length plays.**

One-Act Plays.   Although Samuel Beckett once wrote a 35-second play, one-act plays run anywhere from 10 minutes to an hour long, with most having a playing time of about a half hour. Performed without intermissions, one-act plays reached their heyday in the pre-cinema nineteenth century when they were performed as **curtain-raisers** and **afterpieces** to the evening's full-length attractions. In the twentieth century, the curtain-raiser function fell to the 10-minute cartoons and 20-minute "two-reelers" of the early cinema and then eventually to television's "half-hour" programs. In the theatre, one-act plays experienced a resurgence of popularity in the 1960s in the short absurdist dramas of Eugene Ionesco, Samuel Beckett, Jean Genet, and Edward Albee. Today, aspiring playwrights often find the discipline of writing a complete comprehensible play in one act an im-portant developmental exercise. Annual festivals and competitions such as the National One-Act Play Contest of the Actors Theatre of Louisville solicit the short plays of developing dramatists as a way of discovering new talent and properties to produce. Even accomplished dramatists have written complete "evenings" of one-act plays strung together thematically. Among the most successful are Har-vey Fierstein's *Torch Song Trilogy,* George C. Wolfe's *Spunk,* Terence McNally's *Bad Habits,* Brian Friel's *Lovers,* and David Ives' *All in the Timing.*

The first four plays of Edward Albee (1928–   ), the award-winning author of Who's Afraid of Virginia Woolf?, *were all one-acts. His first and most enduring,* The Zoo Story *(1958), is a violent, two-character drama of modern alienation in which the near-derelict Jerry provokes middle-class Peter into killing him with a knife. Besides the two actors, the play requires only a park bench, a book, and a knife.*

Full-Length Plays. Over the centuries "full-length" plays have varied in the number of acts and the time required to perform them. From the Renaissance to the nineteenth century, most plays had five acts and a running time of about three hours. By the end of the nineteenth century, three acts became standard. Today, because of decreasing leisure and the more complex logistics of "getting home," "full length" means two acts and a shorter running time. Conventional wisdom on Broadway, for example, is that serious plays should be two and a half hours long (a comedy should be at least a half hour shorter) because audiences will not sit still for more. Any longer, it is felt, and boredom, inattention, and stiffening of the joints set in.

Boredom is not strictly a function of length. A seemingly "lengthy show" is often a psychological effect, a function of the relative proportions of suspense and predictability. If a playwright has succeeded in taking out the "dull parts," full length may take an extraordinary amount of "real time." August Wilson's *The Piano Lesson* runs three hours. Eugene O'Neill's autobiographical drama of family dysfunction, *Long Day's Journey into Night,* runs three and a half hours. In his Pulitzer Prize-winning dramatic saga *The Kentucky Cycle,* Robert Schenkkan takes six hours to depict six generations of turbulent family history in the "dark and bloody land" of rural Kentucky. The two parts of Tony Kushner's *Angels in America* take seven hours to perform. "The need to take a certain amount of time to tell a particular story in whatever way is appropriate—those things are what determine the running time," says Benjamin Mordecai, a producer and general manager involved with *Angels in America, The Kentucky Cycle,* and all of August Wilson's plays. "I think it's the artistry that should define these issues."[28]

Limited Space

With its park bench and two actors, just about any theatre space can accommodate Albee's *The Zoo Story.* But only the largest can accommodate such extravaganzas as *Les Misérables, The Phantom of the Opera,* or *Sunset Boulevard.* Thus, while playwrights record their plays on paper, they must imagine them on stages, which vary in size from small "black box" spaces of about 240 square feet to huge proscenium houses with stages ten times as large. The ancient Greek dramatists wrote for large amphitheatre spaces (2,800 square feet) and accordingly filled their plays with large dancing choruses and dialogue written to be declaimed loudly by vocally strong, masked actors. Conversely, contemporary playwrights like Sam Shepard and David Mamet, whose works are often produced in small Off-Broadway houses, write plays with small casts favoring actors adept at playing extended, intimate scenes that rely on subtle facial expression and body language. For most playwrights, smaller spaces—under 800 square feet—are the rule. Part of the reason we see more bedrooms than battlefields in contemporary plays is because, as David Edgar notes, "Battlefields are bigger than bedrooms."[29] Bedrooms are also cheaper to build and populate.

Costs

Arthur Miller spoke for all playwrights when he described the escalating costs of theatrical production as "the heart of the beast."[30] Cost, even more than time and space, may be a playwright's severest limitation on imagining dramatic action. Limited budgets lead playwrights to make plays with ever smaller casts and scenic requirements. Playwright Diane Ney laments the 90 percent of theatres that "no-way-no-how" can produce a play having more than two characters.[31] Marie Irene Fornes, the Cuban-born author of *Promenade, Fefu and Her Friends,* and a contemporary English version of Ibsen's *Hedda Gabler,* claims that she tries to write without restrictions, but the reality of the situation is probably much different. "It may be," she admits, "that I limit my plays unconsciously

LIMITATIONS
*Eduardo Machado's social
drama* Broken Eggs, *produced by
New York's Repertorio Español
under the title* Revoltillo.
*Machado believes small cast
sizes limit the abilities of
playwrights to imagine dramas
of social activism and
consequence. "That's why we
have so many psychological
plays," Machado theorizes—
because of cast limitations. "I
would love to write plays with
17 people. My plays are about
people whose worlds are highly
populated, but my casts keep
getting smaller. That's the
toughest thing to deal with. In
the last five years, without even
thinking about it, I've been
keeping people from coming in
the door."[32]*

because I know that if I demand too much in sets and so on, the theatres may not be able to do them. I've never had 20 characters and then cut it down. But there's an instinct to keep the cost down."[33]

The Rules of the Live Audience

Unlike the literary artists who imagine readers silently scanning their words on a page, playwrights imagine the audience hearing and seeing *their* actions from the seats of the auditorium. The theatregoer cannot call for a "replay" of dramatic action the way a reader can "reread" prose. Therefore, playwrights observe the **rule of three** when writing dialogue. The rule was most succinctly stated by **Jacinto Benavente** (1866–1954), author of over 150 plays and the most successful Spanish playwright of his day, who received the Nobel Prize for Literature in 1922:

Everything that is of importance to the writing of a play must be said at least three times. The first time one half of the audience will understand it, the second time the other half, only on the third occasion may we be sure that everybody understands, except for deaf persons and certain critics.[34]

Shakespeare seems to have been especially observant of the rule of three, but it may have had more to do with *where* his audience was sitting than with their ability to absorb and comprehend spoken language. Shakespeare's audience sat on three sides of the Elizabethan **thrust stage.** Therefore, according to a theory advanced by Patrick Spottiswoode, education director of London's Shakespeare Globe Museum, an actor had to have lines—especially the important ones—that could be addressed to the three sides of the house. Imagine—as Shakespeare did— Richard Burbage speaking Hamlet's most famous line. With stage directions, the acting edition of the play might have read like this:

HAMLET: *[facing left]* To be *[he turns to the center]* or not to be, *[facing right]* that is the question.

"Friends, Romans, countrymen," he wrote for Marc Antony. "Tomorrow and tomorrow and tomorrow" was for Macbeth. Even the death of Pyramus as hilariously enacted by Bottom in *A Midsummer Night's Dream* is a three-sided affair: "Thus die I, *thus, thus, thus. [Stabs himself.]*" It is no accident of writing that so many of Shakespeare's most memorable scenes and quotable lines seem structured for delivery to the requirements of the audience at the Globe.

Limitations Versus Possibilities

The conundrum of the creative imagination is that the possibilities are limitless, within limits, of course. Samuel Beckett populated his plays with casts of one to four characters on ever-barren wastelands requiring a single withered tree *(Waiting for Godot),* a pile of dirt *(Happy Days),* a couple of garbage cans *(Endgame),* or a table and tape recorder *(Krapp's Last Tape).* Ever the pessimist, Beckett once said, "The best play is one without actors, text only. I'm trying to find a way to write one."[35] The rules and limitations of drama, like an existentialist's angst at the absurdity of existence, can be imaginatively debilitating. For the passionate playwright, however, the conventions of dramatic art define the possibilities and actually free the imagination. Like comic strip artists with lines, inches, and a few words, playwrights also have their menu of artistic ingredients and the formulas for mixing them creatively. Lanford Wilson, who has written small-cast plays like the intimate two-character *Talley's Folly* (1979) and larger works like *Balm in Gilead* (1965), relishes the process of imagining dramas according to the rules he has learned so well. "With each new work," he once said, "a writer discovers he has learned nothing. The process begins all over again: I have space, light, time, sound, music, and perhaps actors with which to work. What can happen here? How can I employ these elements to say what I want to say?"[36]

Dramatic Structure: The Elements of Drama

Aristotle—logician, philosopher, scientist, teacher, critic, and theatre lover—applied his formidable analytical skills to an examination of the nature and structure of drama. In the *Poetics* he determined the basic elements of drama to be six constituent parts: plot, character, thought, diction, melody, and spectacle.

Plot

In playmaking, many things get left out while a select few things get put in. There is, after all, only so much time. Leaving out the "dull parts" is a process of exclusion. Choosing which actions to *include* and the order of their occurrence is the primary business of dramatizing. The **plot** is the total arrangement of the action. Although the terms are often confused, *plot* is not the same as the "story," which is the *complete* chronological telling of an event. The plot is a *selective* portrayal of an event that may or may not be strictly chronological.

Intrigue Plots.   The most traditional arrangement of dramatic action is the intrigue plot in which the episodes are arranged chronologically in a careful cause-and-effect relationship. The result of a well-made intrigue plot is increasingly suspenseful, unpredictable, but entirely probable action. The formula has been used successfully since Sophocles perfected it in *Oedipus the King:* a careful **exposition** in which prior events are revealed and the characters are introduced is followed quickly by an **inciting incident** that actually begins the action of the play by setting up the basic conflict and its unpredictable outcome. In Mastrosimone's *Extremities,* the inciting incident occurs when Raul, after entering Marjorie's house ostensibly looking for a friend, makes his move:

RAUL: House full of people, and when you holler, nobody comes.

[She bolts for the door; he cuts her off.]

MARJORIE: Get out!
RAUL: You got a lousy bunch of friends.
MARJORIE: Get out right now!
RAUL: Take it easy, lovely. I saw the other two chicks leave this morning. The one wit the ratty car should get here about five-thirty. The one wit the specs, bout six. Today's gonna be a triple header.
MARJORIE: Get out!

[Long pause, RAUL goes to the door, looks at MARJORIE, laughs, goes to phone, rips the wire out.]

RAUL: Your move.[37]

The plot then proceeds through a series of invented **complications,** events the playwright constructs that force the characters to act under increasingly difficult circumstances. In *Extremities,* once Marjorie has overpowered Raul, her plan to kill him is complicated by the arrival of her roommates, who try desperately to talk her out of what would amount to murder. The complications build suspensefully to a **crisis** or final confrontation in an **obligatory scene** in which motives are revealed. The conflict is settled in a **resolution** of all lines of action. Mastrosimone builds his plot to an emotional climax in which Raul breaks down and confesses at knifepoint to the attempted rape of Marjorie as well as to other unsolved sexual assaults, resolving the legal and emotional dilemmas of the characters.

Playwrights often find resolving an intrigue the most difficult part of plotting. *Deus ex machina* (literally, "a god from a machine") was the name given to a device in ancient Greek drama by which the play ended with a god descending from Olympus to sort out the complications of the plot by divine fiat. Ever since, the term has been used derisively to refer to complicated intrigues that end summarily or illogically.

Episodic Plots.   Often referred to as **"nonlinear," episodic plots** are those in which the incidents are selected and arranged according to a unifying idea, character, or image. Since Einstein and Freud theorized alternatives to the strictly linear progression of time and thought, playwrights have realized that audiences are capable of perceiving in sequences other than the strictly chronological. Flashback, flash-forward, discontinuity and juxtaposition of images and events evident in dreams, memories, and thoughts are all plotting techniques used by modern playwrights. In *Death of a Salesman,* Arthur Miller's plot is a series of memories and fantasies that insinuate themselves into Willy Loman's futile fight for his job, respect, and love of his son. In the musical *You're a Good Man, Charlie Brown,* the plot is an episodic series of vignettes unified around a day in the lives of the "Peanuts" characters. The exact sequence of scenes is not nearly as important as their emotional juxtaposition and variety. The logic of the plot would not be ruined if the order were switched or if a scene were cut. Similarly, in George C. Wolfe's *The Colored Museum,* the sequence of eleven "exhibits," depicting various aspects of the African American experience, is not unified by chronology but by an idea. Episodic plots are used extensively by contemporary playwrights who have been influenced by modern psychology, which holds that human thinking is not strictly linear, but associational, imagistic, and spatial. In the last fifty years, playwrights have also been heavily influenced by commercial television, which arranges its episodes in ten-minute scenes separated by commercials and other nonconnectives such as "Now, this . . ."

Character

Characters in plays should not be confused with personalities in real life. Characters are the agents of the action, the dramatic elements that carry out the plot. In real life, we play many different roles: infant, child, adolescent, young adult, senior citizen, parent, spouse, lover, employee, student, teacher—the list goes on. Characters in plays, however, play a very limited number of roles. Shakespeare's

EPISODIC PLOT   *George C. Wolfe's* The Colored Museum *is a series of eleven sharply satirical sketches called "exhibits" on the history of the African American experience. In this "exhibit" called "The Hairpiece," two talking wig stands caustically criticize their fashion-fickle owner and then turn viciously on each other.*

Hamlet, for instance, has only young manhood—he is 30 years old for the entire action of the play—his total existence. To serve the intrigue, Shakespeare made him a son, companion, erstwhile lover, prince, and rival to his uncle, but that's all. Any other qualities or roles would have been extraneous to the plot.

Character Traits.   Characterizing is the process by which playwrights assign certain traits to their "agents" that distinguish one character from another. The categories of traits from which they choose include:

> *Biological traits* distinguish male agents from female agents, or human characters from nonhuman characters.
> *Physical traits* include details of age, health, physical appearance, clothing, and deportment.
> *Professional traits* indicate a character's profession, station in life, or relationship to other characters.

Psychological traits reveal emotional and intellectual qualities, attributes of thinking and deliberation, as well as motivating desires.

Decisions are the choices characters make. Plots move forward through the decisions of the main characters. When characters make decisions, characters, in effect, become action.

Minor characters are those that have been given only biological, physical, and perhaps rudimentary psychological traits. Supporting and leading characters have the most complex makeup with contrasting and conflicting psychological traits. So rich in assigned traits are characters like Sophocles' Oedipus, Shakespeare's Hamlet, Ibsen's Hedda Gabler, and Miller's Willy Loman that they are studied and analyzed as if they were living psychological subjects. But they are creations with the briefest of existences. Observation of others is a playwright's richest source of character traits. Neil Simon spent his youth writing character sketches of his friends, trying to predict what they would be when

AN ASSEMBLAGE OF DRAMATIC CHARACTERS   *In the famous "mousetrap scene" from* Hamlet, *Shakespeare has assembled a cast of characters with varying traits that denote their status and complexity within the play: the guards and ladies and gentlemen-in-waiting are* **supernumeraries** *assigned only biological, physical, and professional traits.* **Supporting characters** *such as Ophelia, Polonius, and Horatio have additional psychological traits—desires, attitudes, intellect, and emotions. The plot of the play, however, moves forward through the decisions of the* **antagonist** *Claudius and of the* **protagonist** *Hamlet, one of the most complex characters ever invented for the stage.*

they grew up. Wendy Wasserstein observes others, but also claims that she puts aspects of herself into her characters—male and female:

> I mean, I can't wait to leave myself. It's a very happy experience. To me, there's something very enjoyable about writing men, writing characters who are so distant from me—like, for instance, an aggressive male journalist. And I find that to get to become him for a while, and to take whatever part of me is like that, and put it into him, is basically fun, and an interesting thing to do. So I think when you're talking about leaving yourself, that becomes very personal.[38]

Thought

Thought, as an element of drama, means the thoughts of the characters, a structural feature not to be confused with theme or meaning. Theme and meaning are debatable qualities—as much the opinions of the viewers as any intention of the playwright. After all, what is the theme of *Death of a Salesman?* The answer or answers are as complex as the psychological makeup of the characters: "man's inhumanity to man," "the conflict of the generations," "truth and illusion," "an exploitive and impersonal society," "the senseless pursuit of material success," "the need for love." All of these "themes" can be discerned in Miller's play as well as in those of many other great dramatists. If the play is an accurate imitation of human action, those essential human aspects will be evident.

The thoughts of the main characters are the motivating forces of the play. Playwrights reveal characters' thoughts, which are for the most part silent activities, through the use of such classic devices as **soliloquies** (in which characters, alone on stage, speak their thoughts directly to the audience in monologues); **asides** (in which they speak their thoughts to the audience in short confidences that the other characters cannot hear); and **confidantes** (minor characters whose primary function is to listen to major characters pouring their hearts out). In many modern plays, complex psychological traits are inferred in the **subtext,** or thoughts suggested by the disparity between the way a character behaves and what the character says.

Diction

Diction is patterned words intended to be spoken by the characters. Spoken diction requires certain theatrical conventions each playwright must observe. One of the first requirements for effective dramatic diction is a dynamic **dramatic language.** Ancient Greek and Latin were excellent dramatic languages, universally understood by the theatregoers, suitable for a variety of verse and musical forms, and using colorful metaphorical expressions. With a vocabulary of only 60,000 words, the English of Shakespeare's England was not nearly so accommodating to spoken drama, so Shakespeare made up his own words and phrases whenever he needed to decorate his diction: "assassination," "dexterously," "dislocate," "indistinguishable,"

THESIS PLAYS   *George Bernard Shaw wrote what some refer to as "thesis plays," in which he sought to promote his specific beliefs about socialism and other intellectual concerns. In* Major Barbara, *a play about the moral conflict between a Salvation Army officer and her arms-merchant father, his thesis is "poverty is the root of all evil." The play, of course, is much more than its intended argument. It endures because Shaw was adept at choosing and arranging all the dramatic elements including a good intrigue, memorably original characters, sparkling comic dialogue, and entertaining spectacle.*

"obscene," "pedant," "premeditated," "reliance," and "submerged" are just a handful of words that make their first appearance in Shakespeare.

Second, dramatic language is of the present: "*Now* is the winter of our discontent," Shakespeare wrote for Richard, duke of Gloucester. "Oh, what a rogue and peasant slave *am* I," he gave to Hamlet to express an intolerable inner rage. In addition, the diction must be user friendly for actors; it must roll "trippingly" off the tongue and be easy to memorize. The regular rhythms and often the rhymes of dialogue written in verse meet these requirements.

As for style and pattern, playwrights choose either verse (the preferred form for serious drama until the eighteenth century) or prose (the more realistic diction that most closely approximates everyday speech). But even when written in prose, dramatic diction is not merely the recorded conversations of real persons. It is as selected and artificial as the characters who speak it. Conventional patterns include **monologues,** long speeches spoken by individual characters, and **dialogue,** in which two or more characters alternate shorter speeches, sentences, and phrases.

August Wilson is one playwright who begins working with diction rather than plot, characters, or thought. He takes a notepad to local bars, sits in a booth, and writes down snatches of dialogue he hears. He then ponders who would be saying it, then to whom someone would be saying it, and finally why the person would be saying it.

Melody

Melody refers to the total sound of the play, from the sounds of the actors speaking the diction, to any musical component (songs or underscoring), and any required sound effects. Such were the melodic qualities of classical verse plays that theatregoers commonly spoke of going to "hear" a play. Much of the melody of the dialogue is rendered by the actors—the loudness or softness of the utterance, the pitch, rate, and quality of the voice. Playwrights make melody choices when they craft their dialogue in accents, dialects, regionalisms, and musical selections of vowels, consonants, and phrases. For instance, in Sam Shepard's *Suicide in B-flat*, the character Louis speculates on the motivation for a murder. Note how Shepard used the sound of the words to create the effect of a solo instrument in a jazz combo. For the full effect, it must be read out loud.

LOUIS: *[piano behind]* A boy hears sound before he has a name. He hears gurgling, pounding underwater. He hears an ocean of blood swimming around him. Through his veins. Through his mother. He breaks into the light of day. He's shocked that he has a voice. He finds his voice and screams. He hears it screaming as though coming down through ancient time. Like it belongs to another body. He hears it that way. He hears the crack of his own flesh. His own heart. His skin sliding on rubber mats. Squeaking. He hears his own bones growing. Stretching his skin in all directions. Bones moving out. Organs expanding. The sounds of cells booming through his brain like tiny intergalactic missiles. Atoms. Nuclear rushes of wind through his nose holes. Toenails rubbing blankets in the dark. Books falling on pianos. Electricity humming even when the lights are off. Internal combustion engines. Turbo jets. Then one day he hears what they call music. He hears what they call "music" in the same way he hears what they call "noise." In the same stream. Music is an extension of sound. An organization, another way of putting it. He's disappointed. He's disappointed and exhilarated at the same time. Exhilarated because he sees an opening. An adventure. A way inside. He sees that putting any two things together produces sound. Any two things. Striking, plucking, blowing, rubbing, dropping, kicking, kissing. Any two things. He has a revelation. Or rather, a revelation presents itself. Stabs at him. Enters into him and becomes part of his physiology. His physiognomy. His psychology. His paraphernalia. His makeup. He puts it to use. He's driven toward it in a way most men consider dangerous. And suicidal. His production is abundant. Nonstop. Endlessly winding through unheard-of-before symphonies. Concertos beyond belief. He organizes quintets. Soloists rush to him to be in his presence. The best ones are rejected. He only takes apprentices. He only plays nightclubs although he could pack out the Garden in a flash. He shakes the sidewalks with his compositions. Every city in the world is calling his name. He invents totally new chord progressions and scales. New names for notes that not even Chinese have heard of. Instruments that he makes in the bathtub. His music is sweeping the country. And then one day he disappears. Just like that.[39]

Spectacle

Just as surely as drama is an auditory art, it is also a visual one. **Spectacle** is the totality of visual elements of a play. It includes the settings, costumes, lighting effects, properties, the actors, and their movements. Playwrights select and combine elements of spectacle to convey crucial information concerning aspects of time, place, character, and style more effectively than description or dialogue alone. In the cinematic age, visual images are so dominant that today's theatregoers speak of going to "see" rather than "hear" a play. Under less than favorable circumstances, manipulating the visual elements can cover a multitude of playwriting failures. "When all else fails," the saying goes, "play up the spectacle."

By emphasizing spectacle it is possible to make an effective play that is lacking in spoken diction of any consequence or merit. Farces that rely on physical comedy, melodramas that manipulate suspense through shocking disasters and terrifying special effects, and musicals that promote large-scale choreography are spectacle-intensive plays.

The last two elements, melody and spectacle, are as much constituent parts of theatre art as they are of dramatic art. Many playwrights make only token efforts to delineate the sound and spectacle in their scripts, preferring to leave those choices to the imaginations of the theatre artists. The challenge of "writing" melody and spectacle into scripts demonstrates the need for testing the playwright's choices on stage before the play can be completed.

Finishing the Script

Preproduction Staging

Plays are not finished when the writer emerges from isolation with a cleanly word-processed script in hand. Before it can be submitted for production, the first draft (or the **foul papers,** as they were called in Shakespeare's day) must go through the preproduction component of playwriting. To complete the play, each dramatist must have opportunities to see and hear what has been written—to make sure it is, in fact, stageworthy.

The usual methods for testing the preliminary choices are **staged readings** and **workshop productions.** In staged readings the script is given to a director for a few days of minimal rehearsal with a small group of actors who "perform" the play by walking through an approximation of the required action while reading the dialogue from hand-held scripts. August Wilson, whose big break came in 1982 when the National Playwrights' Conference accepted his play *Ma Rainey's Black Bottom* for a staged reading, calls the process "standing the play up on its feet."[40]

Workshop productions are more fully mounted with longer rehearsal periods of up to two weeks for a straight play and four weeks for a musical. Still, there are no sets or costumes—only the actors on their feet, but with memorized lines. Whether at staged readings or workshops, the playwright is in close attendance, watching, listening, and testing the choices and collaborating with the performers and director on new ones.

The rewriting process continues in rehearsals for the first full-scale production as well as preview performances. In an interview, actor Patrick Stewart (Jean-Luc Picard of *Star Trek*) described how Peter Shaffer (author of *Equus* and *Amadeus*) worked with the cast in rehearsal to finish the script of his Biblical play *Yonadab:*

> One of the things that made a significant difference with *Yonadab* was that Peter Shaffer attended every minute of every rehearsal for eight weeks. It's what Peter Shaffer calls and I think it is a wonderful phrase, "carving the play with the actors." What he does is—I used to watch him in rehearsal—he would sit somewhat like a bird, with his ear half-cocked towards the action, half looking, but with his ear turned in the way that a musician would listen to an ensemble.
>
> And he would write, and he would write and write. In that way, the play would undergo significant changes. And he would talk to the actors, and at breaks he would discuss with them what was going on. Because he is one of our very finest writers, he had enough self-confidence and assurance to be able to listen. . . . Shaffer [is] a relentless and obsessive rewriter. I've seen Peter toss aside pages of writing that most actors would have given a limb to have created.[41]

Only after the production of a play has successfully "opened" is the script considered ready for publication in either **acting editions** meant for theatre artists or in commercially available general readership versions.

SUBMITTING A PLAY FOR PRODUCTION

Playwrights without residencies at established theatres or who have not been commissioned to write specific plays must submit their unsolicited works to producers and theatres for consideration. To sort through the various submission guidelines, contests, fellowships, grants, agents, and publishing opportunities, many playwrights, translators, composers, lyricists, and librettists rely on annual publications such as The Dramatists Sourcebook. The following submission procedure for the not-for-profit American Place Theatre, famous for its productions of new plays, is typical. Note the warnings of limitations in length, subject matter, and space.

The American Place Theatre
111 West 46th St; New York, NY 10036; (212) 840-2960
Literary Department

Submission procedure: accepts unsolicited scripts from agents only; others send synopsis, first 20 pages of script and letter of inquiry. Types of material: full-length plays, adaptations, performance pieces. Special interests: works by living American playwrights only; works that are innovative in form and perspective; less interested in "sentimental naturalism" and commercial material. Facilities: Main Stage, 180–299 seats, flexible stage; Cabaret Space, 75 seats, flexible stage; First Floor Theatre, 75 seats, flexible stage. Best submission time: Sept.–June. Response time: 2 months letter; 3–4 months script. Special programs: American Humorist Series: works by or about American humorists. Jubilee: annual festival celebrating the history and experience of minority and ethnic Americans (black, Hispanic, Irish, Polish, etc.). First Floor Theatre: program of new experimental writing and performance pieces.[42]

The American Place Theatre receives approximately 800 unsolicited 20-page submissions each year of which 5 to 10 receive further consideration, a few being given "in-house" readings.

Protecting Choices

For any playwright, having a work accepted by a producer is validation of dramatic imagination. But finally turning the play over to the theatre artists for production can be an act of mixed emotions. Considering all of the artists—not to mention managers, staffers, and technicians—who will subsequently interpret, stage, and perform the play, protecting the original choices throughout the production process can be a high-anxiety affair. Once rehearsals begin, playwrights can look forward to more interference than can any other artists. Instead of collaboration, the process can seem sometimes like a battle. Directors and producers may demand, rather than recommend, changes. Actors may read lines to shade or substantially alter the intended meaning and even redefine characters. At the very least, the creative tension makes for an uncertain romance with the stage itself. Arthur Miller, who has been through many stellar productions of his plays, recommends the personal armor of reptilianlike skin to protect against the theatrical onslaught:

> You know, to be a playwright you not only have to be a writer, you have to be an alligator. A lot of writers are not alligators. I mean, in my lifetime I've known 10 or 12 people who were really talented people but they couldn't take the abuse. You know, a playwright lives in an occupied country. He's the enemy. And if you can't live that way you don't stay.[43]

To be fair, the perception of interference can exist on both sides of the footlights; production anxiety works from either direction. Theatre artists are protective of their own artistic prerogatives and are naturally wary of being told what to do at every turn. After all, the playwright makes choices, for better or worse, that are dictated in writing to other artists; they are not creative suggestions. Actors and directors often refer to them as the **given circumstances** of the play. Robert Brustein, who has produced many new plays in his long career, provides a reasoned analysis of the performers' "resistance" to playwrights:

> The actor's resistance to the playwright is traditional. Perhaps it is influenced by a residual memory of the most primitive form of the theatre, when thespians, not playwrights, dominated the attention of the audience; when mimes, interpolations, scenarios, and improvisations held the stage, and not plays. This resistance reflects the feeling every person has about hardening into a fixed character determined by others which others are then in a position to analyze, to catalogue, and possibly to dismiss. It is a resistance to cause-and-effect thinking, to predestination, to determinism, to the sense that people are not free.[44]

In light of this creative tension, it is not surprising that playwrights make concerted efforts—legal and otherwise—to protect their works. The playwright is the only working artist in the theatre whose choices are protected by copyright, although this protection has to do mainly with unauthorized publication and abuses of royalty payments. By agreement between the Dramatists Guild and professional producers, playwrights have retained for years the contractual power of veto over the casting of roles in the original productions of their works. In a major change, the 1991 contract for members of the Guild prohibits anyone from changing even a letter of a playwright's work without permission.

None of these strategies can fully protect a playwright's work against undeveloped theatrical imaginations or even developed ones making ineffective choices. The best chance of a good production of a play is with a skilled producer who has the ability to facilitate the collaborative efforts of the best theatre artists.

CREATIVE TENSION *Anton Chekhov (with beard, center) reading his play,* The Seagull, *to directors and actors of the Moscow Art Theatre, 1898. The Moscow Art Theatre's productions of Chekhov's plays made both the playwright and the acting company famous. Yet there was always an acute creative tension (note their facial expressions) over the company's interpretations of the plays. Chekhov complained that artistic director Konstantin Stanislavsky (at far right) took them much too seriously, failing to bring out the humor the author intended.*

 THE PLAYWRIGHT AT WORK ······················

From Page to Stage: How a Playwright Guards His Vision

by Terrence McNally
[Excerpts reprinted from the *New York Times*][45]

Terrence McNally is a successful dramatist known for his comedies, The Ritz, Bad Habits, *and* It's Only a Play, *and more*

recently for his tragicomedies, Frankie and Johnny in the Claire de Lune, Lips Together Teeth Apart, A Perfect Ganesh, Love! Valour! Compassion!, *and* Master Class. *He also wrote the book for the musical* Kiss of the Spider Woman. Frankie and Johnny *had successful runs both off and on Broadway and then was made into a major motion picture starring Al Pacino and Michelle Pfeifer. In the following article, written while* Frankie and Johnny *was still in "development,"* McNally described the frustrations of protecting his choices through the rehearsal and tryout phase of "writing" his play.

Room 407 at the New School on West 12th Street in Greenwich Village is a long way from Broadway. In fact, it's a long way from anything resembling a working theater anywhere. There are no sets, no lights, no anything to create a theatrical illusion. It is a classroom with hard seats, fluorescent lighting and a green blackboard where the cyclorama should be. It's where the play I'm working on had its first hearing not long ago.

Twenty years ago my first play, *And Things That Go Bump in the Night,* opened at the Royale Theater on West 45th Street. We had stars onstage, celebrities out front, and it seemed like the most momentous evening of my life.

In room 407 we had two actors on plastic chairs reading from scripts, an audience of "civilians" with a keen interest in theater and a tolerance for first drafts, and it still seemed like the most momentous evening of my life.

Twenty years ago, all I asked God for was a hit. He didn't give me one. Now I'm hoping I can guard the vision of my new play, *Frankie and Johnny in the Claire de Lune,* a contemporary romance, as it begins the arduous rounds of what has come to be known as the "development process." It's up to me.

In the weeks, months, maybe years ahead, my new play will be read by dramaturgs, directors and producers. It will have cold readings, semi-staged readings, fully staged readings and workshop productions. In the best of all possible worlds, it will one day "open" somewhere, meaning that my work on it is done and a producer or theater has deemed it worthy of a full production, meaning that the plastic chairs have at last been replaced by the Louis XIV pair they were meant to be ever since room 407.

And once again I will undergo still another most momentous evening of my life. By now, I'm an old hand at them.

It's what's going to happen between now and then I worry about. I worry that in the process of developing my new play I lose it. This is the truly momentous period of any play's creation and I often wonder if I will ever get the knack of it.

People will tell me they don't like the title. Fair enough. An actor will suggest I make a role more sympathetic. Is Iago sympathetic? Was Lady Macbeth? But if this is the actor I dreamed of in the role when I wrote it, perhaps he has a point. Directors will insist on structural changes they are positive will make all the difference to the play's success. If it's a good director, I'd be a fool not to listen, especially if you're of the Nobody's Perfect (Including Playwrights Named McNally) School of Theater. Producers will tell me I can't have those Louis XIV chairs after all. No one reviews furniture, I remind myself. Total strangers will tell me it's the worst play they've ever sat through while I just count my blessings they're not a critic for The New York Times.

A play is lost not on the IRT but when the original impetus behind its writing is misplaced or forgotten during its metamorphosis from typescript to that living organism we call a play.

A good play convinces us for a couple of hours that this is how the world is. The right actor for that play inhabits it fully. If directing is 90 percent casting (and I have heard at least one great director aver this), then the fate of a play is almost surely sealed when those troops first assemble.

Even in the earliest stages of a play's development, the wrong cast can thoroughly derail a playwright's intentions, often through no fault of their own except that they were not well cast in the first place. I have never been able to resist the temptation to cut or rewrite a role because of an actor's unsuitability for it. I kick myself for doing it every time and I swear never again but if you hire Mr. X and Miss Y to create your character you are wedded to Mr. X and Miss Y. After a while, they become your characters and you are only the author of them. . . . The quickest way I know to lose your bead on your play is to start rewriting to accommodate the actors. Either hire the cast you can 100 percent commit to, or don't even allow a demi-semi-staged performance.

The rewards of the development process can be immeasurable. An intelligent, feeling actor can make a permanent contribution to the play. If I were to thank every actor who has given me insight, inspiration and just plain joy in creating a character (not to mention a line here and there and some terrific business) the list would include just about every actor I've ever worked with. Last night I learned something invaluable about the new piece from Miss Stein and Mr. Abraham. They read with an intuitive insight that made me relieved to know that what might have seemed underwritten in other hands was just right. The point is, of course, it wasn't in other hands last night and I'm not rewriting this morning for all the wrong reasons. . . .

There is nothing less spontaneous than the invited audience of "professionals" who regularly see workshop productions and whose reactions are supposed to inspire producers and investors to go ahead with the project. And, too, there is the temptation to let any audience's response become a tyrant dictating to you. The desire to please seems to go hand in hand with working in the theater. It's your play. Don't let them take it away from you. Bring them to their knees or feet but don't ever let them bring you to theirs. Pandering to an audience is the second quickest and certainly the best way I know to lose your play—and just a bit of your soul maybe. I know.

Come to think of it, losing your play is a distinct possibility right up until the last rehearsal and the final preview. You're either working in the pressure cooker of going right into rehearsal and opening after a few previews in New York or in the slow simmer of the development process. Either way, you're not home free until the reviews are in. The only thing you can be sure of if you write a play is the number of people eager to tell you how to rewrite it. It's staggering. Hang in there. It isn't easy.

●●

SUMMARY

1. The status of playwriting and playwrights has varied throughout history—from that of esteemed artists to hacks.

2. Playwrights, like other artists, are creatures of their times who reflect the shared perceptions, manners, conventions, and values of their age.

3. Like the solitary literary artist, many dramatists write in seclusion, enjoying periods of inspiration and fighting writer's block. Playwrights also collaborate with co-authors, writing teams, and developmental ensembles.

4. Writers turn to drama in order to work out their own "uncertain romance with the universe." Writing plays becomes a way to play out the inner conflicts, desires, and agitating ideas that remain unresolved.

5. A playwright's primary source of dramatic action is personal experience. Other sources include real-life events and personalities, novels, films, paintings, comic strips, other plays, and the theatre itself.

6. The conventions of playwriting include limited time, limited space, limited production budgets, and the conditions of live performance.

7. The elements of drama determined by Aristotle are plot, character, thought, diction, melody, and spectacle.

8. Before a play can be considered complete, the written choices must be tested on stage.

9. A creative tension exists between playwrights and theatre artists. Playwrights are protective of their choices, while theatre artists resist intrusions on their artistic license.

CHOICES

1. Devise alternate endings for well-known plays such as *Hamlet, Romeo and Juliet,* or *Death of a Salesman* that would alter the implications of the play, yet maintain the tragic nature of the action.

2. Write out a scenario for scenes that do not appear, but could be logically included or substituted for others in the plays suggested in number 1. Imagine, for instance, scenes that could precede the beginnings of these plays as presently structured.

3. Scan the daily newspaper and create a scenario for a play based on a real-life event. It does not have to be a headline or front-page story. The event may be reported in the sports, financial, or lifestyle sections. The source might be printed in capsule form under the headings "arrests," "legal notices," "social clubs," or even "recipes."

4. Using the Plots Unlimited "Masterplots" menu on page 178, mix and match the characters, conflicts, and resolutions to create a scenario based on an "uncertain romance" of your own. Base all of your characters on persons you know well.

5. Do a survey and description of currently showing plays, movies, and TV shows that are based on real-life events and personalities. Are any controversies associated with the way in which these personalities or events are depicted? In your opinion are the depictions accurate portrayals or are they distortions?

6. Write a thirty-five-second play.

A THEATRICAL HIGH ROLLER   *Broadway producer Rocco Landesman at Belmont racetrack: when playing the ponies or searching for hit shows, a love of risk.*

Hath all his ventures failed, what not one hit?

The Merchant of Venice, *Act III, scene ii*

CHAPTER 6

The Theatrical Catalyst

THE PRODUCER'S CHOICES

PREVIEW

The Theatrical Catalyst

The History of Producing

The Art and Business of Commercial Producing

The Art and Business of Not-for-Profit Producing

The Passion for Playmakers

Previewing Part 3

The Producer at Work

Andrew Lloyd Webber certainly does make musical plays that audiences everywhere love: *Jesus Christ Superstar, Joseph and the Amazing Technicolor Dreamcoat, Evita, Cats, Starlight Express, Sunset Boulevard,* and, of course, *The Phantom of the Opera,* one of the hottest tickets worldwide. Almost singlehandedly, Webber invented the concept of techno-pop musicals. But a concept for a play is one thing. Its creation as a theatrical production is quite another endeavor. Consider the human facts of *The Phantom of the Opera.*

It took just three people to put *The Phantom of the Opera* on paper. Andrew Lloyd Webber came up with the idea of turning Gaston Leroux's novel into a spectacular, romantic musical melodrama. Webber also composed the music and co-wrote the book with Richard Stilgoe. Charles Hart wrote the lyrics.

However, it took more than 400 theatre people and $8.5 million to put it on the stage for its Broadway opening in 1988. Listed in the program for the Broadway production are 125 individual artists: 36 actors, 31 musicians, 1 director, 2 choreographers and their assistants, 5 primary designers, 4 associate designers, 4 assistant designers, 20 consultants, and 22 specialty artists. Also listed are 170 individual production staff professionals including construction and running crews—it takes 37 backstage specialists just to operate the highly mechanized scenery and computers that coordinate the special effects—as well as administrative personnel involved in public relations, legal counsel, insurance, banking, travel, customs, payroll, photography, facilities management, and maintenance. In addition, more than 50 companies were subcontracted for their specialty services, running the theatrical gamut from the worldwide computer power of the Shubert Organization's telemarketing system to Costume Armor, Inc., which is credited with making "the newel post statues and elephant."

This is all quite a distance from the far-off time when Thespis packed a few masks and robes into a cart and traveled the Attic countryside of Peloponnesia playing all the parts in his one-actor plays.

The Theatrical Catalyst

A theatre production does not generate itself. That which is needed to mount *Phantom,* to stage a summer festival of Shakespeare, or to present a season of community theatre is not a self-starting or self-sustaining mechanism. Every script, if it is to see the light of the stage, requires a **producer**—a theatrical visionary and catalyst—who joins the script with the artists and their production with its appropriate audience. The producer's imagination ignites the creation of theatre art.

Seminal Choices

In the modern theatre the word *producer* conjures up often contradictory meanings and a variety of classic images. The Hollywood stereotype is a cigar-chomping, fast-talking operator, feet up on a desk, phone glued to an ear, casting couch at the

OPENING NIGHT: JANUARY 26, 1988

MAJESTIC THEATRE

A Shubert Organization Theatre

Gerald Schoenfeld, *Chairman*   Bernard B. Jacobs, *President*

CAMERON MACKINTOSH and
THE REALLY USEFUL THEATRE COMPANY, INC.

present

The
PHANTOM
of the
OPERA

starring

MICHAEL CRAWFORD
SARAH BRIGHTMAN

STEVE BARTON

CRIS GROENENDAAL   NICHOLAS WYMAN
LEILA MARTIN   DAVID ROMANO   ELISA HEINSOHN
and
JUDY KAYE

At certain performances
PATTI COHENOUR
plays the role of Christine

Music by
ANDREW LLOYD WEBBER

Lyrics by **CHARLES HART**

Additional lyrics by RICHARD STILGOE
Book by RICHARD STILGOE & ANDREW LLOYD WEBBER
Production Design by MARIA BJÖRNSON   Lighting by ANDREW BRIDGE
Sound by MARTIN LEVAN   Musical Supervision & Direction DAVID CADDICK
Orchestrations by DAVID CULLEN & ANDREW LLOYD WEBBER
Casting by JOHNSON-LIFF & ZERMAN   General Management ALAN WASSER

Musical Staging & Choreography by GILLIAN LYNNE

Directed by **HAROLD PRINCE**

Travel arrangements furnished by Pan American World Airways, Inc.

**The Producers and Theatre Management are Members
of The League of American Theatres and Producers, Inc.**

FIGURE 6–1   *The title page of the program is a schematic of the seminal function of the producer in initiating the production of a play. Appropriately, the producer's name appears above the authors', the stars', the actors', the director's, designers', and even the title. (PLAYBILL is a registered trademark of Playbill Incorporated, N.Y.C. Used by permission.)*

ready, making and breaking careers and cutting deals—in show business lingo, "blowing smoke." There are the **impresarios** like the late Ed Sullivan and Sol Hurok, master presenters of the world's greatest performing artists. There are the artistic, social, and educational missionaries like George C. Wolfe of the New York Shakespeare Festival, Stan Wojewodski, Jr., of the Yale Repertory Theatre, and Sharon Ott of the Berkeley Repertory Theatre, more concerned with addressing the needs of society than with making profits. The newest breed may well be the global arts managers like Cameron Mackintosh and Garth Drabinsky who orchestrate productions throughout the world. Whether making deals, making money, or remaking society, all producers are in the business of making theatre art. The success of their creations depends on the most fundamental choices of theatre art.

Whatever their missions, theatrical producers choose:

1. the play to be produced
2. the space in which to produce it
3. the artists who will conceive, design, and perform it
4. the timetable for its conception, design, rehearsal, performance, length of run, and closing
5. the staff to package, promote, and administer it
6. the strategy for financing it
7. the target audience that will (hopefully) attend it

This chapter examines the history and modern practice of producing—both the art and the business of knowing when, where, what, and who work best on stage.

The History of Producing

From the very beginning of the theatre, the art and business of producing have been determined largely according to who pays for the production, who owns it, and thus, who controls it. Two basic production models have predominated: theatre offered as a **subsidized service** having a religious, civic, or artistic mission in which profit is not the primary motive, and theatre produced as a **commercial enterprise** in which profit is the major motive.

Theatre with a Mission

The first 2,000 years of theatrical play production were wholly noncommercial and subsidized, and producing evolved accordingly.

Producing as a Service.   In ancient Greece, theatre was produced as a competitive celebratory activity at joyous festivals honoring Dionysus, the god of wine and fertility. Production responsibilities were divided between the city-state government and wealthy citizens who so coveted the honor of financing plays that they had to be chosen by lot. The producer, a government official known as the **archon,** chose the plays that were to compete for prizes, assigned actors, and chose each play's **choregus,** the wealthy citizen with the civic obligation to be the major financial backer. The *choregus* underwrote the training, costuming, and salaries of the chorus, musicians, and supernumeraries, and paid for the properties as well. The state was responsible for paying the actors, playwrights, and all costs of the theatre building. It was crucial to each competing dramatist that a munificent *choregus* be assigned, since the success of the play's production could depend on the amount the benefactor was prepared to spend. The prize for the best play, like today's Tony and Academy Awards, went, appropriately, to the *choregus* as well as to the playwright. It was, after all, the playwright who generated the script, but the *choregus* who owned the production.

In Europe during the Middle Ages, local churches produced the community-wide mystery cycles that dramatized the Bible as a way of teaching Christian doctrine. Each play within the cycle was financed and mounted by individual trade guilds according to the appropriate subject of the play. Under this system the fishermen's guild would produce the play about Jonah and the whale, while the bakers would be assigned the play about Christ and the loaves and fishes. Since production of these cycles involved from twenty-five to fifty plays requiring hundreds of amateur actors and complicated special scenic effects, the Church and guilds usually subcontracted the overall planning, casting, and staging of the production to a professional organizer called a **pageant master.**

In Service to the Nation.   Play production in the Renaissance was largely a commercial enterprise. But in 1680 Louis XIV established the **Comédie Française** as the world's first national theatre in which a sharing company of actors performed in a state-subsidized theatre and received annual pensions upon retirement. Over the last three centuries, the Comédie Française served as a model for the establishment of national theatres throughout the countries of Europe, Asia, and Africa that consider their subsidized theatres as repositories for culture in the same way that governments fund museums, libraries, and symphony orchestras. Among the leading national theatres of the world today are Great Britain's Royal National Theatre and The Royal Shakespeare Company, Ireland's Abbey Theatre, Germany's Berliner Ensemble, Russia's Moscow Art Theatre, Ghana's Drama Studio, Nigeria's Duro Ladipo National Theatre, the Turkish State Theatre and Conservatory, The National Theatre of Egypt, China's Beijing People's Theatre, the Chilean National Theatre, and Israel's Habimah Theatre.

Despite several attempts, a centralized national theatre in the United States has yet to become a reality. In fact, subsidized theatre of any kind was not firmly established in America until the mid-1950s. American theatre practice evolved primarily from the commercial tradition of producing plays.

Artistic Missionaries.   In the late nineteenth century, commercial theatre production dominated by catering to the faddish tastes of the general population, while national theatres such as the Comédie Française staunchly preserved classical traditions. In response to new artistic philosophies such as **naturalism** and

AN AFRICAN NATIONAL THEATRE   *A recent production at Nigeria's Duro Ladipo National Theatre. The company is named for* **Duro Ladipo** *(1931-78), a pioneer of Nigerian theatre who wrote operas inspired by Yoruba oral tradition, music, myth, and masquerade. The theatre company he founded is one of 120 now operating in Nigeria, the most theatrically active country in Africa.*

symbolism, theatrical innovators in Europe founded their own theatres to practice their art. The model for these **independent theatres** was established by **André Antoine** (1858-1943), an artistic producer who founded the Théâtre Libre ("Free Theatre") in Paris in 1887 to produce the naturalistic plays of Henrik Ibsen, August Strindberg, and Henri Beque, plays that would not be considered for production by established commercial theatres. Inspired by Antoine, other committed producers founded theatres with similar artistic missions in London, Germany, Moscow, and America. Among the most important were the Freie Bühne, founded by Otto Brahm in 1899 in Berlin; J.T. Grein's Independent Theatre Club, established in London in 1890; Konstantin Stanislavsky's Moscow Art Theatre, which opened in 1898; and the Provincetown Players, founded by Susan Glaspell in 1916 to produce the experimental works of Eugene O'Neill, Edna St. Vincent Millay, and others.

THE FEDERAL THEATRE PROJECT   *The most notable American attempt to establish a national theatre was the Federal Theatre Project. Chartered and funded by Congress as part of the Works Project Administration (WPA) by Congress in 1935, this nationwide establishment of theatres was an attempt to put unemployed actors and playwrights to work during the Depression. Organized and administered by* **Hallie Flanagan,** *the Federal Theatre Project encouraged experimental writing and avant-garde productions such as Orson Welles and John Houseman's famous "voodoo"* Macbeth *at the Mercury Theatre in 1936. (See Langston Hughes' poem, "Note on Commercial Theatre," Chapter 4, p. 129.) The Federal Theatre Project was closed by the government on political grounds in 1939.*

Theatre for Profit

Commercial play production began in the sixteenth century as formerly itinerant professional actors settled into newly built permanent theatres such as the **Hôtel de Bourgogne** (1548) in Paris and **The Red Lion** (1567) in London. Organized like other profit-making commercial enterprises, these acting companies had their stockholders, called "sharers"; junior interns, called "apprentices"; and management executives, called "householders." In companies such as Shakespeare's at the Globe, the actors were joint owners, and as a collective enterprise made decisions about both artistic and financial matters. Rival companies such as those at the Fortune, Hope, and Swan theatres worked for a single powerful theatre owner. One of the most successful of the Elizabethan householders was the impresario **Philip Henslowe** (?–1616), who built three theatres in the newly established entertainment districts outside London, and who managed the Lord Admiral's Men, a rival of

Shakespeare's company. Henslowe ruled the Lord Admiral's Men with an iron hand. He demanded deposits from actors in order to hold them to their agreements to remain with the company, and he fined actors for being drunk during rehearsals and performances or for missing them. Henslowe was constantly involved in litigation with actors, such as the 1615 *Articles of Grievance, and Articles of Oppression, against Mr. Hinchlowe,* in which members of his company accused him of embezzling their money and unlawfully retaining their property.

Despite his troubles with actors, Henslowe's theatrical ventures demonstrated the fundamental principles of commercial producing. First, theatre production could be a profitable business with the potential to appeal to a huge market. Second, sound organizational principles were needed to efficiently manage a people-intensive enterprise like the theatre. Third, a theatre's location was as important as its offerings. Fourth, legal disputes with his actors demonstrated the importance of understanding the personalities of theatre artists and their creative needs. The need for diplomacy and artistic sensitivity became even more apparent by the end of the seventeenth century.

In 1689 **Christopher Rich** (?–1714), an English lawyer with no theatrical experience or artistic inclinations whatsoever, was sufficiently impressed with the profit potential of commercial theatre to buy a share in the Drury Lane theatre company. By 1693 he had acquired complete control of the company. Without regard for his performers, he became a veritable tyrant, slashing salaries and expenses and spending more time in litigation than in production. More than anyone before him, Rich gave commercial producing a bad name, setting the tone for adversarial relationships with actors. The infamous Rich management of Drury Lane demonstrated the need for commercial producers to be schooled in essential theatre practice.

The Actor-Manager System.   The most successful producers of the eighteenth and nineteenth centuries were the **actor-managers,** leading actors who ran major theatre companies in which they also played the starring roles. In England, **David Garrick** (1717–79), considered by many to have been England's greatest actor, was the most successful actor-manager of the eighteenth century. The first American actor-manager was **David Douglass** (?–1786), who built the first permanent theatre in the United States, the Southwark in Philadelphia in 1760, as well as three others in New York City. Producers who had no theatrical experience hired **acting-managers** to supervise the artistic aspects of theatre management for them.

The Birth of Show Business.   Commercial producing became big business in America during the westward expansion and Industrial Revolution. Following the examples of such monopoly-building tycoons as John D. Rockefeller and J. P. Morgan, an association of New York booking agents formed the **Theatrical Syndicate** in 1896. Concerned only with making huge profits, the Syndicate gained absolute booking control over the nation's theatres—in effect a stranglehold on American entertainment. So complete was the Syndicate's control of American entertainment, that the great international star **Sarah Bernhardt** (1845–1923), who refused to sign with it, had to perform in a tent during her second tour of the United States (see photo,

p. 286). The Theatrical Syndicate was finally put out of business by the even more powerful **Shubert Theatre Corporation,** which gained booking control by acquiring ownership of most of the theatres in New York and in most other major American cities, giving it a virtual monopoly on all commercial legitimate theatre in the country. In 1950 the U.S. government filed a successful antitrust suit against the Shubert Corporation, forcing it to sell twelve of its theatres outside of New York. The corporation still owns sixteen Broadway theatres and is considered among the most powerful commercial producers in the world.

Modern Producing

The essential requirements of theatre production—the product produced (plays for the stage), the personnel needed for production (actors, designers, technical staff), the facility needed for presentation (empty space), and the consumers (an audience assembled in the space)—are the same today as they were 2,500 years ago. Producing for today's theatre is not fundamentally different from the way it has been practiced for many centuries.

Modern theatrical production still falls into the two basic categories of profit-making ventures and not-for-profit services. The distinction is defined by whose pockets the money goes into. In commercial theatre the money goes to the investors; in the not-for-profit theatre the money goes back into the organization to defray the expenses of continued existence. Closer examination reveals other, more fundamental differences as well.

The Art and Business of Commercial Producing

Commercial producers today work in a variety of venues, from the big time of multinational markets, the bright lights of world-class theatre districts like Broadway, and big-city tours, to more modest local productions, one-night stands, summer stock star packages, and even dinner theatres. Regardless of scale or location, most commercial producers are in the business of **single-play production,** sharing the common goal of hitting it big one venture at a time. The potential for complete failure is great. The odds of success are minimal. The required artistic and financial risks are not for the faint of heart.

If the big-time commercial theatre were a case study at the Harvard School of Business, students would recommend filing for Chapter 11 receivership. The core market is aging; costs are soaring out of control; five out of six new products lose money; and the most talented workers look to competing industries for their livelihoods. Quipped Jerry Sterner, the author of the Broadway hit *Other People's Money,* "There's no business in show business."[1] So what is the attraction that keeps potential investors lining up to sink their money into the latest ventures of commercial theatre producers?

There is much truth to the old saying that in the theatre you can't make a living, only a killing. The payback on a blockbuster show can be astronomical, returning three to ten times the original investment in half as many years. But in light of sky-rocketing costs, the results of putting on a failure are so catastrophic that commercial producers are not in the business of putting on plays, but of producing "smash hits." Therefore, producers have developed certain strategies designed to lessen the risks. Making choices based on minimizing risks and maximizing audience appeal may seem like good *business* sense, but in a business where the risks can never really be minimized, good *theatrical* sense is more important. The talent and enthusiasm for taking on this challenge are the essence of the art and business of the commercial producer in today's theatre.

Who They Are: Profiles of Theatrical High Rollers

It was Morton Gottlieb, the producer of such hits as *Same Time Next Year, Sleuth,* and *Tribute,* who once remarked, presumably tongue firmly in cheek,

> Anyone can be a producer. It's the only business I know where you can start at the top. You don't have to know how to read or write or count to ten. You don't have to have experience or talent. No license or degree is required, nor is any sense of honesty or honor. If you can separate fools from their money, you can be a producer.[2]

On the contrary, the most successful commercial producers working today are those who learned the business by coming up through the ranks, having worked at a variety of artistic and administrative theatrical jobs. While they all have proven business acumen, all are, in a sense, high rollers, willing to risk other people's millions on their passions for plays—betting each time out that the audiences will like what they like.

The names of a select group of twentieth-century producers are synonymous with the profession, demonstrating aptly how this high-stakes game is played. **Florenz Ziegfeld** (1867–1932) turned his taste for the scenic splendor, beautiful choruses, and comic sketches of Paris' *Folies-Bergère* into his own Americanized versions, the *Ziegfeld Follies,* which opened in 1907 and continued annually until 1932. Apart from the *Follies,* he also produced straight plays and musicals, the most successful of which was *Showboat* in 1927. In the 1940s and 1950s, **Kermit Bloomgarden** (1904–76) was the most successful producer in New York, demonstrating not only his understanding of the musical comedy formula for success with shows like *The Most Happy Fella* and *The Music Man,* but also an uncanny sense for recognizing the potential of that rarest of Broadway commodities, important serious dramas such as *Death of a Salesman* (1949), *The Diary of Anne Frank* (1957), and *Equus* (1973). In the 1950s and 1960s, **David Merrick** became virtually synonymous with a flamboyant flair for promoting his productions. When his *Subways Are for Sleeping* opened to devastating reviews, he found seven people with the same names as the drama critics and ran full-page ads quoting their rave reviews. Nicknamed the "Abominable Showman," Merrick was the most prolific producer of musicals in the history of Broadway. His string of hits included such blockbusters as *Oliver, Hello, Dolly!, Gypsy,* and *42nd Street.* In the 1960s and 1970s, **Harold Prince** won eight of his sixteen Tony Awards for producing before he switched to directing (for which he has won eight more). Among commercial producers, he has distinguished himself as a theatrical catalyst with a mission: to promote a more serious, alternative form for musical theatre. Almost singlehandedly he changed the perception of "musical comedy" to "musical theatre," producing plays that expanded the range of a very tradition-bound form. Among his innovative productions are *Fiddler on the Roof* (1965), *Cabaret* (1971), *Company* (1971), *Candide* (1973), and *A Little Night Music* (1973).

The most successful commercial producer in the world today is **Cameron Mackintosh.** Born in North London, the son of a Scottish timber salesman, he decided to become a producer of musicals at the age of 8. He studied stage management at the Central School of Speech and Drama, worked for several years as a stagehand for West End musicals, and in 1969 produced his first show, a revival of *Anything Goes* that closed in two weeks. Over the next ten years he built a record of successes with touring productions and small London shows. His big break came in 1980 when the superstar composer Andrew Lloyd Webber asked him to discuss production of a show based on a book of T. S. Eliot poems. Webber wanted to call it *Practical Cats.* Mackintosh agreed to produce it, shortening the title to *Cats,* and the show went on to become the first of the British techno-pop megamusicals. Since then, one Mackintosh hit seems to follow another as he continues to produce the most highly publicized, successful musicals of recent times, including *Les Misérables, Little Shop of Horrors, The Phantom of the Opera, Miss Saigon,* and the revival of *Carousel.* From his theatrical enterprises he has amassed a fortune estimated at more than $120 million.

Mackintosh accounts for his success by having developed a producer's most essential instinct: knowing what the public will flock to see. "My own tastes happen to be in tune with what the public wants," he claims. "I think that's the reason my batting average is so high, not because I've discovered some brilliant formula."[3] He also cites as crucial to his success his passion for stage musicals: "I suppose it has to be the very heightened theatrical experience it provides. The musical is the one area of the theatre that can give you the biggest buzz of all. I'm still as mad about it as I was when I started, indeed when I was a schoolboy dreaming about it."[4] Like other successful artists and entrepreneurs, Mackintosh has found success in translating his dreams into reality.

In addition to on-the-job theatrical experience, unerring audience instincts, and a passion for a specific kind of drama, Mackintosh identifies one other element important to his success: the ability to take charge of everything. "I'm a terrible interferer," he says. "There isn't an element of the show, from the design of the poster all the way through, that I don't have a go at some point."[5] Or as one of his staff members puts it, "He does like to have his thumbprint on everything."[6]

Choosing Plays

Finding the Right Property.   In the single-production ventures of commercial theatre, a play is referred to as a **property** to which a producer acquires the contractual **option** for professional production, subsequent productions in other

THE PRODUCER'S IMPRINT   *For the opening of the San Antonio production of "Les Miz" (as it is popularly known), Cameron Mackintosh's advertising and promotion staff drew up an ad that showed a drawing of Cosette, the young waif who has become the logo for the show, wearing a Davy Crockett coonskin cap with a caption that reads, "Remember the Alamo." "The Alamo," he responded. "Everyone was killed there, weren't they?"[7] He rejected it in favor of a more upbeat rendering—an idea of his own that he thought up on the spot.*

media such as print, film, and television, as well as **subsidiary rights** that cover all merchandising tie-ins such as books, soundtrack recordings, T-shirts, souvenirs, and trademark reproductions (see Figure 6–2).

For most producers, finding the right property is a never-ending search. Successful producers constantly receive hundreds of scripts from hopeful playwrights. They read many themselves, but often employ **play readers** to recommend the best ones out of the huge stacks of scripts that become part of the furnishings of their offices. Other strategies for finding the right play include (1) commissioning new plays on specific subjects, (2) traveling the country and the world to see new plays being staged in the not-for-profit theatres, and (3) forming collaborative relationships with specific playwrights. Emanuel Azenberg has such a relationship as the sole producer of Neil Simon's plays, and Cameron Mackintosh has produced most of Andrew Lloyd Webber's musicals. Significantly, Mackintosh passed on the option to produce Webber's 1990 small-cast, low-tech, "intellectual" musical *Aspects of Love;* it must have been missing the "buzz." In New York, the play had a "mixed" reception, closing after barely going into profit. Recognizing a play that will

FIGURE 6–2 MERCHANDISING BROADWAY *Selling theatrical keepsakes has become a multimillion-dollar business, with some shows like* The Phantom of the Opera *and* Tommy *earning more than $1 million per year on merchandising.* Tommy *even marketed a pinball machine to arcades that at $4,500 per unit completely sold out.*

"work" on stage is perhaps a producer's most essential talent. As Kermit Bloomgarden once remarked, "Even people intimately involved with the theatre often cannot tell from reading a script what will work and what will not."[8]

The strategy for choosing plays for commercial production is that proven properties lessen risks. Much of commercial producing today might be characterized as the **import business:** picking up properties that have had great success in other venues such as London's West End, Off-Broadway, the regional professional theatres, or—as in the case of star-studded revivals—on Broadway itself. Lloyd Webber's shows were all part of the so-called "British invasion" that took over Broadway in the 1980s. In turn, national tours and summer musicals are virtually all remounted versions of New York hits.

For Broadway productions conventional wisdom holds that big spectacle musicals, light comedies and romances, farces, and the occasional melodrama are the safest bets. John Kenley, one of the most successful producers of summer musical "star" packages, put it this way: "Audiences like high kicks and high C's."[9] Nothing serious, classical, strange, or sentimental, please. Conventional wisdom, however, might best be defined as that which is waiting to be proven wrong.

Stuart Ostrow is a gambling impresario who bets against accepted orthodoxies of his profession. He likes to build productions of new, unorthodox plays from scratch, such as *1776,* his historical musical about the signing of the Declaration of Independence, and *Pippin,* a soft-rock musical about the flower-child son of Charlemagne. In 1988 he produced on Broadway David Henry Hwang's *M. Butterfly,* a nonmusical play based on a true story about a French diplomat who, unbeknownst to him, married a person who was a male transvestite spy for the People's Republic of China. (See color plate 5.) The author had never had a play produced on Broadway, the show got disastrous out-of-town reviews, and the advance sale was only $36,000—enough to keep the show running for only four performances. Ostrow, relying on his producer's instincts, opened the show anyway. The New York audiences and the critics raved, the production played for two years (including a national tour and a hit London production), it went on to win the Tony Award as the best play of the season, and became a motion picture starring Jeremy Irons.

Choosing a Theatre

Most commercial producers do not own theatres. In the single-play production business, being tied to one theatre limits a producer's creative options of putting the "property" into its appropriate space—a most crucial theatrical choice. *Driving Miss Daisy,* a three-character play with minimal suggestive scenery (two stools and a chair), requires a theatre with small stage space and an intimate relationship between auditorium and the acting area. *Miss Saigon,* on the other hand, requires a theatre large enough that a helicopter must appear to land on stage.

Theatre Owners.   Common theatre practice is for producers to rent spaces from theatre owners. In effect, what is rented is an empty shell: a stage, auditorium

A BROADWAY MISS   *Not all of Stuart Ostrow's long shots finished in the money. His 1991 Broadway production of David Hirson's* La Bête *seemed to violate not only conventional wisdom, but common sense as well. Ostrow spent $2 million (one of the most expensive nonmusical productions in Broadway history) to produce the first play by a novice playwright—a Molière-like intellectual comedy written in rhymed couplets about the backstage squabbles of a seventeenth-century French acting troupe. Opening to unenthusiastic reviews, Ostrow closed it after less than a week of performances.*

with seats, lobby, rest rooms, dressing rooms, box office, and marquee. As a rule, rented theatres have no shops or other production-generating space. They come without lighting equipment or sound systems. They provide no stock of scenery, props, or costumes. A producer brings in what is essentially a complete production. In New York City there are three major theatre-owning organizations: the **Shubert Organization,** which owns and operates sixteen of Broadway's most desirable theatres as well as a half interest in one other (the Music Box Theatre, which it co-owns with the estate of Irving Berlin); the **Nederlander Organization,** which owns ten Broadway theatres (as well as several others in major cities throughout the country); and **Jujamcyn Theaters,** which owns five.

Theatre owners naturally want to rent to blockbuster productions; the length of rental lasts only as long as the length of run. Standard practice is for owners to engage in fierce bidding against each other for productions that show signs of

CREATING ITS OWN PROPERTIES *The Disney corporation has built an empire by taking fairy tales in the public domain and reinventing them as corporate properties. In 1994 it extended this practice to the legitimate stage when it remodeled an old 42nd Street movie theatre to mount stage adaptations of its full-length cartoons. The stage version of* Beauty and the Beast *is Disney's incarnation of the classic children's story, which has been a megahit animated film, an even bigger hit on video, a soundtrack, a theme-park attraction, and an ice show. Similar stage treatments are planned for* Aladdin, Mary Poppins, *and* The Little Mermaid.

being "sure" hits. **Rocco Landesman,** the president of Jujamcyn Theaters, described the bidding war among himself, the Shuberts, and the Nederlanders to acquire the 1989 revival of the Bertolt Brecht/Kurt Weill musical *The Threepenny Opera* starring the rock singer-turned-actor Sting:

> I wanted *Threepenny Opera* more than any show since I've been at Jujamcyn. *Threepenny Opera* was a layup. It was a lead-pipe cinch. In horse racing we call it a walkover. Only one horse running. How could it possibly miss? You had Sting, who was a huge international star. You had John Dexter, an internationally renowned director who had just come off a huge success in one of our houses with *M. Butterfly.* You had a classic show with classic music. You had all the elements of a hit. You couldn't possibly lose.
>
> So I moved heaven and earth. I did everything a human being could do to get that show. I went toe to toe with the Shuberts. We were scratching each other's eyes out. And, of course, the Shuberts won it, for the Shubert theatre. I was devastated.

> [Then] the Shuberts couldn't get *A Chorus Line* out of the Shubert soon
> enough. . . . So they brought it to the Nederlanders . . . which was devastating. I re-
> member feeling so down at the time. So I had to settle for *Gypsy* . . . this roadshow re-
> vival [starring Tyne Daly] which would come in and play maybe a couple of months.
> The rest is history.[10]

The Threepenny Opera closed after a two-month run and disastrous critical notices. *Gypsy* turned out to be the long-running, Tony Award-winning blockbuster.
It was a classic case of the theatre owner losing the battle, but winning the war.
"So tell me there's no luck involved in this business," said Landesman. "It's the
luck of the draw. What theatres are available."[11]

Because the theatre owners have such an interest in renting to hit shows, they
often become involved as producers and investors in the productions that play in
their facilities. The Shubert Organization, called the "700-pound gorilla of Broadway," is the largest single investor in new productions, having co-produced
Dreamgirls, Ain't Misbehavin', Dancin', Amadeus, and *The Gin Game,* among
many others. Among the Nederlander's successful production ventures was the
megahit *Annie.* Jujamcyn's co-production hits include *Big River, Into the Woods,*
and *City of Angels.*

Theatre Districts.   It has been said the three most important factors for a successful
business are "location, location, and location." The same is true for theatres. Producers seek out those facilities positioned to best attract large audiences. When
the first commercial producers built permanent theatres in the sixteenth century,
they erected them in areas noted as entertainment sectors. In Elizabethan England,
theatres were built in the Shoreditch and Bankside areas—outside the city limits
and noted as centers of bearbaiting, bullbaiting, and other large-draw spectator diversions. Today, major metropolitan areas all have their theatre districts. London's
commercial theatre district is the **West End,** in Chicago the major commercial
houses are near the downtown Loop. A common practice for smaller metropolitan
areas is to build civic center complexes that contain exhibition halls, an arena
adaptable to sporting events as well as large-scale performance spectacles, and a
theatre used by symphonies, dance troupes, and tours of Broadway productions.

The most famous theatre district in the world is **Broadway;** the very name suggests a mystique of success in the theatre just as "Hollywood" does for the movies.
Geographically, Broadway is the longest street in the world, extending 150 miles
north from the foot of Manhattan Island to Albany. The street is a main traffic artery
in New York City, running through the nation's financial center at Wall Street and
entering the theatre district at Times Square. As a theatre district, Broadway refers
to the area in midtown Manhattan from about 42nd Street to 50th Street, bisected
by Broadway itself. Of the thirty-two Broadway theatres, only two (the Wintergarden and the Broadway Theatre) are actually on the famous street. Broadway theatres are those in this area with a capacity of more than 499. Producers and owners
have negotiated contracts with theatrical unions that result in the highest production costs anywhere in the world. High costs and high risks lead Broadway producers to choose the "safe" formula of musicals, light comedies, and proven hits for the

"Great White Way," so called because of the marquees that light up this most famous of theatre districts.

Off-Broadway is not so much a theatre district as a contractual reference to those theatres anywhere in Manhattan with a capacity of 499 or less, for which the League of Off-Broadway Theatres has been granted less stringent union operating terms and city regulations. These concessions have helped to keep production costs lower, leading to more adventurous choices in play selection and production style. For example, after opening twenty-nine shows on Broadway, Neil Simon and his longtime producer Emanuel Azenberg decided to open *London Suite* at the Off-Broadway Union Square Theatre. The cost of loading in the play Off-Broadway was $8,000. On Broadway, with union scale, the cost was estimated at $175,000.

The crucial event in attracting producers to the Off-Broadway option was the successful 1952 production at the Circle in the Square Theatre of Tennessee Williams' *Summer and Smoke,* which had been a recent failure on Broadway. The concept of "Off-Broadway" theatres actually began in the eighteenth century in Paris, when enterprising producers began to challenge the monopoly of the Comédie Française by establishing **boulevard theatres,** smaller, alternative houses on the Boulevard du Temple, a popular recreational district. Today, most major metropolitan centers have such alternative theatrical districts as London's Fringe theatres, Chicago's Off-Loop, and Los Angeles' Theatre Row.

The Road.   As in the days of the Theatrical Syndicate, the real story of today's commercial theatre is the road: big-budget tours of Broadway hits playing limited engagements in big cities, small cities, university towns, and regional arts centers. The attendance at touring shows in the United States during the 1994 season was 16.7 million—about twice as many people who attended Broadway shows in New York. The reason is size. Broadway theatres with capacities averaging about 1,000 are limited in relation to today's skyrocketing production costs. Many hit shows do not make real profit until they go on tour where they can play in civic center and roadhouses with capacities ranging from 2,000 to 4,500 or in arenas with capacities of 10,000 or more. Total box office receipts for 1994 topped $1 billion for the first time, with the road representing two thirds of the gross. The total economic impact of commercial touring companies on American cities in which they performed was estimated at $2.5 billion.[12]

Global Markets.   The road, of course, does not end at the North American borders. There is a global market for Broadway properties that is rapidly expanding to the world's proverbial "four corners." The driving forces in the globalization of Western theatre are Cameron Mackintosh and Andrew Lloyd Webber. *Cats* has been performed over 45,000 times in twenty-one different countries since it first opened in 1981. The many (up to forty at one time) productions of *Les Misérables* playing around the world include one in Reykjavik and one in Oslo that has been seen by a third of Norway's population. *Sunset Boulevard* and *Joseph and the Amazing Technicolor Dreamcoat* are playing throughout Europe and as far away as Sydney.

The Phantom of the Opera has been on stage in Singapore and Hong Kong, with negotiations in the works for productions in Korea, Taiwan, and Vietnam.

Broadway is not welcomed everywhere. *Les Misérables, The Phantom of the Opera,* and *Miss Saigon*—all of French origin in one form or another—were short-run flops in Paris. France's leading musical theatre composer, Louis Dunoyer, explains that "since the days of Molière, the French have aggressively maintained their "cultural sovereignty."[13] Theatre is a matter of taste and tradition, but the government has fought for strict import quotas to protect the French film industry from the incursion of American movies.

Once the property and a space in which to mount it have been secured, producers turn their attention to choosing the theatre artists who will actually bring the play to life.

Choosing Artists

Perhaps a producer's greatest talent lies in understanding—and loving—the theatrical imagination. On the wall of Rocco Landesman's office hangs a self-portrait of **Antonin Artaud** (1896–1948), the provocative, influential French writer, director, and actor. Beside the drawing are the author's words, written at the mental institution where he spent the last ten years of his controversial but productive life:

> I want the last friends that I may have on this earth to understand and be enlightened that I was never mad or ill, and that my incarceration is the result of a frightful occult plot in which all sects of the initiated Christians, Catholics, Mohammedans, Jews, Buddhists, Brahmins, plus lamas of the Tibetan monasteries have participated.[14]

The paranoia evident in the quote is an admittedly extreme, but nevertheless blunt reminder that a certain degree of megalomania—passion, inspiration, imagination—is part of the creative energy of artists. Landesman, like all successful producers, knows you have not only to tolerate, but to appreciate and to nurture the megalomania if you are going to get the art.

Like the managers of sports teams, theatrical producers may not play the game themselves, but they are talented at putting together winning combinations of players at their appropriate positions. The producer hires the entire production team, and in the single-play projects of the commercial theatre, the "lineup" is different each time out. For his production of *Death of a Salesman* in 1949, Kermit Bloomgarden chose his players unerringly when he picked a group of artists noted for their experience with intense psychological American dramas. To direct, he hired Elia Kazan, who had scored a recent hit with Tennessee Williams' *A Streetcar Named Desire* in 1947. To design the expressionistic scenery and lights, he signed Jo Mielziner, who had designed not only Williams' *Streetcar,* but also *The Glass Menagerie* and *Summer and Smoke.* For his actors, he prudently settled on a cast of veterans including Mildred Dunnock, Arthur Kennedy, and Cameron Mitchell, and took a big risk with an unknown 36-year-old actor named Lee J. Cobb to play the 60-year-old Willy Loman.

Choosing Actors.   Producers understand that the audience comes to the theatre primarily to see the actors. To fill supporting, chorus, and supernumerary roles, producers usually hire casting agencies or rely on the recommendations of their directors. But in the commercial theatre, raising money, especially for a serious drama or other nonformula property, often depends on the availability of a star actor. British producer/director Peter Hall was able to bring a 1989 revival of Shakespeare's *The Merchant of Venice* to London's West End and to Broadway because he signed Dustin Hoffman (who had no previous experience acting Shakespeare) to play Shylock. Broadway revivals of *Cat on a Hot Tin Roof* with Kathleen Turner, *Orpheus Descending* with Vanessa Redgrave, and the ill-fated *The Threepenny Opera* with Sting were likewise able to draw investors largely because of the presence of stars.

Theatrical stars, like those in any field, cost a lot of money. Salaries for actors like Hoffman, Redgrave, and Turner range from $15,000 to $35,000 per week plus 5 to 10 percent of the gross. For playing the Devil in the 1994 revival of *Damn Yankees,* Jerry Lewis became the highest paid Broadway actor ever with a weekly salary said to be at least $40,000 plus a percentage of the box office. With potential weekly ticket sales of $700,000 on Broadway, the cost of a star does not seem exorbitant to most commercial producers.

What It Costs: Financial Choices and Strategies of the Commercial Producer

There is no doubt about it—commercial theatrical ventures cost a lot of money to produce, and the production expenses increase faster than inflation. The pre-opening cost of mounting a nonmusical play on Broadway in 1995 was $1 million to $2.5 million. The cost of a musical was $5 million to $12 million. Even the smallest commercial show in an Off-Broadway venue can seem exorbitant. The 1990 production of the campy satire *Vampire Lesbians of Sodom* (minimal scenery, small cast, and piano accompaniment only) at Chicago's Royal George Cabaret Theatre, a tiny theatre seating only seventy-five people, required $50,000 in pre-production costs and $10,000 per week in operating expenses.

According to William Baumol, an economist who has studied performing arts finances, there are good reasons why live theatre production costs so much. First, theatre is a people-intensive business in which most of the cost of the product is labor. Other businesses can manage labor costs through the efficiencies of automation. But in the theatre, the potential for saving labor and production time is limited. It takes just as many hours today to build a balcony for Juliet and for an actor to recite the "Romeo, Romeo" monologue as it did 400 years ago. Attempts by producers to introduce the use of labor-saving technology have been countered by theatrical unions seeking to protect their members.

The second reason, according to Baumol, that commercial producers have little control over their skyrocketing costs, is the competition from the film and television industries. Even though Hollywood also suffers from exploding costs on a scale that far exceeds Broadway's, once a movie has been "wrapped," its multimillion-dollar costs can be amortized with tens of thousands of showings on thousands of screens worldwide. With video sales and subsidiary spinoffs, the risks on even a modestly received film can be virtually eliminated.[15]

For a clearer picture of the costs involved in producing a major commercial property, consider the breakdown of preopening expenses of Stuart Ostrow's Broadway failure, *La Bête:*

Sets	$ 300,000
Costumes and wigs	70,000
Lighting	35,000
Sound	10,000
Fees and advances*	130,000
Rehearsal salaries	225,000
Administration**	561,000
Bonds***	209,000
Advertising and publicity	200,000
SUBTOTAL	**1,740,000**
Built-in reserve	260,000
TOTAL BUDGET****	**$2,000,000**

*includes the author's advance and fees for the director, producer, and designer
**includes audition costs, insurance, travel, theatre rent, and legal fees
***two-week pay guarantee for union employees
****very expensive Broadway play has budget that is 2% of budget for a very expensive Hollywood film.
(*Source:* Stuart Ostrow)

La Bête also had to make $150,000 a week in ticket sales just to break even. Unfortunately (or fortunately, depending on your point of view), the producer closed the show before the first week of performances was completed, resulting in a loss of virtually the entire original investment of $2 million.

Obviously, the risk of such failure is too much for any one individual or even corporate producer to undertake. Most plays that are optioned are never even produced because the producers cannot raise the capital needed to bring them to the stage. Sharing the risk is the most common way to produce plays in the commercial theatre.

The Limited Partnership Agreement.   For legal, economic, and theatrical reasons, the limited partnership agreement has become the favored arrangement for raising the money needed to finance a commercial production. Under this agreement, a company is formed for the sole purpose of producing a single play. The agreement stipulates two kinds of partners: **general partners** and **limited partners.** The general partners assume all artistic, administrative, and legal control. In other words, the general partners make all the decisions. The limited partners, also called *angels* or *backers,* buy shares in the company that cover the *total* preproduction costs, but receive only half of the profits in proportion to their investments. The general partners receive the other 50 percent. Backers are classic silent partners.

To clarify liabilities assumed by the backers, every limited partnership agreement contains a section called "The Risk to Investors," which states that most commercial theatrical productions fail, rarely recouping production costs, let alone making a profit. Most investors are lucky just to break even. If a commercial show gets bad reviews, the general partners will close it quickly to minimize operating losses to the limited partners.

On the other hand, hit shows can multiply the return on an investment quicker and in larger proportion than any other in the business world. The Globe Theatre recouped the production costs of a play in one week, which is the reason Shakespeare saw thirty-eight of his plays produced. Today, the payback time is longer, but the payback dollars can be huge. For example, the cost of bringing *Miss Saigon* to Broadway was in excess of $10 million, but it recouped its entire investment in thirty-nine weeks, the usual commercial theatre payback period for a hit. *Les Misérables,* which cost $4 million to produce in 1985, recouped in twenty-four weeks. So far, it has returned more than $5 for every $1 invested. *Cats* has already earned $50 for every $1 put up by its limited partners—a return on investment of 4,900 percent. The $1,000 invested in the original 1943 production of *Oklahoma!* would have yielded $2.5 million by 1994, a return of 249,900 percent.

Of course, these great hits must be balanced against such monumental multimillion-dollar flops as *Shogun* ($10 million), *Carrie* ($7.5 million), and the long-awaited, but never materialized, *Annie 2: Miss Hannigan's Revenge* ($8 million). Failed productions constitute near total losses for the investors. There are no assets to liquidate. The sets, costumes, and props of a commercial theatrical failure have little resale value.

The high costs, high prices, and high risks of commercial theatre production attract a special breed of artistic gamblers. Rocco Landesman puts it this way: "I enjoy being tested. . . . If there's not the risk of real failure, of looking bad, of embarrassing yourself, what's the point? I think you have to be able to step up to the plate and take your cut, and if you strike out, you strike out. But maybe you'll connect. Maybe you'll hit one."[16] But others view the consequences of this commercial system as limiting artistic options and stifling rather than promoting theatrical imagination. For these theatrical missionaries, only the not-for-profit system of play production can accommodate their passion for being creative catalysts.

The Art and Business of Not-for-Profit Producing

In the 1920s, a young actor named **Eva Le Gallienne** (1899–1991) declared "the theatre should be free to the people just as the Public Library is free, just as the museum is free." She went on to lament the fact that "the theatre had fallen into the hands of real estate owners and syndicates and those who have no love or interest in the stage or its life, but who have considered it principally as a means to make money."[17] In 1926 this young woman who became a renowned actor, director, and

PRODUCTION CAPITALIZATION   *One of Off-Broadway's biggest commercial hits is the participatory production of* Tony 'n Tina's Wedding, *in which the paying audience take the parts of guests at a staged marriage ceremony. To capitalize the production, producer Joseph Corcoran raised $112,000 among twelve limited partners. The show opened in February 1988, and recouped its original investment by the end of April. It now grosses close to $4 million per year, and, according to Corcoran, the investors are making more than a 100 percent return annually.*

producer founded the Civic Repertory Theater, devoted to producing populist productions of Shakespeare, Ibsen, and Chekhov at low ticket prices. By 1935, however, she had to close her theatre for lack of money and patrons. Le Gallienne, it seems, was twenty-five years ahead of her time.

Since 1950, other artistic visionaries have developed the diverse alternatives to the commercial theatre in America that Le Gallienne dreamed of. Not-for-profit theatres are now an essential part of the entire theatre establishment. There are more than 400 such professional theatres in municipalities across the country; local school districts establish magnet schools for the performing arts that prepare students for study in more than 600 college and university theatres; and more than 8,000 community theatres support widespread amateur participation.

*Eva Le Gallienne in the 1931 revival of
Alexandre Dumas' fils* Camille.

The Not-for-Profit Theatre Profile

Despite the diversity of the goals, constituencies, and expertise of the participants, not-for-profit theatres share unifying characteristics that distinguish them
from their commercial counterparts.

Organizational Identity. Not-for-profit theatres are organized as tax-exempt public
corporations under charters issued by the states as opposed to limited partnerships organized for profit and registered with the Securities and Exchange Commission. Under section 501C3 of the Internal Revenue Code, such corporations
can achieve tax-exempt status if they are organized for charitable, religious, or educational purposes. Those involved in the administration of such organizations
usually prefer the term **not-for-profit** to describe their status, as opposed to "nonprofit," which can be construed to mean losing money. Many not-for-profit theatres actually make money, but the surpluses are not profits that are distributed to
investors. Rather, they are "positive fund balances" that are reinvested in the corporation for its future projects.

Mission Statements. Not-for-profit theatres are organized to serve a specific mission
that must be stated in their charters. Mission statements may be either broadly
worded or narrowly specific. For instance, the La Jolla Playhouse in California adheres to a broad statement that permits a great variety of production projects:

The La Jolla Playhouse provides a home for theatre artists to gather, share ideas and extend themselves. At the heart of each project we produce is a director, playwright or performer who can impact the development of our art form and help define the course of American theatre. We encourage a variety of genres and styles, believing that the vitality of the American theatre is bound to our rich and diverse theatrical and cultural heritage. We produce new works and classics side by side. . . . This juxtaposition allows artists and audiences alike to examine contemporary issues in a historical context.[18]

In contrast, the Living Stage in Washington, D.C., is a professional, multiracial, improvisational company that was created in 1966 by Robert Alexander with the

A FOCUSED MISSION *A performance workshop of the Living Stage Theatre Company. Expanding on the mission of the theatre, founder Robert A. Alexander explains that "the theme of racism runs constant throughout our work—the causes, the results, and the possible means of annihilating this disease which is an intrinsic part of the soil of our land. . . . Our company [also] intends to strengthen our American Sign Language skills and learn to speak Spanish so we can continue to work with deaf audiences and extend our work to Spanish-speaking children and teens."[19]*

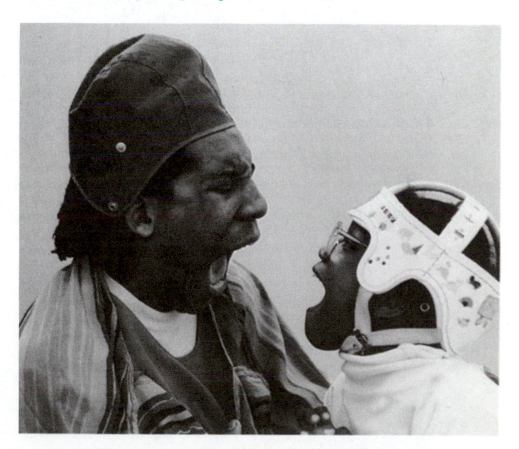

specific "outreach" mission to "provide access to theatre for the disadvantaged, the handicapped, the incarcerated, and the elderly."

Such mission statements make the theatre organizations more responsible to their community constituencies—responsible to the consumers as opposed to investors.

Subsidized Financing.   Not-for-profit theatre companies may have artistic missions that extend beyond their abilities to earn sufficient money from the sale of tickets alone. Therefore, they require subsidies in order to accomplish their missions. Subsidies are provided by individual donors, charitable organizations such as the Ford Foundation (which began its extensive program of giving grants to professional theatres in 1959), corporations, and local, state, and federal governments.

Federal funds have been dispersed to qualified not-for-profit theatres through the **National Endowment for the Arts** (NEA), an important but not

CORPORATE SUBSIDY OF THE THEATRE   *In 1985 communications giant American Telephone and Telegraph created* AT&T: Onstage *to encourage performing arts organizations to develop and present original new works for the stage. Since its inception, the program has presented fifty-one productions including plays, operas, and musicals in partnership with premier cultural institutions worldwide. One such new work was the Berkeley Repertory Theatre production of* The Woman Warrior, *adapted by Deborah Rogin from two novels by Maxine Hong Kingston. Scenic design by Ming Cho Lee.*

COMMUNITY THEATRE   *An amateur production of* The Music Man *at Ohio's Youngstown Playhouse, one of the oldest community theatres in the United States. The word* amateur *is taken from the Latin root word* amat, *which means "to love." Amateur productions are produced literally by theatre lovers. The community theatre mission is participation.*

overly generous source of federal government support compared to that of other countries. The $7 to $10 million theatre program budget (6 percent of the NEA total budget) is less than the amount the British Arts Council appropriates annually for the Covent Garden Opera.

Although each theatre tries to sell as many tickets as possible, a standard of success among not-for-profit theatres of all types is a 60 to 40 ratio of earned (ticket sales) to unearned (subsidies) income.

Producing a Season.   Unlike the temporary partnerships that produce the single-play projects of the commercial theatre, not-for-profit theatres are organized to exist in perpetuity. As a result, their thinking is long term. They produce seasons with play choices determined according to their missions. Their repertories are distinguished by commitments to plays that do not necessarily fit proven commercial formulas. Not-for-profit theatres, therefore, are the primary sources of productions of classics, serious dramas, and new plays on the cutting edge of experimental diversity.

Theatre companies like the La Jolla Playhouse with broad-based missions ("We encourage a variety of genres and styles") produce eclectic seasons that are mixtures of styles, genres, and subjects; no one particular type of drama is emphasized. La Jolla's 1994–95 season was typically eclectic: Mary Chase's *Harvey* (a classic American comedy); Pierre Marivaux's *The Triumph of Love* (an eighteenth-century French neoclassical comedy); Emile Zola's *Thérèse Raquin* (a nineteenth-century naturalistic tragedy); Bertolt Brecht's *The Good Person of Setzuan* (an episodic political allegory); *Mump and Smoot* (a two-person clown show); and Abe Burrow's and Frank Loesser's *How to Succeed in Business Without Really Trying* (a revival of a big-book musical). Theatre companies with narrow missions like the Living Stage ("the theme of racism runs constant throughout our work") produce strictly homogeneous seasons.

While producing a season of plays has the advantages of diverse offerings and artistic challenges, it also has one significant drawback. Once begun, the season rolls on without a mechanism for the theatre to capitalize on its successes or to close its failures. Thus the theatre's best and worst works get equal play in the same space.

Owning Theatres. Unlike commercial producers who rent theatres from owners, not-for-profit organizations usually own their theatres. In a theatre practice of long-standing historical tradition, many begin their existence in converted **found spaces** in churches, barns, storefronts, train stations, or abandoned factories. Theatres with names like the Mule Barn Theatre and the Cider Mill Playhouse give evidence of their humble origins. Others are able to capitalize on years of success and build new fully equipped facilities with two or more theatres. Houston's famous Alley Theatre played for years in an abandoned fan factory; today it is housed in a multimillion-dollar theatre complex in downtown Houston. Some of the best equipped and most comfortably appointed theatres in the country are university theatres that are used almost exclusively by student actors.

Lower Operating Costs. Compared to the high-risk, high-cost, high-life glamour of commercial show business, the not-for-profit theatres display more "middle-class" values that define permanence, continuing service, and tradition. Collectively they have a long-term interest in keeping operating expenses and ticket prices as low as possible. Professional not-for-profit theatres have negotiated concessions from theatre unions that enable them to pay lower scales of salaries and benefits.

The Divided Responsibilities of Producing. The emphasis on an artistic mission defines not only the character, but the titles of the producers in not-for-profit theatres. State charters require that each company have a board of trustees that oversees the operation of the theatre. Entirely voluntary, the unpaid board members agree to serve because they identify with the mission of the theatre. They are, first and foremost, advocates for the theatre in the community at large—protectors of a theatre's idea. The board then hires professional executives who actually run the companies according to policies established in the charter. The traditional job of producer is usually divided between two individuals having separate responsibilities for the artistic functions of the company and for the administrative activities.

The **artistic director** is charged with carrying out the creative mission of the theatre. Like the commercial producer, the artistic director chooses the season's plays, selects the directors, actors, and designers, and approves artistic choices. Unlike their commercial counterparts, artistic directors usually direct one or more plays each season. The **managing director,** sometimes called the "producing director," is in charge of staff administration, facilities management, contractual negotiations, ticket sales, fund-raising, and audience development.

While many not-for-profit theatres thrive under this management system, the triangle of governance can foster creative tension. A theatre's artistic needs can appear vague and impractical when compared to the complex and absolute demands of the so-called bottom line. Anne Bogart, who resigned in 1990 after one year as artistic director of the Trinity Repertory Company in Providence, Rhode Island, described the frustration of small disputes that can become major aesthetic/managerial conflicts such as when a manager "insists that an intermission must occur at a certain point because that is where the subscribers are used to an intermission, and the artist feels 'NO' that is wrong, that is not where it feels right."[20]

Success in business is measured in results, not process, a commercial attitude that equates artistic accomplishment with box office sales. **Robert Brustein,** the founding artistic director of the Yale Repertory Theatre in New Haven, Connecticut, and the American Repertory Theatre in Cambridge, Massachusetts, warns that not-for-profit theatres can thrive (as opposed to merely survive) only through a passionate commitment to their artistic missions: "If the management of an artistic institution does not love the imagination, first and foremost, if it does not dedicate itself to the growth of its artists and the development of its public, if it prides itself only on being a self-perpetuating machine, then it might as well be running a processing plant or a fast-food chain."[21]

The Decentralization of American Theatre.　Theatres aren't as ubiquitous as McDonald's restaurants, but they are fast becoming popular fixtures of American culture. There are thriving not-for-profit theatres in New York City, but the real story of subsidized play production is the decentralization of the American theatre, with professional theatres now in nearly every state and the District of Columbia. Considering the range of their offerings and the diversity of their missions, it is not so appropriate to refer to the "modern American theatre" as it is to describe modern American theatres.

Not-for-Profit Theatre in the Big Apple

More than fifty not-for-profit professional theatre organizations in New York City exist as alternatives to the formidable commercial competition. They come in all sizes, missions, and locations.

The New York Shakespeare Festival.   The largest not-for-profit professional theatre in the country is the **New York Shakespeare Festival** (NYSF), founded by **Joseph Papp** (1921–91) in 1954 with the ambitious goal of producing free performances of Shakespearean plays in New York City. Unlike the separate artistic and managing directors who run most not-for-profit theatres, Papp was for thirty-seven years the sole producer of the Shakespeare Festival. The scope of his accomplishments made him an impresario who rivaled—many would say exceeded—those of the legendary commercial producers. He certainly surpassed by far his original ambition. From a humble beginning with a single truck for touring modest productions of Shakespeare to parks and playgrounds, the NYSF has grown into a theatrical

FREE SHAKESPEARE   *The 1962 NYSF production of* The Merchant of Venice *in the Delacorte Theatre in Central Park. In 1987 the Festival embarked on a six-year marathon to produce all thirty-six of Shakespeare's plays with the foremost American actors in the leading roles.*

conglomerate with a $17 million budget that supports a mission of "providing the-atre of the greatest range, rooted in the classics but with new American plays as its primary focus using artists of the highest professional standards for a broadly based public."[22]

Today, the NYSF produces everywhere throughout the city. Since 1962, the Festival has presented free outdoor summer productions of the classics at the Delacorte Theatre in Central Park. NYSF's permanent home is the Off-Broadway Public Theatre, a six-theatre complex in the landmark Astor Library building where new American plays encompassing the country's multicultural heritage are produced. The Festival continues to bring Shakespeare to the playgrounds and parks, administers educational programs like Playwriting in the Schools, and presents annual international festivals of theatre, film, music, and dance such as Festival Latino. Papp even brought his productions uptown to Broadway itself. *Hair, The Pirates of Penzance* (with Linda Ronstadt and Kevin Kline), *The Two Gentlemen of Verona,* and the record-breaking *A Chorus Line* were all NYSF productions that began life at the Delacorte or the Public and became hits on Broadway. The resulting "positive fund balance" generated by such productions is channeled back into the NYSF to underwrite its many projects.

Other important not-for-profit theatres that produce successful New York seasons and have transferred productions to the commercial stage include the

RENAISSANCE PRODUCER   *Before succeeding to the position of producer of the New York Shakespeare Festival, George C. Wolfe had already established a formidable record as a dramatist and director of major commercial productions including* Jelly's Last Jam *and* Angels in America. *With* Angels *he became the first black director in the history of Broadway to direct a major play that was not about people of color. As for the multicultural mission of the NYSF, Wolfe reflects by way of a question: "Is it possible to come up with a system, a management team, and a play department and a press department that can address the specific needs of different artists, that can try to appeal to the five or six different communities that we're actively cultivating? It's much easier to appeal to the 'traditional theatre audience,' but we're trying to get as many different kinds of people in here as possible. . . . If you can engage imaginations, then hearts come along. If you can engage hearts, then minds come along. In theatre, on one level, you gotta seduce. You're tickling with one hand and then you're stabbing with another."[23]*

Lincoln Center Theatre, the Manhattan Theatre Club, the Circle Repertory Theatre, and Playwrights Horizons. Increasingly, the theatre unions have begun to withdraw their concessions for Off-Broadway productions, making it less and less a place to produce daring or experimental works.

Off-Off Broadway.   The New York venue for the most adventurous not-for-profit theatre is **Off-Off Broadway,** a term coined in 1960 by Jerry Talmer, then drama critic of the *Village Voice.* Originally an amateur movement that was long on enthusiasm but short on experience and know-how, Off-Off Broadway theatres are now organized primarily as **showcases** for new talent, especially playwrights and actors. Plays are produced in very small spaces (fewer than a hundred seats) with minuscule budgets and minimal production elements. The "showcase," or "equity waiver" contract permits union actors to work for no pay, although reimbursement of carfare expenses is recommended. The narrowly defined showcase missions of Off-Off Broadway theatres are evident in names such as the Equity Library Theatre (for showcasing the work of union actors and directors); the New Federal Theatre ("to bring minority playwrights, actors, and directors to national attention"); INTAR Hispanic American Arts Center ("presents and develops contemporary Latin and Hispanic artists living in the U.S. and throughout the world"); the Women's Project & Productions ("to encourage women to write for the theatre and to help establish credibility for both women writers and directors in American theatre"); and the Pan Asian Repertory Theatre ("to produce the works of Asian-American playwrights, Asian masterworks translated into English, and innovative adaptations of Western classics").

Cities with similar waiver agreements include Chicago, San Francisco, and Los Angeles—all theatre centers with large resident populations of actors, writers, directors, and designers in need of places to showcase their work and of artistic directors who have the know-how to produce these works on a shoestring.

The Regional Theatre Movement

More than anything else, the establishment of more than 400 regional professional theatres in the last fifty years demonstrates the real vitality of the decentralized American theatre. Calling the phenomenon of the American regional theatre a "movement" is an apt description of the not-for-profit theatre's migration to every American metropolitan or tourist area with a population of 500,000 or more (see Figure 6–3).

Founding Mothers.   In the 1920s and 1930s, Eva Le Gallienne and Hallie Flanagan blazed the trail. In the 1940s, the first regional theatres in the country were founded by theatrical pioneers such as **Margo Jones**, who started Theatre 47 in Dallas in 1947; **Nina Vance,** who established the Alley Theatre in an abandoned fan factory in Houston in the same year; and **Zelda Fichandler,** whose Arena Stage (established in 1950) is still one of Washington, D.C.'s most important arts institutions. Not immodestly, Zelda Fichandler considers the fact that the

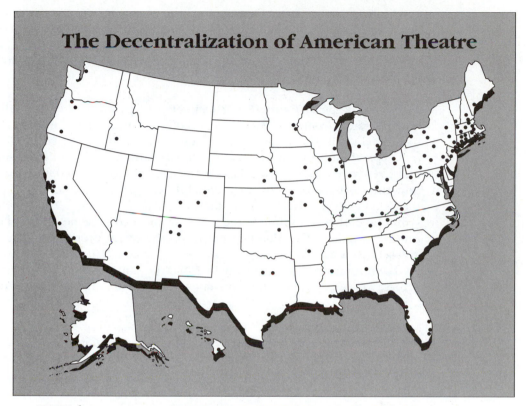

FIGURE 6–3 Locations of regional professional theatres in the United States.

regional theatre movement was invented by female artistic directors to be more than coincidental:

> *Founding* a theatre is different from *going* into the theatre. It's a big deal. It's taking on a tribe. George Tabori once said to me while we were working on *Mother Courage* that he thought the impulse to found a theatre was the same impulse as founding a family. Perhaps women channeled the creative abilities that couldn't be channeled into the commercial theatre into making our own kitchens so we could cook the dishes we wanted. In the early years, we didn't know what we were doing. We didn't know what forces were going to come along. We all started our theatres whimsically, capriciously even, and they were small. It was a way to do our work, direct plays. Then it got to be very large and complex economically and our responsibilities ramified to constructing buildings and raising funds and charting courses through these very treacherous economic and social waters.[24]

Despite the efforts of these pioneers, the regional theatres that were established across the country in the 1960s, 1970s, and 1980s were run mostly by men. In the 1990s, however, artistic direction of regional theatres has become a gender-neutral endeavor. Creative, visionary women like Sharon Ott (Berkeley Repertory Theatre), Carey Perloff (American Conservatory Theatre), Lynne Meadows (Manhattan Theatre Club), and Libby Appel (Indiana Repertory Theatre) joined their male counterparts in taking charge of some of the country's largest not-for-profit theatres.

The Cost of Regional Theatre Play Production.   Regional theatre annual operating budgets range from a low of about $50,000 to a high of $10 million for theatres like the Guthrie Theatre in Minneapolis and the Mark Taper Forum in Los Angeles. Typical budgets, however, are in the $3 million to $7 million range. The average cost of a single nonmusical production is about $300,000. For a picture of how this cost compares to commercial theatre production, consider the case of the Yale Repertory Theatre's production of August Wilson's *The Piano Lesson,* a symbolic drama of lost and found values in succeeding generations of an African American family. The Yale Rep produced the world premiere of the play in its 489-seat New Haven theatre in 1989 for $300,000. When it moved the Pulitzer Prize-winning work to Broadway in 1990, the same production—with the same actors, director, sets, and costumes—cost $1.1 million in preproduction

SUMMER THEATRE FESTIVAL   *More decentralized than even the regional theatres are the summer theatre festivals that locate in tourist areas. Many are produced in outdoor, open-air facilities. A large number in England, the United States, and Canada are Shakespeare festivals (more than fifty in the United States) such as the famous Oregon Shakespeare Festival in Ashland.*

expenses. Having recouped their original $1.1 million investment in the Broadway production, Yale Repertory Theatre artistic director Lloyd Richards and managing director Benjamin Mordecai agreed to share 7.5 percent of future weekly net profits with the show's six original cast members. The unusual profit-sharing plan harkens back to the days of the Globe Theatre, when the actors, not silent investors, reaped the profits of their creative labors.

As for the cost to the public, single tickets at regional theatres range from $20 to $30, but most try to market their product through season subscriptions that reduce the cost of a ticket to between $13 and $20 per show. Tickets for students, seniors, and groups can usually be purchased for $5 to $10.

The successful regional theatres have achieved the coveted status of essential institutions in the communities that support and patronize them. Like libraries, museums, symphony orchestras, and dance troupes, they have become prized emblems of cultural and creative vitality. Regional theatres are true repositories of classical drama as well as laboratories of performance experimentation. Their commitments to diverse missions are unified by social, civic, and artistic responsibility. Increasingly, the work of these theatrical institutions is an important source of "properties" for the commercial theatre. Regional theatres are changing the face of Broadway itself with a repertory of works that is thought provoking, nontraditional, less safe, and culturally diverse. Jack Kroll, theatre critic for *Newsweek,* predicted that if the current trend continues, the "Great White Way" may become the "Great Rainbow Way."[25]

The Passion for Playmakers

Business schools teach that the classic models for managers are the "consulter," the "teller," the "seller," and the "joiner." The modern theatrical producer must be all of these at once. Regardless of the management hat worn at any particular moment in the process of generating new theatre art, the producer's primary resource is the individual theatre artist. As Richard Hopkins, artistic director of the Florida Studio Theatre, said, "Our first responsibility is to the artist: to protect the artist and to allow the artist's whisper to become a voice."[26]

The art and business of producing become the art of theatre when the artists sign their contracts and proceed to give voice, action, and structure to their imaginations. In the theatre today, it is the director who speaks first.

Previewing Part 3

Part 2 examined forces, both external and internal, that shape the conception, writing, selection, and preproduction planning of a play—the initial artwork. Part 3, "The Production," focuses on the choices of the company of artists assembled by the producer for the staging of the play. The imaginations of directors, actors, and designers are the subjects of the chapters in this section.

THE PRODUCER AT WORK

In Residence: One Man's View of '90s Regional Theatre

[Reprinted from *Backstage*.][27]

Arvin Brown, artistic director of the Long Wharf Theatre in New Haven, Connecticut, talks about how the role of resident theatres has changed.

I think the main change that I sense is that what we hoped and what we predicted would be true all those years ago, has in fact become true—that we in the regional theatre, or whatever you want to call us, are the chief suppliers of whatever new material comes to Broadway, particularly in the area of serious drama or the serious play. That's no longer a supposition. It really is the way it is. There are very, very few plays that come to Broadway, particularly in the area of the serious drama with a genesis other than our various theatres around the country . . . or England.

Another change that we've been responsible for has been the level of experience for the American actor, because there have been places around the country for young actors to at least begin to experience classical theatre of various kinds and improve their skills in those areas—playing Shakespeare, playing Molière, so that you have a generation of actors, like Kevin Kline, who can become naturalistic movie actors, and yet still have that larger-than-life scale, which comes from their theatre training.

We have also educated an audience to the possibilities of theatre, which again was something we hoped would happen. Now I think we're left with the problem that that audience we've educated is getting older, and we now have to start again to find a way to reach the younger audience, which has so many other distractions, and try to create a theatre audience out of them. And that's turning out to be a fairly major challenge for all of us around the country.

[Our audiences are] fed by a lot of academic institutions, and there's a very large and wide professional population in New Haven—doctors, lawyers—so our audience, overall, has been extremely literate. So it has tended to be a sophisticated audience, and one in which the idea of participation is pretty strong—the audience is able to meet the actors halfway. I don't always find that true in New York, where there's that sense of settling back: "Entertain me." Which is fine—great theatre is entertaining—but I think it takes some effort.

SUMMARY

1. The producer is a creative catalyst who joins the script with theatre artists who will bring it to life, then unites the theatrical production with its potential audience.

2. Historically, one type of theatre production has had social, civic, or religious missions that have resulted in financial subsidy for these theatre organizations.

3. Commercial theatre in Europe began in the 1600s. It has included the "share system" in which actors form a partnership for both artistic and financial rewards. However, the dominant model has been of a single entrepreneur with both artistic experience and strong business know-how.

4. Modern producing falls into one of two basic categories: profit making and not for profit.

5. The profits from commercial theatre can be substantial. However, both the investment required and the risk are extremely high, forcing commercial producers to seek proven properties that have great audience appeal and a greater chance of success.

6. Commercial producers rent theatres for their single-play ventures. The producer hires the artists who bring the play to life and finds investors who will put up the money. Finally, the producer finds the audience that will enable the production to make a profit.

7. The not-for-profit theatres reinvest excess income into the organization rather than return profits to investors. Generally, the not-for-profit theatre relies on subsidies from corporations, government grants, and private donations to accomplish its artistic goals.

8. Not-for-profit theatres usually offer a season of plays rather than the single-show enterprises of the commercial theatre. The play choices are made to carry out the missions of the organizations.

9. Not-for-profit theatres usually own their own facilities.

10. Responsibilities in the not-for-profit theatre are divided between the artistic director and the managing director, both of whom are hired by a board of trustees.

11. Since the 1950s, the American theatre has been characterized by its decentralization or movement away from New York City. Regional professional theatres are now valued institutions in the cultural lives of their communities.

CHOICES

1. Imagine you are the artistic director of a not-for-profit professional theatre in a culturally diverse metropolitan center. Drawing on your knowledge of books, films, current affairs, and historical events, use your imagination to conceive of three new plays for an eclectic season that would attract the widest possible audience. Write a short scenario that describes the basic action and genre of each play. Explain the appeal of your season of new works.

2. To get your ideas for plays on the page, decide which playwright mentioned in Chapter 5 you would commission to write each of the new works. Explain your choices.

3. Create a season brochure that promotes these plays to your intended audience. Create a headline, sketch artwork, and write a one-paragraph description of each play that will make people want to come and see it.

4. Consider your most important, deeply felt political, religious, or social conviction. Create an imaginary theatre group organized to promote the idea in which you believe. Write a mission statement defining the purpose and function of your intended theatre company. Then, drawing on your knowledge of books, films, current affairs, and historical events, use your imagination to conceive of three new plays that will fulfill the specific mission of your intended theatre company. Defend your choices. Write a short scenario that describes the basic action and genre of each play.

THE PRODUCTION

Ariane Mnouchkine directing a dress rehearsal of Euripides' fifth century B.C. tragedy,
The Eumenides.

Come, sit down, every mother's son,
and rehearse your parts.

A Midsummer Night's Dream, *Act III, scene i*

CHAPTER 7

The Primary Theatre Artist

THE DIRECTOR'S CHOICES

PREVIEW

A Brief History of Directing
The Current Practice of Directing
An Imprint of Directorial Choices
The Necessity of Entrusting
The Director at Work

BARD IN THE BUFF!

The headline was provocative. A theatrical controversy over an artist's choice in England had gone out over the world wire services and made the papers in middle America: Sir Bernard Miles, artistic director of London's Mermaid Theatre, decided Desdemona should appear nude in the final death scene of his company's production of *Othello*. Sir Bernard claimed the idea had come to him in a flash of inspiration, and he could not understand why nobody had thought of it before. It was, he said, perfectly clear in the text of Shakespeare's play. In Act IV, scene iii, Emilia, the nurse, asks, "Shall I fetch your nightgown?" Desdemona replies, "No, unpin me here."

"That is obvious justification from this fantastic man Shakespeare that she is going to win her husband back that night," concluded Sir Bernard. His decision, of course, went against nearly 400 years of traditional theatre practice and, as might be expected, caused a bit of a stir. The person originally cast as Desdemona refused to appear in the "buff" and quit the show nine days before opening. She was replaced by a respected young player who was quoted as saying, "I would not have done it just for a sensation. The fact that she takes her clothes off adds to the scene."[1]

What is going on here? Can this one theatre artist so flagrantly disregard tradition and impose such a naked choice not only on Shakespeare (who, conveniently, is not in a position to object) but on everyone else involved from audience to actors—not to mention the costume designer? Did he have the right? Does anybody? Did Shakespeare intend *Othello* to be *that* flexible as to permit one theatre artist to imagine ink on the page to be this kind of display on the stage?

The answer to all of these questions is "yes."

The artistic license to peer into the theatrical codes of a written play and discern clues that will affect the choices of all other involved artists belongs to the director. The artistic authority to exercise the theatrical imagination in such crucial choices makes the director the primary theatre artist.

Like the other performing arts, delivering drama requires a master artist to organize the entire performance into a unified whole. For orchestral performances and dance recitals such artists have been a necessity for thousands of years. Only in the last hundred years or so has the theatre placed such artistic authority in the hands of one person. In that short time, the emergence of the stage director as an artistic force has become a distinguishing characteristic of the modern theatre. This chapter examines the most recent addition to the theatrical imagination, contrasting historical traditions with the modern practice of directing, and examining the controversies concerning the scope of the director's choices.

A Brief History of Directing

Someone in the theatre has always been responsible for the multiple tasks involved in mounting the play on the stage. For the first 2,400 years of theatre history, however, a strict separation was maintained between those who made the artistic choices and those responsible for the organizational logistics.

Playwrights in Control

In the classical theatres of ancient Greece and Rome the playwrights themselves held the responsibility for mounting their own plays. Following the example of the pioneering performer Thespis, the earliest tragic dramatists trained the chorus, invented the music, conceived the choreography, taught it all to the actors, and even acted in their own plays. It was Sophocles who may have established the playwright's retreat from such total domination and control. It seems the fifth century B.C. audiences ridiculed his performances because of his high-pitched, ineffective voice. He quit acting. Comic playwrights also withdrew from the process of play production and turned over the mounting of their works to an actor in the play. By the time this system was adopted by the Romans, actors were in complete command of their performances.

Actors in Control

In the prosperous commercial theatre of the Renaissance actors were the primary theatre artists. European theatre companies—Shakespeare's in England, Molière's in France, Lope de Vega's in Spain—were acting companies with no one person in control. Theatre people spoke always of "acting a play," never "directing" or "staging" one.

Staging conventions were based on the etiquette of actors sharing the stage and taking turns featuring themselves. Casting was an automatic consequence of parts either written for them or of a contractual system that allowed them to own or "possess" their roles as long as they remained with the company. Since they knew all the lines for the parts they possessed, little rehearsal was needed. Besides, actors preferred to "save" themselves for their performances. Stage movement amounted to little more than entering, exiting, and taking turns delivering speeches downstage center in front of—never within—the scenery that served as a backdrop.

From 1750 to 1850, as sharing diminished and the star system developed, the actor's primacy solidified into a rigid system of conventions. The final manifestation of this system was the **actor-manager,** the leading actor who tended to retain the best roles, the most sumptuous costumes, and the down-center area of the stage. It is not surprising that the great English and American theatrical personalities of the eighteenth and nineteenth centuries—David Garrick, Edmund Kean, Ira Aldridge, William Charles Macready, Charlotte Cushman, Edwin Booth, and Ellen Terry—were actors. Their control was absolute. It was not something they willingly relinquished.

Organizational tasks such as calling rehearsals, posting entrances and exits, and handing out scripts were left to **prompters,** hirelings similar to modern stage managers. They could start and stop actors in rehearsal, even fine them for infractions of established rules, but to impose or even suggest an artistic choice would have been unthinkable.

The Need to Control Actors

The need to impose some restrictions on the actors' freedom of choice in moving about the stage became obvious as the public began to favor new forms of drama in the nineteenth century. The elaborate and dangerous stage machinery needed to produce the catastrophic effects of the new and wildly popular melodrama (forest fires, floods, earthquakes, stampedes, and avalanches) could imperil the actors' safety if they were not placed in precise positions on stage.

By the end of the nineteenth century, the fidelity to life required by the new realistic dramas of Ibsen, Strindberg, and Chekhov could be realized on stage only if actors could be persuaded to change their domineering ways. They would have to give up their down-center acting to become part of a stage picture that was to resemble a slice of life. The need became apparent for someone outside the cast to be in charge: to keep things safe and picture perfect.

The First Directors

Acquiring artistic control over actors was not easy. It began in earnest in the 1860s and involved legal authority, autocratic personalities, and training a new generation of actors unencumbered by tradition.

Legal Authority over Actors.   **George II, the Duke of Saxe-Meinengen** (1823–1914), was the first influential director in the modern sense. A theatre enthusiast, he established a state-supported acting company in his small German duchy and appointed himself its artistic head. By virtue of his position as absolute ruler of his subjects—actors and designers included—he was able to impose his choices in acting and staging to achieve completely unified, historically accurate, realistic productions. He was the producer and the director, but never an actor. Among his many innovations were blocking, strict supervision of long rehearsals, realistic staging of crowd scenes, historically accurate costumes and settings for each production, and orchestration of theatrical elements and artists into a unified play. Favoring melodramas and Shakespearean revivals, he exerted a worldwide influence by touring with his company to thirty-eight cities in nine countries.

Autocratic Personalities.   **Richard Wagner** (1813–83) was one of the most autocratic persons ever to have total control of staging his own works. He preferred opera to theatre, since the musical form afforded complete control of production elements—especially performers. By setting their dialogue to music he could control even the pitch, rate, and rhythm of their utterances. He was also his own librettist and scene designer in an innovative theatre built for him at Bayreuth (see photo p. 388). He anticipated modern directors by seeking to control and unify all of the production elements into a *Gesamtkunstwerk,* or master artwork that included music, acting, dance, scenery, and costumes.

George Bernard Shaw (1856–1950) achieved international fame as a playwright with a monstrous ego. He even proclaimed himself a better writer than Shakespeare. Shaw sought to protect his creations from the whimsy of actors by writing detailed character descriptions that covered everything from their appearance to their psychology.

Shaw invariably cast his friends in his plays that he staged for private theatre clubs. These clubs were part of an international effort called the **Independent Theatre Movement** founded to test on a small scale the most recent artistic philosophies and methods, of which the new art of directing was a crucial part.

The Naturalistic Directors.   Directing pioneers **André Antoine** (1858–1943), **Otto Brahm** (1856–1912), and **Konstantin Stanislavsky** (1863–1938) were European theatre artists who understood that achieving the illusion of life on stage required great attention to every detail. Any whiff of theatricality such as an actor breaking character, looking at the audience, or speaking in an artificial manner would destroy the lifelike illusion. In their quests for a completely natural effect, they stood back to unify the theatrical action in every detail. They recruited inexperienced amateur actors unencumbered by any theatrical tradition.

The small-scale experiments of these nineteenth-century directors demonstrated the theatrical virtues of unified productions. They were followed by others who refined their methods, explored the creative potential of the new art, and helped establish the director as an indispensable artist for every production of a play. The model for the modern director is **Max Reinhardt** (1873–1943), an eclectic not devoted to any one particular artistic style. Reinhardt staged plays from all periods and styles, analyzing each one carefully before deciding on an appropriate theatrical approach. Called the "great organizer," he created detailed promptbooks to record his choices for over 385 productions for both stage and film. Perhaps the clearest indication of his authority was the accusation that he treated "his" actors "like puppets." With Reinhardt, the evolution of the new theatrical order was complete: actors had gone from the etiquette of sharing to the preeminence of starring to the subservience of being directed.

The model of the modern director had been established: the theatre artist charged with the responsibility of interpreting each play, developing an appropriate concept for its staging, and supervising the work of the other artists into a unified production that supports that concept.

The Current Practice of Directing

A theatrical art that achieved universal recognition and became widely practiced only sixty years ago has hardly had time to develop a system or even a technical language. To speak of a tradition of directing would be absurd; there is barely even an etiquette.

No two directors "direct" in the same way. For every one who practices the art one way, another directs exactly opposite. For every expert who proclaims the

A DIRECTOR BY ANY OTHER NAME

The use of the term *director* has only recently achieved what can be called universal acceptance. Saxe-Meinengen, of course, was "his royal highness." As a theatrical designation—even for the primary theatre artist—this would be going too far. Wagner preferred *Gesamtkunstwerker,* or "master art worker," which is too long for most marquees and programs. The French coined the word *régisseur,* which the Russians accepted verbatim, but the Americans translated as "director" and the British translated as "producer." The British began to use the American terminology in the 1960s.

qualities that make a good director, another will declare contradictory attributes. Alan Schneider, the director who staged the first American production of *Waiting for Godot,* once said, "There are no secret formulas, there are no rules. There's only yourself and your talent and your taste and your choices."[2]

Agreement exists only on what a director *is* and, in general, on what the director *does,* but not on how the director does it or on how far the director may go in making choices that affect the art, careers, and enjoyment of so many.

The Director as Interpreter

In the new theatrical order, playwrights need directors. Marshall Mason, the artistic director of the Circle Repertory Company in New York, described the artistic symbiosis of his working relationship with Lanford Wilson, the award-winning author of *Talley's Folly, The Fifth of July, Burn This,* and *The Redwood Forest:* ". . . we agree that the words are his responsibility and anything else is mine. Usually he does not have a visual concept for the play. The characters just talk somehow in his head, and the ultimate visual design we arrive at for a production is a revelation to him."[3] In a sense, playwright Wilson is the architect, and director Mason is the builder working from a flexible set of blueprints. The flexibility of a dramatic text, however, is a virtue only when the decisive step is taken to settle on a specific interpretation of it for a theatrical production. Interpreting the overall action of the play is the director's first and most crucial choice.

The unified vision of the dramatic action of a play is called different things by different directors. Konstantin Stanislavsky referred to it as the **super-objective** of the play. Harold Clurman, who staged the original production of Clifford Odets' *Awake and Sing,* sought to imagine what he called the **spine** of the play. Zelda Fichandler, the founding artistic director of Washington's Arena Stage, uses the Russian word ***zamissel,*** which means "the pervading thought." As Fichandler explains,

It's the thought that binds together all elements of the idea. The *zamissel* accounts for the whole—explains every action, every breath, every pulse, every second of the life of the play. It's like looking at a tree. The sap is in every leaf and it's also in the roots. I can spend months looking for the exact *zamissel* or idea or superobjective that will set a play in motion, unlock its hidden conflict.[4]

In *A Streetcar Named Desire,* playwright Tennessee Williams pits longing for a genteel old South in the character of Blanche Dubois against the realities of a modern society in which brutish men such as Stanley Kowalski struggle to survive, and women struggle to discover new relationships. For the original 1947 Broadway production of the play, director Elia Kazan determined the unifying idea to be a violent dramatic action: "This little twisted, pathetic confused bit of light and culture puts out a cry. It is snuffed out by the crude forces of violence, insensibility and vulgarity which exist in our South—this is the cry of the play."[5]

Research and Analysis.   In an eclectic theatre that draws its inspiration from an ever-shrinking, multicultural global village, new directorial preparation is required for every production. A stage director who may go from mounting *Julius Caesar* (the Roman Empire) to *Terra Nova* (the South Pole) to *A Flea in Her Ear* (1910 Paris) to *Waiting for Godot* (the existential wasteland) has cultures, manners, languages, history, and philosophies to absorb. Extensive research is required.

Analysis of the structure of the play itself requires multiple readings, both silent and out loud. For revivals, researching a play's **stage history** reveals the pitfalls and successes of other productions. For instance, the stage history of Shakespeare's *The Tempest* reveals that in over 350 years of continuous productions, most major actors (John Gielgud is a notable exception) have avoided playing the leading role of Prospero. Why? Because many actors recognize Prospero as a rather boring part. In light of this shortcoming, most actor-managers and directors have compensated by playing up the fantasy and spectacle elements of the play.

"Knowledge," Zelda Fichandler said, "releases my imagination. Imagination is what is there after you know everything; without knowledge, one's imagination may be too thin—lacking in strength and too fragile to build on."[6] For directors, knowledge gained through research coalesces into imagination in terms of sights, sounds, and emotions. They begin to see the play, to hear it, and to feel it. At this point in the interpretive process, *zamissel* begins to solidify into a **directorial concept,** a total vision of the stage action.

The Director's Imagination.   While directing may be an art too young to have developed strong traditions, it has had sufficient time to generate a major ideological dispute. The disagreement is an artistic schism not unlike the argument over whether art is, in fact, imitation or something more intangible.

On one side are those who believe the director is essentially an *interpretive* artist whose primary task is to serve the playwright's original intent as written in the script. Opposed are those who maintain a director is an entirely *conceptual* artist who is free to use script and actors as well as other theatrical elements in order to present an original and altogether personal theatrical vision. The debate is

DIRECTORIAL CONCEPT   *For his production of* The Two Gentlemen of Verona *at the Clarence Brown Theatre, Jeffrey Huberman conceived the play as "Happy Days" in the sixteenth century. "I saw the play as a comedy about bumbling young kids on the make, rather than the usual interpretation of the play as a mannered piece about sophisticated noblemen," said Huberman. "It's about Richie and Potsie and Fonzie. Except for clothes and hairstyles and cars, there's not much difference between the 1550s and the 1950s."*[7]

similar to that waged between liberal and conservative jurists who either respect or discount the "original intent" of the framers of the U.S. Constitution. Interpretive directors would be cast as "strict constructionists"; the conceptual directors (also called ***auteur* directors** because they author a production in much the same way as an author writes a text) take on the roles of artistic "activists."

Interpretive Directors.   Fundamental respect for the playwright guides the imaginations of interpretive directors. Gregory Mosher, who has served as artistic director of Chicago's Goodman Theatre and New York's Lincoln Center Theatre, defines himself in this theatrical mold: "I'm one of those people who think that everyone involved in the collaborative process is there to support the intentions of the playwright."[8] Not surprisingly, the productions of the great interpretive directors are often associated with the works of particular dramatists. Jose Quintero, cofounder of Off-Broadway's Circle in the Square Theatre, has directed the original productions of Eugene O'Neill's later plays including *The Iceman Cometh, Long Day's Journey into Night,* and *A Moon for the Misbegotten.* Mike Nichols is regarded as the major stage interpreter of the plays of Edward Albee and of David Rabe; Marshall W. Mason has staged all of the original productions of Lanford Wilson's works; Joan Littlewood achieved fame as the director who brought to the stage the works of the mercurial Irish genius Brendan Behan; Franco Zefferelli has been hailed for his robust but respectful stage and film interpretations of Shakespeare; and Gene Saks has directed the Broadway premieres of most of Neil Simon's plays. These interpretive directors are dedicated, skilled collaborators who have forged artistic symbioses with playwrights.

Conceptual Directors.   By contrast, conceptual directors are artistic loners often at odds—legally as well as artistically—with living playwrights and at the center of swirling theatrical controversies over their treatments of the classics. For his 1964 Royal Shakespeare Company production of Peter Weiss' *The Persecution and Assassination of Jean Paul Marat as Performed by the Inmates of the Asylum of Charenton Under the Direction of the Marquis de Sade,* director Peter Brook rewrote the script, music, and lyrics to deemphasize Weiss' predominantly political drama in order to stage his own dark and perverse "theatre of cruelty" extravaganza. When legal remedies sought by Weiss failed to halt the production, the author disassociated himself from the Brook version of his play.

Even the terminology used by the conceptual directors sounds disrespectful of playwrights and their texts. Instead of the "interpretation" of plays they speak of "reinterpretation" and the **deconstruction** (which sounds a lot like "destruction" or "desecration") of celebrated classical works. In fact, deconstruction refers to the intriguing process of exceeding a drama's built-in flexibility by breaking up the play into separate parts—such as episodes of the plot, lines or words of dialogue, or the traits of the characters—and then recombining them in experimental ways to create new theatrical possibilities. The eminent international director, Romanian expatriate Liviu Ciulei, describes his process of rewriting and rearranging classical plays as "cutting into the flesh."[9] Some trace the beginnings of conceptual directing to Orson Welles' controversial 1937 production of *Julius Caesar,* which he based more on the fascist regime of Benito Mussolini than on Shakespeare's Roman emperor.

Welles' groundbreaking production was relatively tame by current standards of conceptual directing. Peter Sellars, who started doing deconstructions of Shakespeare while a student at Harvard in the early 1980s, has put King Lear in a Lincoln Continental, staged *Antony and Cleopatra* around a swimming pool, and "cut into the flesh" of *Macbeth,* digesting it down to a play with three actors. When asked why he would want to manipulate plays so radically, he replied,

> Because I wanted to get at another way of reading the text. I wanted to remove the received associations that we have of . . . all of the Shakespeare plays. You see, I've never really believed in plot that firmly because a play is about content. It's not about the story. Plot is the hook on which the playwright hangs what interests him. By entirely removing the plot I wanted to treat the play line by line, literally, for "what does this mean?" In America we are totally at the mercy of the plot. Everything is synopsis. Like listening to the abbreviated plots at the beginning of the Metropolitan Opera broadcasts. American theatre has Milton Cross on the brain. As long as you can reduce it to a plot synopsis it must be sensible.[10]

And on the specifics of his working method, Sellars explained,

> When I direct Shakespeare, the first thing I do is go to the text for cuts. I go through to find the passages that are real heavy, that really are not needed, places where the language has become obscure, the places where there is a bizarre detour. [And then] I take those moments, those elements, and I make them the centerpiece, the core of the production.[11]

Some view Sellars' productions as distortions—perversions of the theatrical process that amount to little more than arrogant ego-tripping. Others, however, see him as refreshingly original—an *auteur* who breathes new life into old plays, replacing what was "classic" with something thoroughly modern.

Are these *auteur* productions in any way reflective of the playwright's imagination or merely images of the director's personal visions? Furthermore, is one

CONCEPTUAL DIRECTING   *In Shakespeare's* Merchant of Venice, *auteur director Peter Sellars saw a play that spoke to the racial and economic divisions that set off the Rodney King riots. To translate his concept to the stage of Chicago's Goodman Theatre, Sellars transplanted the action from the multicultural world of fifteenth-century Venice to the multicultural world of 1990s Venice Beach, California. To diffuse the anti-Semitism in the play and to call attention to racial stereotyping Sellars cast African American actors as Shylock and the Jews, Latinos as Antonio and the Venetian merchants, and Asians as Portia and her retinue. Some actors also used camcorders to shoot the action, adding simultaneous close-ups to the full-stage view.*

view preferable to the other? Can both a "conceptual" production and an "interpretive" production of the same play stand as individual works of art, each with its own validity? Such are the questions in this ongoing theatrical controversy.

Ironically, among directors in other media there is little debate on the subject of the director's prerogatives. Film directors are universally recognized to be *auteurs* with absolute primacy over the script, while television directors go almost unnoticed in their total subservience to actors, producers, and sponsors.

It is inevitable that young, eclectic stage directors working in today's theatre have been influenced by both the interpretive and the conceptual approaches as they seek to follow their own developmental paths in this newest of theatre arts.

Whichever imaginative path is chosen, the resulting directorial concept must be conveyed with a clarity and completeness to other artists who must render it in concrete, living form. At this point, the director's job changes from the solitary task of interpreter to the challenge of collaboration.

The Director as Unifier: Guarding and Guiding the Concept

Richard Thomas, star of screen (John Boy of *The Waltons*) and in recent years of stage *(Hamlet, Peer Gynt, The Count of Monte Cristo, Tom Paine, Richard III)*, sought once to try his hand at directing. He imagined the creative excitement of guiding an entire production from his own concept. It was, according to Thomas, not quite the intellectual experience he had imagined. He recounts one particularly unsettling moment: in the midst of coaching actors on the fine points of a complex, intense scene, a costume assistant holding two baseball caps ran onto the stage, frantically interrupting Thomas' intense rehearsal:

"Which one do you want the actor to wear, Mr. Thomas, the red hat or the blue hat?"

Thomas was taken aback. This was directing? This was guarding and guiding a concept that emerged from months of research and analysis? A red hat or a blue hat?[12]

In fact, Thomas' experience is indicative of two definitive aspects of the art of directing. First, myriad choices must be made, from the big picture to the smallest details. From the actors' motivations to the color of the hats they wear, the director chooses from the largest menu of choices of any theatre artist. Second, the choices—no matter what the category and no matter how long the list of possibilities—*must* be made. A subtitle might well be printed on the back of the classic director's chair: "The choice stops here."

The Director's Two Hats.   Most conceive of the director as a giver of orders, the supreme ruler of the production, an artistic dictator. Certainly this is a part of the job description—taking charge and *giving directions*. ("Wear the red hat.") There is, however, another, more subtle aspect of the job. Peter Brook, considered by many to be the greatest director in the world, describes this other aspect as being a guide in the sense of *"maintaining the right direction."*[13] In today's theatre the director cannot and does not do everyone else's job; the skills and imaginations of the other artists must be brought to bear, but the director must point the way. Combining the two approaches means walking a thin line between dictator and diplomat. The power to choose so much for so many is an enormous responsibility.

Promoting Unity Through Collaboration.   By definition, then, the director is the chief practitioner of the art of collaboration—working together to achieve a common artistic goal. Promoting collaboration takes a diplomat's skill at interpersonal communication and the ability to articulate visual as well as visceral images. The goal is to get from each artist a refinement and extension of the directorial concept. "The worst thing that can happen," Hal Prince once said, "is to get back from artists exactly what you ask for."[14] Zelda Fichandler put it this way: "You have to be able to use other people as your instrumentality. This is an art in itself—to make your imagination proceed through the imaginations of other people."[15]

UNIFYING THE ELEMENTS   *In Richard E. T. White's production of* Twelfth Night *at the California Shakespeare Festival, all of the theatrical elements including the costumes, settings, music, and the regional accents of the actors upheld his Louisiana bayou concept of the play.*

CONTRACTUAL CASTING CONTROVERSY   *After rocky tryouts in London and Los Angeles, Andrew Lloyd Webber's* Sunset Boulevard *became a hit with Glenn Close in the role of Nora Desmond, the forgotten film star trying to make a comeback. To cast Close, Lloyd Webber had to settle lawsuits totaling $3 million filed by the two previous actors who had been given contracts for the role. After seeing them perform—and reading their reviews—Lloyd Webber decided they were "not right" for the part.*

In a typical production, **concept meetings** are held between the director and designers at which the director's interpretation of the play is discussed and the director's concept for a production is presented. At subsequent concept meetings, designers respond with renderings of the concept for the director's approval. When the actual work of mounting the play begins, regular **production meetings** ensure that the unity of the concept is maintained by all. As the work of the individual theatre artists compartmentalizes, the director proceeds to work with the actors.

Casting: Choosing the Actors

A director's work with actors begins with choosing them. Most directors would agree their most critical choice is casting the right actors. It can also be the most permanent choice, since casting means committing in advance to certain results that, unlike the color of a hat, are very difficult—financially, contractually, and personally—to change.

In most cases the choice of actors is the director's, but there are some exceptions. Producers with an eye on the box office and artistic directors who must maintain the missions of a resident company often cast the leading roles themselves. For the original productions of their new works, playwrights may retain a contractual veto over a director's casting. Still, most directors exert considerable influence over casting.

They choose from a large palette of human types and talents to portray the dramatic personages sketched in theatrical code. Some playwrights give detailed descriptions of the characters in their plays. George Bernard Shaw's lengthy character descriptions attempt to restrict the choices of subsequent actors and directors. Tennessee Williams was more circumspect in his character descriptions. Consider his sketch of Amanda Wingfield in *The Glass Menagerie:*

> A little woman of great but confused vitality clinging frantically to another time and place. Her characterization must be carefully created, not copied from type. She is not paranoiac, but her life is paranoia. There is much to admire in Amanda, and as much to love and pity as there is to laugh at. Certainly she has endurance and a kind of heroism, and though her foolishness makes her unwittingly cruel at times, there is a tenderness in her slight person.[16]

Shakespeare, on the other hand, gives only hints concerning character traits in the dialogue: "Yon Cassius," he wrote in *Julius Caesar,* "hath a lean and hungry look." Consider the approximately 25,000 members of the stage actors' union (Actors' Equity Association) in New York alone competing for an estimated 1,500 available roles per year. Finding the right actor from the many who compete for the part is the challenge. As is usual for their art, directors cast in traditional and nontraditional ways.

Auditions: The Mechanics of Casting.   Most directors choose actors from **auditions** at which the would-be performers present prepared monologues or do brief readings from a script. This system was supposedly invented by **George Abbot** (1887–1995), the director/playwright whose life spanned virtually the entire history of directing. Before Abbot started directing, there were no casting calls, callbacks, or prepared monologues. Actors were hired based on a personal meeting and often fired the day after the director heard them read the parts. Actors' Equity Association disapproved of this erratic system, so Abbot came up with the idea of having actors meet the director and read from the play beforehand. Using Abbot's system of readings, directors progressively delineate their choices of actors based on talent as well as type.

Casting by Type.   Assuming an equally talented pool of actors, **casting by type** means choosing actors who by age, physique, ethnicity, and attitude most closely resemble the roles they are to play. According to this system, a director would need young, beautiful lovers to play Romeo and Juliet; a brooding 30-year-old, Danish-looking (blond) actor for Hamlet; and a woman of dark, tall, mysterious

CASTING BY TYPE   *Franco Zefferelli was hailed for casting according to perfect types when he chose the youthful and beautiful Olivia Hussey and Leonard Whiting to play these most famous of teenage lovers. Hussey, like Juliet, was just 13 years old at the time of her casting. (Photo courtesy of Paramount Pictures.* Romeo and Juliet *copyright 1968, 1992 by Paramount Pictures. All rights reserved.)*

CASTING AGAINST TYPE   *For his production of* Romeo and Juliet *at Minneapolis' Theatre de la Jeune Lune, director Dominique Serrand was praised by critics and audiences alike for casting against type when he chose actors Marti Goetsch and Vincent Gracieux as Shakespeare's young lovers. Serrand's bold choices proved the intense passions of the play transcend expected physical appearance.*

stature for Hedda Gabler. In casting his production of *Julius Caesar* at the New York Shakespeare Festival, director Stuart Vaughan needed to find an actor for Brutus who would contrast sharply with the "lean and hungry" Cassius: "Brutus can look like a stuffed shirt and a cold-blooded nincompoop if he isn't played by someone whose essential goodness doesn't shine through." Vaughan chose film actor and social activist Martin Sheen despite Sheen's lack of classical stage experience. He explained that Sheen, who had been arrested in demonstrations for his involvement in the causes of the homeless and the antinuclear movement, was a man "of conviction and personal integrity."[17]

Casting Against Type.   Choosing an actor who is the opposite of what the role seems to require is **casting against type.** The very idea of it seems absurd—artistically suicidal, like casting Michael J. Fox as Rambo. Why would any director even think about doing it? Yet adventurous directors have cast actors against type with often startling results that reveal unperceived flexibility in roles thought to be entirely defined by type. To cast the role of Lestat, the debonair, blond eighteenth-century vampire in the film version of Anne Rice's *Interview with the Vampire,* the author and producers considered tall, mature actors like John Travolta, Mel Gibson, and Richard Gere. Daniel Day-Lewis was offered the part but turned it down. When young, short, American heartthrob Tom Cruise was picked by the producers, Rice denounced the selection, saying the actor "is no more my vampire Lestat than Edward G. Robinson is Rhett Butler."[18] After the show became a box office hit, Rice declared Cruise was perfect for the part. Similarly, comedian Whoopi Goldberg, cast by Stephen Spielberg to star in *The Color Purple,* revealed a touching pathos and innocence; there was not a laugh to be heard. In the 1987 New York Shakespeare Festival production of *Richard III,* Kevin Kline, noted for his swashbuckling good looks, brought a dimension of suave, hypnotic romance to the traditionally repulsive Richard.

Nontraditional Casting.   Casting actors against age, demeanor, and physical appearance may be adventurous and risky, but only in artistic terms. In an increasingly diverse society, casting plays now takes on new ethical implications. Can Hamlet, the Dane, be appropriately played by an African American, Asian, Native American, or other non-Caucasian actor? What about a woman as Willy Loman? Or a wheelchair-bound actor as Stanley Kowalski? Increasingly, directors throughout the world are adopting **nontraditional casting** policies called variously **color-blind, gender-neutral,** or **cross-societal casting** whereby the director casts a play based on the best possible *talent* for a part regardless of the actor's gender, physical condition, cultural heritage, or racial characteristics.

Advocates of nontraditional casting believe the benefits are artistic as well as social. First, nontraditional casting promotes the employment of minority actors by offering opportunities to perform previously unavailable roles in plays written almost exclusively by and for western European men. It is only natural for all actors to want to expand their artistic horizons and personal repertoires beyond their own types. In Carlyle Brown's play *The African Company Presents Richard III* (see Chapter 4, p. 129), the character James Hewlett eloquently

DEATH OF A SALESPERSON

Drawing by Mike Twohy © 1989 *The New Yorker* Magazine, Inc.

expresses this desire when he explains why he persists in playing parts written for Europeans:

> I get to be loved and accepted. To be openly admired. To feel myself, to be full of myself. To breathe air and give it back again. To make myself as if I were clay. . . . The makeup, the costumes, the robe. It's all glass that I know how to polish and make clear. So that any man can see that I am any man.[19]

In this vein, African American actor James Earl Jones makes no secret of his desire to play the tyrannical southern aristocrat and plantation owner Big Daddy in Tennessee Williams' *Cat on a Hot Tin Roof.* Second, theatre, as a powerful reflector of society, can increase understanding of the universality of the human condition. For his production of *Julius Caesar* at the Indiana Repertory Theatre, director Tom Haas sought to "tap the energies of many cultures to create something of the feeling of melting pot culture that was characteristic of the Roman Empire." Haas cast Japanese American actor Koji Okamura in the role of Octavius Caesar and African American actor Andrea-Michelle Smith in the traditionally white male role of Messala. According to Haas, Okamura created a "sense of urgency, a presence within a military matrix that summoned up subconscious thoughts about the Asian rise to power in our own world," while Smith created "new and striking readings of scenes within the play."[20] As walls between nations and peoples, both real and imagined, continue to fall, and as the world consolidates into a global village, nontraditional casting may become the most accurate way to reflect the human condition on stage. It is, says critic David Richards, the definitive aspect of the most essential theatre art:

The art of acting operates on the assumption that in any man there is, indeed, an everyman. At the same time that performers are depicting the thousand and one faces of humanity, they are also showing us how much alike we are under the skin. For all the debates it has provoked, the current push in the theater for nontraditional casting is really saying nothing more. If the talent and insight are there, black should be able to play white, young play old, even female play male. And vice versa.[21]

In historical terms, nontraditional casting is the biggest change in theatre practice since the ascendancy of the director. Changing theatrical conventions is difficult, but yesterday's impossibility has a way of becoming today's tradition. Consider the public outrage that initially greeted such events as the banishing of spectators from the stage in the eighteenth century, the darkening of the auditorium in the 1870s, or the racial integration of major league baseball in the 1940s. Until recently, ethnic and minority actors were often "ghettoized" by working primarily within their own enclave theatre companies. Today, barriers between actor identity and the role continue to break down.

Ironically, the loudest objections to unconditional policies of nontraditional casting have come primarily from minority playwrights. August Wilson points out the absurdity of using a color-blind policy for his plays that examine the African American experience in all its ethnic richness throughout the decades of the twentieth century. Caucasian actors in *Fences?* Asians in *The Piano Lesson?* According to Wilson, such choices would ruin, not illuminate, the dramatic

NONTRADITIONAL CASTING CONTROVERSY   *The casting crisis of the 1990s occurred when Cameron Mackintosh, the producer of the mega-theatrical event* Miss Saigon, *cast the British Caucasian actor Jonathan Pryce in the starring role of the Eurasian pimp. Actors' Equity, in an attempt to promote affirmative action in the casting of American productions, ruled the producers had to abide by ethnic-specific casting and hire an Asian actor for the part. The union, which had received complaints about the casting from actor B.D. Wong and author Henry David Hwang, said it could not "appear to condone the casting of a Caucasian in the role of a Eurasian."[22] Claiming an infringement of artistic freedom, Mackintosh abruptly cancelled the multimillion-dollar production rather than cast the role as dictated by Equity. The union rescinded its decision, and the play opened with Pryce (made up as a Eurasian) in the role.*

world he is trying to imitate. Therefore, Wilson claims the artistic caveat of **ethnic-specific casting** for his plays.

Nontraditional casting strikes at the very nature of artistic freedom and theatrical choice. Is it a restriction of the imaginative impulse, or does it open a rich new menu of opportunities for creative directors to reimagine the plays they stage? Nontraditional casting adds a new dimension to the fundamental concept of the flexibility of dramatic texts.

Staging the Play

Zelda Fichandler remarked that one of the greatest compliments she received as a director was from a theatregoer who told her, "When I see your work, I see the feeling."[23] Such praise meant she had successfully staged the play beyond mere arrangement and traffic control of entering and exiting actors and had created a physical rendering of the dramatic action.

If the director "paints" with actors, then the director's canvas is the stage, a space for placing dramatic action throughout its dimensions of height, width, and depth. To work within such an environment a director must have a visual imagination that is at once three dimensional and kinesthetic.

Staging plays—the fundamental business of the theatrical imagination—means using actors, scenery, light, costumes, and sound to create moving pictures that illustrate and punctuate the action and reveal details of character that perhaps even the playwright did not imagine.

The director's first step in staging is to secure a set from the scene designer that, whatever else it may be, is a machine for acting with multiple levels, entrances and exits, acting areas, and moving parts that allow for the greatest variety of spectacle. The second step involves arranging the actors on the set to create picturization, movement, and stage business. Only rarely can an actor do all of this without assistance. Actors cannot see themselves, and history proves that, left to their own devices, they will arrange themselves into a straight line across the stage, a convention more appropriate to earlier historical periods.

Picturization.   The well-worn cliché, "a picture is worth a thousand words," could not be more true for directors. **Picturization** is the director's visual interpretation of each moment of the play. It must accomplish sharply directed focus as well as emotionally charged storytelling. **Focus** is the arrangement of the stage picture so as to direct the audience's attention to the appropriate actor, object, or event. Nothing is quite as frustrating for a theatregoer as looking at a stage full of talking actors and being unable to tell who is speaking. Achieving focus in relatively uncomplicated for screen directors. Point the camera, and the audience has no choice but to look at what the camera reveals. For stage directors the task is more complex, involving a larger menu of choices for achieving compelling focus.

Storytelling.   An audience can take only so much exposition unrelieved by action, therefore storytelling is carried out by the director through stage pictures. In

A MENU OF DIRECTORIAL CHOICES

Achieving Focus

1. **By body position**—The actor who is most "open" or "full front" to the audience will have the focus.
2. **By stage area**—The actor placed in the most central stage area will have the focus.
3. **By level**—The actor placed highest on the stage space will have the focus.
4. **By plane**—The actor placed farthest upstage will have the focus.
5. **By triangulation**—The actor placed at the apex of a triangular arrangement will have the focus.
6. **By contrast**—The performer who acts apart from the group will have the focus. For instance, if everyone on stage stands, the actor who sits will have the focus.
7. **By movement**—The moving actor always has the focus.

drama the diction reveals intent and emotion, but the actual words often mask the truth that lurks beneath the lines in the so-called **subtext.** For the director, stage pictures are the primary means for revealing the truth of the dramatic action.

Consider the complex relationships that must be revealed at the crucial moment of the "mousetrap" scene in *Hamlet.* To discover if his uncle and mother are guilty of his father's murder, Hamlet has a troupe of actors perform a play with a plot not unlike the suspected assassination before the entire assembled court of Elsinore including the King, Queen, their adviser Polonius, and their unwitting spies Rosencrantz and Guildenstern, Hamlet's would-be lover Ophelia, his true friend Horatio, and the lords, ladies, and soldiers of the castle. As everyone watches the play, Hamlet watches for his mother's reaction to it, while Horatio watches for King Claudius'. The moment of the "mousetrap" murder, where the truth of Claudius' guilt is revealed, is considered to be one of the most difficult stage pictures to create. If you can stage the picture that tells *that* story at *that* moment, directors say you can stage anything.

Stage Movement.   The stuff of drama—action—in its most physical form means stage movement, the blending of one stage picture into another. Directors understand their art is about *moving* actors, not sitting actors or talking actors. Their most powerful means of staging a play is through stage movement that is bold, dynamic, and naturally motivated in sufficient variety so nothing is repetitive or boring.

Specifically, directors use movement as visual punctuation marks for the spoken dialogue and unspoken subtext. The author's written punctuation marks in the text are the director's cues for inventing a variety of moves. Strong moves that reveal aggressive motivations include those that increase the size of the actor within the stage picture: standing or jumping up, turning to face the audience,

PICTURIZATION   *In this famous stage picture from the Broadway production of the musical* Cabaret, *director Harold Prince created sharp focus on Joel Grey as the emcee through a strong combination of body position, stage area, level, triangulation, and contrast.*

moving from upstage to downstage, or from a lower level to a higher one. For example, when Romeo challenges Tybalt to a duel, Shakespeare wrote the young lover's challenge to his villainous cousin as a weapon-brandishing shout, "This shall determine that!" To a director this may mean to position Romeo as far away from Tybalt as possible so he can charge Tybalt at full attack speed for a fight to the death. Weak moves that decrease the size of the actor and reveal submissive intentions are just the opposite: sitting or falling down, turning away from the audience, moving farther upstage, or from a higher level to a lower one.

Blocking.   Blocking is positioning the actors into the entire scheme of the staging. It is so called because early directors conveyed their staging instructions to actors

"MOUSETRAP" MOMENTS   *These two pictures attempt to tell the same story from the crucial "mousetrap" scene in* Hamlet. *Above is a 1932 Old Vic production in London directed by Harcourt Williams, who placed Hamlet and Horatio in clear positions to watch the King and Queen, but the assembled court is bundled together in an*

by drawing a grid on the stage floor and labeling each stage position or "block." Some directors preblock their plays before rehearsals begin by working with a ground plan or model of the set provided by the designer. By contrast, other directors prefer to develop blocking on the spot at each rehearsal. A few directors even let the actors "find" their own blocking from which the directors pick and choose the most effective moves. Regardless of the method, most directors agree that blocking is one of the most difficult parts of staging a play. JoAnne Akalaitis, noted for her innovative staging of *avant-garde* plays, speaks for many directors on the subject:

> To me the mark of a real director is blocking, where people are in space. . . . Even among so-called "great directors," I see a real messiness, the inability to use space. Actors block themselves more often than one is aware. Once I have blocked the play, I say, "Oh, thank God, I did the hardest thing. It's over. Now I can work on it." That doesn't mean that I don't change the blocking, because I do that a lot.[24]

Blocking is part of the larger process of helping actors learn to behave naturally in the stage environment created by the setting, costumes, and action of the play. They do not learn it in a day. It takes practice. It takes rehearsal.

unfocused crowd that fails to reveal much of their individual motives. Above is a 1948 production directed by Hugh Hunt, clearly delineating the various character relationships through their sharply focused positions on the stage. The picture tells the entire story.

Rehearsing the Play

Until the first rehearsal, directing is mostly imaginative—theoretical images of what the stage reality might be. With the first rehearsal, the theatrical manifestation of the concept begins.

The amount of time required for rehearsals varies from director to director, production to production, even country to country. An improvisation may need only five seconds of preparation. On the other hand, it is not uncommon for European directors working in government-supported theatres to spend several months to a year rehearsing a play.

In the American professional theatre the usual rehearsal period is 3 to 4 weeks (8 hours per day/6 days per week) for a straight play (140–200 hours), and 6 weeks for a musical (290 hours). A rule of thumb says the cast should rehearse through the entire play 12 times. Like all other directing jobs, individual choices on how to use this time vary from director to director.

Working with Actors.   Successful directors develop a sensitive understanding of the special "co-laboring" required for working creatively with actors. Such

STAGE BUSINESS *From the picturization to the seemingly mundane: Gene Saks staged this famous scene from Neil Simon's* The Odd Couple *that involved the creation of detailed prop movement and handling called* **stage business.** *It required the careful working out of an ongoing poker game, food serving, food eating, and food fighting.*

understanding must have diplomatic awareness of the actors' essential role in the theatre as well as respect for the actors' talent, including the solitary risks they take by standing alone on stage with all of the theatrical choices. Since many actors feel vulnerable in rehearsal, they prefer, especially in the early stages, not to be watched, even by other actors.

Respect for this working relationship leads some directors to practice an "indirect" approach to working with actors. For Marshall Mason, such a working method requires maintaining "an atmosphere of creativity that will stimulate the best work from the actor, to be a mirror, tell them what they are doing and what we see."[25] Ed Stern puts it this way: "My job in rehearsal is to give actors the right to fail—that is, to create a rehearsal atmosphere that cultivates their personal exploration of the best choices from which I can pick the most effective."[26] Such directors would never think of giving an actor a **line reading** ("Stand like this, hold your hand out, and say your line like this . . ."). Most actors consider such inflexible directives to be insensitive intrusions on their imaginative prerogatives.

Other directors are much more "direct" in working with actors and exercise control in the autocratic tradition of Max Reinhardt. George Abbot believed "a director wastes his time in rehearsal when he talks endlessly to an actor about who his mother was, what did she want, what does he want and why it has led him up

REHEARSAL SCHEDULE

For a straight play rehearsing for a total of four weeks, a typical schedule breaks down into the following sessions:

Read-through and discussion: One to five rehearsals. Takes place in a conference room. Some directors, like JoAnne Akalaitis, hate them. They find them boring and depressing. Others, especially directors of Shakespeare, find them indispensable for clarifying language and action.

Blocking: Five rehearsals. In a rehearsal room with tape on the floor to indicate the locations of walls, platforms, doors, and other scenic units. The actors carry scripts in which they record the blocking given by the director.

Business and polishing: Five rehearsals. In a rehearsal hall or on stage. All lines are memorized. The director and the actors refine the blocking, and substitute props are provided.

Technical rehearsals: One or two rehearsals. On stage with full sets, lights, sound, props, crews, and actors.

Dress rehearsals: Three or four rehearsals. On stage with full performance conditions.

to this moment when he asks for the salt." Abbot preferred that the director get right to the point and tell the actor, "C'mon, Johnny, just pass the salt."[27] Line readings were always a frequent occurrence at his rehearsals. Actors who wanted to work in a George Abbot show accepted them willingly. With over eighty years of directing experience (he died in 1995 at the age of 107), Abbot's choices—line readings included—were usually right.

Working with Technicians: Technical Rehearsals.   Usually no more than two rehearsals are devoted to setting lighting, sound effects, and scenery shifting. Patience and organization are the director's indispensable virtues for these rehearsals. To the casual observer it may seem the activities of technical rehearsals are nonartistic, but it is not unusual for a modern production to have over a hundred lighting and sound cues alone—each one a specific choice that will either add to or detract from the director's overall concept for the play.

Working with Everybody: Dress Rehearsals.   The most anticipated rehearsal is the dress rehearsal at which everybody and everything is finally assembled on stage as the first complete test of the directorial concept. From the vantage point of the audience, the director can finally see if the play has been created as it was imagined. Has unity been achieved? Has the ink on the playwright's page become the director's art

DIRECTING ASSISTANTS AND ASSOCIATES

In the modern theatre, the jobs of a director are often too numerous and too demanding for one person to carry out effectively. Musicals, period plays, and large spectacle dramas require many directing associates and assistants with training and certification in their specialties. A sampling:

Dramaturg: A literary adviser, play reader, and expert in theatre history, the dramaturg researches past productions of the play and provides information on its cultural and artistic milieu. Essential employees of European theatres since the eighteenth century, dramaturgs have been adjuncts to directors in the United States only in the last twenty years.

Musical Director: Teaches actors required songs during rehearsals and usually conducts the orchestra and singers during performances.

Choreographer: Creates dances based on the music and the director's concept. Teaches the choreography to the actors during rehearsals. Some directors who have achieved fame for staging musicals choreograph their own productions. Bob Fosse, Michael Bennett, Jerome Robbins, and Tommy Tune are among these director/choreographers.

Voice/Dialogue Coach: Coaches actors in special vocal requirements of certain roles such as speaking verse in classical plays and using foreign accents and dialects.

Fight Director: Stages fights and stunts, both armed and unarmed. American fight directors are certified in the stage use of period weaponry and safe combat techniques by the Society of American Fight Directors. Fight directors are essential for staging Shakespearean tragedies and histories and for modern plays requiring combat such as *The Colored Museum, Oleanna,* and *Extremities.*

Casting Director: Consults with the director on the concept and roles and then screens possible actors and sets up auditions for the director and producer.

Stage Managers: Organize rehearsals, maintain promptbook, and supervise the performances. The *production stage manager* (PSM) is responsible for maintaining the director's concept after the show opens, the *stage manager* (SM) calls the cues during the performance. The *assistant stage manager* (ASM) remains backstage for traffic-control purposes. Members of Actors' Equity Association, stage managers often consider their work as an apprenticeship to professional directing.

on the stage? Peter Brook describes the first dress rehearsal as a revealing experience at which "the coherence explodes" (as in "into view," not "apart").[28]

Dress rehearsals, however, are not performances; there is still time for polishing what works and for "cutting away the garbage," as Peter Brook calls it.[29]

Rehearsing the Audience: Previews.   There is an old saying in the theatre. (Any institution that has existed for 2,500 years is bound to have many old sayings.) "You learn a show in performance, not in rehearsal." The chance to test their productions under actual performance conditions are in **previews,** a series of performances in advance of the official opening. As Harold Clurman would announce to his casts on the evening of the first preview, "Tonight we rehearse the audience."[30] Scheduling previews has spread to almost every professional theatre in the country; amateur and educational theatres often use the final dress rehearsal with an invited audience as a onetime preview.

The rehearsal process reveals the director as an artist with one eye on the script and the other on the stage from the vantage point of the audience.

The Director as Ideal Audience

Directors are successful in exact proportion to the empathy they have with the audience. If there is one skill that directors work at developing above all others, it is reacting to dramatic action like a theatregoer sitting in the audience. Television directors manipulate the camera shots, not from the studio floor, but from control rooms where they can watch TV monitors in order to see exactly what their audiences see. Likewise film directors constantly check the takes through the camera lens or the viewfinder they carry around their necks, and then view each day's rushes in screening rooms. Stage directors use nothing more high tech than seats in empty theatres to verify the calculated effects of their productions.

Arousing and Manipulating Emotional Responses.   From the director's perspective, making an audience laugh, cry, scream, or think requires enhancing the action of the play with emotionally truthful acting, rhythmically paced staging, evocative scenery and lighting, and sound.

Being the ideal audience also means a director must have pedestrian, not elitist tastes in the sense of being susceptible to the same sentiments as the audience. If tears are called for, a director must be able to feel the pathos and tragedy of the action. If laughter is to be the response, the director must have the same sense of humor as the expected theatregoers. If the purpose of the play is to make them think, then the director must have a clear understanding of the intellectual disposition of the audience.

Comprehending Stage Action.   The director as surrogate audience checks to see if the play as staged is understandable. Will the audience know what is going on? The rule of thumb: Do not overestimate the perceptive powers of the audience. They have not read the play ten times, delved into the milieu of the play and playwright, or watched it twelve times in rehearsals. Therefore, the director must always verify the clarity of sights and sounds. Can the audience see clearly? Are the actors open to the audience? Is there enough light to see faces? Does the staging work? Is the language as spoken understandable? Are the actors loud enough? Too loud? Inarticulate? Unremedied, these obstacles remain insurmountable by even the most brilliant directorial concept.

Comprehending Dramatic Action.   A more intriguing question for directors is whether or not the language *as written* is understandable. If not, the production requires a more artistically intrusive remedy from the director as ideal audience: changing the very text of the play.

For a variety of reasons, directors have changed portions of scripts to suit the tastes, morals, language, and comprehension of the audience. The sexually explicit passages of *Romeo and Juliet* are often edited for secondary school audiences. In response to modern sensitivity to racial and ethnic stereotyping, directors sometimes delete or rewrite derogatory references to Jews, Arabs, Africans, and other groups in Shakespeare's and other classical plays.

After cutting, the most frequently practiced directorial script alteration is rewriting for the purpose of clarity. Such changes range from simple word substitutions to the creation of major passages of new dialogue. For his production of *Much Ado About Nothing* at the Royal National Theatre of Great Britain, Franco Zefferelli changed one word to clarify an entire character. In Act II, Beatrice, who swears she will never marry, asks rhetorically if it "would not grieve a woman to be overmastered by a piece of valiant dust? To make an account of her life to a clod of wayward *marl?*" "Marl?" Zefferelli changed the word to "clay," and the meaning and Beatrice's scathing wit became clear.[31]

Only the most pedantic scholar or remote, theatrically unengaged closet dramatist would seriously object to these kinds of directorial script alterations. Still, the question might be asked: At what point do they stop being adaptations to clarify and become alterations of such magnitude that they fundamentally change the playwright's vision?

An Imprint of Directorial Choices

Like an athletic coach's playbook, the **promptbook** is a graphic representation of the director's imagination. In form it is an overlay of the director's choices on those of the playwright. Each page demonstrates fundamental organizational skills. On page 270 an excerpt from Steve Rothman's promptbook for Rupert Holmes' comedy thriller *Accomplice*[32] records 37 directorial choices that include:

3 cuts
1 rewrite
2 lighting effects
1 sound cue
1 scenery shifting cue
5 special effects

CHANGING THE NAMES   *For his 1988 production of Georges Feydeau's 1910 French "bedroom" farce* A Flea in Her Ear, *director Frank Galati changed the names of the characters and the setting to give the audience a sense of the author's playfulness with his dramatis personae: Feydeau's Hotel du Minet Galant (literally, the Hotel of the Mannerly Kitten) was changed to the Hotel Pussy à Go-Go. Dr. Finache was renamed Dr. Panache; the womanizing Romain Tournel became Maurice Blasé; the old alcoholic Baptistin was changed to Benedictine; and the hotel porter Poche (literally, a stupid person) was renamed Goche, with intentional assonance with "gauche," as in "awkward." As Galati put it, "The names have been changed to prolong the innuendo. Any resemblance to persons living or dead is strictly facetious."[33]*

  2 pieces of costume business
  1 note on characterization
  2 major stage pictures
  1 choice of audience reaction
  4 pieces of prop business
 14 blocking moves

To conceive as well as convey such choices, Harold Clurman once said, a director must be "a great lover" in the sense of being "an organizer, teacher, politician, psychic detective, lay analyst, technician, a creative being knowing literature, acting, the psychology of an actor, visual arts, music, history, and simply understanding people"[34]—this last trait being, perhaps, the most important.

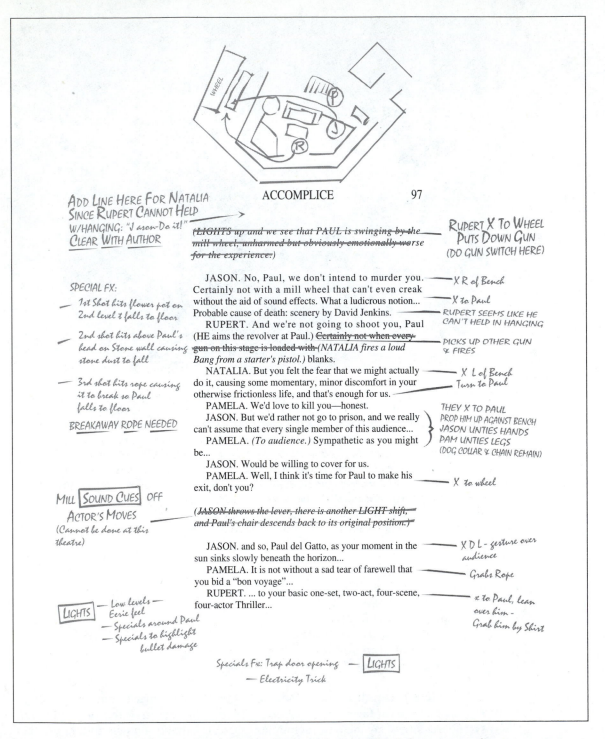

ACCOMPLICE   97

ADD LINE HERE FOR NATALIA
SINCE RUPERT CANNOT HELP
W/HANGING: "Jason-Do it!"
CLEAR WITH AUTHOR

RUPERT X TO WHEEL
PUTS DOWN GUN
(DO GUN SWITCH HERE)

~~(LIGHTS up and we see that PAUL is swinging by the~~
~~mill wheel, unharmed but obviously emotionally worse~~
~~for the experience.)~~

SPECIAL FX:

JASON. No, Paul, we don't intend to murder you.
Certainly not with a mill wheel that can't even creak
without the aid of sound effects. What a ludicrous notion...
Probable cause of death: scenery by David Jenkins.

— X R of Bench

— X to Paul

RUPERT SEEMS LIKE HE
CAN'T HELP IN HANGING

— 1st Shot hits flower pot on
2nd level & falls to floor

— 2nd shot hits above Paul's
head on stone wall causing
stone dust to fall

— 3rd shot hits rope causing
it to break so Paul
falls to floor

BREAKAWAY ROPE NEEDED

RUPERT. And we're not going to shoot you, Paul
(HE aims the revolver at Paul.) ~~Certainly not when every~~
~~gun on this stage is loaded with~~ (NATALIA fires a loud
Bang from a starter's pistol.) blanks.

PICKS UP OTHER GUN
& FIRES

NATALIA. But you felt the fear that we might actually
do it, causing some momentary, minor discomfort in your
otherwise frictionless life, and that's enough for us.

— X L of Bench
Turn to Paul

PAMELA. We'd love to kill you—honest.

JASON. But we'd rather not go to prison, and we really
can't assume that every single member of this audience...

PAMELA. (To audience.) Sympathetic as you might
be...

JASON. Would be willing to cover for us.

THEY X TO PAUL
PROP HIM UP AGAINST BENCH
JASON UNTIES HANDS
PAM UNTIES LEGS
(DOG COLLAR & CHAIN REMAIN)

PAMELA. Well, I think it's time for Paul to make his
exit, don't you?

— X to wheel

MILL SOUND CUES OFF
ACTOR'S MOVES
(Cannot be done at this
theatre)

~~(JASON throws the lever, there is another LIGHT shift,~~
~~and Paul's chair descends back to its original position.)~~

JASON. and so, Paul del Gatto, as your moment in the
sun sinks slowly beneath the horizon...

— X D L - gesture over
audience

PAMELA. It is not without a sad tear of farewell that
you bid a "bon voyage"...

— Grabs Rope

RUPERT. ... to your basic one-set, two-act, four-scene,
four-actor Thriller...

— x to Paul, lean
over him -
Grab him by Shirt

LIGHTS — Low levels -
Eerie feel
— Specials around Paul
— Specials to highlight
bullet damage

Specials Fx: Trap door opening — LIGHTS
— Electricity Trick

A page from director Stephen Rothman's promptbook from Accomplice.

The Necessity of Entrusting

Directors are usually hired only through opening nights of "their" productions. While they can supervise to completion the work of designers and technicians, the actors' work has barely begun when the production opens. It is, as JoAnne Akalaitis describes it, a necessary, but unsettling process of letting go. "The actors," she says, "have to be able to possess the show. . . . I'm the outsider after the show has opened, and I *should be* the outsider."[35]

Many directors experience this moment of separation with a sense of loss—like being an uninvited guest at a feast to which only the performers, stage crew, and audience have been invited. Film directors, by contrast, are notorious for holding on to prints of their movies and reediting them into new versions. Directors are only occasionally (if ever) asked to return to view their productions in performance and give notes to the actors.

Letting go is an intrinsic part of the interdependent process of *entrusting.* Just as a playwright must entrust the personalized dramatic work to a producer, the producer entrusts the considerable financial investment in the play and its conceptualization to the director. The director must entrust the concept to the scenographic artists for design and construction, and to the actors for public presentation to the audience. When the house lights dim and the curtain rises, the actors rule.

 THE DIRECTOR AT WORK ··

Blood and Bones of Tragedy: Ariane Mnouchkine's Epic Cycle of Greek Plays Is Thrilling Entertainment by Any Standard

by Jack Kroll
[Reprinted from *Newsweek*][36]

Center for Theatre Research. In 1992 Ariane Mnouchkine brought her Théâtre du Soleil company to the United States to perform ancient Greek tragedies in a monumental transcultural production (see photo p. 240). Newsweek critic Jack Kroll offers an insightful look at this director's provocative theatrical imagination.

Despite its official policies of cultural sovereignty, France has always been a center of artistic fusion. In the Renaissance, French royals imported Italianate neoclassical ideals, opera, and scenic art. Through the renowned work of their own artists, they spread the new culture throughout the world. In the twentieth century the Cannes Film Festival is a convergence of international cinema. In the theatre Peter Brook assembles actors from all over the world to work at his International

No more electrifying theater will be seen in the United States this season than "Les Atrides," the 10-hour, four-play cycle of Greek theater by the brilliant French director Ariane Mnouchkine and her celebrated Théâtre du Soleil (Theatre of the Sun). This production is so huge that the Brooklyn Academy of Music, which is presenting the company in its first New York appearance, has had to appropriate the Park Slope Armory, an arena the size of two football fields. The troupe's only previous

U.S. appearance was the Los Angeles Olympic Festival in 1984, where its Kabuki-style versions of Shakespeare's "Richard II" and "Twelfth Night" demonstrated the originality that has earned it international fame. Before its Brooklyn run, "Les Atrides" traveled to Montreal, where it played a sold-out engagement at a sports stadium. Such vast spaces are perfect for these plays, which were first seen by Athenians in the fifth century B.C. at the theater of Dionysus, which held 14,000 spectators.

Hey, that was entertainment. And it still is, at least in the thrilling version created by Mnouchkine and her gifted performers. Mnouchkine has taken the "Oresteia," Aeschylus's trilogy on the accursed house of Atreus, and preceded it with Euripides' "Iphigenia in Aulis" to make the story complete. It is, simply and overwhelmingly, our story, the story of the human race in its attempt to shake off the endless cycle of violence and replace it with the rule of law.

The ancient Greeks would have laughed at our debates over violence in the arts. Their theater was awash in blood. The myth of the house of Atreus is an epic sideshow—infanticide, regicide, matricide, patricide, every kind of -cide, plus cannibalism and assorted horrors. In the first play, the Greek king Agamemnon sacrifices his daughter Iphigenia to propitiate the gods as he embarks on the Trojan War. In "Agamemnon," his wife Clytemnestra takes vengeance by killing her husband and his Trojan captive, the prophetess Cassandra. In the next play, "The Libation Bearers," Agamemnon's son Orestes, supported by his sister Electra, keeps the vengeance cycle going by killing his mother and her paramour Aegisthus. In the final play, "The Eumenides," the Olympian deities Apollo and Athena engage in a trial of Orestes, who's opposed by the dark forces, the Furies. Orestes is acquitted, and the murderous cycle is ended.

Such are the bare and bloody bones of these complex and potent dramas. Mnouchkine's

staging brings to life that old saw, "total theater." Drama, music, dance, brilliant costumes and makeup, but above all, energy, galvanize the huge stage space. Mnouchkine does wonders with the chorus, who constitute from play to play a microcosm of the body politic. It's a dancing, chanting body politic, swarming like acrobats over the high walls that flank the stage, leaping down again to reform in a battalion of blazing color.

The Théâtre du Soleil, founded in 1967, is based in the Cartoucherie in Paris, an 18th-century munitions factory. The company is a theatrical General Assembly from more than 20 nations. The leading players speak French with a passionate precision (in Brooklyn there will be headsets transmitting an English translation). Simon Abkarian, an Armenian, takes the roles of Agamemnon, Orestes, a *coryphaeus* (Chorus Leader), even Orestes's old Nurse. Juliana Carneiro da Cunha, a Brazilian, plays Clytemnestra and Athena. Indian-born Nirupama Nityanandan plays Iphigenia, Cassandra, Electra, and a leader of the Furies. Catherine Schaub, the chief *coryphaeus* throughout the cycle, is astonishing as she moves from powerful speech to eloquent song to sensual ecstatic, shoulder-shaking dancing. Schaub alone is total theater.

Mnouchkine has boldly grafted an Oriental performing style—mainly the precise, ritualized gestures and masklike makeup of the Indian *kathakali* theater—on to this bedrock work of Western theater. In a time of burgeoning ethnic enmity, the stage becomes a synthesis of East and West. This feeling reaches a climax in the final play, "The Eumenides," when Athena imposes a new harmony on the family whose internecine war is a symbol of all human conflicts: Mnouchkine turns the three chief Furies into bag ladies, dressed in tattered duds and sneakers, and costumes their Chorus as hellish dogs, snarling, growling, cowering and cavorting. It's an unforgettable image. These Furies want blood, but Athena cajoles them into accepting a new identity—Eumenides, the "kindly ones," who take their place in a new civic order of democracy and justice. As the cycle ends, the dogs, fearful and confused, slowly rise on their hind legs. Animal bloodlust has become human understanding.

The Greek plays are profoundly political and spiritual. That's the theatrical idea of Mnouchkine, 53, a handsome woman of passionate intellect. For her these 2,500-year-old works have a sharp relevance to today's social traumas. "As artists our mission is to warn—to yell, to shout and to celebrate any small victory," she says. "What's happening in Eastern Europe is terrible. These Greek plays train the intelligence and the senses. They're full of demons, and today a big demon has been defeated, but all the small ones have been let loose." "Les Atrides" evokes, identifies and dispels those demons.

SUMMARY

1. The emergence of the director in a dominant artistic role is a distinguishing feature of the modern theatre.

2. Directing, as a theatre art, has been fully integrated into the theatrical process only for the last hundred years. In the classical period, playwrights staged their own works.

3. There is virtually no agreement among directors concerning an effective system for practicing the art, a methodology, terminology, or etiquette.

4. The director chooses from the largest menu of choices of any theatre artist.

5. The process of directing involves not only the decisive, take-charge process of "giving directions," but also the more subtle responsibility of guiding other theatre artists in the sense of "maintaining the right direction."

6. Directors cast actors primarily according to type, although some have achieved unique success by casting against type. Nontraditional casting has become a hotly debated issue in the theatre as directors come to grips with the demands of an increasingly multicultural world community.

7. Staging involves directorial choices that seek to achieve effective focus, picturization, business, and movement.

8. Directing assistants and associates include the dramaturg, musical director, choreographer, voice coach, fight director, casting director, stage managers, and assistant director.

9. The dress rehearsals are the director's first test of the viability of the concept. A director must be the ideal or surrogate audience for every production.

10. Directors often manipulate the text to accommodate the audience's understanding of the play.

11. There is a major dispute between those who conceive of the director as essentially an interpretive artist and those who believe the director is an independent conceptual artist.

12. Entrusting the production to the actors for performance is the director's final, inevitable activity in connection with a production.

CHOICES

1. Richard Thomas had to make the choice, so you give it a try: imagine you are directing a production of Tennessee Williams' *The Glass Menagerie*. Tom, who narrates the play, makes his first entrance as an itinerant seaman of the Merchant Marine of the 1930s. Should he wear a red hat or a blue hat? What type should it be? Justify your choice.

2. Choose a favorite TV show or a currently playing movie of immense popularity. From the famous actors in film, television, or the theatre, recast *against type* all the leading roles so as to reveal other aspects perhaps not considered. Your choices should not lead to a burlesque or spoof of the original. Provide the reasoning that led to your decisions.

3. Based on the indications of character given by the respective authors as quoted in this chapter, cast Cassius and Brutus in a production of *Julius Caesar* and Amanda in a production of *The Glass Menagerie*. Choose from among the famous actors working in film, television, or on stage. Justify your choices.

4. Refer to the examples of strong and weak moves on page 260 and create "visual punctuation" from a playwright's written punctuation in a brief passage from a play of your choosing.

5. The Casting Problem:[37] In real-life amateur productions, directors don't have the 25,000-person membership of Actors' Equity Association from which to choose their actors. Casting in these situations invariably is based on factors other than type. Imagine you are a first-year instructor at a large high school and are preparing to direct your first production for entry into a play competition. Your principal has asked you to do *Romeo and Juliet,* which would be the first Shakespearean play you have ever directed. At the play competition there will be several major colleges and universities offering scholarships to the best student actors. None of the students at your auditions, except one, has ever acted in Shakespeare before. After auditioning all the students who wanted to read for the play, you narrow the selection of the leading role, Juliet, down to one of these three students:

MARY: A senior who has played many leading roles in past productions at your high school and is president of the Drama Club. She has played leads in *Barefoot in the Park* and *Dracula,* and most recently, she was Laura in a very good production of *The Glass Menagerie.* She is also a cheerleader and a member of the National Honor Society. Last year in *Dracula* she played opposite her boyfriend, Jonathan, with whom she had been going steady until last month when she broke up with him. You have, by the way, decided to cast Jonathan as Romeo because you have no other choice. Mary is of average height and very attractive. Her reading was OK but she seemed a little preoccupied during the callbacks. You know she can do better and have been told she is a fine performer. Mary wants to be a professional performer.

JULIE: A sophomore, whose interests so far have been in musicals. She has been doing community theatre since she was a little girl, appearing in the local production of *Annie* when she was only 3. You, in fact, worked with Julie in a production of *My Fair Lady* two years ago when you were acting a role, and she was in the chorus. You were happy and surprised to see her come to audition for *Romeo and Juliet.* Julie is a member of the chorus, of which she is vice president, and also very active on the yearbook and school newspaper. Her grades are not very good, but she does try hard. She is short (5'1"), very busty, and wears braces. She is the only one you have worked with before, and you believe her callback reading is the best of the candidates.

NANCY: A senior who just entered your high school this year when her family moved across town. At her old school Nancy played several big roles, including Katherine in *The Taming of the Shrew,* Annie Sullivan in *The Miracle Worker,* and Beneatha Younger in *A Raisin in the Sun.* She has studied ballet since she was a little girl and tells you she comes from an artistic family that has always encouraged her to excel in the arts. Nancy plays piano (classical) and will probably major in either drama or dance in college. Physically she is the tallest of the three women (5'9"), and is the only African American student who has auditioned for the play. (Jonathan, who will play Romeo, is 5'8½".) She has done some modeling work for local department stores, and is the most attractive of the three women you are considering. For reasons unknown to you, no one at the audition seems to like her very much. She sits alone in the auditorium, and you overhear snide comments about her made by others. During one of the breaks during the auditions you ask one student why Nancy is sitting alone and are told, "She's too stuck-up to be with anybody else."

Probably all three of these students are capable of learning the role. Your problem is to cast Juliet. Who will you cast and why? What specific factors did you use to make your choice?

Award-winning actor Anthony Hopkins and Michael Bryant in the Royal National Theatre of Great Britain production of King Lear.

Is it not monstrous that this player here,
But in a fiction, in a dream of passion,
Could force his soul so to his own conceit
That from her working all his visage wann'd,
Tears in his eyes, distraction in's aspect,
A broken voice, and his whole function suiting
With forms to his conceit? And all for nothing!

Hamlet, *Act II, scene ii*

CHAPTER 8

Artistic Impersonation

THE ACTOR'S CHOICES

PREVIEW

The Imitative Instinct and the Need to Perform
Historical Perspectives on Acting
Modern Acting and the Stanislavsky System
Other Modern Styles of Acting
The Demand for Skills: Making Choices Possible
Standing Publicly with Their Choices
The Actor at Work

Perhaps you have seen one of the following:

> Horribly disfigured—in body as well as soul—he hides both with practiced desperation: a stark white mask covers the distortions of his face, and an ardent comportment obscures the murderous emptiness of his heart. But tonight, deep in the candlelit caverns beneath the teeming city, romance rises to fill the void. He bends tenderly toward the alabaster perfection of the face of his captive love and sings to her of transcendent beauty, imploring her to "LISTEN TO THE MUSIC OF THE NIGHT."

> On an oppressively humid Louisiana summer night, a powerfully built man, emotionally shattered, stands alone and wails for the return of his pregnant wife who has just fled his drunken abuse. Oblivious to the stifling heat, his muscles tighten with anguish under his sweat-soaked T-shirt. He uses every fiber of his brutish being to raise his voice in ferocious, convulsive screams of desperation: "HEY STELLA! STELLLLLLAAAAAAAAA!"

> The tall city cop sights coolly along the sleek barrel of the most powerful handgun ever made, looking, at point-blank range, directly into the darting eyes of the desperate fugitive and his frightened hostage. Suddenly, the murderous thug moves to kill his terrified prisoner. Seemingly unperturbed, the detective raises his weapon slightly to a target point just above the fugitive's nose. His eyes narrow to a squint, his lip curls up from clenched teeth, and the words seethe from his throat: "GO AHEAD . . . MAKE MY DAY!"

Michael Crawford in *The Phantom of the Opera?* Marlon Brando in *A Streetcar Named Desire?* Clint Eastwood in *Sudden Impact?* No. It's just one unknown person performing alone in front of a mirror, trying to find out what it feels like to be somebody else. Aristotle maintained that this urge to impersonate is innate in human beings. He wrote that human beings are the most imitative creatures on earth, and that we all want to know what it is like to be someone else. This chapter examines acting as artistic impersonation in psychological, sociological, and aesthetic contexts. Historical styles of acting are contrasted with contemporary practices, and the skills required of professional actors are reviewed. The chapter explains where and when, in the continuum of given circumstances, the actor makes the choices.

The Imitative Instinct and the Need to Perform

Social Role Playing

From early childhood, we are asked to consider—and we daydream about—what we want to be when we grow up. We spend our youths playing "cops and robbers," "superheroes and villains," "doctors and patients," "monsters," and "house." Supposedly such child's play is bounded only by the limits of our young imaginations.

Actually, even as children, the fanciful roles we choose reflect the values of our society. Only recently, for example, did little girls begin to imagine themselves as doctors or little boys as cooks. Still, we know the fantasies of child's play are over when we are warned sternly and repeatedly to "stop acting like a child. Act your age!"

In his essay "The Shadows of the Gods," Arthur Miller maintains that "the man is in society and the society is in the man."[1] It is a way of saying that succeeding as an adult involves learning to imitate the socially accepted behavior for the real-life roles we choose to play. Thus society dictates the rules for becoming a mature adult, a responsible citizen, a successful student, or a parent. For other roles we undergo long and difficult courses of study in order to become doctors, lawyers, engineers, nuclear physicists, philosophers, or artists. Social role playing means a doctor must exhibit a good bedside manner, a top salesperson must be persuasive

JOHN MALKOVICH, ACTOR

IF THE WORLD IS A STAGE, WE CAN HELP YOU DRESS FOR ALL THE GREAT ROLES. BUT WE'RE BEST AT HELPING YOU PLAY YOURSELF. WE'VE MASTERED OUR CRAFT TO MAKE YOURS EASIER. MR. MALKOVICH IS WEARING OUR OWN ITALIAN TAILORED SUIT. WE ACCEPT BARNEYS NEW YORK, AMERICAN EXPRESS AND OTHER MAJOR CHARGE CARDS. 212-929-9000

B A R N E Y S
N E W Y O R K

THE NEW YORK TIMES MAGAZINE · APRIL 24, 1988   13

SOCIAL ROLE PLAYER *Actor John Malkovich appears in an advertisement designed to appeal to upscale social role players.*

and aggressive, a politician must be telegenic, parents must be good role models, and comedians must "never let 'em see you sweat." Everybody, of course, must "dress for success."

Consider, for instance, what it means to act like a college student. A variety of socially acceptable roles can be imitated by the aspiring undergraduate: Frat Rat, Suzie Sorority, Top Jock, "A" Student, Hacker, Revolutionary, Preppie, BMOC. If you are dissatisfied with your part, you can always "change your image." In this sense, we can all understand the implications of Shakespeare's poetic observation:

> All the world's a stage,
> And all the men and women merely players:
> They have their exits and their entrances;
> And one man in his time plays many parts . . .
>   (*As You Like It,* Act II, scene vii)

Such are the consequences of ineffective social role playing that we even seek out advisers, counselors, and analysts to help us adjust to the demands of our parts. This role playing is anything but "play." For adults, the harmless, uninhibited fantasies of childhood are rarely played out in real life as we perform our social roles. The need to maintain maturity prevents us from achieving the exhilarating, creative freedom displayed by children.

Artistic Role Playing

For a select group in our society, however, such adult restrictions have never applied. They are determined to continue the playing. These are the actors who, within the confines of the theatre, impersonate multitudes of the most fascinating characters. They play kings, queens, vagrants, murderers, cops, fops, sex maniacs, nuns, priests, presidents, despots, and dentists, to name just a few. For each role, they live a brief, imaginary life, about as long as a child's playtime. Even better, they play only the most passionate moments of the lives they impersonate without having ever to suffer the emotional, physical, or legal consequences of their behavior. In William Mastrosimone's intense drama *Extremities,* the protagonist Marjorie retaliates violently against a would-be rapist. Yet neither of the actors who plays these parts gets hurt, and nobody goes to jail. Likewise, actors who play lawyers never have to endure the tedium of filling out the endless forms, writing long briefs, or spending hours in the law library. The great stage lawyers, like Henry Drummond in *Inherit the Wind* or Barney Greenwald in *The Caine Mutiny Court-Martial,* argue only the most consequential court cases in which they do mesmerizing opening statements, intense cross-examinations of crucial witnesses, and fiery closing arguments. And they never have to be in court on the day nothing much happened. In a whimsical perspective, Academy Award-winner Meryl Streep says she likes her life in the countryside with her husband and children, but acting has its enjoyable moments also: like doing love scenes with Robert Redford, the best kisser I ever met in the movies. It's a terrible job, you know. I mean, loving all those handsome men. Come on! It's fun! It's fun to re-create those feelings—and not have any of the repercussions. Just think of what lives I've lived vicariously. I've been poisoned by radiation, sent a child to the gas chamber, lost custody of another, lost husbands and lovers. God! If it weren't for the moments when I fall in love, I'd go nuts![2]

Thankfully, dramatists do not give actors plays about the time Lady Macbeth got angry and pouted until she felt better, or about the night Willy Loman came home from a boring road trip and fell asleep reading the newspaper. Instead, playwrights invent the most emotionally potent situations the characters will ever face. In *Death of a Salesman,* Arthur Miller created the one brief episode in Biff Loman's life when he faces the truth about himself and his father. That particular moment of maximum intensity is what the actors get to play when Biff breaks down sobbing in his father's arms:

WILLY: *[with hatred, threateningly]* The door of your life is wide open!
BIFF: Pop! I'm a dime a dozen, and so are you!
WILLY: *[turning on him now in an uncontrolled outburst]* I am not a dime a dozen! I am Willy Loman and you are Biff Loman!
BIFF: I am not a leader of men and neither are you. You were never anything but a hard-working drummer who landed in the ashcan like the rest of them! I'm one dollar an hour, Willy! I tried seven states and couldn't raise it. A buck an hour! Do you gather my meaning! I'm not bringing home any prizes anymore, and you're going to stop waiting for me to bring them home!
WILLY: You vengeful, spiteful mut!
BIFF: *[at the peak of his fury]* Pop, I'm nothing! I'm nothing, Pop. Can't you understand that? There's no spite in it anymore. I'm just what I am, that's all.[3]

The opportunities to play—and replay—such once-in-a-lifetime moments account for the intoxicating need actors have to perform. At the same time, the rest of us can live out vicariously our own needs to "play" through them.

The actors who are best at playing these "great moments" hold a special place in our society. Often we grant high celebrity status as well as huge salaries to the actors who excel at capturing our imaginations. It is that way today, and it has been that way throughout history.

Historical Perspectives on Acting

The Social Status of Acting

In ancient Greece, actors were so highly valued as members of society that they were exempted from military service and arrest and were occasionally granted

THE NEED TO PERFORM   *The members of the Off-Off Broadway acting company
Naked Angels are actors who have successful careers in film, television, or on
Broadway. They formed their company, which plays in a dilapidated former picture-
frame shop in Manhattan, as an antidote to the restricted roles they get in the
commercial venues. Between engagements they return to Naked Angels to perform in
serious, brooding plays that provide them with the kind of juicy parts television or the
movies rarely offer. After ten years of performing to please themselves, they are
becoming one of the hottest "unknown" theatres in New York. (Clockwise from left
above) Jennifer Estess, Nancy Travis, Fisher Stevens, Merril Hotzman, Ron Rifkin, and
Rob Morrow.*

diplomatic immunity to serve as ambassadors between states. The great Roman actor **Roscius** (125–62 B.C.) raised himself out of slavery through acting and, according to Cicero, earned a vast fortune. Even during the 1,200 years from the sixth century through the Renaissance when the theatre was banned and actors had the legal status of "rogues, vagabonds, and prostitutes," people sought out clandestine performers and legal loopholes so actors could perform among them. In seventeenth-century England, for instance, the performers in Shakespeare's company called themselves **The King's Men** so they could be designated as servants in the royal household, not as actors playing in a theatre.

With the end of most legal and religious prohibitions against theatre in the eighteenth century, the status of some actors soared so high that they began to be referred to as "stars," and some attained positions of the greatest respect in the world. In England, **Henry Irving** (1838–1905) was the first actor to be knighted, in 1895. **Onoe Baiko** (1916–95), one of Japan's greatest Kabuki actors, was designated a "Living National Treasure" in 1968 by the government. And, **Sir Laurence Olivier** (1907–89) was raised to the House of Lords in 1970.

The First Actors

Acting officially debuted in 534 B.C. when **Thespis** separated himself from a singing and dancing chorus to speak a prologue and impersonate a character. In Greek, the actor was called *hypokrites,* "the answerer," from which we derive the modern English word *hypocrite,* meaning one who is not what one pretends to be. The effect of this dramatic impersonation was so powerful in its ability to create illusion that Plato wanted to ban plays from his ideal Republic.

The Question of Realism.   The fictional impersonations of these **early thespians** were so lifelike in their portrayals that audiences—philosophers and lawmakers notwithstanding—viewed them as realistic and truthful. But "realistic" and "truthful" are relative theatrical designations. Their meanings vary greatly from culture to culture and age to age and are determined by the conventions of theatre practice that are necessary to create illusions in the minds of the people. For instance, today we consider the most truthful acting to be that in which the actor accomplishes a total impersonation of the character based on the most lifelike kinds of behavior: actors eat, drink, move, talk, and behave on stage much as they do in real environments. More often than not, we believe so strongly in the performances of our greatest actors that we forget they are acting. As lifelike as such acting seems to be, modern stage actors still take great care to practice such unlifelike conventions as "holding" for a laugh and keeping their bodies turned toward the audience as much as possible so they can be seen by everyone.

But consider the "truthfulness" of ancient Greek acting that looked like this:

Wearing a mask with a shockingly high headdress, a long, flowing, brightly colored robe, and large thick-soled boots, a male actor playing an ancient Greek god majestically enters the outdoor performing space where 17,000 spectators sit expectantly.

With symbolic gestures and studied, dancelike movements, he sweeps his arms high over his head, then suddenly falls dramatically to the ground. In a booming voice that embodies all of the emotion he cannot show with his masked face, he recites the lyrical, poetic cadences of the dialogue. Sometimes declaiming loudly, usually singing to the accompaniment of a flute, he speaks of the great moral issues of human existence—in a manner not unlike that of grand opera. As the chorus sings an interlude, the actor exits to change his costume and mask and then reappears as a mighty warrior king, changing his talented voice to sing the dialogue of the new, more human character. Before the play is over he will change his costume, mask, and voice twice more to play not only a lowly messenger, but also the queen.

Such were the conventions of the ancient Greek theatre that actors imagined their characters almost totally in terms of formalized, nonconversational vocal impersonations.

The Declamatory Style of Acting

In the larger-than-life manner of performing established in the ancient Greek theatre, the actor is called on to be an orator and demonstrator who displays artistic gifts to impress an audience. This **declamatory style of acting** defined theatrical performances for the next 2,400 years—until the late nineteenth century. With the addition of some energetic miming and instinctive impersonation, the declamatory style of acting was very similar to the kind of oration practiced by flamboyant public speakers: politicians behind their rostrums, preachers in their pulpits, and lawyers in their courtrooms. Movements and gestures were all predetermined and practiced like classical dance steps. Declamatory actors deliberately rejected *natural* utterances and motions, since these were considered to be crude—unshaped by *artistic* choices. Although the particular conventions of this manner of performing varied and evolved in different historical periods and cultures, the declamatory style of acting was distinguished by several important characteristics:

1. Declamatory acting is more presentational than representational in that actors demonstrate or *show* the audience idealized versions of the characters rather than try to convince the audience they *are* the characters.
2. Declamation as an acting style is particularly well suited to the speaking of the heightened dialogue of verse, the dominant language of drama until the eighteenth century.
3. It is also well suited to the impersonation of larger-than-life characters such as gods, kings, queens, and great warriors, as well as broad comic types.
4. The focus of declamatory acting is primarily toward the audience rather than toward other characters. As such it encourages the practice of actually *breaking character* for such reasons as asking the prompter for a forgotten line, taking a bow in the middle of a scene, repeating well-received stage business (such as a dramatic death), or even carrying on an argument with a heckler.

DECLAMATORY ACTING   *The Guthrie Theatre's production of* The House of Atreus, *a modern adaptation of Aeschylus' fifth century* B.C. *tragedy,* The Oresteia. *The stylized masks and costumes of these actors severely limit their physical creativity. Such choices as scratching their noses, wrinkling their eyebrows, leaping, or crying real tears would be impossible. Broad gestures and vocal virtuosity are their options.*

Women on the Stage

For the first 2,200 years of theatre history—until just 300 years ago—women were not permitted to act on stage. Ancient Greeks and Romans considered the female voice too weak to project effectively in large amphitheatres and too highly pitched to impersonate multiple characters. Therefore, all the female roles were played by men.

In the Renaissance, the legal status of male actors was questionable enough; religious and civil law held them to be rogues and vagabonds. For women to act on

ROLE REVERSAL *Sarah Bernhardt (1844–1923)*, considered by many to be the greatest female actor who ever lived, was an artist ahead of her time. She was the first-ever international superstar—fifty years before Hollywood existed, with as huge a following in America and England as in her native France. And in one of the first efforts at "gender-neutral" casting, Bernhardt took on centuries of role reversal by playing Hamlet in an acclaimed 1899 world tour.

stage would have constituted a moral outrage. Thus, in the theatre of Shakespeare's time, most female roles, including such characters as Juliet, Desdemona, and Lady Macbeth, were written for and played by adolescent boys called **apprentices.** Unlike the mature men who specialized in playing the comic old female characters, the apprentices did not play broad burlesques in "drag." They were artistically precise impersonations intended as convincing portrayals.

Following European practice, England's Charles II finally granted women the right to act in plays. In 1661 he officially decreed "that all women's parts to be acted . . . for time to come may be performed by women." At least in matters of gender, acting took a step toward a style of playing that could be recognized as

"realistic" by everyone regardless of differences in culture, country, historical period, or theatrical practice.

Portraying Emotions and the Paradox of Acting

For all their larger-than-life histrionics, declamatory actors always understood
their primary job was to portray convincingly the intense emotions inherent in
the lines they recited. Great passions have always been the essence of live theatre;
they are what brings audiences to the theatre. During the eighteenth and nineteenth centuries, many theatregoers left during the unexciting parts and returned
when passions were displayed.

We have all seen examples of passionate acting so emotionally compelling
that we sit in awe of the performers' abilities to lose themselves in their parts. But
does this really happen? Is it possible for actors actually to experience the emotions they portray?

Throughout the history of the theatre, actors have held two diametrically opposed views as to the best way to portray emotions on stage. One view holds that
actors should indeed become emotionally involved in the imaginative lives of the
characters through personal inspiration. Aristotle called this involvement that
"certain madness" by which actors truly experience the feelings they portray. The
opposite view holds that actors should feel nothing and seek only to imitate the
outward signs—gestures, postures, and facial expressions—of their characters'
emotions.

The belief that the actor should "feel nothing" was argued most convincingly
by the French philosopher **Denis Diderot** (1713–84) in a famous essay called "The
Paradox of Acting." Diderot maintained that inspiration is unreliable, since the very
spontaneity that defines it, renders it uncontrollable. What, Diderot asked, would
happen to an actor deserted by inspiration in the middle of a performance? For instance, the actor who plays Othello must portray a jealousy so intense as to become
livid with rage and smother the life out of his wife Desdemona, and then must express the most searing anguish when Othello realizes he has destroyed the only
woman he ever loved. In a professional production of this play, the actor would
have to re-create this emotional intensity for up to eight performances per week.
Diderot maintained that to try to feel as Othello does performance after performance would be impossible. Some nights the actor would be inspired and highly
emotional, while on others the audience would see an Othello who was burned out,
cold, and boring. Devoid of any true passion, such an actor would probably try to
force the emotions by resorting to a kind of loud, empty overacting called **rant,** as
in "rant and rave." Finally, proponents of the "feel nothing" view maintain that
since emotionally inspired acting cannot be controlled, it could ultimately prove
dangerous in the hands of an actor "lost" in the part. Caught up in the "madness" of
a truly murderous Othello, might not such an actor do real harm to the one playing
Desdemona?

To Diderot and great actors like Garrick, Bernhardt, and Irving, the very idea
of *choosing* to be inspired seemed a dangerous contradiction in terms. On the

PAUL ROBESON AND PEGGY ASHCROFT IN *OTHELLO* *The portrayal of the most extreme theatrical passion is called for in the life-shattering intensity of the climactic moment when Shakespeare has Othello strangle Desdemona, stab himself, and in his dying words say, "I kiss'd thee ere I kill'd thee—no way but this,/Killing myself, to die upon a kiss."* **Paul Robeson** *(1898–1976) was the first black actor to play Othello in London (1930) since Ira Aldridge sixty years earlier.*

other hand, choosing to portray the outward, physical signs of emotions was not only much safer and more reliable, it was artistically appropriate to the declamatory style of acting required for the classical plays and melodramas in which they performed. Sarah Bernhardt, her contemporaries noted, always gave "the picture of an emotion, never the emotion itself."[4] Legendary film producer Samuel Goldwyn put it this way: "The most important thing in acting is *honesty;* once you learn to fake that, you're in."[5]

Naturalistic Acting

The paradox-of-acting argument intensified at the end of the nineteenth century when interest in scientific methodology, the ascendency of the working and middle classes, and the popularity of photography promoted a new standard of imitation in the arts. **Naturalism** called for art to be a "slice of life" as opposed to the classical goal of the "idealization of life." Adopting this view, nineteenth-century dramatists began to write plays that demanded stage life look and sound exactly like real life, a demand never before placed on declamatory actors. Thus the naturalistic style of acting differs substantially from declamatory acting in several important ways:

1. Naturalistic acting is more representational than presentational in that the actors portray the total impersonation of the characters in order to experience the emotions called for in the script and to make the audience believe they *are* the characters.
2. Naturalistic acting is particularly well suited to the speaking of everyday prose dialogue as opposed to the heightened style demanded of verse.
3. It is also well suited to the portrayal of characters in the everyday domestic situations depicted in naturalistic plays.
4. Most importantly, the naturalistic actor must always be *in character*. The actor's focus is always within the confines of the stage set and on the other characters in the play. Any contact with the audience or breaking character would ruin the naturalistic effect.

If this new style of acting were to succeed in creating the illusions of real life, then all vestiges of artificially demonstrated emotions would have to be eliminated. For the modern actor, the spontaneity of personally inspired, emotional portrayals became an absolute necessity. However, in order to change the traditions of acting that had held the stage for 2,500 years, an entirely new method of creating characters had to be invented.

Modern Acting and the Stanislavsky System

The methodology that unlocked the secret of naturalistic acting—that is, "living the part"—was developed by the innovative Russian director, actor, and teacher, **Konstantin Stanislavsky** (1863–1938). Through his work with actors at the **Moscow Art Theatre,** Stanislavsky perfected a method for achieving the goal of naturalistic acting: the total impersonation of the character by the actor—in effect, a theatrical truth beyond declamation. The Stanislavsky system of acting has been so widely accepted by actors throughout the world that it is referred to simply as "the method."

Stanislavsky and Freud.   Stanislavsky's ideas were consistent with the revolutionary theories of his contemporary **Sigmund Freud** (1856–1939), whose analytical approach to psychology established a new science of human behavior. Stanislavsky recognized the key to naturalistic acting was finding a reliable, scientific technique for the actor repeatedly to stimulate and unleash unconscious feelings, urges, and desires. The goal was to "make the unconscious, conscious," as Stanislavsky said, "to seek those roads into the secret sources of inspiration."[6] Thus his approach to acting is not unlike the process of psychoanalysis in which the actor, in effect, puts the character on the couch to discover the motivations behind the character's actions. The system, therefore, is divided into two basic phases: the process of **character analysis** by which the actor seeks to make the appropriate psychological, physical, and vocal choices; and the life-giving techniques for making those choices believable to the actor and the audience.

The Essentials of Character Analysis

Determining the Given Circumstances.   According to Stanislavsky, an actor's first task is to determine all of the circumstances that affect the character in the imaginary world of the play. Stanislavsky called them *given circumstances* because they do not originate with the actor, but rather are imposed by the playwright and the director. The playwright gives the actor the imaginary world in which the character exists: the who, what, where, when type of circumstances. For instance, it is Arthur Miller who provides the actor playing Biff Loman with the details of a frustrated, athletic, 35-year-old drifter who returns to his father's New York home. Miller also furnishes the rich history of the tortured relationship between father and son and the unspoken secrets that are the source of their conflict.

The director provides the actor with the how: those aspects of concept and interpretation that will particularly affect the character's behavior. Orson Welles' decision to set Julius Caesar in fascist Italy, Frank Galati's resetting of *A Flea in Her Ear* from 1910 to 1966 (p. 269), Richard E. T. White's Cajun concept for *Twelfth Night* (p. 252), and Peter Sellars' race-skewed, multimedia *Merchant of Venice* (p. 250) were directorial circumstances that predetermined significant choices for the actors—from their costumes to their vocal accents.

The Magic If: The Actor's Choices.   Stanislavsky found an important key to naturalistic acting in the simple word *if.* He understood that actors who try to lose themselves in their parts are attempting to accomplish the artistically impossible. To go on stage and try to believe through some sort of trancelike self-hypnosis that the actor *is* actually the character is a lie, and unless the actor is mentally ill, impossible to do. Instead, Stanislavsky directed actors to go on stage and simply *do what you would do* **if** *you were that character in those given circumstances.* In this way the actors are in the truthful situation of playing themselves in the circumstances of their characters. Thus the question the actor asks is not "what would Biff Loman do?" (which is unknowable), but "what would I do if I were Biff in Miller's imaginary world of *Death of a Salesman?*" The answers to this basic question are not stated directly in the script or dictated by the director. They come from the personal creativity of the actor. At the point when the performer begins to provide specific answers to this fundamental theatrical question, the actor's job as an independent creative artist begins.

WHAT I WOULD DO *IF* I WERE . . . (Top) *Marlon Brando was a Broadway sensation in 1947 when he created the role of Stanley Kowalski in Tennessee Williams'* A Streetcar Named Desire. *His Stanley was at once powerful, crude, sensual, and aggressive, yet childlike and innocent in his consuming need for his wife. Brando's performance defined the role and American method acting for a generation. (Bottom) Forty-years later Alec Baldwin brought Stanley Kowalski back to Broadway in a performance characterized by his own unique choices. Baldwin emphasized more suspect motivations in the character, portraying a Stanley more driven by greed and scheming than by an all-consuming need to satisfy basic physical and emotional urges.*

This filtering of the character through the mind and body of the actor is what is meant by **creating a character.** When the object of imitation is as detailed as the naturalistic, everyday activities of human beings, the possible choices are as unlimited as life itself. The talent of great actors lies in making astonishing, original, and personal choices from this vast palette. The fact that each actor brings an "I" to the magic "if" means no two actors will make exactly the same choices for even the most popular, often performed roles.

The Superobjective and the Through-Line of Action.   The most consequential choice a modern actor makes is a psychological one, deciding the character's overriding emotional desire or intention in the play. Stanislavsky called this primary motivating force the **superobjective** and defined it as that which the character must do more than anything else in the play. For instance, an actor playing Biff Loman in *Death of a Salesman* might choose this for a superobjective: "No matter what the cost, I must force my father to face the truth of our failed lives." An actor playing Marjorie in *Extremities* might see the superobjective as this: "Even if it means killing Raul and convincing my roommates to help me do it, I must stop him once and for all from ever hurting me or anyone else." Another actor playing the role might choose a different, but still entirely justifiable superobjective: "I must punish and torture to death this animal for what he did to me."

Superobjectives compel the actor to make an ever-building sequence of desperate attempts to accomplish the motivating goal. Stanislavsky called this sequence the **through-line of action,** since it is the sum total of each actor's own unique choices for the play. Consider the artistic options available to the actor playing Marjorie at the precise moment in the first scene of *Extremities* when Raul viciously attacks her, pins her down, and at knifepoint demands, "Kiss me and tell me that you love me. Tell me!" The script indicates that Marjorie's response is "Please don't."[7] The actor playing the role could choose to whisper those words—barely audibly—through a throat dry with terror. She could sob the words incoherently or scream them hysterically. In a firm voice, she could even order him to stop. Each of these options would be appropriate. The actor must make the choice. To do nothing would ruin the dramatic potential of a great moment. Because of artistic opportunities like this one in *Extremities,* modern, naturalistic actors often speak of "playing the moment."

Making Choices Believable

After a careful character analysis has led to making appropriate choices, the actor's next challenge is to take the imaginative creation to the stage and make it believable, both personally and for the audience. Stanislavsky's solutions to this difficult task lay in the unbreakable relationship between inner desires and outward actions. Stanislavsky recognized that each physical action, no matter how large or small, is motivated by a psychological desire, and that, in turn, psychological needs are carried out by physical actions. You open a door (a physical action) because you want to leave the room (a psychological desire). Conversely, if you want to leave the room, you will go to the door and open it. This relationship between emotional states and outward activities led Stanislavsky to develop two different, but equally valid techniques for making the "unconscious conscious."

Emotional Recall: The Inner Technique.   Stanislavsky's first method for making stage actions emotionally truthful starts with the psychological desire, hence the designation "inner" technique. The process asks the actor to recall from memory a personally compelling emotional experience that will serve to make the stage actions natural and psychologically appropriate. We all have memories of very strong emotional moments in our lives that can be triggered by often accidental, but nonetheless conscious means. For instance, you may have had the experience of encountering sights or smells that instantly returned you to a time and place in the distant past. Or perhaps you remember a time when you heard the radio playing a long-forgotten song that was very important to you and some special person. The power of these **sense memories** to overcome you and let you actually relive for a moment—even after many years—a strong emotional time in your life illustrates the potential for this inner technique.

Since most actors have seldom lived through the specific extreme conflicts of stage characters (for example, murder, attempted rape, torture, teenage suicide), the method of emotional recall asks actors to remember and use strong *analogous* feelings while on stage: the death of a loved one, the anguish of a broken relationship, a funeral, even the trauma of having a pet put to sleep—all such moments are important tools for the naturalistic actor.

The inner approach to acting has been most popular in the United States, where it is called simply **method acting.** For more than forty years it has been taught at the famous **Actors Studio,** founded by Stanislavsky disciple **Lee Strasberg** (1901–82). Among its students have been some of America's greatest actors, including Marlon Brando, James Dean, Paul Newman, Jane Fonda, Robert Duvall, Jack Nicholson, Marilyn Monroe, Anne Bancroft, Sidney Poitier, Rod Steiger, Roscoe Lee Browne, Al Pacino, Lee J. Cobb, Robert De Niro, and Dustin Hoffman, all of whom are famous for their honest and emotional acting.

The Method of Physical Actions.   Disillusioned by overreliance on emotion memory, Stanislavsky developed an alternative "outer technique" based on the observation that the most honest things an actor can do on stage are simple physical actions. An actor who walks across the stage floor, sits down, and drinks coffee is really doing, not faking these activities. Thus the appropriate physical action—sometimes called a **psychological gesture**—can be an effective stimulus for an emotional state. For example, an actor playing Richard III who pounds violently on a table and says the famous line "I am myself alone" will be forced to an entirely different emotional reading of the line than saying the words while settling slowly into a chair. The method of physical actions gives the actor a tool for choosing a variety of emotional responses. This outer technique has been popular among British actors who are noted for the great physical control of their characterizations.

Both emotional recall and the method of physical actions lead actors to relive publicly what for most of us are private—Freud would say suppressed—emotional experiences. Actor Shirley Knight put it this way,

> The constant need to take yourself to the center of all pain, joy and despair, the looking into and experiencing emotion, raw, the public bleeding, exposing your secrets unashamedly, is both the curse and blessing of the actor-artist. It forces you to deal every day with insanity, tamper with your own psyche and enter into a world beyond your control. For this commitment society should be grateful. A true and visionary actor can expose the best and the worst of us, and if we are able to accept his perception, we can make the next step toward enlightenment.[8]

It is a way of saying that, in order to make the most compelling choices, modern, naturalistic actors must learn to invade their own privacy.

Other Modern Styles of Acting

Since realism, especially in performing, is still a very popular theatrical style, naturalistic acting is the most widely practiced form of the art—it is the norm. On the other hand, the eclectic nature of modern theatre has led to a need to develop alternative styles of acting more suitable for plays and productions in which total illusionism is not the goal. For these overt departures from realism, the total impersonations of naturalistic acting are inappropriate, and the Stanislavsky system is not at all suitable for creating what are often very unlifelike characters.

Avant-Garde Acting

Avant-garde is an all-inclusive term that refers to the newest, most original, and experimental approaches to art. In the theatre, the *avant-garde* refers to those forms defined primarily by their intentionally nonrealistic techniques and philosophies. Examples range from the symbolist and expressionistic works of the early twentieth century to the absurdist and existentialist plays of the 1950s and 1960s, and the performance art and postmodernist creations of the last forty years.

The characters in *avant-garde* plays, rather than being the idealized or naturalized imitations that are the traditional focus of dramatic action, serve instead merely as parts of an overall fragmented impression or as aspects of a larger symbol. As they seek to portray the often bizarre creations of *avant-garde* playwrights and directors, actors end up making vocal, physical, and psychological choices that are more mechanistic and abstract than real. For example, in Eugene Ionesco's famous one-act play *The Bald Soprano* (1950), actors must create a through-line of action made up entirely of non sequiturs: lines and actions that, by definition, do not follow. It is Ionesco's choice for depicting the absurdity of modern discourse made up entirely of meaningless clichés. By the end of the play the characters are reduced to speaking only in nonsense words and syllables.

AMERICAN REPERTORY THEATRE PRODUCTION OF ROBERT WILSON'S *CIVIL warS*
Perhaps the most radical avant-garde *theatrical creations have been the so-called*
postmodernist *productions in which actors become mere objects and human mobiles*
to be integrated spatially and kinesthetically into an overall multimedia spectacle.
Robert Wilson's CIVIL warS *(1983–84), a postmodernist reflection of conflicts that*
inhibit human relationships, utilizes twelve languages to address a multicultural,
global audience. Its time-warped characters include Voltaire, Abraham Lincoln,
Frederick the Great, Karl Marx, and a Native American tribe. Each audience member,
Wilson maintains, must construct a personal experience from the discontinuous
images and sounds.

Mrs. Martin, Mr. Smith:	Robert Kipling!
Mrs. Smith, Mr. Martin:	Rudyard Browning.
Mrs. Martin:	Silly gobblegobblers, silly gobblegobblers.
Mr. Martin:	Marietta, spot the pot!
Mrs. Smith:	Krishnamurti, Krishnamurti, Krishnamurti!
Mr. Smith:	The pope elopes! The pope's got no horoscope. The horoscope's bespoke.
Mrs. Martin:	Bazaar, Balzac, bazooka!
Mr. Martin:	Bizarre, beaux-arts, brassieres!
Mr. Smith:	A, e, i, o, u, a, e, i, o, u, a, e, i, o, u, i![9]

Such vocal and psychological abstractions are part of Ionesco's larger pattern of nonsequential illogic.

Modern directors have also sought to manipulate actors into new styles of performing to suit their *avant-garde* visions. For example, an extreme departure from realistic playing was required for the Kennedy Center production of the classic melodrama *The Count of Monte Cristo,* staged by the *auteur* American director Peter Sellars. In this controversial production, Sellars forced his actors to find ways of playing highly emotional and intimate scenes without ever looking at each other, a form of naturalistic communication he considered overly sentimental and redundant. In rehearsal, whenever the actors would relate to each other in instinctively sensitive ways, Sellars would object by jumping up and yelling, "Care Bears! Care Bears!"[10]

As these examples illustrate, in the *avant-garde* styles of acting, the creativity of the performers is often at the mercy of playwrights or directors, to be manipulated as part of a personal, nontraditional artistic vision. At the opposite end of the creative spectrum are other modern styles of acting that rely almost solely on the performer as an independent artist who must make choices from individually developed methods and expertise.

Improvisation

The most performer-dominated style of acting is improvisation in which the players provide virtually all of the theatrical and dramatic choices. By inventing the given circumstances, the actor becomes the playwright, the director, *and* the performer. In this style, dramatic action is created when a group of actors invents a performance by instantly reacting to each other's choices. Unlike the methodically analyzed rehearsed creations of naturalistic acting, improvisation is, by definition, never planned. Spur-of-the-moment creativity is its very essence.

Instead of an existing script and a directorial concept, improvisational acting begins with little more than a general idea, situation, or scenario for action. A typical example for four actors might be "Thinking your parents are away for the weekend, you and your companion decide to get romantic. Just at the most intimate moment, your parents return unexpectedly." The dramatic results of such an improvisation can be quite serious, and, in fact, such scenarios are often used in clinical settings to create **psychodramas** for therapeutic purposes. Mostly, however, improvisations are humorous and require actors with the comic inventiveness to react quickly to their partners. For this reason, great improvisational acting has traditionally been associated with comedy troupes.

The vogue for improvisation extends back to the sixteenth-century ***commedia dell'arte,*** Italian "professional comedy" troupes, which were extremely popular throughout Europe until the middle of the eighteenth century. Using minimal scenery and props, *commedia dell'arte* actors improvised broadly farcical plays. Their scenarios were domestic love stories for which they invented dialogue as they went along, and to which they added generous amounts of standard comic

STOCK CHARACTERS   Commedia dell'arte *actors always played well-known stock characters in all of their improvised performances. Among the favorites were Capitano, the braggart warrior, and Pantalone, the duped father. Notice the slapstick in Pantalone's hand and the standard masks that all comic* commedia *characters wore.*

business called *lazzi.* These were mostly routines of physical comedy such as pratfalls and often involved the use of a **slapstick,** a hinged piece of wood that created the loud "whack" of comic violence. It is from this 400-year-old device that we derive the modern designation for physical humor called "slapstick comedy."

The modern vogue for such comedy cooperatives can be traced to the success of Chicago's Second City Troupe, a group devoted entirely to improvisation. Founded in 1959, Second City boasts alumni who are among America's most inventive comedians including Mike Nichols, Elaine May, Shelley Berman, Robert Klein, Danny DeVito, Chevy Chase, John Candy, John Belushi, Dan Akroyd, Jim Belushi, Ed Asner, and George Wendt.

Because of the intimate sense of ensemble playing that results from improvisation, its techniques have often been used as exercises for improving the sensitivity and spontaneity of naturalistic actors.

Clowning

As an acting style, clowning is derived from the broadly physical comic traditions of vaudeville, circus, and burlesque. In these all-but-extinct variety entertainments, the performers created their own **stage personas,** identities through which they did their "acts" such as dance numbers, animal routines, comedy sketches, juggling, or acrobatics.

When such acts are integrated into a play, clowning becomes a distinct acting style in which the characters are filtered through the minds and bodies of the performers' stage personas rather than their real-life personalities. Thus great physical comedians like Laurel and Hardy, Abbott and Costello, the Three Stooges, W.C. Fields, and the Marx Brothers—all of whom started as vaudeville or burlesque acts—played only their well-known stage personalities, no matter what play or film they happened to be doing. Few people, for instance, were ever aware of the real-life personalities of Julius, Arthur, and Leonard ("Groucho," "Harpo," and "Chico") Marx.

Conventional wisdom is that film, radio, and television combined to kill vaudeville. Recently, however, a number of exceptional performers have begun once again to practice the art of theatrical clowning. Taken together, their work constitutes a revival of sorts that has been referred to as the "new vaudeville." Among the most notable of these performers who have created strong stage personas for their acts are (1) Larry Pisoni, who as Lorenza Pickle claims he can juggle any three things he is given; (2) New York-based clown Avner the Eccentric; (3) Geoff Hoyle, who is famous for his marvelous Mr. Smith and his three-legged man routine; (4) Bill Irwin, shtick artist extraordinaire; (5) Dario Fo, the internationally sensational Italian mime, playwright, and political agitator; (6) Penn and Teller, an outrageous duo of *faux*-magicians; and (7) the amazing Flying Karamazov Brothers. Having adopted the names of Dostoyevsky characters, Howard Jay Patterson (Ivan), Paul David Magid (Dmitri), Michael Preston (Rakitin) and Sam Williams (Smerdyakov) present wildly ridiculous, but brilliantly skillful routines of juggling, gravity-defying slapstick comedy, and nonsensical one-liners.

Most new vaudevillians are content to perform as solos on variety specials, in comedy clubs, or even in the streets. Some, however, like the zanies of old, have taken opportunities to integrate their acts into legitimate theatrical productions and perform actual roles in plays. The vogue for such performing was established when the Flying Karamazov Brothers starred in Chicago's Goodman Theatre's 1983 clown-crazy production of Shakespeare's *The Comedy of Errors,* which eventually had a successful Broadway run. Bill Irwin has starred in his own clown shows on Broadway, performed in several major studio films as well as appearing as Lucky in the Lincoln Center production of *Waiting for Godot* with Robin Williams, Steve Martin, and F. Murray Abraham.

Transformations

Transformational acting refers to the playing of many different characters by one actor in a single play. Like improvisation, this type of acting relies on the individual inventiveness of the performers, who transform themselves from one character to another, often in full view of the audience. Using a minimum of costume and makeup changes, transformational actors make choices based primarily on

CLOWNING *The Flying Karamazov Brothers at the Brooklyn Academy of Music where they clowned their way through Stravinsky's famous ballet-drama* The Soldier's Tale, *in a production that included their famous juggling, fire-eating, and ladder balancing.*

voice, posture, and attitude to distinguish an often broad range of characters. In a single play, they are called on to act roles that can span the spectrum of types in terms of age, sex, and even species.

A good example of a play requiring transformational acting is Barbara Danashek and Molly Newman's musical drama *Quilters,* which depicts the struggles of a

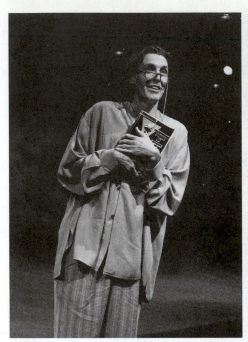 

TRANSFORMATION   *In Terrence McNally's play* Love! Valour! Compassion!,
*John Glover played twin brothers—one gentle and kindhearted, and the other cold,
calculating, and almost sadistic in his ill temper. Glover sometimes changed characters
in full view of the audience by merely sitting in a chair or standing up. Other times he
accomplished the transformation with the help of a dresser who stood in the wings for
lightning-quick costume changes. McNally's award-winning play, about eight gay men
who meet at a country house over one summer, originated at the not-for-profit
Manhattan Theatre Club and then transferred to Broadway.*

pioneer woman and her daughters to settle the American West. Each actor plays
not only a specific member of the family, but a variety of other characters associated with the westward expansion such as small children, adolescent school-
girls, fathers, preachers, cowboys, and even cows. In a historical context,
transformational acting is traditional. The ancient Greeks, limited by rule to just
three actors in each production, relied on the versatility of their performers to
play up to five or six roles in one play.

Modern variations of transformational acting evolved out of the improvisational exercises of the **Open Theatre,** an Off-Off Broadway cooperative of actors
founded in 1963 by *avant-garde* directors Joseph Chaikin and Peter Feldman. Their
best and most characteristic work was their 1968 production of Jean Claude
Van Itallie's *The Serpent,* a transformational exploration of humanity's fall from
genesis through the assassination of John F. Kennedy. While the Open Theatre's
work was primarily experimental and politically partisan, its transformational
techniques have been incorporated into the mainstream of the modern theatre,

especially in musicals. Popular musicals requiring transformational acting include *Hair, The Robber Bridegroom, Nine,* and *Candide* in which 24 actors play more than 120 roles.

Multicultural Alternatives

The very popularity and longevity of the Stanislavsky system have prompted the development of variations on it and alternatives to it that have their origins in other countries. Like the naturalistic method, these multicultural variations have been articulated by influential theorists whose work has been published in manifestos.

Grotowski.   The first widely influential theorist since Stanislavsky was **Jerzy Grotowski.** Having studied Stanislavsky's method in Moscow, he returned to his native Poland in the 1960s to found the Polish Laboratory Theatre where he evolved his alternative ideas, published in *Towards a Poor Theatre* (1968). For Grotowski, "poor theatre" was a reaction against the "wealth" of contemporary theatre with its lights, scenery, costumes, and music. He wanted to strip the theatre of its inessentials and rely completely on the brain and body of the actor. In Grotowski's method, the goal is to find new theatrical expressions beyond realism, to make use of the physical and mental powers of the actor for new theatrical expressions. To make his actors rely on their own resources, Grotowski forbade the use of makeup or changing costumes to portray a change in role or character, insisted that actors produce all music with their own voices, and required that they gain absolute physical control over every part of their bodies. Grotowski's actors are famous for the astonishing vocal and physical virtuosity of their performances.

Though his company toured to major world capitals in the late 1960s and early 1970s, actual live performances of his work have been seen by relatively few people. His company has remained a fixture of Polish experimental theatre. His primary influence has been through his book and through the work of such major directors as Peter Brook and Jerome Robbins who have employed his methods in some of their productions.

Suzuki.   More visible has been the new acting methodology of Japanese master teacher **Tadashi Suzuki.** Through his resident company in Japan, his book *The Way of Acting* (1968), and committed disciples in the United States, the Suzuki style of acting has been seen on many contemporary stages.

Unlike Stanislavsky, who emphasized the mind, Suzuki's style is defined by what he calls "BodyVoice," a commitment to the physical—in the extreme. Suzuki's method seeks to push actors to the limits of human physical and vocal expression. Training, rather than focusing on mental techniques like emotion memory and the magic *if,* emphasizes ferocious physicality: kicking, screaming, shuffling, pounding the earth, and especially feet stomping. "Modern theatre," writes Suzuki, "is so tedious to watch because it has no feet. Stomping spreads physical energy up through the body to the center: the pelvis, as opposed to the Western center of expression: the face."[11]

SUZUKI ACTOR *Kelly Maurer as Hamlet in Eric Hill's Suzuki-style production at StageWest. By casting a female actor in his production of* Hamlet, *Hill emphasized the* zamissel *that identity and gender are discontinuous, ambiguous, multiple, and contradictory. "To be or not to be" evoked an entirely new ironic dimension. Maurer compared her nightly encounter with the Danish prince to a "car crash."*

Suzuki has found his way to American stages through the work of committed directors like Anne Bogart and Eric Hill, who trained with Suzuki for eight years. As artistic director of StageWest in Springfield, Massachusetts, Hill built a resident not-for-profit professional theatre around Suzuki's principles. For Hill, the speed and emotional intensity of the modern world make Suzuki the definitive acting style:

> The old style of stage acting, realism, belongs to the age of the luxury ocean liner, sailing smoothly and leisurely across the Atlantic. Today we live in the jet age. Actors have to be top-gun pilots, flying over the Pacific, turning right angles on a dime. Now we experience enormous emotional shifts in a split second. Chaotic experiences crowd our consciousness, and our world, like Hamlet's, is falling apart at the seams.[12]

Histrionic Convergence. The "chaotic images" that crowd our consciousness are reflected in the cultural convergences on the world's stages, making new demands on actors and audiences alike. National acting traditions share the spaces at global institutions like Peter Brook's International Center for Theatre Research and Ariane Mnouchkine's Théâtre du Soleil where Kabuki actors, Kathakali dancers, Yoruban storytellers, British classical actors, and Polish mime artists perform together. The National Theatre of the Deaf employs both hearing and deaf actors who incorporate sign language and speech to fulfill their promise that audiences will "see and hear every word." Multilingual plays are being written and performed everywhere. As a citizen of the global village, the modern actor must be histrionically diverse in order to perform on today's stage where all cultures converge.

Of necessity, modern actors must become adept at playing all styles of impersonation including the idealized mannerisms appropriate to classical plays, the psychological techniques and real-life choices of naturalism, the mechanistic stage behavior of the *avant-garde,* and multicultural alternatives, as well as the performer-intensive arts of improvisation, clowning, transformation, and performance art.

The Demand for Skills: Making Choices Possible

Imagine yourself as a basketball star making the most spectacular slam dunk of all time.

> Running at full speed, you take a bullet pass at center court. As you approach the top of the key, you take two powerful steps that launch you into the air. Arching upward and forward, you twist your body into a vertical spin—one complete revolution and then another half-turn. With fingertip precision you flip the ball from your right to your left hand, and then, with a sudden, lightning-quick, but perfectly graceful motion of your arm, you scoop the ball forward, up, above your head, and behind your back—jamming the ball hard through the net. The entire backboard shudders in response to your athletic virtuosity. Magnificent!

Imagining yourself making such a shot is relatively easy. Actually doing it is something else altogether. Unless you are very tall, have phenomenal strength, a finely honed rhythmic sense, great leaping ability, an instinctive sense of distance, pinpoint peripheral vision, and a body in perfect physical condition, such a shot will be forever the stuff of daydreams.

Or, imagine you had been lucky enough to have attended one of the rarest of all twentieth-century artistic events:

> The tall octogenarian, greeted by thunderous applause, strode purposefully across the stage of Carnegie Hall. Without so much as a bow, he sat before his polished, perfectly tuned, $50,000 custom-made Steinway concert grand piano. A sudden hush fell over the capacity crowd as he placed his large powerful hands over the keyboard. Anticipation became performing art when Vladimir Horowitz, one of the greatest pianists who ever lived, began to play. Astonishment was the only possible reaction to the way in which his fingers moved in fast and complicated combinations over the keys in another of his aggressive, signature renditions of a great classical composition.

Like all virtuosos, Vladimir Horowitz (1904–89) had to have the finest and most perfectly tuned instrument—and the physical, rhythmic, and tonal skills to play it—in order to display the astonishing choices of his musical imagination.

It is the same for actors. Without a finely tuned instrument and the attendant skills at playing, the most brilliantly conceived theatrical choices will remain only conceptions locked forever in the imaginations of the performers. The actors' instruments are the body and voice. Ultimate effectiveness as artists depends on how well the actors can, in effect, play upon themselves. An actor whose body and voice are not up to the demands of stage acting will be as ineffective as a piano that is out of tune or an athlete who is out of shape.

The Technical Demands of Stage Acting

Compared to film and television acting, stage acting is far more demanding of skills and much less forgiving of "instrumental" weaknesses. Screen actors, for example, require only limited stamina for doing short takes that can be reshot as often as necessary, until all the mistakes are eliminated. Since their performances are recorded on film or tape, screen actors have to perform it right only once. If screen actors lack the specialized skills demanded of their roles, doubles such as stuntpersons and stand-ins are routinely used. Finally, technological solutions such as electronic amplification, dubbing, and digital imaging can be used to correct and compensate for weaknesses in the skills of screen actors.

By contrast, stage actors are allowed no doubles, few technological enhancements, and no retakes to correct mistakes. Stage acting requires a kind of one-take-per-performance perfection that must then be repeated for up to eight performances per week. A long-running hit of several years can require actors to play a schedule that even professional athletes do not endure. In fact, the physical rigors of performing live theatre invariably force actors to retire from the stage when they no longer possess the strength and stamina for the intensive and unforgiving playing. Take the case of Laurence Olivier, considered to be the greatest actor of his time. In 1946 at the age of 39 he played Shakespeare's King Lear—as demanding a part as has been written for an actor, and one for which he was more than forty years too young. In 1982, when he was finally the same age as the character, he played Lear again. Although he had gained the maturity necessary to fully understand the part, he no longer possessed the strength and endurance for even one stage performance. Therefore, the production was done on film according to a schedule in which Olivier's scenes were shot in five-minute takes, and for which such tricks as wires were used for suspending the actor he had to appear to carry.

The actor who expects to work consistently in today's theatre, in which plays from all genres and styles are produced, must train like a cross between an athlete and a musician to develop the skills of stage acting. Consider, for example, a typical American repertory season that includes an eclectic selection of plays such as the big-book musical *West Side Story;* the Shakespearean tragedy *Hamlet;* the wild British farce *Noises Off;* Tennessee Williams' American "classic" *A Streetcar Named Desire;* and the rock-opera spectacular The Who's *Tommy.* To be hired for just the five plays of this hypothetical season, a stage actor would need, at a minimum, to be accomplished at the following kinds of skills.

Vocal Skills

Voice Production.   Nothing is more frustrating than sitting in the theatre and being unable to understand what the actors are saying. Therefore, an actor's first responsibility to an audience is to be clearly heard and easily understood. In large theatres with imperfect acoustics and noisy ventilation systems, not to mention the living presence of an audience, this is not as easy as it may seem.

Stage actors must be skilled at the techniques of vocal production, especially **articulation,** which is the use of the jaw, tongue, teeth, lips, and palate for the clear enunciation of each word; **projection,** which is speaking loudly through strong diaphragmatic support so as to be heard clearly even in the last row of the theatre; and **relaxation,** which is speaking loudly while keeping the vocal cords (larynx) and all the muscles used for speaking free from the strain that would cause loss of an actor's voice. In everyday speech the voice production of stage actors would sound as if they were constantly yelling and spitting and would look as if they were "chewing" their words. From the stage, the effect is that of dialogue that sounds like normal conversation—but conversation that can be clearly understood from anywhere in the theatre.

Speaking Dialogue.   A skill unique to actors is making written dialogue sound like natural speech being spoken for the first time.

For *Hamlet* and most other plays written before the eighteenth century, actors must be adept at speaking verse—especially the five-stress poetic line of **iambic pentameter,** the most common form of English **blank verse.** To make the verse comprehensible, actors must not only identify the rhythmic stresses of each stanza, they must also speak the dialogue according to the actual sentence structure and punctuation. It is a process not unlike that of reading music and diagramming sentences.

It is not an exaggeration to claim that Shakespeare's plays have stayed alive for so long because actors love to speak his verse.

Prose dialogue, which sounds more like natural speech, can be just as challenging to an actor as verse. Over the course of a long play (or even a long speech), actors must avoid monotone and sing-song, repetitious patterns of speaking by varying the rate, volume, pitch, and emphasis of the dialogue. Actors who are best at giving the **illusion of the first time** to prose and verse dialogue gain a valued reputation for their original line readings.

Accents and Dialects.   Three of the plays in the hypothetical repertory season being considered require actors who can speak with a variety of specialized accents and dialects. **Accents** refer to a second language spoken with the melody and lilt of a foreign tongue. **Dialects** are regional varieties of the same language distinguished by features of vocabulary, grammar, and pronunciation. *West Side Story* requires Puerto Rican accents for the immigrant street gang, the Sharks, and Upper-West-Side, lower-class New York dialects for the Jets. In *A Streetcar Named Desire,* Blanche affects the sophisticated dialect of southern gentry; a

"TRIPPINGLY ON THE TONGUE"

An actor playing Hamlet would **scan**—or see—the stresses of iambic pentameter in the following passage like this:

> Is IT not MONstrous THAT this PLAYer HERE,
> But IN a FICtion, IN a DREAM of PASsion,
> Could FORCE his SOUL so TO his OWN conCEIT,
> That FROM her WORKing ALL his VISage WANN'D,
> Tears IN his EYES, disTRACtion IN'S asPECT,
> A BROken VOICE, and HIS whole FUNCtion SUITing
> with FORMS to HIS conCEIT? and ALL for NOTHing!

He would understand the same passage for meaning as if it were printed like this:

> Is it not monstrous that this player here, but in a fiction, in a dream of passion, could force his soul so to his own conceit that from her working all his visage wanned, tears in his eyes, distraction in his aspect, a broken voice, and his whole function suiting with forms to his conceit? And all for nothing!

variety of British dialects—cockney, midlands, and the Queen's English—are appropriate for *Noises Off*.

Singing. Since musicals are the most popular form of theatrical entertainment, singing has become an indispensable skill for modern actors, even though some never master it. The demanding musical style of Leonard Bernstein's *West Side Story* requires actors skilled at **legitimate** (sometimes called "head voice") **singing,** which has the clear, perfectly placed tones of opera. For the pop-rock score of Peter Townshend's The Who's *Tommy,* the "chest voice" style called **belting** is more appropriate. Rather like yelling on pitch, belting is the kind of singing for which Judy Garland, Ethel Merman, Liza Minnelli, Madonna, and Jennifer Holliday are known. To stay in shape vocally, even accomplished singing actors continue expensive voice lessons with master teachers.

Physical Skills

Every play requires actors to perform specialized physical tasks. The physical side of acting runs the gamut from habitual idiosyncrasies of the characters and the

TO THE MANNER BORN   *The costumes require special skills of modern actors in Molière's scathing seventeenth-century comedy of manners,* Tartuffe.

mannered behavior of historical periods to activities so extreme and demanding that they require the expert assistance of specialists.

Period Style.   If a director chooses to set *Hamlet* in any period except the modern one, the particular historical milieu will dictate many aspects of stage behavior. Period costumes, for instance, strictly define how an actor can walk, stand, sit, or gesture. In addition, actors must use such nonmodern accoutrements as canes, wigs, riding boots, corsets, hats, hooped skirts, bustles, capes, fans, and snuff-boxes. Especially foreign to American actors are the various bows and curtsies that must be learned for plays with kings, queens, and an abundance of lesser nobility. On the other hand, even relatively modern plays like *West Side Story* have aspects of period style that must be mastered: walking and dancing on spike-heeled shoes take much practice if they are to look natural.

Ultimately, "looking natural" is the goal of all period movement on stage. Actors must behave as if they were born to the style, and give the impression they have worn such clothes and displayed such mannered idiosyncrasies all of their lives.

Stage Combat.   Physical violence is a common climactic outcome of the intense conflicts at the heart of many plays. For the attempted rape in *Extremities,* the knife fights and rumbles in *West Side Story,* and the flashing swordplay in *Hamlet,* stage actors—who do not have stunt doubles—must be proficient at safe, but dangerous-looking armed and unarmed combat.

Training in all types of stage combat is provided by **fight directors** certified by such professional organizations as the Society of American Fight Directors (SAFD). These combat specialists choreograph stage fights as if they were dances in which every step, jump, cut, thrust, and parry are planned as part of the overall dramatic action and then carefully rehearsed.

Slapstick and Circus Tricks.   Under the general heading of slapstick are the techniques, tricks, and routines of physical comedy that are the stock-in-trade of madcap farces like *Noises Off.* Specifically, modern actors need skills in several types of slapstick:

> *Knockabout:* the comic violence of the type made famous by the Three Stooges.
> *Pratfalls:* the slip-on-a-banana-peel tricks that are the ultimate comic humiliation.
> *Shtick:* the classic category of comic bits and business that includes such favorites as double takes, slow burns, hat flipping, pie throwing, and such signature routines as Groucho's leering walk.
> *Comic timing:* the innate sense of setting up, trapping, and delivering the "punch" to stage humor.

The revival of clowning has led to renewed interest in such traditional circus skills as juggling, stilt walking, comic tumbling, and acrobatics. The Ringling Brothers Clown School in Florida is one of the few places that teaches

The drawing illustrates the tricky technique involved in the "fast food roll" in which an actor playing a waiter is walking along with a plate of food in each hand, suddenly trips, does a forward roll, and ends up standing without spilling a morsel of the food.

circus routines, but the techniques of physical comedy can also be learned by watching the great screen comics and zanies like Harold Lloyd, Charlie Chaplin, the Marx Brothers, Lucille Ball, Carol Burnett, Dick Van Dyke, Jackie Gleason, Jerry Lewis, and Jim Carrey.

Dancing.   Musicals, of course, require actors who not only can sing, but dance as well, usually at the same time. The most common style of musical theatre dance is jazz in which the performers' feet trace geometric patterns that are repeated or opposed by the upper body. But *West Side Story* also features ballet, marenga, and rumbas. Also essential to an actor's repertoire is tap dancing, which has enjoyed a revival in such hit shows as *No No Nanette, Anything Goes, 42nd Street, The Will Rogers Follies,* and *Crazy for You.*

Accomplished dancers, like singers, continually take lessons to stay in shape and maintain proficiency in this highly technical physical skill.

Performing.   Performing is the conventional behavior of actors in the stage space and consists of the technical adjustments they make in order to be seen and heard by the audience as well as to be protected from unintentional harm by other actors. Performing dictates certain rules of behavior for working and living in the stage environment, such as:

Eating: Take small bites to keep the voice free for speaking and to avoid awkward swallowing (not to mention choking).

Sitting: Since it breaks focus and always looks silly, never glance back at a chair before sitting in it.

Talking on the phone: Keep the mouthpiece under your chin so as not to cover up the face and muffle the voice.

Firing a blank gun: Aim the gun slightly upstage of the person being shot, and no matter how strong the inclination to do so, never aim toward the audience. It makes them very nervous.

YOU ROTATE AROUND YOUR ARMS
(AND THE SOUP)

©1987 Christopher Agatino

WHAT THEY DID FOR LOVE   *Prior to the opening performance of* A Chorus Line, *the members of the original company collectively appeared in 72 Broadway shows, 17 national companies, and 9 bus and truck tours in which they gave a total of 37,095 performances. They had 612 years of dance training with 748 teachers, counting duplications. They spent approximately $894 a month on dance lessons. While performing they sustained 30 back, 26 knee, and 36 ankle injuries. (Source:* Playbill *magazine)*

Since the face and voice are an actor's primary means of conveying emotion, **staying open** to the audience is an important skill. On a proscenium stage (with the audience all on one side), actors stay open by **cheating out** into more full-front positions than they would take for the same activities in real life. In addition, small but important techniques (such as always gesturing and holding objects with the upstage hand) keep actors' bodies more open to the proscenium audience. On arena and thrust stages (where they always have their backs to someone in the audience) actors stay open by moving in circular patterns, looking slightly past each other, and never staying in one body position for too long.

The potential for smudging makeup as well as possible illness from communicable infections are the reasons actors learn to fake deep passionate kisses on stage. The logistics of faked romantic contact are not as simple as they may seem. The following textbook description of the technique of a stage embrace and kiss illustrates the demand for skill at performing:

If the embrace is to be performed while both actors are standing, the correct position is arrived at by first taking what amounts to a natural dancing position. The right hand of the boy is placed under the left arm of the girl and around her back toward her right shoulder. Instead of taking the girl's right hand, the left hand of the boy either goes around the girl's waist or high on her upper arm or on her right shoulder blade. The girl then puts her right hand on the boy's left shoulder, or on the lapel of his coat, or around his neck, or she may smooth his hair. Her left arm is around his right shoulder. . . . The covered kiss is executed by the boy's turning the girl's head slightly upstage and bringing his own directly below hers. His head will cover and mask the process, as his face will be directly upstage and his shoulders and the back of his head toward the audience. From the waist down he will be in profile. When the head is in this position he can either not kiss at all or can put his lips on her cheek or chin, or he can put his face to the side and back of her neck.[13]

Mental Skills

Concentration.   For actors, the distractions of the live theatre can be overwhelming. Backstage is the hustle and bustle of cast and crew in constant motion. Onstage are shifting scenery, other actors who may or may not remember their lines,

STAYING OPEN   *The actors in the Missouri Repertory Theatre production of James Costin's* Jekyll *are "cheating out" into more open positions than would be natural.*

and blindingly bright lights, which can make the edge of the stage all but invisible. In the audience are rustling programs, late arrivals trying to find seats in the dark (or worse, early leavers trying to find the exits), and the very irritating beeping watches, coughing patrons, and crying babies.

Staying in character—pursuing a single-minded superobjective over the course of an entire play—requires that actors have substantial skill at concentration. Stanislavsky developed a technique for achieving the mental state he described by the oxymoron **public solitude.** He recommended that actors create imaginary **circles of attention** around themselves in which to focus their concentration. When they feel secure in a very tight circle around their bodies, they may gradually widen it to the boundaries of the stage. If they feel their attention wandering to focus on offstage distractions, they should focus back down to a smaller circle until they regain their concentration.

Memorizing Lines.   Any one of the many distractions of live theatre can cause an actor to commit the potentially disastrous sin of **blanking**—suddenly forgetting the next line or action. Therefore, memorizing lines is a mental skill that comes easily to some actors and is excruciatingly difficult for others. Nothing holds up the creative growth of a production as much as a slow line learner. Quick studies, on the other hand, are valued for their ability to memorize their parts within the first few days of a rehearsal period and thus are able to spend more of the production process on the imaginative aspects of creating their characters. Even quick studies face a challenge when memorizing the role of Hamlet, who in the uncut version of Shakespeare's play speaks 1,530 lines, one of the longest parts ever written.

Listening and Adaptation.   Academy Award-winner John Wayne once said, "I don't act, I react." It was "the Duke's" way of saying that the spontaneity of acting comes from actually listening to what the other characters are saying and from watching what they are doing *without anticipating* what everyone on stage already knows will happen. Actors who plan every move or try to protect themselves from blanking by always thinking ahead to their next lines will look like they are doing just that—anticipating rather than "living" the part. Listening and watching for a **cue,** the line, phrase, or stage business of another that prompts a response, are a much more effective aid to learning lines and acting spontaneously than rote memorization and meticulous planning.

Obviously, listening and adapting, or *acting in the moment,* as it is called, involve the risk of trusting the other actors to give the right cues. When they do, and spontaneous interplay among all the actors occurs on stage, the result is a creative chemistry of playing together called *ensemble.*

Perception.   John Gielgud tells the following story:

> Once when I was rehearsing *Crime and Punishment*—it was a very hot day, I was walking through St. James's Park—I saw a tramp lying down, with his head buried in

ENSEMBLE PLAYING IN *THE GRAPES OF WRATH*   *Members of Chicago's Steppenwolf company, many of whom have worked together since college, are famous for the effective ensemble of their performances.*

the dirty grass, filthy hands and everything, and he was absolutely relaxed. I thought, "This is the way that Raskolnikov must lie on the bed," and immediately it gave me a kind of line on the part.[14]

Unlike Gielgud, most of us who passed the tramp would not even look at him. We would probably avert our eyes, too embarrassed to observe, let alone examine him closely. Prolonged and overt staring at others, society teaches us, is extremely rude. But Gielgud, like all great actors, had spent a lifetime learning to stare at others in order to perceive all aspects of human behavior—from the most complex to the seemingly simple—and then adding the perceptions to his mental catalog of possible choices.

What they do not have stored in their memories, actors must learn through specific observation and practice. Actors who have played hookers have walked the streets with real prostitutes, actors who have played police have pounded beats with real officers, and actors who have played convicts have checked themselves into prisons. To portray an Irishman falsely accused of terrorism in the film *In the Name of the Father,* Daniel Day-Lewis locked himself in a cell. To play an

PERSONALITY ACTOR *Alan Alda has achieved award-winning recognition as a gifted personality actor in stage, TV, and film roles. He has refined the portrayals of self-absorbed, intelligent, neurotic, successful, middle-aged characters such as the title role of Neil Simon's* Jake's Women.

artist with cerebral palsy in *My Left Foot* he was carried around off camera. The point is, actors cannot play what they have not in some way experienced.

Job Skills

The most employable actor is the one with the most skills and versatility to play a variety of styles. But actors, like everyone else, tend to specialize according to their particular talents. Some, like Liza Minnelli, Bernadette Peters, Patti Lupone, Michael Crawford, and Gregory Hines, make careers out of doing musicals; others, like Jason Robards, James Earl Jones, and Al Pacino, work primarily at naturalistic acting. John Gielgud and Laurence Olivier built reputations based on their classical portrayals, and Robin Williams, Whoopi Goldberg, and Billy Crystal are among the very best at improvisation.

CHARACTER ACTOR
Robert De Niro in the New York Shakespeare Festival production of Cuba and His Teddy Bear. *With a reputation as an accomplished character actor, Robert De Niro is virtually unrecognizable in roles as various as Al Capone (in* The Untouchables)*, Jake LaMotta (in* Raging Bull)*, Rupert Popkin (in* King of Comedy)*, and Max Cady (in* Cape Fear)*.*

Personality vs. Character Actors.   Actors also tend to be cast according to the types of characters they are good at playing. **Personality actors** are those who trade on the natural attributes of their own physical and psychological makeup to play only one particular type. Personality actors are "typecast" to play themselves. As a consequence, all the characters they play are very similar, virtually indistinguishable from each other. John Wayne earned his living as a tall-in-the-saddle American hero; Marilyn Monroe always played a seductive, but alluringly vulnerable woman; Clint Eastwood's cops and cowboys are always a variation of Dirty Harry; and Jim Carrey has made a specialty of hyperkinetic misfits. How much of what personality actors project is actually themselves and how much is created stage persona is never quite clear. The performances, however, never vary, and personality actors are employed by being cast as they are.

On the other hand, **character actors** constantly manipulate their skills in order to submerge their real selves and take on hundreds of different voices, bodies, and psyches. They earn their livings based on their abilities to play a great variety of types. The best character actors, such as Laurence Olivier,

Dustin Hoffman, Meryl Streep, Anthony Hopkins, and Robert De Niro, are almost unrecognizable from role to role.

Auditioning.   An actor's primary means of getting cast in a show is by auditioning for parts. Some actors, fortunate enough to be represented by agents and managers, get private auditions with producers and directors. Most, however, must attend **open calls** in which so many actors are seen (up to 600 per day at New York or Los Angeles auditions) that the auditions are derisively referred to as "cattle calls." These opportunities—all of which are very brief—can take one of several forms. Actors must be skilled at all of them if they want to work.

Principal interviews are the most perfunctory and mechanical, and are not really auditions at all. They are merely brief opportunities for actors to present their pictures and résumés to a production assistant. No opportunity to display talent or ability is offered. In **standard auditions**, also called "generals," each actor has three to four minutes to present two contrasting monologues taken from plays—a classical verse piece and a modern prose piece, one of which should be serious and one of which should be comic. The actor stands alone on an empty stage without a costume or props and pretends to carry on a scene with an imaginary character. **Chorus auditions** for a musical consist of a chance to sing a maximum of sixteen bars of a song from a Broadway show. Sixteen bars from the *West Side Story* song "Somewhere" would be:

There's a place for us.	There's a place for us.
Somewhere a place for us.	A time and place for us.
Peace and quiet and open air	Hold my hand and we're halfway there.
Wait for us somewhere.	Hold my hand and I'll take you there—[15]

That's it.

Dance auditions, made famous by the record-breaking hit *A Chorus Line,* consist of learning a jazz, tap, or ballet combination with a large group of up to fifty other aspiring "hoofers." **Cold readings** are the standard procedure for casting new plays. In this duet audition, the actor, often knowing nothing about the play or characters, is given a script, little or no time to prepare, and then must play a scene in which the other character is "read" by an often untalented production assistant.

The challenge for actors in these audition situations is to show off all of their talents in order to demonstrate that they are just what the producers are looking for, whatever that is. The high anxiety involved in auditioning is achingly expressed by Iris Parodus, a character in Lorraine Hansberry's play, *The Sign in Sidney Brustein's Window.* An aspiring young performer, Iris has just returned from an audition:

Iris: You don't know what it's like though—God, to walk through those agency doors . . . There's always some gal sitting at a desk, you know, with a stack of pictures practically up to the ceiling . . . And they're always sort of bored, you know . . . They've seen five million and two like you, and by the time you come through that door they are *bored.* And when you get past them, into the waiting room, there they are—the five million and two sitting there, waiting to be seen, and they look scared and mean and as competitive as you do. And so you all sit there, and you don't know anything: how you look, how you feel, anything. And least of all do you know how they *want* you to read. And when you get inside, you know less. There are just those faces . . . All I ever see are those blank director-producer-writer faces just staring at you . . . waiting for you to show them something that will excite them, get them arguing about you . . . And you just stand there knowing that you *can't,* no matter what, *do* it the way you *did* it at home in front of the mirror, the brilliant imaginative way you did it the night before. No matter what.[16]

Rejection.   Actors lucky enough to get noticed at a cattle call can look forward to a series of **callbacks,** further auditions from which they can be cut at any time. Actors know they have been rejected when they hear the words, "Thank you very much." It is just a more polite euphemism for "Don't call us, we'll call you." Both phrases are inelegant testimony to the fact that actors lead largely passive lives filled with daily rejection by others who are in control of their artistic, not to mention financial, destinies. Betty Buckley, an actor who stepped into the *Sunset Boulevard* casting controversies (see Chapter 7, p. 253) when she took over the part of Norma Desmond in London, knows about rejection:

> You don't steel yourself for disappointment. You are disappointed continually. You're rejected continually. People have great things to say about you one day and the next day they don't. . . . If you are not prepared to look realistically at the fact that rejection and disappointment are a huge part of this business, then don't go into it. And to fully realize that it will never end, no matter how successful or acclaimed you become.[17]

Employment statistics prove the absolute necessity of standing out from the crowd at auditions. According to the Actors' Equity Association (which represents professional stage actors) and the Screen Actors' Guild, more than 81 percent of all their members (70,000) earn less than $5,000 per year. Worse yet, more than 30,000 performers earn less than $1,000 per year. The big money—over $50,000 per year—is earned by fewer than 2,000 of the performers who comprise only 2.6 percent of the membership. TV commercials provide the performers with more than half of their income. According to union officials, about 85 percent of their members are unemployed on any given day of the year.

So, why go through it? Why choose such a career? Actors do it because they are addicted to the intoxicating thrill of being the only theatre artists who stand before live audiences and present the creations of not only their own imaginations, but the choices of *all* the other theatre artists as well.

Standing Publicly with Their Choices

After the character has been analyzed, the choices made, the appropriate skills engaged, the costume fitted, and the makeup applied, the actor must take the creation to the stage for presentation to the audience. In this final phase, the ultimate success of the artistic impersonation depends on infusing the performance with qualities as difficult to acquire as talent itself.

Stage Presence

Stage presence is the quality of commanding poise that the best actors bring to the stage. Actors who have it seem to fill the empty space with an exciting, even dangerous unpredictability that rivets the attention of everyone watching, while those with a less significant presence seem to fade into invisibility. Ask theatre people to define stage presence and they are usually at a loss for words: "It's intangible," they say. "It's that certain *je ne sais quoi* . . . you've either got it or you don't."

Still, examined closely, certain traits common to actors with great stage presence can be discerned. First, they seem to stand slightly off balance, holding their breaths perhaps moments longer than is normal. Second, their muscles appear tense with a kind of pent-up energy and passion fighting to be released. In fact, they are manipulating a kind of moment-to-moment suspense that grips the attention of an audience that is never sure how the held-back energy will release itself. What will they do next? What surprising choices will they make? Predictability kills stage presence. Energy, suspense, and passion are its essence.

Passion

Lope de Vega said it: All one needs to create theatre art are "four trestles, four boards, two actors, and a *passion.*"[18] The first three ingredients are in plentiful supply, but passion, some would say, is a rare artistic commodity in today's theatre.

It remains a reality of American life that publicly expressing real human passion is socially unfashionable. Not surprisingly, the same is true in the performing arts. We all have been influenced by television, which conditions us to value certain personality traits over others. A long list of media heroes from Madonna to David Letterman and Jerry Seinfeld are emulated because they seem to be "sophisticated," "strong," "witty," "aloof," "cool," and above all and in all things "together." What they definitely do not seem to be are "innocent," "vulnerable," "open," "childlike," "intense"—in a word, "emotional." Yet these are the very qualities most needed by actors. The willingness of an actor to publicly expose vulnerability and surrender to extreme passions—whether they be those of a violent rapist, an insane murderer, an enraged but powerless father, or a feverish young lover—is the only pathway to successful and compelling theatre art.

Risk

To throw the full weight of passion and emotional commitment behind all their choices takes courage and daring. Making choices that are both public and emotionally potent is risky business. There is no scientific formula for making successful choices, so actors understand that only by risking everything on a daring choice can they hope to succeed greatly. Such risks also imply they could fail greatly. And stage failure is never private. It is reported in all the media, often with an accompanying photograph.

One measure of the elusive nature of stage success can be seen in the number of superstitions observed by actors in their attempts to impose some reliable control on the volatility and unpredictability of live theatre. Among the most widely practiced are:

1. Never whistle in the dressing room.
2. Never wish an actor "good luck." It will jinx the entire performance.
3. Never utter the name of Shakespeare's play about the tragically ambitious highland king ("Mac - - - h") in the theatre. Refer only to the "Scottish play."
4. Ensure a good performance only by giving out negative encouragements such as "Break a leg!" or the French expletive *"Merde!"*

Another measure of the degree of public risk required of actors is the utter terror—the **stage fright**—that grips even the most seasoned actors as they wait in the wings for their first entrances. Paradoxically, most actors learn to value this rush of adrenaline-induced excitement as an essential part of getting them "up" for a show.

Great actors understand there is no virtue in making safe, timid, or mediocre choices. Such words are just artistic euphemisms for "boring." And the greatest sin you can commit in the theatre is to bore an audience.

Like all the great actors before him, Stanislavsky understood this principle, and he urged his students to the highest levels of daring in every exercise, rehearsal, and performance. As his students prepared to stand before him with their

PEANUTS® by Charles M. Schulz

PEANUTS reprinted by permission of UFS, Inc.

choices, he liked to take a seat in the dark recesses of the Moscow Art Theatre and, speaking in French for audiences everywhere, challenge his young actors to *"Etonnez-moi!"* It means "Astonish me!"

Design for Acting

Standing alone on stage does not mean, and never has meant, abandoned. Since the time of Aeschylus, most actors have had at least one other performer with whom to share the performance. Together they bring to the stage the combined choices of the playwright, producer, and director to which they add their own. More often than not, the actors stride "the boards" that are designed by visual artists who create inviting, evocative stage environments. And the actors are rarely naked; they play in special clothing, styled and tailor-made to the needs of their characters. These design elements can be powerful components of the theatrical imagination that enhance the performers' concentration and the audience's belief in the dramatic action.

 THE ACTOR AT WORK

Enchanting, Colorless, Glacial, Fearless, Sneaky, Seductive, Manipulative, Magical Meryl

by Brad Darrach
[Excerpted from *Life* magazine][19]

There is a standard joke in the theatre directed at those actors who claim that while they are on stage, they truly experience the exact emotions of the characters they are portraying. The punch line is: "Of course you do. But how about when you die?" Dying is the one obvious experience actors cannot be counted on to have stored in their emotional memories. Brad Darrach reports that the woman who is one of America's finest actors sought a way to add even death to her catalog of choices. Although she claims never to have read Stanislavsky, it is obvious that Streep's intensively imaginative

and systematic way of creating a character is genuine "method" acting.

Meryl Streep is gray with cold. In the film *Ironweed* she plays a ragged derelict who dies in a cheap hotel room, and for more than half an hour before the scene she has been hugging a huge bag of ice cubes in an agonizing effort to experience how it feels to be a corpse. Now the camera begins to turn. Jack Nicholson, her derelict lover, sobs and screams and shakes her body. But through take after take—and between takes too Meryl just lies there like an iced mackerel. Frightened, a member of the crew whispers to the director, Hector Babenco, "What's going on? She's not breathing!" Babenco gives a start. In Meryl's body there is absolutely no sign of life! He hesitates, then lets the scene proceed. Yet even after the shot is made and the set struck, Meryl continues to lie there, gray and still. Only after 10 minutes have passed does she slowly, slowly emerge from the coma-like state into which she has deliberately sunk. Babenco is amazed. "Now *that,*" he mutters in amazement, "is acting! *That* is an actress!"

That in fact may well be the most extravagantly creative actress now at work in a world that swarms with leading ladies of redoubtable talent. Vanessa Redgrave, Liv Ullmann, Jessica Lange, Kathleen Turner, Jane Fonda, Diane Keaton, Glenda Jackson, Hanna Schygulla, Sigourney Weaver, Sissy Spacek—each has stocked her résumé with brilliant performances. Yet none has assembled a gallery of portraits that displays the depth and power and finesse of Streep in her supreme interpretations: Joanna in *Kramer vs. Kramer,* Sarah in *The French Lieutenant's Woman,* Sophie in *Sophie's Choice,* Karen in *Silkwood,* Baroness Blixen in *Out of Africa*—and now Helen in *Ironweed.* . . . "Helen," says Nicholson, "is one of Meryl's greatest transformations. She's done something extreme but impeccable—and as good as it gets. This one is for history."

Like most things that rate such adjectives, Helen was not built in a day. Meryl constructed the character, as she constructs every character, pore by pore. "I have no Method, you know," she explains a little sheepishly. "I've never read Stanislavsky. I have a smattering of things I've learned from different teachers, but nothing I can put into a valise and open it up and say, 'Now which one would you like?' Nothing I can count on, and that makes it more dangerous. But then the danger makes it more exciting."

Danger was written all over Helen. In William Kennedy's 1983 novel she shuffled like a wounded roach through the streets of Depression-era Albany, N.Y., a thing of the gutter looking for a drain to die in—how could Meryl possibly make audiences care about such a dingy entity. She found a way. In a flash of intuition she heard a melody in Helen's life and instantly transformed it into a symbol. "My image for Helen," she says, "was the sign of the treble clef. It expressed for me her passion for music and her inner grace, and it gave the sad, drooping line of her body." Inspired by this resonating hieroglyph, Meryl imagined in acute detail Helen's hair, hands, feet, eyes, mouth, clothes, ways of moving, ways of speaking, how it felt to be in her body, what went on in her mind, how the world looked through her eyes. "These things trigger me," she says. "They help me to build up a being." Once the being was there, Meryl stepped into her skin and lived for hours at a time as if she really were Helen, wrung with her sorrow, fleeing through her nightmares, inhabited by her fate.

SUMMARY

1. Role playing—from the games of children to the careers of adults—is an instinctive, necessary human activity. Actors, as artistic role players, enjoy a valued position in society for their abilities to impersonate a great variety of intensely emotional characters in the most extreme circumstances.

2. The declamatory style of acting dominated the theatre for 2,400 years, having more in common with heightened oratory and flamboyant public speaking than with everyday discourse.

3. Legal, religious, and social restrictions prohibited women from acting for more than 2,000 years.

4. Throughout history actors have put forward two opposing views of how they should portray emotions. The traditional view holds that actors should feel nothing, but should portray only the outward physical signs of emotions. The opposite view holds that actors should give themselves over to the characters and rely on the inspiration of the moment to actually experience the emotions they must portray.

5. Naturalistic acting is necessary for the "slice-of-life" realism of late-nineteenth-century drama. Its goal is to create stage life that looks and sounds exactly like real life.

6. Konstantin Stanislavsky created a widely practiced, modern system for achieving the naturalistic total impersonation of the character by the actor.

7. The eclectic nature of modern theatre and drama with its many nonillusion-istic genres requires a variety of alternative acting styles including the experimental *avant-garde,* improvisation, clowning, transformations, and multicultural alternatives.

8. Without the specialized skills for playing the actor's instrument—namely the voice and body—the most brilliantly conceived theatrical choices will never see the light of the stage.

9. Most actors usually choose careers in which they play "personality" parts or "character" parts. To get these roles, all actors must learn the crucial skills of auditioning. A part of all auditions is the possibility of rejection.

10. Actors must ultimately rely on intangible talents such as stage presence, the instinct for passionate playing, and a willingness to take substantial risks in order to make acting choices that are at once original, memorable, and astonishing.

CHOICES

1. Imagine you have been cast in *Extremities* as either Raul or Marjorie. Since you probably have never experienced the terrible things they do to each other, how can you play the role convincingly? What choices could you make to prepare this role? What sort of research would you undertake? What skills do you personally need to acquire?

2. Cast *Extremities* with your friends or persons from your class. Justify your choices in terms of type and talent. Are the ones you picked "personality" or "character" actors?

3. Observe closely for at least a week the daily behavior of a friend, classmate, or teacher. Create and perform a five-minute artistic impersonation of the person of your choice. Do not do a mere caricature or impression, but try to act

the role with as much attention as possible to details of body, voice, clothes, mannerisms, and disposition.

4. With a partner, rehearse the performing technique for a romantic, intense stage kiss as described on page 311. Perform the resulting illusion, and solicit reviews from the audience as to whether the kiss was, at the least, believable.

The Hartford Stage Company production of A Midsummer Night's
Dream.

. . . can this cockpit hold the vasty fields of France?

King Henry the Fifth, *Prologue*

Pray you, undo this button . . .

King Lear, *Act V, scene iii*

Give me some light . . .

Hamlet, *Act III, scene ii*

. . . and let the sounds of music creep in our ears.

The Merchant of Venice, *Act V, scene i*

CHAPTER 9

Sights and Sounds

THE DESIGNERS' CHOICES

PREVIEW

Setting the Stage

Suggestion vs. Illusion: A Brief History of Theatrical Design

Scenic Choices: The Imagination and Skills of the Set Designer

Costume Choices: The Imagination and Skills of the Costume Designer

Lighting Choices: The Imagination and Skills of the Lighting Designer

Noises Off: The High and Low Technology of Sound Design

Design Unity

Previewing Part 4

The Designer at Work

His name is Whitney White, but his friends call him "Whiz." He is a scene designer by trade. When he talks about his art, he speaks in a fervent mix of metaphors that are at once dramaturgical, theatrical, technological, and metaphysical. His is an imagination overflowing with visual choices. Consider his description of the way in which he imagined and created the scenery for a production of *Salem's Daughters,* a play about the New England witch-hunts of the seventeenth century:

> This is a play with an attitude. It's about the nightmarish imaginations of children overloading on witch stories. It's got these 23 scenes that keep alternating between interior and exterior settings, and between stark realities and brutal psychotic fantasies. It was originally written to be done outdoors in a park at night—trees, rocks, shadows, moonlight—the usual witch stuff. I had to put it into a theatre. And I don't like clichés.
>
> My first concept was a gigantic tree that revolved on an off-center pivot—a big, hulking, ominous, enveloping arboreal mass. Everybody liked it. But then I had a dream. I realized this is not a play about a tree, it's about people. You can never diminish the role of a person in the stage picture.
>
> So I thought, "How do I get the audience in a scary mode from the beginning, take them back in time, yet make a contemporary point?" Since the director decided the props and costumes should be very real and authentic, I figured I could go very *unreal* with the set and lights.
>
> I was in a rock-and-roll mood, so I got this incredible, fabulous idea of using a big floating platform attached to four rock-and-roll motors—you know, those one-ton electric chain hoists. I mean, these things are incredible; in full view of the audience they can go from flat-horizontal to completely vertical, and to any angled rake in between! This was a set that could warp, rise, fall, crash, and rip! That's how you stage a nightmare.
>
> And get this—I attached yards of erosion cloth to the bottom of the platform, and underneath them I mounted 60 MR-16's, which are these fabulous high intensity 12-volt lamps that when you run them in a series of 10, don't need any transformers! Well, anyway, they shoot these incredible beams of light up from the floor, and . . .
>
> The effect was like we ripped up the earth right from under the feet of the characters.
>
> It worked. The reviewers went nuts. The audience applauded—the scenery![1]

The actors, of course, took the bows. Whiz and those who helped him create and operate his ingenious spectacle remained backstage, out of sight. Like all theatre designers they understand the prime directive of the other, more well-known "Wiz," the exposed charlatan at the end of the 1939 film, *The Wizard of Oz:* "Pay no attention," he commands Dorothy and her companions, "to the man behind the curtain."

This chapter looks behind the curtain at the women and men who imagine and create the stage environment that facilitates the playing out of dramatic action before live audiences. The ongoing debate over the appropriate functions of stage spectacle is analyzed in historical and modern contexts. Separate sections examine the methods of the scenery, costume, lighting, and sound designers.

Setting the Stage

Before a play becomes sights and sounds on stage, it was words on the play-wright's page, then a concept in the director's mind. The designers translated the concept into visual images, first rendered in crude sketches, which were trans-formed into painted renderings or perhaps scale models. From these, technical drawings, plans, and patterns were drafted. Finally, with the aid of skilled techni-cians, the designs were built, assembled, painted, hung, cabled, focused, colored, programmed, cut, sewn, fitted, altered, accessorized, composed, synthesized, and recorded into a visual and aural display that actors could appear in, wear, hear, and play upon. The required combination of time-art sensibilities and space-art skills constitutes the **designers' imaginations.**

Aesthetic Goals

Theatre artists make choices—theatrical suggestions—that prompt the audience to understand and accept the imaginary context of the play. After the auditory clues of preshow music, the first theatrical suggestions of a performance are vi-sual choices—light, scenery, and costumed actors that **set the stage** in the sense they "set up" the context for what will follow. Through their choices, theatrical designers suggest essential aspects of location, style, genre, time period, charac-ter traits, and interpretive ideas. Scenery, lighting, costume, and sound designers create the audiovisual context that joins the concrete reality of the stage space with the kinesthetic choices of the director and the histrionic impersonations of the actors. French set designer Denis Bablet describes the fundamental goal of his creations as the "interplay of line, color, objects, and lighting effects [that] pro-duces in the public a *visual* emotion which is in harmony with its auditory emo-tions and which strengthens it."[2] The question for theatre artists has always been just how much of the stage space must be filled with their creations in order to prompt an audience to experience appropriate "visual emotion": a minimum of suggestive visual elements, or a stage space arranged with all of the details of a complete, illusionistic portrayal of reality?

Suggestion vs. Illusion: A Brief History of Theatrical Design

The Art of Theatrical Suggestion

From the time of the first Greek plays in the sixth century B.C. to the development of indoor theatres in the sixteenth century, stages were set almost entirely by sug-gestion rather than illusion. During this 2,000-year period, the resources of the theatre were invested primarily in the actors. The entire production, therefore, was designed to display their histrionic art. Playwrights relied on actors to speak lines that suggested location, time, and atmospherics. In effect, the audience had to *hear,* rather than see, where a play was set. For example, in the second line of *Romeo and Juliet,* the character called Chorus refers to "fair Verona, where we lay our scene." The title of *Hamlet, Prince of Denmark* declares the country in which the dramatic action is set, and the opening lines of the first scene of the famous tragedy tell the audience the time of day and the weather:

BERNARDO: Tis now struck twelve; get thee to bed, Francisco.
FRANCISCO: For this relief much thanks; 'tis bitter cold . . .

For the theatregoers at the Globe, such verbal suggestion was sufficient to set the stage. By contrast, modern audiences assume for *Hamlet* at the least a cold-hued, dimly lit, heavily shadowed, foreboding stage. At the most, a stage construction that appears to be the high escarpments of a medieval Danish castle would not be an unreasonable expectation.

Auditory theatrical suggestion has always relied on the art of the actor and the resulting strong imaginative participation of the audience to overcome what the spectators do not see. *Designing* the light was, quite naturally, impossible in open-air theatres like the ones used in ancient Greece, Rome, and medieval Europe and Asia where performances took place in the full light of day. The darkness of night had to be declared by a character perhaps appearing with a lantern or candle. It was left to the imagination of the audience to accept such suggestions and envision something other than sunlight. The dialogue could even suggest the most delicate, romantic atmospheric effects as in the tender scene in Act V of *The Merchant of Venice* when Lorenzo "paints" a most exquisite setting for his beloved Jessica:

> How sweet the moonlight sleeps upon this bank!
> Here we will sit, and let the sounds of music
> Creep in our ears: soft stillness and the night
> Become the touches of sweet harmony.
> Sit, Jessica: look, how the floor of heaven
> Is thick inlaid with patines of bright gold:

Keep in mind: this was originally acted in the sunlight of a bustling summer day in London. To stage this scene today, lighting designers would be called on to set the stage with a beautiful shaft of moonlight that bathes the reclining lovers in the fading light of evening.

Since actors had the major responsibility for suggesting the settings, visual clues were mostly generic and occasionally symbolic. The architecture of outdoor theatres included permanent **facades** that served as generalized backgrounds for entrances and exits. The acting area of ancient Greek theatres was backed by a **skene,** or scene house that suggested the palace or temple before which most Greek tragedies are set. The scene house most probably had a large central doorway and smaller doors on either side, allowing the actors to suggest they were moving between different environments. The roof of the scene house was used to suggest remote places and the dwelling of the gods. The facades of Roman the-atres were made up of an ornate series of doorways and arches, suggesting multiple dwellings along the street locations where the popular comedies were set. Medieval European stages displayed a line of small **mansions** suggesting the continuum of the universe with those on the left (stage right) locating heaven (God's ornate throne) to a king's palace (a less ornate throne), humble earthly abodes, and finally, at the extreme right (stage left), the gigantic open jaws of a demon—the **hell mouth**—meant to depict the horrors of eternal damnation (see color plate 16). The facades of Renaissance theatres were comparatively simple with doors and balconies that could, with verbal suggestion, become any interior or exterior needed. (See photograph, Chapter 6, p. 230.) The insides of such scene buildings and mansions were convenient places for changing costumes and storing set pieces and properties.

Symbolic visual elements included small set pieces and properties that could be easily and quickly carried on or off, such as shields and spears to indicate an army camp, a tree to suggest a forest, or a rock to locate a cliff or seashore. In

GREEK THEATRE   *In this performance of a tragedy in the reconstructed ancient Greek theatre at Epidaurus, the* **orchestra,** *or circular acting area is bare; the skene provides a generalized background. The architectural emphasis is clearly on the human beings and the struggle with social forces far greater than the physical environment.*

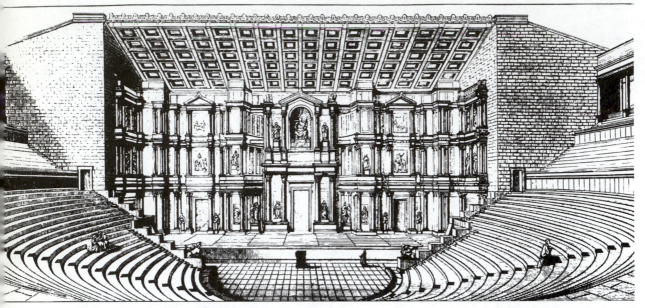

ROMAN THEATRE   *The Roman theatre, such as this one in Orange, France, featured a neutral scene house in front of which actors performed on a high bare stage. Location was* suggested *by the various doors in the facade (called the* **scaenae frons***) of the scene house.*

Asian theatrical traditions, actors often used hand props to create "scenic" effects symbolically. The stately Noh dramas, which flourished from the fifteenth to the eighteenth centuries, followed the Japanese principle that finds beauty in the absence of everything unnecessary. Accordingly, Noh dramas were set on conventionalized stages with a templelike roof supported by four pillars and a symbolic background; there was no other scenery. Actors used the pillars for conventionalized locations and symbolic fan movements set to music to suggest such effects as the rising moon, rippling water, falling rain, or the blowing wind.

The facades and set pieces of these classical theatres were never main features of a theatrical performance. They were backgrounds at best. All of the outdoor theatres—Greek, Roman, European, or Asian—were built around large unadorned acting areas surrounded on at least three sides by spectators. Actors, not scenery, occupied the playing space—transforming it through their art as the playwrights wished.

The Visual Splendor of Costumes.   The most important source of visual splendor on the scenery-bare stages of the actors' theatres were the costumes. Leading actors always chose and paid for their own costumes, often investing substantial sums in dazzling wardrobes. Like modern pop-music performers, the emphasis was on choosing costumes for their form-enhancing resplendence, rather than as accurate

JAPANESE NOH THEATRE   *A modern Noh stage, bare of scenery except for the symbolic backdrop. To enhance the spectacle created by the costumes, gold-leafed paper strips were woven into the cloth that shimmered in the light of the open-air theatres. During performances, folded around moving actors, they created patterns of light on stage.*

reflections of characterization or historical period. In fact, in medieval Europe and Renaissance England, all characters, regardless of the time period of the play's action, wore dressy, often opulent contemporary clothing. For instance, in medieval cycle plays, any character with theological significance (such as God, angels, saints, or ancient Hebrews) wore Roman Catholic priestly vestments. The suggestion, not the illusion, of holy characters was sufficient. The splendor and colors of the moving actors themselves created the spectacle.

IMAGES OF THE WORLD
*Perhaps more than any other
playwright, Shakespeare relied
on the imaginative changeability
of his theatre's bare stage to set
his dramas in a dizzying series
of "global" locations. In fact,
Shakespeare's visual
imagination far exceeded the
capacity of any theatre to depict
it. The third act of* Antony and
Cleopatra *calls for thirteen
scenes in nine different locations
on three different continents. If
full-scale scenery were used for
each of these locations,
Shakespeare would have
bankrupted his theatre company
by the sheer tonnage and labor
needed to build and change it. In
this production of the play at
Stratford-on-Avon's Royal
Shakespeare Theatre, Cleopatra's
palace in Alexandria is suggested
by her ornate throne and royal
garments.*

The Magic of Scenic Illusion

For the better part of 2,000 years, theatrical playing space was inseparable from architecture. It was impossible to talk of theatrical design as if it were like any other work of visual art that could be independently analyzed by its qualities of form, beauty, and craft. Whereas the outdoor theatres of classical Greece and Rome, medieval Europe, Asia, and Elizabethan England provided architectural spaces devoted to the vocal and physical expressiveness of the performers, the new indoor theatres of the Italian Renaissance were the sources of possibilities for visual decor. An art of illusionistic scene design emerged in which very little spectacle was left to the imaginations of the spectators.

The Magic of Perspective Drawing.   Invented by Italian architects in the fifteenth century, **perspective drawing** is a graphic technique for creating the illusion of three-dimensional space by showing the spatial relations of objects as they actually appear to the eye. When drawn in perspective, objects and structures in the foreground are larger than those in the background. In the distance, objects seem to diminish progressively in size as they fade toward **vanishing points.** It is difficult to appreciate the almost magical effect of painted perspective on the Renaissance mind. More than any other factor, painted perspective demonstrated the potential for creating complete pictorial illusions of a single location in its entirety.

PERSPECTIVE SCENERY   *Early **linear** or **single-point perspective** setting designed by Ludovico Burnacini in 1662. Note the receding vista that angles in and up toward the distant vanishing point. The proscenium arch frames the design, giving reference points to the stage picture. The scenery is behind this arch and forms a background in front of which the actors performed. Unlike earlier practice, the visual emphasis is not just on the actor, but also on the illusion created by the scenic designer.*

The techniques were soon adapted to the horizontal stages of the new indoor theatres: the receding walls of exterior and interior edifices were painted on flat surfaces called **wings** that diminished in size and spacing as they were arranged on a **raked stage** that angled up toward the back of the theatre, away from the audience. A framing device called a **proscenium arch** was used to set boundaries on the perspective, hide stage machinery, and focus the eyes of the audience on the stage picture. The first theatre with a permanent proscenium arch was the **Teatro Farnese** built in 1618 in Parma, Italy. Performers played in front or **downstage** of the scenery, since to stand **upstage** (farther away, which was progressively higher because of the rake) would destroy the perspective illusion; the actors would appear to be taller than the scenery.

Illusionistic scenic creations in perspective could not be fashioned by dramatic language or by the interpretive skills of the actors. Trained scenic artists, ample dedicated stage space, numerous technicians, and substantial financial investment were required. By the sixteenth century, architects published manuals that explained the techniques of the new art of scene design. By the seventeenth century, professional full-time scene designers were in demand to set the stages of indoor theatres throughout Europe. Realistic scenic effects were all the rage.

The Rage for Realism

The importance of the change from visual suggestion to visual illusion cannot be overemphasized. It was one of the most important theatrical developments in the last 500 years. Once exposed to the magic of scenic illusion, audiences had little use for the former suggestive conventions of theatre art. It was similar to the way in which twentieth-century audiences rejected black-and-white films and television when the color versions became available.

What took place was a shift in the imaginative requirements placed on the artists and audience alike. On classical stages anything added to the fixed facade merely suggested a place; its actualization took place in the imagination of the audience. With the adoption of perspective scenery, locations began to be *represented* as they would actually appear. Thus the art object shifted from the imagination of the spectator to the skills of the new visual artist, the scenic designer. By the nineteenth century the term *realism* became part of the theatrical vocabulary to describe the artistic style based on the illusions of the scenic artists.

Technological evolution is the inevitable result of technological revolution. As theatregoers demanded more convincing "realistic" scenic illusions, designers invented new methods for improving their stage pictures. The changes affected theatre practice in every area from architecture to playwriting.

Theatre Architecture.   The new commitment to visual representation required theatres built to feature the new stage illusion. Huge indoor theatres seating in excess of 3,000 were built in England, Europe, and America by the end of the eighteenth century. While the actor was diminished in the overall stage picture, the scenery was in full display. As the size of stages grew, the available acting area shrank as it was taken up with more and more scenery.

PLATE 15. A MODERN METAPHOR FOR AN ANCIENT PLAY   *In both time and space Indiana University's proscenium stage is far from the Theatre of Dionysus where* The Trojan Women, *Euripides' tragedy depicting the suffering of innocent victims in the aftermath of a bloody war, premiered 2500 years ago. Designer Frank Silberstein used a modern metaphor to make the play's universality speak clearly to his 20th-century audience: "The design concept was derived from the principal theme of the script—the horrors of war and by extension the fact that throughout history mankind has seemingly been sucked inevitably into these catastrophic events as into a whirlpool. Thus it was we settled on the visual image of a vortex—a receding series of blasted rings that drew the eye of the beholder and, by inference, mankind into a black hole. Some of the audience reactions were gratifyingly responsive. Some saw it as reminiscent of a burned out World War II bomber, while others saw it as a gigantic spider's web. Both of these responses are appropriate."[1]*

PLATE 16. SUGGESTING THE UNIVERSE   *A medieval stage used for a French passion play in the sixteenth century. The heaven mansion is at left, and the hell mouth is at the right. Because the people observing these biblical plays had such strong imaginative connections with the realities of heaven and hell, the suggestive scenery simply unlocked what already existed in their own minds.*

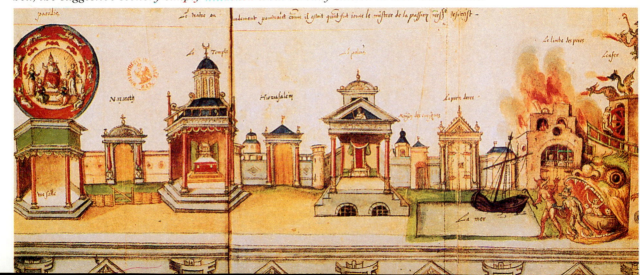

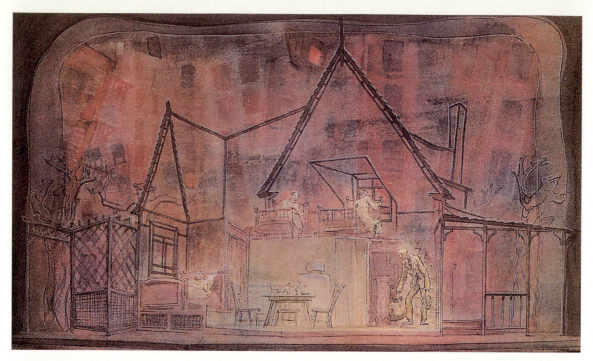

PLATES 17–18. MODIFIED REALISM *Jo Mielziner's set design for the original production of* Death of a Salesman *illustrates the conventions and the flexibility of modified realism. The skeletal walls, projections, and lighting effects permit scenes to fade and bleed from one to another as they might occur within Willy Loman's mind. The scene at the top shows the intrusion of a dreary urban landscape; the scene below it, accomplished by the slow fade of a lighting effect, regresses to an earlier time of youth and optimism. The realistic furnishings such as the table, refrigerator, and beds establish the illusionistic contexts for the play, indicating specific aspects of time, place, and social class.*

PLATES 19–20.   VISUAL IMAGES OF TRAGEDY IN THE HIMALAYAS   K2, *Patrick Meyers' harrowing drama of climbers stranded on the world's second highest mountain as imagined by two different designers: (Left) Ming Cho Lee envisioned a towering (55-foot), realistic crystal precipice for the production at Washington's Arena Stage. (Right) For the smaller space and smaller budget of the Syracuse Stage, Charles Cosler created a totally abstract rendering of the setting with steel and fiberglass to suggest a frozen existential desolation.*

PLATE 21.   DESIGN METAPHOR   *The arrival of Air Force One in the opening scene of John Adams and Alice Goodman's* Nixon in China. *Designed by Adrianne Lobel. Directed by Peter Sellars.*

PLATE 22.   RENT: A MUSICAL FOR THE '90s   *Jonathan Larson's* Rent *moved uptown in 1996 to take over Broadway. Inspired by Puccini's* La Bohème, *Larson transformed the opera's end-of-the-19th-century Paris Bohemians into turn-of-the-20th-century struggling artists of New York's multicultural East Village. * Rent *is not about scenery: This concept musical relies on a cast of exuberant, talented unknowns performing a fusion of popular forms including rock, reggae, salsa, gospel, and tango. * Rent *won the Pulitzer Prize for drama and four Tony awards including Best Musical.*

PLATES 23–24.   APOCALYPTIC LANDSCAPE   *J. B. Priestley's 1946 mystery drama,* An Inspector Calls, *is about a police inspector who interrupts the dinner of an upper-middle-class family to apprise them of their individual complicity in the death of a young woman. In reimagining this typical "drawing-room" drama, designer Ian MacNeil and director Stephen Daldry made two fundamental changes: whereas Priestley set his play in the England of 1912, they placed it in an indeterminate postapocalyptic wasteland of rain-swept ruins, above which rises the family's house perched precariously on stilts. They also decided the inspector would never enter the house, but rather call the family members outside one by one. As their world becomes progressively undone, the house itself collapses, tips forward, and spills its contents onto the cobblestone street.*

PLATE 25.   A CINEMATIC ERA ONSTAGE   *Andrew Lloyd Webber's* Sunset Boulevard *is a musical stage version of Billy Wilder's classic 1950 film about the psychotically narcissistic silent-film star Nora Desmond who has been long forgotten by her public. The script consists of 22 scenes requiring 15 different settings, including swimming pools, offices, gloomy garages, Schwab's drugstore, and a Cecil B. DeMille studio. The centerpiece of the design is Nora's opulent residence, which the script describes as "a preposterous Hollywood mansion." Set designer John Napier (who also designed scenery for* Cats, Starlight Express, Les Misérables, *and* Miss Saigon*) created an immense, ornate drawing room of a 1930s Hollywood mansion that is reminiscent of old baroque-style movie palaces. He enhanced the play's dark atmosphere by creating eerie recesses in elaborately carved panels, adorned columns, a pipe organ, and an imposing curved staircase, all covered in gilt. The size and sweep of the staircase, Napier explains, were inspired by Desmond's line, "I am big. It's the pictures that got small."*[1]

PLATE 26.   COSTUME RENDERINGS   *Maria Bjornson's rendering for the male singers in the "Hannibal scene" from the Broadway production of* The Phantom of the Opera. *Designers prepare such color renderings of each character in the play to demonstrate to the director that clothing choices are consistent with the overall production concept. Fabric swatches attached to the renderings are samples of the actual materials to be used. Bjornson's handwritten notes identify specific costume pieces and quick-change requirements.*

PLATES 29–31.   PAINTING WITH LIGHT   *For a production of Chekhov's* The Seagull, *scenic and lighting designer William J. Langley, Jr., used dramatic changes in the colors, intensity, direction, and focus of the lights to create evocative atmospheric effects that literally change the setting. Notice how the first photograph shows the set under work lights as flat and lifeless.*

PLATE 27.   HIGH-TECH THEATRICAL MAGIC   *The gondola scene as designed by Maria Bjornson for the Broadway production of* The Phantom of the Opera.

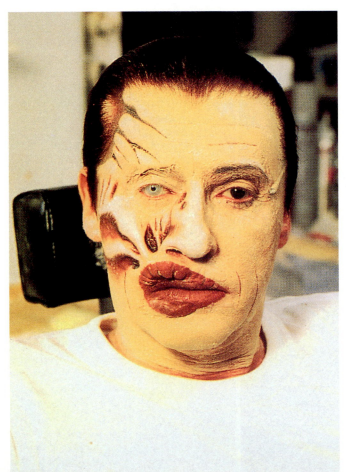

PLATE 28.   MAKEUP DESIGN   *Makeup design has been a natural extension of costume design ever since actors discarded the painted masks of the ancient Greek and Roman theatres in favor of painted faces. The makeup designed to transform actor Michael Crawford into the hideous* Phantom of the Opera *demands more than traditional greasepaint. Requirements include latex foam prosthetics, one white and one dark blue contact lens, a plastic bald pate, two wigs, and a wireless radio microphone attached near his eye. The application procedure takes about two hours.*

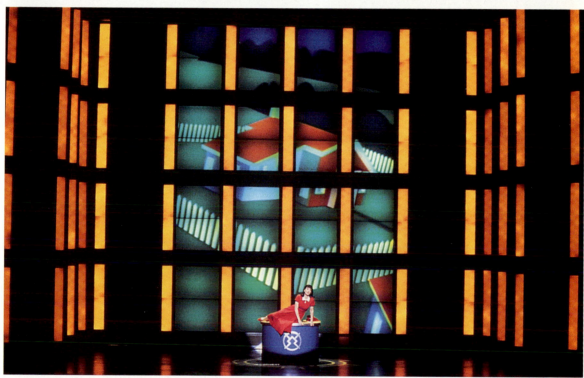

PLATES 32.   VIRTUAL SCENERY   *The computer-controlled video wall was used as a digitized background for the 1995 Broadway revival of* How to Succeed in Business Without Really Trying, *a musical comedy satire about a mail-room clerk who climbs to the top of the corporate ladder. The bank of thirty-two large-screen monitors was arranged to suggest the windows of a glass and steel skyscraper. With images recorded on a laser disk, the virtual scenery could be changed instantaneously: from a basement mail room with the screens revealing hundreds of slots for holding letters to a plaza-level lobby to the Manhattan skyline from the upper floors. When one character sings an ode to domesticity called "Happy to Keep His Dinner Warm," the wall becomes the visual embodiment of her fantasies, as the view zooms over Manhattan and lands on her suburban house (shown above). During the "Coffee Break" number, the caffeine-addicted chorus watches in agony as a blimp passes by bearing an ad for Eight O'Clock Coffee. Scenic designer John Arnone believes the fusion of recorded and live scenic techniques is inevitable: "Video is an important part of our lives. We were raised on it. It's your vocabulary as a child and adolescent. You have to go back and see it as a raw tool for communication. And that's exactly what the theatre is, in its most primal, mythical, tribal sense. To me, any resistance to any sort of new idea is a quick trip to the graveyard."[1] Directed by Des MCanuff, video wall by Multi-Image Systems, Inc., with installation and programming by Scharff Weisberg.*

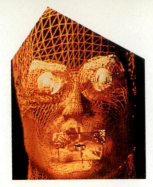

PLATE 33. SYNTHESPIANS *Experts predict that within a few years they will be able to create computer-generated actors who will look so real, you will not be able to tell the difference between the graphic images and human actors. In film and television, recognizing what is real and what is computerized will become more complex. Not only could new film and television stars be manufactured, but dead human stars might be "resurrected" and counterfeits of living personalities could be created as well. There are those who are even predicting the invasion of the legitimate theatre by these digital performers. "Coming soon," says computer scientist Raymond Kurzweil, are "artificial people . . . life-size, three-dimensional images . . . indistinguishable from real people. Such spectral citizens might become actors in a computerized drama or musical ('I Got Algorithm') or act as teachers, entertainers, and companions."[1]*

PLATE 34. DRESS THE STAGE *The ability to "see" a play while reading a script is one of the most important aspects of the theatrical imagination. The artistic choices of the director, actors, scene designer, costume designer, and lighting designer combine to dress the bare boards of the Oregon Shakespearean Festival's Angus Bowmer Theatre for a production of Shakespeare's* The Two Gentlemen of Verona.

The development of the proscenium arch began an architectural trend that has continued to the present day. Of all the existing theatres in the Western world, by far the most common type features a proscenium stage with the audience arranged for a single-sided, straight-on view. The proscenium not only serves as an ideal framing structure for stage pictures, it is also an ideal masking device for stage machinery and additional scenery placed above, below, and off to the sides of the stage.

CUTAWAY VIEW OF COVENT GARDEN THEATRE IN 1824   *This nineteenth-century theatre is typical of the large structures built to accommodate great, realistic scenic spectacles. Note the enormous spaces above, below, behind, and to the sides of the stage for storing and shifting multiple sets and operating complex mechanical machinery. Note also the grooves cut into the stage floor for shifting the perspective-painted flat wings. The acting area is the relatively small section of the stage in front of (or "downstage" of) the grooves.*

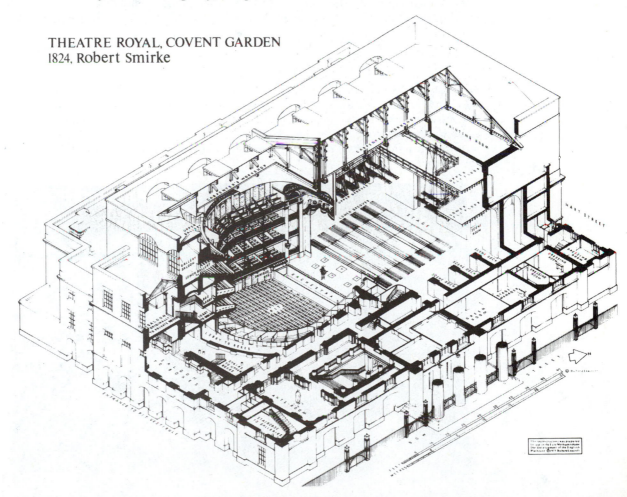

THEATRE ROYAL, COVENT GARDEN
1824, Robert Smirke

Theatre Technology.   Illusion in the theatre depends on technological devices and tricks. Among the earliest innovations in theatre technology were shifting mechanisms for depicting more than one locale in a production. Designers invented complex systems of ropes, pulleys, and counterweights to shift and manipulate painted flat wings, flying pieces, wagons, substages, elevators, and lifts. In the nineteenth century, scenery underwent another transformation as painted details were replaced by three-dimensional decorations and forced perspective was abandoned in favor of **free plantation** (in which the stage floor was leveled and scenery was placed as needed across the stage) and the **box set** (in which wings were replaced by enclosed walls and ceilings). All of these innovations and devices are still in use today.

Historical Accuracy.   The discovery of the ruined cities of Pompeii and Herculaneum in 1747 set off a craze for depicting historical and geographical accuracy in scenery and costumes. People worldwide developed new interests in learning about and *seeing* other lands, cultures, and historical periods. Playwrights and theatre designers met their needs. In Paris, for instance, one of the most popular plays of the eighteenth century was Voltaire's *The Orphan of China*, a melodrama that purported to depict Chinese architecture, customs, and dress. By the middle of the nineteenth century, historical accuracy in costumes and scenery was the

BOX-SET NATURALISM   *The naturalistic plays, with their central concern for the effects of heredity and environment, also depended on the skills of the scenic artist. The naturalists wanted to create the illusion of a "slice of life"—not spectacles of earth-shaking catastrophe. In this 1902 production of Emile Zola's* The Earth, *the naturalistic details adorn the scenery, costumes, lighting, and properties (including live chickens).*

norm as designers used their art to create a veritable travelogue of scenes that took theatregoers from Asia to Africa to the American frontier.

Lighting.   Lighting evolved from the dim, flickering, hazardous candelabra of the seventeenth century to safer, more controllable, brighter oil lamps in the eighteenth century. In the nineteenth century gas lighting made more complete control possible, and such inventions as the gas-fired **limelight** and the electric-powered **carbon arc** produced beam-generating spotlights making illusionistic moonlight and sunlight effects possible. By the end of the nineteenth century, electric incandescent lighting made darkening the auditorium as well as variable control of the color and intensity of the stage illumination possible.

Reallocated Finances.   Scene design added new expense to theatrical productions; resources were reallocated to scene designers and away from actors. To recoup investments required for multiple realistic settings, managers looked for plays that they could "run" for many consecutive performances.

New Drama.   Among the most popular of the new spectacle-intensive plays were melodramas that depended on creating spine-tingling suspense through the use of shocking, realistic visual effects such as shipwrecks, storms, earthquakes, avalanches, forest fires, and horse races. (The chariot race in *Ben Hur* was a perennial favorite.) The theatre technology invented to produce the illusions for these

HORSE RACE AT UNION SQUARE THEATRE, 1889   *By combining a moving panorama, treadmills powered by electric motors, and live animals, scene designers and technicians created the illusion of a full-speed horse race at New York's Union Square Theatre in 1889. The theatrical illusion, however, pales in comparison to the location effects of horse races, stampedes, and chases in films.*

special effects was almost entirely mechanical, incorporating ever more complex systems of ropes, counterweights, pulleys, treadmills, and scrolling background vistas called **moving panoramas.**

The legacy of pictorial realism remains with us today and retains a strong hold on the imaginations of spectators. We are so visually oriented that we now refer to going to *see* a play, not to *hear* one. Likewise, today we *watch* the news and even *watch* some music.

Cinematic Illusion

Large-scale realistic theatrical illusion was dealt its first serious setback at the end of the nineteenth century. Ironically, the setback resulted from a new invention that altered the visual imaginations of audiences and artists alike—just as the introduction of perspective had done 400 years before. Cinema was the "magic lantern" that could record and project changing panoramic pictorial illusion more convincingly than even the largest, best equipped theatres. For a time it seemed the movies might eventually replace live theatre because of film's superior ability to depict changing visual images. Because film "cuts" instantly to different "locations," no time for scene changes is required. Film technology allows the epic sweep of Shakespearean drama and the illusions of the best pictorial realism. Almost overnight, theatre artists were forced to reevaluate the conventions of scenery, costumes, and lighting. Theatre had to adjust once again to new artistic realities.

The Retheatricalization of the Theatre

The first theatre artists to call for a return to suggestive conventions of scenic decor were designers. **Adolph Appia** (1862–1928) and **Edward Gordon Craig** (1872–1966), working independently, maintained that theatrical spectacle should not be employed to "lie" through illusions. Rather, designers should rely on the evocative effects of three-dimensional, *nonrepresentational* scenery. Steps, ramps, platforms, and soaring vertical shapes should all be tied together with strong atmospheric lighting to create powerful visual images and emotions. A return to its suggestive roots—the "retheatricalization of the theatre," as Craig called it—would remove theatre from competition with the cinema and refocus the theatrical imagination on dramatic action. Appia and Craig pursued limited careers as designers, but the influence of their ideas on the imaginations of modern designers has been great.

Modern Nonrealistic Scenic Conventions.   In the twentieth century new perceptions of reality reinforced the trend toward nonrealism in theatrical design. Albert Einstein demonstrated new relationships between time and space that were not limited to a single fixed observer at one moment in time. Visual concepts such as *simultaneity* (the depiction of two or more events occurring at the same time)

RETHEATRICALIZATION   *Czech designer Josef Svoboda's set for the National Theatre of Prague's production of Sophocles'* Oedipus Rex *shows the influence of Appia and Craig. There are no representative details of illusionistic setting. The design is completely suggestive, yet very different from the ancient Greek* skene *facade; the set creates a strong sense of the protagonist's tragic fall from greatness and power.*

and *juxtaposition* (contrasting images displayed in contiguous space) of objects and events proceed from Einstein's new realities. Sigmund Freud found reality in dreams and other symbols of the subconscious and unconscious. As the environment of plays shifted from the social to the psychological, the visual requirements changed from the literal depictions of observable phenomena to the symbolic, metaphorical, and fluid processes of the human mind. Scenic depictions of these nonrealistic environments range from completely symbolic settings to those incorporating both suggestive and illusionistic elements that allow for the visual transformation of one mental state to another, from memory to fantasy, and from

SURREALISTIC SETTING   *Josef Svoboda's setting for* The Insect Comedy, *a satire on the horrors of regimentation by Karel and Josef Capek, suggests a nightmare world as seen from the faceted eyes of a bug. The sharp, angular lines create a sense of conflict and crisis. Note the way in which the actors on the stage floor are reflected in the facets above.*

one time frame to another. **Modified realism** is the popular visual style that permits such a combination of suggestive and illusionistic effects (see color plates 17 and 18). Typical features include skeletal or cutaway see-through walls, selective, highly focused lighting, and projections mixed with realistic scenic pieces and furnishings.

Modern Design Choices

Scene designers of the past imagined theatrical spectacle from one frame of reference for all plays, but contemporary design choices reflect the eclectic views of today's theatre. Designers choose from a large diverse menu of styles and playing spaces in which to envision their productions: from actor-rendered total suggestion to the illusionistic details of complete realism; from nonrealistic depictions to designs that require little suspension of disbelief to recognize reality; from very sparse scenic decor like that called for by Beckett's *Waiting for Godot* (a small tree), Uhry's *Driving Miss Daisy* (two stools and a chair), or *A Chorus Line* (a white line and a back wall of mirrors) to the immense spectacle requirements of so-called industrialized, techno-pop extravaganzas like *Miss Saigon* (in which a helicopter must appear to land on stage in full view) or *Starlight Express* (50 tons of scenery engineered from space-age materials, 11,350 lights, 22 miles of fiber optics, and laser beams, all controlled by six computer systems). Modern designers must be able to imagine and create it all.

Scenic Choices: The Imagination and Skills of the Set Designer

Theatrical designers must imagine and create within certain limits imposed by the productions' predetermined choices—the "given circumstances." Beginning with printed words on a page and a production concept from the director, the scenic designer transforms empty space into a usable environment that fulfills what the playwright and the director have only suggested.

Specifically, the designer's choices must accommodate the playwright's needs for locations, time, and exits and entrances, the director's choices for staging and style, and the performers' needs for a safe "machine for acting." The production must also stay within the producer's budget and fit within the space and technological capabilities of the theatre and its staff.

The Design Elements

Just as a dramatist crafts a play from the dramatic elements of plot, character, thought, diction, melody, and spectacle, the scene designer shapes and mixes visual elements to create the stage environment:

> *Line: The silhouette made by the scenery and action on the stage which projects emotional values that enhance mood and dramatic action.* Sharp angular lines create a sense of conflict, crisis, and suspense; graceful, smooth, curving lines and shapes generate feelings of warmth, romance, and serenity. Mielziner's skeletal outline of the set for *Death of a Salesman* (color plates 17 and 18) clearly demonstrates the ethereal effect of line.

> *Mass: The overall bulk or weight of the scenery on the stage.* High towering pillars may communicate the power and majesty of a king while a single tree on an otherwise bare stage might suggest alienation or despair. On the other hand, the large mass of Air Force One (color plate 21) tends to dwarf the actors on the stage.

> *Color: The traditional palette of hues from which visual artists choose.* The live theatre has always thrived on the colors of its spectacle. "Black and white" has never

been a limitation or much of a choice. As a consequence, colors in set design—as in life—are associated with everything from emotions (red with anger, green with envy), to gender, to food flavors. (Why else "artificial colors"?) Yellow candle flames against blue mist set the atmosphere of foreboding in *The Phantom of the Opera* (color plate 27).

Texture: The look and feel of the surfaces of the stage scenery. An interior covered with rough, dirty, peeling wallpaper and plaster contrasts sharply with a room of dark polished oak walls, bookcases, and brass fixtures. Sharp, complex, craggy, shadowed ice is represented efficiently in two versions of a mountain in *K2* (color plates 19 and 20).

Space: The area defined by stage structures and boundaries in which line, mass, color, and texture are arranged. Scene designer Thomas Leff describes stage design as concentrating on the arrangement of the space *between* the objects and not exclusively on the objects themselves. A performer's life in space is the only source for a space's expressive value. Therefore, stage space must be designed to shape and channel direct movement. "In all cases," explains Leff, "if action is to be considered the life and soul of the drama, and the performer is the bearer of this dramatic content, then space will be its measure, a visual index against which the action is perceived."[3] Notice how the figures fill the space on an open design of *The Two Gentlemen of Verona* (see color plate 34).

Composition: The balance achieved by the scenic elements arranged on stage. A perfectly symmetrical stage setting reinforces feelings of stability, well-being, and order; asymmetrical arrangements of scenic elements project images of imbalance, precariousness, disruption, and suspense. Compare, for example, the order inherent in the symmetrical perspective design on page 340 with the disruptive effect of Svoboda's off-balance setting for *The Insect Comedy*.

As Appia noted, the moving bodies of the performers complete and unify the kinesthetic arrangement of these static elements.

The Design Metaphor

The intelligence of a scene designer is based on the ability to see the world in terms of objects and spatial relationships and not just words and actions of human beings. Proceeding from the playwright's dramaturgy and the director's concept, the set designer selects and arranges the scenographic elements to contrive a **design metaphor,** the visual statement that expresses the totality of theatrical imaginations. The translation of the verbal and intellectual ideas into a single design metaphor that unites all the visual elements into an idea that can be both seen by the audience and used by the actors is the primary imaginative task of the set designer. In a sense, the statement of visual unity for the production is not unlike the playwright's plot, the director's concept, or the actor's superobjective.

A Monumental Metaphor.   The awesome grandeur of Air Force One taxiing to a halt on a runway lined with foreign dignitaries is the stuff of television news and fictionalized movies. But on stage? Scene designer Adrianne Lobel imagined just such an amazing sight—complete with red-carpeted flight steps and the deplaning president and first lady—as the centerpiece of her design metaphor for *Nixon in China* (see color plate 21). Lobel's conceptual process illustrates her choices from given circumstances as well as from her own scenographic imagination.

Nixon in China is an operatic drama of President Richard Nixon's historic 1972 state visit to the People's Republic of China. Director Peter Sellars wanted to emphasize the contrast between the simple humanity of the political figures and the extraordinary, larger-than-life importance of the historical event. It was left to Lobel to set the action in the specific time and location of the play as well as in the theatre space and to reinforce visually the director's concept. Sellars gave her an idea that was not yet an image. The stage was her "canvas" for creating the physical reality.

Lobel's reading of the script led her to the conclusion that *Nixon in China* was "part documentary, part fairy tale, part James Bond adventure." She also concluded that the sets had to be very simple because the show had to tour, and the environment should be "serious," so as not to compete with the humor of the text.[4] By studying photographs of the actual trip, Lobel formulated specific visual images that corresponded to scenes in the dramatized version of the event. She then connected these images into a design metaphor in which the sets would "dwarf the principal characters in relation to the historic events" because the people were so much less significant than their mission.[5] The design metaphor became the visual organizing principle that would guide all her other choices. The final design consisted of six life-size, illusionistic replicas of the actual locations that, when placed on stage, visually overwhelmed the characters in the scenes. In addition she chose to use very saturated pure colors to intensify the visual impact of the scenic elements. The result was a stunning display of scenographic images that has become an inextricable part of the opera's notoriety.

Crafting the Vision: Scenic Skills and Training

An examination of Lobel's creative methodology reveals that successful designers must possess an uncommon variety of skills, experience, and training in both the fine and applied arts.

Theatrical Skills.   Certainly scene designers must possess the theatrical skills of play analysis and productive collaboration—especially with the director.

Research Skills.   Designers formulate design metaphors only after extensive research into the fashions, architecture, and visual styles of the periods and locations depicted in the plays.

Spatial Art Skills.   Scene designers must be skilled in the essential theory and practice of the space arts. Required graphic arts skills include sketching, drawing, and especially painting—on a small scale for the **renderings** presented to the cast and director, and on a large scale for painting full-stage sets. Required plastic art

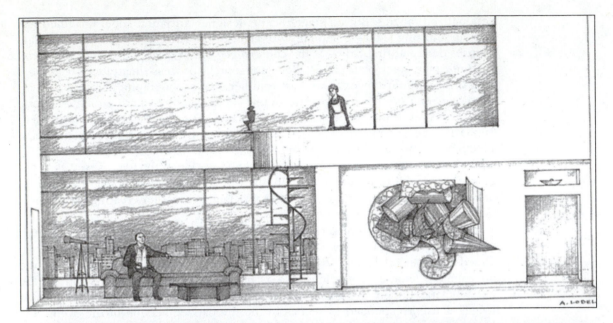

MODERN METAPHOR *Designer Adrianne Lobel set Mozart's eighteenth-century opera* The Marriage of Figaro *in modern New York City. She visualized the world of the play as existing in a penthouse of New York City's Trump Towers, a modern metaphor for the glitter and* glitterati *of upper-class eighteenth-century Spain.*

LIGHTER-THAN-AIR METAPHOR   *For the Royal Shakespeare Company's production of Shakespeare's* The Winter's Tale, *Anthony Ward used balloons as the central image of his design metaphor: "The whole notion is that we never leave childhood—it's always with us, and we behave incredibly childishly," Ward explained. "We see a gorgeous little kingdom shaken up by the boy." Ward believes every production requires a "click moment" when the playwright's, director's, and designer's ideas coalesce "into this land of air and light."*[6]

skills include small-scale model making and larger scale creating for statues, trees, and other three-dimensional set pieces.

Architectural Skills.   Architecture is the oldest, most traditional of required scenographic skills; scene design began with the imaginative perspective constructions of Renaissance architects. Just as architects make design choices for new buildings, scene designers make similar, albeit less permanent, choices on a smaller

ARCHITECTURAL SKILL   *Both research and architectural skills are evident in Herbert Andrews' design for the original Broadway production of George and Ira Gershwin's* Porgy and Bess, *set in the Catfish Row ghetto of South Carolina in the 1920s. Note how the space and structures are designed to facilitate the presence and activities of the performers on the multilevel set of building exteriors.*

scale for stage buildings. They must be able to depict a sense of logic in these buildings not only for what can be seen onstage, but for what must be imagined offstage. Architectural choices also define the relationships among stage space, structures, and people moving in the space. Finally, understanding the dynamics of theatre architecture affects such considerations as scene shifting, storage, size, and the sight lines and safety of the audience. A scene design is wasted effort if the technical staff cannot build it, the theatre cannot hold it, or the audience cannot see it.

Interior Design.   Since there are "more bedrooms than battlefields" in plays, designers must be well versed in interior styles of room arrangement, furnishings, and decor consistent with the time period, location, and socioeconomic status of the characters.

DREAM HOUSES   *Theatre critic David Richards theorizes that audiences applaud sets in the theatre because they want to live in them. For example, John Lee Beatty's design for Terrence McNally's dark comedy,* Lips Together, Teeth Apart, *is an ultramodern Fire Island beach house with sliding-glass doors opening onto a cedar deck, with a working shower, portable grill, expensive patio furniture, an ocean view, and a water-filled swimming pool downstage center. Such a home would cost $800,000 on the open market.*[7]

Applied Arts Skills.   The feasibility of the design and its actual creation by a staff of technicians depend on the designer's skills at such applied arts as drafting, engineering, construction (especially carpentry and welding), the use of special materials (such as plastics, foams, pigments, and adhesives), and even chemistry required for the creation of special effects (such as smoke, fog, and pyrotechnics). **Computer assisted design (CAD)** is a necessary skill not only of engineers, but of scene designers. The CAD programs are great time-savers allowing scene designers to test their ideas before committing them to blueprints, renderings, and models. Computers have also been used to create "virtual scenery" in which traditional flats and backdrops have been replaced with a **video wall.** In The Who's *Tommy* and in the 1995 revival of *How to Succeed in Business Without Really Trying,* banks of up to thirty-two integrated big-screen monitors are used to display preprogrammed, computer-generated and controlled images of still scenes and full-motion sequences. (See color plate 32.) Increasingly, scene designers also must comply with environmental regulations by designing with friendlier materials.

The Walt Disney corporation refers to the persons who conceive their wondrous, entertaining high-tech attractions as *Imagineers©*. The copyright-protected term is also a fitting designation of theatrical scene designers, artists whose imaginations directly depend on their knowledge of highly technical materials and procedures.

GIANT TECHNOLOGY   *For the Seattle Children Theatre's production of* Jack and the Beanstalk, *set designer Robert Gardiner based his concept for the giant on eighth-century Celtic carvings on the Irish Isle of Erin. A combination of high and low tech, the creature is a soft sculpture made of plastic fencing over a frame of PVC and steel, topped with upholstery batting treated with paint and glue to create a warty, puckered, ugly surface. The giant is mechanized by a counterweighted, pivoting, lever-controlled system that enables it to swivel, nod, lift its head, roll its eyes, raise its eyebrows, move its mouth, and tap dance with its monstrous fingers. A puppeteer inside the head monitors the movements on a video screen. Kids who saw the production frequently asked, "Is the giant real?"[8]*

Costume Choices: The Imagination and Skills of the Costume Designer

Like the scene designer, the costume designer also begins with the dramaturgical and directorial circumstances to create a different part of the stage picture. The costume designer begins making choices by imagining the clothing, makeup, and hairstyles of the particular characters who will live in the stage environment.

The purposes of clothing go beyond protection from the elements for the human creatures anthropologist Desmond Morris called "the naked apes." Clothes are an important means of expressing many aspects of personality. Costume designers, such as Romanian-born Smaranda Branescu, recognize that what a person wears is an important statement about who the person is: "A fashion designer creates beautiful clothes. A costume designer creates clothes to reveal character. Making a dress that is only pretty serves no dramatic purpose. The challenge for a costume designer is how to use color, line, and fabric to project the emotional life of characters."[9]

The Creative Potential of Costumes

Designers use costumes to define and convey characterization. For the audience, the costume designer's choices become immediate visual clues to the world of the play and its inhabitants.

Projecting Physical and Social Traits.   Costumes are the most immediate indications of the physical and social traits of the characters. Designers use costumes to define and convey size, age, and the strength of the characters. The costumes also make important statements about the characters' professions. For instance, Willy Loman's hat, suit, polished shoes, and briefcase mark him as a traveling salesman. The women he meets at the restaurant wear provocative and alluring clothing and makeup that indicate their intentions. Linda Loman's housedress, apron, lack of makeup, and unfashionable hairstyle define her domestic endeavors. In this regard, costumes can be an important dynamic force to underscore visually important character changes. For example, in Bertolt Brecht's sociopolitical drama *The Life of Galileo*, a crucial confrontation occurs between the Pope and Galileo, who has been a victim of the Inquisition for his heretical views of the cosmos. As the scene begins, the Pope appears in simple undergarments as an ordinary man as he protests the Inquisition's desire to silence Galileo. As the scene progresses, attendants dress the Pope in layer upon layer of religious vestments. By the end of the scene, the Pope stands in full papal attire, transformed into the supreme, official symbol of authority. As such, his initial sympathy turns to condemnation. The costume designer's choices not only define the professional station of the character, but also serve as visual statements underscoring the important personality change. Costumes become politics.

A SPRITE BY PROFESSION   *Shakespeare calls for supernatural sprites in both* A Midsummer Night's Dream *and* The Tempest. *Conventional wisdom is that they fly, or as Shakespeare wrote, "ride on the curled clouds." For director Kent Thompson's sci-fi production of* The Tempest *at the Alabama Shakespeare Festival, designer Beth Novak based her costume for Ariel on the fervent imaginations of Leonardo da Vinci and Jules Verne.*

Reflecting Psychological and Ethical Traits.   In Anton Chekhov's *The Seagull,* a young suitor asks the forlorn Masha why she always dresses in black clothes. She responds, "I'm in mourning for my life." The fact that clothes reflect psychological states is an important creative reference for costume designers. The colors of the costumes are often the audience's first clues to the mood of a scene. Similarly, costumes can also project symbolic, even ethical aspects of characters and actions. Dressing the heroes in white and the villains in black has always been a cliché of melodrama. More complex ethical conflict can also be reflected in costume choices. For his production of *The Death of Klinghoffer,* an opera based on the hijacking of the *Achille Lauro* cruise ship by Palestinians and their brutal murder of a wheelchair-bound, elderly Jewish passenger, Peter Sellars dressed all of the male characters in the same neutral costumes: white shirts and dark slacks. His idea was to use the costumes to neutralize any emotional predisposition to identify with one side or the other according to appearances. By eliminating

EXAGGERATION AND ORNAMENTATION   *Costumes take center stage in Kristi Zea's designs for Jean Genet's cruel satire* The Balcony *at the American Repertory Theatre. The play is set in a bordello that caters to perverted customers seeking release through the act of role playing. Shown here are the general who takes pleasure in imagining acts of courage, the bishop who enjoys forgiving sins, and the sadomasochist judge who delights in being humiliated by thieves. The exaggerated silhouettes and ornamentation of the costumes also reflect the play's satirical genre.*

stereotypical indications of national origin or politics, Sellars intended to illustrate there are no heroes or villains, no easy answers. The costumes made it difficult to take sides and fall back on reflexive reactions.

Conveying Time and Place.   Costumes are often the first indications of the historical period, geographical locations, and climate of the play. In the Broadway production of *Porgy and Bess* (see photograph on p. 346), the hot, 1920s South Carolina "summertime" (the subject and title of one of the musical's most famous songs) is as evident in the characters' costumes, designed by Paul DuPont, as in the scenery

COSTUMES INDICATE PLACE   *For the New York Shakespeare Festival production of*
The Caucasian Chalk Circle, *Bertolt Brecht's epic saga of greed and motherhood,
director George C. Wolfe relocated the action of the play from the Caucasus Mountains
to a Caribbean island reminiscent of Haiti. Toni-Leslie James' flamboyantly
ornamental costumes had the look of a Mardi Gras parade; Barbara Politt and
Stephen Kaplin's half-masks made theatrical caricatures out of the political
stereotypes Brecht created.*

and lighting. The usual assumption is that historical plays require historically accurate costumes, but this is not always the case. Many directors and designers of
classical or period plays opt for **modern dress productions** to emphasize the
contemporary relevance of the action. Some designers choose to mix costumes
from different historical periods in the same production to underscore a more universal significance of the play that endures across history and cultures. (See photos of *Hamlet,* Chapter 9, p. 359, and of *Romeo and Juliet,* Chapter 12, p. 433.)

Practical Considerations.   Costumes are more than clothing and must be designed
and constructed to accommodate the visual unity and technical flow of the

production. Besides reflecting aspects of character, color choices must interact with those of the scenery; the performers must stand out from, not fade into, the set. The scene-by-scene costume changes for a character are primary clues to the passage of time within a play. Finally, costumes, more than any other design element, must accommodate—even adhere to—the actors. Therefore, each costume must be designed in terms of the actor who will wear it. Designers must ensure that the costumes facilitate rather than hinder the performers' physical actions. In this sense, stage costumes have a certain technology:

- They must be constructed to last through repeated, extremely physical usage and cleaning.
- They must be fabricated to create certain illusions. For the Antarctic drama, *Terra Nova* (see photograph on p. 141), the costumes must appear to be made of thick insulated skins and furs, but must actually be constructed from lightweight ventilated materials so the actors will not sweat under hot stage lights when they are supposed to appear to be freezing to death.
- The continuous action of stage plays often requires that costumes be designed for **quick changes.** In Georges Feydeau's French bedroom farce *A Flea in Her Ear* (see photograph on p. 269), the wild plot turns on the complications that arise from two different characters who look exactly alike. Both parts are played by the same actor, who accomplishes the trick with the aid of under- and overdressing costumes constructed with Velcro fasteners and other quick-change features. Offstage "dressers" are also vital to the design of the costumes for this show.

Dressing a Chekhovian Protagonist.   Smaranda Branescu's design of the title character's costume for the American Repertory Theatre production of Anton Chekhov's *Platonov* demonstrates the dramaturgical, emotional, and practical considerations that influenced her choices:

Chekhov's characters have remained close to us because he penetrated the wrinkles on the soul and saw people as they are with virtues and vices all mixed up. You don't have heroes and villains in Chekhov. You have human beings of flesh and blood with their little defects, little virtues, little neuroses. Whenever you see Chekhov's characters up on stage, there's always a pang of recognition.

Take Platonov, the title character. I have to design a costume so the audience feels his sense of failure. The audience must see in his behavior and clothes that he was a brilliant student, on fire with ideas and ideals. Now he is trapped in a mediocre life—that's a real Chekhovian touch. But Platonov has given up his dreams. His environment dragged him down. He's become a provincial school teacher eking out a miserable existence, saddled with a not too intelligent wife and child. He's aggressive and nasty with other people because he's lost his self-respect. When people become malicious, they are unhappy about themselves. So Platonov drinks too much and starts to torture other people. So you cannot make a beautiful new suit and drape it on the actor. That's not Platonov. His self-disgust must show in his clothes. He doesn't take care of himself. He's not as you say in America clean cut. He's going

COSTUMES REFLECT CHARACTER   *Smaranda Branescu's costume design reflects the abandoned dreams and disillusion of the title character of Chekhov's* Platonov *in the A.R.T. production.*

to seed and doesn't bother to wash himself or change his clothes very often. We'll have to age our fabrics to get the right crumpled look we need. He must look as if he has slept for a month in the same jacket.[10]

Costume Design Skills

In order to imagine the stage clothing, communicate the vision to the other artists, and assist in the creation of the costumes, costume designers must possess a number of important skills. The creative imagination that allows the designer to envision these characters is informed by knowledge of the history of clothing and stage costumes, which are not always the same things. The ability to communicate the design to the other theatre artists requires the skills of a fashion designer and graphic artist. Costume designers imagine their creations in three dimensions, but plan and test them in two-dimensional sketches and painted color renderings. Therefore, life drawing skills are essential.

Like all theatre artists, costume designers must have the ability to work within prescribed limits of facilities, available personnel, and budgets. Theoni

Aldredge, the award-winning costume designer of such Broadway hits as *A Chorus Line, Hair,* and *Annie,* as well as hundreds of other plays and films, testifies to the economic and diplomatic skills required for communicating costume choices to producers:

> Anybody can tell you what a costume designer does in the theatre. Almost anybody, that is, except producers and their "angels." When examining the sometimes enormous budgetary demands of a Broadway play or musical the eyes of the producer and his backers dilate and tear when they come upon the costume costs. The question that follows is one that I have actually heard so often that I am no longer amused at its naivete, "Good heavens! Why so much money for clothes?" From that moment on the designer will spend the better part of her working days on the phone trying to explain basic economics. It is during these times that a degree in cost accounting seems more useful than any design talent. Even after the enormity of the task is made clear to them, and the costumes are finally designed, constructed and on the stage, the wardrobe is still singled out as the root of all evil. The following are comments heard during the try-out period of a musical deeply in trouble: "The show would be so much better if her dress was blue, her shoes beige and, please, no hat." "And you know this dance number would bring the house down if the dresses were just a little shorter." "Oh darling, remind me to bring my sweater from home—it would make this actor look much more comfortable." "Don't you think we can shop for some of these things tomorrow." (The show was, mind you, a 1905 period piece.)[11]

Finally, the actual construction of the garments necessitates a facility with fabrics, pattern making, cutting, cleaning, shop machinery, tailoring, stitching, accessorizing, wig making, and makeup. On the other hand, many costumes that are a part of the total design are not built from scratch, but are bought off the rack, rented, or pulled from stock. Costumes are, in fact, the theatre's most valuable, recyclable resource.

Only when the actor dons the costume is the design complete. Patricia Zipprodt, the award-winning costume designer of the original productions *Fiddler on the Roof, Sweet Charity, Cabaret, Pippin,* and *1776,* describes the sometimes difficult moment of letting go. Her mixed emotions are reminiscent of director JoAnne Akalaitis' feelings about entrusting "her" productions to the performers: "There is a funny point when the costumes are no longer yours. The actors start saying, 'Where is my costume?' and the wardrobe department starts to absorb them, and they become their property physically. And you have to give them distance. You've turned over your creative results to the world. It can just be wrenching."[12] As with everything else in the theatre, the performer on the stage defines the art object.

Lighting Choices: The Imagination and Skills of the Lighting Designer

Unlike the outdoor playing spaces of Sophocles, Plautus, and Shakespeare, today's indoor theatres are built to completely shut out the light of day, requiring the creation and design of artificial light. This fundamental visual requirement, however, goes beyond mere illumination to make possible an array of theatrical choices of substantial potential and effect.

The Creative Potential of Stage Lighting

The first experiments to explore the creative potential of stage lighting were undertaken in the eighteenth century. In England, **Philippe-Jacques de Loutherbourg** (1740–1812) used dyed and painted gauzes, silks, and other translucent materials lit by oil lamps to create amazing atmospheric effects at London's Drury Lane Theatre. His celebrated stage illusions included fire, volcanoes, sunlight, moonlight, clouds, mist, and fog effects. He even built a small-scale model theatre he called the **eidophusikon** in which to carry out his experiments before committing them to productions. The success of de Loutherbourg's techniques not only fed the public appetite for ever more realistic stage spectacle, his new techniques added substantially to the theatrical designer's menu of choices.

Focusing Attention.   Focusing the attention of the audience on the stage has always been the first order of business at the start of a performance. On the open playing spaces of ancient Greek, English Renaissance, and seventeenth-century Japanese theatres, playwrights got the noisy audiences to pay attention with formal entrances or processions, a prologue, or with a loud sound. Having all of the performers leave the stage was the only option for an ending. The Romans began the attention-grabbing practice of using a front curtain called an **auleum** that could be dropped or raised to suddenly reveal or conceal the spectacle. "Curtain time," even for theatres that do not use curtains, is still a universal designation. Since widespread electrification of theatres in the late nineteenth century, focusing and releasing the attention of the audience have been done primarily with lighting: house lights dim and black out to silence the audience, and when the stage lights come "up," the play begins. Fading to black at the end of the production means the play is over. No exits, epilogues, or curtains are necessary.

Atmospheric Effects.   As de Loutherbourg demonstrated, stage lighting can create convincing visual atmospheric effects. The time of day, the season, the weather, and even fantasy effects can be conveyed with theatrical lighting through the use of variations in "warm" light (reds, yellows, ambers) and "cool" light (blues, greens, and grays). Through illumination of the set punctuated by beam effects, lighting the curved neutral background called the **cyclorama,** and enhancing the illusion that light appears to come from practical sources (such as candles, torches, and lamps), lighting designers can transcend the dark confines of the theatre. The results are a major source of visual wonder and magic in today's theatre. "We can," writes lighting designer Richard Pilbrow, "fill a space with the atmosphere of a dull day or sparkling morning; we can use this three-dimensionally as if creating the air that the actor breathes."[13] It is to wonder if Shakespeare would ever have written "moonlit" poetry if the Globe Theatre had possessed moonlight-generating lighting equipment.

FOCUSING ATTENTION WITH LIGHT
Lighting is used to focus audience attention on particulars of action and character. For this moment from You Can't Take It with You, *lighting designer Doug Grekin focuses attention on the actors with the effect of natural sunlight through the window and with the light from the lamp. Note the curving lines and soft textures of the set pieces and costumes, which help create a wistful, romantic feeling. Set design by Craig Wolf.*

Mood and Emotion.   The primary creative potential of scenery is to suggest place and that of costumes is to define character. The power of lighting is its capacity to intensify moods and emotions. Lighting designer Jennifer Tipton compares the power of what she creates to another performing art with great emotional potency: "Light affects the same way music does," she says. "Wordlessly. Fluidly. People are very aware that they hear, but they're not so aware of what and how they see. Light is just as powerful as music in a subliminal way."[14] It is no wonder, therefore, that after the musicians, the most important artist of a live pop-music concert is the lighting designer, many of whom create such fantastic visual displays that their spectacles are referred to as "light shows."

Painting with Light.   The technology of lighting is so sophisticated that designers can control the direction, intensity, color, focus, and movement of the stage lights. During a performance the light can change much more easily, quickly, and frequently than either scenery or costumes. This visual mutability enables designers to use lighting to "change" the setting to such a degree that they often speak of "painting with light." Patrick Spottiswoode, education director of the

CREATING THE AIR   *Howell Binkley's award-winning lighting seems to create the very air for this production of Shakespeare's* Richard III *starring Stacy Keach at the Shakespeare Theatre at the Folger. Lighting is the primary visual means for changing Derek McLane's suggestive set for the play's sixteen interior and exterior locations. Costumes designed by Merrily Murray-Walsh.*

Shakespeare Globe Museum, observes that today "we lighting design Shakespeare because scene designing Shakespeare is too expensive."[15] For Jules Fisher, the Tony Award-winning lighting designer of many Broadway productions, change-ability is a distinguishing characteristic of his art: "Stage lighting and photography depend on knowing the effects of light on a subject—and what that implies emotionally. However, the theatre requires the light to change continually—a living breathing portrait—a million photographs."[16]

Technology and Skills

Of all the scenographic arts, lighting design is the most technology dependent. Today's lighting equipment has been developed beyond the mere electric lamps

LIGHTING SHAPES CHARACTER   *In this modern-dress production of* Hamlet *at the Tyrone Guthrie Theatre, lighting focuses attention on Hamlet while the other characters are silhouetted by* **backlighting** *the screens behind them. Note how the lighting actually sculpts the figure of Hamlet, emphasizing the ominous nature of the action as well as the complex turmoil of the character. Note also the way in which the scenic designer and the lighting designer have collaborated to produce the reflections of the characters on the highly polished floor. The horizontal lines of the screens seem to extend beyond the barrier of the stage. Lighting designer, Jim Ingalls; set designer, Doug Stein; costume designer, Ann Hould-Ward; director, Garland Wright.*

and dimmer boards to electronic computer-controlled systems that can generate an incredible variety of changing effects. It is not uncommon for modern productions to have hundreds of lighting cues produced by hundreds of instruments linked by microcircuitry, memorized and imprinted on disk, and controlled by a single **board operator** in a lighting booth.

To imagine the visual possibilities, a lighting designer must not only understand the creative potential as well as the technology of the equipment, but must also have a strong emotional sensitivity to the dramatic action. "I'm playing with all those things," Jennifer Tipton explains, "and I'm responding with my gut."[17] "The art," Jules Fisher emphasizes, "is still in the designer; the equipment palette just broadens the options."[18]

Noises Off: The High and Low Technology of Sound Design

Sound Effects

Before there was sound design, there were only "sound effects," produced mechanically—and some would say, more reliably. The sound of galloping horses was simulated by clattering empty coconut shells. The sound of howling wind was produced by a **wind machine,** which was a drum with thin wooden ribs that was rotated at various speeds against a sheet of thin cloth. Dried beans added to the drum would simulate the sound of rain. Thunder was produced by shaking a suspended sheet of metal called a **thunder sheet,** or by rolling heavy iron balls down inclined wooden troughs called **thunder runs.**

Aural Manipulation of Emotional Response

While sound effects create illusions of natural sounds, music is used to manipulate the emotional response of the audience. **Preshow music** sets the initial mood, and transitional **scene change music** comments on previous action and prepares for what is next. **Underscoring** is theme music that plays under dialogue and pantomimic action. Such music is indispensable in film and television. One need only think of the music used to underscore the shark attack scenes in *Jaws,* the final love scene in *Ghost,* or the training sequences in *Rocky* to understand the direct link between the empathic response of an audience and music. In the seventeenth century, Shakespeare's company at the Globe Theatre understood the creative potential of underscoring even the Bard's great dialogue. They kept a permanent group of musicians under contract for all of their productions. Feel the intensity of the love scenes, fights, and death scenes in Franco Zefferelli's film version of *Romeo and Juliet* as underscored by its variations on the stirring and memorable love theme "A Time for Us." In the twentieth-century theatre, using music to underscore action had been somewhat of a lost art; the process of composing, recording, cuing, and playing music for live performance has been technically complex and costly. But accessibility of high-tech sound reproduction put the art at the forefront of a theatrical comeback.

Designing Sound.   "Sound design" is a very recent addition to theatre art. Only since tape-recorded sound and amplified playback replaced phonographs have sound systems become standard aspects of theatre architecture. It was not until 1971 that a person was listed in a Broadway program as a "sound designer." The digitization of sound in the 1990s certified sound design as a legitimate art. Digi-Carts, computer-controlled hard drives that stack sound cues and play them back at the press of a button, have rendered tape decks obsolete. Today, everything from musical underscoring to atmospheric effects like rain, thunder, wind, crowds, traffic, airplanes, and battles can be created on digital audio work stations as easily as a playwright creates dialogue on a word processor.

Design Unity

The final step in executing the complete visual design is unifying the scenery, costumes, makeup, lighting, and sound effects with the actors on stage. As Royal Shakespeare Company lighting designer Chris Parry puts it, the "ideal is that the finished production [design] should look like it was all done by one very talented person."[19] It is the performers, however, who activate the design. The scenery is, after all, an environment and machine for the actors; the costumes are their character-defining clothes; and the lighting is focused on the actors, not the scenery. The logistical complexity of assembling all of these components requires special, often lengthy **technical rehearsals** followed by several **dress rehearsals.**

As flawless as a show may run in rehearsal, a production is incomplete without the presence and participation of theatregoers. "It is," the master scene designer Donald Oenslager said, "like a still life on the stage and does not come to life until it becomes animated with actors before an audience."[20]

Previewing Part 4

Part 3 examined the choices of artists assembled to stage the play. Part 4, "The Performance," focuses on the play as enacted live before an audience. Since they are not active or present parts of the conceptual or rehearsal processes, the audience and certainly the critics are the least predictable participants in the creative process of theatre. Yet their reactions to the performance can affect the very life span of a production.

THE DESIGNER AT WORK ·····················

High-Tech Magic: Follow That Gondola
by Jack Kroll
[Reprinted from *Newsweek*][21]

"Techno-pop" and "industrial" are two of the designations used to describe shows such as Cats, Les Misérables, The Phantom of the Opera, Miss Saigon, *The Who's* Tommy, *and* Sunset Boulevard: *"techno" because of the high technology needed to operate the famous special effects that are so central to the theatrical impact; "pop" because of the pop music, pop art, and overwhelming popularity of the shows; and "industrial" because of the sheer factorylike weight, scale, and personnel needed to build and operate the spectacle. In his account of the Broadway opening of* The Phantom of the Opera, Newsweek *critic Jack Kroll profiled the new-age creator of* Phantom's *visual wonders.*

Maria Bjornson is as much the star of *The Phantom of the Opera* as Andrew Lloyd Webber, Hal Prince, or Michael Crawford. As designer of sets and costumes, she presides over one of the most dazzling and complex shows ever mounted on any stage. *Phantom* is her first musical, and to it she brought the same passion for detail that marks her work in opera and at the Royal Shakespeare Company. With her assistant Jonathan Allen, Bjornson went to the Paris Opera House and explored the legendary building from its rooftop to its catacombed cellar, taking hundreds of photographs of everything from the famous lake to the stable where 100 horses were kept to haul the scenery.

One of the technical marvels of the show is the "travelator," which is essentially a bridge suspended between two towers. As the Phantom spirits Christine down to his lair, they move on this bridge, which tilts one way and another, creating various levels as the automated towers move up- and downstage. The magical moment is the arrival at the underground lake, the illusion of which is created by fumes from dry ice machines in the basement. The gondola that the Phantom apparently rows is actually moved by a stagehand in the wings operating a radio-controlled device [see color plate 27]. This eternally anxious fellow must steer the boat through the one hundred candles that rise through underground traps. Such technical complexity seems to invite disaster, which has sometimes accepted the invitation. Jonathan Allen and Dana Kenn, Bjornson's chief American assistants, recall such a gala occasion. "Something caught in the lighting board," says Allen, "which went down. A flustered technician then cued the travelator which moved into some scenery, trapping a bed onstage. A drape flew up the set from a previous scene. The Phantom's throne and organ came on, crunching the candles while the boat got stuck upstage." As this Rube Goldberg foul-up escalated, the stage manager had to decide whether to stop the show. He decided not to. "Michael and Sara did their scene," recalls Kenn, "dancing around all those trapped and crunched candles. It was brilliant. They got a standing ovation."

***

SUMMARY

1. Designers are the artists who make the choices that create the visual and aural elements of theatrical production.

2. The choices of the designers set the stage by establishing the essential aspects of location, style, genre, time period, character traits, atmosphere, mood, and ideas. The visual design unifies the stage space with the director's concept and the actors' performances.

3. It is the particular intelligence of the visual artist to create the relationship between human beings and the space that surrounds them.

4. The history of theatrical design is the story of two different conceptions of what stage spectacle ought to do. Visual suggestion relies on the imagination of the audience to create the particular reality that is only prompted by the visual aspects of the production. Visual illusion utilizes scenery, lights, and costumes to make the audience believe they are seeing the actual locations, furnishings, and historically accurate clothing depicted in the play.

5. The inventions of recorded drama, particularly the cinema, prompted theatre artists to reintroduce suggestive conventions. New perceptions of reality also led to increasing nonrealism in theatrical design.

6. The imagination of the scenic designer manifests itself in translating the verbal and intellectual ideas of the playwright and the director into a single design metaphor.

7. The costume designer creates clothes that reveal physical, professional, emotional, and intellectual traits of the characters.

8. The creative potential of stage lighting includes focusing the attention of the audience, simulating atmospheric effects, enhancing mood, and instantaneously changing the setting.

9. High-tech recording and playback equipment has made sound design a recent addition to the theatrical imagination.

10. The audience gives final validity to the choices made by all of the theatre artists.

CHOICES

1. Imagine that both directorial concept and budget constraints require a setting that "suggests" the rooms called for in *Death of a Salesman* or some other play with which you are familiar. What choices could you make in abbreviating the realistic representation of a room and its furnishings? What are the essential elements that define each interior location?

2. Consider the design for a play in which the characters are locked in a barn that catches fire and burns to the ground. While it would be impossible to actually burn the place down, what could be designed to suggest this action? Is there a way to create the realistic illusion of the fire without actual pyrotechnics? Consult with local theatrical designers or peruse books to determine the possibilities.

3. The director decides to visually update Sophocles' tragedy *Oedipus the King* to a modern context, although the director has not, as yet, determined the specific setting. What might you suggest as an environment that would visually accommodate the fall of Oedipus from his position of great power?

4. Research the historically accurate style of clothing and furnishings (tables, chairs, refrigerators, typewriters, pens, wire recorders, briefcases, cheese spread containers) for a production of *Death of a Salesman* (or of some other play with which you are familiar). Compile a selection of sketches and photographs from a variety of sources that could be presented to the director for a production of the play.

5. Elements of design include line, mass, color, and texture. Describe the settings for a popular film or television show in these terms to determine the intentions of the designers. How does the design support the serious or humorous intentions of the play? Identify a design metaphor for the screenplay or teleplay you have chosen. In what ways do the costumes define the characters?

6. Analyze the design elements of a particular rock concert you attended. What were the emotional connections between the meaning of the music and the visual details?

7. Choose four photographs of theatrical productions from this book that show contrasting scenic and/or costume designs. Compare and contrast the designs in terms of the design elements of line, mass, color (optional), texture, space, and composition.

8. From the popular or classical music with which you are familiar, choose the appropriate music to underscore the suicide scene in *Romeo and Juliet* and the epilogue in *Death of a Salesman*. Justify your choices on the basis of the desired empathic response of the audience. Prepare an audio recording of the music to underscore an in-class reading of the scene.

PART 4

THE PERFORMANCE

The audience at and in *the performance of the Trinity Repertory Theatre production of* Tom Jones. *Environmental design of scenery and audience seating by Eugene Lee.*

All for your delight . . .
The actors are at hand: and by their show,
You shall know all that you are like to know.

A Midsummer Night's Dream, *Act V, scene i*

CHAPTER 10

The Audience Plays Its Part

THE PUBLIC IMAGINATION

PREVIEW

Imaginations Captured
A Brief History of the Audience in the Theatre
Modern Audiences
The Audience at Work

It is one of the most well-known pleas for help ever uttered. On stage, Peter Pan helplessly gazes down on the dying Tinker Bell, and the audience in the theatre—on the edges of their seats, but powerless to help—shares the pain. Then, in a moment of inspiration, Peter looks up, and his gaze breaks the proscenium barrier. He stands, runs to the edge of the stage, and focuses on the spectators. "Her light is growing faint," he tells them, "and if it goes out, that means she is dead! . . . She says—she says she thinks she could get well again if children believed in fairies! . . . Do you believe in fairies? Say quick that you believe! If you believe, clap your hands!"[1]

At first, the audience hesitates, unsure how to respond to Peter's direct appeal for help. Then, a few unself-conscious children and self-conscious adults begin to clap. Others join in. Peter desperately works the now willing crowd to a

"IF YOU BELIEVE, CLAP YOUR HANDS" *Only in the theatre can the audience be called on to play a part integral to the drama. James M. Barrie's original play was intended as much for adults as for children. His designation of Peter Pan's country as "Never Land" reflects his cynical view of adults. The musical version (shown here in the Broadway production starring Cathy Rigby) was intended primarily for children, hence the more childlike designation, "Never Never Land."*

fever pitch until Tinker Bell, "played" by a flickering, fading light, revives to robust brightness. The audience cheers.

Like the actor playing Peter and the light board operator, the audience members played their roles perfectly. The implication, at least in the case of the classic fantasy by James M. Barrie, is that if they had not, Tinker Bell—and by extension the play itself—would have died.

What can account for this irrational behavior? Certainly grown men and women, if not the children, do not believe in fairies. The spectators obviously see that Tinker Bell is only a light, Peter Pan is an actor who flies on a wire, and Never Land is a cartoonlike stage set. Yet there they are, clapping wildly to save the life of something that does not even exist.

It happens all the time.

The explanation lies in the timeless satisfaction human beings derive from forming a connection with actors. The role of an audience at a performance is as important as that of the theatre artists. The spectators, like the other theatre artists, accept an imaginary premise, the given circumstances of the play and production. Like the actors, they form psychological connections with the characters, and they must collaborate with the artists working on stage. In a kind of aesthetic communion, the audience validates or rejects the histrionic choices, which are the external means by which the possibility of theatre is created. The audience makes internal connections and decisions that complete the creation of theatre.

This chapter examines how the imagination works in the audience—those assembled in the theatre at curtain time who are prepared to take an active part in the creation of theatre art. Topics include connecting with the theatrical imagination, historical perspectives on the changing roles of the theatre audience, group dynamics, and new roles for the contemporary theatre audience.

Imaginations Captured

Getting caught up in the actions of Tinker Bell, the Phantom of the Opera, Oedipus, Willy Loman, or the feuding families and lovers of "fair Verona" begins when theatre artists succeed in capturing the collective imagination of the audience.

Theatrical imagination is an interactive process of suggestion and acceptance. Theatre artists suggest an imaginary world through actions, characters, words, sounds, and visual displays. If the suggestions are clear and stimulating, audience members return the favor by accepting the suggestions and engaging their own imaginations to proceed along the theatrical journey. The members of the audience become willing captives. They are primed to accept all suggestions. They have paid for the ride. They are not in the mood to reject. They possess imaginative muscle that enables them to leap over such obvious fictions as spotlights as fairies, actors on wires, houses with missing walls, and traveling from one place to another without leaving their seats. The process of capturing the imagination of the audience is at the same time delicate, depending on certain psychological realities of the collective imagination.

Group Psychology

Various psychological theories have sought to explain the behavior of groups. "Mob psychology," "group think," "the collective imagination," and "peer influence" are all terms that acknowledge the altered states of an assembled group. Is the crowd really the sixth player on the home basketball team? Is it possible for a supportive and cheering grandstand to influence the outcome of a forward pass or a baseball pitch? Can a laughing audience make an actor performing a comedy funnier? Many athletes and actors would answer all of these questions with an unqualified "yes."

Most experts in social psychology agree that assembling into a group reinforces individual power, leading participants to act differently than they do when they are alone. Mob violence is the most extreme example of such reinforcement. Joining the shouting to urge on the home team is a more controlled but equally fervent example. Laughing uproariously and clapping loudly for actors almost never occur if you are a lone observer; such behavior erupts spontaneously when reinforced by a full house.

Assembling individuals into a group provides one of the most distinguishing characteristics of the theatre. From an aesthetic viewpoint, groups agree to suspend disbelief in order to empathize with fictional portrayals; they participate in dramatic irony and experience emotional release; and they maintain an all-important aesthetic distance.

Willing Suspension of Disbelief: The Imaginative Agreement

There have always been those like Plato, who, when confronted with convincing stage portrayals, have doubted the audience's ability to recognize them as fictions—to distinguish them from reality. However, spectators at a play performance have no trouble making the distinction. Dramatic portrayals on stage are not mistaken for reality. No matter how good the illusion, the theatre experience is full of omnipresent reminders and conventions of the artificial nature of the portrayal: the theatre setting, the exit signs, the stage, the program, the shared decorum, and characters who break into song, dance, or verse at the slightest emotional prompting. In live performances of James M. Barrie's *Peter Pan* every member of the audience can tell the "flying" actors are suspended by wires and Tinker Bell is played by a lighting effect. Yet no one stops the show to point this out to others. No one sits restlessly through the performance in total distraction at this unbelievable and obvious contrivance. At the same time, audience members would not describe their reaction as one of absolute belief in either the special effects or the fantasy world of the play in which children never grow up, can fly, detach from their shadows, and have winged fairies for companions. No one is moved to immediate action by what occurs on stage. No one dials 911 when a crime is committed in a play. No one rushes to the stage to administer CPR to the fallen Hamlet. On the other hand, few in attendance are indifferent to these actions. There is a degree of involvement that may even prompt extreme, heartfelt

INTENTIONAL DISBELIEF   *Some playwrights intentionally disrupt the willing suspension of disbelief to discourage deep emotional involvement by the audience. Bertolt Brecht believed the role of the audience was to contemplate and judge the action on the stage, not believe in its truth. In the American Repertory Theatre production of* Threepenny Opera, *his cynical play about class struggle, technicians were purposely shown shifting scenery, setting props, and hanging crude signs to tell the audience the locations of the action. The purpose was to "distance" or "alienate" the audience from any emotional or imaginative connection to the action, substituting an entirely intellectual connection. Brecht's intention was constantly to remind the audience that they were in a theatre. No suspension of disbelief required. (Directed by Ron Daniels.)*

emotional responses: not belief, but certainly not disbelief either—a curious imaginative state. The English romantic poet, critic, philosopher, and closet dramatist **Samuel Taylor Coleridge** (1772–1834) described this phenomenon as an unwritten agreement called *"the willing suspension of disbelief."* Under the terms of this aesthetic contract, the audience, rather than agreeing to believe in the theatrical fiction, agrees *not to disbelieve* it. The distinction is semantic, but nonetheless important. The theatrical imagination depends on this agreement remaining in force throughout the performance. From the actors' point of view the agreement is only slightly different. Speaking for the performers, noted stage and screen director Mike Nichols put it this way: "I'll pretend this is really happening if you pretend you believe it."[2]

The agreement, of course, can be broken easily by unwarranted occurrences in the audience or on stage. Actors forgetting lines or breaking character, stage props that do not work on cue, shaking scenery, flubbed lighting cues, intrusive noise, movement, or other disturbances in the audience can focus the attention of the audience or performers on that which must not be "disbelieved." Only after their disbelief has been suspended can the audience form emotional and intellectual connections with the performance.

Empathy: Emotional Connections

Empathy is the human capacity for identifying with and vicariously experiencing the feelings of another to the point of participation in a shared emotional experience. *Sympathy* means "to feel for"; *empathy* means "to feel with." In life, empathic responses to the emotions of others are considered normal human reactions; one of the most popular conceptions of "alien" is the inability to respond empathetically, like *Star Trek*'s Mr. Spock. Empathy in the theatre is engaged primarily by the truthful portrayals of the actors, but it is also promoted by the sound, lighting, staging, and costumes. If the actors form emotional connections with their characters, the audience will empathize accordingly.

Eliciting empathy is crucial to understanding the larger significance of a play. In *Widows,* Chilean playwright Ariel Dorfman depicts a village where most of the men have been taken away by government troops. When a man's decomposed body is found on a riverbank, the women of the village claim it, defiantly refuse it burial, and stoically accept the oppression that results from their desperate actions. Dorfman wanted his audiences to confront the fates of the thousands of "disappeared" victims of tyranny. The confrontation, however, is possible only if the audience empathizes with the characters in the play. The success of the production depends on the audience sharing the women's suffering for their lost men and their anger at the military regime. Through empathy, the imaginative world of the play and the imaginative lives of the audience members intersect.

As in life, empathic responses from others tend to intensify and heighten the original emotional experience. Actors feel the response of the audience and depend on it for their own creative energy. When the sustaining emotional energy of the audience is lacking, actors refer to the awful experience of "dying" on stage.

Dramatic Irony: Intellectual Connections

Just as empathy is necessary for the audience's emotional connection to the characters, dramatic irony is the basis for the spectator's cognitive connection to the stage action. **Dramatic irony** is a technique in which the audience is given knowledge the characters of the play do not have. The observers understand the implications of actions of which the characters remain unaware.

Dramatic irony is a function of the live audience and their secret knowledge of the stage action. The audience, like the theatre artists, knows more than the characters who are aware only of what they glean and experience from the scenes in which they appear. The audience, on the other hand, sees and hears it all. Consider the formal definition of dramatic irony:

a remark or event for which there are two hearers or observers. The first hearer (the characters in the play) fails to understand the remark or event. The second hearer (the audience in the theatre) understands not only the remark or the event, but also the characters' incomprehension of it.[3]

Playwrights know the effective manipulation of dramatic irony is critical to the audience's enjoyment of drama. Much of the suspense of melodrama is generated by ironic effects. *Ghost,* one of the most successful film melodramas of all time, depends for its effectiveness on the ironic convention that the audience can see and hear the young lover's ghost (played by Patrick Swayze), while none of the other characters can. **Mistaken identity,** a staple of many comedies, is pure dramatic irony. Shakespeare was a master at using it. In his romantic comedy *Twelfth Night,* two fraternal twins, Sebastian and Viola, become separated in a shipwreck,

CREATING EMPATHY   *Empathy can be created in many ways. In the Mark Taper Forum production of Ariel Dorfman's* Widows, *empathy was achieved by the emotionally realistic portrayals of the actors, the evocative music, the suggestive stage setting, and the shockingly realistic "properties" created by Michael Key.*

and each supposes the other dead. To survive in the foreign land where she is washed ashore, Viola disguises herself as a man. Hilarity ensues as both a woman and a man fall in love with Viola and with Sebastian whom everyone believes are the same person. Only the audience members, with dramatic irony on their side, know who is who—much to their amusement. Dramatic irony also intensifies the effect of tragedy. Since Sophocles' *Oedipus the King* was first performed in c. 430 B.C., audiences have always known the outcome of the tragic hero who obsessively hunts down the murderer of the former king without realizing he himself committed the crime. Oedipus' desperate search makes virtually everything he says ironic, and only the audience knows his vow of vengeance will eventually cause his own destruction. The frightful moment of truth, when Oedipus finally learns what the audience already knows, makes the tragedy as horrifying for the spectators as it is for the character.

Catharsis

When empathy and dramatic irony combine to arouse intense emotions in the audience, **catharsis** is the purgation or release of those emotions through the concluding events of the play. Aristotle used the word to describe the sensations of being spent of emotion, worn out, and relieved at the end of a play. It is not unlike the effects of finishing a thrilling roller-coaster ride.

Releasing emotions through art suggests a therapeutic experience for the audience. According to this view, releasing overwhelming thoughts and emotions in the relative safety of the theatre allows spectators control and relief from potentially destructive proclivities. **Antonin Artaud** (1896–1948), the influential French actor, director, and poet, went so far as to suggest a near psychiatric function for theatrical catharsis. Artaud called for a **theatre of cruelty** that would assault not the physical, but the moral sensibilities of the audience. The world, he maintained, was sick and in need of shock treatment. The theatre, he felt, was its medicine. "The theatre," he wrote, "has been created to drain abscesses collectively."[4] By assaulting their senses with extreme, emotionally charged sound, spectacle, and dramatic action, Artaud wanted spectators to leave the theatre exhausted and transformed. Do not wait until it happens in society, he warned. Avoid it by doing it first in the theatre.

There are those, however, who believe the vicarious experiences of spectators at a play or musical concert serve to engender rather than to purge aberrant tendencies and behavior. As an example, such critics point out that the violent confrontation over accusations of sexual assault that ends David Mamet's *Oleanna* has caused shouting matches and fistfights in some audiences. Mamet, on the other hand, rejects any notion that he or his play is responsible for such behavior:

> It is just dead wrong to suggest that my work incites—or supports—violence. My job is exactly the contrary. My job is to show human interactions in such a way that the synthesis an audience takes away will perhaps lead to a greater humanity, a greater

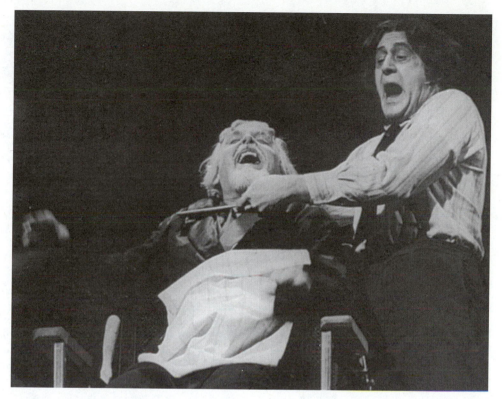

CATHARSIS OR CARNAGE? Sweeney Todd, the Demon Barber of Fleet Street, *a "musical thriller" by Stephen Sondheim and Hugh Wheeler (that was directed on Broadway by Harold Prince) depicts the bloody revenge of a man who returns from twenty years of brutal imprisonment to murder those responsible (as well as many who were not responsible) for incarcerating him under false charges. Under the guise of a barber, Sweeney Todd slits his victims' throats and dispatches them to a basement bakery where his paramour and accomplice, Mrs. Lovett, butchers and bakes them into meat pies, which she sells to an unsuspecting clientele. Called* grand guignol, *these plays that specialize in graphic scenes of violence, murder, rape, and suicide go back to the time of Seneca, who wrote a particularly bloody version of* Oedipus. *Shakespeare tried his hand at it in* Titus Andronicus, *a play full of rape and dismemberment. Today,* grand guignol *is primarily the province of such "slasher" films as* Friday the 13th *and* Nightmare on Elm Street. *The debate as to their harmful or therapeutic effects remains unsettled.*

understanding of human motives. I don't know how successful I am at it, but that absolutely is my job. If the net effect is otherwise, which I don't think that it is, then they should throw me in jail.[5]

The ongoing debate—which is being waged in the halls of Congress—about possible dangers from the portrayals of graphic violence on television and on film or in the lyrics of songs is primarily an argument over catharsis.

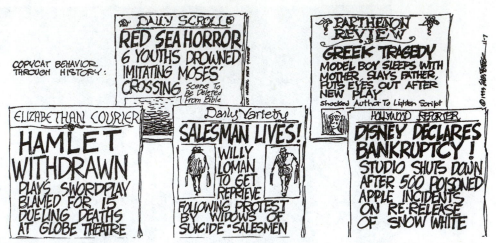

COPYCAT BEHAVIOR THROUGH HISTORY   *The implication of playwright/cartoon artist Jules Feifer's editorial drawing is that catharsis rather than emulation is the result of watching violence portrayed in ethically complex tragedies. In such dramas, violence is never the solution to the moral dilemma, and its consequences are always tragic. On the other hand, the incessant, repetitive, "mindless" violence of movie and film melodramas, depicted without ethical context or consequences, leaves the question of catharsis in doubt.*

Aesthetic Distance

In the theatre the best seats in the house are the ones in the orchestra section, those closest to the stage. They sell out first and often cost the most. In the movies, because of the huge size of the screen, all the seats, except those in the front rows, are regarded as equally good. Watching television is a matter of a few feet from the tube to the seat. But consider your *actual* distance from the performers when you are at the movies or watching TV: physically and psychologically the screen actors could not be farther from you. In reality, the performers are not where you are—only their recorded images flicker in your presence.

In the theatre, the psychological as well as the physical distance between spectator and performer is comparatively very short. The proximity—the **aesthetic distance**—defines the imaginative theatrical connection. Controversial portrayals of events such as violence, nudity, or sexual activity are more provocative than the same depictions on film, the difference being that of watching human actors perform these acts in your presence rather than watching pictures of the acts. While film and television drama search for ever more graphic (literally) ways of depicting these acts, the physical presence of live human beings on stage makes conventional portrayals histrionically acceptable. In addition, the close aesthetic distance in the theatre makes possible—even demands—communication among audience members and between the audience and the performers.

A Brief History of the Audience in the Theatre

Unlike an actor who develops a complete character, the role of the audience at theatrical performances is not strictly prescribed. The question of exactly how much active participation is appropriate or permissible has varied throughout theatre history. Like styles of acting, scenic design, and the interpretation of plays, the role of the audience has changed with the times.

Active Audiences

For most of theatre history, very active audiences have crowded into outdoor and indoor theatres to play assertive, vociferous, and physical parts in almost all aspects of the performance. Theatres were built for audience participation—the playwrights wrote for it, and the actors played to it (some would say, *endured* it).

Crowd Control.   When the collective mind of a crowd replaces the mind of the individual in isolation, behavior is reinforced and emboldened according to the size of the group. Because of their large capacities and relative freedom from claustrophobic confinement, outdoor theatres were very conducive to demonstrative audience participation. Crowd control at outdoor theatres was a necessity. As in modern sports arenas, there was much coming and going of spectators throughout the performances.

In ancient Greece and Rome, officials were kept on hand to maintain order. In Athens, fines were imposed on the most unruly people, and outright violence,

Calvin and Hobbes   by Bill Watterson

AN AUDIENCE LEXICON

The derivation of audience terminology refers directly to active participation.

Audience: From the Latin *audire,* literally "to hear." In Rome, financial accounts were given orally, and the people who listened were hearing an "audit." "Audience" grew to mean *any* group of "people listening."

Spectator: From the Latin *spectaculum.* The verb *speculari* means "to watch from a distance." Those who watched from a distance and guessed what was happening were called "speculators." People sitting in a theatre, watching players on stage and puzzling out what was happening, were called "spectators."

Auditorium: Also from *audire,* "to hear." The ancient Greeks called the audience's seating area the **theatron,** or "seeing place." In English, "auditory" and "spectatory" were early references to the part of the theatre building designed to accommodate people hearing and watching the play. "Auditorium" became the common designation in the eighteenth century.

Applause: From the Latin *plaudere,* which means to "explode with sound." In ancient Greece, the audience clapped and cheered to express their endorsement of a performance. In Rome, audience members waved with the pointed ends of their togas (by the fourth century strips of material were distributed for the purpose) in appreciation of a performance. The material at the end of the toga made a snapping sound, which was eventually replaced with the snapping of fingers. In the Renaissance, clapping with hands became standard practice throughout Europe. While most audiences applaud in a random cacophony, some, such as those in Russia, respond in a unison series of claps, which allows for longer, sustained applause. In some countries, whistling, stamping feet, and shouting are customary. In Southeast Asia, applause is rare. More typical are variations of the Indian convention of *namaskara* in which an actor stands on stage with folded hands and bows slightly to the silent approval of the audience.

Boo, Hiss: To express disapproval the ancient Greeks made animal sounds: "boo" was the imitation of oxen, and "hiss" mimicked the sound of geese.

ironically, was punishable by death. The Romans were more concerned with comfort than decorum. By the Empire period, they had perfected a system of air conditioning that involved air blowing over streams of water and an awning to protect spectators from the sun. Roman audiences reflected their sensational entertainments: boisterous and demonstrative. These classical thrill seekers felt they had the right to render their "thumbs up/thumbs down" judgments immediately and energetically. By the sixth century the theatre was banned throughout the Roman Empire, and the large audiences vanished, dispersed by imperial and religious decree.

As long as medieval religious dramas were performed in the church as part of the worship services, European Christian audiences maintained decorum appropriate to the surroundings. When religious plays were removed from the churches in the thirteenth century and performed outdoors, the behavior of the theatre audience changed accordingly from a reverent group of worshipers to an enthusiastic crowd of revelers. In England, the community event included observing a procession of wagons upon which religious plays were staged. Everybody, of course, loves a parade.

The procession lasted the entire day, and spectators watched from windows and rooftops. A festival atmosphere was created as people moved freely between viewing places, followed the wagons, left to eat or drink, and returned at any time. Serious punishment befell any observer who disrupted the performance, carried weapons, or engaged in violence.

Accommodating Architecture. An important aspect of the audience-performer relationship in the medieval period was the close proximity of the actors to the spectators. Unlike Greek and Roman theatres where substantial distance separated audience and actors, medieval spectators crowded around the playing area, greatly reducing the formality of the event. From the medieval period until the nineteenth century, a common feature of both outdoor and indoor theatres was relatively unrestricted access of the audience to the stage. In Elizabethan public theatres, rowdy standing spectators called **groundlings** or **pennystinkers** surrounded the thrust stage, which was raised only about five feet from the ground, or **pit** as the area closest to the stage was called.

In the seventeenth, eighteenth, and early nineteenth centuries, backless benches were installed in the pits of indoor proscenium theatres. Rather than settling the spectators, these seats served as platforms for increasingly exhibitionist and disruptive behavior. (Keep in mind that until the advent of electric lighting, the stage and auditorium were both illuminated throughout the performances.) While more demure and reserved patrons sat in private boxes and galleries, the pit was occupied by rowdies and noisy **orange wenches** of questionable virtue who hawked oranges as refreshments, contending for both the attentions of other spectators and actors alike. Roaming freely throughout the theatres, especially in the eighteenth century, were prostitutes and pickpockets, the former quite noisy and the latter surreptitious in pursuing their livelihoods. Audience acceptance of these criminal aspects of theatregoing is evident in the doggerel verses written by a young boy attending his first play at Drury Lane in 1765.

THE REFRESHMENT TRADITION   *Being invited to the great hall of a medieval nobleman for a night of eating, drinking, and entertainment was much like attending a modern **dinner theatre**. While seated for a lavish feast, spectators were entertained by itinerant professional players who performed short plays called **interludes** between courses of the banquet. An evening of dinner and theatre among friends was born, at least among those privileged enough to be invited to the house of an important person. This drawing of the typical medieval great hall shows the layout of the audience with the best seats reserved for the nobles of the castle and side seats for guests. The interlude players performed between the kitchen doors, using them as well as the aisles for entrances.*

> When on a sudden some one cries:
> Pickpocket! And attracts all eyes;
> Men, women, boys, cry toss him o'er!
> Thy art thou ne'er shalt practice more:
> Amidst this hubbub, and this din,
> Fiddles and fiddlesticks come in.
> Seated in slips with practis'd art,
> The town lass wins the sailor's heart.[6]

The actors were much less tolerant of these criminal interruptions, although their solution was similar. One Restoration dramatist directed the epilogue of his play to the noisy prostitutes, called "masques," in the gallery:

> Our Galleries too, were finely us'd of late,
> Where roosting Masques sat cackling for a Mate:
> They came to not see Plays but act their own,
> And had throng'd Audiences when we had none.
> Our Plays it was impossible to hear,
> The honest Country Men were forc't to swear:
> Confound you, give your bawdy prating o'er,
> Or Zounds, I'le fling you i' the Pit, you bawling Whore.[7]

Most intrusive was the common practice of allowing members of the audience in English and continental theatres to sit on the stage itself. These seats were usually taken by jabbering fops, much to the chagrin and acute irritation of both playwrights and actors. Voltaire succeeded in expelling them from the stage at the Comédie Française in 1759, and David Garrick removed them from the Drury Lane boards in 1762. But the practice lingered in other theatres until 1840.

Despite the banning of spectators from the stage, there was never a push to quell into total passivity and silence the theatre audiences of the seventeenth, eighteenth, or nineteenth centuries. In fact, when guards were posted in Parisian theatres in the 1750s to keep the unruly pit in check, many respectable theatregoers such as the encyclopedist Denis Diderot objected to the regimentation of an art dependent on passionate imaginations:

> Fifteen years ago our theatres were tumultuous places. The coldest heads became heated on entering, and sensible men more or less shared the transports of madmen. . . . There was movement, bustle, and pushing; the soul was beside itself. I know of no frame of mind more favorable to the poet. The play began with difficulties and was often interrupted. But when a fine passage arrived there was an incredible din; encores were demanded unceasingly, the actor and the actress aroused enthusiasm. . . . People had arrived heatedly, they went away in a state of drunkenness. Some went to the brothels, others went into polite society. That is enjoyment! Today, they arrive coldly, they listen coldly, they leave coldly, and I do not know where they go afterward. I am singularly shocked by these insolent fusileers posted to left and to right in order to moderate my transports of admiration, sensibility, and joy, and who turn our theaters into resorts more peaceful and more respectful than our churches.[8]

The Audience in the Play.   While decrying the more disruptive behavior of the public, pre-twentieth-century playwrights recognized the ever-present, ever-visible, and ever-active role of their audiences and accommodated their participation in their plays. Dramaturgical devices that played directly to the audience included **prologues** and **epilogues,** short introductory or closing speeches written in verse that explained or commented on the action, made witty or biting observations of political or social conditions, or solicited the indulgence or applause of the spectators; **soliloquies,** speeches written for characters alone on stage for the purpose of expressing their private thoughts to the ever-visible spectators; **direct address,** such as Peter Pan's solicitation for help in saving Tinker Bell; and **asides,** "confidential" comments by a character intended for the audience.

Actors and Their Public.   As long as there was as much light on the spectators as there was on the actors, performers wasted little time or space playing to each other; they performed down center and focused on *their* public. Their declamatory performances were larger-than-life portrayals; they had to be in order to command the attention of the boisterous theatregoers. Disruptive fops, rakes, pickpockets, prostitutes, orange wenches, and groundlings notwithstanding, actors have always known that they have no art, let alone livelihood, without an audience. Quiet, decorous passivity is deadly, a function of boredom. Actors crave full houses of energized, alert spectators willing to demonstrate approval of their art by literally cheering them on. "Sit back, relax, and enjoy the show" are erroneous suggestions for an active, participatory audience.

The desire for applause has stimulated inventing ingenious—if not altogether legitimate—ways of obtaining it. In the seventeenth century, European actors refined the technique of **claptrap,** concluding a scene or speech with a great vocal display, gesture, or physical flourish that could inspire or *trap* the audience into applauding. Molière, among many other great actors, viewed the practice with disdain as the cheap tricks of actors who could not earn legitimate applause through talented portrayals.

In the nineteenth century, some star actors negotiated contracts that specified the amount of applause they would receive at their first entrance in each play. To assure audience response many theatres in Europe and America employed secret full-time professional clappers called **claques** who were paid to start ovations, bravos, cheers, whistles, and other enthusiastic responses to the play and performers. The modern electronic equivalent is television's ubiquitous "applause" sign.

The benefits to actors of either spontaneous or engineered approval were balanced, if not outweighed, by the destructive effects of active, overt disapproval. By the nineteenth century, booing and hissing, almost unknown in today's theatres, were accepted as appropriate behavior. Hounding inept and otherwise unfavored actors from the stage with loud catcalls and insults was common. And it was not unusual for spectators to come to the theatre armed with throwable produce for pelting the worst histrionic offenders. The spectators never sat silently; they always voiced their opinions and were upheld in 1853 when a New Orleans

MODERN CLAPTRAP   *A contemporary equivalent of planned claptrap is the **kickline** of modern musicals in which a chorus of synchronized high kicks is guaranteed to "stop the show" with applause. Pictured here: high kicks for the Broadway production of* Legs Diamond!

judge ruled that ticket holders have a legal entitlement to hiss and stamp in the theatre.[9]

Confrontation, Conflict, and Riots

High emotions, engaged empathy, crowded spaces, little climate control, and short aesthetic and physical distance between spectators and the stage action made pre-twentieth-century indoor theatres cauldrons of often explosive elements. The theatre is a place where the emotions of an audience are always engaged over

CLAQUE IN ACTION *A nineteenth-century painting of a claque at Paris' Odeon Theatre.*

imaginary conflicts on the stage. But real conflicts are not unknown to theatre. The highly charged responses to drama set the stage for emphatic audience expressions about real events. In fact, some of the most destructive riots in history have occurred at theatrical performances. From 1743 to 1776, eight riots broke out at London's Drury Lane Theatre over such issues as opposition to the appearance of French dancers (three-day riot); the elimination of half-price admissions (two-day riot); a feud between fans of rival actors David Garrick and Charles Macklin (two-day riot); and offense taken by certain theatregoers over controversial plays such as *The Chinese Festival* (six-day riot), *The Platonic Wife* (two-day riot), *A Word to the Wise* (three-day riot), and *The Blackamoor Wash'd White* (four-day riot). And these were considered by most observers to be years of relative harmony and tranquility at Drury Lane.[10]

The Astor Place Riot.   Theatrical rivalry touched off one of the bloodiest riots in American history. In May 1849 the popular American star, Edwin Forrest, and the aristocratic English Shakespearean actor, William Charles Macready, appeared in competing productions of *Macbeth* in New York City. To the American public, the rivalry symbolized much more than Forrest's earthy, physical, proletarian manner versus Macready's reserved, patrician eloquence. To the angry mob of 15,000 that attacked the Astor Place Opera House where Macready performed on May 10, the two actors had come to represent the growing split in American society between the wealthy who were sympathetic to English culture and the underclass who resented the affluence of the new aristocracy and sought to fight back with American values and customs. Real socioeconomic conflict found its violent expression in the artificial, but confrontational confines of the theatre. A pamphlet written at the time describes the reaction of the public inside and outside of the theatre:

When May 7, the first night, arrived, the house was crowded, and there was an ominous looking gallery. When Macready appeared on the stage, in the character of Macbeth, he was assailed by a storm of hisses and yells. He stood his ground, and the play went on, but not a word could be heard. It was a dumb show. The clamor rose higher and higher and as it was not enough to drive the actor from the stage, less legitimate means were resorted to. Rotten eggs were thrown, pennies and other missiles; and soon, more outrageous demonstrations were made, and chairs were thrown from the upper part of the house, so as to peril life. There was nothing to do but stop the performance. The curtain went down and the crowd dispersed.

Three nights later, Macready tried to perform again. As the hour for the opening of the Opera House approached, excited crowds began to gather from all parts of the city. Soon the curtain rose and the mock tragedy commenced. The entrance of Macready was the signal for a storm of cheers, groans, hisses, and yells. The whole audience rose, and the greatest part, who were friendly to him, cheered. But when these were spent, the noise had not subsided. A large body in the parquet hissed and groaned, and the contest was kept up. When the chief of police decided to quell the disorder, and when the noisiest of the rioters were arrested, the play went on in comparative quietness.

MISSILES OF DISAPPROVAL   *An unpopular actor is pelted with fruit and vegetables at Baldwin's Theatre, San Francisco, c. 1870.*

But by the time the tumult was suppressed in the house, it had gained its height on the outside. A vast crowd numbering ten or fifteen thousand had gathered around the building. As a probable consequence of learning of the arrest inside, the house began to be assailed with large paving stones. These crashed against the windows, and in some instances broke through the barricades. Upon the firing by the military the alarmed and excited audience left the theatre under cover of the military, while Macready got away in the disguise of an officer; mounting a horse, escorted by a party of his friends, he left the city and a few days afterward sailed to Europe.

The National Guard and the entire New York police force were required to restore order. At least twenty people were killed in the riot, and more than a hundred were wounded. The anonymous pamphleteer's concluding comments are particularly haunting in their contemporary relevance:

> The dead are sleeping in their quiet graves. But has society no lesson to learn?
>
> A zeal for the rights of Macready and for law and order is commendable—but it must not be forgotten that other rights must have been violated, or this riot could never have taken place. Society by its unjust distribution of the avails of industry, enables a few men to become rich, and consigns a great mass to hopeless poverty, with all its deprivations and degradations.
>
> Those ignorant men had a right to education, and to such conditions of cultivation as would have made them intelligent men and good citizens. It would be better to provide ten thousand schoolmasters to instruct people, than ten thousand soldiers to prevent the result of their ignorance.[11]

Restoring Order

For the theatre to have any chance of fulfilling its artistic function, civilized behavior and assurance of safety are mandatory. The philosopher and playwright **Johann Wolfgang von Goethe** (1749–1832) instructed audiences at his theatre in Weimar on proper behavior in the autocratic German theatrical tradition. He demanded that approval be expressed only by applause and disapproval by silence. From his private box he publicly scolded inappropriate responses of audience members and ordered the arrest of those who misbehaved. His success at establishing decorum never extended beyond the borders of his small duchy.

Ultimately, safety and decorum in the audience came about by changing the architecture of the auditorium. In the 1870s the area nearest the stage (the pit) was filled with comfortable chairs and renamed the **orchestra.** Not only did this reconfiguration restrict access to the stage, it did so with a buffer of affluent theatregoers willing to pay higher prices for the privilege. As the status of sitting in the most expensive seats in the orchestra gained acceptance, the entire dynamic of audience behavior in the theatre changed.

The Audience in the Dark.   Many modern conventions of audience decorum were pioneered by **Marie Wilton Bancroft** (1839–1921) and her husband, **Squire Bancroft** (1841–1926) during their joint management of London's Prince of Wales'

Theatre from 1880 to 1885. The Bancrofts introduced chair-style seating and the novel idea of numbering and reserving seats, thus reducing the often chaotic rush and crush to get the best seats. With reserved seating, plays could run longer because seats could be sold in advance. The Bancrofts were also leaders in the use of the box set and of realistic costumes, properties, and acting, which helped the audience become absorbed in the world of the play, instead of the reality of themselves watching a play.

Their most important innovation was darkening the lights in the auditorium at the start of the performance, forcing the audience's attention on the stage rather than on each other. Several factors combined to give this practice wide acceptance after 1880. First, the desire to create the total illusion of a real place on the stage meant the audience would need to disregard that they were part of a group of spectators watching a play. Second, the invention of gas lighting (and later electric lighting) provided the technology for dimming and brightening the house lights without disrupting the performance. Third, in the twentieth century, the growing popularity of motion pictures, for which a darkened theatre is a must, made the practice familiar and acceptable to new generations of theatregoers inexperienced in the ways of their rowdy predecessors.

Modern Audiences

Diderot would have abhorred it, but passive theatregoers sitting quietly in a darkened auditorium observing a play describes the contemporary audience experience. In today's theatres, the etiquette of acceptable responses dictates that audience members not disturb each other or acknowledge any activity on the stage except through the appropriate communication of laughing, crying, applauding, or silence. Compared to the clamorous, exhibitionist, and physically volatile audiences of the past, today's theatregoers are safer, but much less engaged than the generations who preceded them. Lawrence W. Levine characterizes modern theatre audiences as "mute receptors" cowed into passivity by design and custom.[12] This condition has led to the development of a strict code of audience behavior, as well as to experiments in creating new roles for modern theatre audiences that balance safety and decorum with more active participation.

Audience Etiquette

According to psychology professor Brian Mullen, an expert on group behavior, a theatre is "one of those settings tailor-made for a breakdown in self-regulated behavior," primarily because of the dark, which increases anonymity.[13] So many people in such close proximity for extended time can be detrimental to each other. A certain etiquette is essential if everyone is to have a good time at the theatre.

A survey of theatre- and concertgoers commissioned by the Warner-Lambert Company, manufacturer of Hall's cough suppressant tablets, revealed that whispering, coughing, and sniffling—in that order—were considered the worst annoyances

DEMOCRATIC SEATING *Built between 1872 and 1876, Richard Wagner's Bayreuth Festival Theatre was designed to be democratic and civilized in its seating layout. Note how the horizontal rows restrict access of the audience to the stage. Note also the elimination of the box, pit, and galleries that previously separated the audience into classes. Center and side aisles have also been eliminated to improve sight lines for all. In a classless theatre all seats are equally good, and the same price is charged for every seat. Like the Bancrofts, Wagner darkened the auditorium to focus the imagination of the audience on the stage. Auditoriums built on this model are referred to has having* **continental seating.**

at live performances.[14] Other nuisances included crying children, seat kickers and nervous rockers, overpowering aromas, latecomers, food crunchers, tinkling jewelry, and armrest hogs. Electronic watch alarms, message beepers, and pocket-sized cellular phones also have become scourges of theatregoers and theatre artists. The Alley Theatre in Houston has instituted a policy of "phone sweeps" by ushers who intercept all beepers and portable phones. The Alley now employs a "phone check" person with whom a busy executive can park the portable phone

UNRULY AUDIENCE   *Concerts in modern arenas are conducive to the active, vociferous, demonstrative behavior of pre-twentieth-century theatregoers. The lights usually remain on throughout the arena. Bleacher seating and temporary seats arranged on the arena floor allow access to the stage. In fact, incidents of injuries and even fatal tramplings have occurred at some concerts as the crowds crushed forward toward the performers. Festival seating, which is general admission rather than reserved seats for ticket holders, has been outlawed in several cities. In 1979, eleven people were killed and twenty-two injured in a rush of fans outside Cincinnati's Riverfront Coliseum at a general admission concert by The Who.*

for the duration of the performance. A recent story making the rounds concerns the night a prominent actor reached an emotionally critical scene only to be jarred by the sound of a beeper going off in the audience. Waiting until the noise ceased, the actor pointed an accusing finger at the flustered patron and said, "I think it is time for you to go."

And finally, there are the popping flashbulbs. Even though playbills clearly state that the taking of pictures is strictly prohibited for actor safety, audience courtesy, and copyright protection, during the opening week of *Sunset Boulevard* on Broadway flashbulbs literally stopped the show. Glenn Close, who played the tempestuous Norma Desmond, was making her magnificent entrance down the grand staircase when someone snapped a flash photo of her. Close ignored the interruption and sang her show-stopping number, "With One Look." When she finished,

GOLDEN RULES

"The art of acting consists of keeping people from coughing"
—*Sir Ralph Richardson*[15]

In 1984, the Chicago theatre magazine *Stagebill* commissioned a one-page article called "Audience Etiquette." To this day they get at least one phone call a week from orchestras, theatres, opera and ballet companies all over the United States and Canada asking for reprint rights. The message seems to be an S.O.S.: American audiences are out of control. Are they? At the least, *Stagebill*'s "Golden Rules" reflect the institutionalizing of passive decorum at the live performing arts. Read on.

Part of one's pact as an audience member is to take seriously the pleasure of others, a responsibility fulfilled by quietly attentive (or silently inattentive) and self-contained behavior. After all, you can be as demonstrative as you want during bows and curtain calls.

1. Go easy with the atomizer; many people are highly allergic to perfume and cologne.
2. Unwrap all candies and cough drops before the curtain goes up or the concert begins.
3. Make sure beepers and watch alarms are OFF. And don't jangle the bangles.
4. The overture is part of the performance. Please cease talking at this point.
5. Note to lovers: when you lean your heads together, you block the view of the person behind you.
6. Force yourself to wait for a pause or intermission before rifling through a purse, backpack, or shopping bag.
7. **THOU SHALT NOT TALK,** or hum, or sing along, or beat time with a body part.
8. Coughing. Re item #2: have your lozenges unwrapped and your handkerchief in your hand. If you are really sick, the civic-minded thing to do is to release your ticket to the box office and nurse your cold at home.
9. If you bring a child, make sure etiquette is part of the experience. *Kids love learning new things.*
10. The old standby: Do unto others as you would have them do unto you.[16]

more cameras flashed. This time, in the condescending voice of her egotistical character, she declared, "We can either have a press conference, or we can go on with the show. But we cannot do both."[17] The audience cheered.

No audience experience will ever be disturbance free. Theatre artists understand it as just another factor in the creative process. They learn to deal with the dynamics of the live audience, both beneficial and disruptive. "It's just the price we pay for an audience," maintains playwright Rita McDonald Bleiman. "When we become such perfectionists that this is intolerable, perhaps we should sit by ourselves in our living rooms, noise- and people-free, listening to CDs and watching videos. Then the only distraction we will have is our own loneliness."[18]

Nontraditional Roles for the Audience

In a typical theatre experience, the audience sits passively in the dark and applauds at the end of the play. Their domain is **front of house**—the auditorium, lobby, and rest rooms. The actors have the stage and backstage areas; trespassing by members of either group is forbidden. But in many contemporary productions the audience has much different, nontraditional relationships with the performance. New ways of casting the audience in more active roles are being tried in a variety of intriguing experiments. In several notable productions, the audiences are surveyed for their opinions on how the plot of the play should be resolved. In the musical adaptation of Charles Dickens' unfinished novel, *The Mystery of Edwin Drood,* the cast surveys the audience via a show of hands in order to determine "whodunit." The cast then plays out the appropriate ending based on the *audience's* choice. Similarly, in the long-running murder mystery *Shear Madness,* the cast stops the play to poll the audience members about which of four endings they would like to see (see photo p. 438).

In the improvisational plays found in Chicano theatre, the desired result is not applause, but rather the audience members responding emotionally to the situation and spontaneously creating plays called *actos* from their own experiences. In other productions, playwrights and directors have actually called for the audience to get up from their seats, and as the play proceeds, move to different locations within the theatre space. In Marie Irene Fornes' feminist play, *Fefu and Her Friends,* small groups of audience members are escorted to different rooms to watch scenes being played simultaneously in the house that makes up the set. In the murder mystery "total evening" event *Tamara,* the audience is free to move throughout the setting (there is no auditorium) to watch suspicious goings-on in their attempts to solve the puzzle. The event is catered, so there is no need for intermissions, the purchase of refreshments, or for pre- or postshow dining. Playwright Jean Claude Van Itallie takes the unanchored audience one step further. He imagines a "Theatre of Transportation," which would involve "taking audiences out of their usual habitats, flying or driving them somewhere."[19]

In the long-running Off-Broadway hit *Tony 'n Tina's Wedding* (see photograph on p. 223), the audience actually plays roles as invited guests to a dramatized

THE AUDIENCE AS DETECTIVE   *The audience adds up the clues as the action proceeds throughout the "house" in the New York production of* Tamara.

wedding ceremony in which professional actors play the family and friends of the title characters. Actor, director, writer André Gregory, who has always loved the plays of Anton Chekhov, organized a group of actors for an experiment in playing *Uncle Vanya*. He leased an old broken-down New York theatre and the group did the play for fifteen people who sat on stage for each performance, as if in a living room. Except for a table and chairs, there was no scenery. The actors wore their own clothes and spoke in normal, conversational voices. The purpose was to make the characters seem like an ordinary American family. "I was not interested in Russia in the nineteenth century," Gregory explained. "I am fascinated by our own time. Stripping away the set and costumes, you allow the audience to be an active participant rather than a passive observer."[20] Whether playing their traditional roles or newer active parts, theatre audiences always have more to do than observe and respond in politely passive ways to what they see and hear.

THE FARM WORKERS THEATRE   *Teatro Campesino (Farm Workers Theatre) was founded in 1965 by Luis Valdez, for the sole purpose of allowing the workers (not actors playing workers) to express their own experiences through improvisation. In this* **acto,** *called* Las Dos Caras del Patroncito (The Two Faces of the Boss), *members of the audience re-create what happened at work, and the audience becomes both playwright and performer. In creating these improvisational skits the audience participates directly in theatrical performances that express the day-to-day realities of the people's lives. Like the* campesinos *themselves, the performances alternate among three languages: English, Spanish, and Calo (an urban dialect).*

Passing Judgment

Passing judgment is one way in which the public imagination of the audience interacts with the performers. Such judgment is rendered as both audible and visible responses to what occurs on the stage. The performers can feel, see, and hear these responses. Very often backstage conversation among actors centers on the audience reaction: "They're a hot crowd tonight." "They're really with us—they're getting everything." "I know they're out there, I can hear them breathing." The audience communicates imaginative responses by silent attention or bored restlessness, by laughter, tears, and applause. Such responses are outward signs of the degree to which the performance has captured the public imagination.

The **curtain call,** or bows, in which actors return to the stage to receive the applause of the audience, provides the final structured opportunity to communicate with the performers. The curtain call marks the formalized passage from the imaginary world of the theatre back to reality. For some participants it is not always an easy transition. Some theatre artists feel the issues portrayed in very serious plays make the shared warmth of a curtain call inappropriate, so they dispense with bows altogether. The resulting confusion on the part of the audience left clapping for nobody can be disconcerting and can even engender resentment. The majority of theatre artists maintain that no matter how serious the play, it is still a play—an artistic creation—not reality. The curtain call restores the mind to its proper context. Catharsis is assured.

Perhaps most importantly, the curtain call is the formal giving and acceptance of appreciation: from the audience to the actors through their applause and from the actors to the audience by their bows. Theatrical protocol is opposite to that of film and television, in which credits roll from the leads to the extras in order that the exiting audience, which does not remain to applaud, may at least see the names of the major artists. In the theatre, supernumeraries or the chorus bow first as a group, followed by the actors in supporting roles, then the leads and stars. The idea is to build the applause. The final bow is considered the most prestigious. In today's theatre, audiences respond with degrees of approval from polite clapping to thunderous applause with whistles, cheers, and shouts of "bravo," to the standing ovation, the most coveted of all affirmations of a superior shared experience.

The Audience as Critics

When the performance ends, theatregoers inevitably turn to one another and ask, "Well, what did you think of the show?" It is an obligatory period of informal discussion and analysis, and most patrons will give their opinions to anyone who will listen. The essential word-of-mouth process has begun. "Everyone," actors note with chagrin, "is a critic."

Many theatres—especially the not-for-profit and academic theatres—have formalized the critique in **postshow discussions** at which interested audience members are invited to remain in the theatre for a question, answer, and comment session with the artists. While many participants claim to receive constructive comments and advice from their patrons, not everyone believes in the beneficial effects of such discussions. Some theatre artists, especially playwrights, find the sessions frustrating due to a perceived lack of critical acumen from audience members. The audience, they maintain, is best at rendering a judgment as a group in attendance, as opposed to individual analysts after the fact. Laughter, tears, applause, disinterest, and even hurled fruit are appropriate and allowable responses. Word-of-mouth endorsements to friends and acquaintances are appreciated. Hugs and other backstage affectations are tolerated. But formal public analysis and criticism—either praiseworthy or otherwise—are best left to professional critics, the only participants in the theatrical process whom many theatre people find entirely dispensable.

THE AUDIENCE AT WORK ·················

The Post-Play Discussion Fallacy
by Michael Bloom
[Reprinted from *American Theatre*][21]

The value of postshow discussions is debated by a director and a producer.

Although I haven't acted in some time, I recently spent three hours over the course of one week on stage, in front of an audience, without the benefit of fictional characterization. My cameo wasn't voluntary; my contract required me to be there. I spent much of the time listening to and making redundant comments, "explaining" a play I'd just directed. The playwright, actors, audience and myself had become victims of the post-play discussion.

"Why not let an audience voice its opinion?" say some producers. "After all, they've paid their way. What harm can they do?" But is it harmless when in a post-play discussion an actress hears her performance criticized without substantiation, or when a spectator mistakes a playwright's considered perspective on race relations for his own prejudices? No matter how a majority of the audience feels, ill considered criticisms can adversely affect writers and performers, especially in the fragile environment of a new play process. Discussion leaders often only add to the muddle and mischief.

With the new play process, the discussion can take an especially noxious form. Audiences are told too often that they are watching an unfinished product which they are helping to shape. They are asked to become fellow artists in the collaborative process. Is it any wonder that audiences take this to mean there are weaknesses in the play that they must ferret out? I heard one recent discussion introduced this way: "The playwright is here to listen to your comments and use them in reworking the play." Naturally the audience unleashed a barrage of criticisms that distorted both the play and their generally positive response to it.

The new play, post-production discussion (which I distinguish here from discussions among professionals after play readings or workshops) implies that theatre professionals, unlike other artists, need special advice from laymen to complete their work. A visual artist would never think to include a casual observer's reaction in the development of a work; it would seem only natural that theatre artists should take credit and responsibility for their plays. An audience's participation is crucial, but it is its moment-to-moment responses as a *group,* not individual comments immediately following a performance that affect the artists. Specific comments rarely make a difference in the development of a play, but one is always aware of and attentive to the hush of an audience, its fidgeting at ineffective moments, its laughter and tears. Even in a country that tries to hold its arts up to democratic procedures, the vision of the artist cannot be subject to audience complaints or to a majority vote.

Post-play discussions—with or without artistic personnel—can be far from harmless. At a recent discussion the most eloquent remark was made (from the audience) by a playwright. He said he found it extremely dispiriting that theatre artists work so hard for two or three hours to create an epiphany—only to have it dispelled by a 20-minute question-and-answer session. In other words, a play is a work of art, not an academic exercise; plays aren't lectures that can be distilled. Good plays bear their own conclusions. Discussions violate the final moment of a production and dilute the power of performance by insisting that a play is "finished" only when it is followed by a critique. At best a discussion merely summarizes a play's ideas, reconstituting it into a lesser form.

As most playwrights, actors and directors will testify, audiences will use discussions inevitably to seek clarification, to attempt to secure a simple, brief meaning that will encapsulate the experience. Since only poor plays can be boiled down to an epigram, discussions can be anathema to the artistic process. They inherently assume that plays should provide answers, when we should be conveying to audiences that plays pose questions. Discussions foster the need for resolution instead of encouraging the acceptance of ambiguity.

I recently fled in haste at the start of a discussion of a complex, highly ambiguous new play. But before I could reach the door, I heard audience members shouting angrily at the discussion leader: "What did it mean?!" Is it possible that because they knew a discussion would follow the performance these spectators didn't work as hard as they might have to grasp the play? It's hard to imagine any answer to their question that could help them develop their skills of appreciation and do justice to the play.

My opinions obviously are those of an artist involved in creating a work; theatre educators and those not directly involved may see value in post-play discussions, especially if they focus on questions about the theatrical process. While I acknowledge the value of educating an audience, I believe that both performance and education would best be served by the separating of the two. Just as we wouldn't expect to ask a violinist how he accomplished a difficult passage immediately following a concert, we should separate theatrical performance from questions about process. This would not only respect the integrity of a performance but also increase the value of a discussion held later.

Discussions could serve a real educational purpose if we were willing to take them more seriously. As a possibility, a core group of spectators could be introduced, in a series of meetings, to the reasons for producing the play, its dramaturgical background, and the key concerns of the actors, director and designers. Then a post-play discussion, held on a day other than the performance, might provide a valuable opportunity for an audience to apply its understanding. Most important, it would educate the audience to the necessity of knowledge and understanding as prerequisites for responsible criticism.

Letter to the Editor
[Reprinted from *American Theatre*][22]

Michael Bloom's essay hints dangerously at an ivory-tower elitist perception of the artist-aesthete, the gifted figure performing on a pedestal strewing his pearls before the swinish common man. Mr. Bloom is absolutely correct in insisting that if the production does not communicate on its own merits, no further discussion is going to validate the experience: It is a failure, pure and simple. Theatre is, as he points out, a work of art, but it is a uniquely ephemeral form that differs from the performance of a Beethoven quartet or a study by Georgia O'Keeffe in that it exists only because of the direct involvement of the audience at the time of performance. A portrait may hang in some forgotten gallery of the local museum, but it exists for us whenever we decide to return to it, the interpretation unchanged from the moment it was recorded on canvas. Theatre requires communion, community, a forum in which ideas are shared. Mr. Bloom's argument to the contrary, it is a catalyst for discussion.

I suppose we can ask theatregoers to keep their thoughts to themselves, to just sit down, watch the play and shut up ("You're in the presence of an artiste . . .!"), but this seems to undercut the very nature of the theatrical experience. Theatre artists are passionately committed to ideas and attempting to communicate them to a group of individuals in this two- or three-hour performance. If those ideas are worth expressing, they are certainly worth discussing. If, as Mr. Bloom insists, plays pose questions, should an audience not be given the opportunity to formulate the answers?

I don't deny that post-play discussions can be destructive. Telling an audience that their comments will help the playwright complete and refine his work leads to a barrage of subjective, often poorly thought-out statements that reflect upon the speaker more than they do upon the work being discussed. On the other hand, suggesting that a production, either classical or new, deals with issues that are worth some discussion implies that theatre can and does have an effect on our lives, that it is not just a rarified art form that exists only within the confines of the auditorium walls.

Yes, these discussions are an educational experience for the participants, but I take great offense at Mr. Bloom's placing art and education at opposite ends of some higher aesthetic spectrum, with education on the lowest possible rung. I believe, as many of my colleagues do, that we presently make theatre for approximately 10 percent of the population. If we do not struggle to expose that other 90 percent to the pleasures—and the educational and mind-expanding potentials—of the theatre, then we are going to lose our audiences

to the easier art forms of television and film, which can be enjoyed in the comfort of one's own home without having to deal with 499 other strangers sitting with you in a dark, cavernous space.

And there is no reason why this educational process must pare down the complexity and ambiguity of a performance. The ultimate educational experience is one which reveals a multiplicity of meanings to be found in an event, meanings that even the director may not have considered. When asked "What does it mean?" by a discussion participant, turn it around on the interrogator: "What do you think it means?" is exactly what he wants to hear, anyway, and he will be more than happy to provide an answer to his own question. If theatregoers are made to understand that their responses are only valid if they are based solely upon what the play has given to the viewer and not what the audience has brought to it, then a series of seemingly contradictory but equally valid meanings will arise. Surely Mr. Bloom, as an artist, is in support of any audience that struggles to find a variety of meanings?

Finally, as to Mr. Bloom's proposed discussion format in which a core group of spectators is introduced "to the reasons for producing the play, its dramaturgical background, and the key concerns of the actors, director and designers," I can only respond by saying, "Who cares?" Personally, I don't want to know why a production was mounted. I merely want to know what it's saying to me, four months after all of those decisions were made. And I want to talk about it and find out what other people think about what it says. And I want to argue about it.

And if Mr. Bloom wants to join in on that argument, he may feel free. If not, he can leave the room.

—Greg Leaming, artistic director
Portland Stage Company, Portland, Maine

SUMMARY

1. The role of an audience at the performance of a stage play is as imaginative as that of the theatre artists. The imagination of the audience is captured when theatregoers make psychological connections with the actors and their portrayals.

2. The willing suspension of disbelief is the unwritten agreement in which the spectators agree not to disbelieve the imaginary world of the play.

3. Empathy is the capacity to identify emotionally with characters in the play. Unlike *sympathy*, which means "to feel for," *empathy* means "to feel with."

4. Dramatic irony describes the audience's knowledge of events that are unknown to the characters.

5. Catharsis is the safe release of heightened emotions brought about by the concluding events of the play.

6. *Aesthetic distance* refers to the psychological proximity of the audience to the play.

7. For most of theatre history, very active audiences have played vociferous and demonstrative roles in almost all aspects of the performance, leading to disruptions and occasionally riots. In the nineteenth century, theatre practice underwent changes that transformed theatregoers into more passive observers.

8. New roles are being sought for audiences in experiments involving more active participation.

9. The curtain call provides the final structured opportunity to communicate with the performers.

CHOICES

1. Make a list of differences and similarities of going to the theatre and going to a sporting event. What is the relationship between spectators and players? What are considered appropriate responses to the players in each situation? What is considered appropriate etiquette vis-à-vis other spectators? How does the theatrical effect of dramatic irony compare to the unknown outcome of a sporting event?

2. Imagine you are at a postshow discussion of a theatrical production you have recently attended. But instead of being invited to discuss the play or the artists and their choices, the producer asks you to review the audience experience including the behavior of the group, its reactions, the café accommodations and events, comfort, and facilities. When called on for constructive

criticism, what comments, suggestions, compliments, and complaints would you offer to the producer?

3. Compare and contrast preparations you make for attending live theatre, going to a movie, or watching a video at home. Consider dress, travel, companion, prior planning, costs, etc. How does the complexity of preparations affect your reactions to the performance itself?

An actor's nightmare: the scowling countenance of theatre critic
George Bernard Shaw.

This is the silliest stuff that ever I saw.

A Midsummer Night's Dream, *Act V, scene i*

CHAPTER 11

Judgments on the Theatrical Imagination

THE CRITIC'S CHOICES

PREVIEW

Critics! Who needs them? Just ask Arthur Miller. In his autobiography *Timebends,* Miller testifies to the power of theatre critics over both creative artists and the public. He describes the moment when he first realized he was famous. It was the overnight review—one person's written opinion—of his play *Death of a Salesman* that changed his life forever.

An hour or so later, at the opening night party, Jim Proctor grabbed my arm and pulled me to a phone. On the other end was the whispered voice of Sam Zolotow, that generation's theatrical inside dopester and a reporter for the *Times,* who was actually reading our review directly off Brooks Atkinson's typewriter as the critic wrote it—I could hear the clacking of the typewriter over the phone. In his Noo Yawk voice he excitedly whispered word after word as Atkinson composed it under his nose—"Arthur Miller has written a superb drama. From every point of view, it is a rich and memorable . . ." and as one encomium was laid upon another Sam's voice grew more and more amazed and warm, and he seemed to reach out and give me his embrace. The conspiracy that had begun with me and spread to Kazan, the cast, Mielziner, and all the others now extended to Zolotow and Atkinson and the *Times,* until for a moment a community seemed to have formed of people who cared very much that their common sense of life in their time had found expression.

Driving homeward down lower Broadway at three in the morning, Mary and I were both silent. The radio had just finished an extraordinary program, readings of the play's overwhelmingly glowing reviews in the morning papers. My name repeated again and again seemed to drift away from me and land on someone else, perhaps my ghost. It was all a letdown now that the arrow had been fired and the bow, so long held taut, was slackening again. I had striven all my life to win tonight, and it was here, and I was this celebrated man who had amazingly little to do with me, or I with him.

In truth, I would have sworn I had not changed, only the public perception of me had, but this was merely fame's first illusion. The fact, as it took much more time to appreciate, is that such an order of recognition imprints its touch of arrogance, quite as though one has control of a new power, a power to make real everything one is capable of imagining.[1]

Did Arthur Miller really need a critic to tell him his play was good? Did he, his cast, and the producers of *Death of a Salesman* have to wait to hear it from *New York Times* critic Brooks Atkinson? Didn't the opening night audience and their stunned reaction after the curtain fell tell him? Didn't the theatre artists tell him? Didn't they know? Didn't he?

Everyone involved in the creative process of theatre—theatregoers, playwrights, theatre artists, investors, restaurateurs, parking lot attendants, ushers— needs the critics. Like it or not, theatre critics can have a greater impact on the success of a theatrical production than the artists themselves. Often the opinions of a few critics may persuade people not to attend the production. No one wants to take the chance of seeing a bad show.

"Theatre," Robert Brustein points out, "is the only art that depends so heavily on the press for its survival."[2] Good reviews can ensure tremendous box office, long-term employment, fame for the playwright and leading players, and enormous profits for investors. Unfavorable reviews can torpedo box office sales and put an entire company out of work. Therefore, as soon as the curtain falls on opening night, *everybody* waits for the word.

Need, of course, breeds resentment as well as the finer sentiments of appreciation. The relationship between artists and critics, especially in the theatre, is at best constructive and at worst adversarial. The ancient Greeks had a phrase that describes this ambivalent attitude toward critics: *philos/aphilos,* meaning "love in hate." Clive Barnes, the theatre critic for the *New York Post,* described the relationship this way: "The critic is a symbiotic parasite on the underbelly of art. Not totally essential—but hopefully helpful."[3] In today's theatre, for better or worse, the critic, purposely isolated from the production process, practices an art in which the comments of one are of extraordinary importance to the choices of so many.

This chapter examines the symbiosis of theatre critics with theatremakers and theatregoers. Types of theatrical criticism are defined, and the skills of professional critics are "reviewed."

Critics and Criticism

In general, **criticism** endeavors to evaluate experiences. The purposes of theatrical criticism are to describe the production for potential audiences and to articulate a public response for the theatre artists. Not really theatremakers and much more than theatregoers, critics serve an important function by bringing the two constituencies together or by keeping them apart. The evaluations of theatre critics can range in form from the briefest recommendations to the most detailed analyses.

Reviews

A **review** is the immediate response of a person who has just seen a production and recounts the experience—usually in daily newspaper columns or, increasingly, on television news programs. Theatrical reviews are short. Because they work under strict deadlines and within the constraints of limited column space or air time, reviewers must have a talent for capsulizing their experiences. At a minimum, reviews describe the plot, assess the quality of the production elements, and recommend whether or not to attend. The **media reviewers** deliver their judgments on radio or television broadcasts and are often confined to sixty-second "spots." Reporters who cover the "arts and leisure" beat for local newspapers review many amateur productions and occasional professional touring shows. Local boosterism of the community arts scene is often a part of their charge and is evident in their generous reviews. **Local reviewers** may or may not be qualified as theatre experts or even as theatre lovers.

POLITE LIES

Gary Panetta was a young copy editor for the *Peoria Journal Star* when he was promoted to the theatre beat as a replacement for retiring arts editor Jerry Klein. Almost immediately he discovered that the job of "local reviewer" demanded he make difficult choices in evaluating what truly "plays in Peoria."

Jerry Klein once joked that some local theater people had made a doll of him and stuck pins in it. Given some letters I received about a recent review, I suspect the same thing is happening to me.

Critics who write about local, nonprofessional theater have two choices: They can tell polite lies or tell the truth.

The first choice is easy. It doesn't require thinking about a show or drawing comparisons. It doesn't even require attending a show; just plug in the adjectives and disengage the brain.

The second choice is much harder. It means taking local theater seriously. It means having modest expectations of quality. It means having faith that the local arts community has even more talent and potential than its members realize.

Make no mistake about it. "Nice" reviewers—those who pass over blunders and blemishes and rhapsodize about how magical it all was, even if it wasn't—believe the local arts are capable of only mediocrity or worse.

In the long run, an honest critique will benefit theater.

And in the short run, it benefits readers. Depending on what you see, ticket prices can run anywhere from $9 to $20 apiece. Why shouldn't potential viewers get a frank assessment of what's out there?

But how does a critic decide what's good? After all, what plays in Peoria won't fly on Broadway. But this is no excuse to suspend judgment on everything. Community theater should be held to community standards. Local productions should live up to the best of what's been done locally.[4]

The **daily reviewers** for large metropolitan papers who cover the openings of professional theatrical productions have more certifiable qualifications and seek to maintain a judicial distance from those they review. The *New York Times,* which devotes more space to theatrical coverage than any other daily paper, employs two full-time daily reviewers to cover the many openings in their theatrical metropolis: a "first-string," or "chief" critic who covers Broadway and major Off-Broadway productions and a "second stringer" who reviews Off-Broadway, Off-Off-Broadway, and out-of-town productions. Daily reviewers write under the high-pressure deadlines of next-morning early editions. Their

CAPSULE REVIEWS

Capsule reviews of everything from restaurants and nightclubs to books, films, and theatrical productions are popular features of many publications. In three sentences, *The New Yorker* magazine digests Mimi Kramer's full-length review of Herb Gardner's *Conversations with My Father* into a capsule that evaluates the play and the performances, recommends attendance, and gives the address and phone number of the theatre.

Conversations with My Father—If you're looking for a totally satisfying theatrical experience, try the new Herb Gardner, a bittersweet memory play about a Lower East Side barkeep, his two sons, and the patrons of his tavern. As staged by Daniel Sullivan, with an ace cast led by the wonderful Judd Hirsch, the play does what "Jake's Women" and "Dancing at Lughnasa" would probably do if their authors were, respectively, more sophisticated and less sentimental. Grab this one. (Royale, 242 W. 45th St. 239-6200.)[5]

Judd Hirsch in his Tony Award-winning role in Herb Gardner's Conversations with My Father.

immediate reactions to what they have seen carry tremendous weight in the theatre community.

Theatrical Criticism

Theatrical criticism refers to longer commentaries written by experts in the field of theatre. Because their articles appear in weekly or monthly publications, these theatre critics have more time for thoughtful analysis and insight. The *New York Times* reserves space for a third theatre critic in its "Sunday View" column, a regular feature of its weekly "Arts and Leisure" section that also contains several pieces of theatre criticism by contributing experts. Among the leading theatre critics are John Lahr (*The New Yorker*), Jack Kroll (*Newsweek*), Robert Brustein (*The New Republic*), Matt Wolf (Associated Press and *American Theatre*), John Simon (*New York Magazine*), and Walter Kerr, who has written everything from daily reviews for the now defunct *New York Herald Tribune* to thoughtful commentaries for the *New York Times*. Lahr, Brustein, and Kerr have also achieved the status of **analyst critics,** who by virtue of their theatrical erudition have written influential book-length studies of theatre and drama.

With an admittedly smaller readership than daily reviewers, writers of theatrical criticism are less immediately influential, but they serve longer range purposes of raising the level of literacy among theatregoers and challenging conventional practice among theatre artists. They function much like political commentators who do more than just report the news; columnists like Ellen Goodman, William Raspberry, and George F. Will focus on particular news stories and attempt to probe the larger significance of events as they relate to the nation and the world. Whether readers share the conclusions of these commentators or not, their function is validated if perspective has been widened and opinions clarified.

As is true of political commentators, the best theatre critics are sought out for opinions that are more discriminating than those of the average audience member. In his book *The Critic's Canon,* Richard Palmer insists that critics can "improve theatrical standards by educating an audience to a level of taste more receptive to ambitious theatre and less tolerant of mediocrity."[6] The critic seeks to improve the state of the art by sensitizing playgoers to theatrical values that may otherwise remain hidden: the deeper meaning of the play, the unrecognized quality of the writing or production values, historical similarities, or new trends. In this way, critics keep the public informed of the latest developments in theatre. Who are the up-and-coming playwrights? What are the innovations in staging, and who is responsible for them? What people and events influence the kinds of plays that are successfully presented? What will be important to future audiences?

Critical Skills

To maintain credibility, theatre critics must have certain skills. In addition to familiarity with traditions and modern practice of theatre and drama, effective critics possess a love of the theatre, an open-minded impartiality, and the writing skills of a literary artist.

Love of the Theatre

There is nothing sentimental about the critics' love of the theatre. It is an absolute necessity. It has to be. They spend most of their nights in fold-down seats watching plays, surreptitiously writing notes on small pads. Both Glenna Syse, retired after 33 years as performing arts critic for the *Chicago Sun Times,* and Eliot Norton, who stepped down in 1991 after 56 years as the "dean" of Boston's critics, estimated that they had each seen and reviewed 6,000 theatre, opera, music, and dance performances. Nationally known author and critic Jerry Klein characterized his career-long romance with the stage as the opportunity to live his life "not only among such people as Beethoven, Shakespeare, and Monet, but those who interpret or recreate them . . . who bring Hamlet back from his grave, and who make Beethoven live again through his music."[7]

Of course, not every performance is a masterpiece; for every *Salesman,* Tony Award-winning performance, or Ming Cho Lee setting there are hundreds that are mediocre, barely competent, derivative, repulsive, and worst of all, boring. Nineteenth-century analyst-critic William Archer maintained that "the first qualification for a dramatic critic is the capacity to sleep while sitting bolt upright."[8]

The Question of Impartiality

There is a degree of self-contradiction in the qualities of good theatre critics. On the one hand they must maintain a reporter's objectivity about the events they cover, but on the other hand they are asked to render subjective judgments on those events—a kind of oxymoronic calling. Robert Brustein characterizes himself as a "professional opinionator hired to pass judgment regularly on the state of the theatre."[9] Certainly, a set of standards and personal viewpoints are requirements for making aesthetic judgments. Yet strictly enforced impartiality is required to give those judgments credibility. George Bernard Shaw began his theatrical career as a reviewer for various London publications. He had a reputation for using his formidable wit to write scathing attacks on the popular entertainments and entertainers of his day. But what many theatre artists characterized as an intolerant adversarial bias, Shaw defended as passionate objectivity.

> People have pointed out evidences of personal feeling in my notices as if they were accusing me of a misdemeanor. The artist who accounts for my disparagement by alleging personal animosity on my part is quite right: when people do less than their best . . . I hate them, loathe them, detest them, long to tear them limb from limb and strew their gibbets about the stage or platform. . . . If my own father were an actor-manager, and his life depended on his getting favorable notices of his performance, I should orphan myself without an instant's hesitation if he acted badly.[10]

Glenna Syse cautioned that professional distance is the only way to prevent even the perception of a conflict of interest: "Do not socialize with the people you are reviewing. It is," she adds, "a lonely life."[11] Syse's characterization is not entirely negative. Isolation is an essential aspect of being a writer.

Literary Skills

Critics are writers whose choices—judgments on the theatrical imagination—are rendered as literary art. Their particular kind of writing is characterized by brevity, evocative description, and entertaining wit.

Except for analyst critics who write book-length studies, most theatre critics are restricted to 400 to 800 words. Within these confines, they must be adept at verbally characterizing theatrical effects. Summarizing plots is one thing, but

THE FAMOUS HELICOPTER SCENE FROM *MISS SAIGON*   *The critic's literary skills render such art on the stage as descriptive prose on the page.*

more challenging are written descriptions of the audible effects of music and voice; the visual impact of scenery, costumes, lighting, and staging; and the emotional veracity of the acting. In a reversal of the theatrical imagination, the critic renders art on the stage as description on the page. In his *Wall Street Journal* review of the megamusical *Miss Saigon,* critic Edwin Wilson displayed his descriptive talents to convey the dazzling lighting and scenic effects:

> The subtlety and shading of lighting are orchestrated like a visual musical score. One moment Kim and her son will be on stage alone, isolated by a pale, white light; the next moment the stage will be awhirl with movement and color—a bright red glow encompassing everything as spotlights swivel from above like tracer shells piercing an infernal landscape. And then there is the helicopter, which descends with its motor roaring and its rotor blades sending smoke and fog swirling across the stage.[12]

For many, the real art of critics is in their facility with clever, entertaining phrasemaking. While theatre artists are remembered for their stage choices, critics achieve fame for their written witticisms. In his review of the shoot-'em-up comedy/adventure film *Lethal Weapon 3,* Jack Kroll described Danny Glover's detective Murtaugh as a cop who "shies away from violence as he gets closer to retirement. Only under extreme provocation does he unlimber his arsenal and make kerflooey on the various scumbags that litter his path to peace." About the film's director he wrote, "Richard Donner choreographs violence like Busby Berkeley with Uzis instead of floozies."[13] In this case, Kroll's cheekiness was complimentary, but the most memorable critical passages are the slams. As Glenna Syse explains, "Complimentary adjectives are so overused they just lie there. It's far easier to write pans than raves."[14] It is no wonder that critics seem to be at their best when they are finding fault.

For many theatre artists who have been the targets of critics' literary assaults, it seems that finding fault is the only thing the critics ever do. Some artists have tried to respond in kind, usually without effect, because the artists do not have reserved column space or air time. Performers cannot "close" a critic the way a critic can close a show. But they try. Critic bashing is one of the theatre's favorite pastimes. Less reserved theatre artists have punched critics and filed defamation lawsuits against them. In 1932 one would-be playwright, who was also a U.S. representative, even called congressional hearings to investigate them. Beyond bruises, such desperate efforts have never stopped the critics from writing about the theatre.

History of Theatrical Criticism

Critics of the Theatre

The theatre has always had its critics. Not *theatre critics,* but critics *of* the theatre—those who opposed the existence of the institution itself. In ancient Greece,

LEGENDARY CRITICAL ZINGERS

John Mason Brown on Tallulah Bankhead in *Antony and Cleopatra:* *"Tallulah Bankhead barged down the Nile last night as Cleopatra and sank."*

Dorothy Parker on Katharine Hepburn in one of her early stage appearances: *"Katharine Hepburn ran the gamut of emotions from A to B."*

Walter Kerr on the eminently forgettable drama *Hook and Ladder:* *"It is the sort of play that gives failure a bad name."*

Robert Benchley on an unfunny British comedy, *Perfectly Scandalous:* *"It is one of those plays in which all the actors unfortunately enunciated very clearly."*

George S. Kaufman, taking time out from his own playwriting to review a comedy: *"There was scattered laughter in the rear of the theater, leading to the belief that somebody was telling jokes back there."*

Eugene Field, writing for *The Denver Post,* on the actor who played the title role in a production of *King Lear:* *"All through the five acts of the Shakespearean tragedy he played the King as though under the premonition that someone was about to play the Ace."*[15]

The critic for the London *Evening Standard* on the opening of *Sunset Boulevard:* *"Andrew Lloyd Webber has done it again and I wish he had not."*[16]

Roger Ebert on Rob Reiner's film *North:* *"I hated this movie. Hated hated hated hated hated this movie. Hated it. Hated every simpering stupid vacant audience-insulting moment of it."*[17]

Frank Rich on the National Actors Theater production of Chekhov's *The Seagull:* *"Superior to last season's National Actors Theater productions only in the sense that mediocrity is superior to catastrophe."*[18]

CRITIC BASHING

Mark Twain: *"The critic's symbol should be the tumblebug; he deposits his egg in somebody else's dung, otherwise he could not hatch it."*[19]

Brendan Behan: *"Critics are like eunuchs in a harem. They're there every night, they see it done every night, they see how it should be done every night, but they can't do it themselves."*[20]

Christopher Hampton: *"Asking a working actor what he thinks about critics is like asking a lamp-post how it feels about dogs."*[21]

David Merrick: *"Mr. Rich made many contributions to the American theatre, none more great than to leave his post as theatre critic."*[22]

Thespis suffered Solon's antitheatrical tirades, and Aeschylus, Sophocles, Euripides, and Aristophanes withstood Plato's philosophical objections. Roman theatre artists were unable to survive the religious criticisms of theologians like St. Augustine of Hippo (354–430) and the empirewide bans of the Council of Carthage. Shakespeare and his contemporaries had to perform outside the London city limits to avoid the antitheatrical regulations of civil magistrates and sermons of religious fundamentalists. (By 1642, there was nowhere left to hide when Cromwell's republicans took over England and closed down every London theatre until the monarchy was restored twenty years later.)

One of the most infamous, but nonetheless effective critics of the theatre was the Anglican deacon **Jeremy Collier** (1656-1726). In 1698 Collier penned a widely read pamphlet titled *A Short View of the Immorality and Profaneness of the English Stage* that attacked the writers of the comedies of his day as archenemies of religion.

> Show, music, action, and rhetoric, are moving entertainments; and right employed, would be very significant. But force and motion are things indifferent, and the use lies chiefly in the application. These advantages are now in the enemies' hand, and under a very dangerous management. Like cannon seized, they are pointed the wrong way, and by the strength of the defense the mischief is made the greater. That this complaint is not unreasonable I shall endeavor to prove by showing the misbehavior of the stage with respect to morality and religion. Their liberties in the following particulars are intolerable—viz. their smuttiness of expression; their swearing, profaneness, and lewd application of Scripture; their abuse of the clergy; their making their top characters libertines, and giving them success in their debauchery.[23]

Collier's fanatical diatribe was instrumental in suppressing the glittering, titillating Restoration comedies of manners that were popular with the English aristocracy and replacing them with the more platitudinous sentimental variety favored by the middle classes. Contemporary railings against alleged immorality and profanity in films and on television are nagging echoes of Collier's harangue.

Philosopher Critics

Aristotle, writing in response to Plato's antitheatrical reasonings, became the first true theatre critic. He loved the theatre, understood the form, documented its short history, and possessed formidable literary skill, which he used to set forth standards of excellence by which plays and productions could be judged. Much modern theatre and film criticism is based on the ideas found in Aristotle's *Poetics,* a discourse on the structure of drama that provides an aesthetic context for judging the quality of a theatrical production.

In the Aristotelian tradition, Roman writers carefully scrutinized what they saw on the stage. The poet **Horace** (65 B.C.–8 B.C.) was critical of the depiction of brutality and violence on the stage and set down clear stylistic limitations for comedy and tragedy. The stoic philosopher **Epictetus** (born c. 60 A.D.) wrote a critical thesis attacking the governor of Epirus for showing favoritism toward a certain comic actor. In his treatise, "Concerning One Who Made Himself Improperly Conspicuous in the Theatre," he chided the governor for not setting an example to others as to how they ought to behave in the theatre. The Roman poet **Lucian** (fl. second century) was one of the first critics to attack the quality of acting and costuming:

> Let us consider . . . the hideous, appalling spectacle that the actor presents. His high boots raise him up out of all proportion; his head is hidden under an enormous mask; his huge mouth gapes upon the audience as if he would swallow them; to say nothing of the chest pads and stomach pads with which he contrives to give himself artificial corpulence, lest his deficiency in this respect would emphasize his disproportionate height. And in the middle of it all is the actor, shouting away, now high now low— chanting his iambics as often as not; could anything be more revolting than this sing song recitation of tragic woes.[24]

In the Renaissance, the works of philosopher critics circulated widely among Europe's educated elite influencing others to take up the practice of theatre criticism. Their subject was theatre in general, not judgments on individual plays or productions.

Critical Standards

Standards for reviewing individual productions were suggested by the eighteenth-century poet, playwright, and stage director Johann Wolfgang von Goethe. He maintained that a good theatrical review should answer three fundamental questions:

> *What is the play or production trying to do?* Goethe recognized it serves no purpose to judge a play with very serious intentions by the same criteria as one that intends only to entertain. Both purposes are legitimate artistic goals, but must be held to different standards of excellence. Criticizing a melodrama that intended only to shock and generate spine-tingling suspense because it failed to illuminate complex moral issues would be unfair, serving neither the needs of those looking for pure entertainment nor the desires of theatregoers who prefer more ethically complex drama.

> *How well was it done?* The most familiar critical pursuit is determining the quality of the artwork in terms of its execution (no critic's pun intended). In the theatre, Goethe suggested the question be answered in terms of the ways in which the various theatrical elements either contributed to or detracted from the overall quality of the production. Many great plays have been ruined by bad acting, substandard design, or technical ineptitude. Conversely, mediocre plays have been saved by great productions.

WHAT IS THE PLAY TRYING TO DO?   *In 1992,* Falsettos, *by William Finn and James Lapine, and* Crazy for You, *by Ken Ludwig with songs by George and Ira Gershwin, received wide critical acclaim and were both nominated for the Tony Award as best musical.* Falsettos *(above) is a minimalist production of a bittersweet play about the effects of AIDS on a contemporary New York family. Frank Rich praised it as an "exhilarating and heartbreaking musical" about a "modern family divided in sexuality but finally inseparable in love and death."* Crazy for You *(below) aspired to nothing more than musical comedy fluff. Rich called it a "riotously entertaining show" that "uncorks the American musical's classic blend of music, laughter, dancing, sentiment and showmanship that has rarely been seen during the 'Cats' decade."[25]* Crazy for You *won the Tony.*

Was it worth doing? The most subjective and perhaps the most important of Goethe's critical criteria, this question addresses the broader issues of the value of the work. A production may be conceived for a specific, well-fulfilled purpose, be endowed with excellent direction, acting, and designs, but serve only redundant, imitative, or even destructive ends.

It is the critic's job to articulate answers to these questions.

Play reviews became regular features of weekly newspapers and magazines in the late eighteenth century and of daily newspapers in the nineteenth century. Goethe's reasonable standards, however, were not universally adopted, especially by reviewers in the big cities of Europe and America who used more suspect standards to determine their written opinions.

The Puff System

When theatre became big business, managers used every legitimate and illegitimate means possible, including bribing critics, to get audiences into their competing productions. **Puffers** were newspaper critics who wrote favorable reviews in exchange for outright payoffs, free tickets, and other under-the-table amenities. Legitimate critics like American poet Walt Whitman, who wrote for the *Brooklyn Eagle,* were convinced the puffers often wrote their reviews *before* the performances. Playwright George Colman the Younger lampooned this disreputable practice in the epilogue to his 1788 comedy, *Ways and Means:*

> I am a critic, my master, I sneer, splash and vapour.
> Puff parties, damn poets, in short, do a paper.
> My name's Johnny Grub—I'm a vendor of scandal,
> My pen like an auctioneer's hammer I handle.
> Knocking down reputation by one inch of candle.
> I've heard out the play, yet I need not have come.
> I'll tell you a secret, my masters, be mum!
> Though rammed in amongst you, to praise or to mock it,
> I've brought my critique—cut and dried—in my pocket.

The puff system was reinforced by such powerful entertainment cartels as the Theatrical Syndicate and the Shubert Corporation, which pressured publishers for favorable reviews in exchange for lucrative advertisements in the papers. The system came to an end in 1915 when the *New York Times* stood behind its theatre critic Wolcott Gibbs who had been banned by the Shuberts from their theatres for giving one of their productions a bad review. The Shuberts, as have all producers since, realized that the attendant free publicity of good reviews is indispensable to their business. The *New York Times* and all other major publications now pay for their critics' tickets and adhere to strict policies that proscribe even the appearance of conflicts of interest.

Artistic Symbiosis: Critics in the Modern Theatre

Power to the Critics

American producers often lament the life-and-death power that critics wield over their productions. But it was the producers who were initially responsible for this state of affairs. In 1917 theatrical producers capitulated to the critics by, in effect, designating them as the chief arbiters of theatrical quality. Producers began the now common practice of using favorable comments from reviews as banner advertisements for their productions, prominently displaying the quotations in newspaper ads, on marquees, and in theatre lobbies. The practice made critics powerful allies in certifying hits and in designating failure. Unanimous critical praise, referred to by the producers as **money reviews,** means long runs and huge profits. **Mixed reviews** promise the possibility of running long enough to break even, and **pans** mean cutting losses and immediate closing.

Theatregoers have come to depend on these featured quotations as a time-saving way of cutting through the thicket of reviews to identify the best shows. Even critics themselves have found certification of their professional reputations in the attention their words receive. "A critic has arrived—at least he has arrived on Broadway—," *New York Times* second stringer Mel Gussow wrote, "when his name goes up in lights. Sometimes it appears as if the critic were playing at the theatre."[26]

The Critical Authority of the *New York Times*.   Since the early years of the century, critical power has accrued to the daily reviewer of the *New York Times*. In 1920 there were seventeen daily newspapers in New York City. Today there are only three, of which only the *Times* has a reputation as a national newspaper with a respected tradition of theatre arts coverage. The other two, the *New York Daily News* and the *New York Post,* are metropolitan tabloids given to more sensational reporting. This situation has resulted in a consolidation of critical influence whereby the daily critic for the *New York Times,* regardless of the person's identity, critical acumen, or experience, is perceived to have virtually absolute power to proclaim theatrical hits and misses.

Over the years the critic's chair at the *Times* has been occupied by greater and lesser talents. The most distinguished was the venerable **Brooks Atkinson** (1894–1984) who served as daily reviewer from 1926 to 1960, achieving a reputation for supportive, yet honest and intelligent observations on the American theatre. Atkinson and Walter Kerr are the only critics to have Broadway theatres named after them.

Frank Rich, the *Times'* chief drama critic from 1980 to 1993, was a more controversial occupant. Because of what many feel was an overly negative and intolerant, if elegant, style, he engendered as much resentment as respect; he even earned the nickname "the Butcher of Broadway." Arthur Miller referred to Rich's tenure as "a dictatorship as effective as any cultural control mechanism in the world."[27] British playwright David Hare took his dispute with Rich public. After Rich gave the Broadway opening of Hare's *The Secret Rapture* a bad review, and the play

A CERTIFIED HIT   *This* New York Times *full-page ad is made up exclusively of favorable quotations from reviewers. Notice that the reviewer for the* Times *is featured first.*

immediately folded, Hare wrote an angry letter to the critic attacking him for closing his show. "You know as well as I do," wrote Hare, "that without in any way changing or compromising your view you could have written an identical notice which made the identical points to the one you did, but which supported and extended the play's life in New York." In his own open letter, Rich responded that he was well aware of the consequences of his reviews, but that his "responsibility is to be honest with the *Times* readers, not 'to ensure the survival of the theatre' or to support the 'continuance of the serious play on Broadway.' . . . The *Times,*" he added, "did not close your play. . . . The producers closed your play."[28] What made the situation so difficult is that they were both right. When the judgments of the *Times* are *the* ruling opinions for Broadway shows, the critic has an obligation to the highest standards, careful prose, and strict impartiality. On the other hand, it is the producer's choice to heed those judgments or ignore them.

It has been suggested that since the producers started this system, they could end it by stopping the practice of using critics' quotes for advertising. While it seems unlikely to happen, there is some evidence to give credence to the idea. Cameron Mackintosh, the producer of the megahits *Les Misérables, The Phantom of the Opera,* and *Miss Saigon,* shuns critics' quotes, preferring his own logo-centered, catch-phrase campaigns. His shows, referred to as "critic-proof," have achieved record-breaking, long-running success despite less than enthusiastic reviews from the *Times* and other publications.

Critics and Playwrights

Critics and playwrights have a more complex symbiotic relationship than the Hare-Rich dispute might indicate. Critics measure new plays against a canon of drama going back thousands of years. They look beyond the current production to speculate on a play's suitability and flexibility for other stage incarnations. In addition to pointing out that which is "not worth doing," they must be able to distinguish what is innovative from those plays that are merely idiosyncratic and gimmicky.

As often as they seem to close plays, the best critics have also used their literary skills to open stage doors for unknown or unfairly criticized dramatists. George Bernard Shaw, for instance, stood against the raging critical tide that labeled Ibsen's social dramas such as *Ghosts* and *A Doll's House* as "wretched," "deplorable," "loathsome," "rank," "deadly," "a disease," and "an open cesspool" to urge productions of the plays of this now-celebrated writer. Playwrights are quick to point out, however, that while Shaw was prescient about Ibsen, most critics of the time were wrong about him. There is ample evidence, they maintain, that critics fail to recognize the value of that which is new and different. The initial critical consensus was negative on such masterpieces as Anton Chekhov's *Three Sisters* and *The Seagull,* John Millington Synge's *Playboy of the Western World,* Eugene O'Neill's *The Iceman Cometh,* and Samuel Beckett's *Waiting for Godot.* Viewed from a different perspective, however, there is no denying these dramatists survived their initial encounters with reviewers, prospered, and in so doing irrevocably altered the standards of theatrical criticism itself.

The "standards," of course, keep changing. In an increasingly eclectic, diverse theatre, cultural sensitivity has become a requirement not only of the critics, but of their employers. Diversity in the theatrical judiciary is as necessary for the health of the American theatre as is diversity in the civil and criminal judiciary.

For playwrights, what may seem like a critics' war on theatrical risk taking and originality in the short run can be seen as beneficial in the long run. Despite a successful career as a writer for stage and screen, playwright Michael Weller has received his share of bad reviews. Weller put his ambivalence toward critics on the stage. In his play *Lake No Bottom,* a critic gets his comeuppance after a lifetime of literary invective. Weller insisted he was not out for revenge:

> It just seemed to me that the unspoken feelings that exist in any art between the critics who discuss it and the people who make it are so wonderfully loaded with layers of subterfuge and deception. Through their professional gestures, they enter each other's fantasy lives in a very profound way, so that in critical statements you will find a sudden savage outlashing or a sudden loving embrace that is so astonishing in the context of the rest of the review that, for a second, the curtain is lifted on what is going on in the critic's innermost life. And in the artist's awareness and fear of the critic, there is something major going on also.[29]

No less an authority than Benedict Nightingale, chief critic for the *Times* of London, cautioned his colleagues not to neglect their interactive relationship with those they judge: "So often criticism seems to be a courtroom in which theatre practitioners are arraigned. If that is so, then perhaps the critic should think of himself as court recorder and defense attorney at least as much as a prosecutor and judge."[30]

Critics and Actors

Judging actors is more of a generational thing. Historical perspective is not particularly relevant. Critics do not measure actors against the historical parade of performers who have trod the boards before them. Critics judge actors only against what is current according to the latest conventions. Critical reactions are more immediate and psychological. Critics look to identify believability, subtlety, passion, skill, and astonishing choices. They shun exaggeration, phoniness, and that which is inarticulate.

Referring to reviews as "notices," stage actors depend on critics for the wider attention good reviews can give them. Without the instant access to millions of viewers available to television and film actors, stage actors have come to depend on critics for essential career boosts. Ian McKellan, one of Great Britain's most renowned Shakespearean actors, states the case bluntly:

> I'm working in a very, very old-fashioned industry which depends on direct communication between people in relatively small spaces. . . . If you're crucially a theatre

actor you can't expect to have more than a very, very small group of people who know a sizable body of your work. I mean how many people have seen Vanya? Iago? Macbeth? Those are my finest performances.[31]

A critic's favorable notice can assure that more people will see an actor's work. For instance, Jack Kroll brought deserved national attention to actor, playwright, and Stanford University professor Anna Deavere Smith when he reviewed her one-person show in *Newsweek*. In *Fires in the Mirror*, Smith played twenty-seven characters in a "human collage" depicting the race riots that occurred in the summer of 1991 in Crown Heights, Brooklyn. Among her portrayals were Hasidic rabbis, African American ministers, Jewish housewives, street kids, Angela Davis, and a woman rapper. Wrote Kroll, "Watching the electrifying Smith is like seeing

CRITICAL NOTICE *Anna Deavere Smith as a woman rapper, one of twenty-seven characters she plays in her one-person show,* Fires in the Mirror.

these events in a series of lightning bolts that illuminate the protagonists at their quintessential moments. . . . Smith is an ideal theatre artist for the '90s, as America attempts to synthesize an increasingly diverse culture."[32] The notice Smith received propelled her show to national prominence and a network television broadcast of *Fires in the Mirror.* Her next project, *Twilight: Los Angeles, 1992,* a similar one-person montage on the riots caused by the aftermath of the Rodney King beating, was produced on Broadway by Benjamin Mordecai and directed by George C. Wolfe.

Critics and Theatregoers

While theatregoers may be susceptible to clever advertising and word-of-mouth endorsements, their need for critics remains undiminished. The degree of dependence on critics by today's patrons of the performing arts varies directly with the required investment in time and money. Most major newspapers, entertainment weeklies, and viewers' guide publications have television critics, but their recommendations often go unread and unheeded. Since television shows are free or prepaid, abundant, and instantly accessible, watchers need invest little effort, time, or money to tune in, surf through, or tune out.

Movie reviews get more attention, since the requirement for planning and the cost of going are slightly greater, and the leisure time available for attending is more scrupulously allotted. Movie critics help sort through the multiplex choices. A weekly glance at the number of "stars" or "thumbs-up" bestowed by the critics is common practice, but not always decisive. Box office appeal and word of mouth are equally persuasive with moviegoers.

The investment of time and money required for theatregoing is so much greater than for television or the movies that audience dependence on critics rivals that of producers. As a once-a-month activity (rather than a nightly ritual or weekly diversion), theatregoers plan their choices more carefully. Even patrons subscribed to a season of plays have passed on certain offerings based on a critic's negative judgments. For theatregoers, both casual and dedicated, theatre critics have become art brokers. When reviewers talk, people listen.

Critics vs. Critics: A Matter of Opinion

When critics agree, the choices are easy. Unanimous raves mean keep the show running; the theatregoers will line up. Unanimous pans mean close the show quickly; the theatregoers will not invest. But critics do not always agree. Sometimes their judgments on the theatrical imagination are so divergent and contradictory, it seems as if they had not attended the same production, let alone the same performance. Such was the case concerning Ralph Fiennes' performance of Hamlet. A classically trained former member of the Royal Shakespeare Company, Fiennes received raves and Academy Award nominations for his performances as the sadistic Nazi commandant in *Schindler's List* and as game-show cheat Charles Van Doren in

Quiz Show. When he arrived on Broadway as the famous Dane, critical anticipation was high. Here are excerpts of reviews by two of the best—writing for the same newspaper:

Ralph Fiennes as a Thoroughly Modern Hamlet

by Vincent Canby

[*New York Times,* May 3, 1995]

It's an intelligent, beautifully read and set production that serves the new star as much as he serves. Mr. Fiennes, who slipped into our collective consciousness through *Schindler's List* and *Quiz Show,* is in command at the Belasco from beginning to end.

****

He doesn't intone the lines with the velvety resonance of a Richard Burton. There's no suspicion here that, at the end we'll be treated to an encore of highlights from Dylan Thomas.

****

His Hamlet is utterly contemporary in execution and concept . . .

****

. . . his passion naked.

The Primal Struggle, Familiar and Familial: *Hamlet*

by Margo Jefferson

[*New York Times,* May 7, 1995]

But here's the rub: Mr. Fiennes goes slightly dead in the soliloquies, in his "O that this too too sullied flesh would melt," in his "O, what a rogue and peasant slave am I!" and in the endlessly quoted "To be, or not to be."

****

His voice takes on those generic British "I have been beautifully trained to project blank verse" tones. The words roll out and cushion us with their richness; the meaning shrinks and subsides.

****

Is he temporarily paralyzed by the ghosts of all the great actors who have gone before?

****

Maybe he is best, at least for now, when he plays characters who are shriveled, empty or rotten at their core.

The Critical Conundrum of Theatre Arts

If you have ever attended the opening night of a Broadway show, you probably saw a curious phenomenon at the final curtain: while most of the audience remained to applaud, several theatregoers sprang up from their orchestra-section aisle seats and sprinted for the exits. They were the critics scrambling to their desks to write reviews for the next morning's editions. What's the rush? Film critics do not behave that way.

Unlike recorded drama, reviewing live theatre involves reporting an event that does not last and can never be exactly repeated. Critic John Mason Brown likens his job to "tattooing soap bubbles."[33] David Richards identifies this critical conundrum as the challenge of his profession:

Since the push is on for accuracy in labelling these days, it occurs to me that theater criticism ought to come with a cautionary warning. Somewhere in the notices—rapturous or otherwise—shouldn't it be recorded, "perishable contents" or "Invalid after June 1"?

We like to think—we who produce it, especially—that criticism is timeless. But its shelf life is probably not significantly longer than that, say, of a carton of yogurt. The reason is plain. Critics bear witness to a singular event, destined by the conditions of its making never to be the same again. The theatregoer rarely sees what the critics see, and by that I don't mean what the critics *perceive*. (That's another, thornier, issue.) I mean what they actually, physically, see. . . .

From the first day of rehearsal until the final performance of a long run, evolution of some sort is unavoidable. Desirable even. After all, if a play could be duplicated precisely every night, it wouldn't be a play, it would be a machine. Mutability is the theater's survival mechanism.

If a film is out of sync with the times, its only recourse is to wait for a more receptive age. A play can change *with* the times. With the weather. Overnight. For better. For worse. It even changes imperceptibly because *you*—and not another—are watching it.[34]

Perhaps that is why the life of a theatrical production is called the "run" of a show. Even the critics have to race to keep up.

 THE CRITIC AT WORK

Exit the Critic After 13 Years of Drama and Farce . . . Humming the Music and Settling Scores

by Frank Rich
[Excerpts from *New York Times Magazine*][35]

When Frank Rich retired in 1993 after thirteen years as chief drama critic of the New York Times, *he took the opportunity to reflect on his career of rendering judgments on the theatrical imagination. In a wide-ranging comprehensive memoir, the person his targets dubbed "the Butcher of Broadway" does his best to bury the hatchet. Some excerpts:*

On His Love of the Theatre

The stage was my obsession from age 6—an idiosyncratic one, to put it mildly for a child growing up in the sleepy provincial Washington of the 1950's. . . . By my early teens, I had become so conspicuous a Stage Door Johnny that the manager of the National Theater, Washington's one Broadway tryout house in the pre-Kennedy Center era, took pity on me and hired me as a ticket taker, at $4 a show. (Plus all the performances I could watch free of charge.) . . . The Times was also inextricably bound up with my passion. From earliest memory, it was Al Hirschfeld's drawings of plays and the imposing full-page advertisements heralding them in the Sunday Times drama section—and then the Brooks Atkinson reviews the morning after—that had transported my imagination to the New York theater while I impatiently languished 200 miles away.

On His Literary Technique

I gradually aspired to write reviews as stories evoking the play's impact rather than as merely report cards leaning on adjectives and plot. This, I felt, was a way to engage the majority of readers, who never went to the theater no matter what the reviews, and to reach those readers like my younger self, who wanted to go to the theater but couldn't, for reasons of finances or geography. I also learned that if I had anything positive to say, say it first, because the artists who do valiant work in a mediocre enterprise are, in the journalistic sense, the real news—the lead.

On Championing New Talent

Yet the talent in the American theater was still considerable, if often young and not widely known. I found a mission championing new voices—David Henry Hwang, Beth Henley, William Finn, Marsha Norman, Eric Bogosian, among others, early on—even as I delighted in charting established talents like Sam Shepard, Michael Bennett, David Mamet, Lanford Wilson, and Athol Fugard.

On Impartiality

I never reviewed plays written by friends I had in the theater before I became a critic.

On David Merrick

His shameless promotion of his productions, often at the expense of critics he baited through practical jokes and irrational public ravings, had always struck me as part of the essential romance of Broadway. . . . When I once happened to walk past Merrick's table at Elaine's restaurant, he intercepted me, then dressed me down in a low, snide voice out of Victorian melodrama—as his stricken dinner guests, one of them Mary Tyler Moore, looked on.

On Reviewing Bombs

Broadway was not all *Amadeus* and *Dreamgirls.* At a time when production costs were still low enough for first-time producers to indulge their most catastrophic theatrical whims, covering the theater was as madcap as going to the circus. It became a running gag . . . that many of the biggest bombs on Broadway had titles beginning with the letter M. . . . There was *Marlowe,* a rock musical in which the titular playwright joined Shakespeare and Richard Burbage to smoke dope backstage at the Globe Theater, and *Merlin,* in which the on-stage animals outnumbered the audience at the Mark Hellinger Theater on a snowy matinee day, and *Marilyn,* a musical biography of Marilyn Monroe that had 16 producers. (Favorite line, spoken by Marilyn: 'But you're Arthur Miller. How can you be so boring?') *Moose Murders* was a special case. It is the worst play I've ever seen on a Broadway stage. A murder mystery set in a hunting lodge in the Adirondacks, it reached its climax when a mummified quadriplegic abruptly bolted out of his wheelchair to kick an intruder, dressed in a moose costume, in the groin.

On Writing Slams

While it can be fun to write a joke-strewn pan of a venal or lunatic theatrical catastrophe, whether *Moose Murders* or *Carrie,* there is no pleasure in writing about a failure in which artists commit no crime other than fallibility in pursuit of high theatrical ambitions. But neither was there any point in pulling punches for Times readers who know better. It was a no-win situation.

On Responsibility to Readers

Like most of Woollcott's successors, I felt ambivalent about the paper's weight. If a review of mine could convince people to check out the work of an exciting new playwright, The Times's influence seemed worthwhile. If it had the opposite effect, who could take pleasure in that? Yet was the alternative to write waffling reviews, imploring readers to go to some well-meaning mediocrity for the good of the theater and those who worked in it? If I did that, I'd become the boy who cried wolf: those same readers would not believe me when I praised the really good play that came along. I was writing for the reader who did not want to waste a night or a hundred bucks on a dull evening—and who did not want a patronizing critic to trick him into doing so. I was hardly writing for the producer who might lose a million dollars on *Merlin*.

On the Power of the New York Times

While I would not dispute some areas of The Times's influence—especially its critics' ability to encourage extended runs . . . the power to control the fate of that most endangered species, the drama on Broadway, is close to nil. Serious dramas enthusiastically greeted by me and most other critics, whether *The Grapes of Wrath* or *Joe Turner's Come and Gone* by August Wilson, or Royal Shakespeare Company imports like the Trevor Nunn *All's Well That Ends Well,* routinely fail on Broadway. The marketplace now only accommodates one drama per season—one *Dancing at Lughnasa* or *Angels in America*—unless there is a Madonna or Jessica Lange on another marquee.

On the Profound Effect of Great Theatrical Choices

One show that exemplified my stubborn faith was the . . . Sondheim musical, *Sunday in the Park with George.* . . . As the first act ended, with the re-creation of a Georges Seurat canvas, I felt that tickling sensation on the back of my neck that always speaks to me at a level so deep that my spirit responds before my mind.

SUMMARY

1. Theatre criticism has become an indispensable part of the theatrical process, in part because of the substantial investments of time and money required to attend and produce theatre.

2. The critic may have a greater impact on the choices and perceptions of theatregoers than any theatre artist. The opinions of just a few critics may persuade people never to attend a production. On the other hand, a favorable review can ensure lasting success for a production.

3. A review is the immediate response of a person who has just seen a play; simple recommendations and ratings are the goals. Theatrical criticism is more in-depth analytical commentary on the significance of the production.

4. Theatre critics assess a production in terms of its impact on society and culture, its intellectual significance, and its artistic quality.

5. Essential critical skills and talents include impartiality, descriptive literary ability, and wit.

6. Theatremakers have vied with critics *of* the theatre since the ancient Greek theatre. Philosopher critics set the foundations, and Goethe established critical criteria for specific productions. The impartiality of some eighteenth- and nineteenth-century critics was suspect, but current standards proscribe any conflicts of interest.

7. By using excerpts of reviews to advertise their productions, producers designated critics as the primary arbiters of theatrical success and quality. For better or worse, theatre artists and theatregoers have symbiotic relationships with critics.

8. Effective theatrical criticism describes the overall effect of the play, analyzes the ways in which the various theatrical elements either contribute to or detract from the overall effect, and makes judgments on the value of the production to art and society.

CHOICES

1. What if the audience reaction to a play in production is directly opposite to the critic's reactions? Should the critic take the audience reaction into account in formulating the review? Should the more informed and sensitive critic resist the unschooled demonstrations and spontaneous reactions of the theatregoers? Is "unschooled" a fair characterization of today's audiences?

2. If you were spending a weekend in New York and had time to see three plays, how would you make your selections? Pick a hypothetical weekend in which you plan to attend one Broadway show, one Off-Broadway show, and one Off-Off-Broadway production. Collect an assortment of reviews for each category including word-of-mouth recommendations, advertisements with excerpted review quotations, capsule reviews, and in-depth written criticism. Make your choices and explain the primary critical factors that helped you decide.

3. Imagine you are the director of a play that receives a review that points out some mistakes you made without realizing them. Since you have most of the planned run remaining to be played, would you make changes because of the review? How would you explain the changes to the cast?

4. Critics wield enormous power over the careers of theatre workers and the financial well-being of investors. How may the power of the critic be balanced? Should newspapers and television stations provide "equal time" for answering critics? Are there other business ventures that so heavily rely on the subjective opinions of so few?

5. Write two reviews of a play or movie you have seen recently. First, whether the production deserves it or not, write a "gee-whiz-community-service-flattery" review of a play you have seen. Next, write a condescending, sadistically gleeful slam full of scathing one-line putdowns.

6. Analyze a recent theatre review in a major daily newspaper (such as the *New York Times*) or a journal (such as *The New Yorker*) for evidence of what playwright Michael Weller referred to as "a sudden savage outlashing or a sudden loving embrace that is so astonishing in the context of the rest of the review that, for a second, the curtain is lifted on what is going on in the critic's most innermost life" (p. 418).

New York Times *ad for the final performances of* A Chorus Line.

Life's but a walking shadow; a poor player,
That struts and frets his hour upon the stage,
And then is heard no more . . .

Macbeth, *Act V, scene v*

CHAPTER 12

The Life Cycle of the Theatrical Imagination

THE RUN OF A SHOW

PREVIEW

A Brief History of Playing Time
A Century of Long Runs
Revivals: New Choices for Old Ink
Adding It All Up: A Formula for Success?
Closing a Show
The Art of the Present
A Reviver at Work

The words appear in advertisements that scream in large, boldfaced fonts set off by quotation marks and an exclamation point.

"THE LONG-RUNNING, AWARD-WINNING, BLOCKBUSTER SMASH HIT!"

They have an explosive connotation that seems to catch the ear as well as the eye. The *sine qua non* of success in the theatre, the headline triggers an unavoidable urge to go—to be present at the event—get in line—forget the cost—see it now—while you can—while it lasts.

The opposite terminology is equally loud but apocalyptic, comprising not an invitation, but a warning.

"AN ABSOLUTE DISASTER! A REAL BOMB! A FLOP! A TURKEY!"

The euphemisms of theatrical failure are never found in advertisements, only in reviews that are ignoble obituaries that report the sudden death of productions whose time has run out, or even worse—never was. Save your money—forget it—don't waste your time.

Obviously, the theatrical imagination is consumed by a quest for the former—the designations of success and the prospect of long life—and by avoidance of the latter.

The theatre dies after each performance, only to be reborn before a new audience. This regenerating life cycle—the run of a show—continues as long as the production draws an audience. The number of performances reflects important characteristics of the audience, the times, the performers, and the quality of the work. The run of a show is a definitive aspect of theatre, the most ephemeral of the time arts. But, the run is not perpetual motion. Many factors, some of them nonartistic, can interrupt it.

This final chapter of *The Theatrical Imagination* examines the life span of a play after its opening in the theatre. The book concludes with a discussion of the elusive measures of success in the theatre.

A Brief History of Playing Time

Demographics, mission, current events, culture, economics, and the fitness of the performance—not to mention the quality of the work—are factors that have determined how theatre is played out before its audiences. Throughout history, theatre artists have developed a variety of effective strategies for keeping a show running.

The Limited Run

The **limited run** is the system of presenting a play a few times and then closing it for good. For limited audiences, this limited calendar of performances works best. The ancient Greeks, for example, used the most limited runs of all. With a theatre on the Acropolis seating 17,000, a one-day, one-performance run of a play was sufficient to accommodate the entire theatregoing public. With 3 drama festivals per year, each presenting 4 new plays per day for 4 days (16 plays per festival), the ancient Greek theatregoer could see 48 plays per year. Converted to modern "weekend" leisure, it was like going to the movies once a week. Throughout the classical and medieval periods, the limited run well accommodated the theatregoing needs of these civic- and religious-minded cultures.

Touring

Touring, the system of taking a play to the audience, rather than the other way around, is as old as traveling minstrels. Thespis is said to have toured using a wagon to carry his props, masks, and costumes. Touring was especially widespread during the Dark Ages when theatre was banned in European cities. Historical records are filled with references to *histriones* (storytellers), *cantores* (singers), and *jongleurs* (jugglers, acrobats) who traveled the countryside and passed the hat.

Touring became an important part of show business with the birth of the commercial theatre in the sixteenth century. Small troupes of traveling actors brought highly entertaining, but educational **interludes** to the castles of nobility eager for literate diversions (see drawing p. 380). Even after permanent theatres were built in Europe's capital cities in the sixteenth century, most companies continued to tour the provinces whenever they were forced to close due to inclement weather, legal restrictions, religious observances, or outbreaks of the plague.

In the nineteenth century touring became big business with the invention of railroads. In the United States, regular theatrical circuits were established by a few powerful producers who controlled tours throughout the entire country. Under this system, "one-night stand" and "played in Peoria" entered the theatrical lexicon.

The Repertory System

By the beginning of the seventeenth century, daily commercial performances of plays had been sanctioned throughout Europe. Keeping seats filled in the new

permanent theatres was a matter of creative scheduling for professional performers accustomed to touring. For instance, in Shakespeare's time, London had three
theatres with a yearly total seating capacity of up to 2.14 million. Competing for
60,000 theatregoers, the only feasible strategy for commercial viability was the
repertory system of play production, which was designed to keep the same theatregoers returning to the theatre for new plays as often as possible.

Under this system, each acting company acquired a sizable number of new
plays from authors commissioned to turn them out quickly. Each new play was performed once and then placed in the "repertory" where it was occasionally replayed
until its popularity waned. Successful troupes needed a large repertoire to keep
drawing the same theatregoers back to see a variety of new plays and "old" favorites. Most companies owned a range of 175 to 200 plays of which 45 to 50 were
in active rotation. Daily rotating repertory was the standard operating system of
play presentation for 275 years from the seventeenth century to the late nineteenth
century.

In the repertory system, theatrical versatility was prized above all. Actors
were hired based on their abilities to play **stock characters,** standard types they
could outfit from their personal **stock of costumes;** designers created **stock
scenery and props**—generic palaces, drawing rooms, castles, forests, and street
scenes—that could be made appropriate to just about any play. The advantages of
the repertory system are that it (1) involves low technical/design costs, (2) provides long-term financial security to actors, (3) promotes ensemble playing, (4)
provides a system of effective training for apprentices, and (5) promotes the alle-
giance of a regular theatregoing public. The disadvantages are that the actors may
tend to become too familiar and predictable to the audience, and the security of
the system can breed complacency.

The Evolution of the Long Run

The idea of the **long run**—many consecutive performances of a single play—was
virtually unheard of throughout the seventeenth and eighteenth centuries. In the
1600s only a few London productions were given *consecutive* showings before
joining the repertory, the longest being Thomas Middleton's *The Game of Chess*
(1624), which ran for nine performances. By 1850, a run of fifteen performances
was considered standard. In the latter half of the century, the urban population
explosion brought on by the Industrial Revolution made mass marketing of theatre and lengthening the run possible. In the 1860s the run of a new play ranged
between 14 to 40 performances; in the 1870s the range was 20 to 50; and by 1880
no play was considered a success unless it ran for at least 100 performances. A few
plays, the first "blockbusters," had truly long runs, even by modern standards:
Uncle Tom's Cabin (1852) ran for 300 performances in New York; *Our Boys,* a
sentimental comedy by H. J. Byron, was the first play to have more than 1,000 performances during its three-and-a-half-year London run; and Brandon Thomas'
Charley's Aunt, the most popular play of the nineteenth century, had a four-year,
1,469-performance run beginning in 1892.

LONG-RUN RECORD HOLDER
W. S. Penley, the first of many great comic actors to star in Charley's Aunt. *The original production of* Charley's Aunt *defined the modern concept of the long run. In the final years of the nineteenth century, this riotous farce about a young man who masquerades as his friend's dowager aunt ran simultaneously in 48 productions worldwide in 22 different languages, including Zulu and Esperanto. The author's descendants claimed as recently as 1964 that the play was performed somewhere in the world every day.*

In long runs, specialization is a more valued commodity than versatility. Actors are hired for their specific talents and types as opposed to the range of stock characters they can play. The most secure working agreement is a **run-of-the-play contract.** The long run also permits recovery of large investments for plays requiring multiple sets and big casts. Consecutive playing became associated with large metropolitan centers with sizable populations—both permanent and transient—that can keep a show running for a long time.

The Life Cycles of Modern Productions

In the modern theatre, all the traditional playing systems are practiced with a variety of modifications. Limited runs are primarily the province of amateur and academic theatres in which the avocational or educational commitment of the personnel limits performances to a weekend or two.

Modern Repertory Systems.   The repertory system is practiced today by the appropriately named *summer stock companies* and by professional repertory theatres.

Modern repertory is based on presenting a theatre season, but the system is played out in two different versions.

Real, or **rotating repertory** is most similar to the historical variety, but on a smaller scale where two to five plays are rotated daily. It is practiced by resident or stock companies catering to tourist audiences who can see several different plays in a few days. Rotating repertory is especially popular with summer theatre festivals such as the Shaw Festival in Canada, the Utah Shakespearean Festival, and the Spoleto Festival in South Carolina. At the Shakespearean Festival at Stratford, Ontario, the summer playing schedule is arranged so visitors to the popular tourist attraction can see six different plays in five days or three different productions on weekends. The Festival's season runs from May to November, produces twelve plays and eight special events at three different theatres, and plays to more than half a million persons annually. Theatre artists favor rotating repertory because of the potential for playing a variety of roles over the course of an entire season. Rotating repertory is also quite familiar to subscribers of premium cable channels such as HBO, Cinemax, and Showtime, which rotate a monthly selection of films on a daily basis.

Relying on a permanent audience of subscribers, not-for-profit regional theatres present plays in shorter, prescheduled runs known as **weekly, fortnightly,** or **monthly repertory.** Weekly and fortnightly repertory, in which a new play opens and closes every one or two weeks, is most common in European provincial theatres. Monthly repertory is the favored system in the United States. Although many U.S. resident theatres call themselves "repertory" companies (e.g., the Berkeley Repertory Theatre, the Indiana Repertory Theatre, the Seattle Rep, the Repertory Theatre of St. Louis), they are only so in the most modern, "limited" sense of the word.

Modern Troubadours: Life on the Road.   The huge national touring companies of "Broadway" blockbusters that fill civic centers around the country are provincial extensions of today's commercial long runs. A thriving industry of smaller touring troupes, however, finds its identities and audiences exclusively on the road. As such, they have much in common with their medieval and Renaissance counterparts. Like their theatrical ancestors, these modern troubadours fill their performance calendars with a year's worth of one-night stands. Many play at the performance-ready fine arts facilities of colleges and universities, centers of learning not unlike the castles of the knowledge-hungry nobility where interlude players found nightly employment in the sixteenth century. Most travel light and focus on the wit, talents, special skills, and personal missions of the performers rather than the art of theatrical design and technology, which travels heavy. Cost per performance among these troupes ranges between $5,000 and $40,000. Among the best are:

The National Theatre of the Deaf—A world-class theatre troupe of deaf and hearing actors who have taken their unique productions to the great international theatre centers. Using a combination of mime, signing, and dialogue, the NTD is a creative personification of the international language of the theatre. In recent years they have toured such highly praised productions as *The King of Hearts, Treasure Island,* and *An Italian Straw Hat.*

The San Francisco Mime Troupe—Founded originally as a pantomime troupe to perform silent plays, the Troupe is now famous for its hard-hitting street theatre productions of **agit-prop** (agitation-propaganda) plays dealing with current social,

THE SHOW ON THE ROAD   *One of the most unique touring troupes is the Cornerstone Theatre Company, which collaborates in its productions with the citizens of ethnically and economically diverse communities across the United States. All of its productions are interactions between classic plays and specific American communities. By writing local concerns into the script, by sewing local color into the costumes, and by rehearsing local actors into the roles, they work to open people's minds and hearts to plays that have been traditionally closed to them. They have played out the civil strife of* Romeo and Juliet *(pictured here) in the segregated streets of small-town Mississippi, the ancient rituals of Aeschylus' plays on Native American reservations, the disintegrating family of Molière's* Tartuffe *in the Kansas farmland, and an updated Sanskrit epic performed in English, Spanish, Mandarin, and Korean with thirty residents of a Los Angeles housing project for seniors.*

economic, and political issues. Recent productions by this multicultural company include *Uncle Tom's Cabin, Seeing Double* (a provocative piece on the Arab-Israeli conflict), and *Offshore* (a transcultural production on the economic and social
consequences of Pacific Rim trade policy).

The Reduced Shakespeare Company—A troupe of three zany slapstick actors who
perform a play they call *The Complete Works of Shakespeare (Abridged),* which one
critic described as "all 37 of Shakespeare's plays as written by *Reader's Digest,* acted
by Monty Python, and performed at the speed of the Minute Waltz." For an encore,
the RSC does a five-minute version of *Hamlet,* and for a second encore they do a 15-
second version of *Hamlet*—backward, in which they caution the audience to "listen
for the satanic messages."

Theatreworks/USA—Seeking to develop the next generation of theatregoers, this
troupe specializes in new musicals for schoolchildren. During three decades, it has
played to more than 20 million young people in every state but Hawaii. Its popular
production of *Hansel and Gretel* blends Humperdinck's opera music with a libretto
that softens the grim story by making it a pageant staged by a Salzburg family.

The one-night stands of these touring companies may seem the very anathema
of an extended run, but they do add up. A year or more of performing the same
play every night is a *long* run in any sense of the word. The only difference between these small troupes and those that play out modern long runs is the distance the performers have to go each night to get to the theatre.

A Century of Long Runs

The long run with its attendant tours, spinoffs, and merchandising is the stock in
trade of today's commercial theatre. As it has always been, the long run today is the
exclusive province of large metropolitan areas, from Broadway and Off-Broadway to
London's West End.

While theatrical success was defined in the 1890s as 100 consecutive performances, today no play is considered a hit unless it runs for at least 500 performances. At 8 performances per week, that means a run of 63 weeks (15 months).
Keep in mind that it takes at least 30 to 40 weeks for a Broadway play to return its
original investment; a long run, somebody once said, is when you pay back your
investors.

This emphasis on the length of run may seem a simplistic measure of success,
but the definitive nature of theatre is its identity as a *time* art. Therefore, time or
times played before an audience cannot and should not be ignored. Accordingly,
those plays that have become theatrical phenomena by virtue of their record-
breaking runs are examined here for evidence of those qualities that account for
their success in giving pleasure over such long periods of time. These record-
breaking shows constitute the theatre art of our time that has, like very few others, captured the imaginations of so many.

Broadway Records

All right, you've read the book. Go ahead, take an educated guess. Which of the following had the longest run when it first played on Broadway?

West Side Story, the Leonard Bernstein/Stephen Sondheim musical version of *Romeo and Juliet* staged and choreographed by Jerome Robbins. Even if you were not there for the Broadway opening in 1957, you know the songs: "Tonight," "Maria," "Somewhere."

A Streetcar Named Desire. It is 1947 and New Orleans comes to Broadway. Tennessee Williams, Marlon Brando, and "Stella!" resound through Times Square.

Death of a Salesman. In 1949 nobody said it better than Arthur Miller: "I am not a dime a dozen! I am Willy Loman . . ."

Life with Father, a sentimental comedy by Howard Lindsay and Russell Crouse about a family's amusing struggle to have their father baptized. It opened on Broadway as the world went to war for the second time in 1939.

Guessing by genre, reputation, widespread familiarity, and the number of local revivals, you probably picked *West Side Story.* If you judged by the emphasis of this book—space devoted, number of examples or illustrations—your best bets would be *Streetcar* or *Salesman,* probably a toss-up. But, if you have gained insight into the unpredictable, delicate chemistry of the theatrical imagination (remember *Carrie* and *Fiddler on the Roof*), you would have been correct to choose *Life with Father,* the longest running *nonmusical* Broadway play in the history of the American theatre. With its 8-year run of 3,224 performances, it played almost 2½ years and 1,000 performances longer than the other three choices combined. For the record: *A Streetcar Named Desire* had a 24-month run of 855 performances; *Death of a Salesman* had a 22-month run of 742 performances; and *West Side Story* ran for 21 months with 732 performances.

Records, as everyone knows, are made only to be broken. Our modern age with its teeming, mobile populations, and its multimedia techniques is ideally suited to promote long theatrical runs. Accordingly, the mantle of "longest running theatrical production" is passed to a new play every few years.

Fiddler on the Roof. *Life with Father* held its long-run record for 25 years until Joseph Stein's musical about turn-of-the-century Russian Jews trying to "scratch out a living" in their "little village of Anatevka" closed its 8½-year Broadway run on July 2, 1972, after 3,242 performances—18 more than *Life with Father.* Despite the years and cultural divide that separate the two plays, there is not much imaginative distance between them. They both depict a domestic situation that has been a mainstay of the dramatic imagination since the fourth century B.C. Lindsay and Crouse's play about baptizing a father and Stein's musical about a father trying to marry off his daughters according to his religious traditions are cut from the same dramatic cloth. The universality of such domestic human

Close on the heels of Fiddler on the Roof *was the Jim Jacobs/Warren Casey rock and roll musical,* Grease, *which opened five months before* Fiddler *closed. It ran for nearly nine years on Broadway. Playing against the disillusionment of the Watergate years,* Grease *was a part of the craze for 1950s nostalgia that included the film* American Graffiti *(1973) and the television series "Happy Days" (1976).*

dilemmas, not to mention the artistic excellence of their productions, accounts for the staying power of these works.

In the United States, all subsequent long-run Broadway record holders have been musicals. This is due, in part, to the increasing sophistication of the writers who have refined the art of integrating the musical, dramatic, and theatrical elements of the form well beyond the strange hybrids of the early years of "chorus-girl musical comedies." The overwhelming popularity of this most American dramatic genre is also owing to the sophisticated marketing strategies of today's big-time commercial producers.

A Chorus Line.   Until the winter of 1995–96, the longest running play in Broadway history was *A Chorus Line:* the musical opened July 25, 1975, during the administration of Gerald Ford and closed 15 years later on April 28, 1990, when George Bush was in the White House. It played 6,000 consecutive performances to over 7 million theatregoers in New York, winning the Pulitzer Prize and ten Tony

Awards. It continued its run at the Shubert Theatre while countless tours, summer stock shows, amateur productions, and a major motion picture version played throughout the country. Its long-running productions in 22 other countries attest to the universality of this backstage drama by Michael Bennett, James Kirkwood, Nicholas Dante, Edward Kleban, and Marvin Hamlisch.

The high-energy, low-tech musical drama depicts actors auditioning for the dancing chorus of an unnamed Broadway-bound show. It was recognized by the millions who saw it as a play about needing a job. The earnest desperation of the characters played exceedingly well through the inflation-ridden, recessionary years of the 1970s and early 1980s. Marvin Hamlisch's "God I Hope I Get It" and "What I Did for Love" became pop anthems of the same age that dubbed "Bridge over Troubled Water" the song of the decade. The production conceived by Bennett gave the show to the performers; without a star in the cast it was a pure ensemble in which the actors created their own spectacle effects through their show-stopping dancing. Richard Rodgers recognized it as "something great and new." Henry Fonda said it was "perfection of the stage."[1] Ironically, *A Chorus Line* was produced not by a legendary commercial mogul, but by the impresario of the not-for-profit New York Shakespeare Festival, Joseph Papp. He was the first to recognize it as something great and new and gave the show its premiere production at his Public Theatre. The profits from this longest of Broadway runs helped to fund many other New York Shakespeare Festival productions for more than fifteen years (see photograph on p. 310).

Local Favorites

The staying power of great Broadway hits is best understood in terms of their national and international appeals. In contrast, many municipalities are known for long-running productions of more local, strictly provincial flavor. These local favorites achieve celebrity of their own, becoming part of their cities' "permanent" attractions.

The Mousetrap, a quintessential murder mystery whodunit by Agatha Christie (1890–1976), is London's long-run record holder for now and for the foreseeable future. Originally written as a radio drama, the play opened at London's Ambassador Theatre on November 25, 1952, and has been running somewhere in London ever since. In theatrical terms, no playwright has, as yet, built a better mousetrap.

The Bald Soprano, Eugene Ionesco's absurdist one-act play about middle-class family values, opened in 1950 in Paris to catcalls with the lead actor bolting out of the theatre ahead of the spectators. But seven years later, a Paris theatre produced it on a double bill with another Ionesco play called *The Lesson;* they are still running today after more than 12,000 performances.

The Fantasticks is billed as the "longest running show in the history of the New York stage." It is—off Broadway. This exceedingly simple, small musical by Harvey Schmidt and Tom Jones (eight actors, three musicians, one platform, a cloth, and a cardboard moon) was produced by Lore Noto in 1960 at Off-Broadway's Sullivan Street Playhouse at a cost of $16,000. It took three years to start selling out. The early reviews were so bad that Jones remembers "somebody crying, and I got in a cab and couldn't make it across Central Park, I just got out of the cab and vomited my way through Central Park."[2] It has been running at the same theatre ever since. In more than 35 years it has been performed over 13,000 consecutive times. Some perspective is necessary, however, on this longest of Off-Broadway runs. With a capacity of only 150, the Sullivan Street Playhouse is tiny, like the show. It does not take much to achieve a sellout. (The 2 million theatregoers who have seen the production in 35 years are one third the number who saw *A Chorus Line* in 15 years.) It is also related by subject to *Life with Father* and *Fiddler on the Roof.* Based on a play by Edmond Rostand, *The Fantasticks* depicts the attempts of two neighboring fathers to secure the marriage of their contrary children. "Try to Remember" is the plaintive ballad of young love made famous by the play.

In San Francisco, the outrageous musical satire *Beach Blanket Babylon* opened in the back room of a restaurant in 1974, drew big crowds, and moved to a nightclub where it has been performing ever since—to over 3 million theatregoers. *Tamara,* Los Angeles' long-running favorite, is an audience-participation murder mystery. In Moscow, where commercial theatre is largely unknown,

MURDER MOST POPULAR   *The nonmusical play with the longest consecutive run in American theatre history is* Shear Madness, *the comedy-thriller that asks the audience to help solve a murder in a hairstyling salon. By 1995 the show had been running for over 15 years (over 6,000 performances) in Boston, 12 years in Chicago, 8 years at the Kennedy Center in Washington, and additional long-running productions in St. Louis, Philadelphia, Austin, Montreal, Tel Aviv, Melbourne, Barcelona, Buenos Aires, and Budapest. It has never played in New York City. Originally capitalized in 1980 at $60,000,* Shear Madness *has since grossed over $60 million while playing to more than 4 million people.*

Ivanov has been in the active rotation of the Moscow Art Theatre's repertory for more than 20 years. In Japan, *The Merchant of Venice* is the most popular Shakespearean play, and *Fiddler on the Roof* is the most successful musical.

The Latest Contenders.   The straight play is not yet on the boards with the potential for outrunning *The Mousetrap,* or even *Shear Madness,* for that matter. *A Chorus Line,* however, has a pack of imported techno-pop, musical challengers that are setting record-breaking box office paces in the United States and abroad. If they do not collapse under their own substantial weight, these blockbusters could be the theatrical future. The advertising for such international sensations as *Cats, Les Misérables, The Phantom of the Opera,* and *Miss Saigon* betray such wishful thinking: "I eagerly await my audience with you," "writes" the Phantom. "Now and Forever" boasts *Cats.* Forever, indeed. On January 29, 1996, Andrew Lloyd Webber's *Cats* claimed the title as Broadway's longest running production when its 6,141st performance played at the Wintergarden Theatre. In the 1990s, long runs have given way to theatrical marathons.

Actors in Long Runs

If the long run is the theatrical equivalent of a marathon, then actors are the long-distance runners of show business. Performing the same part, night after night, up to eight times per week, sometimes for years, can present serious challenges to the actor with the prized "run of the show" contract. Keeping the show fresh, or as actors say, "maintaining the **illusion of the first time**" is the psychological challenge. Beyond staying in character, keeping up energy, and finding inspiration, there is also the often arduous physical task of continual live performances. Keep in mind that film and video acting requires that actors do it right only once in order to get it "in the can," after which playback technology takes over the run. The renowned British performer Claire Bloom maintains that she cannot understand how stage actors "slog on" in long-running plays. Bloom says she hates repeating a performance night after night, but she *will* do a "short" six-week run.[3] On the other hand, the American actor Eli Wallach spoke for most actors when a line around the block to the box office prompted him to say, "There's something about a crowd like that that brings a lump to my wallet."[4]

In 1989 Tyne Daly, the television player known for her starring role in the long-running CBS drama "Cagney & Lacey," took on the demanding stage role of Mama Rose in the second Broadway revival of the Jule Styne/Stephen Sondheim musical *Gypsy,* which is based on the real-life career of famed stripper Gypsy Rose Lee and her domineering mother. In all, the 44-year-old Daly played the role on a pre-Broadway tour, on Broadway, and in London's West End for a three-year run. For each of the standard eight weekly performances, she almost never left the stage during its three-hour running time, dancing through Jerome Robbins' choreography and singing most of the score, which ends with a climactic, grueling, five-minute-long solo. Daly described it as "like being in training for a prizefight":

The way the part is written, it allows no letdown, especially on two-performance days—we call them double-headers—that tend to feel more like an athletic event than an artistic experience. [But] you don't catch [baseball] pitchers playing 8 times a week. . . . I thought this was going to be a much easier job than "Cagney & Lacey," because "Cagney & Lacey" meant 14-hour work days, minimum. Each night there were new lines to learn, each week a new script, new director, new actors. It was a life-eating job. I had to make appointments with my family. . . . This one I thought, "You'll know your job, you'll know your words and it's the same play every night." I was warned by the experts it would take all my energy.[5]

Daly took particular cautions when she considered the toll the role (called the "King Lear" of musicals) took on the two performers who preceded her in the

COPING WITH A LONG RUN   *To cope with the role in the long haul of the long run, Daly developed a routine of quiet things—writing letters, reading poetry, listening to music, blowing bubbles, and taking "any kind of vitamin anyone says might work— lots of C, lots of B-12, ginseng, herbal teas of all descriptions."[6]*

part: Ethel Merman, who created the role, burst a blood vessel in her throat singing the score. Angela Lansbury, who won a Tony for *her* Mama Rose in the 1974 revival, strained her voice severely and limited her Broadway run to 15 weeks on the advice of her doctor. Lansbury compared the work to that of a "pile driver."[7]

The great vaudevillian Fanny Brice claimed she never left a play until everybody who wanted to see her had seen her in it. When leading actors reach the limits of their endurance or inspiration in today's longer runs, they are usually replaced by another "fresher" actor of equal stature and ability. In *Gypsy,* Daly was replaced by Linda Lavin. With Lavin as Mama Rose, the show ran for another six months. As for Daly, after a brief vacation she opened a new run of the show in London, where they had not seen the play since Angela Lansbury did it there fifteen years earlier.

Revivals: New Choices for Old Ink

The terminology of show business reveals much about the nature of competing performing arts. In film and television it is almost always "the same thing." The film industry has **rereleases**—or at least it used to. After the original run of a hit movie, it was withdrawn, kept in the can for a suitable period, then rereleased to movie houses amid much hoopla. Of course, videotape recordings have changed all that. Films now go from their original, first-run "theatrical" releases to video sales and rentals, to cable premium channels, to network broadcasts, and finally to local, late-night TV. Except for some censorious editing for broadcast television, all these showings are exact clones of the original. Similarly, television thrives on **reruns,** syndicated rebroadcasts of recorded series that can extend the lives of TV shows into significant profit.

Repeated viewings of recorded drama are, at least for the first few times, intriguing. Eventually the artists and their choices—which never change—become well worn and beyond predictable to outlandish cliché. "I coulda been a contendah," "May the force be with you," "Go ahead, make my day," "Life is like a box of chocolates," and almost every moment of the *Rocky Horror Picture Show* are but a few of the most conspicuous examples.

Theatre, by contrast, produces **revivals,** which, by definition, are never the same thing. Revivals are always new things—new productions of "previously produced" plays. The term emphasizes new life. What is new is virtually everything the playwright has left to the producer, director, and other artists: the theatre, the actors, the staging, and the audience. As theatre critic Jack Kroll said, "You don't revive a great play, it revives you."[8]

Most theatrical productions are revivals. Revivals can be contemporary plays brought back and remounted within a few years of their initial runs. Or they can be **period plays,** those so consistently revived that they achieve the status of classics. *Classic* properly refers to ancient Greek and Roman works of art, but in the theatre the term is now used to designate those plays originally produced much more recently. With the march of time, period and classic plays encroach on the contemporary. The works of Ibsen, Strindberg, Chekhov, Shaw, and even O'Neill are now considered classics.

Several decisive factors can promote or suppress the revival of previously mounted plays.

When the Actors Are Right

Many believe the theatre is primarily actor driven, and that great plays are often revived because actors love to perform the parts. A strong case can be made for this view, especially when it comes to reviving those plays, such as Shakespeare's, with larger-than-life roles that must wait for actors of extraordinary talent. Such thespians must be self-confident in their abilities to take on not only the roles, but the formidable reputations of the legendary performers who preceded them in past runs and revivals.

Hamlet, for example, waits for dashing young stars of great technical facility and psychological complexity. In recent years Kevin Kline, Mel Gibson, Keanu Reeves, Kelly Maurer, and Ralph Fiennes have achieved success in reviving the melancholy Dane.

Why do such actors return to the stage to take on the classics? Compared to film, the pay is poor, and the work is hard. Director Michael Kahn explains it this way: "When an actor does the classics, he uses every muscle he has—all of his imaginative, physical, and emotional resources. It's like the Olympics. It's testing yourself against this great material, and if you emerge triumphant, you feel pretty good about yourself."[9] American actor Hal Holbrook, who fulfilled a career ambition by playing King Lear, maintains the excitement is in the risk: "You're making yourself extremely vulnerable because somebody might tell you that you're lousy. And it's not like being lousy in an inconsequential part. You're standing up there on the high board, taking a big swan dive."[10]

When the Times Are Right

Other plays find new life when events converge to make them relevant, and hence playable again. An example is Rodgers and Hammerstein's *Carousel,* an unlikely candidate for a Broadway revival in the 1990s. In its original 1945 Broadway incarnation, this big-book musical was a bittersweet, fantasy love story about the redemptive powers of parental ties. The play is set in a fanciful New England fishing village between 1873 and 1888. In the opening scene Julie Jordan, a local factory worker, meets Billy Bigelow, a swaggering barker at the town carnival, and in a famous duet—"If I Loved You"—they admit their feelings for each other. They marry, and Billy learns he will soon be a father. Desperate for money, he is killed in an attempted robbery. At this point fantasy takes over: Billy is permitted to return to Earth for one good deed, which he accomplishes by attending his daughter's high school graduation and encouraging her to have confidence in herself and believe that "You'll Never Walk Alone." At a time when many fathers did not return from the war, the overall effect of *Carousel* was triumphant, tearful, heartwarming—life affirming. Fifty years later, Nicholas Hytner, who had staged the international hit *Miss Saigon,* recognized elements in this musical morality play that made it consonant with less romantic times. In his 1994 reincarnation, he saw the play as a contemporary look at class war: small-town snobbery, a violently tender hero, and an abused but understanding wife. Sex and violence became the obstacles to redemption. Hytner's revival started, not with a ride on a glittering carousel, but in the garment factory where the local women work under oppressive conditions watched over by the harsh owner and a gigantic time clock. After work they file out the gate to escape for respite to a seedy amusement park where vulgar boys taunt them. Family values in an age of working parents, fatherless homes, and mindless violence converged in an unlikely play for a compelling production that did not change a line of the original dialogue. The result: the longer journey from oppression, loss, and despair to the redemptive power of faith and love was ethically complex and emotionally rich. The *New York Times* verdict: "*Carousel* lives. Rodgers and Hammerstein are back on Broadway where they belong."[11] Of course, the successful revivals such as *Carousel* have as much to do with culture as with the times. The play was reborn of specifically American experiences.

When the Culture Is Right

In a rave *New York Times* review of a 1968 revival of Molière's 390-year-old comedy of manners, *The Misanthrope,* Clive Barnes wrote, "It might be said that it is always the function of a masterpiece to be timely."[12] Throughout history the most repeatedly revived plays are those of such universality that the times are always right; they are virtually immortal in the truest sense of the word. Such masterpieces are plays with multicultural lives.

In the global village, the need to examine human endeavor from multicultural perspectives has become important in everything from art to sociology. In the theatre, multiculturalism is nothing new. Reworking plays to fit another culture has been part of the production of foreign scripts since the beginnings of the theatre. The Romans did their own versions of 500-year-old Greek tragedies and 400-year-old Greek comedies. Renaissance writers in Europe did their own versions of the Roman dramas by Terence and Seneca. In the eighteenth and nineteenth centuries, the British renamed, "deodorized," and produced as their own what they considered to be scandalous, risqué French bedroom farces.

In 1990 the Bin-Kadi Theatre of Abidjan, the Ivory Coast, produced Sophocles' *Antigone* as *Affaire de Sang d'Antigone! . . . Yako!* ("The Problem of Antigone's Kin"). "Africans refuse tragedy," explained director Marie-Jose Hourantier. "Whenever life is out of balance, one must immediately strive to obtain equilibrium." In his production, Antigone's death was followed by an exuberant dance to expel sorrow and grief. "Sophocles is closer to the African than to the European," Hourantier maintained. "Antigone, with her refusal to submit to tyranny or manipulation, represents all of the qualities needed in Africa to face today's struggles."[13]

WHEN THE TIMES ARE RIGHT   Carousel *as a 1945 bittersweet romance and as a 1994 triumph over oppression, poverty, and violence.*

"TWO HOUSEHOLDS" *The Palestinian/Israeli co-production of* Romeo and Juliet.

Almost every culture in the world has revived the plays of Shakespeare from its own unique perspective. Eighteenth-century German productions were first. In translations by Ludwig Tieck, the Bard's plays were so popular that the Germans claim Shakespeare works better in their language than in English. By the eighteenth century other European and American productions appeared, and by the nineteenth century the word *revival* was virtually synonymous with Shakespeare. In the twentieth century, Asian, African, Indian, and Middle Eastern productions have completed the globalization of Shakespeare's thirty-seven sixteenth- and seventeenth-century English plays.

Such revivals require theatre artists with distinctly global and culturally sensitive imaginations. In 1994 Palestinian director Fouad Awad and Israeli director Eran Baneil attempted a small theatrical step toward peace with a joint production of *Romeo and Juliet.* Shakespeare's romantic tragedy about an "ancient grudge" that breaks "to new mutiny, where civil blood makes civil hands unclean" has always found expression in societies plagued by deep divisions. "Shakespeare wrote this play about Jerusalem," quipped Baneil. "Verona was a computer mistake."[14] In this cross-cultural co-production, one family spoke Arabic, the other Hebrew (with English supertitles projected above the stage). The directors, however, set their play in the sixteenth-century Verona envisioned by Shakespeare. "We didn't want to do a folkloric version of *Romeo and Juliet,*" said Awad, "with the Capulets wearing skull caps and the Montagues wearing kafirs. We wanted bigger themes." Logistics, not to mention security, were difficult. The two troupes worked separately for four months before beginning joint rehearsals. Palestinian actors had to sneak past military checkpoints to attend rehearsals. Mutual suspicion and distrust were all too real, not the fictions of drama. Delicate decisions on word usage and staging were made line by line. Real civil brawls outside the theatre in the cities and territories in which Palestinians and Jews were being killed in continued violent clashes stopped rehearsals for long periods. Months passed before all the actors let down their defenses. "Now all the actors are friends," Baneil observed. "That's the big personal and professional transition. Now they must act on stage the hatred they no longer feel."[15] The production premiered in Jerusalem and toured to Germany, Italy, Belgium, Norway, and the United States. Thus did an archaic Elizabethan romantic tragedy become a bridge for crossing a cultural divide more ancient than anything Shakespeare could have envisioned.

Perhaps more than any other type of theatrical production, the culturally specific reimagining of plays tests, then proves, the ultimate flexibility of great dramatic art. In some cases, the new versions are adapted so far beyond the shape of the original work that the revivals must be considered new dramas with only echoes of the precursor.

When the Times Are Wrong

Just as changing cultural views can serve to promote the revivals of plays, these same factors can also converge to suppress the production of once timely dramas. The situation results in theatrical obsolescence, a kind of artistic dormancy. For instance, the once popular and seemingly innocuous musical *Little Mary Sunshine* was a mainstay of amateur and summer stock repertories during the 1950s and 1960s. It was one of Off Broadway's most successful shows, winning every major award during its three-year run. Today it is seldom produced. According to current standards, Rick Besoyan's satirical operetta about the sweet ingenue who saves the day for the Royal Canadian Mounties and a local Native American tribe is considered by many to be dated and offensive in its stereotypical portrayal of Native Americans: "Me, heap big Indian Chief," one of the characters sings to introduce himself.

PLAYBOYS OF TWO WORLDS   *(Top) A young Gregory Peck stars in a 1946 production of* The Playboy of the Western World, *John Millington Synge's 1907 comedy about the provincial insularity of a small rural Irish village. (Bottom) The play was given new life and a new title in Mustapha Matura's 1984 adaptation,* The Playboy of the West Indies.

REVEALING THE ILLUSION   *The Hartford Stage Company production of* The Illusion. *Modern productions of this "lost" play are being staged across the country in productions enhanced by stage technology unavailable—perhaps unimaginable—to Corneille and his contemporaries.*

Vivian Gornish, writing in the *New York Times* on the thirtieth anniversary of *The Fantasticks'* record-breaking run, described the difference between her cosmopolitan reaction to one particular song and that of the predominantly tourist audience.

Then comes the rape song [called "It Depends on What You Pay"], which made me sit up in my chair. The fathers plot a false abduction in order to let the boy "save" the girl. . . . Along with the hired abductor, they sing a Gilbert and Sullivan-like song called "It Depends on What You Pay." The three men prance about the stage discussing what kind of rape the girl will get: "the drunken rape . . . the military rape . . ." and about 32 other kinds of rape, each one described in some detail. The song went on and on. The word seemed to fill the air for a long time. I stared at the show, thinking, "I've lost my sense of humor about rape, why haven't you lost yours?"

The audience, filled with out-of-towners and high-school children, was hysterical with laughter. I could hear the show answering me, "That's why."[16]

Audience reactions also made the authors sit up in their chairs. Shortly after the thirtieth anniversary performance, Tom Jones and Harvey Schmidt replaced the rape song with a new one titled "Abductions."

Uncovering "Lost" Plays

The urge to revive plays in new productions, whether to provide roles for actors or to address the tenor of the times and culture, has led the theatrical imagination to look to the past for "new" dramas. Uncovering the lost, ignored, or seldom produced plays of dramatists known or unknown has become a kind of theatrical salvage business in pursuit of dramatic treasure that can be restored and polished to playability. The theatrical restoration of lost plays occurs in a variety of ways.

New Translations. The impenetrability of many foreign plays must wait for vital contemporary translations to reveal their stageworthiness. The comic masterpieces of Molière, for example, have been known to the French and to scholars throughout the world since their premieres in the 1660s. Until recently, however, they were never widely produced in English-speaking countries because the brilliance of their glittering dialogue that is rendered in rhymed verse was obscured in dull prose translations. In the 1960s, poet/lyricist Richard Wilbur accomplished the linguistic challenge of translating the 300-year-old plays into rhymed, actable English. In so doing, he made such plays as *Tartuffe, The Misanthrope,* and *School for Wives* regular parts of the repertories of theatres throughout the United States, England, Canada, and Australia. For a clearer picture of Wilbur's English restoration of Molière, compare the following versions of the same passage from *The Misanthrope,* in which the sophisticated Célimène lambastes the play's hypocrite, Arsinoe.

A typical prose translation:

She says her prayers with the utmost exactness; but she beats her servants and pays them no wages. She displays great fervor in every place of devotion; but she paints and wishes to appear handsome. She covers the nudities in her pictures; but loves the reality.[17]

Richard Wilbur's restoration:

> She prays incessantly; but then they say,
> She beats her maids and cheats them of their pay;
> She shows her zeal in every holy place,
> But still she's vain enough to paint her face;
> She holds that naked statues are immoral,
> But with a naked *man* she'd have no quarrel.[18]

Giving such new theatrical life to lost plays can completely realign conventional dramatic wisdom. Molière's contemporary, Pierre Corneille, was considered a playwright of limited vision and skill until 1990 when Tony Kushner "freely adapted" Corneille's virtually unknown *L'illusion de Théâtre* (1637) as *The Illusion.* Unlike the mannered neoclassical French plays of the period, *The Illusion* involves a sorcerer and his apprentice, time travel, magic mirrors, potions, and multiple personalities in a suspenseful comic plot involving love rivals and a father's search for his estranged son. Echoes of this play can be heard in *Cyrano de Bergerac, The Fantasticks,* and *The Princess Bride.* Kushner's new version reveals all of these dramatic and theatrical qualities so well that a play that had not been on the English-speaking stage for three centuries is now being produced in theatres across America.

Adding It All Up: A Formula for Success?

Does the imaginative and creative process described in this book add up to a reliable formula for theatrical success? Not quite. There are too many variables that can be combined to yield an infinite number of possible choices—like the permutations in a chess game, the possible combinations of musical notes, or the variant shades of the colors of the spectrum and their possible arrangement on canvas. The theatrical imagination must encompass not just the individual artists, it must also respond to the audience, the times, the culture, and even unforeseen events.

In a sense, the formula for theatrical success is as elusive as the unified field theory long sought by physicists to explain the fundamental workings of the universe itself. The physicists are getting closer to their goal. A unified theatre equation is much less likely to be found. Even a supercomputer would not be much help in crafting live action for the stage. Theatre art is a handmade thing each time out. The recipe for success is fleeting, dynamic, and must constantly be rewritten.

When the Theatrical Imagination Fails

History proves the biggest theatrical disasters are put together not by the worst in the business, but by the best. It is only the hype of modern marketing and the enormous budgets that magnify the scale of modern flops.

THE FAR SIDE   By GARY LARSON

In light of the current revivals of Molière and Corneille, this map may have to be redrawn.

Bible Belt
People Mag. Belt
Garfield Belt
17th Century French Drama Belt

© 1991 Universal Press Syndicate

There are, of course, many anthologies and critical surveys of dramatic and theatrical masterpieces. A collection of disasters by the masters might include the following.

Introduction. The collection would begin with an obligatory historical perspective on the terminology of theatrical failure. A **bomb,** for instance, originally meant an entertainment success. In the eighteenth century "Go like a bomb" meant an achievement of considerable effectiveness or success accomplished with great speed. It was the destructive power of modern military ordnance, demonstrated with such deadliness in the Civil War, that caused the term *bomb* to become American slang for a huge, instantaneous failure. The theatrical usage of **turkey** had a more benign, but nonetheless logical derivation. To most, it is a bird with stuffing and drumsticks. To people in show business, it is death, disaster, and humiliation. Its origin comes from actors (called "turkey actors") who opened poor shows on Thanksgiving Day in hopes of making money as part of the annual holiday when a healthy attendance might be expected. Except for the pieces by Terence, the magnitude of the following "failures" reveals the daring of the theatrical imaginations behind the attempts.

DISASTERS BY THE MASTERS

Classical Turkeys

Plutus (388 B.C.) by Aristophanes—The comic genius of Athens traded in his poison pen, turning from the brilliance of political and social satire to the boredom of mythological travesty.

All five plays by Terence (second century, B.C.)—Dull adaptations of Greek originals. Mediocre at best. Legend has it that he died of grief over some lost luggage containing some new Greek plays he was planning to translate. Too bad. It would have been nice if the Greek originals had survived.

The Tempest (1611) by Shakespeare—Nobody wants to play the lead. The good parts are the clowns and a creature that's half-human and half-fish. To make this play work takes some major rewriting and the best special effects you can get. "When all else fails, play up the spectacle!" The Bard retired from the theatre after this one.

Don Garcie (1663) by Molière—The French comic genius' one serious play. Except for Louis XIV and his court at Versailles, few have heard of it, let alone seen it—and with good reason.

The Modern Bombs

Breakfast at Tiffany's (1966)—David Merrick produced this can't-lose show written by heavyweight writers Abe Burrows, Edward Albee, and Nunnally Johnson and starring Mary Tyler Moore. It lost. Merrick closed the show in previews, announcing to the press, "Rather than subject the drama critics and the theatregoing public—who invested one million dollars in advance ticket sales—to an

Even failure, however, is not as easily identifiable as it might seem. One theatregoer's flop can be another's hit. After all, *Oedipus the King,* when it competed in the contest for best tragedy in 429 B.C., was runner-up to a now lost play by a nephew of Aeschylus. Harold Prince, who had a string of major hits in the 1960s, some flops in the 1970s, and then hit it big again with *The Phantom of the Opera* in 1988 and with a revival of *Showboat* in 1995, angrily reacted to his hailed "comeback": "When I read in the paper that I'm having a comeback," he told an interviewer, "it tees me off. People used to be able to see the difference between a flop and a failure. Flop is when you lose money. But that doesn't mean failure."[21]

Theatrical Success

No one in the theatre really tries to do a bad show. Success is the goal. The standards of success, however, are at least as complex and open to debate as are those

DISASTERS BY THE MASTERS

excruciatingly boring evening, I decided to close the show. . . . The closing is entirely my fault and should not be attributed to the three top writers who had a go at it."[19]

The Creation of the World and Other Business (1972) by Arthur Miller—A comedy in which God creates the Earth and its inhabitants, including mistakes like the "fish with fur." Miller's unabashed enthusiasm for the play demonstrated yet again why playwrights are not permitted to write their own reviews.[20]

Pacific Overtures (1976)—Harold Prince, Stephen Sondheim, and Boris Aronson teamed up for this seafaring musical about Admiral Perry opening up Japan to Western trade and culture. The show went down with all hands.

Legs Diamond! (1989)—Peter Allen wrote it, directed it, and starred in it. Investors lost $5.2 million on it. Critics called the high-kicking musical about the big-time New York mobster "Tarnished," "Not even a decent piece of costume jewelry," and "Legs Zircon."

On the Waterfront (1995)—Bud Schulberg, who wrote the screenplay for the great 1954 film starring Marlon Brando, adapted his original for the stage. Twenty-one producers and co-producers anted up $2.5 million, the largest sum ever to put a nonmusical play on Broadway. They should have hedged their bets. In rehearsal the show's original director and the two leading actors quit. At the final preview an actor in a supporting role had a heart attack on stage. They opened anyway. The critics asked "Why?" After eight performances they closed up shop for good.

of failure. There is commercial success that can be validated by a positive profit-and-loss statement. Critical success is apparent in good reviews and favorable analyses. Popular success is evident in full houses, sustained applause, and long runs. Universal success is validated by repeated revivals across boundaries of time, cultures, and countries. Local success is a matter of culture-specific micro-theatrics. Artistic success may be gauged by the widespread and enduring influence of one theatre artist's work on the theatrical imaginations of others. All of these measures of quality are indications of creative choices that make the theatrical imagination work on stage.

Theatre Awards.   Perhaps the most visible validations of theatrical success are the various awards given annually by peer or professional groups for outstanding achievement in theatre art. The best known and most prestigious are the **Tony Awards** for Broadway theatre. Given annually since 1947, the statuette was named for Antoinette Perry, founder of the American Theatre Wing, a service

THE SUDDEN, SURE KNOWLEDGE THAT
ONE'S BEST EFFORTS HAVE COME TO NAUGHT

Drawing by Gahan Wilson, 1991, *The New Yorker* Magazine, Inc.

organization that brings performances to hospitals and schools. The night the Tonys are awarded is the only time all the theatres on Broadway are dark.

The **Obie Awards** for Off-Broadway productions have been presented annually since 1956. Award categories vary depending on what is being produced in a given year, reflecting the diverse and more experimental nature of the productions. Even the critics somehow get together and once a year find a unanimity of opinion (which seems to elude them during the rest of the season), to give out their awards. **The New York Drama Critics Circle Awards,** given since 1936, are the most well known.

In 1976 the American Theatre Wing inaugurated a new Tony Award for outstanding achievement over the years by a regional theatre. It is a way of recognizing in a national forum that much important theatre is never seen in New York. This award is for theatre art that is conceived and created for a specific, not a mass audience. Like politics, all the theatre in this category is local. Major municipalities that do not wait for the American Theatre Wing to recognize the quality of their local thespians include Chicago (**Joseph Jefferson Awards**), Los Angeles (**Ovation Awards, Dramalogue Awards,** and **Los Angeles Drama Critics Circle Awards**), San Francisco (**Bay Area Theatre Critics Awards**), and Washington (**Helen Hayes Awards**).

"Success in the theatre," Vivian Gornish wrote, "comes because a play is somehow powerfully consonant with its moment: It presents ideas that stimulate

"NOBODY TRIES TO DO A BAD SHOW" *Mel Brooks' film* The Producers *is a satire on theatrical success. Zero Mostel and Gene Wilder play Broadway producers who try to embezzle money from unsuspecting investors by putting on the worst musical ever conceived, closing it immediately, and taking off with their 50 percent share.* Springtime for Hitler, *however, turns out to be, in typical Mel Brooks fashion, a boffo smash hit.*

and disturb. Sometimes the play outlives the moment and enters the body of lasting dramatic literature. More often than not, its virtues fade when the run is over. Either way, the duration of success depends on the audience feeling itself at one with what is happening on the stage."[22] Success in the theatre, however, whenever, and wherever it is validated is, finally, a fleeting thing—as ephemeral as the art itself.

Closing a Show

Perhaps no phrase is more emblematic of the *temporal* nature of theatre art than "the show must go on." Conversely, nothing is more indicative of the *temporary* nature of theatre art than the certainty that the show must also close. Even *A Chorus Line,* once the longest running production in American theatre history, closed in 1990. As one of the characters in the show says with the clear-eyed vision of every theatre artist, "Even if you get this show, it's gonna close one day. Nothing runs forever."[23] Despite the best intentions of the most experienced theatre artists, there is no available insurance against closing. The risks that must be taken to make effective theatrical choices are unacceptable in actuarial terms. It is a reality of the theatre.

Reality and Theatre Art

In addition to imaginative exhaustion, public satiation, and diminished cash flow, productions also close when reality upstages theatre art. Except for bad reviews, no other factor can so unpredictably affect the life cycle of theatrical productions. In Czechoslovakia, for instance, theatre underwent a sudden and unexpected transformation as radical political changes swept the country. Before the fall of the authoritarian government in 1989, the theatres were always full. Theatre was a refuge, not only for preserving culture, but for veiled, yet vigorous political dialogue in plays by such dramatists as imprisoned activist Václav Havel. According to Lida Engelova, the country's leading director, "Everyone knew the symbols, the code. It was a kind of defiance, a Czech defiance, quiet and subtle."[24] With the "velvet revolution," however, reality became more exciting and unpredictable than any script. Havel was not only released from prison, he became the president of the new Czech Republic—expressing his views outright in eloquent speeches before the heads of governments. The effect on the theatre was sudden. "It all happened in a month," said Engelova. "The theatres [had been] full of people who led the Revolution, but administrators were caught off guard. There is no way to change the repertory so quickly. The shows seemed out of date. Now people stay at home and watch what is happening politically on TV."[25]

Former *New York Times* critic Frank Rich described another vivid example of reality upstaging art in the United States—the closing of *The Grapes of Wrath,* Frank Galati's epic adaptation of John Steinbeck's Depression-era novel as performed by Chicago's Steppenwolf Company (see photograph on p. 313).

> Watching this work, one could not ignore the parallels between the homeless Okies of the 1930s and the homeless New Yorkers of 1990, some of whom were begging for change outside the theater at intermission. But *The Grapes of Wrath* itself soon became a sad casualty of hard times, despite winning the Tony Award for best play, traditionally a sure box-office boon to any production in any year. The audience for the show, though by no means meager, was simply not big enough to support its populous payroll, and within weeks of its Tony victory, *The Grapes of Wrath* closed.

June 11, 1991

To The Cast & Crew:

FIDDLER ON THE ROOF will close at the Gershwin Theatre after
the Sunday Matinee performance on June 16, 1991. Please
accept this as one weeks notice of the closing of the show.

It has been a pleasure working with you.

       Sincerely,

       The Fiddler Broadway Co.

BY: _____
       Charlotte W. Wilcox
       General Manager

Employer I.D. 13-3577565
Unemployment I.D. 27-01186

cc: AEA
     IATSE, Local One
     IATSE, International
     ATPAM
     TWAU, Local 764
     AF of M

THE CLOSING NOTICE   *After 25 years and two Broadway revivals, the third closing
notice for* Fiddler on the Roof. *In an open-ended run, the closing of a show is
announced officially to the cast and crew by the posting backstage of a* **closing
notice.** *This theatrical version of the ubiquitous pink slip is not just a layoff notice,
but a statement saying that the imaginative and creative energies from both sides of
the curtain that sustained the production have run out. The creative circle has been
broken. All who wanted or were able to see it did.*

Thus did a play about a distant depression become in death a symbolic victim of a new economic tailspin, adding its own large company at least temporarily to the ranks of the unemployed and leaving another darkened midtown marquee to serve as a makeshift shelter for New York's destitute. Where did art end and real life begin?[26]

Theatre creators and theatregoers know that artistic values are never more important than human values. While art can inform and alter our views of what is valuable in life, life inevitably and profoundly affects what is important to us in art.

The Art of the Present

Spatial and literary artists are fond of the Latin epigram, *Vita brevis, ars longa:* Life is short, but arts lasts long. Once created and with the proper care, works of spatial and literary art can be preserved indefinitely. Recorded performances of musical, choreographic, and dramatic art also "last long." They are images of art of the past.

Not so for theatre art. There is no satisfying way to record or preserve the actual aesthetics of live stage performances. Video recordings of them invariably look like bad television made on the cheap.

The Memory of Choices

In the theatre, we are left only with the ephemera of productions—programs, reviews, posters, souvenirs—only enough for memories of what transpired on stage, "walking shadows" as Shakespeare called them. What remains is not the whole work, only indelible mental images of great choices. The process is direct aesthetic transference from the theatrical imagination to ours.

Thus no canon of past great works of theatre art (as opposed to *dramatic* art) can be collected and put on display in a gallery, in an anthology, or in a retrospective film festival. There are only new productions, handmade each time out, always new, always live, always round. In our recorded society, this impermanence might seem a severe limitation and source of frustration. Quite the contrary. To theatre artists, it is the primary source of renewal and regeneration. Peter Brook put it this way: "Thank God our art doesn't last. At least we're not adding more junk to the museums. Yesterday's performance is by now a failure. If we accept this, we can always start again from scratch."[27]

An idea for filling the empty space of a vacant theatre is the spark that ignites the theatrical imagination.

◼ A REVIVER AT WORK ·······································

Undiscovered Treasure

An Actor's Search Brings Machinal *to Life*

[Reprinted from *American Theatre*]

Frustrated with the limited range of contemporary roles available to her, 31-year-old actor Jodie Markell set out to discover overlooked plays with strong female leads, intent on sharing her enthusiasm with New York-area theatre companies and audiences. The play she rediscovered—Sophie Treadwell's 1928 Broadway expressionistic drama *Machinal*—not only provided her with the role of a complex, tragic antiheroine, but also became the first production of the New York Shakespeare Festival's 1990-91 season and set in motion the reevaluation of an obscure literary career.

Machinal—loosely based on the 1927 murder trial and conviction of the first woman executed in the electric chair—explores the tragic life of Miss A., an everywoman who marries a man she doesn't love because, in the character's words, "All women get married, don't they?" Caught in a downward spiral of emotional submission, Miss A. escapes momentarily into an affair with a mysterious man who spends much of his time supporting rebels in Mexico (a role played by Clark Gable on Broadway). When he confesses to her of having killed a man—viewing it only as a means to an end—she becomes obsessed, and eventually kills her loutish husband in a desperate bid for personal freedom. The play's expressionistic language and staging set Miss A.'s fate against the background of a machine-, money- and male-dominated society and its brutal and impersonal machinations (hence the title).

"Seven years ago, I was given a copy of *Machinal* in an anthology," says Markell, referring to *Plays by American Women:*

1890-1930, published by Applause Theatre Books. "I was astounded by Sophie Treadwell's style. Here was writing that was clear, precise, focused—and contemporary. I thought, 'Why haven't people been doing this play for the last 60 years?'"

Markell saw her mission clearly: She'd found a "lost" woman playwright with an extraordinary vision that she knew she had to share. Having worked with several small theatre companies, she knew the steps for getting a production off the ground: "I needed to secure the rights, but I discovered they weren't held by Samuel French or Dramatists Play Service. So I went on a treasure hunt." She traced Treadwell's estate to a Catholic service organization in Arizona and discovered that the late playwright, author and journalist's will stipulated that all subsequent royalties were to benefit Native Americans. "When I learned that, I burst into tears. It was a cause I had been supporting for a while. Suddenly I felt an incredible kinship."

Armed with the rights to New York production, Markell set out to produce *Machinal* herself. "I brought the play to director Michael Greif, who had worked with me on Theatre of the Film Noir at New York's New Arts Theatre Company. We sent it around to the theatres across the city, and everyone said, 'It's too old. The cast's too large.'" During this time, Markell took numerous other stage and film jobs, but her interest kept returning to *Machinal* and Treadwell. "I'd finish a job and think, 'But what about *Machinal?* It's so much greater a play than what I've been working on.'"

Finally, she and Greif collected a team of actors and designers who agreed to work for little or no pay, secured a space and set out to stage the piece on their own. Just prior to opening, however, the space became unavailable. "I had been working with the Naked

Jodie Markell as Miss A. and Rocco Sisto as a Priest in the New York Shakespeare Festival production of Machinal.

Angels company in Manhattan," Markell says, "so I called them and said, 'Emergency!' They agreed to let us use their theatre, but only for a two-week run."

Even without press coverage, word spread about the exceptional production, which quickly sold out. One of the lucky few who managed to see it—New York Shakespeare Festival producer Joseph Papp—was so impressed that he later asked Greif to join him as one of the theatre's three new directors-in-residence.

Through this long process of living with and working on the play, Markell realized that Treadwell's accomplishments have been sadly underestimated in the history of the American theatre. "As we rehearsed, we discovered the true richness of Sophie's language and the inventiveness of her varied techniques. Someone would say, 'Oh, this is the Clifford Odets scene. And here's a Tennessee Williams scene.' Then we'd stop and remember that both of these playwrights began writing after *Machinal*."

SUMMARY

1. The theatre exists in a series of regenerating life cycles in which plays run as long as they continue to draw an audience. The times played before an audience reflect important information about the culture, the performers, and the quality of the production.

2. Theatrical runs are played out in a variety of forms including limited runs, tours, repertory, long runs, and revivals.

3. Among the longest running shows in history are *Life with Father, A Chorus Line, The Mousetrap,* and *The Fantasticks.*

4. Film and video dramas extend their runs with recorded clones of the original in the form of rereleases, reruns, remakes, and reedits. In the live theatre, revivals emphasize the new lives given to previously produced plays.

5. Multicultural revivals of plays have been standard theatre practice since the fourth century B.C.

6. Unpredictable events, changing times, and evolving cultural standards can suppress as well as promote the revival of plays.

7. Uncovering lost or unknown plays can lead to new productions that can realign conventional theatrical wisdom.

8. There is no single, sure formula for theatrical success. The number of variables and the infinite number of possible choices they yield make such an equation elusive.

9. Theatre is entirely an art of the present—ephemeral and impermanent—a source of renewal and challenge for the theatrical imagination.

CHOICES

1. Let your imagination run riot. Reimagine your favorite Shakespearean play into an adventuresome, bold, even outrageous contemporary context. Consider how such a concept might be rendered by all of the required theatre artists beginning with a playwright who may be needed to adapt the text. Consider the theatre space required, the directorial concept, the actors and acting style, the design metaphor, period, style, and the appropriate audience for the production.

2. Consider a film, television, or stage production in which the actors have become so identified with the characters that it is difficult to imagine any others in the roles. Imagine the actors in the production have played out their runs in the show and leave for other opportunities. Choose their replacements with well-known actors who would maintain the integrity and original intent of the production. The actors you choose should also have sufficient box office appeal to keep attendance up. Explain your choices.

3. Which of the period plays referred to in this book do you think are especially relevant to the current times, affairs, events, and cultural constituencies? Explain your choices.

4. Which of the contemporary plays referred to in this book do you think have the kind of universal appeal that will endure for the next twenty years? For the next hundred years? Why?

5. Recall and recount your most vivid memories of theatrical choices. They may be broad and conceptual including entire interpretations, metaphors, or performances. Or they may be small, precious, insightful—moments of a performance, ornamental details of a design, a line of dialogue written, spoken, or staged magnificently.

THEATREGOER'S GUIDE

Essential Theatregoing Strategies

When you go to the movies, you step up to the window, buy a ticket, and walk in. Getting a ticket to the theatre is a different matter. Following are some essential strategies for obtaining the best tickets to the best shows at the theatre of your choice.

Finding Out What's Playing

Most newspapers and local magazines publish entertainment guides with separate theatre listings. Out-of-towners should avail themselves of:

Travel Guides and Services. Motor clubs, travel clubs, and travel agents provide booklets and brochures describing entertainment attractions for each city.

Hotel Concierges. Lobby attendants at major hotels provide guest services and recommendations such as restaurant and shopping suggestions, tours, sightseeing, and theatregoing arrangements. Some may even have tickets to "sold out" hits. A gratuity is usually expected, and a service charge may apply.

On Line Services. The World Wide Web is an increasingly accessible and easy way to find out what's playing and to even make reservations for individual performances in the world's professional theatres. Just log on to your favorite search engine and type in either the name of the show or even a category such as "Broadway" and you will be able to surf through full-color descriptions (often with video and sound clips) of what's playing.

Regional Theatres. For a complete up-to-date listing of not-for-profit professional theatres in the United States, including personnel, budgets, missions, and repertory, consult *Theatre Profiles,* New York, Theatre Communications Group, 1996.

Getting Tickets

Before going to the theatre, always call ahead. Theatre is not a drop-in activity.

The Box Office. If you are in the vicinity of the theatre, start by calling the box office to make reservations for the show you want to see. Phone reservations usually require credit card payment or payment as much as a week prior to the actual performance. Be sure to ask about:

Special Discounts. Check on the availability of student and senior citizen discounts, pay-what-you-can performances, twofers, and rush tickets, which are unsold tickets put on sale at greatly reduced prices just prior to the performance.

Season Subscriptions. For residents in the area of the theatre, season subscriptions are a good strategy. Subscribers get the best seats at the best prices, sometimes up to a 33-percent savings over single admissions. Other benefits include newsletters, discussion sessions, parking concessions, ticket exchanges, and memberships in clubs.

Group Rates. With savings of 10 percent to 50 percent, group discounts may apply to as few as ten tickets. Clubs and organizations as well as company parties and even families should ask for group rates.

Matinee, Week-Night, and Preview Performances. Because of supply and demand, matinee and week-night performances are almost always less expensive than weekend evening performances. Substantial savings are available at previews, the intermediate performances between dress rehearsals and the actual opening night.

Perquisites. Special benefits offered by the theatre can include free or reduced-rate parking while at the theatre; mass transit coupons; park-and-ride transportation; child-care arrangements; pre- and post-show restaurant discounts; special offers for coming productions; and discounts on merchandise, books, refreshments, and souvenirs offered by the theatre itself.

Ticket Agents.   Licensed ticket agents that operate in large metropolitan theatre districts purchase tickets on speculation and may have their own tickets to "sold out" performances. There is a service charge for each ticket, but it may be worth the extra cost for tickets that suit your travel plans, rather than having to make travel plans that suit your tickets.

Ticketmaster.   The computerized international reservation system sells tickets by phone to nationally listed events and to certain local offerings. Tickets to major commercial and not-for-profit theatre productions can be purchased through this convenient, advance planning service. There are many regional Ticketmaster offices, each handling tickets for a specific area. The Ticketmaster office listed in local phone directories can direct the caller to the correct regional phone number to make a reservation. Ticketmaster provides the best available tickets right at the time you call. Payment is by credit card, and there is a service charge for each ticket.

Scalpers.   Also called "touts," these unlicensed individuals purchase tickets on speculation and may be found hovering around the half-price booths and the theatres just before performances. They charge double or more the face value of the tickets for high demand sell-outs. Scalpers offer no guarantee. *Caveat emptor:* Beware of scalpers who may be selling worthless pieces of paper that only look like tickets. They will be hard to find after the show starts, and so may be your seats. In most locations, reselling tickets without a license and without paying proper taxes is illegal. It may also be illegal to sell tickets on public streets or on the private property of the theatre.

Discount Day-of-Performance Outlets. A not-to-be-overlooked service of metropolitan areas with major theatre districts. Theatres turn over unsold same-day tickets to a centralized location where they are made available at discounts up to 50 percent. Located near tourist attractions, these discount offices provide a service for theatres with unsold tickets and for patrons who are flexible enough to take advantage of the availabilities. Transactions must be made in person at specified hours. Be prepared to stand in line. It's worth the wait. Important "hot tix" locations:

Boston	BOSTIX	Faneuil Hall Plaza (617) 723-5181
Chicago	HOT TIX	The Loop: 108 N. State Street Magnificent Mile: 700 N. Michigan Ave., 6th Floor of Chicago Place Evanston: 1616 Sherman Ave.
Denver	TICKET BUS	16th and Curtis
London	TICKET BOOTH	Leichester Square
New York	TKTS	Midtown: 48th and Broadway Downtown: World Trade Center
San Diego	TIX BOOTH	701 B Street, Suite 225
San Francisco	STUBS	Union Square, Stockton Street
Seattle	TICKET/TICKET	401 Broadway East Pike Place (206) 324-2744
Toronto	5 STAR TICKETS	#1 Dudas Street West
Washington, DC	TICKETPLACE	730 21st St. and 8th St. (202) 842-5387

Appendix B

THE STUDY OF THEATRE ARTS

HAMLET:	My lord, you played once i' the university, you say?
POLONIUS:	That did I, my lord, and was accounted a good actor.
HAMLET:	And what did you enact?
POLONIUS:	I did enact Julius Caesar. I was killed i' the Capitol. Brutus killed me.

Hamlet, III, ii

For some students, the course for which *The Theatrical Imagination* is written introduces an immensely satisfying art form. For others, it confirms an interest already developed through previous experiences. Many will want to continue a relationship with the theatre beyond what has already has been established. You have many choices.

Using any search engine on the Internet, you need only type in the words "theatre" or "actors" or "Broadway" or "drama" or any other subject term, and you will be led to almost overwhelming information about the theatre. Even easier, using links, click through "entertainment" to "theatre" to more specific sites about the theatre. Production companies have home pages announcing plays and performers. Playbills list actors and their roles. The reconstructed Globe Theatre in London is described in detail, as are innumerable programs and sources to expand and explode a mind in search of information. Spend an hour surfing through the files hurling themselves at the screen when you enter the inquiring words and phrases.

More traditionally, you can take another course; beginning acting or stagecraft offers experience with the actual practice of theatre, while survey courses in drama and theatre history offer the challenges of theoretical and critical thinking. You can act in or work backstage on productions. You can pursue a major in theatre arts. Or you may make theatre part of your entire life, either as a career or as an avocation. For those on the stage and for those in the seats, theatre can provide the means of a course of study, a livelihood, or a counterpoint to the stresses of another occupation.

Values of a Theatre Education

The introductory theatre course is often offered as one option on a menu of arts courses required in a general education program. *The Theatrical Imagination* presents theatre as a series of intelligent and informed choices made by talented, skillful, and knowledgeable artists who transform drama from its written format to the live stage. The book directs its focus toward potential audience members as well as potential theatre artists. The purpose is to help students learn to appreciate theatre and to know a good play when they see one.

But why does there have to be a course in theatre appreciation? Is there some mystery about the theatre to be revealed only to the educated? Is theatre appreciation simply explaining the bag of tricks artists use to astound us with their personal images of reality? There are few if any college courses in football appreciation or comedy club appreciation or rock music appreciation. In another era, it was thought necessary to require students to study exercise, diet, and physical education, but these subjects have found their way into the popular culture and are rarely compulsory courses anymore. Currently, sexuality, multiculturalism, and substance control are subjects for university study by those who are expected to become leaders in the twenty-first century.

Theatre appreciation enhances the quality of life for educated people who might otherwise overlook an exceptionally satisfying art form that provocatively illuminates our understanding of the human condition. To elaborate upon Goethe's critical criteria of art, it takes a certain knowledge of "what they are trying to do" before we can judge "how well they are doing it" and "if it is worth doing."

Studying the choices artists make to create theatre leads to an understanding facilitating closer contact with the substance of theatre arts—the human condition. Influencing world affairs is tempered by realizations about human reactions to events. The lessons of history may be taken not from a chronology of conflicts, but from the series of changing relationships among people and their gods, their governments, their contemporaries, and themselves.

Further, at a time of stupefying technology, understanding theatre leads to understanding the tremendous power of mass communications. Success in the new millennium will depend upon dealing with highly emotional calls for action, contained in confusing combinations of information and advocacy, where the difference between what is real and what is imagined becomes less distinct.

Educational Theatre in the United States

The United States government is often chastised for its meager support of the arts. The National Endowment for the Arts finds itself underfunded and regularly steeped in controversy over its goals and mission. Compared to Great Britain, with its magnificent national and provincial theatres, or to the state theatres of Europe, America, we are told, neglects the arts and fosters a nation of culturally deficient citizens.

Is the only educational system to require theatre appreciation the one with the least theatre to appreciate? The answer to these seeming irregularities may be found in one of the most important, though underestimated and unappreciated, theatre delivery systems in the United States: the academic theatre.

While Americans are skeptical of centralization, federalization, and nationalization of the arts, every state in the Union is deeply in the arts business through an elaborate and well-funded higher education system including outstanding facilities, resident colonies of artist/teachers, adequate if not generous operational budgets, and a built-in captive group of students who make up the potential theatre audience of the future. And because of the competition for able and talented students, private colleges and universities offer similar cultural and artistic opportunities for their constituencies.

The strength of American theatre is at least partially found in the significant work of the academic theatre. College and university theatres are ideal places to learn and to be exposed to an art form central to the cultural complexity of world civilization.

Beyond the Introduction

The study of theatre arts is not unlike the study of other areas of inquiry, such as history or literature or political science. Theatre has its own history, its own contemporary practice, and its own criteria for evaluation. Taken as a college major in a liberal arts context, theatre provides a focus for study and a tangible application for broadening knowledge. Math and science, psychology, literature, technology, writing, sociology, marketing, management, and advertising—indeed, the entire list of college departments—all can be applied to theatre in one way or another.

Each play production is a case study in which the problems are identified in terms of objectives and methods for solutions. An organization is constructed to accommodate the manufacturing of the play through actual rehearsal and preparation. A delivery system presents the product of the play to its potential consumers. And post-production analysis provides the opportunity for evaluation and improvements.

All of the knowledge and skills and experiences gained through coursework and activities in higher education can be applied to play production. For this reason, many volunteers in academic theatre are non-theatre majors who have discovered its value as an outlet for the creative use of their skills. Engineers, business administration students, artists, and liberal arts students all can find creative and satisfying outlets in theatre. Theatre study also provides training and practice in the arts of the theatre, which leads to graduate study and direct employment in the profession. The educational system used for discovering and developing professional athletes in an elaborate network of intercollegiate sports also provides the training ground for theatre professionals as well.

Professional Training

The conservatory approach to theatre study is intended for students who want to prepare for professions in the theatre. While an overview of the theatre arts is part of the conservatory program, specific concentrations emphasize performance areas of acting and directing or the technical areas of scene design, lighting, costuming, and sound.

Accreditation by the National Association of Schools of Theatre (NAST) assures suitable faculty, resources, and organization are directed to the program. Professional training programs in theatre lead to a Bachelor of Fine Arts (B.F.A.) degree or a conservatory certificate. Such programs usually require two-thirds to three-fourths of coursework in theatre, with the remainder of courses in general education.

Circumstances much like those in the professional theatre are replicated in both performance and study. Auditions, rehearsals, and performances are conducted as nearly as possible to contemporary practice in the real world of theatre. Strongly motivated and talented students with a commitment to careers in professional theatre develop their skills in conservatory theatre programs.

Liberal Study

Another valid approach to theatre study is provided by the more traditional liberal arts theatre major in which from one-fourth to one-third of the total courses are in theatre and drama, with the remaining courses selected from the general catalog. This major provides a firm grounding in the areas of theatre with more opportunities to study a wider variety of subjects offered by the institution. Students take at least one course in each of the disciplines of acting, technical theatre and design, directing, and history. Additional courses create a specialization in performance or production. Carefully selected college work may lead to second majors, minors, and structured patterns and combinations that fulfill individual goals.

Communications skills, self-assurance, presentation skills, group interactions, and problem solving, which are components of theatre, are also elements that may be applied to any number of career opportunities. Certification in language arts and theatre for teaching at the primary or high-school level couples theatre study with professional education requirements. Completion of a liberal arts theatre program provides the basic intellectual skills and the knowledge necessary for further study or work in a wide variety of occupations and graduate schools.

Graduate Study

Completing courses does not necessarily lead to success in the theatre. The elusive element of talent, and the even more elusive factor of good luck, soon intrude upon the hopeful aspirations of the most dedicated students. Experience and maturity come together at about the age of undergraduate graduation. The more demanding rigors of graduate schools present the testing and training place for theatre professionals.

A Master of Arts (M.A.) degree includes one or two years of academic study leading to intermediate accomplishment in research, usually in theatre history/criticism. The master's degree prepares students for advanced work in doctoral programs and also is important for progress of high-school teachers.

For those interested in college and university teaching, the Doctor of Philosophy (Ph.D.) degree requires two or three years of coursework plus an original research and writing project, the dissertation, which is looked upon as a major accomplishment and contribution to the field of study. The doctorate in theatre is a required terminal degree for those intent on a career as a college or university professor with expectations of research and publications.

The Master of Fine Arts (M.F.A.) degree recognizes the development of a practicing professional theatre artist in areas of acting, directing, or design. Two- or three-year graduate-level conservatory programs foster specialization within the disciplines of theatre and provide opportunities for students to have their work seen by potential employers. An M.F.A. in theatre is considered a terminal degree and is accepted, along with the Ph.D., as a qualification for college teaching.

While academic credentials are seldom criteria for employment in professional theatre, they are essential for educational theatre appointments. Moreover, the skills, knowledge, and maturity gained through graduate study are desirable at every level of theatre practice from the local amateur group to the most glamorous commercial venture.

Onstage, Backstage, or in the House

Those who discover they have an affinity for the theatre can find ample opportunities to get involved. Employment options include the professional and educational theatres as well as advertising, industrial and entertainment films, videos and live presentations, and arts management.

For those whose occupations are found elsewhere, almost every community supports an active amateur community theatre. These cultural centers use performers, technicians, and managers from all walks of life who have learned to find satisfaction from theatrical production.

As the work week changes and more employees become disenchanted with banal entertainments, community theatres will continue to provide highly creative outlets for talented people. For many, work will be only a part of life, and constructive leisure, which satisfies creative and imaginative needs for expression, will become extremely important.

As an art form, theatre is to be enjoyed, its controversy savored, and its excellence admired. As audience members, we not only enjoy theatre, we influence its direction and its outcome. We willingly embrace the responsibilities of an educated life when we recognize the importance of the arts to the fabric of cultural life and provide continuing financial, moral, and personal support.

Theatre professor Howard Stein observes: "If you don't know where you're going, any road will take you there. If you know where you are going, why not take the scenic route?"[1] Educated, active, aware, and sensitive people know where they are going. And their scenic route takes them along the alluring ways of the theatre.

The options are many. The choices are yours.

THEATRE STUDENTS AT WORK

For students intent on pursuing a life in the theatre, summers present much sought after work-study opportunities in one of the oldest forms of American show business: summer stock. The pay is often non-existent and the work is invariably menial. There's not much applause either for these "interns" who, if they are lucky, play the least noticeable of "bit parts." But the study—the opportunities to apprentice with professional theatre artists—is what makes young people with the intoxicating need to perform compete for these prized positions. Lawrence Biemiller describes a day in the life of theatre students who learn, rehearse, and perform Shakespeare among the redwoods that surround Shakespeare Santa Cruz's outdoor theatre.

Where Drama Students Explore Some of the Most Exquisite Language Known to Man

by Lawrence Biemiller

SANTA CRUZ, Calif.—We grow up dreading Shakespeare. Reading that first play—*Julius Caesar* in the seventh grade, or *Romeo and Juliet* in the eighth— is a torture of apostrophes and strange syntax, a racking prolonged by the thousand footnotes that explain "fathom" and "foil" and "forfend." The fortunate among us, dragged to a moving *Hamlet* at 19, chided at 20 to take the drama department's Shakespeare survey—the fortunate come to love those same strange lines, whose "cataracts and hurricanoes" of language represent, indeed define, the emotions of our vainglorious race.

Which is why these 400-year-old plays are staged in summer festivals, such as the one on the University of California's campus here, and why drama students clamor to be festival interns, even when the internships are unpaid and professional actors get the good parts. It's why Clark Huggins is sitting on an outdoor staircase in the middle of the afternoon with Jennifer Falt and Carrie Burriss, the three of them surrounded by *Love's Labour's Lost* scripts, and by their knapsacks, and by shreds of skin from a bright-red apple that Ms. Falt is eating only the flesh of.

"Welcome to our apple-strewn lair," Ms. Burriss tells Ian McConnel. Mr. McConnel will play the King, who banishes women from his court for three years so that he and his fellows can make it "a little academe." It's odd, hearing phrases like "apple-strewn lair" out of people who in the next breath sound, like, totally young. But here language is as thick, and as mutable, as the fog that steals into the redwoods from the Pacific. "So, kingie-poo," Ms. Burriss says, rocketing centuries forward with just a few syllables, "how are you feeling about where you are with this guy?"

"Oh, kinda lost," Mr. McConnel says. "I'm not sure what kind of ruler he is."

"So why is he president of the fraternity?" asks Ms. Burriss. The comic potential of the frat-house conceit is considerable, and its contemporary edge fits right in at Shakespeare Santa Cruz. This year's *Tempest,* for example, is set on an island a lot like Gilligan's, with Prospero as a mad scientist and the gayest Ariel you ever saw. Last year's *Merry Wives of Windsor* was set in a trailer park. This year's other Shakespeare play, *King Lear,* is more traditional, but it's paired with *The Dresser,* a play about a performance of *Lear* in Britain during World War II. Tony Church, a member of the Royal Shakespeare Company, has the Lear role in both productions. The point of Shakespeare Santa Cruz, its administrators say, is to make Shakespeare's language and plays relevant to modern audiences.

Of course, producing *Love's Labour's Lost* is not why the interns are here—they're here to work and to learn. Mr. Huggins plays Francisco in *The Tempest* and has 10 lines to speak at the beginning of Act II; he's also a dresser for *King Lear,* making sure four cast members' costume changes come off without hitches. Mr. McConnel is in the ensemble for *Lear* and is a dresser for *Tempest.* Ms. Falt and Ms. Burriss are assistant directors of *The Tempest,* in charge of the troupe of schoolgirl nymphs who run through lawn sprinklers in tutus and spell out Shakespeare's songs with words arranged on beach balls.

SHAKESPEARE SANTA CRUZ presents almost 70 performances between mid-July and the beginning of September—not counting *Love's Labour's Lost,* to which the public is not invited. In addition, the 20 or so interns attend acting and voice classes. The acting classes are taught by Jack Zerbe, a Guilford College theater professor who plays *The Tempest's* Caliban (wearing only some straps and a few electrodes—in this production, Prospero has enslaved his monster through science). The voice classes are taught by Ursula Meyer, *Lear's* Goneril, who is leaving Yale University to teach at the University of California at San Diego.

"Voice class is hard—you find out you don't know how to talk," says Mr. Huggins. "She'll hammer at you till you can make simple sounds well." But *hammer* may not be quite the right word for it. Ms. Meyer cajoles, murmurs, exclaims, even sings—all while using language inventively enough to make any writer envious: "Hum as if a car is driving up from your tailbone and over your head and down to the ground." "Now change it to an E, as though there's a little insect flying around, and trace the insect with the E." "Now, four huge, gargantuan, true-blue, genuine, hopefully pleasurable sighs of relief."

An hour before the evening's *Lear,* Mr. Huggins gathers armloads of Edwardian coats off a rack in the dressing room to carry down to the glen. "Hold this a minute?" he asks, handing off a top hat. "Everybody has at least two costume changes, and some as many as four or five. Some of them are pretty speedy—like, you have to be there holding the shirt. I place everything so the actors can get to it. I have to be backstage for Edmund's quick change, after he shoots himself. Things heat up for about four minutes, and then I have a lot of time to learn lines."

He heads off down a narrow, dusty path among the redwoods. Evening is falling: the path is illuminated with strings of tiny Christmas-tree lights. The raked stage, which appears spacious and simple from the front, looks cluttered and unbelievably cramped from the back—too cramped, certainly, for a member of the Royal Shakespeare Company. "Is there new blood mixed up?" asks Mr. Huggins, who is responsible for bloodying Gloucester after Regan and Cornwall pluck out his eyes. In odd corners are the wind machines for *Lear's* big storm scene, and the *Tempest* nymphs' beach balls.

"Life is about trying not to get hit," Mr. Huggins said earlier, "but acting is about walking through life asking to get hit." It does seem a strange compulsion, asking to get hit four nights a week or more—and for so little money, in so little space, with so little certainty about the year to come, the decade, the life. Beyond the stage, though, the audience is gathering under the dark redwoods, chatting, laughing, pouring wine. Soon actors will appear to speak some of the most exquisite language known to man—actors understandably eager to pretend, on this sloping stage for these few hours, that words in their mouths are really their own.

Lawrence Biemiller, *The Chronicle of Higher Education,* 8 September 1995, p. A79.

Appendix C
TIME LINES

Art does not exist in a vacuum but flourishes in the context of the most complex interactive global events. These Time Lines provide a sampling of major developments related to the theatre, in parallel with a listing of hallmarks in the history of world civilization. The theatrical imagination at work reflects the world. These events have been selected to suggest the influences that have shaped the definitions of our culture and ourselves. Events mentioned in *The Theatrical Imagination* are listed in **boldface**.

The Theatrical Imagination at Work

The World Reflected

	The Theatrical Imagination at Work		The World Reflected
		4241 B.C.	Egyptian calendar
		3400	Egyptian central government
		2700	Pyramid Texts
2500 B.C.	Memphite Drama		
1868	**Abydos Passion Play—Egypt**		
1850	**Ikhernofret**		
1500			
1400	Canaanite, Hittite, and Babylonian rituals		
		1257	Temple of Ramses II
		1250	The Exodus
		1200	*The Epic of Gilgamesh*
		1193	**Destruction of Troy**
		1027	Zhow Dynasty begins
		900	Homer's *The Iliad*
		800	Homer's *The Odyssey*
		776	First Olympic Games
		753	Founding of Rome
		660	Founding of Byzantium
		630	Zoroaster born
		604	Lao Ze born
		594	Solon archon of Athens
		581	Pythagoras born
		563	Buddha born
560	**Thespis first actor in Greece**	560	Pisistratus archon of Athens
		551	Confucius born
534	**Thespis wins first dramatic contest**		
525	Aeschylus born		
		509	Roman Republic
		500	Battle of Persepolis
		497	Pythagoras dies
496	Sophocles born		

The Theatrical Imagination at Work

493   **Theatre of Dionysus**

486   Comic competition at City Dionysia
480   Euripides born

472   **Aeschylus' *The Persians***
471   **Second actor introduced**

468   Third actor introduced
458   Aeschylus' *The Oresteia*

449   **Acting competition at City Dionysia**
448   Aristophanes born

441   Sophocles' *Antigone*
431   Euripides' *Medea*
430   **Sophocles' *Oedipus the King***

415   **Euripides' *Trojan Women***
411   **Aristophanes' *Lysistrata***
405   Euripides' *Bacchae*

365   **First Roman theatrical
         performance**

350   **Theatre at Epidarus**
335   **Aristotle's *Poetics***

316   Menander's *The Grouch*

240   Livius Andronicus' plays performed

205   Plautus' *Miles Gloriosus*
191   Plautus' *Pseudolus*
161   Terence' *Phormio*

75   Theatre at Pompeii

55   **First permanent Roman theatre**

The World Reflected

490   **Battle of Marathon**

483   Battle of Salamis

470   Socrates born
469   Pericles born

456   Temple of Zeus Olympia

447   Parthenon begun

431   Peloponesian War begins

429   Plato born

411   Peloponnesian War ends

384   Aristotle born
370   **Plato's *The Republic***

356   Alexander the Great born
350   *Mahabarata*

323   Alexander the Great dies

303   Yayoi period begins
264   First Punic War begins
         First gladiator contests

218   Second Punic War begins
214   Great Wall started
206   Han Dynasty begins

150   "Venus de Milo"
149   Third Punic War begins

73   Spartacus slave revolt

44   Julius Caesar assassinated

The Theatrical Imagination at Work

The World Reflected

	37 Anthony marries Cleopatra
	27 Virgil's *Aeneid*
15 Vitruvius' *De Architectura*	
4 Seneca born	
	1 A.D. Jesus born
	5 Ovid's *Metamorphoses*
	30 Jesus dies
	54 Emperor Nero
	64 Fire destroys Rome
	65 *Gospel of Mark*
	80 Colosseum built
	124 Pantheon built
	135 Diaspora of Jews
300 Shudraka's *The Little Clay Cart*	312 Emperor Constantine converts
	320 Gupta Dynasty begins
	396 Augustine becomes Bishop of Hippo
400 Kalidasa's *Shakuntala*	476 Fall of Rome
	552 Buddhism introduced to Japan
568 Lombards stop Roman spectacles	570 Mohammed born
	600 Chinese book printing
	632 Mohammed dies
	701 Li Po born
	715 Gret Mosque, Damascus
	732 Moors defeated at Tours
	742 Charlemagne born
	800 *Book of Kells*
925 *Quem quaeritis* trope	
935 **Hroswitha born**	960 Sung Dynasty begins
	961 Cordoba mosque
965 Ethelwold's *Regularis Concordia*	980 Cologne Cathedral
	1000 *Beowulf*
	1002 Leif Ericson explores North America
	1027 Omar Khayyam born
	1040 Macbeth kills Duncan
	1054 Christian Church splits East and West
	1066 Battle of Hastings
	1096 **First Crusade**
	1100 Angor Wat
1150 *The Play of Adam*	1209 Cambridge University founded
	1210 Charles Cathedral
	1215 *Magna Carta*
	1220 Amiens Cathedral

The Theatrical Imagination at Work

1350	*The Chalk Circle*
	Lute Song
1375	**Second Shepherd's Play**
1398	*Confrerie de la Passion* produces plays
1425	*The Castle of Perseverance*
1465	Fernando de Rojas born
1469	Juan del Encina born
1470	*Pierre Pathelin*
	Mankind
1474	Lodovico Aristo born
1475	Sebastiano Serlio born
1486	Vitruvius' *De Architectura* printed

The World Reflected

1225	Thomas Aquinas born
1233	Inquisition established
1256	Gunpowder invented
1264	Feast of Corpus Christi first ordered
1271	Marco Polo visits Kublai Khan
1279	**Yuan Dynasty begins**
1307	Dante's *The Divine Comedy*
1325	Aztec Tenochtitlan
1337	100 Years War begins
1347	Black Death begins
1348	*The Decameron* begun
1368	Ming Dynasty begins
1387	*The Canterbury Tales*
1399	Richard II deposed
1411	Hus excommunicated
1412	Brunelleschi's *Rules of Perspective*
1415	Henry V at Agincourt
1431	Joan of Arc executed
1432	Van Eyck, Ghent altarpiece
1434	Cosimo di Medici rules Florence
1438	Inca Empire in Peru
1451	Christopher Columbus born
1452	Leonardo da Vinci born
1453	Turks take Constantinople
	100 Years War ends
1454	**Movable type press invented**
1469	Ferdinand marries Isabella
1473	Sistine Chapel built
1474	Michelangelo Buonarroti born
1478	Spanish Inquisition begins
1483	Richard III's rule begins
	Martin Luther born
1484	Botticelli's "Birth of Venus"
1485	**Richard III killed**
1492	Columbus in West Indies
	Leonardo draws flying machine
1495	Michelangelo's "The Last Supper"
1498	Michelangelo's "Pieta"

The Theatrical Imagination at Work

1500	*Everyman*
1510	Lope de Rueda born
1520	Machiavelli's *The Mandrake*
1530	James Burbage born
1533	Heywood's *Johan Johan*
1534	*Ralph Roister Doister*
1545	Serlio's *De Architecttura*
1557	Thomas Kyd born
1548	Frances bans religious plays **Hotel de Bourgogne built**
1561	Preston's *Cambises* Sackville and Norton's *Gorboduc*
1562	**Lope de Vega Carpio born**
1564	**William Shakespeare born** Christopher Marlowe born
1567	**Richard Burbage born**
1572	**Ben Jonson born**
1576	The Theatre Opens **Blackfriars opens**
1590	Spenser's *The Faerie Queen*
1592	**Kyd's *The Spanish Tragedy***
1593	Christopher Marlowe dies
1595	**Shakespeare's *A Midsummer Night's Dream*** **Shakespeare's *Romeo and Juliet***

The World Reflected

1501	Michelangelo's "David"
1503	**De Vinci's "Mona Lisa"**
1504	Michelangelo begins Sistine Chapel ceiling
1509	Henry VIII's rule begins John Calvin born
1513	Machiavelli's *The Prince*
1516	Aristo's *Orlando Furioso*
1517	Luther's 95 Theses
1519	Leonardo da Vinci dies
1522	Magellan circumnavigates the globe
1526	Mongol Empire begins
1533	Pizarro conquers Peru Queen Elizabeth born Henry VIII heads English Church Society of Jesus founded
1545	Council of Trent begins
1547	Ivan the Terrible becomes first tsar Cervantes born
1558	**Elizabeth I begins reign**
1563	Council of Trent ends Index of Prohibited Books
1564	Galileo Galilei born
1588	Spanish Armada defeated
1590	Microscope invented

The Theatrical Imagination at Work

1599	Shakespeare's *Henry V*
	Shakespeare's *Julius Caesar*
	The Globe erected
1600	Calderon born
1601	**Shakespeare's *Hamlet***
	Shakespeare's *Twelfth Night*
1605	**Shakespeare's *King Lear***
1606	Jonson's *Volpone*
	Shakespeare's *Macbeth*
1608	Giacomo Torelli born
1611	**Shakespeare's *The Tempest***
1613	**The Globe burns**
1614	Webster's *The Duchess of Malfi*
	Lope's de Vegas' *The Sheep Well*
1616	**William Shakespeare dies**
	Ben Jonson first poet laureate
1618	*Teatro Farnese* **built**
1622	**Molière born**
1623	**First Folio of Shakespeare's Plays**
1636	Calderon's *Life Is a Dream*
	Corneille's *Le Cid*
1656	Jeremy Collier born

The World Reflected

1597	El Greco's "Resurrection"
1602	East India Company
1603	**James I begins reign**
1606	Cervantes' *Don Quixote Cervantes'*
1607	The Virginia Colony
1608	Telescope invented
1610	Louis XIII begins reign
	Galileo sees Jupiter's satellites
1611	***King James Bible***
1615	Inigo Jones named England's architect
1616	**Galileo ordered to cease research**
1618	Thirty Years War begins
1619	African slaves arrive in Virginia
1620	Massachusetts Bay Colony
	Submarine invented
1625	Charles I begins reign
1628	Taj Mahal
1632	John Locke born
1635	Rubens's "Landscape with Rainbow"
1636	Harvard College founded
1640	English Civil War begins
	Sir Isaac Newton born
	Rembrandt's "Night Watch"
1643	**Louis XIV begins resign**
1644	Jing Dynasty begins
1646	English Civil War ends
1648	Thirty Years' War ends
	English Commonwealth ends
1651	Hobbes' *Leviathan*

The Theatrical Imagination at Work

1662	Molière's *L'Ecole des femmes*
1663	**Drury Lane theatre opens**
1664	**Molière's *Tartuffe***
1666	**Molière's *Le Misanthrope***
1668	Molière's *L'Avare*
1670	Molière's *Le Bourgeois Gentilhomme*
1673	Molière dies
1675	Wycherley's *The Country Wife*
1676	Etherege's *The Man of Mode*
1677	Dryden's *All for Love*
	Racine's *Phèdre*
1679	***Comédie Francaise* founded**
1694	Voltaire born
1698	**Collier's *A Short View of the Immorality and Profaneness of the English Stage***
1700	Congreve's *The Way of The World*
1703	*Scena per angolo*
1722	Steele's *The Conscious Lovers*
1728	Gay's *The Beggar's Opera*
1731	Lillo's *The London Merchant*
1732	**Covent Garden Opera House opens**

The World Reflected

1660	**Restoration/Charles II**
1665	Newton's Laws of Gravitation
1667	Milton's *Paradise Lost*
1678	Bunyan's *The Pilgrim's Progress*
1682	Peter the Great named tsar
1685	James II begins reign
1687	Newton's *Philosophiae Naturalis Principia Mathematica*
1689	Peter the Great begins reign
1692	The College of William and Mary founded
	Salem witch trials
1707	Henry Feilding born
1710	**Georg Wilhelm Friedrich Hegel born**
1711	Addison and Steele's *The Spectator*
1712	Jean-Jacques Rousseau born
1714	George I begins reign
1715	Louis XV begins reign
1719	Defoe's *Robinson Crusoe*
1721	Walpole first Prime Minister
	Bach's "The Brandenburg Concerto"
1724	Immanual Kant born
1726	Swift's *Gulliver's Travels*
1727	George II begins reign
1732	*"Poor Richard's Almanac"*

The Theatrical Imagination at Work

1737 Licensing Act

1741 **David Garrick's London debut**

1746 Goldoni's *The Servant of Two Masters*
1748 Izumo's *Chushingura*
1749 **Johann Wolfgang von Goethe born**

1759 **Spectators banished from French stage**

1765 *Autos sacramentales* banned in Spain
1766 Southwark Theatre opens
1769 **Diderot's *The Paradox of Acting***

1773 Goldsmith's *She Stoops to Conquer*

1777 Sheridan's *The School for Scandal*
1779 Sheridan's *The Critic*

1784 Beaumarchais' *Le Marriage de Figaro*
1785 **Argand lamp**

1787 Tyler's *The Contrast*
       Edmund Kean born
       Louis Jacques Mandé Daguerre born

The World Reflected

1737 **Herculaneum excavated**
1739 Methodism
1741 Handel's "The Messiah"
1743 Hogarth's "Marriage à la Mode"

1748 **Pompeii excavated**

1750 **Voltaire's *Candide***
       Peking Forbidden City
1755 Dr. Johnson's *Dictionary*
1756 Wolfgang Amadeus Mozart born
1757 England rules India
1761 Mongol Empire ends

1762 Catherine the Great begins reign
       Rousseau's *The Social Contract*

1769 Napoleon Bonaparte born
1770 Beethoven born
       Boston Massacre
       Gainsborough's "The Blue Boy"
1772 Slavery abolished in England
1773 Boston Tea Party
       J. B. P. Du Sable founds Chicago
1774 First Continental Congress
1775 Steam engine invented
1776 Declaration of Independence
       Gibbon's *Decline and Fall of the Roman Empire*

1781 Kant's *Critique of Pure Reason*
1783 Stendhal born

1786 Mozart's *The Marriage of Figaro*
1787 Steamboat invented

1788 "Auld Lang Syne"
1789 French Revolution
       George Washington becomes President
1791 Paine's *The Rights of Man*
       U.S. Bill of Rights

The Theatrical Imagination at Work

The World Reflected

	1792 — *A Vindication for the Rights of Women*
	1793 — Louis XVI decapitated / Reign of Terror begins / Marat killed
1794 — Chestnut Street Theatre opens in America	
	1797 — Coleridge's *Kubla Khan*
	1798 — Auguste Comte born
	1800 — Electric battery invented / Jefferson becomes President
1802 — Victor Hugo born / Alexandre Dumas père born	
	1803 — Louisiana Purchase
	1804 — Emperor Napoleon Bonaparte / Steam locomotive invented / Haiti independence
	1805 — Beethoven's *Fidelio*
1806 — Edwin Forrest born	
1807 — **Ira Aldridge born**	1807 — England stops slave trade
1808 — Goethe's *Faust, Part I*	
	1809 — Charles Darwin born
	1810 — P. T. Barnum born
	1811 — Harriet Beecher Stowe born
	1812 — Grimm's *Fairy Tales*
	1813 — Austen's *Pride and Prejudice*
	1815 — Battle of Waterloo
1816 — Gas lighting introduced at Chestnut Street Theatre / **Limelight invented**	1816 — Rossini's *The Barber of Seville*
	1817 — Frederick Douglass born
	1818 — Karl Marx born
	1819 — Walt Whitman born / Herman Melville born
1821 — **The African Company**	1821 — Napoleon Bonaparte dies / Mexico independence / Fedor Mikhailovich Dostoyevsky born
1823 — Stendal's *Racine and Shakespeare*	
1824 — **Ira Aldridge leaves America**	1824 — Beethoven's "The Ninth Symphony"
1826 — **Edwin Forrest debuts** / **Duke of Saxe-Meiningen born** / Bowery Theatre opens	1826 — Cooper's *The Last of the Mohicans*
	1827 — Beethoven dies
1828 — Henrik Ibsen born	
	1829 — Chopin debuts
1830 — Hugo's *Hernani*	
1831 — Goethe's *Faust, Part II*	1831 — Darwin sails on H.M.S. Beagle

The Theatrical Imagination at Work

1833	Edwin Booth born
1835	Büchner's *Danton's Death*
1836	Gogol's *The Inspector General* Büchner's *Woyzeck*
1838	Henry Irving born
1843	Gas lighting installed at *Comédie Français*
1845	Mowat's *Fashion*
1845	Sarah Bernhardt born
1849	**Astor Place Riots** August Strindberg born Edwin Booth debuts
1850	Turgenev's *A Month in the Country*
1851	Labiche's *The Italian Straw Hat*
1852	Boucicault's *The Corsican Brothers* Dumas fils' *Le Demi-Monde*
1856	George Bernard Shaw born
1863	Konstantin Stanislavski born

The World Reflected

1834	Hugo's *The Hunchback of Notre Dame*
1835	Mark Twain born
1836	The Alamo
1837	Queen Victoria begins reign Telegraph invented
1838	Dickens' *Oliver Twist*
1839	Poe's *Fall of the House of Usher* **Photography (Daguerreotype) invented**
1841	Emerson's *Essays*
1842	Hong Kong taken by England
1846	Segregation in South Africa
1848	Republic of Liberia Marx's *The Communist Manifesto* California Gold Rush Seneca Falls Women's Convention
1849	Mendelssohn's "Elijah"
1850	Hawthorne's *The Scarlet Letter*
1851	Melville's *Moby Dick*
1852	**Stowe's *Uncle Tom's Cabin***
1853	Verdi's *La Traviata*
1854	Thoreau's *Walden* Light bulb invented
1855	Whitman's *Leaves of Grass*
1856	Flaubert's *Madame Bovary* Sigmund Freud born Booker T. Washington born
1859	**Darwin's *On the Origin of Species***
1861	U.S. Civil War begins Dickens' *Great Expectations* Russian serfs freed Machine gun invented
1862	**Hugo's *Les Misérables*** Bismarck Prime Minister of Germany
1864	Tolstoy's *War and Peace* U.S. Purchases Alaska

The Theatrical Imagination at Work		The World Reflected	
		1865	Lewis Carroll's *Alice in Wonderland* Wagner's *Tristan und Isolde* U.S. Civil War ends Slavery abolished in the U.S.
1866	**Henry Irving debuts** Ibsen's *Brand* **The Black Crook**	1866	Dostoyevsky's *Crime and Punishment* Trans-Atlantic cable laid
1867	Ibsen's *Peer Gynt*	1867	Marx's *Das Kapital* Howard University founded
		1869	Suez Canal opens
		1870	Franco-Prussian War Vladimir I. Lenin born
		1871	Kaisar Wilhelm I Verdi's *Aïda* Barnum's *"Greatest Show on Earth"*
1872	Gordon Craig born Nietzsche's *The Birth of Tragedy*	1872	Whistler's "Mother" Monet's "Impression of Sunrise"
1873	Max Reinhardt born		
1874	Vsevelod Meyerhold born **Paris Opera House**	1874	Degas' "Ballet Rehearsal"
1875	Bizet's *Carmen*		
		1876	Wagner's *The Ring of the Nibelung* Bayreuth *Festspielhaus* opens Telephone invented
1877	Ibsen's *The Pillars of Society*	1877	Phonograph invented
1879	**Ibsen's *A Doll's House*** Gilbert and Sullivan's *The Pirates of Penzance*		
		1880	Dostoyevsky's *The Brothers Karamazov* Rodin's "The Thinker"
1881	Gilbert and Sullivan's *Patience* **Ibsen's *Ghosts***	1881	Tuskegee Institute
1882	John Barrymore born Becque's *The Vultures*	1882	Tchaikovsky's "1812 Overture"
1883	Buffalo Bill's Wild West Show	1883	James Joyce born Franz Kafka born Munch's "The Scream" The Metropolitan Opera House
1884	Ibsen's *The Wild Duck*		
1885	**Henry Irving knighted** Gilbert and Sullivan's *The Mikado*	1885	Twain's *Huckleberry Finn*
1887	***Théâtre Libre* founded** Strindberg's *The Father*		
1888	Strindberg's *Miss Julie* Eugene O'Neill born	1888	Kaiser Wilhelm II Rimsky-Korakov's *Scheherazade* Jack the Ripper

The Theatrical Imagination at Work

1889	***Freie Bühne* opens**
1890	**Ibsen's *Hedda Gabler***
1891	The Independent Theatre
1892	Hauptmann's *The Weavers*
	Charley's Aunt
1893	Shaw's *Candida*
1894	Shaw's *Arms and the Man*
1895	Wilde's *The Importance of Being Earnest*
1896	**Chekhov's *The Seagull***
	Antonin Artaud born
1897	Rostand's *Cyrano de Bergerac*
1898	**Moscow Popular Art Theatre founded**
1901	Chekhov's *The Three Sisters*
	Harold Clurman born
	Shaw's *Man and Superman*
1902	**Gorky's *The Lower Depths***
	Strindberg's *A Dream Play*
1904	**Checkhov's *The Cherry Orchard***
	Barrie's *Peter Pan*
1907	**Synge's *The Playboy of the Western World***
	Ziegfeld Follies

The World Reflected

1889	Motion Picture invented
1890	Frazer's *The Golden Bough*
	Cézanne's "The Card Players"
1892	Tchaikovsky's *"The Nutcracker"*
1895	Yeats' *Poems*
	Tchaikovsky's *"Swan Lake"*
	X-rays invented
	Strauss' "Thus Spake Zarathustra"
1896	Olympic Games revived
1897	Debussy's "Nocturne"
1899	Veblen's *The Theory of the Leisure Class*
1900	**Freud's *The Interpretation of Dreams***
	Quantum Theory formulated
1901	Washington's *Up From Slavery*
	Commonwealth of Australia proclaimed
1903	First opera recording
	Airplane invented
	The Great Train Robbery
	Du Bois' *The Souls of Black Folk*
1904	**Cohan's *"I'm a Yankee Doodle Dandy"***
1905	**Einstein's *Special Theory of Relativity***
1906	Matisse's "The Joy of Life"
1907	**Picasso's "Desmoiselles d'Avignon"**
	Frank Lloyd Wright's Robie house
	John Wayne born
1909	Assembly-line automobile production introduced
	Mahler's "Ninth Symphony"
	Stravinsky's "The Fire Bird"
1910	N.A.A.C.P. founded

The Theatrical Imagination at Work

1912	**Actors' Equity Association**
1915	Neighborhood Playhouse opens
	Provincetown Playhouse opens
	Cleveland Playhouse founded
1916	Arthur Miller born
1918	Brecht's *Baal*
1919	The Theatre Guild
1920	O'Neill's *The Emperor Jones*
1921	Pirandello's *Six Characters in Search of an Author*
	O'Neill's *Beyond the Horizon*
1922	O'Neill's *The Hairy Ape*
1923	**Rice's *The Adding Machine***
1924	O'Neill's *Desire Under the Elms*
	Stanislavski's *My Life in Art*
	Marlon Brando born
1925	Yale Drama School
	Peter Brook born
1926	Dario Fo born
1927	**Hammerstein and Kern's *Showboat***
	George C. Scott born
	Robert Brustein born
1928	**Brecht's *The Threepenny Opera***
	Edward Albee born

The World Reflected

1912	*Titanic* sinks
1913	Mann's *Death in Venice*
	Proust's *Remembrance of Things Past*
	Stravinsky's "The Rite of Spring"
1914	Panama Canal opens
	World War I begins
	Louis Armstrong band
1915	*The Birth of a Nation*
	Morton's "Jelly Roll Blues"
	Einstein's *General Theory of Relativity*
1917	Russian Revolution
	Jung's *The Psychology of the Unconscious*
	Duchamp's "The Fountain"
1918	World War I ends
1919	League of Nations
	The Bauhaus
1920	Lewis' *Main Street*
	Television invented
1921	Lawrence's *Women in Love*
1922	Union of Soviet Socialist Republics
	Eliot's "The Waste Land"
	Joyce's *Ulysses*
1923	Secretary General Stalin
	Fascist Italy
	Gerschwin's "Rhapsody in Blue"
	Bessie Smith's "Down Hearted Blues"
1924	Lenin dies
	Forster's *A Passage to India*
1925	Kafka's *The Trial*
	Malcom X born
	Leo Chaney version of *Phantom of the Opera*
1926	First Teaming of Laurel & Hardy
1927	**Al Jolson's *The Jazz Singer***
1928	Penicillin discovered
	Ravel's "Bolero"
	First Mickey Mouse cartoon

The Theatrical Imagination at Work

1930	Harold Pinter born
	Lorraine Hansberry born
1931	James Earl Jones born
	Group Theatre founded
1933	Jerzy Grotowski born
	O'Neill's *Ah, Wilderness!*
1934	Wole Soyinka born
	Hellman's *The Children's Hour*
1935	Gershwin's *Porgy and Bess*
	Odets' *Awake and Sing*
	and *Waiting for Lefty*
	Federal Theatre Project
1938	Konstantin Stanislavski dies
	Artaud's *The Theatre and Its Double*
	Wilder's *Our Town*
	Hellman's *The Little Foxes*
	Brecht's *The Good Woman of Setzuan*
	Brecht's *Mother Courage and Her Children*
1940	Al Pacino born
	Eliot's *The Cocktail Party*
1941	Coward's *Blithe Spirit*
	Green and Wright's *Native Son*
1943	Vladimir Nemirovich-Danchenko dies
	Rodgers and Hammerstein's *Oklahoma!*
	Wilder's *The Skin of Our Teeth*
	Robeson's *Othello*
	Robert DeNiro born
	Sartre's *The Flies*
1944	Sartre's *No Exit*
	Robert Wilson born
	Brecht's *The Caucasian Chalk Circle*
1945	**Williams' *The Glass Menagerie***

The World Reflected

1931	Dominion of Canada proclaimed
	Dracula & *Frankenstein* released
1933	Franklin Roosevelt becomes President
	Reichstag fire
1934	**Hitler leads Germany**
1935	Radar invented
1936	**Spanish Civil War begins**
	Chaplin's *Modern Times*
1937	Xerox invented
1938	**Orson Welles' *The War of the Worlds* broadcast**
1939	Spanish Civil War ends
	World War II begins
	Gone With the Wind
	The Wizard of Oz
1941	*Citizen Kane*
1942	Battle of Stalingrad
	Casablanca
1943	Transistor invented
	Camus' *The Myth of Sisyphus*
1944	Normandy invasion
	Copland's *Appalachian Spring*
1945	Atomic bombing of Japan
	World War II ends
	United Nations
	Orwell's *Animal Farm*

The Theatrical Imagination at Work		The World Reflected	
1946	O'Neill's *The Iceman Cometh* Living Theatre founded Cameron Macintosh born	1946	Electronic computer invented
1947	Williams' *A Streetcar Named Desire* Genet's *The Maids* David Mamet born Marsha Norman born Kevin Kline born **Actors' Studio** **Alley Theatre** **First Tony Awards**	1947	India independence
1948	Porter's *Kiss Me, Kate* Andrew Lloyd Webber born	1948	Ghandi assassinated State of Israel founded **Olivier films *Hamlet***
1949	**Miller's *Death of a Salesman*** **Arena Stage** The Berliner Ensemble **Ionesco's *The Bald Soprano*** Meryl Streep born	1949	Chinese Communist Revolution **Cable television inaugurated** Orwell's *1984*
1950	George Bernard Shaw dies	1950	"Un-American activities" investigated *Rashomon*
1951	Ionesco's *The Lesson*	1951	Libya independence
1952	***The Mousetrap* opens in London**		
1953	Miller's *The Crucible* Eugene O'Neill dies Beckett's *Waiting for Godot* Stratford Shakespeare Festival	1953	Skinner, *Science and Human Behavior* DNA structure determined *The Robe* introduces CinemaScope®
1954	New York Shakespeare Festival	1954	Golding's *Lord of the Flies* U.S. segregation declared unconstitutional in U.S. Tolkien's *Lord of the Rings*
1955	Miller's *A View from the Bridge*	1955	Albert Einstein dies
1956	Osborne's *Look Back in Anger* Lerner and Loewe's *My Fair Lady* **O'Neill's *Long Day's Journey into Night*** **Genet's *The Balcony*** Duerrenmatt's *The Visit* Brecht dies	1956	**"Heartbreak Hotel"** Sudan independence Tunisia independence
1957	**Bernstein's *West Side Story*** **Beckett's *Endgame***	1957	Space satellite launched "Great Balls of Fire" Ghana independence
1958	MacLeish's *J. B.* Pinter's *The Birthday Party*	1958	"Johnny B. Goode"
1959	**Hansberry's *Raisin in the Sun*** **Ionesco's *Rhinoceros***	1959	*La Dolce Vita* Cuban Revolution

The Theatrical Imagination at Work

The World Reflected

Grotowski's Polish Laboratory Theatre founded
San Francisco Mime Troupe

1960	Lerner and Loewe's *Camelot* Bart's *Oliver!* Pinter's *The Caretaker* Soyinka's *A Dance of the Forests*	1960	Updike's *Rabbit, Run* "Let's Do the Twist" Somali independence Central African Republic independence Nigeria independence Cameroon independence Chad independence Congo independence Niger independence Senegal independence **Hitchcock's *Psycho***
1961	**Beckett's *Happy Days*** Royal Shakespeare Company Fugard's *The Blood Knot*	1961	Man in space Bay of Pigs invasion Heller's *Catch-22* **The Beatles** Tanzania independence
1962	Albee's *Who's Afraid of Virginia Woolf?* Duerrenmatt's *The Physicists*	1962	Cuban missile crisis "Blowin' in the Wind" Uganda independence Jamaica independence Rwanda independence *Lawrence of Arabia* **released**
1963	Simon's *Barefoot in the Park* **Open Theatre founded** Clifford Odets dies **The Guthrie Theatre** Olivier heads National Theatre	1963	Nuclear Test Ban Treaty **President Kennedy assassinated** Kenya independence *Dr. Strangelove*
1964	Jones's *Dutchman* **Weiss' *Marat/Sade*** **Bock's *Fiddler on the Roof*** Herman's *Hello, Dolly!* Miller's *After the Fall*	1964	"I Want to Hold Your Hand" Malawi independence Zambia independence
1965	**Simon's *The Odd Couple*** Leigh's *Man of La Mancha* **Pinter's *The Homecoming***	1965	Malcomb X assassinated *Doctor Zhivago*
1966	**Kander and Ebb's *Cabaret***	1966	Chinese Cultural Revolution Botswana independence
1967	**Ragni and Rado's *Hair***	1967	Six Day War "Sergeant Pepper" First heart transplant
1968	Performance Group founded Miller's *The Price*	1968	Tet Offensive in Vietnam Martin Luther King, Jr. assassinated

The Theatrical Imagination at Work

Negro Ensemble Company founded

1969	Fugard's *Boesman and Lena*
	Van Itallie's *The Serpent*
	Jones' *Slave Ship*
	Fo's *Mistero Buffo*
1970	Brook's *A Midsummer Night's Dream*
1971	**Webber and Rice's *Jesus Christ Superstar***
	Schwartz *Godspell*
	Hewett's *The Chapel Perilous*
	Pinter's *Old Times*
1972	Shepard's *The Tooth of Crime*
1973	Sondheim's *A Little Night Music*
	Peter Hall takes over directorship of National Theatre from Olivier
1975	***A Chorus Line* opens**
1976	**Shange's *For Colored Girls Who Have Considered Suicide/When The Rainbow is Enuf***
	Shepard's *Curse of the Starving Class*
	Evita
1977	**Fornes' *Fefu and Her Friends***
	Mamet's *American Buffalo*
1978	Shepard's *Buried Child*
	Pinter's *Betrayal*
1979	**Sondheim's *Sweeney Todd***
1980	**Churchill's *Cloud Nine***
	Henley's *Crimes of the Heart*
1981	*Cats*
1982	Churchill's *Top Girls*
	Fuller's *A Soldier's Play*
	Fugard's *Master Harold . . . and the Boys*
1983	Mamet's *Glengarry Glen Ross*
	Tennessee Williams dies
	Norman's *'Night, Mother*
1984	**Breur's *Gospel at Colonus***
	Starlight Express
1985	Shepard's *A Lie of the Mind*
	Brook's *Mahabharata*
	Les Misérables

The World Reflected

Swaziland independence
Zeffirelli's *Romeo and Juliet*

1969	Men landing on the moon
1971	McLuhan's *Understanding Media*
	A Clockwork Orange
	The Republic of Zaire
1972	Republic of Sri Lanka
	The Godfather
1973	Cease-fire in Vietnam
	Pablo Picasso dies
1974	Solzhenitsyn's *The Gulag Archepelago*
	President Nixon resigns
1975	Videocassette recorders marketed
1976	Mozambique independence
1977	***Star Wars***
	Dijibouti independence
1978	First test-tube baby
1979	Iranian revolution
	Three-Mile Island nuclear accident
1980	Reagan elected President
	John Lennon assassinated
	Zimbabwe independence
	Nicaraguan revolution

The Theatrical Imagination at Work

1986	*The Phantom of the Opera*
1987	**August Wilson's** *Fences*
1989	*Miss Saigon*
	Laurence Olivier dies
1993	*Sunset Boulevard*
	Angels In America
	The Theatrical Imagination,
	1st Edition
1995	Augut Wilson's *Seven Guitars*
	George Abott celebrates 107th birthday
1996	**Reconstructed Globe Theatre opens in London**
	Rent

The World Reflected

1986	USSR nuclear accident at Chernobyl
1990	Germany reunited
1992	Clinton elected president
	Gallilio forgiven
1996	George Burns celebrates 100th birthday

Appendix D

SYNOPSES OF SELECTED PLAYS

OEDIPUS THE KING by Sophocles
    First Produced: 429 B.C.
    Genre: Classical tragedy
    Style: Ancient Greek drama
    Time and Place: Antiquity; Thebes

Major Characters
Oedipus, King of Thebes
Jocasta, his wife
Creon, Jocasta's brother
Tieresias, a seer
Messenger
Second Messenger
Shepherd of Laius
Chorus of Theban Elders

The city of Thebes is stricken by a plague, so the people appeal to their great King Oedipus to discover the cause of the disaster and to end their suffering. Creon, brother-in-law of Oedipus, returns from the Oracle at Delphi with the message that the plague will continue until the murderer of the former King Laius is discovered and punished. Oedipus vows not to rest until he finds the killer and expels him from the city. The great irony is that Oedipus has committed himself to an inevitably tragic task; he himself is the murderer. Tieresias, an aged, blind seer, tells Oedipus that he, Oedipus, is guilty both of killing his father and marrying his mother, Queen Jocasta, thus fulfilling a prophecy of patricide and incest proclaimed at Oedipus' birth. In a struggle to avoid the terrible truth, Oedipus desperately tries to prove Tieresias wrong. When an old shepherd who witnessed the death of the former king identifies Oedipus as the murderer and the husband of his father's widow, Jocasta hangs herself in despair and shame. Oedipus puts out his eyes and begs to be banished from Thebes.

ROMEO AND JULIET by William Shakespeare
    First Produced: 1595
    Genre: Classical romantic tragedy
    Style: Elizabethan
    Time and Place: Fifteenth century; Verona, Italy

Major Characters
Romeo, son of the house of Montague
Juliet, daughter of the house of Capulet

Friar Lawrence, a Franciscan, friend of Romeo
Mercutio and
Benvolio, Romeo's friends
Tybalt, Juliet's cousin
The Nurse, Juliet's confidant

Romeo and Juliet are teenagers whose passionate love for each other is eventually destroyed by the ancient hatred between their families, the Montagues and the Capulets. With the help of Friar Lawrence and the Nurse, the young lovers secretly marry in defiance of their families. The family feud reaches a bloody climax when Romeo, to avenge the death of his friend Mercutio, kills Juliet's cousin Tybalt. Romeo is banished from Verona, but the Friar devises a plan to use a secret potion to fake Juliet's death and steal her away to Mantua to be with Romeo. Romeo, unaware of the plan, gets word that Juliet has died, and returns to Verona where he finds Juliet, seemingly dead, in her tomb. To join her he commits suicide with poison. Juliet awakens, finds Romeo dead, and in despair kills herself with his dagger. The two families arrive to discover the tragic consequences of their ancient, senseless feud.

HAMLET, PRINCE OF DENMARK by William Shakespeare
First Produced: 1602
Genre: Classical revenge tragedy
Style: Elizabethan
Time and Place: c. 1200; Elsinore Castle, Denmark

Major Characters
Hamlet, Prince of Denmark
Ghost of Hamlet's father, the former King
Claudius, the present King
Gertrude, Hamlet's mother
Polonius, adviser to Claudius
Ophelia, his daughter
Laertes, his son
Rosencrantz and
Guildenstern, Hamlet's schoolmates

The thirty-year-old Danish Prince Hamlet grieves for the recent death of his father, the king, and is disturbed over his mother's immediate marriage to his uncle Claudius, now the king. Hamlet is visited by the ghost of his father who names Claudius as his murderer and demands that Hamlet avenge his death. Hamlet affirms the truth of the ghost's accusation by having a troupe of actors put on a play about fratricide, trapping Claudius into revealing his guilt. As Hamlet agonizes over his desire for revenge, his realization of the immorality of his potential actions, his hesitation at proceeding, and his mother's possible transgressions, Claudius plots Hamlet's murder. As the action proceeds, Polonius, Ophelia, Rosencrantz, and

Guildenstern die as a consequence of the conflict between Hamlet and Claudius. Their struggle culminates in a fatal duel that results in the deaths of Laertes, Claudius, Gertrude, and finally Hamlet himself.

TARTUFFE by Molière (Jean Baptiste Poquelin)
First Produced: 1664
Genre: Comedy
Style: Neoclassicism
Time and Place: Seventeenth century; Paris

Major Characters
Orgon, a wealthy Parisian
Elmire, his wife
Madame Pernelle, his mother
Damis, his son
Mariane, his daughter
Valere, Mariane's lover
Dorine, Mariane's maid
Cleante, Orgon's brother-in-law
Tartuffe, a hypocrite

Tartuffe is the consummate religious hypocrite who has gained the confidence of Orgon, a wealthy but gullible man who seeks his salvation by honoring the seemingly pious clergyman. Tartuffe moves into Orgon's house where he schemes to get Orgon's money, seduce his wife, and gain power over the entire household. In a desperate attempt to convince Orgon of Tartuffe's treachery, Elmire hides her husband under a table before inviting Tartuffe into the room. Tartuffe attempts to seduce her until Orgon reveals himself. In the end it requires the intercession of the King in order to subvert Tartuffe's hold over the family and restore peace to the household.

HEDDA GABLER by Henrik Ibsen
First Produced: 1890
Genre: Tragedy
Style: Realism
Time and Place: 1880s, Norway, a drawing room in the Tesman house

Major Characters
George Tesman, a thirty-two-year-old scholar
Hedda Tesman, his wife
Miss Juliana Tesman (Tesman's aunt)
Mrs. Thea Elvsted
Judge Brack
Eilert Lovborg

Hedda Gabler, a frustrated, seemingly destructive person, has married the meek, reclusive Tesman, not out of love, but for security. She becomes pregnant, but refuses to acknowledge her condition. Tesman, now heavily in debt from marrying the aristocratic Hedda, wants to obtain a professorship, but his hopes are jeopardized when the brilliant Lovborg completes a monumental book on the history of civilization. Lovborg, who once had a relationship with Hedda, remains obsessed with her. Frustrated with her own life, Hedda at once spurns Lovborg and tries to gain influence over him—even plotting to drive him to drink and commit a grand suicide. Lovborg does indeed shoot himself to death, but in a miserable, not grandly romantic, way. Judge Brack, also infatuated with the beautiful, enigmatic Hedda, threatens to reveal her role in Lovborg's death unless she has an affair with him. Dispirited and fearful of the judge, Hedda shocks everyone by killing herself with one of her father's pistols.

WAITING FOR GODOT by Samuel Beckett
    First Produced: 1952
    Genre: Tragicomedy
    Style: Existentialism
    Time and Place: The present; a country road

Major Characters
    Vladimir, a tramp
    Estragon, a tramp
    Pozzo, a slave master
    Lucky, Pozzo's servant
    A Boy, a messenger

Two tramps, Estragon and Vladimir, engage in a variety of meaningless activities while they await the arrival of Godot, who apparently will tell them what to do next. It gradually becomes apparent that Godot will never come, and thus the two are waiting for nothing. They pass the time by talking about life, considering suicide, arguing, and engaging in slapstick games. Two others, Pozzo, a kind of slave master, and Lucky, a kind of slave, pass by and engage Vladimir and Estragon in idiotic discussions of political and theological subjects. Pozzo and Lucky, one blind and the other dumb, return near the end of the play, having no idea of who they are. The play ends with Godot sending a message that he will not come, leaving Vladimir and Estragon with nothing whatsoever to do.

DEATH OF A SALESMAN by Arthur Miller
    First Produced: 1949
    Genre: Modern tragedy
    Style: Expressionism and realism
    Time and Place: Past, present, fantasy; New York

Major Characters
Willy Loman, a salesman
Linda, his wife
Biff and
Happy, his sons
Uncle Ben, his brother
Charley, his friend
Bernard, Charley's son
Howard, Willy's boss
The Woman

Willy Loman is a traveling salesman in his sixties who has reached the end of his rope, both emotionally and professionally. He feels guilty and angry about his inability to achieve what he considers success. His mind wanders back and forth between his present failures and memories of happier days with his devoted wife, Linda, and his two sons. Like his business career, his relationship with his sons has also failed. The oldest son, Biff, seemed destined for great things until he discovered his father in a hotel room with another woman. The incident opened Biff's eyes to the hypocrisy and emptiness of his father's principles, and Biff has spent the past fifteen years drifting aimlessly from job to job. The younger son, Happy, is a cynical, materialistic womanizer who remains in his brother's shadow.

Faced with the realization that he no longer can travel, Willy asks his boss for a desk job, but he is promptly fired. Meantime, Biff, after a futile attempt to secure a position in business, decides to confront his father and force him to realize that they are both failures. Unable to accept the fact that he has based his life on false values, Willy determines to kill himself and leave the insurance money to Biff. At Willy's funeral Biff concludes that his father's failure was not so much as a salesman, but as a man who never knew who he really was.

EXTREMITIES by William Mastrosimone
First Produced: 1980
Genre: Modern tragedy
Style: Realism
Time and Place: The present, September; a New Jersey farmhouse

Major Characters
Marjorie, a young woman
Terry and
Patricia, her roommates
Raul, a rapist

Marjorie, a young woman, is attacked in her home by Raul, who intends to rape her. While being verbally and physically tormented by him, Marjorie manages to stun the man with insect spray and repel his attack. She binds him and imprisons him in the fireplace while he screams obscenities and threats. Faced with the fact that she cannot prove a case of criminal sexual assault against Raul, as well as the fact that he threatens to return to attack her again, Marjorie resolves to kill him and bury him in the garden. When Marjorie's roommates return, they are shocked by her vengeful hysteria and come to believe the man in the fireplace who declares his innocence. Despite the pleas of her roommates, Marjorie resists their efforts and proceeds with her preparations to kill Raul until the climactic moment when Raul confesses his attempted rape of Marjorie and his assaults on other women. Emotionally and physically spent, Marjorie allows her roommates to call the police as a beaten Raul crawls back into the fireplace.

FENCES by August Wilson
    First Produced: 1985
    Genre: Modern tragedy
    Style: Realism
    Time and Place: 1957–1965; the yard in front of the Maxson household in a big-city neighborhood

        Major Characters
        Troy Maxson, a garbage man
        Jim Bono, Troy's friend
        Rose, Troy's wife
        Lyons, Troy's oldest son by a previous marriage
        Gabriel, Troy's brother
        Cory, Troy and Rose's son
        Raynell, Troy's daughter

Troy Maxson is a garbage man who was once a great baseball player in the Negro leagues. He has had to live with the bitterness of the many barriers (fences) he has faced in life, especially the inability to play major-league baseball. When his son desires to pursue a career as a professional athlete, Troy fights the attempt and is forced to realize that he is doing to his son (putting up a fence) what was done to him.

    Troy also works to support his long-suffering wife, Rose, and his brain-damaged brother, Gabriel. Troy's sexual infidelity produces a child that Rose stoically cares for after the child's mother dies. After a climactic battle against his unseen enemy, Death, Troy dies. His son, now an enlistee in the Army, returns for his father's funeral, having gained a perspective on his father's lifelong struggles and on his own achievements as well.

BROADWAY BOUND by Neil Simon
    First Produced: 1986
    Genre: Tragicomedy
    Style: Realism
    Time and Place: 1949, the Jerome household in Brighton Beach, New York

Major Characters
Eugene Jerome, an aspiring comedy writer
Ben, his grandfather
Kate, his mother
Jack, his father
Stanley, his brother
Blanche, his aunt

Broadway Bound is the final play in Neil Simon's autobiographical trilogy that depicts his journey from adolescence in Brooklyn to his breakthrough to a career as a comedy writer in the early days of live television. In the first play, *Brighton Beach Memoirs* (1982), Eugene (the young Neil Simon) narrates the action of two Jewish families crowded into a lower-middle-class house in Brooklyn and struggling to survive the pre-war depression. The teenage Eugene is consumed with fantasies of baseball and pubescent dreams of girls, all the while observing with a writer's sense of wit and irony the complex relationships of his blended family.

In the second play, *Biloxi Blues* (1985), Eugene narrates his comic and serious experiences as a young army recruit in World War II, struggling through basic training, falling in love, and confronting the diverse, funny, and often hostile world outside his Brooklyn enclave.

In *Broadway Bound,* the time is 1949 and Eugene and his brother, Stanley, are about to leave home to pursue careers as professional comedy writers. Their leaving, however, exposes a terrible rift between his father and mother, which ends with his father confessing to an extramarital affair and leaving the house. The boys' struggle to come up with an idea for a salable TV comedy sketch is the source of most of the humor in the play. Comic and serious actions converge when their sketch is broadcast on the radio, and the family is dismayed to hear that their own trials and tribulations are the sources of the hilarity. Eugene strikes a bittersweet note as he explains that while he and Stan went on to successful writing careers, his parents divorced. The final image is his mother, Kate, alone in the house that was the source of so much "material," polishing the dining room table, a symbol of family pride and endurance.

OLEANNA by David Mamet
First Produced: 1992
Genre: Modern Tragedy
Style: Realism
Time and Place: The Present, a faculty office at an American college

Major Characters
John, an untenured professor
Carol, a student in his class

Carol is a college student struggling in a class taught by John. In the first act, Carol seeks John's help in grasping the nature of the course. What is at first a formal discussion of the course, gradually broadens to a deeply personal series of mutual revelations about their feelings and their social and professional positions. The act ends with John's somewhat ambiguous offer to help Carol overcome her insecurities.

Act II begins with Carol's return to John's office where she declares that she has joined a "group" which has convinced her that John had sexually harassed her in their first meeting and that she has filed a complaint with the college tenure committee. John realizes that every word of their previous discussion has been interpreted to characterize his motives as exploitive and insulting. He unsuccessfully attempts to persuade Carol to retract her accusation. In their final meeting, the hostility escalates to a violent conclusion.

NOTES

Preface

1. Jack Kroll, "Her Majesty the King," *Newsweek,* 15 January 1996.

Chapter 1

1. Michael Crichton, *Sphere* (New York: Knopf, 1987), pp. 348–349.
2. Carl Reiner, dir., *Oh God!,* Warner Bros., 1977.
3. Joyce Kilmer, "Trees," in *Anthology of Catholic Poets,* eds. Joyce Kilmer and James Edward Tobin (Garden City, NY: Image Books, 1955), p. 300.
4. Henry Wadsworth Longfellow, *Hyperion* (Cambridge, MA: Riverside Press, 1869), p. 236.
5. Christopher Gray, "Monarchs of the Forest Rise to a Dramatic Occasion," *New York Times,* 28 March 1993, sec. 2, p. 5.
6. Gene Siskel, *Siskel and Ebert at the Movies,* Broadcast, 21 May 1989.
7. "Challenge Met, and Then Some," *Peoria Journal Star,* 8 November 1993, p. C8.
8. Howard Gardner, *The Arts and Human Development* (New York: Basic Books, 1983), pp. 25–26.
9. Ibid., pp. 25–26.
10. William Shakespeare, *A Midsummer Night's Dream,* V.i.
11. Neil McAleer, "On Creativity," *Omni,* April 1989, p. 100.
12. Ibid., p. 100.
13. Ibid., pp. 101–102.
14. Cathleen McGuigan, "At Home with the Picassos," *Newsweek,* 12 December 1988, p. 72.
15. Neil Simon, *Broadway Bound* (New York: Random House, 1987), p. 62.
16. "Heartbreak Career," *Peoria Journal Star,* 12 January 1989, sec. C, p. 14.
17. Paul McCartney, interview on *Today,* NBC, 18 March 1979.
18. McAleer, p. 44.
19. Jacques Maritain, *Creative Intuition in Art and Poetry* (New York: Meridian Books, 1955), p. 61.
20. Brewster Ghiselin, ed., *The Creative Process* (New York: New American Library), p. 16.
21. Sigmund Freud, *A Study in Psychosexuality* (New York: Vintage Books, 1967), p. 119.
22. McAleer, p. 98.

23. Joe Morgenstern, "More Than a Shtick Figure," *New York Times Magazine,* 11 November 1990, p. 87.
24. "Musical Mind Is Nature's Gift," Associated Press, *ClariNet,* 16 February 1995.
25. "Brain Scans Find Sport Is Really 80% Mental," Associated Press, *St. Louis Post-Dispatch,* 24 January 1995, vol. 117, no. 24, p. 4A; and K. M. Stephan, G. R. Fink, R. E. Passingham, D. Silbersweig, A. O. Ceballos-Baumann, C. D. Firth, and R. S. Frackowiack, "Functional Anatomy of the Mental Representation of Upper Extremity Movements in Healthy Subjects," *Journal of Neurophysiology,* vol. 73, no. 1, January 1995, pp. 373–385.
26. Phone interview with Christopher Owens, 20 March 1995; and Jack Kroll, "Computers and Creativity," *Newsweek,* 27 February 1995, p. 68.
27. B. Miles, "The Lennon View," *The Boston Globe,* 11 December 1980, p. 1.
28. Howard Gardner, *Frames of Mind* (New York: Basic Books, 1983).
29. J. P. Sartre, *The Words: The Autobiography of Jean-Paul Sartre* (New York: George Braziller, 1964), p. 153.
30. Kenneth Tynan, "Profile of Nicol Williamson," *New Yorker,* 15 January 1972, p. 56.
31. Gardner, *Frames of Mind,* p. 224.
32. Janet Hopson, *Psychology Today,* July–August 1988, p. 33.
33. Ibid.
34. *Newsweek,* 20 December 1993, p. 114.
35. *Forbes,* 26 September 1994.
36. Amy Hersh, "Arts' Impact Is $9.8 Billion for NY-NJ Economy," *Backstage,* 8 October 1993, pp. 1, 30.
37. Joanne Kelley, "Creators of Copyrighted Works Growing," Associated Press, *Clarinet,* 19 February 1995.
38. Ann Greer, "Imagine It First," *American Theatre,* 8 July 1988, p. 28.
39. "Dramatic Evidence," *Entertainment Weekly,* 23 December 1994, p. 75.
40. Ellen Goodman, "More Realistic Message," *Peoria Journal Star,* 17 February 1995, p. A4.
41. John Robert Colombo, ed., *Popcorn in Paradise: The Wit and Wisdom of Hollywood* (New York: Holt, Rinehart and Winston, 1979), p. 11.

42. "Group Warns of Culture War," Associated Press, *Clarinet,* 6 March 1995.

43. Elizabeth Blumberg Polley, panel discussion on "The Humanist and the Artist," in *The Role of the Research University in a Changing Society* (Bloomington: Indiana University Institute for Advanced Study, 1986), vol. 3, p. 11.

44. *Peoria Journal Star,* 11 March 1995, p. C4.

45. Louis Harris, *Americans and the Arts VI,* Louis Harris and Associates, 1994, p. 4.

46. Elmer Rice, *The Living Theatre* (New York: Harper, 1959), p. 236.

47. *New York Times,* 22 March 1992, sec. 2, p. 22.

Chapter 2

1. "David Mamet," *Playboy* Interview, April 1995, vol. 42, no. 4, p. 59.

2. Neil Simon, *The Odd Couple* (New York: Samuel French, 1966), pp. 76–77.

3. Richard Katz, "Make Believers," *Omni,* November 1987, p. 128.

4. Oscar G. Brockett, *History of the Theatre,* 5th ed. (Austin, TX: Allyn and Bacon, 1987), p. 225.

5. Frank Rich, "Burn, Baby, Burn!" *New York Times Magazine,* 28 November 1993, sec. 6, col. 3, p. 40.

6. See G. W. F. Hegel, *Aesthetics or the Philosophy of Fine Art,* trans. Henry Paolucci (New York: Frederick Ungar Publishing Co., 1979), p. 179.

7. Julia Braun Kessler, "Stage Presence: Wendy Wasserstein," *Vis à Vis,* 3 May 1991, p. 78.

8. Ralph G. Allen, "Lysistrata," Lecture, Bradley University, 24 February 1995.

9. Daryl H. Miller, "Neil Simon Gets Serious in Latest Play, But It's Funny," *The Cleveland Plain Dealer,* 22 March 1990, sec. D, p. 11.

10. Bernard Beckerman, "The Play's the Thing—But What's a Play?," in *Master Teachers of Theatre,* ed. Burnet M. Hobgood (Carbondale: Southern Illinois University Press, 1988), p. 26.

11. Elmer Rice, *The Living Theatre* (New York: Harper, 1959), p. 27.

12. Beckerman, p. 30.

Chapter 3

1. John F. Gilligan, "Illusions of Reality," *Peoria Journal Star,* 27 December 1992, p. A7.

2. From personal correspondence, 27 August 1992.

3. Robert Brustein, "The Humanist and the Artist," in *The Role of the Research University in a Changing Society* (Bloomington: Indiana University Institute for Advanced Study, 1986), vol. 3, p. 2.

4. Ibid., p. 1.

5. A. M. Nagler, *A Source Book in Theatrical History* (New York: Dover, 1952), p. 3.

6. Diana Rigg, *No Turn Unstoned* (Garden City, NY: Doubleday, 1983), p. 9.

7. Ibid., p. 10.

8. Ibid., p. 12.

9. Strossen, Nadine, "Academic and Artistic Freedom," *Academe,* November–December 1992, p. 15.

10. Alex Witchel, "Jule Styne's Music to Live By, Composed in the Key of Gee," *New York Times,* 23 December 1990, sec. 2, p. 5.

11. Ron House, from personal interview with Jeffrey Huberman, 3 November 1989.

Chapter 4

1. Aristotle, *The Nicomachean Ethics, Book X,* in *The Complete Works of Aristotle,* Jonathan Burns, ed., vol. 2 (Princeton, NJ: Princeton University Press, 1985), p. 1861.

2. Witold Rybczynski, *Waiting for the Weekend* (New York: Viking, 1991), p. 6.

3. *Americans and the Arts V,* National Research Center for the Arts (American Council for the Arts, 1988), p. 13. The survey, the fifth in a series that began in 1973, was conducted by the Harris organization in 1988. The conclusions were based on telephone interviews with 1,501 randomly selected men and women age 18 and over. Its purpose was to probe Americans' perceptions of and participation in the arts.

4. Juliet Schor, *The Overworked American: The Unexpected Decline of Leisure* (New York, Basic Books, 1991), p. 163.

5. *Americans and the Arts V,* p. 8.

6. Louis Harris, *Americans and the Arts VI,* Louis Harris and Associates, 1994, p. 21.

7. "Harris Poll Is at Odds with Arts Statistics," *American Theatre,* May 1988, p. 36.

8. Joseph Papp and Elizabeth Kirkland, *Shakespeare Alive* (New York: Bantam Books, 1988), p. 142.

9. Montague Summers, *The Restoration Theatre* (New York: Humanities Press, 1964), p. 68.

10. Report from "Select Committee on Theatrical Licenses and Regulations," London, 1866.

11. Ibid.

12. John Robert Colombo, ed., *Popcorn in Paradise: The Wit and Wisdom of Hollywood* (New York: Holt, Rinehart and Winston, 1979), p. 9.

13. Ibid.

14. Aljean Harmetz, *The Making of the Wizard of Oz.* Quoted in *Peoria Journal Star,* 20 February 1994, p. B2.

15. *Americans and the Arts,* p. 13.

16. Sources: Theatre Attendance—Compilation of Data from Theatre Communications Group, League of American Theatre Producers and Owners, *Americans in the Arts* Survey, Entertainment Data, and Neilsen ratings.

17. Source: Theatre Communications Group.

18. *The Finances of the Performing Arts,* vol. 2 (New York: Ford Foundation, 1974), p. 13.

19. Lawrence W. Levine, *Highbrow Lowbrow: The Emergence of Cultural Hierarchy in America* (Cambridge, Mass.: Harvard University Press, 1988), p. 17.

20. Association of College and University and Community Arts Administrators, *Value and Lifestyle Segments* (New York: Young and Rubicam, 1988).

21. Gallup Poll reported in Juliet B. Schor, "Workers of the World Unwind," *Technology Review,* 26 November/December 1991, p. 29.

22. Survey courtesy of the Goodman Theatre.

23. Robert Brustein, "The Humanist and the Artist," *The Role of the Research University in a Changing Society* (Bloomington: Indiana University Institute for Advanced Study, 1986), vol. 3, p. 7.

24. Matt Wolf, "In Britain, the Play Really Is the Thing," *American Theatre,* May 1988, pp. 42–44.

25. Guthrie Theater general policies, Minneapolis, Minnesota.

26. Wolf, pp. 42–44.

27. Cynthia Mayeda, "The Presence of the Future," *American Theatre,* October 1991, p. 54.

28. Arthur Miller, *Death of a Salesman,* in *Stages of Drama,* eds. Carl H. Klaus, Miriam Gilbert, and Bradford S. Field, Jr. (New York: St. Martin's, 1991), p. 845.

29. Israel Zangwill, *The Melting Pot* (New York: Macmillan, 1920), pp. 184–185.

30. Quoted in Richard Reeves, "To Be an American," Universal Press Syndicate, 25 June 1991.

31. Richard Bernstein, "The Arts Catch Up with a Society in Disarray," *New York Times,* 2 September 1990, sec. 2, p. 12.

32. Frederic Ohringer, *A Portrait of the Theatre* (Toronto: Merritt, 1979), p. 159.

33. Misha Berson, "Between Worlds," *American Theatre,* March 1990, p. 22.

34. Richard Schechner, "An Intercultural Primer," *American Theatre,* October 1991, p. 30.

35. Leslie Allen, *Liberty: The Statue and the American Dream* (New York: The Statue of Liberty-Ellis Island Foundation, 1985) p. 211.

36. Harold Clurman, from personal interview with Paul Kuritz, January 1977.

37. Langston Hughes, *Selected Poems* (New York: Random House, 1987), p. 190.

38. Robert Brustein, "A House Divided," *American Theatre,* October 1991, pp. 141–142.

39. Michele Pearce, "Alien Nation," *American Theatre,* March 1994, p. 26.

40. David Savran, "In Their Own Words," *Onstage,* The Goodman Theatre Series, vol. 3, no. 2.

41. Cathy Madison, "Writing Home," *American Theatre,* October 1991, pp. 40–41.

42. Mervyn Rothstein, "Women Playwrights: Themes and Variations," *New York Times,* 7 May 1989, sec. 2, p. 42.

43. Jack Kroll, "Mambo King of Comedy," *Newsweek,* 14 December 1992, p. 87.

44. Jack Kroll, *Newsweek,* 1993.

45. Ohringer, p. 91.

46. Sam Coale, "Growing Up on the Aisle," *American Theatre,* February 1988, p. 35.

47. Thomas Walsh, "Equity Council Begins Protest vs. 'Maiden' Casting," *Back Stage,* 13 March 1992, p. 42.

48. Jean Prescott, "Bringing 'Pub Mentality' to TV," *Peoria Journal Star,* 26 October 1991, sec. "TV Week," p. 1.

49. Robert Putnam, "Bowling Alone," *The Journal of Democracy,* January 1995, pp. 3–9.

50. Clifford Stoll, "The Internet? Bah!," *Newsweek,* 27 February 1995, p. 41.

51. James Leverett, "Who's There," *American Theatre,* October 1991, pp. 20–22.

52. Association of College and University and Community Arts Administrators, *Value and Lifestyle Segments,* pp. 18–19.

53. Jan Kott, *Theatre Notebook 1947–1967,* trans. Boleslaw Taborski (Garden City, NY: Doubleday, 1968), p. viii.

54. Laura Shamas, "Watching the House," *American Theatre,* September 1990, p. 7.

55. Anna Quindlen, "Bringing Up Babies to a Broadway Beat," *New York Times,* 19 March 1989, sec. 2, p. 5.

56. Harry William Pedicord, *The Theatrical Public in the Time of Garrick* (Carbondale: Southern Illinois University Press, 1954), p. 134.

57. Reprinted from *Playbill,* April 1987, vol. 87, no. 4.

Chapter 5

1. Mike Bailey, "Gorbachev's Drama: Only a Scriptwriter Might Have Told a Better Story," *Peoria Journal Star,* 26 August 1991, sec. A, p. 3.

2. Joseph Papp and Elizabeth Kirkland, *Shakespeare Alive* (New York: Bantam Books, 1988), p. 137.

3. John Gassner, *A Treasury of the Theatre from Henrik Ibsen to Eugene Ionesco* (New York: Simon & Schuster, 1963), p. 205.

4. Frederic Ohringer, *A Portrait of the Theatre* (Toronto: Merritt, 1979), p. 80.

5. Gwen Gibson, "Playwright George S. Kaufman's Classic Works Live On," *Peoria Journal Star,* 18 February 1990, sec. B, p. 3.

6. Jodi Royce, ed., *Fanfare* (Chicago: Court Theatre, September 1991), p. 1.

7. Neil Simon, *Broadway Bound* (New York: Random House, 1987), p. 42.

8. Howard Stein, from personal interview with Jeffrey Huberman, 23 September 1979.

9. Elmer Rice, *The Living Theatre* (New York: Harper, 1959), p. 1.

10. William Faulkner as quoted in *Onstage* (Chicago: Goodman Theatre, no. 1, 1989), p. 1.

11. Christopher Durang, *Christopher Durang Explains It All for You* (New York: Avon Books, 1983), pp. xv–xvi.

12. David Mamet, *The Cabin: Reminiscence and Diversions* (New York: Vintage Books, 1992), pp. 7–8.

13. Mervyn Rothstein, "Women Playwrights: Themes and Variations," *New York Times,* 7 May 1989, sec. 2, p. 42.

14. Andrea Stevens, "A Playwright Who Likes to Bang Words Together," *New York Times,* 6 March 1995, sec.2, p. 5.

15. Samuel Beckett, "The Calmative," in *The Collected Works of Samuel Beckett: Stories & Texts for Nothing* (New York: Grove Press, 1946), p. 27.

16. Simon, p. 37.

17. "Neil Simon," *60 Minutes,* interview by Lesley Stahl, 8 March 1992, Don Hewit, executive producer.

18. Amlin Gray, "The Big If," *American Theatre,* June 1989, p. 19.

19. William Mastrosimone, *The Making of Extremities* (New York: Samuel French, 1985), pp. 65–66.

20. Ibid.

21. Bill Night, review of 1969, *Peoria Journal Star,* 7 April 1989, sec. B, p. 3.

22. "Stone Raps Report on 'Nixon,'" Associated Press, *Clarinet,* 13 March 1995.

23. Vera Sheppard, "August Wilson: An Interview," *Theatre Forum,* Summer 1990, p. 10.

24. Edward Rothstein, "Hard Up for a Plot? Get with the Program," *New York Times,* 22 September 1991, sec. 2, p. 13.

25. Plots Unlimited, distr. Ashleywilde, 1991.

26. Edward Stern, from personal interview with Jeffrey Huberman, Bloomington, Indiana, 1970.

27. Aristotle, *Poetics,* trans. Kenneth A. Telford (Chicago: Gateway, 1968), p. 11.

28. Michael Kuchwara, "Broadway Audiences Tested by Long Plays' Journey into Night," *Peoria Journal Star,* 19 December 1993, p. B3.

29. Gray, p. 19.

30. "Why Write for the Theatre?" *New York Times,* 9 February 1986, sec. 2, p. 5.

31. Diane Ney, "Re: Readings," *American Theatre,* January 1992.

32. Gray, p. 21.

33. Ibid., p. 20.

34. Jacinto Benavente.

35. Walter Kerr, "The Love Between Beckett and Actors Isn't Mutual," *New York Times,* 13 November 1988, sec. 2, p. 3.

36. Ohringer, p. 45.

37. William Mastrosimone, *Extremities* (New York: Samuel French, 1984), p. 10.

38. Rothstein, "Women Playwrights: Themes and Variations," p. 42.

39. Sam Shepard, *Suicide in B-flat,* in *Fool for Love and Other Plays* (New York: Bantam Books, 1984), pp. 196–197.

40. Sheppard, p. 10.

41. Patrick Stewart, "An Actor's Own Persona Should Inform And Embrace the Role," as told to Ira J. Bilowit, *Backstage,* 20 December 1991, p. 35.

42. Gillian Richards and David Boyse, eds., *The Dramatists Sourcebook* (New York: Theatre Communications Group, 1991), p. 8.

43. "Why Write for the Theatre?" p. 30.

44. Robert Brustein, "The Humanist and the Artist," *The Role of the Research University in a Changing Society* (Bloomington: Indiana University Institute for Advanced Study, 1986), vol. 3, p. 3.

45. Terrence McNally, "From Page to Stage: How a Playwright Guards His Vision," *New York Times,* 7 December 1986, p. 5.

Chapter 6

1. Jerry Sterner, "A Playwright Crunches the Numbers," *New York Times,* 26 January 1995, sec. 2, p. 5.

2. Jan Greenberg, *Theatre Careers* (New York: Holt, Rinehart and Winston, 1983), p. 5.

3. Mervyn Rothstein, "The Musical Is Money to His Ears," *New York Times Magazine,* 9 December 1990, p. 84.

4. Ibid.

5. Ibid., p. 98.

6. Ibid.

7. Ibid., p. 84.

8. Christine Conrad, ed., "The Unfinished Memoirs of Kermit Bloomgarden," *American Theatre,* November 1988, p. 29.

9. John Kenley, from personal interview with Elizabeth Alpert, Warren, Ohio, June 1974.

10. Mervyn Rothstein, "How a High Roller Bets on Broadway," *New York Times,* 3 June 1990, sec. 2, pp. 5, 33.

11. Ibid., p. 5.

12. Source: League of American Theatres and Producers.

13. Louis Dunoyer, personal interview with Jeffrey H. Huberman, March 1993.

14. Rothstein., p. 33.

15. Peter Passell, "Broadway and the Bottom Line," *New York Times,* 10 December 1989, sec. 2, p. 8.

16. Rothstein, "How a High Roller Bets on Broadway," p. 33.

17. Robert A. Schanke, *Shattered Applause: The Lives of Eva Le Gallienne* (Carbondale: Southern Illinois University Press, 1992).

18. Des McAnuff, "The La Jolla Playhouse," in *Theatre Profiles 9, The Illustrated Reference Guide to America's Nonprofit Professional Theatre* (New York: Sarabande Press, 1990), pp. 74–75.

19. Robert A. Alexander, "Living Stage Theatre Company," in *Theatre Profiles 9, The Illustrated Reference Guide to America's Nonprofit Professional Theatre,* p. 77.

20. Anne Bogart, "Incompatible Impulses," *American Theatre,* January 1991, p. 7.

21. Robert Brustein, "The Humanist and the Artist," in *The Role of the Research University in a Changing Society* (Bloomington: Indiana University Institute for Advanced Study, 1986), vol. 3, pp. 8–9.

22. *Theatre Profiles 9, The Illustrated Reference Guide to America's Nonprofit Professional Theatre* (New York: Sarabande Press, 1990).

23. Ed Morales, "Theatre and the Wolfe," *American Theatre,* December 1994, p. 19.

24. Arthur Bartow, *The Director's Voice, Twenty-One Interviews* (New York: Theatre Communications Group, 1988), p. 127.

25. Jack Kroll, "Broadway Unbound," *Newsweek,* 17 February 1992, p. 61.

26. Todd London, "The Artistic Home," *American Theatre,* March 1988, p. 34.

27. *Backstage,* 22–28 October 1993, p. 23.

Chapter 7

1. *Othello* opened at the Mermaid Theatre in London on September 16, 1971.

2. Arthur Bartow, *The Director's Voice: Twenty-One Interviews* (New York: Theatre Communications Group, 1988), p. xvi.

3. Ibid., p. 198.

4. Ibid., p. 116.

5. Toby Cole and Helen Krich Chinoy, eds., *Directors on Directing* (New York: Bobbs-Merrill, 1963), p. 364.

6. Bartow, p. 111.

7. Personal account, Jeffrey Huberman.

8. Bartow, p. 233.

9. Arthur Holmverg, "Liviu Ciulei: Sculpting Shapes for the Stage," *Art News,* November 1988.

10. Bartow, p. 273.

11. Richard Zoglin, "Shylock on the Beach," *Time,* 31 October 1994, p. 78.

12. Richard Thomas, "The Gretchen and Richard Iben Lectureship," Bradley University, Peoria, Illinois, March 1986.

13. Peter Brook, *The Shifting Point* (New York: Harper & Row, 1987), p. 5.

14. Bartow, p. 281.

15. Ibid., p. 108.

16. Tennessee Williams, *The Glass Menagerie* (New York: New Directions Books, 1970), p. 5.

17. Glenn Collins, "Yo Brutus: A Bard for the 80's," *New York Times,* 20 March 1988, sec. 2, p. 36.

18. *Parade Magazine,* 5 December 1993, p. 1.

19. Quoted in David Richards, "When Shakespeare Wasn't for Everyone," *New York Times,* 17 January 1993, sec. 2, p. 5.

20. Tom Haas, "Color Blind Casting and Non-Traditional Casting: Challenging the American Theatre," *Marquee,* Indiana Repertory Theatre, Fall 1990.

21. David Richards, "When Shakespeare Wasn't for Everyone," *New York Times,* 17 January 1993, sec. 2, p. 5.

22. Ellen Holly, "Why the Furor over 'Miss Saigon' World," *New York Times,* 26 August 1990, sec. 2, p. 5.

23. Bartow, p. 116.

24. Ibid., p. 8.

25. Ibid., p. 116.

26. Ed Stern, from personal interview with Jeffrey Huberman, St. Louis, January 1991.

27. Wendy Wasserstein, "Directing 101: George Abbott on What Works," *New York Times,* 8 October 1989, sec. 2, p. 5.

28. Brook, p. 17.

29. Ibid., p. 4.

30. Harold Clurman, *On Directing* (New York: Macmillan, 1972), p. 135.

31. William Shakespeare, *Much Ado About Nothing.* Textual revisions by Robert Graves (London: Radio Corporation of America, 1965).

32. Rupert Holmes, *Accomplice* (New York: Samuel French, 1991), p. 97.

33. *Onstage,* 1987–88 Goodman Theatre Series, Vol. 2, no. 4.

34. Clurman, p. 138.

35. Bartow, p. 12.

36. *Newsweek,* 5 October 1992, p. 70.

37. Suggested by Robert Hetherington.

Chapter 8

1. Arthur Miller, "The Shadows of the Gods," *The Theatre Essays of Arthur Miller,* ed. Robert A. Martin (New York: Viking Press, 1978), p. 185.

2. People," *Peoria Journal Star,* 16 November 1987.

3. Arthur Miller, *Death of a Salesman* (New York: Viking Press, 1949), pp. 132–133.

4. James Fowler, ed., *Images of Show Business from the Theatre Museum, V&A* (London: Methuen, 1982), p. 41.

5. John Robert Colombo, ed., *Popcorn in Paradise: The Wit and Wisdom of Hollywood* (New York: Holt, Rinehart and Winston), 1979.

6. Shomit Mitter, *Systems of Rehearsal: Stanislavsky, Brecht, Grotowski and Brook* (New York: Routledge, 1992), p. 1.

7. William Mastrosimone, *Extremities* (New York: Samuel French, 1984), p. 12.

8. Frederic Ohringer, *A Portrait of the Theatre* (Toronto: Merritt, 1979), p. 115.

9. Eugene Ionesco, *The Bald Soprano,* trans. Donald M. Allen, in *Eugene Ionesco: Four Plays* (New York: Grove Press, 1958), p. 41.

10. Richard Thomas, "The Gretchen and Richard Iben Lectureship," Bradley University, Peoria, IL, March 1986.

11. Arthur Holmberg, "Hamlet's Body," *American Theatre,* March 1992, p. 14.

12. Ibid., p. 14.

13. Alexander Dean and Lawrence Carra, *The Fundamentals of Play Directing* (New York: Holt, Rinehart and Winston, 1965), pp. 58–59.

14. Peter Hay, *Theatrical Anecdotes* (New York: Oxford University Press, 1987), p. 120.

15. Copyright 1957 by Leonard Bernstein and Stephen Sondheim.

16. Lorraine Hansberry, *The Sign in Sidney Brustein's Window* (New York: Samuel French, 1965), pp. 41–42.

17. Michael Kuchwara, "Buckley Makes Role into One of Her Own," Associated Press, *Peoria Journal Star,* 21 August 1994, p. B2.

18. Rosamond Gilder, "Lope de Vega: Super-Man of the Theatre," *Theatre Arts Monthly,* September 1935, vol. 19, no. 9, p. 660.

19. *Life* magazine, December 1987, vol. 10, pp. 72–74.

Chapter 9

1. Whitney White, from personal interview with Jeffrey Huberman, 27 April 1992, Salem, MA.

2. Denis Bablet, "Edward Gordon Craig and Scenography," *Theatre Research,* 1 November 1971, p. 11.

3. Thomas Leff, "Decor or Space: Architectural Stage Design and the Contemporary Theatre," *Theatre Topics,* March 1991, vol. 1, no. 1, p. 68.

4. Ronn Smith, "Brain Food," *American Theatre,* February 1991, p. 16.

5. Ibid.

6. Matt Wolf, "Balloons Make a Statement in *The Winter's Tale,*" *New York Times,* 17 April 1994, sec. 2, p. 5.

7. David Richards, "Rooms with a View . . . of the Audience," *New York Times,* 4 August 1991, sec. 2, p. 1.

8. Amy Reiter, "The Business of Entertainment Technology," *TCI,* March 1994, p. 11.

9. Smaranda Branescu, "Color Tinged with Melancholy," *A.R.T. News,* November 1988, p. 9.

10. Ibid.

11. Frederic Ohringer, *A Portrait of the Theatre* (Toronto: Merritt, 1979), p. 63.

12. Ellen Lampert-Gréaux, "Patricia Zipprodt," *TCI,* March 1994, pp. 33–34.

13. Richard Pilbrow, *Stage Lighting* (New York: D. Van Nostrand, 1971), p. 12.

14. Elizabeth Stone, "Through the Lens Brightly with Jennifer Tipton," *New York Times,* 14 April 1991, sec. 2, p. 5.

15. Patrick Spottiswoode, "Let Me Not Play a Woman, I Have a Beard Coming." Lecture given at Bradley University, Peoria, Illinois, October, 1991.

16. Ohringer, p. 73.

17. Stone, p. 21.

18. Carrie Robbins, "Theatre and Design: Costumes, Sets, and Lights," *Phi Kappa Phi Journal,* Summer 1990, p. 28.

19. Ellen Lampert-Gréaux, "Chris Parry: The Noted LD Lights Shakespeare on Two Continents," *TCI,* January 1995, p. 33.

20. Leff, p. 63.

21. Kroll, Jack. "High-Tech Magic: Follow That Gondola," *Newsweek,* 8 Feb. 1988, p. 70.

Chapter 10

1. J. M. Barrie, *Peter Pan* (New York: Samuel French, 1956), p. 72.

2. Gavin Smith, "Without Cutaways," *Film Comment,* June 1991, vol. 27, p. 27.

3. See H. W. Fowler, *A Dictionary of Modern English Usage* (London: Oxford University Press, 1965), p. 395.

4. Antonin Artaud, *The Theatre and Its Double,* trans. Mary C. Richards (New York: Grove Press, 1938).

5. "David Mamet," *Playboy* Interview, April 1995, vol. 42, no. 4, p. 59.

6. *The Gentleman's Magazine,* March 1765. Also quoted in Harry William Pedicord, *The Theatrical Public in the Time of Garrick* (Carbondale: Southern Illinois University Press, 1954), p. 51.

7. Quoted in Montague Summers, *The Restoration Theatre* (London: Kegan Paul, Trench, Trubner, 1934), p. 89.

8. Denis Diderot, "Réponse à la lettre de Mme. Riccoboni," in *Diderot's Writings on the Theatre,* ed. F.C. Green (Cambridge, England: Cambridge University Press, 1936), p. 216.

9. Lawrence W. Levine, *Highbrow/Lowbrow: The Emergence of Cultural Hierarchy in America* (Cambridge, Mass.: Harvard University Press, 1989), p. 179.

10. Pedicord, p. 52.

11. Excerpts from "Account of the Terrific and Fatal Riot at the New York Astor Place Opera House," 1849. Also quoted in "When 'Macbeth' Shook the World of Astor Place," *New York Times,* 26 January 1992, sec. 2, p. 1.

12. Levine, p. 195.

13. Susan Sloszczyna, "Cinema Sins," *USA Today,* 26 July 1991, sec. D, p. 4.

14. Reported by Associated Press in *Peoria Journal Star,* 19 February 1989, sec. B, p. 3.

15. John Robert Colombo, ed., *Popcorn in Paradise: The Wit and Wisdom of Hollywood* (New York: Holt, Rinehart and Winston, 1979), p. 18.

16. *Stagebill,* January 1994, p. 18.

17. Louis Botto, "Passing Stages," *Playbill,* January 1995, p. 36.

18. Rita McDonald Bleiman, "Shut Up and Get Out!" *Newsweek,* 3 December 1990, p. 13.

19. Amlin Gray, "The Big If," *American Theatre,* June 1989.

20. Margaret Croyden, "Intimate Vanya," *Theatre-Week,* 31 October–6 November 1994, p. 18.

21. *American Theatre,* December 1988, p. 31.

22. *American Theatre,* March 1989, pp. 9, 56.

Chapter 11

1. Arthur Miller, *Timebends* (New York: Grove Press, 1987), pp. 192–193.

2. Robert Brustein, "An Embarrassment of Riches," *The New Republic,* 16 March 1992, p. 29.

3. Frederic Ohringer, *A Portrait of the Theatre* (Toronto: Merritt, 1979), p. 49.

4. Gary Panetta, " 'Polite Lies' Won't Benefit Local Theater," *Peoria Journal Star,* 20 September 1992, p. B3.

5. "The Theatre," *New Yorker,* 8 June 1992, p. 4. Condensed from original *New Yorker* review by Mimi Kramer, 13 April 1992, p. 82.

6. Richard H. Palmer, *The Critics' Canon* (New York: Greenwood Press, 1988), p. 11.

7. Jerry Klein, "Exit Stage Right, Thanks for the Memories," *Peoria Journal Star,* 15 March 1992, sec. A, p. 4.

8. Diana Rigg, *No Turn Unstoned* (Garden City, NY: Doubleday, 1983), p. 13.

9. Robert Brustein, "The Theatre Critic," *National Forum,* Summer 1990, p. 37.

10. Walter Clemons, "From Scarecrow to Celebrity," *Newsweek,* 24 October 1988, p. 75.

11. Jerry Klein, "6000 Plays Later, Critic Still Loves Her Work," *Peoria Journal Star,* 15 November 1987, sec. B, p. 11.

12. Edwin Wilson, "Old-Fashioned Entertainment," *Wall Street Journal,* 12 April 1991, sec. A, p. 10.

13. Jack Kroll, "Signs of Summer," *Newsweek,* 25 May 1992, p. 91.

14. Klein, "6000 Plays Later, Critic Still Loves Her Work," p. 11.

15. All reviews quoted in Peter Hay, *Theatrical Anecdotes* (New York: Oxford University Press, 1987), pp. 273, 274.

16. Jack Kroll, "Sunset Stripped," *Newsweek,* 26 July 1993, p. 42.

17. Roger Ebert, "Reiner's 'North' Loses Its Way," *Chicago Sun-Times,* 22 July 1994, p. 41.

18. *New York Times,* 27 December 1992.

19. Stephen M. Archer, *How Theatre Happens* (New York: Macmillan, 1978), p. 179.

20. Hay, p. 374.

21. Ibid.

22. Frank Rich, "Exit the Critic," *New York Times Magazine,* 13 February 1994, p. 79.

23. Abridgement of Collier by George H. Nettleton and Arthur E. Case in *British Dramatists from Dryden to Sheridan* (Boston: Houghton Mifflin, 1939).

24. Rigg, p. 9.

25. Both reviews quoted from "Arts and Leisure Guide," *New York Times,* 17 May 1992, sec. 2, p. 34.

26. Carol Gelderman, "Critics and How They Got That Way," *American Theatre,* June 1990, p. 64.

27. Klein, "6000 Plays Later, Critic Still Loves Her Work," p. 11.

28. Quoted in Todd London, "Critics Under Fire . . . Again," *American Theatre,* January 1990, pp. 46–47.

29. Patrick Pacheco, "The Critic Tastes Comeuppance," *New York Times,* 25 November 1990, sec. 2, p. 5.

30. Benedict Nightingale, "Utopian Critic," *American Theatre,* November 1992, p. 20.

31. Matt Wolf, "Grueling 'Richard III' Wears Actor Out," Associated Press, *Peoria Journal Star,* 7 June 1992, sec. B, p. 3.

32. Jack Kroll, "A Woman for All Seasons," *Newsweek,* 1 June 1992, p. 74.

33. Gelderman, p. 24.

34. David Richards, "A Cast Changes and, Suddenly, a Play Is Reborn," *New York Times,* 12 January 1992, sec. 2, p. 5.

35. *New York Times Magazine,* 13 February 1994, pp. 32–79.

Chapter 12

1. *CBS Evening News with Dan Rather,* 28 April 1990.

2. Peter Hay, *Broadway Anecdotes* (New York: Oxford University Press, 1987), p. 253.

3. Robert Hurwitt, "The Many Stages of Claire Bloom," *Peoria Journal Star,* 21 October 1990, sec. E, p. 3.

4. Hay, p. 253.

5. Ellen Pall, "In 'Gypsy' a Rose Is a Role Is a Killer," *New York Times,* 13 May 1990, sec. 2, p. 10.

6. Ibid., p. 10.

7. Ibid., p. 5.

8. Jack Kroll, "What Becomes a Legend," *Newsweek,* 27 April 1992, p. 67.

9. *Time,* 28 March 1994, p. 24.

10. Michael Kuchwara, "Actors Like Classic Challenge," *Peoria Journal Star,* 23 December 1990, sec. B, p. 3.

11. David Richards, "A Gorgeous 'Carousel,' A Riveting 'Twilight,'" *New York Times,* 3 April 1995, sec. 2, p. 5.

12. Clive Barnes, review of the APA Phoenix Theatre production of *The Misanthrope, New York Times,* 10 October 1968, p. 59.

13. Deborah Allen, "West African 'Antigone' Speaks a Universal Tongue," *American Theatre,* September 1990, p. 56.

14. Jeffrey Bartholet, "Wherefore Art Thou Palestinian?" *Newsweek,* 20 June 1994, p. 51.

15. Associated Press, *ClariNet,* 28 December 1994.

16. Vivian Gornish, "'The Fantasticks': At 29, a Pacifier More Than a Play," *New York Times,* 14 May 1989, sec. 2, p. 5.

17. Molière, *The Misanthrope,* trans. Henri Van Laun, in *A Treasury of the Theatre from Aeschylus*

to Ostrovsky, ed. John Gassner (New York: Simon & Schuster, 1967), p. 401.

18. Molière, *The Misanthrope,* trans. Richard Wilbur (New York: Harcourt Brace & World, 1965), p. 90.

19. Hay, p. 258.

20. Brant Pope, personal interview, Sarasota, Florida, May 1991.

21. Jack Kroll, "The 'Phantom' Hits Broadway," *Newsweek,* 8 February 1988, p. 69.

22. Gornish, p. 5.

23. Michael Bennett, James Kirkwood, Nicholas Darle, et al., *A Chorus Line* (New York: Tams Witmark, 1985), p. 99.

24. Michael Devine, "The Changing Face of Czech Theatre," *Theatrum,* February/March 1991, vol. 22, p. 18.

25. Ibid., p. 19.

26. Frank Rich, "Reality Nearly Upstaged a Paradoxical Year," *New York Times,* 30 December 1990, sec. 2, p. 5.

27. Peter Brook, *The Shifting Point* (New York: Harper & Row, 1987), p. 56.

28. *American Theatre,* January 1991.

Appendix B
1. Interview with Howard Stein, Peoria, Illinois, September 1990.

Color Plate 15
1. Correspondence with Frank Silberstein, 27 December 1995.

Color Plate 25
1. Ingrid Sischy, "Welcome to 10086 Sunset Boulevard," *New York Times,* 11 September 1994, p. H5.

Color Plate 32
1. David Barbour, "Theatre Production Design: How to Succeed in Business Without Really Trying," *TCI,* May 1995, p. 46–47.

Color Plate 33
1. Jack Kroll, "Computers and Creativity: Culture," *Newsweek,* 27 February 1995, pp. 68– 69.

GLOSSARY

Abstract art   Art that seeks to imitate some aspect of nature with a minimum of recognizable references. Nonrealistic art is often referred to as abstracted because it contains fewer references to observable reality.

Absurdism   Twentieth-century philosophical concept that gave rise to a large number of plays termed by critic Martin Esslin "the theatre of the absurd." The absurdist theory contends that to be human is to strive to understand the world, and yet the world and thus human existence is meaningless. Human beings are therefore "absurd" because they live their lives as if the world made perfect sense. Many absurdist plays are comedies in which the characters use irrational language and engage in meaningless activities without the slightest awareness of their absurd behavior.

Acting edition   Postproduction publication of a play meant for theatre artists. The acting edition incorporates the changes made by the choices of the various artists during the production process, such as setting descriptions and character movements.

Actor-manager   In eighteenth- and nineteenth-century European theatres, leading actors who also ran their own companies in which they played starring roles.

Actors' Equity Association   (AEA) The American stage actors' union, founded in 1913, which represents the interests of the professional actors employed by theatrical producers. As an affiliate of the AFL/CIO, Actors Equity Association stipulates the minimum terms and conditions under which a member of its union can be employed.

Actos   Improvisational plays of the Chicano theatre in which audience members perform skits that re-create events which took place in their work experience.

Ad lib   Improvised bit of dialogue by an actor either in response to forgotten lines on stage or as part of a crowd scene in which many people are talking at once.

Aesthetic distance   Psychological distance between actors and audience members. The aesthetic distance in the theatre is shorter than for film or television, making theatre the most immediate of the delivery systems of drama.

Allographic art   Time arts that are rendered in a code system rather than the medium the audience perceives. Allographic arts include literary art (which is rendered in written words), music (which is rendered in diatonic notation), choreography (which is rendered in laba notation), and drama (which is rendered in the theatrical codes of playscripts). Allographic arts require decoding either by the audience or by other artists who subsequently deliver the art to the audience.

Amphitheatre   Large, outdoor theatre with an open playing area, which originated in ancient Rome and was used for gladiatorial contests and other sensational displays.

Applied arts   Art valued primarily for its practical uses rather than its aesthetic qualities. Also called useful arts.

Arena stage   Theatrical configuration in which the audience sits on all sides of the playing space. Also referred to as theatre-in-the-round.

Artistic director   Producer in the not-for-profit professional theatre who has responsibility for artistic choices including carrying out the creative mission of the theatre, choosing the season of plays, auditioning actors, choosing the directors and designers for each production, and overseeing the artistic quality of the productions.

Aside   Theatrical convention in which a character speaks lines directly to the audience ostensibly without the other characters being able to hear or notice.

Audition   Format in which actors try out for roles by performing brief, prepared monologues and songs, dancing, or reading from the play.

Autographic arts   Spatial arts in which the artist acts directly on the same physical material that is later observed by others. Paintings, drawings, and sculpture are all examples of autographic art.

Avant-garde   All-inclusive term referring to anything that breaks new ground by abandoning traditional norms. In the theatre, the most original and experimental approaches are considered to be *avant-garde*.

Blank verse   Form of poetry in which there is no rhyme and most commonly five stresses per line (iambic pentameter). Dialogue in classical plays, especially in English, is usually written in blank verse.

Blocking   Positioning and movement of actors as worked out by the director in rehearsals. Blocking includes the entire movement scheme including focus, stage pictures, business, entrances, exits, and the position of actors.

Broadway   The most famous theatre district in the world. It encompasses a section of midtown Manhattan in which 32 theatres are located. "Broadway" is also a contractual designation of commercial theatres with a capacity of at least 200 seats. Although the artistic merits of Broadway productions are debated, the symbolic importance of Broadway as a measure of theatrical success remains unquestioned.

Burlesque   Humorous play originally featuring satire and parody of other entertainment forms. In the twentieth century, burlesque came to mean a series of coarse variety acts that often include striptease.

Business   Often unscripted byplay of actors on stage, such as reading newspapers, dressing, comic bits, and preparing food and drinks. Substantial rehearsal is devoted to making stage business look natural and unrehearsed.

Callbacks   Follow-up auditions for a play that are held after the initial tryouts. Callbacks usually involve readings from the script.

Casting against type   Purposely choosing for a role in a play an actor who is opposite in characteristics from the role described in the playscript.

Catharsis   Purging of audience emotions aroused through empathic participation in dramatic action.

Character   Person depicted in a play. In structural terms, characters are the agents of the action. The performer portraying a character is an actor. Aristotle's second part of drama.

Character actors   Actors who specialize in submerging their real selves to impersonate hundreds of different voices, bodies, and psyches. They earn their livings based on their abilities to play a great variety of types.

Chorus   In the plays of ancient Greece, an ensemble representing the general public, who sang, danced, and chanted during interludes in the action or in response to the characters. Shakespeare often used individual characters and small groups to serve as the chorus in his plays. In the twentieth century, a chorus is the singing and dancing ensemble of musicals.

Claptrap   Concluding a speech or scene with such a great vocal or physical display that it would inspire or "trap" the audience into applauding. The technique was popular among lesser actors in the seventeenth, eighteenth, and nineteenth centuries.

Claque   Person paid by nineteenth-century managers and actors to start applause, bravos, and cheers in order to assure enthusiastic audience responses.

Classical drama   Originally meant to identify the great plays of ancient Greece and Rome. Classical drama now is used to refer to period plays from almost any era.

Comedy   Genre of humorous drama that ridicules human foibles. Varieties include comedy of manners, character comedy, farce, burlesque, satire, comedy of ideas, and intrigue comedy.

Crisis   Culmination of the plot in a play when the primary conflict is at the point of highest tension.

Commedia dell'arte   Theatrical form of improvisational slapstick comedy that began in Italy and flourished in Europe from 1600–1750. *Commedia* actors used masks and standardized costumes to create popular stock characters.

Community theatre   Nonprofessional theatre that is produced and staged by and for the benefit of the local community. In America, community theatre is the most popular participation art in the country.

Conflict   The essence of dramatic action. Conflict results from opposing forces working against each other either within a major character or between characters, which leads to the climax of the plot. Understanding the major conflict in a play is the best way to determine the dramatic action.

Conventions   Customary rules and styles of theatre practice that are accepted by the audience as aspects of the willing suspension of disbelief.

Cue   Line, action, or technical effect that prompts a response or another technical effect.

Curtain call   Staged bows at the end of the play in which both actors (through their presence and bows) and the audience (through their applause) acknowledge their mutual appreciation and participation in the theatrical event.

Cyclorama   Cloth or rear wall illuminated to simulate sky effects or other neutral backgrounds.

Declamatory acting   Dominant acting style from the time of the ancient Greeks until the late nineteenth century. Distinguished by great oratorical displays, the declamatory style of acting was audience focused, conventional, and suited to playing the larger-than-life roles of classical verse drama.

Deus ex machina   Scenic effect in the ancient Greek theatre by which a "god" would be lowered onto the stage by a machine. The arrival of the god would resolve the plot and end the play. The term is used in the modern theatre to describe the ending of a play in which resolution of conflicts seems contrived.

Dialects   Regional varieties of the same language distinguished by features of vocabulary, grammar, and pronunciation.

Dialogue   Conversation in a play between two or more characters in which short speeches, sentences, and phrases are alternated.

Diatonic notation   Allographic musical notations (e.g., notes, rests, dynamics, etc.) that are written down by composers to be read and played by musical performers.

Diction   Patterned words intended to be spoken by characters. Aristotle's fourth part of drama.

Directorial concept   Director's personal vision of the play which must be conceived with a clarity and completeness that can be conveyed to other artists who render it in concrete, living form.

Drama   Drama is the play itself, an imitation of human action. When the drama is performed, it becomes theatre art, which is the imitation of an action (the play) by another action (the performance).

Dramatic irony   Audience understanding of the significance of something that the character does not. (For example, Oedipus vowing to hunt down the murderer of his father when the audience knows he himself is that person.)

Dramatis personae   Characters in a play as listed in the front of the script or in the program. The cast of characters.

Dramaturgy   Nature of play construction and production history. A dramaturg specializes in play analysis and theatre history and often assists the director and playwright in making artistic choices.

Dress rehearsal   Final rehearsal of a play in which every element of production is in place. The object is to duplicate the same conditions of the first performance before an audience.

Eccyclema   Stage machine used to bear corpses onto the stage in the ancient Greek theatre. Simulations of violent action were not performed in view of the audience. In Greek tragedies, deaths took place offstage and the bodies were wheeled into view on a rolling platform.

Educational theatre   Academic programs featuring coursework and productions for the purposes of educating and training students and producing plays for campus and community audiences.

Empathy   Act of identifying so closely with someone else that the observer actually participates in the emotional life of that person. In the theatre, audience members empathize when they project themselves into the character or situation from the play and share those experiences.

Enclave theatre   Theatrical works in the cultural terms, conventions, images, characters, subjects of concern, and especially the language of native cultures. This theatre is almost always inaccessible to playgoers outside the confines of the enclave.

Ensemble acting   Mutually created chemistry of acting together resulting in a commitment to serving the play and not the ego of any particular actor.

Epic theatre   Theatrical theory developed by Erwin Piscator and Bertolt Brecht in which the audience is asked to judge rather than empathize with the action on the stage. Devices are used to keep the audience focused on the political significance of the story and not the individual lives of the characters. By judging the action, the audience is then able to draw connections to their own lives and value systems.

Episodic plots   Incidents selected and arranged according to a unifying idea, character, or image, rather than a chronology.

Existential drama   Plays that reflect the philosophical theories developed by Sartre and others. In rejecting the moral and ethical value systems of the past, existentialism argues that the meaning of life is determined by each individual person and the actions each performs. Individuals, as is true with the characters in this kind of play, define existence by what they choose to do or not do.

Exposition   The setting forth of necessary information at the beginning of a play. Prior events are revealed and the characters are introduced to the audience.

Expressionism   Theatrical form of 1920s German origin that dramatizes reality as seen through the eyes of a central character. The world is distorted and time organized by the way in which the central character feels about it. *Death of a Salesman* incorporates elements of expressionism when the past is depicted not as it literally was, but as Willy Loman remembers it to be.

Farce   Humorous form of drama in which laughter is aroused through broad, desperate, irrational, physical action such as mistaken identity, slapstick, stage business, and nonsense language. The protagonist of farce is a victim of capricious circumstance as opposed to the deservedly ridiculed characters of comedy.

Fine arts   Works of art that are valued for their aesthetic, associational, or symbolic, rather than functional, values. The fine arts are contrasted with the applied or useful arts, in which the art object is valued for its practical function.

Focus   Arrangement of the stage picture so as to direct the audience's attention to the appropriate actor, object, or event.

Formal value   Significance of a work of art in terms of the excellence of its structure, design, or composition. Formal value contrasts with functional value, which consists of what the art will generate in terms of enjoyment, instruction, inspiration, or monetary return.

Genre   Distinctive category or class of plays such as tragedy, comedy, melodrama, or tragicomedy.

Gesamtkunstwerk   Master directorial concept described by Richard Wagner that anticipated modern theatrical practice. This organizing concept, or "master artwork," sought to unify all of the production elements including music, dance, acting, scenery, and costumes under the control of the director.

Green room   Lounge where actors may wait before and after a production or when they are not on stage.

Ground plan   Scale drawing of the top view of a stage, showing placement of furniture, large props, and other scenic elements.

Illusionism   Theatrical practice of scenic design that has as its goal the simulation of an actual place in its entirety on the stage.

Imagination   Ability to make mental images of how reality might be. Imagination is linked to creativity, which is the realization—actual or artistic—of these images.

Improvisation   Style of acting in which an actor invents dialogue or physical actions spontaneously. Improvisation can be an art form in itself or it may be used as a rehearsal technique.

Inciting incident   Plot event that sets in motion the major conflict of the play.

Intellectual property   Legal description for a conceptual, revenue-generating idea or object such as a play or a painting.

Interludes   Short didactic plays performed by small troupes of traveling players for medieval nobles between courses of great feasts. By hiring themselves out as servants to noble households, performers were able to avoid legal and religious bans on professional playing.

International Copyright Agreement   The 1886 agreement in which each subscribing nation agreed to uphold the copyright laws of the others.

Interpretive director   Director who strives to identify and serve the original intent of the playwright as written in the script. Diametrically opposed is the view that a stage director is primarily a conceptual artist who is free to use the script and actors as well as any other theatrical element in order to accomplish an artistic vision of the play.

Intrigue plot   Most traditional arrangement of dramatic action in which the episodes are arranged chronologically in a careful cause-and-effect relationship. The result of a well-made intrigue plot is increasingly suspenseful, unpredictable, yet entirely probable action.

Laba notation   Allographic code used by choreographers to record on paper the physical movements, steps, and patterns of dancers. Dancers read these notations in a way similar to reading musical notes or a character's lines in a playscript.

Lazzi   Bits of traditional comic business that are formally inserted into the scenarios of the commedia dell'arte. The term is now used as a synonym for "shtick" or "bit" to indicate unscripted comic situations and business.

League of Resident Theatres (LORT)   The organization of American regional professional theatres that represents such not-for-profit organizations as the Guthrie Theatre, the Hartford Stage Company, the Mark Taper Forum, and the New York Shakespeare Festival.

Legitimate theatre   Theatrical space devoted to the production of live theatre. The emphasis is on the human being as the center of the theatre's focus and ultimate purpose. The term originated during the Restoration period in England when licenses were granted to certain theatres to perform drama. Unlicensed competitors offered musical and variety entertainments.

Limited Partnership Agreement   Contractual document that creates a commercial production company for the purpose of mounting a single play. Limited partners, also called angels, buy shares in the company that cover the total preproduction costs, but receive only 50 percent of the profits, with the other 50 percent going to the general partners, also called producers.

Liturgical drama   Elements of theatre that are performed as part of the liturgy of the Mass. In the medieval church, these were plays chanted or sung in Latin by priests as a regular part of the religious service.

Managing director   Person in charge of the business of "not-for-profit" theatres including staff administration, facilities management, contractual negotiations, ticket sales, fund-raising, and audience development.

Mansions   One of the conventional suggestive scenic units used in the staging of medieval religious plays. Mansions suggested simultaneous proximity of heaven, earthly locations, and hell arranged behind a generalized acting area called the *platea*.

Melodrama   Dramatic genre that imitates temporarily serious action which always upholds conventional morality and poetic justice. Ethical conflicts are simple, with good always triumphing over evil. Characters are drawn in the two-dimensional terms of heroes and villains. Whereas tragedy strives to arouse pity and fear, melodrama creates terror and horror through spine-tingling suspense, great spectacle effects, and evocative music.

Melody   Total sound of the production, from actors speaking the dialogue to any musical component or sound effects that are required. Aristotle's fifth part of drama.

Method acting   Stanislavsky system of acting as practiced in the United States, where the emphasis has been placed on the truthful portrayal of the emotional life of the character. Two primary training philosophies have dominated the teaching of the American "method." The first grew out of the work of Lee Strasberg and the Actors' Studio and places emphasis on the emotion-memory aspect of Stanislavsky's work. The second, which is popular in Great Britain, concentrates on Stanislavsky's concept of physical actions.

Mime   Theatrical form in which actors perform without speaking. Dialogue is replaced by the actors' expressive gestures, movements, and facial expressions. Mime is practiced today by street performers and by such theatre artists as the renowned Marcel Marceau.

Mimetikos   Aristotle's idea, expressed in the *Poetics,* that art is mimetic (*mimetikos*), which means imitative. Thus art, for Aristotle, is the imitation of something natural or imagined.

Musical theatre   Very broad category under which several theatrical forms containing music are grouped. Musical comedy is of American origin and began in the nineteenth century. It came into international prominence with acclaimed productions such as *Showboat, Oklahoma!,* and *South Pacific,* among others. The category also includes operas, operettas, musical revues, rock operas, and concept musicals.

Mystery plays   Medieval religious plays organized into a cycle that dramatized Bible stories from creation to final judgment, and performed annually or biannually by amateur actors throughout the communities of Europe. Staged outdoors in vernacular languages, the purpose was to demonstrate the miraculous nature of the Scriptures. Also common were morality plays in which allegorical good and evil forces strive for the soul of an "everyman" figure.

National Endowment for the Arts   (NEA) U.S. federal agency that disperses government funds (approximately $175 million annually) to various arts organizations.

Naturalism   Late nineteenth-century dramatic and theatrical style that called for the creation of a stage illusion so complete it would appear as a "slice of life." Influenced by the evolutionary and genetic theories of Charles Darwin, naturalistic plays emphasized details of heredity and environment as motivating forces. Ibsen, Strindberg, and Chekhov all wrote naturalistic plays.

Neoclassicism   Dramatic and theatrical style that developed from the Renaissance interest in the classical art of Greece and Rome. Based on the teachings of Aristotle and Horace, neoclassicism set down rules for the writing of plays to conform to what was thought to be the classical practice.

Nontraditional casting   Choosing the most talented actor for a part regardless of the actor's race, gender, physical condition, or cultural heritage.

Obie Awards   Awards given annually to actors, playwrights, designers, and productions of Off-Broadway theatres.

Off Broadway   New York commercial and not-for-profit theatres with a capacity of no more than 199 seats. Because of lower operating costs, the Off-Broadway movement was experimental in nature. In recent years Off-Broadway has become an increasingly commercial, mainstream venue.

Off-Off Broadway   New York not-for-profit theatres with a capacity of no more than 99 seats and prescribed limited budgets. These experimental theatres use many found and converted spaces for their sparse productions and are exempt from many union rules and pay scales that apply to larger houses. In Chicago, nontraditional theatres are called Off-Loop theatres; in Los Angeles, they are referred to as Equity Waiver theatres; and in London, they are called fringe theatres.

Orchestra   In the Greek and Roman theatre, the circular playing space where the actors and chorus sang and danced. In the modern theatre, orchestra-section seats are those closest to the stage.

Pennystinkers   In the Elizabethan theatre, audience members admitted for a penny who stood around the thrust stage while watching the play. Also called "groundlings."

Performing arts   The time arts of music, dance, drama, and their attendant delivery systems such as theatre, film, video, and opera. Performing arts are the only art forms that must be decoded and delivered to the audience by other artists.

Personality actors   Actors who reproduce their natural physical and psychological attributes for every role they play. The character is conformed to the personality of the actor.

Picturization   The director's visual interpretation of each moment of the play realized through the arrangement of scenic units and actors on the stage.

Pit   Historically, the area closest to the stage in which there were no seats, although eventually backless benches were provided. The pit gradually developed into the orchestra, which now contains the most expensive seats.

Play doctor   Specialist who rewrites plays to make them more stageworthy.

Play-followers   Eighteenth-century term for those people who were regular theatregoers.

Plot   Total organization of the action in a play. Although the terms are often confused, plot is not the same as the story, which is the complete chronological telling of an event. The plot is the selective arrangement of the scenes that may or may not be chronological. Aristotle's first part of drama.

Poetics   Aristotle's influential fourth-century B.C. treatise on the nature and structure of tragic drama. The six parts of drama—plot, character, thought, diction, melody, and spectacle—are discussed in detail.

Promptbook   Record of all of the directorial decisions, actors' movements, and technical cues for the production of a play.

Prompter   Predecessor of the modern stage manager. From the seventeenth through the nineteenth centuries, the prompter called rehearsals, posted entrances and exits, distributed scripts, and fed actors forgotten lines during performances.

Property   In the single-play ventures of commercial theatre, a play to which a producer acquires the contractual and exclusive option for professional production. Properties, or "props," also refer to the objects that actors use on stage.

Proscenium theatre   Theatre featuring a stage with a proscenium arch, the architectural framing device that separates the audience from the main playing area. The arch "frames" the stage and focuses the attention of the audience on the often illusionistic events happening in front of them. This type of theatre was introduced in the seventeenth century and is still prevalent today.

Protagonist   Principal character in a play who is set in conflict against the antagonist.

Psychodrama   Improvisational acting exercises that are used for psychotherapeutic purposes.

Public domain   The status of intellectual property first published longer than 75 years ago that is no longer protected by the International Copyright Agreement and is available for use without payment of royalty.

Public theatres   The large open-air theatres of Elizabethan England. Private theatres, which were also open to the public, were indoor structures with higher admission charges.

Raked stage   Stage that is slanted upward from the front to the back of the theatre. Originally used to enhance the perspective, raked stages are now used for a variety of nonrealistic effects. The terms *upstage* and *downstage* literally described the raked stages of the first proscenium theatres.

Realistic art   Art that attempts to reproduce as closely as possible the appearance or sounds of things in nature. Realistic art achieves its proper pleasurable effect through the viewer's recognition of the familiar objects depicted.

Regional theatre   Not-for-profit professional theatres located outside of New York City. The regional theatre movement was started in the late 1940s to decentralize professional theatre in the United States. Also called resident theatre.

Repertory system   System of play production in which a play is performed for a prescribed number of performances, closed, and succeeded by another play. In rotating repertory, the plays are alternated on a daily basis throughout the season, enabling theatregoers to see the entire season's repertory over several days.

Restoration comedy   Sophisticated comedies of manners popular among the English aristocracy during the Restoration period (1661–1700). These ribald plays were famous for their witty dialogue, outrageous characters, and strong sexual content. The term derives from the restoration of the English monarchy after the Puritan rule during the Commonwealth period (1642–1660).

Review   Immediate response of a critic who has just seen the production of a play and writes these impressions in the hours following the performance. A review differs from theatrical criticism, which is more detailed commentary on the significance of the play.

Ritual   Act or series of acts that are honored and repeated for their cultural or religious significance. Many scholars contend that theatre grew out of the ritual performances of prehistoric tribes and early civilizations.

Romanticism   Nineteenth-century theatrical movement that glorified the human spirit and the power of the subjective. It began as an artistic response to the strict rules of neoclassicism and was supplanted by the popularity of realism after 1850.

Royalties   Contractual fees that are paid to playwrights for each production of their plays.

Satire   Play that arouses laughter through the ridicule of actual persons, human vices, follies, beliefs, or social conventions.

Script   Printed text of a play.

Skene   In the theatre of ancient Greece, the large building at the rear of the playing area that served as the scene house for storage, costume changes, and as a palace-like facade for the action.

Slapstick   General term for the techniques, tricks, and routines of physical comedy including knockabout, pratfalls, and other "shtick."

Society of Stage Directors and Choreographers   (SSDC) Independent union organized in 1959 to represent professional stage directors and choreographers in collective bargaining and contractual negotiations with producers.

Spatial arts   Those arts imagined and created primarily through the manipulation of material in space including the graphic arts of drawing, painting, and printmaking—which use line, shape, and color to imitate—and the plastic arts of sculpture, architecture, pottery, and weaving—which manipulate form, mass, and material.

Spectacle   Visual elements of a play including the settings, costumes, lighting effects, properties, and the actors and their movements. Aristotle's sixth part of drama.

Stage areas   Sections of the stage always designated from the actor's perspective including "stage right," "stage left," "center stage," "upstage" (toward the rear of the stage), and "downstage" (closest to the audience).

Stendhal syndrome   Named for author and world traveler Henri Stendhal (1783–1842), the intense emotional and physical reaction that some people undergo in the presence of great inspirational art. Symptoms include dizziness, amnesia, and disorientation.

Stichomythia   Rapid-fire, clipped style of dialogue in which two characters alternate single lines, phrases, or words.

Stock characters   Characters who are recognizable for their conformity to stereotypical dramatic types such as the miser, quack doctor, braggart warrior, clever servant, or country bumpkin.

Style   Distinguishing characteristics of a play, production, or period of history that reflect conventional practice.

Subtext   Unspoken meaning or character motivation in a play, often in contradiction to the actual dialogue. Subtext is the dramatic rendering of modern psychological theories of the subconscious that hold there is often a disparity between what people say and what they mean.

Surrealism Nonrealistic artistic style that attempts to reflect truth through imitations of dreamlike states.

Technical rehearsal Rehearsal prior to the opening of a production during which all of the light, sound, and set-change cues are practiced and perfected.

Theatre art Delivery system for dramatic art. Theatre art is the imitation of an action (the play) by another action (the performance).

Theatrical Syndicate Association formed in 1896 of New York producers and theatre owners, which created a monopoly of American theatres. The syndicate was put out of business by the more powerful Shubert Theatre Corporation, which was weakened, but not eliminated, by federal antitrust suits in the 1950s.

Theatron Literally, "seeing place." In ancient Greece, the place on the side of the Acropolis from which spectators watched plays.

Thought Desires, emotions, reasoning, and decisions of characters in a play, apparent in all they say and do. Aristotle's third part of drama.

Thrust stage Stage that juts out into the audience, who sit on three sides of the playing space. Because they accommodate rapid, suggestive changes of locale, thrust stages were used in Elizabethan England and are found in contemporary theatres that frequently perform the classics.

Tony Awards Awards given annually for outstanding achievements in the Broadway theatres. Short for "Antoinette Perry" Awards.

Tragedy Dramatic genre that depicts predominantly serious action with ethically complex implications resulting in the arousal of pity and fear. Tragedy results from the consequential errors of admirable characters being placed in impossible situations and being forced to make difficult ethical decisions. The philosopher Hegel said tragedy had a disastrous outcome because it involved the life and death struggle between two "rights" or two equally valid sets of conflicting necessities. The tragedy, according to Hegel, was that one of the "rights" could not be realized.

Type casting Choosing actors who by age, physique, ethnicity, and attitude most closely resemble the roles they are to play. Casting against type is purposely choosing someone who is opposite in characteristics from the role described in the playscript.

Unities Requirements imposed by neoclassic critics on the drama. The unities of place, action, and time required that plays take place in one locale, dramatize one single action, and not depict more than one day. These requirements were adhered to most strictly by seventeenth- and eighteenth-century French dramatists such as Molière and Racine.

Vaudeville Theatrical form that was highly popular in the United States from about 1870–1930, featuring short variety acts and comic skits, mixed with singing, dancing, and even animal acts. In recent years a revival of sorts, called

"New Vaudeville," has seen the reappearance of artists who have adopted some of the specialized techniques of the original vaudeville performers.

Virtuality   Visual effect created by computer-controlled video as seen through special goggles.

Willing suspension of disbelief   Imaginative agreement between actors and audience whereby the audience agrees not to disbelieve the dramatic fiction of the events, characters, and places depicted on stage. This imaginative connection allows the audience to become emotionally involved in the action without losing their own sense of what is real.

Workshop production   Limited staging intended to allow the playwright to see and hear the play for the purpose of making rewrites in response to performance conditions.

SELECTED BIBLIOGRAPHY

This bibliography lists some important works on art, culture, drama, and theatre. In addition to sources of general interest, the works are grouped according to the divisions and chapters in the text.

PART ONE
The Creative Imagination

Works of General Interest

Brustein, Robert. *Dumbrocracy in America: Studies in the Theatre of Guilt, 1987–1994.* Chicago: Dee, 1994.

Colombo, John Robert, ed. *Popcorn in Paradise: The Wit and Wisdom of Hollywood.* New York: Holt, Rinehart and Winston, 1979.

Gascoigne, Bamber. *World Theatre.* Boston: Little, Brown, 1968.

Gassner, John, and Ralph Allen, eds. *Theatre and Drama in the Making.* Boston: Houghton Mifflin, 1964.

Fowler, James, ed. *Images of Show Business from the Theatre Museum, V&A.* London: Methuen, 1982.

Hartnoll, Phyllis. *The Concise Oxford Companion to the Theatre.* New York: Oxford University Press, 1986.

Hobgood, Burnet M., ed. *Master Teachers of Theatre.* Carbondale: Southern Illinois University Press, 1988.

Kuritz, Paul. *The Making of Theatre History.* Englewood Cliffs, NJ: Prentice-Hall, 1988.

Nagler, A. M. *A Sourcebook in Theatrical History.* New York: Dover, 1952.

Ohringer, Frederic. *A Portrait of the Theatre.* Toronto: Merritt, 1979.

Prideaux, Tom. *World Theatre in Pictures: From Ancient Times to Modern Broadway.* New York: Greenberg Publisher, 1953.

Reed, Robert M., and Maxine K. Reed. *The Facts on File Dictionary of Television, Cable, and Video.* New York: Facts on File, Inc., 1994.

Schlesinger, Sarah. *Celebrate Theatre!* Reston, VA: Newspaper Association of America Foundation, 1994.

CHAPTER 1: Art and the Creative Imagination

Artistic Freedom Under Attack, Vol. III. Washington, DC: People for the American Way, 1995.

Chipp, H. B. *Theories of Modern Art.* Berkeley: University of California Press, 1968.

Gardner, Howard. *Frames of Mind.* New York: Basic Books, 1983.

———. *The Arts and Human Development.* New York: Basic Books, 1983.

Ghiselin, Brewster. *The Creative Process.* New York: Mentor Books, 1952.

Honour, Hugh, and John Fleming. *The Visual Arts.* Englewood Cliffs, NJ: Prentice-Hall, 1982.

Langer, Susanne K. *Problems of Art.* New York: Charles Scribner's Sons, 1957.

May, Rollo. *The Courage to Create.* New York: Bantam, 1975.

Marquis, Alice Goldfarb. *Art Lessons: Learning from the Rise and Fall of Public Arts Funding.* New York: Basic Books, 1995.

Thompson, William Irwin. *At the Edge of History: Speculation on the Transformation of Culture.* New York: Harper & Row, 1972.

Why We Need the Arts: 8 Quotable Speeches by Leaders in Education, Government, Business and the Arts. New York: ACA Books, 1988.

CHAPTER 2: The Dramatic Imagination

Aristotle. *Poetics.* Trans. Kenneth A. Telford. Chicago: Gateway, 1968.

Beckerman, Bernard. *Dynamics of Drama.* New York: Drama Book Specialist Publishers, 1979.

Bentley, Eric. *The Life of Drama.* New York: Atheneum, 1964.

Bermel, Albert. *Farce: A History from Aristophanes to Woody Allen.* New York: Simon and Schuster, 1982.

Brown, Stuart L., "Animals at Play," *National Geographic.* Vol. 186, No. 6, December 1994, pp. 2–35.

Clark, Barrett H. *European Theories of the Drama.* New York: Crown, 1965.

Esslin, Martin. *The Theatre of the Absurd,* rev. ed. Garden City, NY: Doubleday, 1969.

Granville-Barker, Harley. *The Uses of Drama.* Princeton, NJ: Princeton University Press, 1945.

Heffner, Hubert. *The Nature of Drama.* Boston: Houghton Mifflin, 1959.

Hodgson, Terry. *The Drama Dictionary.* New York: New Amsterdam Books, 1988.

Huberman, Jeffrey H. *Late Victorian Farce.* Ann Arbor: UMI Research Press, 1986.

Kerr, Walter. *Tragedy and Comedy.* New York: Simon & Schuster, 1967.

Lerner, Alan Jay. *The Musical Theatre: A Celebration.* New York: McGraw-Hill, 1986.

Olson, Elder. *The Theory of Comedy.* Bloomington: Indiana University Press, 1968.

Smith, Cecil. *Musical Comedy in America.* New York: Theatre Arts Books, 1950.

Wickham, Glynne. *Drama in a World of Science.* Toronto: University of Toronto Press, 1962.

CHAPTER 3: The Theatrical Imagination

Brockett, Oscar G. *History of the Theatre,* 7th ed. Boston: Allyn & Bacon, 1995.

Brustein, Robert, *The Theatre of Revolt.* New York: Little, Brown, 1964.

Carlson, Marvin. *Theories of the Theatre.* New York: Cornell University Press, 1984.

Fergusson, Francis. *The Idea of a Theater.* Princeton, NJ: Princeton University Press, 1949.

Kirby, E. T. *Ur-Drama: The Origins of Theatre.* New York: New York University Press, 1975.

Lahr, John, and Jonathan Price. *Life-Show: How to See Theatre in Life and Life in Theatre.* New York: Viking Press, 1973.

Laufe, Abe. *The Wicked Stage.* New York: Frederick Ungar Publishing, 1978.

McLuhan, Marshall. *Understanding Media.* New York: McGraw-Hill, 1964.

Winnicott, D. W. *Playing and Reality.* New York: Basic Books, 1971.

PART TWO
The Play

CHAPTER 4: Theatregoers

Mitchell, Arnold. *The Professional Performing Arts: Attendance Patterns, Preferences, and Motives.* Madison, WI: Association of College, University, and Community Arts Administrators, Inc., 1984.

Chinoy, Helen Krich, and Linda Walsh Jenkins, eds. *Women in American Theatre: Careers, Images, Movements. An Illustrated Anthology and Sourcebook.* New York: Crown Publishers, 1981.

Engle, Ron, Felicia Hardison Londré, and Daniel J. Watermeier, eds. *Shakespeare Companies and Festivals: An International Guide.* New York: Greenwood, 1995.

Ettema, James S., and D. Charles Whitney. *Audiencemaking: How the Media Create Audience.* London: Sage, 1994.

Hanson, Bruce K. *The Peter Pan Chronicles.* New York: Brich Lane Press, 1993.

Haskins, James. *Black Theater in America.* New York: HarperCollins, 1994.

Hay, Samuel A. *African American Theatre: A Historical and Critical Analysis.* Cambridge: Cambridge University Press, 1994.

Levine, Lawrence W. *Highbrow Lowbrow: The Emergence of Culture Hierarchy in America.* Cambridge: Harvard University Press, 1988.

Pankratz, David B. *Multiculturalism and Public Arts Policy.* Westport: , 1993.

Park, Robert Ezra. *Race and Culture.* Glencoe, IL: Free Press, 1950.

Plays by Early American Women, 1775–1850. Ann Arbor: University of Michigan Press, 1995.

Postman, Neil. *Amusing Ourselves to Death: Public Discourse in the Age of Show Business.* New York: Viking, 1985.

Rybczynski, Witold. *Waiting for the Weekend.* New York: Viking, 1991.

Schor, Juliet B. *The Overworked American: The Unexpected Decline of Leisure.* New York: Basic Books, 1991.

CHAPTER 5: Imitations of Action

9 Plays by Black Women. New York, 1986.

Cole, Toby, ed. *Playwrights on Playwriting.* New York: Hill & Wang, 1961.

Esslin, Martin. *The Theatre of the Absurd.* New York: Doubleday, 1961.

Gassner, John. *Masters of the Drama.* New York: Dover, 1954.

Miller, Arthur. *The Theatre Essays of Arthur Miller.* New York: Viking, 1978.

———. *Timebends.* New York: Grove Press, 1987.

Methuen Book of Shakespeare Anecdotes, The. London: Methuen Drama, 1992.

Nagler, A. M. *Black Drama.* New York: Hawthorn, 1967.

Nicoll, Allardyce. *World Drama.* New York: Harcourt Brace, 1976.

Smiley, Sam. *Playwrighting: The Structure of Action.* Englewood Cliffs, NJ: Prentice-Hall, 1971.

Weales, Gerald. *A Play and Its Parts.* New York: Basic Books, 1964.

Worthen, W. B. *The HBJ Anthology of Drama.* Fort Worth: Harcourt Brace Jovanovich, 1993.

CHAPTER 6: The Theatrical Catalyst

Atkinson, Brooks. *Broadway.* New York: Macmillan, 1974.

Bell, Marty. *Broadway Stories: A Backstage Journey Through Musical Theatre.*

Bruzzo, James A. *Jobs in Arts and Media Management.* New York: ACA Books, 1990.

Epstein, Helen. *Joe Papp: An American Life.* New York: Little, Brown, 1995.

Ettema, James S., and D. Charles Whitney. *Audiencemaking: How the Media Create Audience.* London: Sage, 1994.

Farber, Donald C. *Producing on Broadway.* New York: DBS Publications, 1969.

Goldman, William. *The Season: A Candid Look at Broadway.* New York: Harcourt, Brace, & World, 1969.

Hay, Peter. *Broadway Anecdotes.* New York: Oxford University Press, 1989.

Kissel, Howard. *David Merrick: The Abominable Showman.* New York: Applause Books.

Langley, Stephen. *Producers on Producing.* New York: Drama Book Specialists, 1976.

———. *Theatre Managements and Production in America.* New York: Drama Book Publishers, 1990.

Little, Stuart. *Enter Joseph Papp: In Search of a New American Theatre.* New York: Cowar, McCann and Geoghegan, 1974.

Marsolais, Ken, Roger McFarlane, and Tom Viola, eds. *Broadway Day and Night.* New York: Pocket Books, 1992.

Papp, Joseph, and Elizabeth Kirkland. *Shakespeare Alive.* New York: Bantam Books, 1988.

Ziegler, Joseph. *Regional Theatre: The Revolutionary Stage.* Minneapolis: University of Minnesota Press, 1973.

PART THREE
The Production

CHAPTER 7: The Primary Theatre Artist

Ball, William. *A Sense of Direction: Some Observations on the Art of Directing.* New York: Drama Book Publishers, 1984.

Bartow, Arthur. *The Director's Voice: Twenty-One Interviews.* New York: Theatre Communications Group, 1988.

Brook, Peter. *The Empty Space.* New York: Atheneum, 1968

Canfield, Curtis. *The Craft of Play Directing.* New York: Holt, Rinehart and Winston, 1963.

Clurman, Harold. *On Directing.* New York: Macmillan, 1972.

Cole, Toby, and Chinoy, Helen Krich. *Directors on Directing.* New York: Bobbs-Merrill, 1980.

Dean, Alexander. *Fundamentals of Play Directing,* revised by Lawrence Carra, 5th ed. New York: Holt, Rinehart and Winston, 1988.

Hodge, Francis. *Play Directing: Analysis, Communication, and Style.* Englewood Cliffs, NJ: Prentice-Hall, 1971.

Saint-Denis, Michel. *The Rediscovery of Style.* New York: Theatre Arts Books, 1960.

CHAPTER 8: Artistic Impersonation

Benedetti, Robert. *The Actor at Work.* Englewood Cliffs, NJ: Prentice-Hall, 1971.

Black, David. *The Magic of Theatre: Behind the Scenes with Today's Leading Actors.* New York: Macmillan, 1993.

Cohen, Robert. *Acting Professionally.* Mountain View, CA: Mayfield, 1990.

Cole, Toby, and Helen K. Chinoy, eds. *Actors on Acting.* New York: Crown, 1980.

Devin, Richard. *Actors Resumes: the Definitive Guidebook.* Universal City, CA.: EMC2 Publishers, 1994.

Gaster, Theodor. *Thespis.* New York: Schuman, 1950.

Grotowski, Jerzy. *Towards a Poor Theatre.* New York: Simon & Schuster, 1968.

Hagen, Uta. *Respect for Acting.* New York: Macmillan, 1973.

———. *A Challenge for the Actor.* New York: Macmillan, 1991.

Parke, Lawrence. *Acting Truths and Fictions.* Hollywood, CA: Acting World Books, 1995.

Shurtleff, Michael. *Audition.* New York: Bantam, 1980.

Spolin, Viola. *Improvisation for the Theatre.* Evanston, IL: Northwestern University Press, 1963.

Stanislavsky, Konstantin. *An Actor Prepares.* Trans. by Elizabeth Reynolds Hapgood. New York: Theatre Arts Books, 1936.

———. *Building a Character.* Trans. by Elizabeth Reynolds Hapgood. New York: Theatre Arts Books, 1949.

———. *Creating a Role.* Trans. by Elizabeth Reynolds Hapgood. New York: Theatre Arts Books, 1961.

Strasberg, Lee. *Strasberg at the Actors Studio.* New York: Viking Press, 1965.

Suzuki, Tadashi. *The Way of Acting.* 1968.

Dudden, Faye E. *Women in the American Theatre: Actresses & Audiences 1790–1870.* New Haven: Yale University Press, 1994.

CHAPTER 9: Sights and Sounds

Barton, Lucy. *Historic Costume for the Stage.* Boston: Baker's Plays, 1935.

Corson, Richard. *Stage Make-up,* 5th ed. Englewood Cliffs, NJ: Prentice-Hall, 1975.

Craig, Edward Gordon. *On the Art of the Theatre.* Chicago: Browne's Bookstore, 1911.

Bay, Howard. *Stage Design.* New York: Drama Book Specialists, 1974.

Fried, Larry K. *Greening Up Our Houses: A Guide to a More Ecologically Sound Theatre.* New York: Drama Book Publishers, 1994.

Jones, Robert E. *The Dramatic Imagination.* New York: Meredith, 1941.

McCandless, Stanley R. *A Method of Lighting the Stage,* 4th ed. New York: Theatre Arts Books, 1958.

Mielziner, Jo. *Designing for the Theatre.* New York: Atheneum, 1965.

Oenslager, Donald. *Scenery Then and Now.* New York: Norton, 1939.

Parker, W. Oren, and R. Craig Wolf. *Scene Design and Stage Lighting.* New York: Holt, Rinehart and Winston, 1990.

Payne, Darwin Reid. *Computer Scenographics.* Carbondale: Southern Illinois University Press, 1994.

————. *Scenographic Imagination.* Carbondale: Southern Illinois University Press, 1993.

Pilbrow, Richard. *Stage Lighting.* New York: Van Nostrand and Reinhold, 1979.

Schechner, Richard. *Environmental Theatre.* New York: Hawthorn, 1973.

Usher, A. P. *The History of Mechanical Inventions.* Boston: Beacon Press, 1959.

PART FOUR
The Performance

CHAPTER 10: The Audience Plays Its Part

Artaud, Antonin. *The Theatre and Its Double.* New York: Grove, 1978.

Beacham, Richard C. *The Roman Theatre and Its Audience.* Cambridge, MA.: Harvard University Press, 1992.

Bennett, Susan. *Theatre Audiences: A Theory of Production and Reception.* New York: Routledge, 1990.

Blau, Herbert. *The Audience.* Baltimore: John Hopkins University Press, 1990.

Brecht, Bertolt. *Brecht on Theatre.* New York: Hill and Wang, 1965.

Davis, Walter A. *Get the Guests: Psychoanalysis, Modern American Drama, and the Audience.* Madison: University of Wisconsin Press, 1994.

Dolin, Jill. *The Feminist Spectator as Critic.* Ann Arbor: University of Michigan Press, 1991.

Le Bon, Gustave. *The Crowd: A Study of the Popular Mind.* London: Benn, 1952.

Raz, Jacob. *Audience and Actors: A Study of Their Interaction in the Japanese Traditional Theatre.* Leiden, E. J. Brill, 1983.

CHAPTER 11: Judgments on the Theatrical Imagination

Booth, John E. *The Critic, Power, and the Performing Arts.* New York: Columbia University Press, 1991.

Burns, Morris U. *The Dramatic Criticism of Alexander Wollcott,* Metuchen, NJ: Scarecrow Press, 1980.

Comtois, M. E., and Lynn F. Miller. *Contemporary American Theater Critics: A Directory and Anthology of Their Works.* Metuchen, NJ: Scarecrow Press, 1977.

Downs, Harold. *The Critic in the Theatre.* London: I. Pitman, 1953.

Stefanova-Peteva, Kalina. *Who Calls the Shots on the New York Stages?* Langhorne, PA: Harwood Academic Publishers, 1993.

Medved, Michael. *Hollywood vs. America.* New York: HarperCollins, 1992.

Palmer, Richard H. *The Critics' Canon: Standards of Theatrical Reviewing on America.* CT.: Greenwood Press, 1988.

Rigg, Dianna. *No Turn Unstoned.* Garden City: Doubleday, 1983.

CHAPTER 12: The Run of a Show

Brockett, Oscar G. *Perspectives on Contemporary Theatre.* Baton Rouge: Louisiana State University Press, 1971.

Brook, Peter. *The Shifting Point.* New York: Harper & Row, 1987.

Engle, Ron, Felicia Hardison Londré, and Daniel J. Watermeier, eds. *Shakespeare Companies and Festivals: An International Guide.* New York: Greenwood, 1995.

Laufe, Abe. *Anatomy of a Hit.* New York: Hawthorn Books, 1966.

———. *Broadway's Greatest Musicals.* New York: Funk and Wagnalls, 1977.

Stevenson, Isabelle, ed. *The Tony Award: A Complete Listing with a History of the American Theatre Wing.* Portsmouth, NH: Heinemann, 1994.

COPYRIGHTS & ACKNOWLEDGMENTS

PHOTO CREDITS

Preview xx, left: Photo by Peter Cunningham. **xx, right:** AP / Wide World Photos.

Chapter 1 2: Photo credit Michal Daniel. **5:** Drawing by Jacob Huberman at age 3. **7:** Angel Franco / NYT Pictures. **10:** © G. Petrov / Washington Stock Photo, Inc. **12:** © 1995 ARS, N.Y./SPADEM. **13:** Melnick / Manhole Covers, (c) The MIT Press. **15:** public domain. **16:** Photo by © Andrew Pothecary, London, 1993. **17:** AP / Wide World Photos. **30:** Billy Rose Theatre Collection, The New York Public Library of the Performing Arts, Astor, Lenox and Tilden Foundations. **32:** (c) Carol Rosegg. **38:** Jim Wilson / NYT Pictures.

Chapter 2 42, left: The Raymond Mander & Joe Mitchenson Theatre Collection Ltd. **42, right:** Photo by Bruce Monk / Manitoba Theater Center. **45:** Martha Swope © Time Inc. **47:** © 1995 Gerry Goodstein. **51:** Martha Swope © Time Inc. **53, top:** VanDamm Collection. **53, bottom left:** public domain. **53, bottom right:** © Joan Marcus. **58:** Martha Swope © Time Inc. **59:** © Carol Rosegg. **60:** © Inge Morath / Magnum Photos, Inc.

Chapter 3 64: © 1977 University of Massachusetts at Amherst. **69:** AP / Wide World Photos. **72, top:** Office for Metropolitan History. **72, middle:** © T. Charles Erickson. **72, bottom:** © Joan Marcus. **73, left:** © Tom Brazil. **73, right:** © Debra LaCoppola / Annex Theatre. **74:** © Carol Rosegg. **81:** Duane Boutte' as Paul, Pamela Payton-Wright as Ouisa in Dallas Theater Center production of "Six Degrees of Separation" photo by Carl Davis. **82:** Chris Harris / Times Newspapers Limited. **84:** Courtesy of The Stratford Festival Archives. Photo by Robert C. Ragsdale, Ltd. **88:** © 1985 Richard M. Feldman.

Chapter 4 92: Reprint Courtesy of The Fort Worth Star-Telegram. **97:** John Haynes / Sports Illustrated. **101:** Shouchiku Co. / Uniphoto Int'l. **106:** Photo by Paula Court. **107:** Martha Swope © Time Inc. **108:** New York Public Library. **115:** © Brigitte Lacombe / Gamma Liaison. **117:** © Gerald Murray. **118:** © T. Charles Erickson. **121, left:** Peoria Journal Star / David Zalaznik. **121, right:** Eliot Elisofon, Life Magazine © 1950 Time Warner Inc. **122:** Photo by Louis Faurer. **125:** George M. Cohan in His Dressing Room—Museum of the City of New York. **126:** public domain. **127:** Peoria Journal Star / Linda Henson. **128:** A Traveling Jewish Theatre / Junebug Theater Project present "Crossing the Broken Bridge" created and performed by Naomi Newman (left) & John O'Neal (right). Photo by David Allen. **129:** © Joan Marcus. **130:** Yale Repertory Theatre, photo by William B. Carter. **131:** © T. Charles Erickson. **134, top:** Martha Swope © Time Inc. **134, bottom:** Martha Swope © Time Inc. **135, top:** © Joan Marcus. **135, middle:** Photo, Terry Shapiro / Denver. **135, bottom:** Sotigui Kouyate (front), Yoshi Oida (back) in "The Man Who," directed by Peter Brook. Photo © Gilles Abegg / BAM. **138:** Living Stage Theatre Company. Photo by Kelly Jerome. **139:** Martha Swope © Time Inc. **140:** Picture Perfect Studio / Ron Corn. **141:** Photo by James G. Brey .

Chapter 5 150: Shakespeare Centre Library; Joe Cocks Studio Collection. **153, top:** © Allan Titmuss, London. **153, middle:** Reuters / Bettmann. **153, bottom:** AP / Wide World Photos. **156:** Yale Repertory Theatre, photo by William B. Carter. **157:** Gjon Mili, Life Magazine © 1946 Time Warner Inc. **159:** © Richard M. Feldman / American Repertory Theatre. **162:** © Ivan Kyncl. **164:** Billy Rose Theatre Collection, The New York Public Library for the Performing Arts. Astor, Lenox and Tilden Foundations. **166:** © Susan Cook. **167:** © Joan Marcus. **168:** Billy Rose Theatre Collection, The New York Public Library for the Performing Arts. Astor, Lenox and Tilden Foundations. **169:** © 1995 Gerry Goodstein. **170:** Seattle Repertory Theatre © Chris Bennion. **172:** Museum of the City of New York Theatre Archives. **174:** © Carol Rosegg. **175:** © James Salzano. **177:** Billy Rose Theatre Collection, The New York Public Library for the Performing Arts. Astor, Lenox and Tilden Foundations. **181:** Billy Rose Theatre Collection, The New York Public Library for the Performing Arts. Astor, Lenox and Tilden Foundations. **183:** © Gerry Goodstein. **187:** © Tim Rue / True Photo. **188:** The Raymond Mander

Harry Ransom Humanities Research Center. The University of Texas at Austin. **388:** Theatre Arts Collection, Harry Ransom Humanities Research Center. The University of Texas at Austin. **389:** AP / Wide World Photos. **392:** Photo by Peter Cunningham. **393:** El Teatro Campesino.

Chapter 11 400: Bettmann Archives. **405:** © 1992 Marc Bryan-Brown. **408:** © Joan Marcus. **413, top:** © Carol Rosegg. **413, bottom:** © Joan Marcus. **416:** Ad designed by Serena Coyne Advertising. **419:** Martha Swope © Time Inc., William Gibson.

Chapter 12 426: Ad designed by Serena Coyne Advertising. **431:** The Raymond Mander & Joe Mitchenson Theatre Collection Ltd. **433:** Cornerstone Theater Company: photo by Benajah Cobb. **436:** Billy Rose Theatre Collection, The New York Public Library for the Performing Arts. Astor, Lenox and Tilden Foundations. **438:** "Shear Madness," from left: Jon Blackstone, Alice Duffy, Michael Fennimore. photo: Marc B. Malin. **440:** Keith Meyers / NYT Pictures. **444, top:** Photo by Vandamm, Billy Rose Theatre Collection, The New York Public Library for the Performing Arts. Astor, Lenox and Tilden Foundations. **444, bottom:** © Joan Marcus. **446:** © Ricki Rosen / Saba. **447, top:** © Eileen Darby. **447, bottom:** Crossroads Theatre Company, Photo by Eddie Birch. **450:** © T. Charles Erickson. **455:** Museum of Modern Art / Film Stills Archive. **460:** Martha Swope © Time Inc.

Color Plates 1: © Jerry Irwin. **2:** © George E. Joseph. **3:** © 1990 Titansports, Inc. All rights reserved. Wrestlemania Photo: Steve Taylor.

4: Martha Swope © Time Inc. **5:** Martha Swope © Time Inc. **6:** Martha Swope © Time Inc. **7:** Tammy Amerson and The Company perform "Kim's Charleston" in Live Entertainment of Canada Inc. production of "Show Boat" directed by Harold Prince. Photo © Catherine Ashmore, London. **8:** Martha Swope © Time Inc. **9:** © Paula Court. **10:** Martha Swope © Time Inc. **11:** Yale Repertory Theatre production, "Niravanov" Yale Cabaret, November 10–12, 1994. Mark Dold. **12:** © 1995 Saban. All rights reserved. **13:** Cirque du Soleil photo by Al Seib. **14:** Martha Swope © Time Inc. **15:** © Frank Silberstein. **16:** Bibliotheque Nationale, Paris. **17:** Reprinted with the permission of Atheneum Publisher, an imprint of Macmillan Publishing Company from *Designing for the Theatre* by Jo Mielziner. Copyright © by Jo Mielziner. All rights reserved. **18:** Reprinted with the permission of Atheneum Publisher, an imprint of Macmillan Publishing Company from *Designing for the Theatre* by Jo Mielziner. Copyright © by Jo Mielziner. All rights reserved. **19:** Martha Swope © Time Inc. **20:** Photo by Susan Piper Kublick. **21:** © 1987 Jim Caldwell. **22:** © Joan Marcus. **23:** © 1994 Joan Marcus / Marc Bryan-Brown. **24:** © 1994 Joan Marcus / Marc Bryan-Brown **25:** © Joan Marcus. **26:** Courtesy of Maria Bjornson. **27:** © Clive Barda / Woodfin Camp & Associates. **28:** © Clive Barda / Woodfin Camp & Associates. **29:** Photo by James G. Brey. **30:** Photo by James G. Brey. **31:** Photo by James G. Brey. **32:** © Joan Marcus. **33:** Digital Actor Ray Tracy from the PBS documentary special Computer Visions Artist: Raul Fernandez © 1991 Digital Vision Entertainment. **34:** Courtesy of the Oregon Shakespeare Festival and Dave Brookman.

INDEX